exceptional
children

inclusion in early
childhood programs

Second Canadian Edition

About the Authors
of the Canadian Edition

Carol L. Paasche is a Professor of Early Childhood Education at Seneca College in North York, Ontario. She has taught both college and university students since 1967 and is the author of *Children with Special Needs in Early Childhood Settings* (1990).

Prior to teaching adults, Carol Paasche taught in an integrated cooperative nursery school; worked with children with special needs; and did counselling with both elementary and junior high-school children. She was a founding member of a community-based parent-participating child-care centre.

Carol Paasche has a B.A. from Antioch University and an M.Ed. from the Harvard Graduate School of Education.

April Cornell is the Executive Director of the Ontario Foundation for Visually Impaired Children and has been active for many years in a number of agencies serving children with special needs.

She worked for 16 years as a Supervisor and then Program Director for the Early Childhood Services of the Metropolitan Toronto Association for Community Living (MTACL), where she developed and implemented community-based integrated services for children with intellectual and multiple impairments.

April Cornell has a B.Sc. from Syracuse University and an M.Ed. from the University of Texas.

Margaret Engel recently retired from the Ontario Ministry of Community and Social Services, where she worked from 1976 to 1993. She was a major contributor to the development of the provincial child-care legislation on services for children with special needs, and she represented the Ministry in working with the community to develop a range of preschool services for children and their families.

Prior to 1976, Mrs. Engel developed individualized programming for children with multiple handicaps at the Centennial Infant and Child Centre. She was also a kindergarten teacher, and was President of the Toronto Kindergarten Association.

She has been a lecturer and instructor on special needs at Humber College, Seneca College, and the University of Lethbridge, Alberta.

Margaret Engel has a B.A. from the University of Toronto and is a Primary Specialist, Toronto Teacher's College.

exceptional
children
inclusion in early
childhood programs

Second Canadian Edition

K. Eileen Allen

Carol L. Paasche

April Cornell

Margaret Engel

with a chapter by
Merylie Wade Houston

ITP Nelson

an International Thomson Publishing company

Toronto • Albany • Bonn • Boston • Cincinnati • Detroit • London • Madrid • Melbourne
Mexico City • New York • Pacific Grove • Paris • San Francisco • Singapore • Tokyo • Washington

I(T)P® International Thomson Publishing

The ITP logo is a trademark under licence
www.thomson.com

Published in 1998 by

I(T)P® Nelson

A division of Thomson Canada Limited
1120 Birchmount Road
Scarborough, Ontario M1K 5G4
www.nelson.com

Canadian Cataloguing in Publication Data

Main entry under title:

Exceptional children: inclusion in early childhood programs

2nd Canadian ed.
Includes bibliographical references and index.
ISBN 0-17-606987-9

1. Handicapped children – Education (Preschool) – Canada. 2. Handicapped children – Canada – Development. 3. Mainstreaming in education – Canada. I. Allen, K. Eileen, 1918–   .

LC4019.2.F87 1998   371.9'046   C98–930338–1

Publisher and Team Leader	Michael Young
Executive Editor	Charlotte Forbes
Project Editor	Evan Turner
Senior Production Editor	Tracy Bordian
Production Coordinator	Brad Horning
Art Direction	Angela Cluer
Cover Design	Bello Studio
Cover Photographs	David Starrett
Composition	VISUTRONX

Printed and bound in Canada
1 2 3 4 (WC) 01 00 99 98

CONTENTS

SECTION IV   PLANNING FOR INCLUSION **199**

SECTION V   IMPLEMENTATING INCLUSIVE EARLY CHILDHOOD PROGRAMS **301**

Preface

BACKGROUND INFORMATION

In the first Canadian edition of *Exceptional Children*, we tried to indicate those aspects of the history of providing for and teaching young children with special needs that are unique to the Canadian experience. At the same time, we sought to include those trends and events in the United States that have influenced the development of legislation and practice in Canada. We adapted the original U.S. text in order to provide information that is important to those learning and working in Canada. We used, wherever possible, examples and photographs that reflected our unique Canadian experience.

In the second Canadian edition of *Exceptional Children*, we have continued to strive to present a comprehensive text that will meet the needs of those who wish to learn more about ways of understanding and working with infants, toddlers, and young children (through age 6) who have developmental exceptionalities. We are aware that there are a large number of school-age children with special needs for whom before- and after-school (and summer) programs are needed. In most instances, we have elected to deal mainly with younger children. However, we feel that some of the material in this edition could lend itself to use with older children.

BASIC APPROACH

An inclusive approach to working with children with exceptionalities has its foundation in knowledge of child development theory. For this reason, we have included basic child development background information throughout this text. Our approach to working with young children focuses on supporting, encouraging, and responding to the developmental needs of *all* children. We advocate inclusion and have tried to provide information that will enable teachers to feel comfortable teaching children with special needs and to be successful in including (integrating) them in their early childhood programs.

Whereas our approach is fundamentally developmentalist—and a developmental interactionist emphasis is advised whenever possible—we acknowledge and support the use of behavioural practices in planning and programming when doing so is in the best interest of the child.

We view the early childhood teacher as a member of a dynamic partnership that involves the teacher, the child, the child's family, other children in the centre, support consultants, the school to which the child will eventually go, and the community in which the child lives.

The historical background of the treatment of children and adults with special needs has been somewhat different in Canada than it has been in the United States. Whereas the United States now has federal legislation that designates specific rights and services for young children with special needs, in Canada the legislation is mainly provincial. At one time, programming for Canadian children with special needs took place in segregated settings. In the 1970s, a trend toward planned inclusion (integration) of children with special needs began. Before then, early childhood teachers often received little or no consultation or support services when children with exceptionalities were enrolled in their programs. Teachers were left pretty much on their own, using a trial-and-error approach in programming for children. In the 1980s, early childhood teachers began to be recognized as valued members of the Individualized Program Plan (IPP) team because of their expertise in child development and the range of developmentally appropriate programming ideas they could contribute. In the 1990s, the team approach is now recognized as the most effective approach for providing support and service to children with special needs and to their families. Early childhood teachers must be equal partners in a coordinated effort to ensure successful inclusion.

CONTENT REVISIONS

As a consequence of our own experience, as well as of feedback provided during the preparation of this text, the content of the first Canadian edition of *Exceptional Children* was rewritten to reflect Canadian society and respond to the needs of Canadian students in the late 1990s. In this second Canadian edition, we have expanded some sections, especially those dealing with giftedness and legislative issues. The content in some chapters has been updated to reflect the findings of recent research and theory; terminology has been altered to reflect recent Canadian usage. As in the first Canadian edition of this text, this second edition includes a chapter on bilingualism and second language development by Merylie Wade Houston. New photographs, charts, and data—all of Canadian origin—have been used wherever possible.

Because of the differences between Canadian and U.S. legislation governing services available to children with special needs and to their families, in this text we have retained only those U.S. references that are useful for comparison purposes. Because Canadian legislation is currently undergoing so many changes, we are able to provide only the information that is available as of this writing.

We refer the reader to government website for current legislative changes.

The glossary and appendices also have been revised and expanded. A new appendix, Appendix F, Current Information on Provincial and Territorial Services and Resources, has been added.

The Review Questions and Answers that were in the first edition are now in the Teacher's Manual. The Student Activities and Mix and Match questions have been retained in the second edition of *Exceptional Children*.

Working on this updated Canadian edition was very challenging. Though research exists, much of it continues to be published and disseminated only on a local or provincial basis. The Child Care Resource and Research Unit of the University of Toronto is making a major effort to obtain and publish Canada-wide research and resource materials on child care. Furthermore, though a number of innovative and interesting education and early childhood programs have been developed in Canada, we have concluded that it has been difficult for these programs to get publicity, ongoing funding, and recognition.

In summary, in this book we have tried to provide as complete a record as possible of current trends in Canada and to include useful information for teachers who will be working with young children with special needs in inclusive/integrated settings.

The Instructor's Manual for this new edition has been revised recently to include more Canadian material, as well as test questions, many of which appeared in the first Canadian edition in the last section of each unit.

ACKNOWLEDGMENTS

We are grateful to K. Eileen Allen and the other authors of *The Exceptional Child* for having written an excellent book on mainstreaming in early childhood education. In addition, we are most grateful for the opportunity offered to us by ITP Nelson to adapt this text to reflect the Canadian experience.

We feel privileged to have been able to work on a text that, we believe, will be of assistance to early childhood teachers working in integrated early childhood settings.

We want to give special thanks to all those who supported us in writing this text, including many agencies that contributed pictures and expertise: Adventure Place, Bloorview Children's Centre; Dr. Judith Bernhard, Ryerson Polytechnic University; the Canadian Hearing Society; Centennial Infant and Child Centre; Cresthaven Nursery School; Delmar Publishers Inc.; Julie Dotsch, Ontario Welcome House Nursery; the Easter Seal Society; Karen Ward at Wayne Preschool and Elizabeth Bowerman at Crescent Preschool; Epilepsy Ontario;

Ruth Fahlman, Early Childhood Multicultural Services, Vancouver; Hedi Gotsche; the Metropolitan Toronto Association for Community Living; the Ontario Foundation for Visually Impaired Children; Maria Ciampani and the staff, parents, and children at the Seneca College Lab School; SpeciaLink; Terry Tan Child Care Centre; Play and Learn (a program of the Bloorview MacMillan Centre); Ontario Ministry of Citizenship; and Victoria Day Care Services.

We also wish to thank the following people for their ongoing help in obtaining information for the Canadian edition: Mike Kucharew and his staff, Daphne Blunden and her staff, Clara Will and members of her staff, Norma Kelly, Margaret Pollard, Jean A. Seligmann, Sharon Hope Irwin, Melanie Panitch and the staff of the G. Allan Roeher Institute Library, Martha Friendly and the staff of the Child Care Resource and Research Unit, and all those other people who have made their personal libraries and resources available to us. A special thank-you goes to Harold Garber for the new photos in the second edition.

The manuscript of this work was reviewed at various stages of its development by a great number of our peers across Canada, and we wish to thank those who shared with us their insights and their constructive criticism. For the first edition we thank Stephanie Dillon, Assiniboine Community College; Karen Fogolin, Confederation College; Paul Fralick, Mohawk College; Leslie Kopf-Johnson, Algonquin College; Malcolm Reed, Red Deer Community College; and Carolyn Simpson, Holland College. For the second edition we thank Rita Barron, George Brown College; Ingrid Crowther, Loyalist College; Kathleen Fischer, Niagara College; Rachel Forster, St. Lawrence College; Leslie Kopf-Johnson, Algonquin College; Donald McKay, Ryerson Polytechnic University; and Eliana Tobias, Kwantlen University College.

We also want to give special thanks to the children, families, and early childhood educators who have permitted us to use photographs of them.

The manuscript for the second edition of *Exceptional Children* was reviewed twice. We want to express our appreciation for the input of the reviewers. Wherever possible, we tried to adapt the text in response to their suggestions.

A final note of appreciation goes to Charlotte Forbes and Evan Turner, both of whom consistently supported us throughout the time we worked on this book.

Carol L. Paasche, April Cornell, Margaret Engel

The National Advisory Committee of SpeciaLink, a Canada-wide mainstream network whose goal is to promote high-quality day care for every child in the country, regardless of special needs. The Committee members are:

Back row (left to right): Elaine Frankel, Ontario; Patricia Canning, Newfoundland; David Young, British Columbia; Donna Michal, Alberta; Steen Esbensen, Quebec; and Josef Kneisz, Manitoba. Front row: Melanie Panitch, Ontario; Sharon Hope Irwin, Nova Scotia; Margaret Brown, Nova Scotia; Debbie Suchy, Alberta. Missing are Marie Battiste, Nova Scotia; Barbara Bloom, Saskatchewan; and Laura Mills, Manitoba. (1992)

section I

EARLY
INTERVENTION

CHAPTER 1

An Inclusive Approach to Early Childhood Education

OBJECTIVES

After studying the material in this chapter, the student will be able to

- trace society's changing attitudes toward children with disabilities
- discuss inclusion in terms of early development, critical learning periods, and teachable moments
- discuss the benefits of inclusion for children with disabilities, for nondisabled children, and for children who are gifted
- explain why decisions concerning program placement should be based on the needs of the individual child and family

INTRODUCTION

This book is about inclusion in the lives of young children. **Inclusion** means that children with special needs attend preschool, child care, and recreational programs with their peers who have no disabilities. Inclusion is about belonging, being valued, and having choices. Inclusion is about accepting and valuing human diversity and providing the necessary support so that all children and their families can participate in the programs of their choice.

INCLUSION DEFINED

Inclusion means

> providing all students within the mainstream appropriate educational programs that are challenging yet geared to their capabilities and needs as well as any support and assistance they and/or their teachers may need to be successful in the mainstream. But an inclusive school goes beyond this. An inclusive school is a place where everyone belongs, is accepted, supports, and is supported by his or her peers and other members of the school community in the course of having his or her educational needs met. (Stainback and Stainback 1990, p. 3)

PHOTO 1–1 *Inclusion supports the right of all children, regardless of individual abilities.*

Inclusion is not a set of strategies or a placement issue. Inclusion is about belonging to a community—a group of friends, a school community, or a neighbourhood. Ehlers (1993) describes three ways to view inclusion: through beliefs and values, through experiences, and through outcomes. We should consider all three views when planning for and implementing inclusive early childhood programs (Photo 1-1).

The *beliefs* and *values* that every family brings to inclusion reflect the unique history, cultural influences, and relationship of that family (Hanson and Lynch 1992; Luera 1993). Family choices must drive the inclusion process. The family identifies the community to which it belongs and in which the child is to be included. The concept of "goodness of fit" (Thomas and Chess 1997) is essential when developing inclusive programs. An inclusive program must consider the unique experiences of every child and family and how it can address the child's strengths and needs as well as family and priorities.

The *beliefs and values* that influence inclusion occur at the levels of the family, the community, and society (Peck 1993). A family's belief system will have direct impact on their views about inclusion. The sociopolitical context in which children and families live and work also affects inclusion. This includes how our society views high-quality early childhood care and education for all children. In other words, if providing high-quality child care for children is not a societal priority, providing high-quality child care for children with special needs will not be a priority either.

The *experience* of inclusion varies from child to child and from family to family. The goal is to create a match between the program and the child and the family. Inclusive classrooms are caring communities that support the ongoing development of participants (Salisbury, Palombaro, and Hollowood 1993). Inclusion requires planning, teamwork, and support. Our values and beliefs will help define our experience with inclusion; in turn, our experience will shape future values and beliefs.

The *outcomes* observed and reported by the parents and teachers of children in inclusive educational programs are broad-based and *holistic*. The outcomes include some of the developmental changes observed in specialized (segregated) special education programs (e.g., improved communication skills, improved motor skills). They also include important changes in social behaviour and a general sense of belonging. Many parents of children in inclusive educational programs report that their child received his or her first invitation to a birthday party or to play at a friend's house after being involved in inclusive education. Some parents report that they feel more included in the community because their child is attending a "regular" school.

Schwartz, Peck, Staub, and Gallucci (1994) propose a three-domain conceptualization of the outcomes of inclusive education. These three interlocking domains are membership, relationship, and development. The membership domain includes the child's interactions with groups. This includes being a member of a class, being a member of a small group within a class, and being a member of non-school-related groups (e.g., children's choir at church). The defining criterion of this domain is that other members of the group are willing to make accommodations for the child with disabilities to support inclusion and membership. The relationships domain describes peer relationships, that is, relationships with playmates and classmates. This domain looks at the different roles that the child plays in her or his relationships with peers. For example, in the majority of interactions with peers is the child with disabilities receiving help? Does the child with disabilities have opportunities to be in a role of helping other children? Are there reciprocal or play and companionship types of interactions? Looking at relationships this way allows us to provide rich descriptions of the peers in the child's social network and the many different roles each peer plays.

The development domain looks at more traditional types of early childhood special education outcomes: changes in participation in classroom routine and rituals, changes in social-communicative behaviour, changes in functional skills, changes in preacademic skills, and other goals that are included on a child's **Individual Program Plan (IPP)** or **Individual Family Service Plan (IFSP)**. Together these three domains provide a tool for teachers and families to use to describe the unique outcomes found in inclusive educational settings. This outcome framework can be used to guide the development of goals and objectives for inclusive educational programs (see discussion of IPP and IFSP in Chapter 11).

The inclusion of young children with special needs into community early childhood programs has gained increased momentum in much of North America. In Canada, inclusion is supported in various ways by the provincial governments, professional organizations, and parent and consumer **advocacy groups**.

RECOMMENDED PRACTICES FOR INCLUSIVE EARLY CHILDHOOD PROGRAMS

The DEC's (Division of Early Childhood, one of the affiliated groups of the Council of Exceptional Children [CEC]) *Recommended Practices: Indicators of Quality Programs for Infants and Young Children with Special Needs and Their Families* (1993) puts forth six general principles. These should be used to identify the *best practices* for meeting the needs of young children with special needs in early childhood programs. The principles are equally useful when discussing quality early childhood education programs for *all* children. To be considered a recommended practice, strategies have to reflect or be compatible with the following principles:

- research based or value based
- family centred
- multicultural in emphasis
- cross-disciplinary participation
- developmentally/chronologically age-appropriate
- normalized

The following is a brief description of each of these principles.

RESEARCH BASED OR VALUE BASED.

Accountability must be a cornerstone practice for teachers working with young children (with and without disabilities) and their families. Practices, strategies, and techniques used in early child education and early childhood special education must be supported by **empirical research**. In some instances (e.g., the inclusion movement) practices are pushed by personal and social values rather than empirical research. In these cases it is necessary to work toward gathering the empirical evidence necessary to evaluate those practices.

FAMILY CENTRED.

In family-centred or family-focused intervention, practices are designed with, rather than for, the child and family. This view of intervention acknowledges that the child is part of a dynamic family system and that any change in the system (e.g., intervention or change in programs) affects all parts of the system.

MULTICULTURAL IN EMPHASIS.

Recommended practices embrace a multicultural perspective and celebrate the concept of family uniqueness. *Family uniqueness* encompasses ethnic and racial differences as well as the unique history and traditions of individual families. This is especially important as our society becomes more pluralistic and families are more commonly unique blends of backgrounds. This multicultural perspective recognizes and respects different needs and value systems of the children and families. This respect must be translated into practice by developing programs that are *culturally sensitive* and supportive of differences.

CROSS-DISCIPLINARY PARTICIPATION.

Early childhood and early childhood special education programs should involve professionals from different disciplines working as a team on behalf of young children and their families. Disciplines, in addition to education and special education, that often are represented on early childhood teams include *speech pathology, audiology, occupational therapy, physical therapy, nursing, medicine, nutrition, psychology,* and *social work.* Team members develop expertise in their own discipline as well as expertise in working cooperatively with other professionals. (Chapter 11 provides additional information about interdisciplinary teams.)

DEVELOPMENTALLY/CHRONOLOGICALLY AGE-APPROPRIATE.

The concept of developmentally appropriate practice can be equated with "the problem of the match" (Hunt 1961) or "the goodness of the fit" (Thomas and Chess 1977) between a child and an intervention technique. With children with developmental disabilities the issue of chronologically age-appropriate practices is crucial (Brown et al., 1979). This principle challenges researchers and practitioners to consider the unique learning needs of an individual child; at the same time they must develop an intervention program that is appropriate within the context of an environment and learning experiences that are chronologically age-appropriate. In other words, a 5-year-old with severe disabilities should be using materials and exploring environments that are typical for all 5-year-olds, regardless of his or her developmental age.

NORMALIZED.

Normalization refers to opportunities for individuals with disabilities to go to school and participate in education experiences as do other children and youth. For young children these experiences may include preschool, child care, swimming

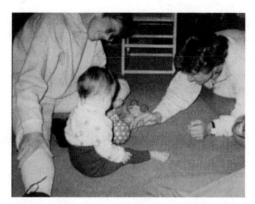

PHOTO 1–2 *A resource teacher models for the parent in an infant development program.*

lessons, play groups, going to the movies, religious training, and dance lessons. A family with a child with disabilities should have the same range of activities and services available to them as any other family (Bailey and McWilliam 1990).

Although these principles were proposed for programs designed to meet the needs of young children with disabilities, they also can be applied to programs for typically developing children and inclusive programs that serve children with a wide range of abilities. These principles are appropriate for all programs across the early childhood period, from infants and toddlers to children in the early primary grades. Although there are many cross-age similarities in quality programming, there also are practices that are age-specific. In the United States, inclusion came about because of the Education for All Handicapped Children Act (PL 94-142; see Chapter 3). This law requires every child with a handicapping condition be educated "in the least restrictive environment."

Since there has been no Canadian federal policy establishing services for children with special needs in early childhood programs, progress in this area has been the responsibility of individual provincial and territorial governments. Early childhood programs for children with special needs were developed in an uneven manner during the 1950s and 1960s, mainly in response to pressure from parent groups. By the 1970s, infant development in-home programs were established along with mainly segregated preschool programs for children with intellectual, physical, and/or emotional handicaps (Photo 1–2).

During this same period, Wolf Wolfensberger at the National Institute on Mental Retardation (now known as the G. Allan Roeher Institute, York University, Toronto) was advocating the integration of persons with special needs into all aspects of the "normal" social system. This movement included advocating the integration of young children with special needs into regular early childhood settings. Wolfensberger stated that "integration is one of the most significant corollaries of normalization" (Wolfensberger 1972).

The concept of normalization was first described by Bank-Mikkelsen, head of the Danish Mental Retardation Services, as "letting the mentally retarded obtain an existence as close to the normal as possible" (Wolfensberger 1972). In 1959 this principle was written into the Danish law that governs services to Danish citizens with "mental retardation."

Bengt Nirje, secretary general of the Swedish Association for Retarded Children, further defined normalization as "making available to the mentally retarded patterns and conditions of every day life which are as close as possible to the norms and patterns of the mainstream of society" (Wolfensberger 1972).

In the mid-1970s, in preparation for the downsizing or closing of its largest institutions for intellectually impaired and emotionally disturbed children and adults, the province of Ontario asked Nirje to come to Canada to assist with the planning of community services to serve residents returning to mainstream society from institutions. It was at this time that the philosophy of normalization and integration was broadened to include all children with special needs, not just those defined as **"mentally retarded."**

During its early years, in the United States the "least restrictive" (under PL 94–142) mandate for children with special needs led to serious misunderstandings. The most frequent misunderstanding was that every child with a disability was to be placed, automatically and full time, in a regular classroom. The result was confusion, inappropriate educational practices, and widespread resistance to the notion of integration/mainstreaming. The situation led to unfounded anxieties.

All provinces in Canada have their own legislation pertaining to the education of exceptional children. Children in the public education system have the right to access to service under the Canadian Charter of Rights and Freedoms. Because early childhood programs are optional, equal access is not guaranteed.

Though some of the problems still need to be addressed, there is fairly general agreement at this time that "the integration of handicapped and nonhandicapped persons of all ages is a sound and ethical policy" (Spodek, Saracho, and Lee 1984, 4).

The Division of Early Childhood (DEC) of the Council for Exceptional Children has developed and adopted a position statement on inclusion. Included in this statement is the following:

> DEC values the diversity of families and supports a family-guided process for determining services that are based on the needs and preferences of individual families and children.
>
> To implement inclusive practices DEC supports:
>
> a) the continued development, evaluation, and dissemination of full inclusion support services and systems; b) the development of preservice and inservice training programs that prepare families, administrators, and service providers to develop and work within inclusive settings; c) collaboration among all key stakeholders to implement flexible fiscal and administrative procedures in support of inclusion; d) research that contributes to our knowledge of state-of-the-art

services; and e) the restructuring and unification of social, education, health, and intervention supports and services to make them more responsive to the needs of all children and families.

INCLUSION: AN APPROACH TO EARLY CHILDHOOD EDUCATION

Since the mid–1990s, in Canada inclusion has been the term most widely used to describe the integration of children with special needs into programs for normally developing children. Inclusive education is used to refer to a unified system that merges special education and regular education systems into one unit. Specifically, the Council for Exceptional Children (1993) has defined inclusion as "a value (that) supports the right of all children, regardless of their diverse abilities, to participate actively in natural settings within their communities." This trend is beginning to appear more and more frequently as a practice in early childhood systems.

PHOTO 1–3 *Inclusion increases awareness and promotes acceptance.*

Reverse integration is the term used to describe programs in which children without handicapping conditions participate in programs originally established for children with disabilities (Photo 1-3). In reverse integration programs, the number of children with disabilities is equal to or more than the number of children without disabilities. Many professionals believe that the optimal situation is one in which the percentage of children with special needs in an integrated program is the same as the percentage found within the specific community.

INCLUSION/INTEGRATION IN PERSPECTIVE

EARLY ATTITUDES

The number of children with disabling conditions participating in community programs has increased steadily over the last 20 years. This is in marked contrast to the way children with special needs were viewed in the past. Caldwell (1973) gives the following description of the stages that North American society has gone through in its treatment of the disabled.

1. Forget and Hide

Until the middle of the 20th century, families, communities, and society in general seemed to try to deny the existence of the disabled. As much as possible, the children were kept out of sight. Families often were advised to institutionalize immediately any infant who was born disabled.

In 1950 the U.S. National Association of Retarded Children (now the National Association for Retarded Citizens) was founded. Efforts to identify "handicapped" and "retarded" children, to bring them out of attics and backrooms, were put in motion. The Kennedy Foundation and members of President John Kennedy's family also were influential through their public acceptance of their own intellectually impaired family member. The Kennedys' acceptance went a long way in breaking down the social stigma that had been attached to a family that allowed a child with a handicap (especially a child with an intellectual impairment) to be seen in public.

In 1958 the Canadian Association for Retarded Children was established. One person in Canada who contributed much to the process of changing attitudes toward those with special needs was Jean Vanier, a son of the Right Honourable Georges P. Vanier, Governor General of Canada. Jean Vanier began by working with people who were intellectually impaired. He was inspired by Gandhi's love and acceptance of the underprivileged and the untouchables in India. In 1964, through Vanier's efforts, a small home known as l'Arche was opened in the village of Trosly-Bureil in France for patients who had lived in local institutions for the mentally retarded. Supported by volunteers from Canada and other countries, the people who lived in l'Arche actively joined in village life and were accepted by its citizens. The l'Arche model became the basis for a movement that developed similar centres throughout Europe and North America. The first Canadian l'Arche community was founded in the early 1970s.

2. Screen and Segregate

The purpose of the "screen and segregate" period was to identify individuals with special needs and provide them with a program separate from their nondisabled peers. This movement grew partly out of the belief that individuals would be better served within the segregated/specialized group setting.

In the 1960s and early 1970s, parents through their local advocacy associations began pressing provincial governments for funding for early childhood programs for their children with disabilities. Legislative action was taken in some provinces.

For example, in 1972, the Day Nurseries Act in Ontario was amended to provide a funding mechanism for service for children with "developmental handicaps." At this time, funding was also provided by the Ministry of Community and Social Services to open programs for school-aged children who were being excluded from local public school programs due to the severity of their intellectual impairment. As a consequence of this process, a system that was separate from the system available to other children of the same ages (therefore, segregated) was developed (Photo 1–4).

It was not until the early 1980s that educational services for all school-aged children were provided through the Ontario Ministry of Education.

3. Identify and Help

The "screen and segregate" period lasted for 20 years or more, at which point the rights of the handicapped began to be recognized. The current "identify and help" period began in the late 1970s because of social and political activities. By 1982, the federal government had adopted the Charter of Rights and Freedoms; this helped to prevent discrimination on the basis of disability (see Chapter 3).

PHOTO 1–4 *Programs designed exclusively for children with disabilities were developed in the late 1960s and early 1970s.*

4. Include and Support

This stage is an addition to Caldwell's stages. It describes our current view of people with disabilities. The underlying assumption of the *include and support* period is that people with disabilities should be included as full members of society and that they should be provided with appropriate supports such as education and accessible environments to ensure their full and meaningful participation.

RATIONALE FOR EARLY INTERVENTION AND INCLUSION

Early childhood education has been gaining widespread acceptance in our society throughout the last half of this century. The formal inclusion of young children with and without disabilities is relatively new to the early education scene, though the acceptance of children with **handicapping conditions** had occurred informally within many programs. The rationale for early childhood inclusion will be discussed in terms of ethical issues, socialization concerns, developmental considerations, and the always pressing issue of cost effectiveness. (See Chapter 6.)

THE ETHICAL ISSUE

The rights of children with a disability to live as full a life as possible has been a major ethical force among inclusion/integration advocates. It was Dunn (1968) who first brought the unfairness of segregated education for the disabled into public consciousness. He asserted that special classes, for the most part, provided inadequate education for children with disabilities and developmental delays. The inclusion of children with disabilities runs parallel to the multicultural approach to early education. According to Derman-Sparks (1988–89), the goal these two movements have in common is to gain acceptance in our educational system for all children—those with noticeably different cultural, intellectual, and/or physical characteristics. Until this is accomplished, ethical issues related to any kind of segregation in our childcare and educational systems remain unresolved.

PHOTO 1–5 *Inclusion increases awareness and promotes acceptance.*

THE SOCIALIZATION ISSUE

Good for both exceptional + non-exceptional

Including young children with disabilities implies that these children will be given equal social status with children who are developing normally. Inclusion promotes awareness (Photo 1–5). Members of the community become more accustomed to children with developmental disabilities; this leads to greater acceptance. It cannot be overemphasized that young children with developmental disabilities are entitled to the same kinds of enriching early experiences as children who are developing normally. As Haring and McCormick (1990, 102) point out, "separating young children with handicaps from normal experiences creates distance, misunderstanding, and rejection ... Moreover, separating these youngsters from the real world means that there must be reentry. Reentry problems can be avoided by not removing the child from normal settings."

Young children with disabilities who play and interact only with other children with disabilities will not learn normal social skills. Play with normally developing children must be an integral part of any program designed to promote healthy development in a young child with a disability (Thurman and Widerstrom 1990).

All children during their preschool years should have the opportunity to get to know children who have disabilities, especially children whose disabilities are obvious—children who are blind, deaf, physically disabled, and those who are cognitively less able. During their very early years, children, unless otherwise influenced, seldom have trouble accepting children who are developmentally different (Photo 1–6). In fact, the disability may not even figure in a child's efforts to describe a classmate with a disability. One parent tells the following story:

PHOTO 1–6 *Young children rarely have problems accepting children who are developmentally different.*

Andrea came back from preschool saying she wanted to invite Katie home for lunch the next day. I could not figure out who Katie was. Andrea tried to describe Katie's hair, then her new jacket, then her paintings. I still couldn't place her. Finally Andrea said, "Katie's the one who comes with shiny ribbons in her hair," and I knew immediately who Katie was. She was the child in the wheelchair who always had big colourful bows at the ends of her braids! Apparently, being confined to a wheelchair was not one of Katie's outstanding characteristics for my child.

Another example also has to do with the ease with which young children accommodate to developmental differences. This parent, Ann Turnbull, who is also a well-known professional in the field of special education, tells of an episode when her son was in his early teens. The Turnbulls' two younger children were preschoolers.

Four-year-old little sister had just been told by a playmate that there was something wrong with her big brother. She denied it vigorously but when the other child persisted she asked her mother about it. Mother explained that big brother could do many things that everybody else could do, only it took him much longer and sometimes it didn't turn out quite the same. The 4-year-old thought about this and then she said, "It's like when I play the old 78 records on my record player." She passed the explanation on to her friend, who accepted it without question.

DEVELOPMENTAL ISSUES

The significance of the early years in laying the foundations for lifelong learning is all but indisputable. As will be described in Chapter 2, it is then that children acquire a broad range of basic skills in all areas of development:

- They learn to move about, to get independently from one place to another, to explore and experiment.
- They become skilled at grasping, holding onto, releasing, and manipulating ever more complex objects.
- They become increasingly able to take care of their personal needs—toileting, dressing, and eating.
- They acquire their native language and use it in a variety of ways to get what they need (and prefer) from others in their environment.
- They develop the ability to think, get ideas, solve problems, make judgments, and influence others.
- They respond with increasingly sophisticated words and gestures when others speak to them or attempt to influence them.
- They discover ways of getting along with and interacting with others—some who are like themselves, and others who are different.

A quality early childhood program can assist all children in acquiring the developmental skills just mentioned. The experience is of special benefit to children with developmental disabilities or children at risk for developmental problems. For these children, it is like opening a door to both the present and the future. The inclusive early childhood program may be their only access to appropriate early learning experiences. Each day they will encounter a variety of challenging materials and equipment, as well as planned and unplanned æ ities. There will be interactions with all types of children who serve as models to imitate and to play with, children who will help and who will need help. There will be teachers who understand the regularities and irregularities of development and will assist each child (with or without a developmental problem) in taking advantage of sensitive learning periods and teachable moments.

Sensitive/Critical Periods

The majority of young children will acquire basic developmental skills on their own. Some of these learnings, however, seem to come about more readily at particular points in time. These are referred to as developmentally *sensitive* or *critical* periods. (Sensitive is the preferred term, though critical periods continues to be in popular usage; see Bee 1989.) During these periods, the child appears to be especially responsive and able to learn from specific kinds of stimulation. The same stimulation at other times is thought to have little impact on development. It is important that all children be in an enriched and responsive learning environment during these periods. For children with developmental problems, it may be even more essential, as we shall see in a moment.

A disabling condition or delay often prevents a child from reacting in ordinary ways during a sensitive period. Parents, especially inexperienced parents, on their own in the home setting, may not recognize signals from their child that a critical learning period is at hand. By contrast, teachers in an integrated setting, where there is a range of developmental differences among children, tend to pick up on all kinds of subtle behavioural variations.

Critical learning periods that are not recognized and not utilized are common among visually or hearing-impaired infants and children. Think of the learning experiences so readily available to nondisabled children: hearing the difference between the doorbell and the telephone; puzzling over a bird call, a flash of lightning, an angry face. The normally developing child turns automatically, dozens of times a day, to look and listen and learn specific things at specific times (Photo 1–7). These same cues, quite literally, are *not there* for the child with a sensory deficit. Without special assistance and opportunities to follow the lead of other children who are responding to what is going on, the child with a sensory impairment is isolated from everyday events.

Language acquisition appears to be especially linked to a sensitive period in development. A child with a hearing impairment may never acquire truly adequate language if the hearing loss is not treated prior to what is thought to be the critical period for language development. On the other hand, a child whose hearing problem is identified early may experience many fewer problems in

PHOTO 1-7 *Normally developing children turn to look and learn dozens of times each day.*

language development. A combination of appropriate treatment and a special education program for the hearing impaired or an inclusive preschool (or a combination, depending on the child's age and severity of loss) allows for building on critical learning periods as they occur.

Children with physical disabilities are also denied critical learning opportunities, but for different reasons. Many cannot move themselves about. They cannot explore their environment. They may not be able to open doors, get into cupboards, run to the window, learn by simply getting into mischief. Contrast this with physically able children who are on the move from morning to night. They are touching, reaching, running, tumbling, climbing, getting into this and that. They try adults' patience at times, especially during critical learning periods when they seem to be in constant motion.

Example:

The infant who is learning to walk is forever on the go. Once walking is mastered, a great cognitive advance seems to take place. Then comes another surge of motor development. The child learns to run, jump, and climb, practising these skills relentlessly, all day long. On the other hand, those who do not walk until late childhood may have continuing problems. They may never become skilled at activities that involve sustained running, jumping, and climbing. Even more serious, they may have missed other critical aspects of early learning during the sensorimotor stage when cognitive development and motor activity are so interdependent.

Teachable Moments

For teachers in an inclusive setting, another concept of developmental significance is that of **teachable moments**. These are points in time (perhaps associated with critical periods) when a child is highly motivated, better able to learn particular skills such as walking, riding a tricycle, learning to count. All children, including those with a severe impairment, have many such teachable moments (Photo 1–8). They occur any time throughout daily routines and activities. It is important that teachers recognize these opportunities and make sure they lead

PHOTO 1–8 *Throughout the program day, all children have teachable moments.*

to developmentally appropriate learning activities. Teachers also can help parents understand the significance of teachable moments and guide parents in recognizing them and finding ways of responding. The inclusive program is an especially suitable place for parents to observe teachers and try out various ways of working with their child.

The infant who is blind and getting ready to learn to walk is a good illustration of teachable moments. First, though, think about developmental sequences and the infant who is sighted. Walking usually is preceded by a period of just standing, then holding onto furniture, and finally cruising about. Most infants do this spontaneously; no teaching is necessary, no special arrangements are needed.

On its own, the baby who cannot see may barely progress beyond the standing stage. What is needed is someone who recognizes pulling-to-stand as a teachable moment and helps the baby build upon it. Experienced parents usually recognize the sign; inexperienced parents may not. The teacher in an infant centre is geared to such moments and ready to provide encouragement. Once standing is mastered, the baby's hands may be moved along the tabletop to teach the fundamentals of cruising. (Usually the baby's feet follow almost automatically.) Teachers should also make sure the environment is safe by keeping things off the floor so the baby does not have frightening falls that may discourage further cruising.

As an infant becomes skilled at cruising, another teachable moment occurs— lifting one hand and one foot as if ready to try a step with less support from the furniture. Again, the infant who cannot see will need special encouragement and a safe environment. Pieces of equipment and furniture, for example, should be left in their regular places. It is frightening to reach for the support of a familiar table or chair to find it no longer there. The infant who is visually impaired also needs someone to give a verbal play-by-play description of what he or she is doing, stimulating further exploration: "You walked to Delia's chair. Can you walk back to the piano?"; "You have your hand on the rocking chair. Let's go find the rocking boat." Simple games such as "Can you find the bells?" (the child can tell from the direction of the teacher's voice) also build upon teachable moments and keep the infant moving.

The more the infant who is visually impaired (or any other infant, disabled or not) moves about, the more the infant progresses in every area of development. In fact, a major reason for utilizing teachable moments as often as possible is to keep the child involved in the process of learning. Hanson and Lynch (1989, 210) put it this way:

> The child learns to be motivated and engaged in the environment and to seek interactions both with the social aspects of the environment—people—and with the nonsocial or physical aspects of the environment of toys, materials, and household items.

PHOTO 1–9 *Young children with disabilities will observe and imitate more advanced skills.*

Imitation

Another important rationale for inclusion is that young children with disabilities will observe and imitate more advanced skills modelled by normally developing children (Goldstein 1993). The logic is sound; imitating others is a major avenue of learning for everyone, old and young alike (Photo 1–9).

Young children learn by doing. If children with developmental problems are to learn to play appropriately they must have children around them who play appropriately and whom they can imitate. If children with behaviour problems are to learn to share and take turns, they must have opportunities to imitate and interact with children who know how to share and take turns. If a young child who is hearing impaired is to learn appropriate speech, the child must have interactions with children who model good speech.

In a segregated setting where there are only children with hearing impairments, it is unlikely that children will do much talking or modelling of appropriate language skills for each other. This is a powerful argument for inclusion of all children in group settings. Totally segregated programs can lead to even greater developmental disruption. When there are no appropriate behaviours to imitate, inappropriate and purposeless behaviours tend to dominate.

Up until the late 1950s, for example, many children with Down syndrome were institutionalized soon after birth. Though they often were in an early childhood wing of a residential building, their playmates were children like themselves. The playmates, too, had been institutionalized at an early age. They, too, had never had opportunities to learn even the most basic developmental skills. And so the myth was perpetuated for generations that children with Down syndrome were unteachable.

What many of these children did learn through imitation was a variety of bizarre or self-destructive behaviours. As noted, their only models were other institutionalized children who had many maladaptive behaviours and few appropriate behaviours. Today, rarely is an infant with Down syndrome institutionalized; many are integrated into community early childhood programs. Most will acquire basic developmental skills and attain varying degrees of academic achievement. (See Peterson 1987, 40, for a comprehensive summary of program results with children with Down syndrome.)

The Cost Issue

The cost of a full-day child-care space varies greatly from province to province depending on a number of variables, including the age of the child. Because of the greater number of adults required for infant group care, infant programs tend to be more costly than group care for preschool and school-age children.

Most programs serving young children with special needs use specially trained early childhood educators or persons with parallel training, as well as consultants, such as physiotherapists, occupational therapists, speech **pathologists**, registered nurses, behaviour consultants, and others, including those trained in signing or orientation and mobility skills. Since the staff required for children with special needs is usually greater than regular staff requirements, the cost of operating these programs is relatively higher. Because of provincial grants, the actual fee paid by parents of children with special needs should be no different from that paid by other parents.

The data in Table 1–1 were compiled by the Childcare Resource and Research Unit of the University of Toronto. The material was collected from provincial officials and child-care organizations. The content is up to date, but the researchers have commented that it is "not as reliable as we would have liked it to be."

As you can see, the fees vary from province to province, as do the program options (for example, full- or half-day, segregated or integrated programs). In 1992, for example, parents of a child with special needs in British Columbia who managed to secure a child-care space were not charged for the service. The fees were entirely covered by the province (Irwin 1992). However, in British Columbia, as in other provinces, there are waiting lists for services for all children, including children with special needs. In Manitoba and Prince Edward Island, the grant money "goes with the child" and the cost paid by the family is

TABLE 1–1

AVERAGE MONTHLY CHILD-CARE FEES BY PROVINCE (ESTIMATED)*

Region of Canada	Infant		Preschool	
	1993	1995	1993	1995
Alberta	$382	$430	$348	$375
British Columbia	$608	$660	$366	$440
Manitoba	$529	$529	$348	$348
New Brunswick	$383	$405	$335	$373
Newfoundland	n/a	n/a	$370	$450
Northwest Territories	n/a	$543	n/a	$536
Nova Scotia	n/a	$500	n/a	$400
Ontario	$792	n/a	$518	n/a
Prince Edward Island	$530	$530	$375	$375
Quebec	$407	$404	$328	$404
Saskatchewan	$418	$431	$328	$358
Yukon	$500	$560	$450	$500

Source: *Child Care in Canada: The Provinces and Territories 1995* (Draft), Childcare Resource and Research Unit, University of Toronto (in press). Reprinted with permission.

* It should be noted that these figures are collected by each province/territory and that collection methods are not consistent.

based on the family's income and ability to pay. In other provinces, the family must pay or be income tested or needs tested for subsidy to cover the cost of the regular child-care fees. The additional costs required to give the child with special needs an individualized program within a centre or home daycare are covered by the province.

Another aspect of the cost issue is the larger number of normally developing children, as well as young children with disabilities, who continue to go unserved or are cared for in unsupervised settings. Simply put, there are not enough integrated, affordable, quality early childhood programs to go around. Investing public money in additional, segregated rather than inclusive, programs would be a setback—philosophically and financially—in meeting the developmental needs of all young children. In the case of children with special needs, it is vital to begin to support parents and begin the intervention process, as well as provide an inclusive environment for the child, at an early age. The cost to the public of a "late start" may be substantial as the child grows older. (See Chapter 9 regarding the role of parents.)

SUPPORTING INCLUSION: IMPLICATIONS FOR TEACHERS

PHOTO 1–10 *Effective inclusion requires specific planning and implementation.*

The mere act of placing children with disabilities and those who have no identified disabilities together in a classroom is not enough to ensure effective socializing and learning among all of the children. Teachers must take that responsibility. Particular skills are needed. Many of these skills stem from knowledge of child development (Photo 1–10). Effective inclusion requires:

- individualizing programs and activities to meet each child's specific needs and abilities (Chapter 11)
- recognizing that there are no well-defined markers between children who are normal, at risk, and developmentally disabled
- remembering that the range of normalcy is broad and that many so-called normal children have developmental irregularities
- avoiding the possibility of limiting children's learning by labelling; as noted earlier, a label often becomes a self-fulfilling prophecy
- recognizing the value of play as an avenue for learning for children with disabilities, as well as for children who are developing normally; at the same time, recognizing that play skills often have to be taught to children with disabilities, many of whom neither play spontaneously nor know how to play
- arranging a balance of large and small group experiences, both vigorous and quiet, so that all children, at their own levels, can be active and interactive participants
- structuring a learning environment in which disabled and nondisabled children are helped to participate together in a variety of activities related to all areas of development
- supporting the development of all children by creating a learning and playing environment that includes a range of materials and activities that will enable the younger functioning children to be independent and the older functioning children to be challenged.

STRUCTURING CHILD–CHILD INTERACTION

The effectiveness of inclusion depends on the interactions between children who have disabilities and those who do not. Such interactions do not necessarily come about spontaneously. Guralnick (1990) and his colleagues have continued to conduct research on this issue. One of their early research efforts (Devoney, Guralnick, and Rubin 1974) indicated that handicapped and nonhandicapped children played together when *the teacher structured the environment so as to promote such interaction* (Photo 1–11). (Chapters 4 and 10 discuss ways for teachers to accomplish this structure.) An interesting sidelight in the Devoney study was that children with special needs, playing with children who are nondisabled, played in a more organized and mature way than had been characteristic of their earlier play.

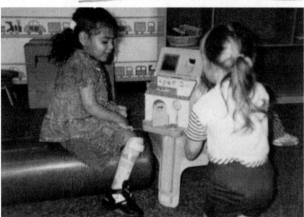

PHOTO 1–11 *The learning environment should be arranged to promote integration between children with disabilities and those without.*

Another classic study also should be mentioned because of its focus on imitation and the teacher's role. It was found that children with developmental disabilities were more likely to imitate nonhandicapped children if they were trained to do so and reinforced for it (Peck et al., 1978). From these and innumerable other pieces of research, it is apparent that teacher structuring of play activities is essential. Curriculum planning for an inclusive early childhood program must focus on activities that lead to all children, disabled and nondisabled, working and playing together. (See Chapter 15.)

Planning Classroom Activities

Curriculum planning for inclusive classrooms also requires teachers to integrate the goals identified on the children's IPP/IFSP into ongoing classroom activities. Using an *activity-based approach* to planning inclusive classrooms draws from the strong tradition of early childhood education and special education to best meet the unique learning needs of young children with disabilities (Bricker and Cripe 1992). This approach allows teachers to use traditional early childhood activities such as dramatic play, art, nature walks, and water play to address specific goals and objectives across developmental domains (e.g., cognitive, social, communication, motor, self help/care) for children with special needs.

PROFESSIONAL COLLABORATION

In addition to classroom practices, integrating children requires integrating fessional efforts. Administrators, teachers, aides, volunteers, health care and social services professionals, and members of the interdisciplinary team need to work

together (Photo 1–12). Professional growth comes with the collaborative search for ways to provide for children who are developmentally disabled in an inclusive setting. Part of the search has to do with looking for paths that lead to a genuine partnership with parents. As will be discussed in Chapters 9 and 21, this means listening to parents, consulting with them, learning from them. In fact, everyone—children, parents, teachers, classroom staff, and clinicians—can learn from each other in an inclusive early childhood setting. Early child-

PHOTO 1–12 *Members of the interdisciplinary team plan together.*

hood teachers, however, receive a special bonus. In learning to meet the needs of children with disabilities they become more skilled at meeting the needs of all children. By learning to build on the capabilities of children with special needs, they become better attuned to the special capabilities of all children.

BENEFITS OF INCLUSION FOR YOUNG CHILDREN WITH DISABILITIES

For children with developmental disabilities, a number of specific benefits are to be derived from the inclusive preschool or child-care setting. Some of these have been touched on in the section dealing with the rationale for inclusion; here they will be summarized. Children with developmental problems are likely to benefit from a good inclusive early childhood experience because it provides

1. more stimulating, varied, and responsive experiences than special classrooms composed of children with limited skills;

2. developmental scaffolding for curriculum activities rather than a **deficit model curriculum**, where major emphasis is on the pathological aspects of development;

3. opportunities to observe, interact with, and imitate children who have acquired higher-level motor, social, language, and cognitive skills;

4. implicit motivation to "try a little harder," in that nonhandicapped children often expect and encourage improved behaviours on the part of less-skilled children; as Peterson (1987, 359) puts it: "A more demanding environment may push the child ahead to develop more appropriate behavioral repertoires";

5. opportunities to learn directly from other children. It appears that certain skills are learned more easily from another child—the explanations and demonstrations often are closer to the developmentally disabled child's capabilities than are the adults' explanations and demonstrations.

BENEFITS OF INCLUSION FOR YOUNG NORMALLY DEVELOPING CHILDREN

Obvious — only advantageous.

DEVELOPMENTAL PROGRESS

Children who are developing normally progress at an appropriate pace in inclusive settings (Photo 1–13). Summarizing a number of studies, Thurman and Widerstrom (1990, 39) suggest that children without disabilities benefit from inclusive programs "at least to the same degree and sometimes to a greater degree than would have been expected if they had attended nonintegrated preschools." There is no evidence of negative effects on children who are developing normally (Odom and McEvoy 1988). Similar levels of achievement occur whether children are enrolled with children who are disabled or with children who are not. (This holds true even in preschool settings where children with disabilities outnumber children who are not disabled.) Another safe conclusion to be drawn from the current research, according to these authors, is that *the developmental outcome for children in inclusive programs depends on the quality of teaching,* and how well the teacher is provided with special supports when needed, rather than on the process of inclusion itself.

PHOTO 1–13 *Parents may wonder, "Will my child receive all the necessary attention and services required?"*

PEER TUTORING

A well-documented benefit of inclusion for children who are developing normally is peer tutoring—one child instructing another. It appears that both the child being tutored and the child doing the tutoring receive significant benefits from the experience (Guralnick 1978). The common sense of this is readily apparent; most of us have discovered that given an unpressured opportunity to teach someone else something we know (or are learning), our own skill and understanding are increased. The same is true of children. As pointed out by Spodek, Saracho, and Lee (1984), voluntary peer tutoring among young children of all developmental levels can promote

- social interactions among children who are disabled and those who are not;
- acceptable play behaviours; and
- appropriate and enhanced use of materials.

Peer tutoring (a child demonstrating to another child how to do something) should not be confused with peer modelling (the unconscious process that occurs when a child observes and interacts with other children). Both peer tutoring and peer modelling enhance the development of children with disabilities.

BENEFITS TO FAMILIES

In general, parents' attitudes about inclusion were influenced by their experiences with inclusion (Lamorey and Bricker 1993). Parents of children with disabilities were most often positive in their responses, although they did identify some concerns (see page 26). Attitudes of parents of typically developing children improved as experience with inclusion increased. In a study involving 125 parents of nondisabled children who attended inclusive preschool programs, Peck, Carlson, and Helmstetter (1992) found that parents perceived their children's experience as generally positive and were supportive of inclusive education. Additionally, Peck and his colleagues found that parents reported that their children were more accepting of human difference and had less discomfort with people with disabilities and people who looked or behaved differently than they did.

BENEFITS TO SOCIETY

Not only does inclusion have positive effects on all types of children, it appears to be of long-term benefit to society. Children who grow up with opportunities to interact with children with disabilities are likely to be more tolerant in later years. They tend to mature into adults with greater understanding and respect for those less able in our society (Bricker and Sandall 1979). Many teachers report that most young children, unless influenced by inappropriate adult attitudes, have a natural acceptance of individual differences. They are unlikely to make negative judgments and comparisons of children who are developmentally disabled. When they do comment or ask questions, they are doing so because they need to learn about whatever it is that is unfamiliar about the child with a disability.

THE CONCERNS AND CHALLENGES OF INCLUSION

As noted repeatedly, the inclusion of young children with disabilities in a preschool setting appears to be of general benefit to everyone. Even so, concerns continue to be voiced. This section reviews arguments for and against the practice. Such arguments, however, must be based on the assumption that the studies were conducted in a quality program with well-trained and caring adults in a ratio appropriate to the number of children enrolled (Bredekamp 1987). A poorly structured, poorly staffed program can have a negative effect on any child, from the most delayed to the most gifted.

In the United States, inclusion is the law. In Canada, though not required by law, the inclusion of young children with disabilities into early childhood community programs is recognized as a preferred practice. The pros and cons of early inclusion continue to be raised and to be the focus of considerable research. The discussion that follows has to do with identifying the most common concerns and providing brief glimpses of research findings that address those issues.

Will Special Needs Be Served?

Parents and teachers have expressed concern that the special needs of children with disabilities may not be met adequately in a community early childhood program (Photo 1–14). They feel that teachers may not have the time or the skills needed. The opposite is of concern, also: If a program is meeting the special needs of children with developmental problems, then what about children who are developing normally? Are they going to be short-changed?

This concern has been addressed in a number of research studies. By and large, the data indicate that most parents believe that their children benefit from integrated programs. (Again, the findings are based on well-structured programs with knowledgeable teachers. Little parent satisfaction is found in poor programs, integrated or otherwise.)

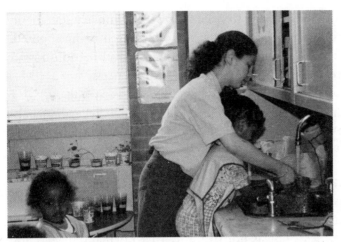

PHOTO 1–14 *Children who are developing normally progress at an appropriate pace in an inclusive setting.*

In a review of a number of research studies, Lamorey and Bricker (1993) state that in general the needs of the children were met in inclusive programming. Some parents were concerned about the quality of training received by teachers in inclusive programs. This indicates that there is a need for different types of training in early childhood education. Professionals need to work on adapting preservice training for teachers in early childhood, early childhood special education, and related therapy fields to prepare professions to work together to deliver quality service to children with special needs in inclusive programs (Odom and McEvoy 1990; Washington, Schwarts, and Swinth 1994).

Many researchers have documented that parents of normally developing children report that their children are learning important social and academic lessons from their experiences in inclusive classrooms (e.g., Guralnick 1994). A similar reaction is found among parents of children with disabilities. They also felt the program helped their children work harder. Bailey and Winton (1987, 86) reported the following:

> Parents of handicapped children felt that the important components—real-world exposure and community acceptance of the handicapped—were being promoted … For parents of nonhandicapped children, prior concerns related to teachers and resources were not realized.

In general, teachers' attitudes are favourable toward inclusion, once they have actually worked with children with special needs in an inclusive setting. In the many studies they reviewed, Odom and McEvoy (1988, 262) conclude:

> … It appears that teacher attitudes toward including children with handicaps in mainstreamed settings were generally positive. In most situations, teachers have the skills for integrating children. However, to integrate children with certain handicaps, additional training and support for the teacher is needed. [This issue is discussed in Chapter 10.]

Thurman and Widerstrom (1990, 40) offer the following summary statement: "There does not appear to be any basis for the fear of children being slighted, as an examination of successful programs at the preschool level demonstrates." The authors then go on to talk about their personal experiences:

> Individualized programming for the children with handicaps often spilled over into better practices with the nonhandicapped children. Teachers who thought mainly in terms of group activities learned, through their work with special children, to plan for individual differences among all children more effectively.

Concerns About Inappropriate Behaviours

Another frequently expressed concern is that normally developing children will learn immature or inappropriate behaviours from classmates with handicaps. Again, this is an unfounded fear. This is not to imply that normally developing children do not imitate other children. They do. They should. As noted earlier, imitation is an important avenue for learning. But normally developing children imitate one another. Rarely (and then only briefly) do they imitate the atypical behaviours of another child. The exceptions are those children who get undue attention from teachers and parents for imitating inappropriate behaviours. Data collected by a group of researchers working with autistic children and reported by Odom and McEvoy (1988, 259) indicate that "normally developing children did not imitate the unusual and stereotypic behaviour of children with autism."

SUMMARY

Including young children with developmental disabilities into regular early childhood programs is the preferred practice in Canada; it is the law in the United States. The degree to which a child is integrated depends on his or her special needs and the intensity of the services that are required. The reasons for inclusion are based on ethical, social, developmental, and cost considerations. No longer is it acceptable, as it once was, to keep children with disabilities out of the social and educational mainstream.

For children with and without developmental problems, the early years are critical years. A variety of learnings seem to be *programmed* in at particular times as a part of the developmental plan. These types of learning may never again be acquired as readily or as well. An abundance of *teachable moments* occur during infancy and the preschool period. These are best used in an inclusive setting with teachers who are trained to recognize such developmental opportunities. An inclusive early childhood program also provides opportunities for children with developmental problems to imitate children who are developmentally normal. At the same time, children who are developing normally at a normal rate are provided with significant learning experiences in helping children who are less able to acquire a variety of skills—motor, social, and intellectual. However, children with developmental problems and children who are developing normally do not necessarily work and play together of their own accord. Teachers should structure the program so that interactions can occur and be reinforced.

advisability of inclusion continue to be
parents and teachers, is that the special
y not be adequately met in an inclusive
veloping children will receive less than
h disabilities are properly served.
ldren who are developing normally will
aviours from children with disabilities.
over the past 10 years demonstrate that
In fact, the opposite is true: the advan-
ho are developing normally as well as for
es, are numerous and well documented.

St

n the pros and cons of inclusion.
ldhood program. Try to identify children
Describe both their problems and their

ntre or early childhood centre. Ask about
1 with disabilities in the program. If there
ry to find out why.
1g. Record any episodes of a child learn-
or peer tutoring.
nce with three other students, two play-
ing the child's parents, the other two the child's teachers. The parents' concern is that their normally developing 3-year-old may not get enough attention because a child who is blind is scheduled to be integrated into the program. Role play a discussion of the situation.

REFERENCES

Allen, K.E. 1972 "Integration of Normal and Handicapped Children: Case Studies." Paper presented at the Third Annual Conference on Early Intervention. University of Kansas at Lawrence.

Bailey, D.B., and P.J. Winton 1987 "Stability and Change in Parents' Expectations about Mainstreaming." *Topics in Early Childhood Special Education* 7, no. 1: 73–88.

Barnett, W.S., and Escobar, C.M. 1990 "Economic Costs and Benefits of Early Intervention." In S.J. Meisels and J.P. Shonkoff, eds., *Handbook of Early Intervention* (pp. 560–582). New York: Cambridge University Press.

Bee, H. 1989 *The Developing Child*. New York: Harper and Row.

Board of Education, Sacramento City Unified School District v. Holland, 7867, Supp. 874 (E.D. Cal 1992).

Bredekamp, S., ed. 1987 *Developmentally Appropriate Practice in Early Childhood Programs Serving Children from Birth through Age 8*. Washington, D.C.: National Association for the Education of Young Children.

Bricker, D., and S. Sandall 1979 "The Integration of Handicapped and Nonhandicapped Preschoolers. Why and How to Do It." *Education Unlimited* 1: 25–29.

Bricker, W.A., and D.D. Bricker 1976 "The Infant, Toddler, and Preschool Research and Intervention Project." In T.D. Tjossem, ed. *Intervention Strategies for High Risk Infants and Young Children*. Baltimore: University Park Press.

Bricker, D., and Cripe, J. 1992 *An Activity-Based Approach to Early Intervention*. Baltimore: Brookes.

Caldwell, B.M. 1973 "The Importance of Beginning Early." In J.B. Jordan and R.F. Dailey, eds. *Not All Little Wagons Are Red: The Exceptional Child's Early Years*. Reston, VA: Council for Exceptional Children.

Childcare Resource and Research Unit 1993 Information Sheet. Toronto: Childcare Resource and Research Unit, Centre for Urban and Community Studies, University of Toronto.

Council for Exceptional Children, Division for Early Childhood 1993. DEC position on inclusion. Reston, VA.

Derman-Sparks, L., and the A.B.C. Task Force 1988–89 *Anti-Bias Curriculum*. Washington, D.C.: The National Association for the Education of Young Children.

Devoney, C., M.J. Guralnick, and H. Rubin 1974 "Integrating Handicapped and Nonhandicapped Preschool Children: Effects on Social Play". *Childhood Education* 50: 360–64.

Dunn, L.M. 1968 "Special Education for the Mildly Retarded—Is Much of It Justified?" *Exceptional Children* 35: 5–22.

Ehlers, L. 1993 "Inclusion in the Lives of Young Children with Disabilities." In S.M. Rehberg, ed., *Starting Point: A Series of Definition Papers* (pp. 33–43). Olympia, WA: Office of the Superintendent of Public Instruction.

The Exceptional Child's Early Years. Reston, VA: Council for Exceptional Children.

Goldstein, H. 1993 "Structuring Environmental Input to Facilitate Generalized Language Learning by Children with Mental Retardation." In A.P. Kaiser and D.B. Gray, eds., *Enhancing Children's Communication: Research Foundations for Intervention.* Baltimore: Brookes.

Guralnick, M.J. 1978 *Early Intervention and the Integration of Handicapped and Nonhandicapped Children.* Baltimore: University Park Press.

Guralnick, M.J. 1990 "Social Competence and Early Intervention." *Journal of Early Intervention* 14 (1), 3–14.

Guralnick, M.J. 1994 "Mothers' Perceptions of the Benefits and Drawbacks of Early Childhood Mainstreaming." *Journal of Early Intervention* 12, 168–183.

Hanson, M.J., and E.W. Lynch 1989 *Early Intervention.* Austin, Tex.: PRO-ED.

Hanson, M.M., and Lynch, E.W. 1992 *Developing Cross-Cultural Competence: A Guide for Working with Young Children and Their Families.* Baltimore: Brookes.

Haring, N.G., and L. McCormick 1990 *Exceptional Children and Youth.* Columbus, Ohio: Charles E. Merrill.

Irwin, S.H. 1992 "So What's an Advocate to Do?" Sydney, N.S.: SpeciaLink (unpublished paper).

Lamorey, S., and Bricker, D. 1993 "Integrated Programs: Effects on Young Children and Their Programs." In C.A. Peck, S.L. Odom, and D.D. Bricker, eds., *Integrating Young Children with Disabilities into Community Programs* (pp. 249–270). Baltimore: Brookes.

Luera, M. 1993 "Honoring Family Uniqueness." In S.M. Rehberg, ed., *Starting Point: A Series of Definition Papers* (pp. 1–9). Olympia, WA: Office of the Superintendent of Public Instruction.

Nirje, B. 1976 "The Normalization Principle." In R.D. Kugel and A. Shearer, eds. *Changing Patterns in Residential Services for the Mentally Retarded.* Washington, D.C.: President's Committee on Mental Retardation.

Odom, S.L., and M.A. McEvoy 1988 "Integration of Young Children with Handicaps and Normally Developing Children." In S.L. Odom and M.B. Karnes, eds. *Early Intervention for Infants and Children with Handicaps.* Baltimore: Paul H. Brookes.

Odom, S.L., and McEvoy, M.A. 1990 "Mainstreaming at the Preschool Level." *Topics in Early Childhood Special Education,* 10 (2), 48–61.

Peck, C.A. 1993 "Ecological Perspectives in the Implementation of Integrated Early Childhood Programs." In C.A. Peck, S.L. Odom, and D.D. Bricker, eds., *Integrating Young Children with Disabilities into Community Programs* (pp. 3–15). Baltimore: Brookes.

Peck, C.A., T. Apolloni, T.P. Cooke, and Raver, S. 1978 "Teaching Retarded Preschoolers to Imitate the Free-Play Behaviors of Non-Retarded Classmates: Trained and Generalized Effects." *Journal of Special Education* 12: 195–207.

Peck, C.A., Carlson, P., and Helmstetter, E. 1992 "Parent and Teacher Perceptions of Outcomes for Typically Developing Children Enrolled in Integrated Early Childhood Programs: A Statewide Survey." *Journal of Early Intervention,* 16, 53–63.

Peterson, N.L. 1987 *Early Intervention for Handicapped and At-Risk Children*. Denver: Love Publishing.

Salisbury, C.L., and Chambers, A. 1994 "Instructional Costs of Inclusive Schooling." *Journal of the Association for Persons with Severe Handicaps*, 19, 215–222.

Salisbury, C.L., Palombaro, M.M., and Hollowood, T.M. 1993 "On the Nature and Change of an Inclusive Elementary School." *Journal of the Association for Persons with Severe Handicaps*, 18, 75–84.

Schorr, R. 1990 "Peter, He Comes and Goes." *Journal of the Association for Persons with Severe Handicaps*, 19, 215–222.

Schwartz, I.S., C.A. Peck, D. Staub, and C. Gallucci. 1994 (October). *Membership, Relationships, and Development: Facilitating Meaningful Outcomes in Inclusive Preschool Programs*. Paper presented at the Division of Early Childhood Conference, St. Louis, MO.

Spodek, B., O.N. Saracho, and R.C. Lee 1984 *Mainstreaming Young Children*. Belmont, Cal.: Wadsworth.

Stainback, W., and S. Stainback. 1990 *Support Networks for Inclusive Schooling: Interdependent Integrated Education*. Baltimore: Brookes.

Status of Disabled Persons Secretariat. 1991 *A Way with Words. Guidelines and Appropriate Terminology for the Portrayal of Persons with Disabilities*. Ottawa: Ministry of Supply and Services Canada.

Strain, P.S., Hoyson, M., and Jamieson, B. 1985 "Normally Developing Preschoolers as Intervention Agents for Autistic-Like Children: Effects on Class Deportment and Social Interaction." *Journal of the Division of Early Childhood*, 9, 105–115.

Thomas, A., and Chess, S. 1977 *Temperament and Development*. New York: Bruner/Mazel.

Thurman, K.S., and A.H. Widerstrom 1990 *Infants and Young Children with Special Needs: A Developmental and Ecological Approach*. Baltimore: Paul H. Brookes.

Turnbull, A.P. 1982 "Preschool Mainstreaming: A Policy and Implementation Analysis." *Educational Evaluation and Policy Analysis* 4, no. 3: 281–91.

Turnbull, A.P., and P. Winton 1983 "A Comparison of Specialized and Mainstreamed Preschools from Perspectives of Parents of Handicapped Children." *Journal of Pediatric Psychology* 8: 57–71.

Washington, K.J., Schwartz, I.S., and Swinth, Y. 1994 "Physical and Occupational Therapists in Naturalistic Early Childhood Settings: Challenges and Strategies for Training." *Topics in Early Childhood Special Education*, 14 (3), 333–349.

Wolfensberger, W. 1972 *The Principle of Normalization in Human Services*. Toronto: National Institute on Mental Retardation.

CHAPTER 2

Normal and Exceptional Development

OBJECTIVES

After studying the material in this chapter, the student will be able to

- describe characteristics of children who are referred to as developmentally normal, disabled, and at risk
- provide three reasons to justify this statement: "To work effectively with children with disabilities, teachers need to have a thorough knowledge of normal growth and development"
- distinguish between developmental sequences and developmental milestones; give examples of each in motor, cognitive, and language development
- discuss developmental disabilities in terms of range and variations as well as factors that determine if a disability will handicap a child

INTRODUCTION

Young children are much alike in many ways. They also are different in just as many ways. Too often, the ways an exceptional child is like other children are overlooked, never put to good use; the focus is on remediation of their delays or disabilities. The following points need to be kept in mind when working with children with special needs:

- A child is first of all a child, regardless of how smart or delayed or troubled that child may be.
- Every child is unique, different, and therefore exceptional in one or more ways.

In small, closely knit societies, the fact that some children are different is not an issue. This seldom holds true in complex societies such as ours. Setting these children apart, even excluding them from society seems to have been built into our system almost from the start. As we have seen, however, change is happening. Inclusive educational programs are a major step in the right direction.

The underlying issue of classification is still with us. Having to distinguish between those children said to be developing normally and those who are developing differently continues to plague us. Policymakers, early childhood teachers, early childhood consultants, and special education administrators often use categories of exceptionality that vary from area to area and province to province.

PHOTO 2–1 *The child with a developmental disability may or may not be easy to recognize.*

Definitions of normalcy and of developmental differences vary among physicians, psychologists, educators, and every other professional associated with the growth and development of young children. The variations come from each professional's training, clinical practices, and traditions. Government policymakers, for example, may use their own specific guidelines to identify particular disabilities, whereas educators may use different guidelines. In other words, there is little consensus as to who are to be classified as developmentally disabled, who are the gifted and talented, and who are the developmentally normal (Photo 2–1). The result is confusion for everyone, and especially for students and newcomers to the field of early childhood education and early intervention.

This chapter will provide practical definitions of normal development and exceptional development. In this book, at-risk, disabled, and gifted children, and children of different language backgrounds will be included in the term exceptional. Normal development will be discussed first, as background. The rationale is obvious: to work effectively with exceptional infants and children, teachers must have a thorough knowledge of normal growth and development. All early intervention programs should have as a main goal the facilitation of a child's overall development. A parallel goal is to implement strategies that prevent or lessen developmental problems. As emphasized by Thurman and Widerstrom (1990, 11), "To improve the development of children with special needs we must understand normal development, including the problems that may occur in normal developmental patterns."

WHAT IS NORMAL DEVELOPMENT?

As noted above, there is little general agreement about the meaning of various terms used to describe the developing child. One of the most common and frequently used terms, *normal development*, has long been the subject of dispute. What is normal for one child may be quite abnormal for another. For example, most early childhood teachers expect children to make eye contact when spoken to. Teachers tend to be concerned if a child fails to do so. Yet, in certain other cultures, such as some North American Aboriginal (Indian) groups, and some areas in the West Indies, children are considered disrespectful if they look directly at the adult who is speaking to them.

In addition to culturally defined differences in what is considered normal, there are individual differences among children. No two children grow and develop at the same rate, even within the same culture. Some children walk at 8 months; others do not walk until 18 months. Most children begin walking somewhere in between. All children within this range, and even a bit on either side of it, are normal with respect to walking. The same is true for every other area of development. Normal development, therefore, shows great variation and significant differences among children.

DEVELOPMENTAL SEQUENCES

In spite of the variations in normal development, certain principles serve as guidelines. One is that the sequences of normal development are predictable. The predictions are based on well-documented developmental norms derived from detailed observations of hundreds of children at various age levels. Well-trained early childhood teachers (and experienced parents) know that each normally developing child can be expected to move step by step toward mastery of each developmental skill, in every area of development. As children do so, individual differences begin to show up. Each child will accomplish the specific steps but will do so at his or her own rate. Furthermore, no matter how quickly or slowly a child is developing, each preceding step is necessary before practice on the next step can begin. A child must roll over before learning to sit, must sit before standing, must stand before walking (Photo 2–2).

PHOTO 2–2 *A child must be able to sit before learning to stand.*

Exceptions are common, even to this basic principle of developmental sequencing. For example, most infants crawl before they walk, but some do not. A few infants move about by sitting up and hitching forward with one foot. Others lie flat on their back and push with both feet. Such self-propelling methods of getting about are quite appropriate, even though atypical.

It must be remembered, too, that no two children grow uniformly and at the same rate. Nor do they move forward in all developmental areas at the same time. Rarely is developmental progress smooth and flowing; irregularities and slowdowns are typical. In fact, progress in one skill may actually stop when the child is attempting to learn a new skill in a different area of development. A common example is the infant who talked early and then quit talking for a time, while learning to walk. Some children even regress, that is, slide backward, under certain conditions—for example, the 3-year-old who temporarily loses bladder control with the arrival of the new baby. Almost all children experience "special needs" on a short-term basis at one time or another.

It may appear that the toddler who walks or talks early is somehow "better" than those who walk or talk several months later. We now know that a developmental lead is not necessarily retained. By Grade 1, the later walkers and talkers are often equally skilled in both language and motor performance.

DEVELOPMENTAL MILESTONES

Regardless of the many variations, certain behaviours or skill sequences can be seen in a fairly predictable order in almost every child who is developing normally. These significant points or events often are referred to as developmental milestones (Photo 2–3). A child who does not reach or is seriously delayed in reaching one or more of these milestones needs attention. It could be a warning signal that something may be amiss in the child's development. Thus, it is necessary for everyone working with very young children to have a thorough knowledge of developmental milestones and sequences in each area of development.

A brief overview of common milestones follows. More detailed profiles are given in the units on physical, cognitive, language, and social development. For a comprehensive account of developmental areas, see Allen and Marotz (1994).

PHOTO 2–3 *Learning to feed oneself is a major milestone.*

Infancy

Recent research reveals that within the first days (even hours) of life, infants react to many things in their environment. They follow a moving object with their eyes. They turn their heads in response to a loud noise. They make a face if they taste something unpleasant. They synchronize their body movements with changes in the voice of the person speaking to them. When the voice speeds up, the baby's arms and legs flail about rapidly. When the voice slows, the baby's movements also slow. From earliest infancy, the human face (especially that of the mother or major caregiver) is of great interest to the baby. Even the very young infant will attempt to imitate various facial expressions, sticking out its tongue, pursing its lips, opening its eyes wider when the caregiver makes such faces (Meltzoff and Moore 1983).

Between 4 and 10 weeks of age babies begin social or responsive smiling (Ontario Ministry of Community and Social Services 1984a, 53). The social smile is considered a major developmental milestone. Lack of social smiling in a 12- to 14-week-old may signal a potentially serious developmental problem. Parents need to consult a healthcare provider should lack of smiling (or any other delay) persist.

Somewhere around 2 or 3 months of age the infant begins to make social kinds of sounds. These sounds, mostly cooing and gurgling, are labelled social for two reasons:

1. They are made in response to the voice of the person talking to the baby.
2. When initiated by the infant, the sounds capture and hold the attention of a nearby adult who usually responds vocally. Thus, the almost totally helpless infant learns that he or she can make things happen, can get people to respond.

PHOTO 2–4 *Given a responsive environment, the infant will learn to smile back.*

Such reciprocity or "give and take" is essential to the **attachment process**. It is also a first major step toward language and social development. Furthermore, this *give and take* demonstrates the basic needs of all infants to have responsive caregivers if they are to develop well. Given a responsive environment, the infant soon is smiling readily at people and discovering, with delight, that most people smile back (Photo 2–4). Three- and 4-month-old infants also smile at objects and even at their own noises and actions. They reach for an object that attracts them and sometimes manage, usually accidentally, to grasp it. These reaching behaviours are significant signals that eye–hand coordination is beginning to develop.

By 5 or 6 months of age, most infants show trunk control and some rolling over. At 7 months, many are sitting, some with support, others without. Nine months finds a few infants walking, and many more crawling or showing readiness to crawl. Cruising, holding onto a low table or other piece of furniture, comes next. Then comes walking. Walking begins at about 12 months, though there are great differences as to when this begins. As noted earlier, anywhere between 8 and 18 or 20 months is considered normal.

Infants' cognitive development is closely interwoven with motor development. In fact, all areas of development are interdependent throughout the formative years. It is true that most child development textbooks present cognitive, social, and language development separately. Necessary as this may be for discussion purposes, such separation is artificial. In real life, all developmental areas are closely interrelated. Early language, cognitive, and social skills are intertwined and mutually supportive. Motor skill development has an impact on all other areas of development.

The importance of good motor skills to overall healthy development cannot be overemphasized. Piaget began to analyze this relationship more than 50 years ago. He described the first 24 months of life as the **sensorimotor** stage of development. During these early months the infant learns by poking, patting, touching, banging, and tasting whatever comes within its grasp. The older infant is on the move every waking moment, crawling and toddling about, experiencing the environment. This early exploring provides an essential foundation for sound cognitive development and intellectual functioning.

PHOTO 2–5 *Most toddlers are able to manipulate small toys.*

Toddlers

Between 18 and 36 months of age most children are moving about freely. In fact, they seem to move about almost too freely, or so it seems to parents and caregivers as they try to keep up with a toddler. Developmental progress is evident in a number of other ways, too. Most toddlers are able to do these things:

- manipulate small toys and a variety of objects (Photo 2–5)
- understand much of what is said to them
- speak in simple sentences
- imitate the behaviour of others (a skill needed in all learning)
- give signs of readiness for toilet training, using the toilet with variable reliability

- feed themselves (usually somewhat messily)
- put on some articles of clothing
- play alone and sometimes with other children

The Preschool Years/Early School

Between 3 and 6 years of age, basic motor skills are perfected. The child learns to run, jump, and climb with assurance. Skill in manipulating a wide range of objects and tools such as paintbrushes, pencils, and crayons grows day by day. Creativity and imagination colour everything from role playing to telling tall tales. Vocabulary and concept development expand rapidly. The result is a dramatic increase in the ability to express ideas, make judgments, solve problems, and plan ahead. During these years, children come to develop a strong belief in the rightness of their own opinions. At the same time, they are beginning to develop awareness of the needs of others as well as some control of their own behaviour in relationship to those needs. All of this combines to allow the child increasing breadth of movement and thought. This, in turn, leads to increasing independence. At the same time, preschool children tend to touch base frequently with important adults. It is as if they need to know that there is someone readily available who will give assistance and comfort, or come to the rescue if need be.

Throughout the preschool years the child's physical growth is slower. Consequently, the amount of food needed to support growth is greatly reduced. Many parents and caregivers are not aware of this biological shift. They think that the child is not well or has become a "picky" eater. Unwittingly, they may try to force the child to eat more than he or she needs. Serious conflict can result. Conflict over food can have an unhappy and lasting effect on the overall parent–child or caregiver–child relationship.

Language skills develop rapidly during the preschool years. It is not unusual, however, for children who were talking well to become a bit less fluent for a while. That is, they may go through a period of stammering or stuttering, which is a perfectly normal or typical developmental irregularity. Usually, this early **dysfluency** will disappear as long as there is no adult pressure to "slow down" or "say it right" (see Chapter 17). Generally speaking, children are talking freely and spontaneously by 6 years of age. In fact, many 6- and 7-year-olds appear to talk all the time, or so it seems to family members and teachers. At this age, a vocabulary of 2500 words is not uncommon, with the child using most of the grammatical forms of the native (home) language (see Chapter 17).

The preschool years are a time of extensive social and emotional development (Photo 2–6). The child is beginning to understand that he or she is a separate

PHOTO 2–6 *The preschool years are a time of extensive social development.*

person, with a separate identity from everyone else, and especially from parents. This growing independence, this sense of self-directing individuality is the essence of **autonomy**. Toward the end of the preschool years most children are sharing and taking turns, at least some of the time. Children who have been in group child care much of their lives may demonstrate these particular social skills considerably earlier. Older preschool children usually are beginning to show empathy— that is, an understanding of how another person feels. The notion of "best friends" is taking hold, too. In summary, it is during the preschool years that children develop the many basic social skills and emotional responses that will help them to be accepted members of their communities.

If all goes well, the developing child passes milestone after milestone in every area of development. Nevertheless, the question posed at the start, "What is normal?" has not been given a truly complete answer. What about a child who is developing normally in some areas but is delayed, even disabled, in others? What about children with severe orthopedic disabilities, for example, who cannot walk, let alone run and jump and climb as normally developing children do? Many children with orthopedic impairments are developing normally otherwise, and can be gifted in language, intellectual, or artistic development. The opposite may also be true: children who are delayed in language or cognitive development may have well-developed motor skills.

WHO ARE THE EXCEPTIONAL CHILDREN?

Efforts to decide which children are exceptional have been going on for decades (Photo 2–7). At times, the term has been all-inclusive. Its use has ranged from children with the mildest of speech differences to those who were outstandingly brilliant (but different).

PHOTO 2–7 *Sometimes it is difficult to determine which children are exceptional.*

CHANGING TERMINOLOGY

Years ago, terms that covered a broader but more individualized range of disabilities came into use. At the time, apparently, the language seemed less demeaning. *Behaviour disordered, learning disabled, mentally deficient*, along with *handicapped, deviant*, and so on, were commonly used to describe both children and adults. Individual identities were locked into differences: *He's Down syndrome; She's autistic; These boys are mentally deficient*. Now we vigorously question the appropriateness of such terms, especially when describing a given individual. Statements such as *She is a learning disabled child* highlights the problem, rather than the child; whereas *This child has a learning disability* puts the focus on the child. The new word order and terminology is referred to as *people first language*. Incidentally, the *people first* approach highlights a fundamental assumption of inclusion—that all children are children and our practices should reflect that reality (Wolery and Wilber 1994).

Historically, the terms handicap and disability were used interchangeably. In recent years, advocacy groups have succeeded in redefining terms. The new accepted terminology reflects a change in attitude, one that promotes "a fair and accurate portrayal of persons with disabilities" (Status of Disabled Persons Secretariat 1991).

The following are some of the attempts that have been made to define terms:

Generally speaking, handicapped children have been categorized on the basis of their major disability ... learning disabled children, children with speech disorders, visually impaired children (Garwood 1979).

Handicap is the burden imposed socially on an individual because of a behavioral or somatic [bodily] deviation (Smith et al., 1983).

Handicap refers to the consequences of a disability that render a person less able to function or perform tasks in the way a normal person can (Peterson 1987).

Handicapped is an environmentally related limitation (Haring and McCormick 1990). [By this the authors appear to be referring to a lack of skills relevant to a particular situation.]

A "handicap" is an environmental or attitudinal barrier that limits the opportunity for a person to participate fully. Negative attitudes or inaccessible entrances to buildings are examples of handicaps (Status of Disabled Persons Secretariat 1991, 3).

A disability is a functional limitation or restriction of an individual's ability to perform an activity (Status of Disabled Persons Secretariat 1991, 3).

Other terms that are frequently used to identify children who are in need of additional support services include the following:

1. *Exceptional.* Extreme ends of what society considers normal development; the term usually includes those who are gifted and talented as well as those with handicapping conditions. Used most frequently in the field of education.

2. *Special* or *challenging needs.* The preferred terms used by early childhood educators, service providers, and advocates for children who

    a. face "barriers to normal development and functioning in one or more of the following areas of development: physical, social, emotional, communication, intellectual, behavioural," and/or

    b. have "increased vulnerability to environmental and non-environmental stresses, including those related to family, social, economic and cultural circumstances" (Ontario Ministry of Community and Social Services 1984b).

3. *Impairment.* Refers to incapacities or injuries, especially those having to do with the sensory and neural systems; thus, we speak of the visually impaired, the orthopedically impaired, the speech impaired, and the hearing impaired.

4. *Atypical.* A much broader term that covers almost any variation from what is considered normal; often it is a matter of degree: How different or how far behind must a child be to be considered atypical? (Seldom is this term used in reference to gifted children.)

5. *Developmental disability.* Usually refers to a variety of conditions that interfere with the child's physical, sensory, or cognitive development, and originate between conception and 18 years of age.

Recognizing a child with a disability is not always easy to do. Whereas a severe spinal cord malformation, present at birth, is easily identified, other disabilities such as a severe hearing loss in a newborn may be nearly impossible to recognize unless the infant is receiving high-quality medical screening or is in an intensive neonatal health care facility.

Identifying a problem also depends on who is describing the child. In the past, the term handicapped was applied to individuals who were noticeably different, either physically or intellectually. Usually, they were referred to as "deaf and dumb," "blind," "crippled," or "retarded." Society provided "homes for crippled children" and "institutions for the mentally retarded" (a common term in those days for individuals who were judged to be of lesser intellectual abilities). For decades, these were the only public services available for the disabled.

The outline presented here reflects the early development of services for children with special needs in Canada (Table 2-1). Further information can be found in Chapter 3.

TABLE 2-1

SOCIETAL CARE AND TREATMENT OF THE DISABLED—A CANADIAN HISTORICAL PERSPECTIVE OF EARLY SERVICES

In 1830, legislation was passed that "allowed the insane to be committed to common jails" (Winzer 1993, 65).

1830–1859:

1831—In Champlain, Quebec, a school for deaf children was opened.

1848—The Catholic Church opened a school for Catholic deaf boys in Quebec. This was followed in 1851 by a school for deaf girls.

1856—The Halifax School for the Deaf was established.

1858—John Barrett McGann opened a school in Toronto to teach deaf children.

1860–1879:

1861—Blind children in Toronto were admitted to the school for the deaf opened by John Barrett McGann.

1866—In Montreal, the Grey Nuns opened a small private school for the blind.

1870—A publicly supported institution for the deaf was opened at Belleville, Ontario.

1870—In Montreal, Thomas Widd established a school for Protestant deaf children. Later, the name of this school was changed to the Mackay School for Deaf and Crippled Children.

1872—Ontario opened a publicly supported school for the blind in Brantford.

1873—In Halifax, a public school for the blind was opened under the auspices of Sir Frederick Fraser.

1876—In Orillia, Ontario, the first Canadian institution specifically for the mentally retarded was established.

1880—1900:

1884—The Winnipeg School for the Deaf was opened by J.B. Watson, a son-in-law of John Barrett McGann.

1888—Nova Scotia and Manitoba gave free education to deaf children.

1888—In Orillia, Ontario, a school was established at the institution for the mentally retarded.

1898—Woodlands, a facility for the mentally retarded, was opened in British Columbia.

SOURCE: Adapted from Winzer 1993, 9, 10.

PHOTO 2–8 *At one time a child who did not speak English or French was considered to be handicapped.*

In the not-too-distant past, some teachers considered a child who spoke a language other than English or French to be handicapped in a classroom where either English or French was the only language used. Haring and McCormick refer to this as an "environmentally related limitation." It should be noted that the same child may well have been highly capable in the language of his home environment (Photo 2–8). (See also Chapter 18.) Note, too, that the child's preschool teacher might have been considered handicapped in the child's own community if the teacher spoke only English or French.

Many early childhood special education texts use the terms handicap and developmental disability interchangeably. In this text, as recommended by the Status of Disabled Persons Secretariat (1991), **developmental disability** will be used. The term developmental disability can be defined as

1. any condition that significantly delays a child's normal growth and development (for example, a 5-year-old whose language development is on a par with a typical 3-year-olds' has a significant language delay);

2. any condition that distorts (makes abnormal or atypical) a child's normal growth and development (for example, fingers missing at birth which may or may not be a handicap); and

3. any condition that has a severe negative effect on a child's normal growth and development, such as extreme neglect or malnourishment during the first years of life.

THE PROS AND CONS OF LABELLING

Convincing arguments can be made for not putting a specific diagnostic label on infants, toddlers, and preschoolers who are developmentally different. Many young children who are developmentally different in one way or another resemble normally developing children far more than they differ from them. With the exception of children with severe impairments, children with developmental disabilities go through the same sequences of development as normally developing children, though at different rates. It should not be assumed

PHOTO 2–9 *Because a child is different in some ways does not preclude one's noting how typical that child is in other ways.*

that a disability in one area of development means that special programming is required in all areas (Photo 2–9). Furthermore, many infants and young children start out with serious problems that they are able to overcome if they receive appropriate early intervention services. Premature infants are a good example. Often they are delayed in acquiring early developmental skills. Yet by age 2 or 3, many of these children, with adequate care and nutrition, are catching up. By age 5, most look and perform like all other 5-year-olds. Freedom from developmental delay does not hold true for all low birthweight babies, though many show no long-term disability. This is in contrast to those born a generation ago when treatment of premature infants was less advanced (Bee 1992).

Some impairments, even though serious, may never be handicapping if the child receives appropriate support and intervention services. The condition may continue to exist but the child finds ways to compensate and so learns to function almost normally in spite of it.

Example:

Bret was a child born with one short arm and a malformed hand. The family, from the start, had referred to this as his "little hand." At preschool, there was nothing Bret could not do as well as any other child, be it puzzles, form boards, or block building. In kindergarten, he was among the first to learn to tie shoes. By Grade 7 he was a champion soccer player.

Individuals like Bret seldom consider themselves handicapped; nor do their families view themselves as having a child with a handicap. It is unlikely that this positive attitude could be maintained if the label handicapped (with the inevitable differences in attitude that accompany the term) had been attached to this child in infancy.

Labelling is useful and at times necessary for

1. gaining access to public funds;

2. advocating support and changes; and

3. clarifying and facilitating communication between professionals—for example, in research.

(See Chapter 4 for a classification of developmental disabilities.)

DEVELOPMENTAL DELAYS AND DEVIATIONS

It can be useful to think of developmental disabilities as taking two basic forms: delays and deviations. What is the difference?

PHOTO 2–10 *Oromuscular dysfunction often leads to speech problems.*

A delay is present when a child is performing like a normally developing child of a younger age. As an example, consider Josh, a 3-year-old just beginning to put together two-word sentences. Josh has moved steadily through each earlier milestone in language development. It is evident that this 3-year-old is experiencing a language delay; normal language will come, though later than for other children his age. By the age of 8 or 10, it is unlikely there will be any hint of Josh's earlier delay.

A deviation is present when some aspect of a child's development is different from what is ever seen in a normally developing child. Another language example will be used, this time a 3-year-old with severe **oromuscular dysfunction** due to **cerebral palsy** (Photo 2–10). The child makes many sounds and tries very hard to talk, but cannot be understood. This is a deviation. It is likely that this child will continue to have speech problems.

Developmental deviations, however, are not necessarily handicapping. Individuals with six toes on each foot have a developmental deviation; yet they most surely would not be thought of as handicapped. On the other hand, what may seem to be an equally nondisabling deviation can be a handicap if it is a source of anxiety for the person. Such things as a large birthmark on the cheek, missing fingers, or a shortened leg might be a handicap for some but of little concern to others. As in the example of Bret, the impact depends on how well the child, especially in the early years, is helped to manage the deviation.

AT-RISK POPULATIONS

Many infants and young children are said to be at risk or at high risk. This means there is reason to believe that serious problems are likely to develop. For example, mothers who were heavy drinkers or chemically addicted during pregnancy often bear children who are at risk developmentally (Photo 2–11). Their new-

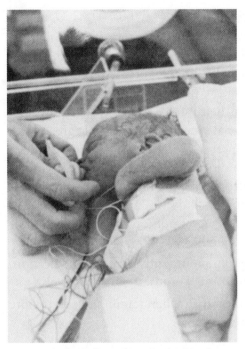

PHOTO 2–11 *Infants may be high risk at the time of birth.*

borns may or may not show immediate problems. Infants who are born both addicted and at a very low birthweight are likely to be considered high-risk babies; they may be in grave developmental danger. These children are more likely than others to exhibit learning problems, emotional disorders, and attention deficits. Another less dramatic, but all too frequent, example of high-risk children is those born into serious poverty. Developmental risk is almost certain in cases of malnutrition, inadequate shelter, and poor health care.

An important characteristic of the at-risk condition is that the potential for healthy development is there. The majority of at-risk infants and children have a good chance of overcoming the initial setbacks. What is required is early and comprehensive intervention services: medical treatment, ample nurturance, and in many cases, family support services (see Chapter 9). Risk factors, including those already discussed, can be grouped into two major categories: *biological* and *environmental*.

Biological Risk

This term applies to infants and children whose systems have undergone some kind of biological insult such as an accident, injury, or severe stress. The incident may have occurred before birth (prenatal), at the time of birth (perinatal), or following birth (postnatal). Consider these examples:

A newborn with **respiratory distress syndrome (RDS)** *is at risk—in serious trouble medically—but likely to recover if given immediate and appropriate treatment.*

Premature birth or low birthweight (5 pounds or 2500 grams or less) are risk factors that require immediate, intensive intervention. Without it, many of the infants affected will suffer **irreversible developmental damage**.

Other biological risk factors include genetic disorders such as Tay-Sachs syndrome and **chromosomal disorders** *such as Down syndrome, which may have accompanying physiological problems, putting the child at greater risk (Photo 2–12).*

PHOTO 2–12 *Chromosomal disorders include Down syndrome.*

Environmental Risk

Poverty is the greatest single factor associated with environmental risk. As noted earlier, families who live in severe poverty often are seriously undernourished and may lack adequate shelter. In addition, they may have little or no way to learn about caring for their infants and may not know how to obtain appropriate social services and medical care. As will become evident in Chapter 4, the effects of poverty produce many biological risk conditions. However, poverty is not the only environmental factor that puts infants and young children at risk. Other factors include

1. child abuse and unfit living conditions due to addicted or dysfunctional family members;
2. family beliefs that prohibit urgently needed medication, medical treatment, or surgery; and
3. inaccessibility of medical care when families live in remote mountain or rural areas.

SUMMARY

Decisions as to who are the children who are developing normally and who are the children whose development is exceptional vary among provinces and the various professions involved with young children. The terminology used to refer to children who deviate from the norm has gone through a series of changes over time, reflecting changes in societal attitudes.

Normal development is difficult to define to everyone's satisfaction because it is so complex a process and includes such a range of developmental skills. Certain guidelines are available. These are based on knowledge of developmental sequences, developmental milestones, and the interrelatedness of developmental areas. A thorough knowledge of normal growth and development is necessary for understanding and working with exceptional children.

STUDENT ACTIVITIES

1. Meet with an advocacy group for exceptional children and find out how and why it was established and what changes have resulted from its actions.
2. Select a specific area of disability and identify how social attitudes and treatments have changed over the past hundred years.

3. Observe a group of preschool children. List any instances of what you feel may indicate development or behaviour that deviates from the norm. Explain.

4. Research legislation in your province and summarize definitions of developmental disabilities.

REFERENCES

Allen, R.E., and L. Marotz 1994 *Developmental Profiles: Birth to Six*. Albany, N.Y.: Delmar.

Bee, H. 1992 *The Developing Child*. New York: Harper and Row.

Garwood, S.G. 1979 *Educating Young Handicapped Children: A Developmental Approach*. Germantown, Md.: Aspens Systems.

Haring, N.G., and L. McCormick 1990 *Exceptional Children and Youth*. Columbus, Ohio: Charles E. Merrill.

Meltzoff, A.N., and M.K. Moore 1983 "Newborn Infants Imitate Adult Facial Gestures." *Child Development* 54: 702–9.

Ontario. Ministry of Community and Social Services 1984a Dellcrest Children's Centre. *A Guide for Parents of Young Children—Infants, Toddlers and Preschoolers*. Toronto, Ont.

Ontario. Ministry of Community and Social Services 1984b Metro Report. *Services for Special Needs Preschool Children in Metropolitan Toronto*. Toronto, Ont.

Peterson, N.L. 1987 *Early Intervention for Handicapped and At-Risk Children*. Denver: Love Publishing.

Smith, R.M., J.T. Neisworth, and F.M. Hunt 1983 *The Exceptional Child: A Functional Approach*. New York: McGraw-Hill.

Status of Disabled Persons Secretariat 1991 *A Way with Words: Guidelines and Appropriate Terminology for the Portrayal of Persons with Disabilities*. Ottawa: Ministry of Supply and Services Canada.

Thurman, S.K., and A.B. Widerstrom 1990 *Infants and Young Children with Special Needs: A Developmental and Ecological Approach*. Baltimore: Paul H. Brookes.

Winzer, Margaret 1993 *Children with Exceptionalities: A Canadian Perspective*. Scarborough, Ont.: Prentice-Hall, Canada.

Woolery, M., and J.S. Wilber 1994 *Including Children with Special Needs in Early Childhood Programs*. Washington, D.C.: National Association for the Education of Young Children.

section **II**

LEGISLATION

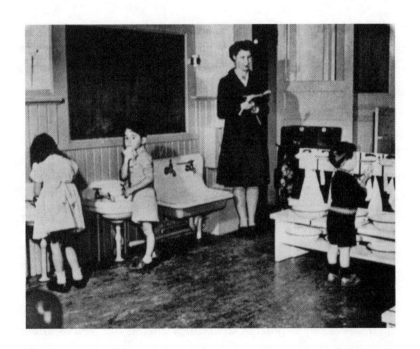

3

Canadian Legislation: Support for Children through Early Intervention

OBJECTIVES

After studying the material in this chapter, the student will be able to

- understand the differences between legislation for children with special needs in the United States and legislation for children with special needs in Canada

- explain how the War Measures Act of 1942 influenced the funding of child care in Canada

- specify how the Medical Care Act of 1966 supported the well-being of young Canadian children

- describe how the Canada Assistance Plan Act influenced the growth of Canadian child care

- recognize the impact of the Canada Health and Social Transfer Act on child care in Canada.

INTRODUCTION

Public policy on behalf of infants and children with developmental disabilities or children at risk for acquiring disabilities during the developmental years has been expanding steadily over the past several decades in North America. Beginning in the early 1960s, the Congress of the United States passed a number of laws that supported early identification, prevention, and treatment of developmental problems. Shortly thereafter, parallel legislative action took place in Canada.

In order to gain an appreciation of the differences that influenced the field of early childhood education in Canada and the United States, it is important to review the historical background against which Canadian early childhood legislation developed. In contrast to their U.S. counterparts, the education and care of young Canadian children are the responsibility of provincial and territorial governments and not the federal government. The following legislative outline shows how this happened.

FEDERAL LEGISLATION IN CANADA

THE INFLUENCE OF THE BRITISH NORTH AMERICA ACT

The legislation of any young country influences the development of the services that it provides to its population. In Canada, the British North America Act of 1867 established that the provinces were to be responsible for local matters. While the act was silent on the role to be played in local services by the federal government, it stated that the federal government should take responsibility for those matters affecting all provinces, such as national defence (Sobsey 1985). Education and social services are identified as "local matters." Therefore, child care and care for children with special needs (when it became available) were regarded as provincial concerns. A variety of child-care centres and related services evolved in an informal manner as the need arose in each province. Examples of these are the following:

- The first day-care centres were founded by Roman Catholic nuns in Quebec, in the 1850s.
- The first Toronto creche (day-care centre), now called Victoria Day Care Services, was founded for the benefit of needy families in the 1890s.
- Edmonton and Winnipeg started day-care centres in 1908–1909.
- Vancouver Children's Hospital opened an infant and preschool centre for children of mothers working in the hospital, in 1910.
- The National Council of Women and the Young Women's Christian Association (YWCA), both advocates for women's rights, were strong advocates for the development of summer camps and child-care programs.

THE WAR MEASURES ACT: ITS IMPACT ON CHILD CARE

It was not until World War II, with the passing of the War Measures Act, that the federal government provided funds for child care. The War Measures Act enabled the federal cabinet to enact specific legislation that it deemed necessary, which potentially limited some freedoms of citizens (for example, gas was rationed in order to ensure appropriate supply).

PHOTO 3–1 *The Dominion-Provincial Wartime Day Nurseries Agreement provided for the shared funding of day-care centres.*

Since more women workers were required to replace men in essential industries, the provision of child care became a priority issue. The provincial governments and the federal (sometimes called Dominion) government were asked to participate in the provision of day care for those children whose mothers were employed in an essential industry.

The Dominion–Provincial Wartime Day Nurseries Agreement, under the War Measures Act, provided for shared funding between the federal government and any province that was interested in developing day care for children (Photo 3–1). Thus, in 1942, a mother working in an essential industry in Ontario paid about 33 percent of the cost of day care for her child or children, while the remainder of the cost was shared on a 50–50 basis between the federal and provincial governments (Stapleford 1976, 2). This was the first time that child care was included in Canadian legislation.

Federal funding for child care was withdrawn after World War II when the War Measures Act expired. With the termination of the War Measures Act and the return of men to the workforce, it was expected that mothers would resume caring for their children. Any continued costsharing for child care was limited to agreements between local municipalities and provincial governments. Provincial legislation evolved as a result of pressures from women wishing to continue to work outside the home. An example was the 1946 Day Nurseries Act in Ontario.

More than 20 years passed before the federal government would once again provide a mechanism for the funding of child care.

THE CANADA ASSISTANCE PLAN ACT (1966–1996): FEDERAL SUPPORT FOR SOCIAL SERVICES

Although there was public interest in continuing some form of cost sharing for child-care services through federal legislation, it was not until the passing of the Canada Assistance Plan Act (CAP) in 1966 that certain welfare programs, including subsidized child care, entered the federal cost-sharing picture. Under this open-ended legislation, the federal government offered to share with any province the cost of up to half of the financial assistance required for children in child care whose families were deemed to qualify through a needs test or income test.

It should be noted that funding specifically for children with special needs was not addressed in this legislation.

The Canada Assistance Plan Act had two major sections:

1. *Assistance programs* that provided funding for the following:
   - food, shelter, clothing, fuel, utilities, household and personal require-ments
   - care in a home for special care
   - health-care services
   - prescribed welfare services purchased by or at the request of a provin-cially approved agency
2. *Welfare services* focused on reducing, removing, or preventing the causes and effects of poverty, child neglect, and dependence on public assistance. These services were included under this legislation:
   - rehabilitative services
   - caseworker, counselling, assessment, and referral services
   - adoption services
   - homemaker, day care
   - community development services

There were other programs available under the Canada Assistance Plan:
- the Indian Welfare Services Agreement
- the Vocational Rehabilitation of Disabled Persons Agreement (VRDP)
- Family Benefits Assistance (FBA)
- General Welfare Assistance (GWA)

For many years after the introduction of the Canada Assistance Plan, there was slow but steady growth within the child-care system and its related services, including specialized programming for infants and young children with special needs. Child care for needy working families continued to be supported across Canada through federal cost sharing. The number of full-day child-care spaces (day care and home day care) for both subsidized families and those paying the full fee rose approximately 600 percent between 1973 and 1984, going from 28 373 to 171 654 (Health and Welfare Canada 1986).

The 1970s saw a movement toward the active involvement of parents through the Parent Cooperative movement and parent associations for the gifted, the

PHOTO 3–2 *Programs for children with special needs developed as a result of the advocacy of parent associations.*

emotionally disturbed, and the physically and developmentally disabled (Status of Day Care in Canada 1990) (Photo 3–2).

The early 1990s saw the establishment of ceilings placed on funds available to some provinces. In 1996 the Canada Assistance Plan Act was repealed and the Canada Health and Social Transfer Act was established.

THE CANADA HEALTH AND SOCIAL TRANSFER ACT (CHST) 1996

During times of economic flux, at both the federal and provincial government levels there is often an impact on funding formulas for health and social services for children and families such as has been revealed in the Canada Health and Social Transfer Act (CHST). The elimination of the Canada Assistance Plan Act and the introduction of the Canada Health and Social Transfer Act has signalled that the federal government has transferred social responsibilities such as welfare and child care to the provinces and territories.

Under the new legislation, the federal government has guaranteed an annual, though shrinking, "lump sum" contribution to each province or territory, to be spent for health and social services, including welfare. Unlike the CAP that refunded provinces 50 percent of the cost for child care to families in need, there is no requirement that any of the annual lump sum under the CHST be allocated to childcare. Some provincial governments with growing child-care services are being forced to consider transferring larger welfare costs, including those for child care, to the local governments. The local government will then be responsible for determining how to obtain enough funding to meet their child-care costs. It is too early to judge the overall impact of CHST on services to children with special needs who are currently supported by provincial child-care systems. However, increasingly, public opinion, especially from working parents, seems to indicate the need for a mid-course correction. This will require the introduction of a new method of federal child-care funding to relieve financial pressure on provincial governments.

Due to the potential changes in provincial child-care services (resulting from CHST), it is important that early childhood educators make a regular effort to read and respond to current provincial planning directions and legislative changes. (See Appendix F for further information on individual provinces and territories.)

THE CHARTER OF RIGHTS: THE IMPACT ON CHILDREN WITH SPECIAL NEEDS

The Canadian Charter of Rights and Freedoms became a part of the Canadian Constitution in 1982. Section 15 of the Charter guarantees equal rights for all citizens. It has been argued that there is a right to education implicit in the Charter (MacKay 1987). Since the responsibility for both school-age and preschool education lies with each provincial government, it is up to the provinces to show that any lack of service that limits these rights (for example, lack of service to a child with special needs) is due to the child's excessive needs, which go beyond the "reasonable limits" clause as stated in Section 24 of the Charter of Rights.

The equality rights in the Charter did not come into force until 1985, providing time for provincial ministries and local school boards to plan for the integration of children with special needs into the regular school system. Although education for school-age children is mandatory under provincial legislation (usually starting at 6 years of age), early childhood education, including kindergarten and/or child care, is not mandatory. Therefore, under the Charter of Rights, parents of school-age children who are disabled or have special needs and are denied access to education have the right of legislative appeal (that is, they are able to take their provincial ministry of education to court and demand equal educational opportunities for their child). However, parents with a preschool child who has a disability are unable to use the power of the courts since early childhood education is optional, not a legislated requirement. Therefore, it cannot be regarded by the courts as a right under the Charter of Rights.

The phrase "least restrictive environment" became popular in the 1970s as part of the development of normalization and integration activities throughout Canada. It was agreed by those who followed the normalization philosophy that children or adults with special needs should not be placed in an institution but should remain in their own community, preferably in their own home. Similarly, children with special needs should not be segregated but should be included in early childhood programs as far as possible in order to experience normal

PHOTO 3–3 *Children with special needs have the right to be included in community early childhood programs.*

preschool activities and to interact with nondisabled peer models (MacKay 1987) (Photo 3–3).

PROVINCIAL AND TERRITORIAL LEGISLATION FOR CHILD CARE

Because there continued to be a lack of any federal child-care legislation beyond the subsidy arrangements in the Canada Assistance Plan legislation, most provinces and territories embarked on developing their own child-care legislation, either through separate acts or through inclusion in existing provincial legislation.

Table 3–1 lists the child-care legislation of each province and territory and notes if the legislation contains a reference to services and/or funding for children with special needs (Childcare Resource and Research Unit 1993). Since 1990 several provinces, including Alberta, British Columbia, New Brunswick, Saskatchewan, and Ontario, have initiated the review and/or revision of their policies and legislation involving services for young children with special needs. (See Appendix F for further information on provinces and territories.)

EDUCATIONAL LEGISLATION IN CANADA

In Canada, the responsibility for the education of students with disabilities lies with the provincial governments. While all provinces recognize the right to education for all children, the legislation varies from province to province.

Differences exist in provincial educational legislation with respect to the diagnostic categories of identified exceptionalities. How an individual student is designated as being eligible for special services also varies from province to province. However, in some provinces diagnostic categories such as "orthopedically impaired," "visually impaired," and "educable mentally retarded" are used for determining program designation.

TABLE 3–1

PROVINCIAL/TERRITORIAL CHILD-CARE LEGISLATIVE CHART

Province/ Territory	Regulatory Body	Title of Legislation	Special-Needs Funding
Alberta	Alberta Family and Social Services, Day Care Programs	Social Care Facilities Licensing Act 1980. Alberta Day Care Regulation 33/90	Grants available to child-care services that integrate children with special needs, to assist with additional costs
British Columbia	Ministry for Women's Equality	Community Care Facility Act. British Columbia Regulation 319/89; Child Care Guaranteed Available Income for Need Act 1979	Funding for children with special needs in specialized or integrated settings
Manitoba	Department of Family Services Child Day Care	The Community Child Day Care Standards Act 1983. Manitoba Child Day Care Regulations 23/87, 62/86, 148/83	Grants available for children with special needs in integrated centres
New Brunswick	Office for Childhood Services, Department of Health and Community Services	Family Services Act 1980. New Brunswick Legislative Assembly, Family Services Act Regulations 1983, amended 1992	Grants for eligible children through the Integrated Day Care Program to help meet the child's specific needs
Newfoundland and Labrador	Day Care and Homemakers Services Division, Department of Social Services	The Day Care and Homemaker Services Act, Newfoundland Regulation 219/82, and as amended to 979/82; Newfoundland Day Care and Preschool Licensing Requirements, Newfoundland and Labrador (1991–92).	Some funding may be available to children with special needs on a case-by-case basis through departments other than Social Services.

Province/ Territory	Regulatory Body	Title of Legislation	Special-Needs Funding
Northwest Territories	Child Day Care Section, Department of Education, Culture and Employment	An Act Respecting Child Day Care Facilities. The Child Day Care Standards and Regulations	Not available as yet (1993)
Nova Scotia	Day Care Services, Family and Children's Services, Department of Community Services	Day Care Act and Regulations, Chapter 6, 1980	Differential subsidy grants to licensed full-time nonprofit centres enrolling children with special needs
Ontario	Ministry of Community and Social Services, Child Care Branch	The Day Nurseries Act, Revised Statutes, 1990; Ontario Regulation 262, 1990	Grants may be available for child-care programs/services for children with special needs who require individual program plans
Prince Edward Island	Early Childhood Services Division of Special Services, Department of Health and Social Services	The Child Care Facilities Act, 1988, Prince Edward Island Child Care Facilities Regulations, 1988	Funding may be available to encourage integration and individual programming for children with special needs
Quebec	L'Office des Services de Garde à l'Enfance	An Act Respecting Child Day Care as amended June 1992; Quebec Regulation Respecting Child Care Centres 411, R2	Subsidy grants for children with special needs in licensed integrated child-care programs
Saskatchewan	Child Day Care Division, Department of Social Services	The Child Care Act 1990, Saskatchewan Child Care Regulations 1990	Includes grants for programs serving children with special needs in integrated settings
Yukon	Child Care Services Unit, Department of Health and Social Services	Child Care Act 1990; Family Day-Home Regulations and Day Care Centre Regulations 1990	A funding formula is used to reflect additional costs when serving children with special needs

Source: Authors, 1993.

Differences also exist across provinces with respect to the age at which each provincial ministry of education assumes responsibility for service to students with exceptionalities. For example, in Ontario, children who are hearing impaired are eligible from 2 years of age for special education services at no extra cost, even though they are much younger than the age at which other children enter the public education system (Council of Ministers of Education 1989).

THE IMPACT OF U.S. LEGISLATION ON CANADA

In contrast to Canada, in the United States the provision of services to young children with special needs is required by federal legislation. Many of the service components required under the U.S. legislation and the extensive research used in the development of program resources and strategies have significantly influenced the services and program practices across Canada. The Portage Guide to Early Education is an early example of the many U.S. resources now widely used in Canada. More recent programs such as the Brigance Diagnostic Inventories, which enable ongoing record keeping of children's development, are also now widely used. (See Appendix A for a list of assessments and program guides.)

The following is a brief overview of major U.S. legislation that has directly influenced the resources and services available to young Canadian children with special needs and to their families.

Handicapped Children's Early Education Assistance Act (PL 90–538)

This 1968 law, most often referred to by its initials, HCEEAA, focuses exclusively on the very young. Its major purpose is to improve early intervention services for children with disabilities, at-risk children, and their families. Federal funds supported experimental centres known as the First Chance Network. These centres continue to demonstrate new and better approaches to early educational practices for children with developmental problems.

Head Start Amendments (PL 92–424)

Amendments related to children with disabilities were attached to Head Start legislation in 1972. Head Start's tradition had always been an "open door" policy: all children, regardless of their developmental status, were to be included in Head Start programs (Photo 3–4). The new law, however, required that 10 percent of Head Start's enrollment be reserved for children with developmental disabilities.

PHOTO 3–4 *Bettye Caldwell has been a prime figure in Head Start since its earliest planning days.*

In 1974, the term handicapped was redefined specifically so as to ensure serving children who were more severely disabled.

In 1990, Head Start was reauthorized at its highest funding level ever through the Child Care and Development Block Grant. This legislative activity endorses recognition of the benefits of providing early education and intervention services for young children. It also points up the need for greatly expanded numbers of early childhood personnel trained to provide the services that have been authorized.

Developmental Disabilities Act (DDA) (PL 93–112)

Another set of rulings related to handicapping conditions was originally authorized in the Rehabilitation Act of 1973. Section 504 focused on reducing discrimination against individuals with disabilities. This law, updated in 1992 as the Developmental Disabilities Act, required that everyone with a disability be given access to jobs, education, housing, and public buildings. This law also ruled that states offering preschool services to nondisabled children must offer comparable services to those with disabilities.

Education for All Handicapped Children Act (PL 94–142)

This legislation was signed into law in 1975. Its popular title is the Bill of Rights for Handicapped Children. It guaranteed (for the first time in U.S. history) all children and youth, regardless of the severity of their disability, the right to a free and appropriate public education. Among other things, the law gives specific support to early education programs for children under 5 years of age. Special funds, called incentive monies, are authorized to encourage states to locate and serve preschool-age children in need of early intervention services.

In addition to the early intervention component, PL 94–142 has a number of rulings that apply to all children with developmental disabilities. These are summarized as follows:

ZERO REJECT.

Local school systems must provide all children, regardless of the severity of their disabilities, with a free education appropriate to each child's unique needs.

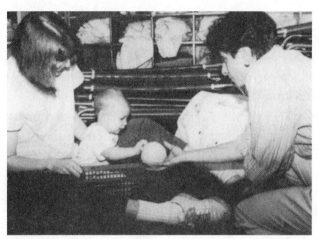

PHOTO 3–5 *The U.S. public law clearly recognizes the importance of parent contributions to the child's progress.*

(Though there is no federal legislation, similar education legislation exists in a number of Canadian provinces.)

NONDISCRIMINATORY EVALUATION. No child may be placed in a special education program without full individual testing. The tests must be nondiscriminatory—that is, appropriate to the child's language and cultural background.

INDIVIDUALIZED EDUCATIONAL PROGRAM (IEP). Every child is to have an IEP tailored to meet his or her unique needs.

LEAST RESTRICTIVE ENVIRONMENT: MAINSTREAMING. To the greatest extent possible, children with a handicapping condition will be educated with nonhandicapped children.

DUE PROCESS. A legal procedure enabling parents to call a special hearing when they do not agree with the process further ensures that a child cannot be removed from a classroom simply because of annoying or inconvenient behaviour.

PARENT PARTICIPATION. PL 94–142 recognized the importance of parents' contributions to their child's progress (Photo 3–5).

Education of the Handicapped Amendments (PL 99–457)

In 1986 the U.S. Congress passed amendments to PL 94–142 that became the most comprehensive legislation ever enacted on behalf of infants and young children. PL 99-457 has several parts or "titles"; only those that focus on the very young, Title I and Title II, will be discussed here.

TITLE I: HANDICAPPED INFANTS AND TODDLERS. Often referred to as Part H, this part of the law is discretionary. This means that a state may serve children from birth through 2 years of age if it chooses, but it is not required by law to do so. (An exception is that any state serving non-disabled infants and toddlers must serve infants and toddlers with disabilities.)

- Individuals to be served: Infants and toddlers who are experiencing developmental delays or are at risk of having substantial delays unless they receive early intervention services.

- Labelling no longer required: Very young children no longer need to be labelled as having a particular kind of disability.

- Individualized Family Service Plan (IFSP): Each infant and toddler and his or her family must receive a multidisciplinary, written assessment of their needs and of the services prescribed. This service will be provided by a team of qualified personnel that includes special educators, speech and language pathologists and audiologists, occupational and physical therapists, social workers, nutritionists, and professionals from other disciplines as deemed necessary. Services will be coordinated by a case manager assigned specifically to each case. One purpose of the case manager is to make sure the family has a part in planning the child's IEP; another is to help the family obtain and coordinate services that ensure identified needs are being met.

TITLE II: HANDICAPPED CHILDREN—AGES 3 TO 5.

Services for 3- , 4- , and 5-year-olds remain much as they were under PL 94-142. Title II of PL 99-457 is now mandatory. States receiving federal funds for early intervention programs must serve young children with developmental disabilities according to the same formula and requirements as before. Furthermore, parent-support services are allowable as "related services."

AMERICANS WITH DISABILITIES ACT (PL 101–336).

In 1990 the Americans with Disabilities Act (ADA) was passed into law. The ADA gives civil rights protection to individuals in private employment, all public services and accommodations, transportation, and telecommunications. For early childhood education, some of the most significant implications are in the area of access to child care and community recreation programs.

INDIVIDUALS WITH DISABILITIES EDUCATION ACT (PL 101–176).

The Individuals with Disabilities Education Act (IDEA) amended and changed the name of the EHA in 1990. This amendment also changed the emphasis of the program from providing segregated programs for specific conditions to providing support to individuals with disabilities in community settings.

NATIONAL HEALTH CARE AND PREVENTION IN CANADA

Although people criticize the lack of child-care legislation and educational legislation at the federal level in Canada, it is to the credit of the federal government

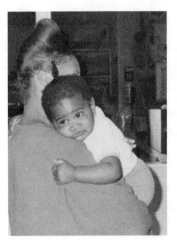

PHOTO 3–6 *Support services for infants may be provided through health or social services programs.*

that a national health care system was introduced for all Canadians in 1966. Legislation known as the Medical Care Act offered medical care whose cost was shared between the federal and provincial governments. Services provided specifically for children included childhood immunization at the request of the child's parents. With this legislation came an increase in the provision of screening and assessment services for children (including those with special needs) at hospitals and health centres in major Canadian cities. Procedures such as amniocentesis and other pregnancy-related health care services became more readily available. Although a variety of funding mechanisms now exist for the provision of health care from province to province, every family is entitled to receive medical assistance and care.

Efforts have been made to establish and implement local prevention programs that encourage families to use the local health services and centres. Therefore, assistance such as support services for infants may be provided through either provincial health or social service legislation (Photo 3–6). The source of funding, whether from the Ministry of Health or the Ministry of Social Services, influences the model of service delivery (medical vs. social services) and the required educational background of the service providers (for example, nurse, early childhood educator, therapist, etc.).

THE PUSH FOR FEDERAL CHILD-CARE LEGISLATION IN CANADA

During the 1980s and into the 1990s, the provinces and territories have continued to struggle to develop sufficient child-care services to meet the needs of a growing population of young children and their families. Many young families have emigrated from other countries to Canada and may need more initial support. Federal and provincial agencies and many advocacy groups representing both parent users and professional staff have come together to demand that the federal government enact specific child-care legislation. This legislation is needed to address universal concerns such as quality of child care, accessibility of care, staff training, affordability, and the full inclusion of children with special needs in child-care centres.

Organizations that have Canada-wide representation through provincial and local chapters and are actively involved in advocating for these concerns include

PHOTO 3–7 *The Canadian Association for Community Living has strongly advocated inclusion of children with intellectual impairments in early childhood/educational programs.*

the Canadian Child Care Federation, the Canadian Association for Young Children, Canadian Rehabilitation Council for the Disabled, and the Canadian Day Care Advocacy Association. Other associations with broad membership such as the Canadian Council for Exceptional Children and the Canadian Association for Community Living (formerly the Canadian Association for the Mentally Retarded) are also working on behalf of children with special needs (Photo 3–7).

Several detailed reports such as the Celdic Report (Robert et al., 1970) have confirmed that existing services do not meet the needs of many young children, including those with special needs. Therefore, the Canadian goal is to have inclusive legislation that would give support to all children within child-care programs rather than, as is currently true in the United States, having separate legislation for children with special needs.

In the *Report of the Task Force on Child Care*, Katie Cooke states that "Child Care centres need to adopt a philosophy and policy of integration and make efforts to secure financial and professional support to transform their policies into workable programs" (Status of Women in Canada 1986, 89). Furthermore, "governments that design and fund programs must be cognizant of the needs of the disabled and give priority to their special needs in the design of programs" (89). In this same publication, the Canadian Rehabilitation Council for the Disabled indicates that, although it is a prosperous country, Canada is failing children with disabilities through the lack of essential child-care services (88). The same report confirms the need to provide financial and professional support to assist integrated child-care centres (89).

It was a great disappointment to child-care advocates that Canadian Bill C-144, the federal Child Care Act proposal of July 1988 based on the Cooke report, failed to become law as a result of a change of government in that year.

Perhaps the most hopeful occurrence in recent years was that in January 1990 the Canadian government signed the United Nations Convention on the

Rights of the Child. This has been interpreted as a sign that the federal government continues to be committed to recognizing the rights of all children (Castelle 1990, 22), including children with special needs. Additional signs of federal support for young children and their families are noted in funding initiatives such as the Child Care Initiative Fund (1988) and the Community Action Program for Children (Brighter Futures 1993).*

SUMMARY

Intervention in the form of early childhood programs has become a popular approach to reducing both the number and severity of developmental problems. In the United States, a number of federal laws have been passed that support the identification, prevention, and treatment of developmental problems in young children. U.S. federal legislation, specifically PL 94–142 and PL 99–457, has influenced the delivery and program approaches used across Canada in working with and caring for young children with special needs. Though there is no comparable federal legislation in Canada, a parallel development has occurred through the inclusion of children with special needs within provincial and territorial educational and child-care legislation.

The British North America Act established a structure whereby each province would be responsible for developing its own childcare and educational legislation. This included responsibility for services for children with special needs. Through the Canada Assistance Plan Act, provinces entered into cost-sharing agreements with the federal government for child-care services. The Medical Care Act ensured health care for all Canadians, supporting the prevention and treatment of developmental disabilities. The above legislation was cancelled in March, 1996 and was replaced by the Canada Health and Social Transfer Act, 1996. Through this legislation the federal government has transferred responsibility for health and welfare to the provinces and territories, along with a guaranteed, but shrinking, annual monetary contribution.

---

* For a list of CCIF publications on children with special needs, contact the National Child Care Information Centre, Social Services Program Branch, Ottawa, Ontario, K1A 1B5.

STUDENT ACTIVITIES

1. Write to the early childhood branch of your provincial or territorial department of education or social services and ask how you might obtain information regarding early childhood education programs for children with special needs in your area.

2. Locate the office of a local advocacy group and arrange to talk to the person working on behalf of children with disabilities about his or her work and the challenges it presents.

3. Choose one piece of legislation mentioned in this unit. Do a detailed research-oriented report on the history and current status of the legislation.

4. Obtain and study a copy of the proposed federal Child Care Act of 1988 (Bill C-144) and decide whether or not it deserved to be passed into law. Give reasons.

5. Form several small groups. Have each group select one of the pieces of legislation described in this unit or describe legislation that the group feels should be enacted. See if you can successfully advocate for this law: convince others in the class that this law should be enacted.

REFERENCES

Castelle, K. 1990 *Children Have Rights Too! A Primer on the U.N. Convention on the Rights of the Child*. Defense for Children International, First Canadian Edition.

Childcare Resource and Research Unit 1993 "Child Care Information Sheets: The Provinces and Territories." Childcare Resource and Research Unit, Centre for Urban and Community Studies, University of Toronto.

Council of Ministers of Education 1989 "Special Education Information Sharing Project: Summary of Responses." Ottawa, Ontario.

Health and Welfare Canada 1986 *Status of Day Care in Canada*. Ottawa: Health and Welfare Canada.

MacKay, A.W. 1987 "The Charter of Rights and Special Education: Blessing or Curse?" *Canadian Journal for Exceptional Children* 3, no. 4: 118–27.

Roberts, C.A., et al. 1970 One Million Children—The Celdic Report, a National Study of Canadian Children with Emotional and Learning Disorders. Crainford, Toronto, Ontario.

Sobsey, D. 1985 "Educational Services: Canada, the United States and Oz." *Canadian Journal for Exceptional Children* 1, no. 4: 126–29.

Stapleford, E.M. 1976 *History of the Day Nurseries Branch—A Personal Record.* Toronto: Ministry of Community and Social Services, Ontario.

Status of Day Care in Canada 1990 Health & Welfare Canada, Ottawa.

Status of Women in Canada 1986 *Report of the Task Force on Child Care.* Ottawa: Minister of Supply and Services Canada.

section III

DEVELOPMENTAL DIFFERENCES

CHAPTER 4

Developmental Disabilities: Causes and Characteristics

OBJECTIVES

After studying the material in this chapter, the student will be able to

- specify underlying causes of developmental problems and give examples
- discuss the correlation between poverty and developmental disabilities in young children
- discuss the arguments both for and against labelling young children as having a particular disability, and support each argument with examples
- explain why it is especially inappropriate to label a young child as mentally retarded or emotionally disturbed
- identify the major categories of disabling conditions that are likely to affect the development of the young child

INTRODUCTION

Determining the cause of a disabling condition is a complex process. Classifying a young child with developmental problems is especially complex, particularly when trying to assign the child to a particular disability category. Both processes are subject to differences of opinion because of problems similar to those discussed in Chapter 2. These include

- individual differences in children;
- differences in knowledge among the professionals; and
- differences in public policy.

Confusion can result, regardless of the child under consideration, whether severely or moderately impaired, or even exceptionally bright. Consider the following examples of questions that might arise when you attempt to determine the cause of exceptionality in a child:

1. Two 3-year-old boys display hearing impairments: one is talking well, the other not talking at all. Why?
   - Do they have different kinds of hearing losses?
   - Has one child had more frequent or more severe ear infections?
   - Is one child in a better early childhood program?
   - Do cultural and family differences account for the developmental differences?

2. An educator is assigned a group of exceptionally bright young children. What accounts for their special abilities?
   - Are they programmed that way genetically?
   - Have they had earlier and better preschool experiences?
   - Have their parents been reading to them and taking them to the library regularly and frequently?

3. What accounts for performance differences among school-age children with high IQ scores? Most of these children do well in school; some do poorly. Why?

Questions such as these are common among child developmentalists, clinicians, and educators. Though the issues are not new, there are no ready answers. The best response, so far, is that the causes of developmental differences appear to be a combination of factors: heredity, biology (physical makeup), temperament (personality style), and a long list of environmental factors that interact in complex ways.

As noted in Chapter 2, the range of both normalcy and individual differences is broad. Furthermore, all children develop at slightly different rates, excelling more quickly in some areas of development than others. It is important to observe children fully and refer them for professional assessments before jumping to the conclusion that an observed deviation from normal growth and development is serious and/or permanent. One thing is certain: more harm than good comes from prematurely labelling a child.

In spite of the difficulties associated with specifying the cause of and assigning categories to developmental problems, some guidelines are available. Practical knowledge about the causes of developmental irregularities is accumulating rapidly. In addition, classification systems have been designed that can be used under prescribed conditions with some types of infants and young children. These issues—causes and classifications—are the focus of this chapter.

CAUSES OF DEVELOPMENTAL DIFFERENCES

Whatever the cause of a developmental disability, the damage can occur at any stage of development: before the child is born (**prenatally**), during the birth process (**perinatally**), or any time following birth (**postnatally**). Any condition present at the time of birth is referred to as congenital. Congenital problems may or may not be genetically related. Deafness, for example, may have been caused in one child by an infection the mother had during early pregnancy. In another child it may be genetically linked to parents who are deaf. Some disabilities can be recognized at birth; others may not be detected or do not manifest until much later. Generally speaking, the more severe the disability, the earlier it is recognized. Exceptions are many, however. A serious hearing loss may not be identified until the child enters group care.

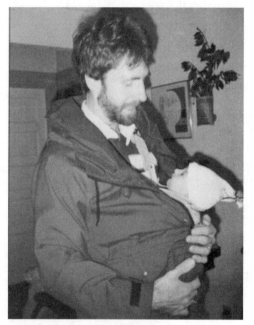

PHOTO 4–1 *A healthy infant "hooks" parents into responding.*

Biology and environment act together to produce both atypical and normal development. It is nearly impossible to isolate one or the other as the single cause of a developmental problem. In every instance, environmental factors act on a child's biological foundation, influencing the developmental outcome. Furthermore, children themselves exert an influence on the environment. A healthy infant, as we shall see, "hooks" parents into responding (Photo 4–1). Strong, early bonding is the usual result. An ill, low birthweight infant may have little or no energy to expend on any activity and so the outcome may be less positive. These complex interactions and transactions, with the child as the pivot point, need to be kept in mind in the discussions that follow.

BIOLOGICAL FACTORS

Biology plays a major role in determining both healthy and less-than-healthy development. **Biological insult** is a term that describes interference with or damage to an individual's physical structure or functioning. The biological insult, as we shall see, may occur at the time of conception, during pregnancy (often within the first trimester, because of health problems in the mother), during the birth process (from complications such as the umbilical cord becoming wrapped around the baby's neck), or following birth (respiratory distress, viral infections, and so on). All of these, singly or in combination, together with environmental factors can lead to developmental disabilities.

Chromosomal Disorders

The genetic makeup of every individual is determined at the moment of conception. Each parent contributes 23 chromosomes on which there are thousands of genes. In a process called cell division (involving two processes, **meiosis** and **mitosis**), the chromosomes from each parent divide and recombine. Physical characteristics such as size, body build, eye and skin colour, sex, and even the shape of the nose are determined at that moment. Genetically determined abnormalities also are programmed at this time.

Various syndromes are a major class of genetic abnormalities. The term *syndrome* refers to a grouping of characteristics, sometimes called **stigmata**. These stigmata, several of them occurring together, can be seen in all individuals with a similar chromosomal error. In many instances, children with a given syndrome have similar physical characteristics, which may make them look somewhat alike.

PHOTO 4–2 *The most readily recognized chromosomal disorder is Down syndrome.*

Down syndrome. The most readily recognized chromosomal disorder is Down syndrome (Photo 4–2). It occurs approximately once in every 900 births, with the risk higher among young teenage mothers and women over 45. The cause (oversimplified) is an addition to the 21st chromosome pair (hence the term trisomy 21). In about one-third of cases, the problem originates in the sperm of the father (Bee 1989, 88).

Children with Down syndrome often are easy to identify because of the following physical characteristics:
- small, round head, with face that appears somewhat flattened
- bridge of the nose is low
- low-set ears, unusually shaped earlobes
- protruding tongue due to poor muscle tone
- short fingers and toes with little fingers and little toes curving inward
- simian crease: a single, almost straight line across the upper part of one or both palms, instead of the usual pair of parallel lines

- curving folds of skin at the inner corners of the eyes, which give an almond shape to the eyes[1]

About 50 percent of children with Down syndrome have heart defects. Hearing impairments and severe cases of ear infections such as otitis media also are common, as is some degree of cognitive delay, ranging from mild to severe.

Fragile X syndrome. Fragile X syndrome is caused by a marker on the X chromosome. The consequences of this are cognitive deficiencies varying from mild to severe, repetitive speech, and autistic-like behaviours.

Metabolic Disorders

In addition to the many syndromes, other genetically associated disorders have been identified (Photo 4–3). Frequently, these are problems of metabolism—that is, interference in one or more of the complex physical and chemical activities that both create and destroy living cells. Various types of errors are possible. Two of the more common genetically related metabolic disorders are PKU and galactosemia. These are described as follows:

PHOTO 4–3 *Metabolic disorders account for some developmental irregularities.*

- **PKU (phenylketonuria)** occurs in infants born without the liver **enzymes** needed to digest the **amino acid** known as **phenylalanine**. As a result, toxic (poisonous) materials build up, leading to irreversible brain damage. Today, blood tests are available and all newborns should be routinely screened for this disorder. If placed immediately on a highly restricted diet, the child usually is saved from serious intellectual impairment. The diet, low in phenylalanine (milk and many other common foods are excluded), must be continued during most of the child's developmental years (Crain 1984).

---

[1] It was this characteristic that led, at one time, to these children being called Mongoloid, a demeaning term that should never be used in describing individuals with Down syndrome. Point of interest: The characteristic folds of skin at the corners of the eyes of individuals with Down syndrome are typical of one stage of prenatal development in all children, regardless of race.

- **Galactosemia** is a metabolic disorder in which milk cannot be digested. Infants with galactosemia tend to appear normal at birth. The moment milk is introduced, vomiting, diarrhea, and enlargement of the liver begin. Without treatment, death usually occurs within the first months of life. Should the infant live, intellectual impairment is inescapable. Again, the problems can be avoided with screening of the newborn. If milk intolerance is detected in the early days of life, a special diet, started immediately, will prevent intellectual impairment.

Sex-Linked Anomalies

A number of diseases are due to sex-linked genetic factors. These include both metabolic disorders and blood composition abnormalities such as:

- **Tay-Sachs disease**—a rapid degeneration of the nervous system from birth on, with death occurring around 3 or 4 years of age. The cause seems to be ineffective metabolism of fats, leading to fatty accumulations in the brain that interfere with critical neurological processes. The disease is most common among children of Eastern European Jewish descent.
- **Cystic fibrosis**—a damaging buildup of mucus in the lungs and digestive system. It is a fatal disease, though children who receive adequate medical care and pulmonary therapy often live into their thirties.
- **Sickle-cell disease**—a disease of the blood that can result in death. The symptoms are severe anemia, painful joints, leg ulcers, and heightened susceptibility to infection. The disease is found mostly among black Americans.
- **Muscular dystrophy**—a fatal disease found almost entirely in boys in which the muscles literally waste away. The most common type is Duchenne's.
- **Fragile X syndrome**—both boys and girls can have Fragile X syndrome, but boys are likely to be more seriously impaired physically, mentally, and behaviourally. An estimated 5 to 7 percent of mental retardation among males may be due to Fragile X syndrome (Zigler and Hodapp 1991); Ho, Glahn, and Ho (1988) suggest it is the second leading genetic cause of retardation, with Down syndrome first.

PRENATAL CONDITIONS, INFECTIONS, AND INTOXICANTS

Most developmental abnormalities, especially those that occur prenatally, cannot be explained by genetics. Less than 3 percent of all birth defects are thought to be purely genetic in origin. Factors that have a negative effect on a mother's health during pregnancy are responsible for 25 percent or more of all developmental deviations. A few of the conditions and infections that can occur **in utero** are listed here:

- **Rubella** (German or three-day measles) can have a devastating effect on the fetus (unborn infant). If contracted during the first trimester, rubella can lead to severe and lifelong disabilities.

- **CMV virus** (cytomegalic inclusion disease), contracted by the mother through intimate contact, is a frequent cause of severe damage to infants. Often the pregnant woman has no symptoms. Ninety percent of infants with CMV are asymptomatic at birth; that is, they show no problems. It is only later that intellectual impairment, deafness, diseases of the eyes, and other disabilities begin to show up.

- **Herpes Simplex** is an incurable disease. Even when it is in **remission**, a woman can pass it on to her unborn infant. Results can be devastating, even fatal, as in cases of inflammation of the infant's brain and spinal cord. Less damaging results include periodic attacks of genital sores.

- **AIDS** (acquired immune deficiency syndrome) interferes with the body's ability to ward off diseases such as respiratory disorders and certain types of cancer. Transmission of AIDS is through various kinds of sexual activities, shared hypodermic needles, and transfusions of contaminated blood. A high probability exists that an infected mother will give birth to an infected infant.[2]

- **Diabetes** in the mother puts the infant at high risk for serious developmental problems, even death. True, today's diabetic woman has a better chance of bearing a healthy baby because of medical advances. Nevertheless, maternal diabetes must be monitored throughout pregnancy.

- **Toxemia**, a frequent complication of pregnancy, produces a variety of symptoms: swelling of the mother's arms and legs, poorly functioning kidneys, and high blood pressure. Women with toxemia often deliver babies who are premature or of low birthweight, and at medical risk.

- **Drugs, alcohol, and other chemical substances** used by the mother for medicinal purposes or as "recreational" substances (for example, crack cocaine, alcohol, and some prescription drugs) often result in serious abnormalities in the unborn infant. These range from deformed arms and legs to mild to severe intellectual impairment. Estimates for the United States "run as high as 375 000 newborns a year who are born hooked due to maternal drug use" (Bliley 1989). Similar problems can be the result of alcohol intake during pregnancy. Children born of these mothers often are described as

---

[2]Knowledge of AIDS is expanding rapidly. The reader is encouraged to check with local organizations for the most up-to-date findings.

having **Fetal Alcohol Syndrome (FAS) and Fetal Alcohol Effect (FAE)**. In addition to some degree of intellectual impairment, the physical abnormalities associated with FAS include small head, droopy eyes, wide space between nose and upper lip, the occasional cleft palate, and heart problems (Schultz 1983).

Years of research by Streissguth and her colleagues (1990) indicate that the potential for subnormal IQ is three times greater among children whose mothers drank during pregnancy. These researchers report that even occasional "binge" drinking can be extremely damaging to the fetus. It is not yet known if there is a "safe" amount of maternal alcohol consumption. In light of such incomplete knowledge about alcohol and fetal damage, the only safe course is to refrain from drinking during pregnancy.

A number of drugs used by pregnant women for medicinal purposes also can cause serious birth defects. *Pregnant women should take no medications without consulting a physician.* This is particularly important in terms of over-the-counter drugs. As for illegal drugs—cocaine, for example, and its many variations—used during pregnancy, these can put the unborn infant at high risk for both short-term and long-range developmental problems. Many such infants are born prematurely, are very low birthweight, or are stillborn; others die of "crib death" during the first year. Many more suffer neurological damage that may not show up until years later as a serious learning disability (Keith 1989). Again, it is not known how much drug use is too much. It is known, however, that "even a single hit can have a devastating effect at any time during pregnancy. In some cases, it appears to cause a stroke in the fetus resulting in partial paralysis" (Bee 1992, 73). As with alcohol, the best thing a woman can do for her baby is to completely abstain from drug use.

- **Rh blood incompatibility** is a situation in which the mix of the mother's blood type and the father's causes serious problems. The mother's body may reject the fetus or the fetus's red blood cells may be destroyed. The danger of Rh incompatibility can be controlled with early medical treatment. Rarely does the problem occur with a first child.

- **Poor diet** (maternal malnutrition and protein deficiency) often results in premature and seriously low birthweight babies. These infants are at high risk for a number of developmental problems, including limited brain cell development. (Note: Many reasons other than poor nutrition also are responsible for premature and low birthweight infants.)

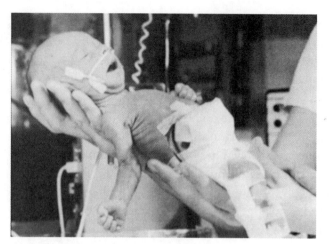

PHOTO 4–4 *Premature and low birthweight infants often are in need of intensive care.*

BIRTH COMPLICATIONS

Birth itself can result in trauma—that is, injury or shock. An infant, perfectly healthy until the moment of birth, can experience damage during the birth process. For example, **anoxia**, lack of oxygen available to the brain cells, can occur because of labour complications. Brain damage or severe neurological problems such as cerebral palsy and/or intellectual impairment may result. Recent evidence, however, indicates that a healthy newborn may be able to withstand a fairly substantial shortage of oxygen without suffering major damage. Bee (1989) suggests that when damage does occur, it may not come from a newborn's inability to breathe immediately. Instead, the failure to start breathing may have been caused by earlier, perhaps unsuspected, damage in utero. (This is one example of how difficult it is to be certain about the cause of a developmental problem.)

Premature infants, especially, are subject to another kind of trauma: hemorrhaging or bleeding into the brain. These immature newborns also are at higher risk for breathing problems, heart failure, and infections (Photo 4–4). Even less severe problems at birth can result in later trouble. It is now thought that some school-age learning disabilities may be associated with low birthweight or seemingly minor disturbances at the time of birth (Hittleman, Parekh, and Glass 1987).

COMPLICATIONS AFTER BIRTH

Following the birth process, other events can lead to developmental problems. Among these are meningitis, encephalitis, lead poisoning, and poor nutrition.

- **Meningitis.** This is a viral or bacterial infection that causes inflammation of the protective covering of the brain and the spinal cord. In newborns (when meningitis-related death is most likely), the cause usually is organisms found in the intestines or birth canal of the mother (Wolraich 1983). Risk of serious damage from contracting the meningitis virus at a later time continues up through age 5. The results of meningitis are unpredictable. Some children show no serious effects; others experience major neurological damage.

- **Encephalitis.** Encephalitis is an infection that attacks the brain itself. The symptoms are so many and so varied that the infection often is not diagnosed correctly. A range of aftereffects is possible, from no damage to identifiable neurological damage and later learning problems.

- **Lead poisoning.** Poisoning from lead ingestion can cause grave damage to young children whose bodies and nervous systems are still developing.

The Canadian Paediatric Society (1996, 781) states:

Since lead may be present in soil, air, water or food, it cannot be avoided. Levels of lead in the body which are not high enough to cause outward symptoms of lead poisoning may nevertheless be associated with developmental and behavioural abnormalities in children. Lead can certainly cause intellectual and behavioural changes in children if they are exposed to it over long periods.

The chief risk to preschool-age children is from the ingestion of lead-based paint, which can be found in older (pre–World War II) homes and buildings. If paint or plaster is peeling or chipped, it should be tested for lead content. To do so, caregivers are advised to contact the local public health agency.

Children who eat well-balanced diets are at less risk of lead poisoning than children with malnutrition or with calcium and/or iron deficiencies.

Further sources of lead cited by the Canadian Paediatric Society (793–94) include

a. lead-glazed ceramics (utensils, pots, etc., made of lead-glazed ceramics should not be used for cooking or serving food or beverages, especially acidic ones such as tomatoes, fruit juice, and so on);

b. old painted toys and furniture (Photo 4–5);

c. folk medicines;

d. cosmetics from Asia; and

e. imported earthenware toys.

PHOTO 4–5 *The lead-based paint used on this radiator would be dangerous to a young child if ingested.*

- **Poor nutrition.** Inadequate protein intake (milk, cheese, grains, eggs, fish, chicken, and meat) can result in low birthweight, illness, and higher risk of death during the baby's first year. Stunted growth throughout childhood is often another consequence. The effects of a poor diet are particularly damaging during the last trimester of pregnancy when significant maturing of the brain and nervous system is taking place. It is now recommended that a pregnant woman gain 25 to 30 pounds during pregnancy, more if she is underweight to begin with.

ENVIRONMENTAL FACTORS

Many developmental problems, regardless of when they occur—before, during, or after the birth of the baby—can be directly or indirectly related to poverty. Families living in poverty experience the highest rates of infant death, failure to thrive, and birth defects. The same holds true for subsequent developmental problems: intellectual impairment, learning disabilities, and social and emotional deviations.

The link between poverty and developmental problems cannot be denied. The reasons are many:

- Family diet tends to be nutritionally inadequate. For example, about 30 percent of women and young children living in poverty suffer from **anemia**.

- Though there is health care available for all Canadian residents, and families in poverty are eligible for health care services, they may not know how to, or be able to, obtain them. Therefore, women from these families may have more health-related complications during pregnancy, which can lead to developmental problems in their infants before, during, and following birth.

- Families tend to be larger, with more unplanned pregnancies.

- Living space is usually smaller, with fewer play materials to promote learning and language development.

- Women often are the sole support of the family. While mothers are at work (often in jobs paying the minimum wage), children are likely to be cared for in substandard and unlicensed daycare homes or centres where learning opportunities and nurturing care are limited.

"Between 1989 and 1994 the rate of child poverty in Canada climbed from 14.5 percent to 19.5 percent. Although the rate of infant mortality has decreased, children in poor neighbourhoods are still twice as likely to die as infants in non-poor neighbourhoods" (Child Poverty in Canada, Report Card, 1996). Furthermore, in their publication "The Determinants of Health," Fraser Mustard and John Frank cite the research of David Barker who notes the importance of childhood environment in determining responses (intellectual and other) throughout life (Barker 1989, 371–72).

We have known for a long time how to stop the costly and devastating effects of poverty on the development of infants and children. It was dramatically demonstrated in a study conducted 25 years ago called the Milwaukee Project. Two groups of mothers with low IQs, living in poverty, were assigned to either a control group or an experimental group. Mothers and infants in the control group received no special services. The experimental group received a variety of services: good nutrition, medical care, parent education, and stimulating infant and child care (Heber 1975). By the time the children in the experimental group were 4 years old, they were scoring significantly higher than the control group in the developmental, intellectual, and language assessments. On average, they were "exceeding the norms generally established by peer groups of the majority culture" (President's Commission on Mental Retardation 1972). Follow-up studies when the children were 9 years old indicated that the gains had held. Furthermore, and surprisingly, the entire family seemed to have profited from the program: brothers and sisters in the experimental group were scoring higher on standardized tests, and mothers were more employable and were earning substantially more money than the mothers in the control group (Heber and Garber 1975).

In the ensuing years there have been many studies taking off from Heber's pioneering work. Researchers such as Craig Ramey and his colleagues have demonstrated repeatedly that children enrolled in enriched programs gain significantly in IQ. These children also do better on achievement tests and are less likely to be held back in school. On the other hand, children in the control groups, those without an intervention program, continue to function in ways generally viewed as subnormal or retarded (Ramey, Lee, and Burchinal 1989). It also has become evident that even prenatally malnourished infants and infants with serious birth complications have benefited markedly through enrollment in stimulating infant and preschool programs, many having significantly higher IQs than similar infants reared at home by poorly educated mothers (Ramey and Ramey 1992).

In summary, there are a range of factors that may influence the development of a child. These include conditions that may result in mild to severe intellectual and/or physical impairment. Some causes of these conditions are:

- accidents (head injuries, burns, car accidents, near drowning, poisoning, etc.),
- certain viral and bacterial infections, as well as parasitic organisms, and
- conditions that occur prenatally, usually caused by problems during the first trimester, as well as some conditions that may be caused by an as yet unidentified deviation in the child's genes or chromosomes.

CLASSIFICATION OF DEVELOPMENTAL DISABILITIES

As noted earlier, disagreement has long revolved around classifying individuals with developmental problems. Should we label children who are developmentally different according to categories such as deaf, blind, emotionally disturbed, and intellectually impaired? Those in favour of categorizing argue that it is necessary in order to make important decisions by asking questions such as these:

- How many individuals have a particular problem? (Is it widespread? increasing? decreasing?)

- How many teachers, clinicians, and facilities are needed to provide services for children of this category?

- What proportion of public money should be allocated to serve each of the different groups of developmental disabilities?

- Which individuals are eligible for government financial assistance?

PHOTO 4–6 *Infants should be provided with a variety of structured and unstructured activities.*

Those opposed to labelling or categorizing argue that it can be harmful. The harm may be especially great where young children are concerned. The very young may get locked into categories that are developmentally unsuitable.

Example:

At 3, Jodie was talking very little, seemed incapable of following simple directions, had few play skills. She scored low on an IQ test and was placed in a preschool for children who are intellectually impaired. It was not until age 7 that a severe hearing loss was discovered. Between 3 and 7, crucial developmental years, Jodie functioned as an intellectually impaired child. Why? Because she had been labelled as intellectually impaired and consequently had not been identified as a candidate for deaf education services; she was not receiving the stimulation needed to develop language and cognitive skills.

In the United States, there is government legislation (PL 99-457) that recognizes the potential harm of prematurely classifying children under the age of 6. For this reason, funding by categories has been discontinued in this legislation for children below age 6. Instead, the more flexible concept of *developmental disabilities* is used to cover all developmental problems. Such an approach is more in keeping with the tremendous variability of development among young children.

There is no comparable federal legislation in Canada. At this time, some provinces are developing and others are adapting legislation that provides for young children with special needs. The current direction in Canada is to focus on providing funding for all children who are experiencing developmental difficulties during their early years. However, in order to qualify for specific treatment programs and services, young children need to be assessed and in many instances categorized. It is in instances such as this that having a classification system becomes important. Classification, labelling, and categorization are also necessary in situations in which medical doctors and other professionals communicate with others in using research and sharing case information. Those doing research into various disabilities need to have a common vocabulary.

DEFINITIONS OF CATEGORIES

In spite of disagreements, categorizing does exist. A major problem is that the systems vary. The medical profession may group the disabled one way, special education programs another way, and government agencies still another.

Brief descriptions of each category are given in the following discussion. In subsequent units the impairments will be regrouped and discussed in greater detail, focusing on early identification, assessment, and intervention.

PHOTO 4–7 *Speech and language problems among children vary greatly.*

Speech and Language Disorders

Speech and language problems among young children vary greatly (Photo 4–7). It is difficult to define clearly what is and what is not a disorder because so many factors affect language development. These include the following:

- individual differences in temperament
- rate of development
- cultural expectations
- general health and well-being

Also, as noted in Chapter 2, there are a number of typical or frequently experienced irregularities that are common in the course of language development. These need not become problems unless the child is unduly pressured.

Speech and language problems are likely to accompany other developmental disorders. Children with cerebral palsy often have serious speech problems, as do children with hearing impairments and severe emotional disturbances. Whatever the cause, it is important that speech and language disorders receive attention as early as possible. Problems in this area can lead to serious disruptions in cognitive and social development. (Note: Do not confuse a language disorder with a language delay resulting from English being a child's second language. See Chapter 18.)

Learning Disabilities

Like speech disorders, learning disabilities are difficult to define satisfactorily. In the school-age child, the label is often one of exclusion—what the child is not: not intellectually impaired, not hearing impaired or visually impaired, not having identifiable neurological problems such as cerebral palsy. In spite of no observable or identifiable disabilities, these children have trouble acquiring basic academic skills.

A normal IQ is characteristic of most school-age children with learning disabilities. Nevertheless, these children have problems in learning to read or write or do arithmetic. The largest group of children characterized as learning disabled are those having trouble with reading. The problem is often referred to as **dyslexia**. Other children may have trouble learning to print and write. This may be referred to as **dysgraphia**. More than 100 different labels have been assigned to children whose learning problems baffle clinicians and educators. The labels, it should be noted, do little to help children with their learning problems.

Intellectual Impairment (Mental Retardation)

Generally speaking, it is unwise to assign the label of intellectually impaired to a young child. Children change; they are evolving. The younger the child, the more likely it is that changes will occur. The range of "normal" intellectual functioning is enormous. Furthermore, a child's family circumstances may change, health problems may clear up, the child may enter an early intervention program. Any one of these has the potential of producing dramatic change in a child's cognitive skills. Recall the remarkable increases in the abilities of the children in the Milwaukee Project. In this text, therefore, intellectual impairment will not be treated as a separate and unique category. Instead, issues related to cognitive development and mental functioning will be addressed in the chapter on cognitive skills (Chapter 19).

A formal definition of mental retardation is stated by the American Association of Mental Retardation (AAMR 1992):

Mental retardation refers to substantial limitations in present functioning. It is characterized by significantly subaverage intellectual functioning, existing concurrently with related limitations in two or more of the following applicable adaptive skill areas: communication, self-care, home living, social skills, community use, self-direction, health and safety, functional academics, leisure, and work. Mental retardation manifests before the age of 18.

This is a complicated definition that needs further defining. Let us look at each concept separately.

- *Intellectual functioning* usually refers to the score an individual gets on a **standardized IQ test** such as the Stanford-Binet or the Wechsler Intelligence Scales.

- *Significantly subaverage* is a score of 70 or below obtained by an individual on one of the standardized tests.

- *Adaptive skill areas* refers to an individual's ability to communicate verbally or nonverbally; to take care of personal needs (bathing, dressing, feeding self, toileting); and to carry out simple but basic social responsibilities expected of individuals of similar age and culture.

- *Mental retardation begins before the age of 18.* The AAMR definition is an important and much-needed advancement in social and educational policy. It changes the way we view those who in earlier times might have been placed in an institution or assigned to classes for the mentally retarded. No longer can any individual be labelled as "mentally retarded" solely on the basis of a low IQ score (Photo 4–8). Individuals who are functioning well in their home and in the community, regardless of their inability to read or write or do well on IQ tests, are not to be labelled as "mentally retarded."

PHOTO 4–8 *No longer is the diagnosis of "mental retardation" made on the basis of IQ score alone.*

Multiple Disabling Conditions

A number of children have more than one disability (Photo 4–9). It has been estimated that 20 to 50 percent of children with serious hearing deficits have additional disabilities. The same is true of children with cerebral palsy. Many of the syndromes are also characterized by several disabilities occurring together. It is not uncommon, for example, for a child with

PHOTO 4–9 *Some children may have more than one disability.*

Down syndrome to have a heart defect, respiratory problems, a marked hearing loss, and hard-to-understand speech.

The number of children with multiple disabilities is rising. Three possible reasons for the increase are these:

1. Excessive use is being made of drugs and alcohol by increasing numbers of pregnant women.

2. Many of the diseases that cause both prenatal and postnatal disabilities in infants and young children have not yet come under modern medical control. In other words, we do not yet know how to treat a number of the medical problems that occur at the same time.

3. Advanced medical practices now allow us to keep seriously damaged or very low birth-weight babies alive. A major problem is that we do not know how to cure many of the disabilities with which the children are born.

Orthopedic Impairments

Developmental problems that interfere with walking or other body movement are considered orthopedic impairments. In many instances, **orthopedic problems** and neurological problems are closely related, one example being cerebral palsy (Photo 4–10). The term *orthopedic impairments* includes

- impairments caused by **congenital anomalies** and structural deformities such as club foot, absence of a limb, or paralysis;
- impairments caused by diseases such as polio;
- **neurological** and spinal cord damage resulting in problems such as paralysis of major muscles; and
- impairments from other causes such as incidents that result in severely fractured bones, amputations, or burns.

It is commonly thought that neurological problems are evident at birth. Often the opposite is true. It may be weeks or months (even well into the first year) before the infant gives evidence of a neurological impairment. The

PHOTO 4–10 *Cerebral palsy is an example of an orthopedic disability.*

problem may become noticeable only when certain of the very early **reflexive** (primitive) **behaviours** do not drop out on schedule and so interfere with the acquisition of new and more mature responses. For example, most newborns automatically grasp a finger placed in their hand. However, unless this primitive grasp reflex disappears between 1 and 4 months of age, infants will not be able to learn to release objects at will.

Emotional Disturbance

Emotional disturbance is a label that *should not be assigned to young children.* The reasons are similar to those given earlier for avoiding the label of intellectual impairment with young children. Alternative terms for emotional disturbance (which are more appropriate, developmentally) might be *behaviour disorders* or, better yet, *behaviour problems.* The term *social adjustment problems* is also used. These terms will be used interchangeably in this text. Even so, they are used with caution. Why? One reason is that children's behaviour during the early years is heavily influenced by child-rearing practices, cultural values, and expectations of the family and community. Parents who are aggressive, for example, tend to have children who also behave aggressively (Hetherington and Martin 1979). Thus, the child's aggressiveness is perfectly "normal" in the light of the family environment.

The social and emotional characteristics of young children also are highly influenced by particular stages of development. (In times gone by, early childhood educators and pediatricians even used such terms as "The Terrible Twos" to describe the toddler's struggle for independence.) Behaviour difficulties often arise out of the frustrations a young child experiences in trying to master basic developmental skills such as learning to feed oneself, learning culturally acceptable bowel and bladder practices, and learning what to fear and what not to fear. In most cases, therefore, a child's behaviour should be judged by what is developmentally appropriate for his or her particular age range and background. The majority of behaviour problems occurring in early childhood do not carry over into adult life.

(Note: There are other developmental disorders that have symptoms that involve severe behaviour disorders. These include **pervasive developmental disorder [PDD] and attention deficit disorder [ADD].** These conditions will be discussed in Chapter 7.)

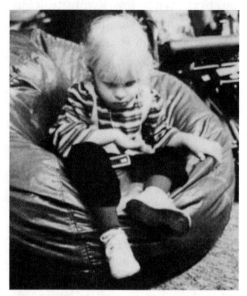

Photo 4–11 *Deafness has an impact on every aspect of a child's life.*

Deafness and Hearing Impairments

As defined by U.S. legislation (PL 94-142), the deaf are individuals whose hearing loss is so severe they cannot process spoken language, even with hearing aids or other forms of amplification. The hard-of-hearing are those whose loss has a negative effect on their education, but not to the same degree as it does on children who are deaf. Hearing impairments have a delaying effect on a young child's cognitive, social, and language development (Photo 4–11). The degree of developmental damage is determined by the severity of the hearing loss and the age of the child when the hearing problem developed.

Generally speaking, the greater the loss, the greater the disabling effects; the earlier in life the loss, the greater the developmental damage. Because of the age factor, deafness and hearing impairments often are labelled according to when the damage occurred.

- **Congenital deafness.** The individual is deaf at birth and never had the benefits of normal hearing.
- **Adventitious deafness.** The individual is born with normal hearing but loses it through injury or disease. If the loss occurs after a child has acquired some language, the developmental problems tend to be less damaging.

In fact, children who have even a short exposure to language before they lose their hearing do a great deal better in developing language skills than do children who are born deaf. Nevertheless, even a mild hearing loss can have negative effects on all aspects of development unless the child receives appropriate early intervention.

Health Impairments

Young children with severe health problems often have limited strength, vitality, and alertness. They also may experience pain and discomfort much of the time.

A normal childhood may be nearly impossible because of frequent hospitalizations or intensive medical treatment.

Health disorders take many forms:

- heart problems (weak or damaged heart)
- leukemia (cancer of the bone marrow)
- asthma (disorder of the respiratory system)
- sickle-cell disease (red blood cell malformation)
- hemophilia (a bleeding disorder)
- diabetes (faulty metabolism of sugar and starch)
- cystic fibrosis (lung and digestive problems)

Health disorders may be described as chronic or acute (although a chronic problem can go into an acute state). In either event, the child's overall development is under constant threat. True, health problems may not be the cause of other developmental disorders, yet they can create situations that lead to other problems.

Example:

A child who is physically weak and unable to run and jump and play with children of the same age may be socially isolated. Brothers and sisters may resent having to play with the child instead of their own playmates. They also may resent that so much of the parents' attention and resources seem to be focused on the sick child. This may lead to the sick child feeling lonely, rejected, anxious, guilty, and even more isolated.

Blindness and Visual Impairments

As with other problems, there is no clear-cut definition of visual impairment. A legal–medical definition proposed by the U.S. National Society for the Prevention of Blindness is currently accepted in Canada (Photo 4–12):

- *Blind.* **Visual acuity** of 20/200 or less in the better eye with the best possible correction; or a much reduced field of vision (at its widest diameter, a visual arc of 20° or less).
- *Low vision* (partially sighted). Visual acuity between 20/70 and 20/200 in the better eye with the best possible correction.

The American Foundation for the Blind offers an educational definition:

- *Blind.* Visual loss is severe enough that it is not possible to read print, requiring the child to be educated through the use of Braille and other **tactile** and **auditory** materials.
- *Low vision* (partially seeing). **Residual vision** is sufficient to allow a child to read large print or possibly regular print under special conditions and to

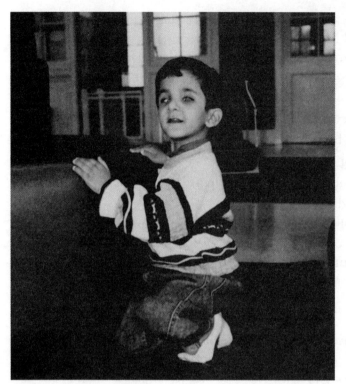

PHOTO 4–12 *Legal blindness is defined as visual acuity of 20/200 or less in the better eye after correction, or a much reduced field of vision.*

use other visual materials for educational purposes.

Total blindness, whether congenital or occurring after birth, is readily identified. The baby simply does not respond to people or objects within its range of vision. Less severe visual disorders may be more difficult to identify. Frequently, the problem does not show up until it is time to learn to read and write. By this time the child may have developed a number of other problems in trying to compensate for the undiagnosed vision loss.

Combined Deafness and Blindness

Children who are described as being both deaf and blind have a combination of vision and hearing problems so severe they require highly specialized intervention programs. Two such serious sensory deficits in combination usually result in a number of other problems in language, cognitive, and social development.

SUMMARY

Determining the cause of a developmental disability can be a difficult process. The same is true of assigning a classification of exceptionality to a young child. Both issues, cause and classification, are subject to varying definitions, depending upon professional perspective.

Biological and environmental factors, in combination, account for the preponderance of developmental problems. Biological factors include genetic disorders, diseases and infections that occur during pregnancy, and poor nutrition. Problems at the time of birth as well as diseases and infections following birth also may cause developmental damage. In young children, especially those raised in old and dilapidated housing, lead poisoning is a common problem. Poverty, in general, accounts for a large percentage of developmental problems, most of which are preventable with early intervention.

Classifying, or categorizing, children in terms of a particular disorder is a common educational and administrative practice. Most child developmentalists argue against categorizing, especially for young children, in that infants and children are changing so rapidly during the early years. Nevertheless, a classification system seems necessary from the standpoint of both informed discussion and professional training. Classifying and labelling disabilities is mainly necessary for medical professionals who must confer with colleagues, and for researchers who are studying and analyzing data.

STUDENT ACTIVITIES

1. Take a poll among the female members of your class to determine how many students are protected against rubella. Consult your public health department for information on preventing prenatal infections.

2. Discuss with your mother your own birth and that of your brothers and sisters to determine the kinds of problems, if any, that she or the infants experienced. (Feel free to carry out this activity with any woman who has given birth and is willing to discuss the issues with you.)

3. Study a copy of your province's guidelines, regulations, and/or legislation for funding services to preschool children with disabilities. Chart your findings.

4. Serve as a discussion leader: invite three or four other students to discuss, before the class, the issue of not labelling a young child as either emotionally disturbed or intellectually impaired.

5. Make a listing of the kinds of services available in your community for pregnant teenage girls; do the same for pregnant women with alcohol- or drug-related problems.

6. Mix and Match

Select the one best match for each item in column I from column II and place that letter in the appropriate space in column I.

I		II	
—	1. classifying	A.	maternal diet
—	2. mitosis	B.	lack of oxygen
—	3. amino acid	C.	difficulty in printing
—	4. rubella	D.	Stanford–Binet
—	5. first trimester	E.	early gestation
—	6. anoxia	F.	chromosome activity
—	7. dysgraphia	G.	club foot
—	8. standardized IQ test	H.	phenylalanine
—	9. low-weight babies	I.	categorizing
—	10. congenital anomaly	J.	German measles

REFERENCES

American Association of Mental Retardation (AAMR) 1992 *Mental Retardation*, 4th ed. Washington, D.C.: AAMR.

Barker, D. J. 1989 "Rise and Fall of Western Disease." *Nature*, March.

Bee, H. 1992 *The Developing Child*. New York: Holt, Rinehart & Winston.

Bliley, T.J. 1989 "Born Hooked: Confronting the Impact of Perinatal Substance Abuse." Opening statement at the hearing before the Select Committee on Children, Youth, and Families. Washington, D.C.: U.S. Government Printing Office.

Canadian Council on Social Development 1996 *Child Poverty in Canada, Report Card 1996, Campaign 2000*. Toronto, Ontario.

Canadian Paediatric Society 1996 *Well Beings: A Guide to Promote the Physical Health, Safety and Emotional Well-Being of Children in Child Care Centres and Family Day Care Homes*. Toronto: Creative Premises.

Crain, L. 1984 *Prenatal Causes of Atypical Development*. Baltimore: University Park Press.

Heber, F.R. 1978 "Sociocultural Mental Retardation—A Longitudinal Study." In D. Forgays, ed. *Primary Prevention of Psychopathology*, vol. 2. Hanover, N.H.: University Press of New England.

Heber, R., and B. Garber 1975 "The Milwaukee Project: A Study of the Use of Family Intervention to Prevent Cultural-Familial Mental Retardation." In B. Friedlander, G. Sterritt, and G. Kirk, eds. *Exceptional Infant*, vol. 3. New York: Brunner/Mazel.

Hetherington, F.M., and B. Martin 1979 "Family Interaction." In H.C. Quay and J.S. Werry, eds. *Psychopathological Disorders of Childhood*. New York: Wiley.

Hittleman, J., A. Parekh, and L. Glass 1987 "Developmental Outcome of Extremely Low Birth Weight Infants." Paper presented at the biennial meeting of the Society for Research in Child Development, Baltimore. April.

Ho, H.Z., T.J. Glahnt, and J.C. Ho 1988 "The Fragile X Syndrome." *Developmental Medicine and Child Neurology*, 30, 252–256.

Keith, L.G., S. MacGregor, S. Freidell, M. Rosner, I.J. Chasnoff, and J.J. Sciarra 1989 "Substance Abuse in Pregnant Women: Recent Experiences at the Perinatal Center for Chemical Dependence of Northwester Memorial Hospital." *Obstetrics and Gynecology* 73, 715–720.

Mustard, F., and J. Frank, 1991 "The Determinants of Health," on behalf of the Canadian Institute for Advanced Research Population Health Program, Toronto.

President's Commission on Mental Retardation 1972 *A Proposed Program for National Action to Combat Mental Retardation*. Washington, D.C.: U.S. Government Printing Office.

Ramey, C.T., M.W. Lee, and M.R. Burchinal 1989 "Developmental Plasticity and Predictability: Consequences of Ecological Change." In M.H. Bornstein, et al., eds., *Stability and Continuity in Mental Development*, 217–234. Hillsdale, N.J.: Earlbaum.

Ramey, C.T., and S.L. Ramey 1992 "Effective Early Intervention." *Mental Retardation*, 30, 337–345.

Streissguth, A.P., H.M. Barr, and P.D. Sampson 1990 "Moderate Prenatal Alcohol Exposure: Effects on Child IQ and Learning Problems at Age 7 1/2 Years." *Alcoholism: Clinical and Experimental Research*, 14, 662–669.

Wolraich, M.L. 1983 "Encephalitis and Meningitis." In J.A. Blackman, ed., *Medical Aspects of Developmental Disabilities in Children Birth to Three*. Iowa City: University of Iowa.

Zigler, E., and R.M. Hodapp 1991 "Behavioural Functioning in Individuals with Mental Retardation." *Annual Review of Psychology*, 42, 29–50.

CHAPTER 5

Sensory Impairments: Vision and Hearing

After studying the material in this chapter, the student will be able to

- discuss hearing and vision problems and their impact on the development of young children
- identify warning signs indicating an infant may have a hearing loss
- identify signs of a possible hearing loss for a child with language
- indicate some strategies useful in helping a child make the transition into an inclusive program
- describe strategies that teachers may use in preschool activities to facilitate the learning of children with visual impairments who are in an inclusive environment

INTRODUCTION

Everything that children learn about themselves and their world comes through their five senses—hearing, vision, touch, taste, and smell. In healthy newborns, the five senses are functioning from the very beginning. Every aspect of development, from the moment of birth, depends on these systems being in good working order. The most serious and most prevalent sensory problems are hearing and vision losses. Most of what infants and children are expected to learn is acquired through these two senses. A child who is both blind and deaf (also referred to as *multisensory deprived* or *MSD*) is at extreme developmental risk. These children are more difficult to include on a full-time basis in a regular early childhood program. As stated by McInnes and Treffry (1982, 7):

> The young or low-functioning MSD child must be exposed to sensory input at the level he can assimilate. As his tolerance grows, the type and strength of the stimulation will be increased until he can function in an open environment.

PHOTO 5–1 *A hearing loss almost always has an effect on language acquisition.*

The normal activity level of an early childhood program may be both confusing and frightening for these children. For successful inclusion to occur, highly specialized support services and teaching staff may be necessary.

A hearing loss almost always has an impact on language acquisition (Photo 5–1). This, in turn, often has a negative effect on cognitive functioning. Cognitive learning, after the first year and a half of age (regardless of the potential level of intelligence), is tied closely to both receptive and expressive language. As noted in earlier chapters, development of cognitive skills is nearly inseparable from development of language skills.

Children who are blind learn language with considerably less difficulty than children who are deaf (though certainly not as easily as normally developing children). Children who are blind can benefit from the many incidental learning opportunities available every day. They hear environmental sounds, footsteps, doors closing, and other sounds that, when tied to the child's concrete experiences, provide the basis for cognitive insight. All of this gives children who are blind a greater potential for academic success. Because of the far-reaching influence of language in forming and maintaining relationships, children who are blind may have more options for social learning than children who are deaf.

Infants and young children with severe hearing or vision problems require teachers and support people who are trained to meet their special needs. Sometimes this special care is first introduced in a segregated setting, and at other times in a regular early childhood centre. As noted in Chapter 1, Turnbull (1982) suggests that the relative restrictiveness of an intensive, highly specialized program may be necessary for some children in the very early years if the child is to have greater freedom in the long run. On the other hand, most early childhood educators argue that many of the developmental needs of children who are blind or deaf are the same as for all children. Children with impairments also need the experiences that are available in a good preschool program. Merit can be found in both arguments. A combination of programs as described in Chapter 10 is a good solution for many children. There is no definitive answer, however, as to what is best. In fact, what is best will vary from child to child and may be dependent on the specific environment (physical and social) of the available child-care program or programs.

DEAFNESS AND HEARING IMPAIRMENTS

As described in Chapter 4, children with hearing impairments may be classified in two ways, as deaf or as hard-of-hearing. Children who are *deaf* are those whose hearing loss is so severe that they cannot process spoken language even with hearing aids or other amplification devices. Children who are classified as *hard-of-hearing* have a lesser loss, but enough to have a definite negative effect on their social, cognitive, and language development.

Two other items from Chapter 4 should be mentioned again at the outset of this discussion. One has to do with severity: the greater the loss, the greater the interference with development. The second reminder relates to timing: the earlier in life the loss occurs, the greater the interference with development. Losses may be thought of as *prelingual* (occurring before speech and language have had a chance to develop) and *postlingual* (occurring after the onset of language). Lowenbraun and Thompson (1994) corroborate that children with a prelingual loss have greater difficulties in all areas of development throughout their growing up years. The most severe developmental damage occurs when a hearing loss is *congenital*—that is, the infant is born with little or no hearing. Generally speaking, there are fewer negative developmental consequences when the hearing loss occurs *after* the child has begun to learn language.

TYPES OF HEARING LOSS

Hearing losses are categorized in various ways, through various kinds of assessments. To ensure valid results, both screening and testing should be done by audiologists who are specially trained to work with infants and young children. The results of hearing tests usually are plotted on what is called an audiogram (Figures 5–1 and 5–2). A hearing loss is classified according to where the loss occurs:

- Problems in the outer or middle ear produce a **conductive hearing loss**.
- Problems in the inner ear **(cochlea)** or auditory nerve produce a **sensorineural hearing loss**.
- Problems in the **higher auditory cortex** produce central deafness.
- A combined loss involves one or more of the above.

In most instances, a conductive hearing loss can be corrected or greatly reduced with appropriate medical treatment. A young child with chronic ear infections such as *otitis media* may suffer a hearing loss that comes and goes a number of times in the course of a year, as the infection flares up and clears up. This is called an *intermittent* hearing loss. Once the infection is cleared up permanently, language is likely to improve.

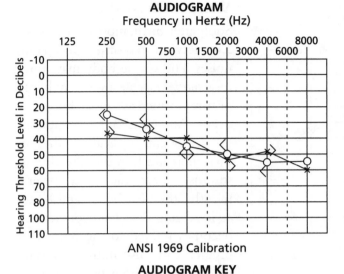

AUDIOGRAM
Frequency in Hertz (Hz)

ANSI 1969 Calibration

AUDIOGRAM KEY

AIR CONDUCTION
O Right ear (red)
× Left ear (blue)
* Free field (black)
With masking:
△ Right ear (red)
□ Left ear (blue)

BONE CONDUCTION
〈 Right ear (red)
〉 Left ear (blue)

With masking:
[Right ear (red)
] Left ear (blue)

AUDIOMETER USED _____
MASKING: _____
    TYPE _____
    AMOUNT _____
RELIABILITY_____

FIGURE 5–1 *Audiogram showing conductive hearing loss.*

Identifying an intermittent hearing loss is difficult. Many times the condition is missed entirely in routine screening tests because the child is hearing adequately and therefore responding appropriately at the time of testing. According to one clinician (Naremore 1979), more than half of the children who came through his clinic had some degree of undiagnosed hearing loss. These children had been diagnosed as having speech problems or had been categorized as learning disabled. Upon careful study of their health records, most of the children had histories of the ear infection, chronic otitis media. Yet the resulting hearing loss *had not been identified* in general screening procedures. For this reason, it is important for early childhood educators to impress upon parents the importance of consulting a pediatrician or physician any time they suspect ear infections. It should be remembered that even after an ear infection has been eliminated, residual fluid may remain, resulting in distorted hearing.

Unlike conductive hearing problems, sensorineural and central deafness do not respond readily to medical intervention. That picture is changing, however, with the coming of microsurgery and such things as **cochlea implants**. For the time being, most children with severe hearing losses are fitted with *amplification devices*, usually in the form of hearing aids. A child often wears a device in each ear.

It is important to examine hearing as early as possible, because when a child is unable to hear, models for verbal language are inaccessible and the development of speech and language is slowed down.

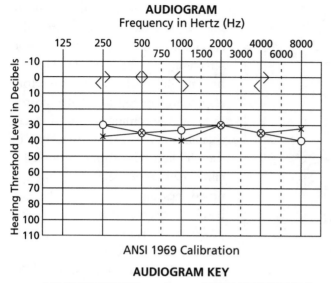

AUDIOGRAM
Frequency in Hertz (Hz)

ANSI 1969 Calibration

AUDIOGRAM KEY

AIR CONDUCTION	BONE CONDUCTION
O Right ear (red)	〈 Right ear (red)
× Left ear (blue)	〉 Left ear (blue)
* Free field (black)	
With masking:	With masking:
△ Right ear (red)	[Right ear (red)
☐ Left ear (blue)	] Left ear (blue)

AUDIOMETER USED _____
MASKING: _____
   TYPE _____
   AMOUNT _____
RELIABILITY _____

FIGURE 5–2 *Audiogram showing sensorineural loss.*

WARNING SIGNS

Soon after birth, most infants make a variety of responses to various noises. The whole body may move in a *startle response*, eyes may blink, or a rapid increase in sucking may occur. At about 3 to 4 months, infants begin to *localize*—that is, turn their heads in the direction of sounds. Over the next several months, they get better and better at localizing. Early use of hearing becomes refined to the point that infants can discriminate among voices and indicate preference for their mother's voice, as contrasted to that of a stranger.

When infants do not make such responses, hearing loss is a definite possibility. On the other hand, all infants make so many random movements that the infant who is hearing impaired may be difficult to identify. Furthermore, if the infant has some **residual hearing**, the loss may be all the more difficult to identify. This infant may be hearing just enough to be able to respond appropriately *some of the time*, and so give the appearance of normal hearing. Another complication is that even infants who are profoundly deaf babble, at least for a while. Nevertheless, parents are usually the first to sense that *something* is wrong. Horton (1976) reported that the majority of the mothers of children who were hearing impaired that she studied had expressed concern before their child's first birthday. Even so, only in a few of these cases had the physician pinpointed the problem.

Infant caregivers and early childhood teachers are in a strategic position for noting possible hearing problems or risk conditions (Photo 5–2). Persistent ear infections, discharge from the ears, or constant poking or banging at the ears often indicate a problem. If a parent or teacher suspects a hearing loss, it should

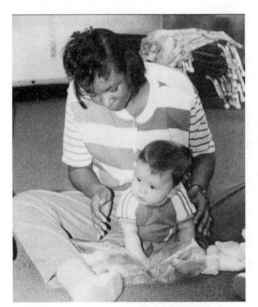

Photo 5–2 *Teacher/caregivers are in a strategic position for noting possible hearing problems.*

be checked into by a medical specialist immediately. The earlier a hearing deficit is recognized, the earlier the child can be treated and, if need be, fitted with amplification devices (hearing aids). It should be emphasized that most children with hearing impairments have some residual hearing. To maximize the use of residual hearing for future language development, it is important that intervention by a trained specialist occur as early as possible. Remember, it is only when the child begins to hear, or to learn to use whatever residual hearing he or she has, that speech will begin to develop.

Children with a conductive hearing loss may drop certain initial consonants (the ones that are described as voiceless: p, h, s, f). They simply do not hear these sounds and so they do not reproduce them. With sensorineural hearing loss, a marked delay in speech and language development is a major warning sign.

With children who have acquired some language, teachers need to be alert to a child who displays these behaviours:

- does not respond when spoken to
- does not understand, or looks puzzled when addressed directly with a simple question or request
- cocks his or her head to one side, studies the speaker's face, or watches the speaker's mouth
- asks for frequent repetitions ("Huh?" "What?")
- turns one ear to the source of sound or speech
- seems overly shy, avoids children and teachers
- is inattentive
- makes inconsistent or irrelevant responses
- complains of ringing or buzzing in the ears
- has an articulation or voice quality problem
- speaks too loudly or too softly

Further signs of a potential hearing problem are shown by a child who

- has a speech delay or slow response to usual sounds
- does not participate and/or concentrate during activities based on speech (for example, story time, show-and-tell), especially if the child is not directly facing the speaker
- persistently withdraws from the other children and is moody
- has an unexplained personality change, especially during a cold or following an ear infection
- always wants the radio, TV, or record player on high volume
- pulls at his or her ear(s)

When teachers become aware of a possible problem, the first step is to confer with parents about seeking clinical help. Because any degree of hearing loss has an impact on speech and language development, early detection is extremely important. For this reason, it is also a good idea to have annual screening of every child's hearing.

AUDITORY BRAINSTEM RESPONSE (ABR)

A frequently used procedure called *auditory brainstem response* (ABR) is now being used effectively to provide an objective measure of the degree of hearing in infants and young children suspected of hearing impairment. This procedure involves placing surface electrodes on the child's forehead, as far back as the ear. It is most effective in determining high-frequency impairment. Whereas other screening devices require a child to respond to stimuli, this process, by monitoring involuntary brain activity, is independent of the child's participation and therefore extremely useful in identifying high-frequency hearing deficits in infants and preverbal children.

THE IMPACT OF HEARING LOSS

The **cumulative effects** of a severe hearing loss on children's cognitive, social, and language development are clearly evident. Many children who are deaf are educationally delayed as much as three to five years. In addition, many have significant social and behavioural problems. As children who are hearing impaired grow older, they tend to fall even farther behind due to the increasing complexity of school and community expectations.

Later developmental problems in children with impaired hearing may be related to restricted play opportunities during the early years (Photo 5–3). Play

PHOTO 5–3 *Hearing problems often restrict children's play opportunities.*

skills seem to develop quite normally up until about 2 years of age. At this point, hearing children begin to use words symbolically. They begin to attach words to play materials and activities.

Effects on Language Development

The most serious and far-reaching effect of a hearing problem is on early speech and language development. It appears that language acquisition may be tied to certain periods in a child's development (the *critical period* idea, Chapter 1). According to this theory, a child who cannot take in sounds and verbal stimulation at certain points in development may never fully master language. In any event, inadequate auditory input during early development almost always leads to serious problems in language acquisition and in speech production. Another reason for faulty early language development may be lack of responsiveness from family and teachers. Unwittingly, they may fall into the habit of not talking to the young child who has impaired hearing. It is easy to see how this happens. The child's range of responses is limited, thus providing inadequate feedback for family and friends. Consequently, the child's language skills become even more delayed.

Effects on Cognitive Development

Once the normally developing child is beyond the sensorimotor stage, cognitive skills, as mentioned at the outset, become inseparably intertwined with language skills. In turn, language skills (including the ability to communicate thoughts) continue to be inseparably related to adequate hearing. Thus, children with hearing problems often do less well than hearing children when it comes to cognitive activities. As noted earlier, many children with severe hearing problems are several grades behind in their education. Their educational retardation seldom is due to poor cognitive potential, however. Usually, the cause is the inadequate auditory input; in other words, the child has been denied a major channel for cognitive development.

Effects on Social Development

Children with hearing problems may experience a high degree of social isolation. They often begin to be left out of things, even within the family, at a very early age. True, a child with a hearing impairment may be in the room where a

PHOTO 5–4 *Someone needs to help the child who has a hearing impairment understand everyday family and school events.*

family activity is going on. Nevertheless, he or she is often unintentionally excluded, for a very simple reason: the child is not able to enter into the verbal give and take and so has no way of figuring out what is going on. Peterson (1987, 197) points out that unless someone takes responsibility for helping the child understand everyday family and school events (Photo 5–4), the child is likely to remain a passive and silent observer.

Even as they get older, many children with severe hearing deficits tend to be less mature socially. Often they have a low frustration **threshold**. This may be related to an earlier inability to make their preferences known. At times, children with hearing impairments also may seem to be uncaring and unaware of the needs and feelings of others. It is unlikely they are truly indifferent. More to the point is that they have not heard, and therefore not learned, the language of sympathizing, a language that most young children acquire almost spontaneously.

METHODS OF COMMUNICATION

With the help of a trained teacher of the deaf, children with hearing impairments, even those with severe limitations, can be taught to speak and to understand speech. In recent years, more and more infants and toddlers are being fitted with special hearing aids as soon as their impairment is identified.

Once a hearing loss is identified, the child, regardless of age, immediately should be fitted for hearing aids and/or other equipment that will maximize the use of any residual hearing. (This may also involve having the child's teachers and caregivers wear special microphones that enhance the sound the child receives through his or her hearing aid.) Speech will begin to develop spontaneously only at the point when a child hears and makes sense out of what he or she hears. It has been found that many children learn lip reading, more accurately called *speech reading*. They learn to read what another individual is saying by watching his or her face, mouth, tongue, and throat movements. Other forms of communication are also available to children who are hearing impaired. McCormick and Schiefelbusch (1990) describe the various systems as follows:

PHOTO 5–5 *Total communication is a system that combines both speech and a sign system.*

- *American Sign Language.* Ameslan (ASL) is the language of the majority of deaf people in the United States and Canada. It is a language with its own words and grammar.
- *Signed English.* This is a sign language that parallels the English language. For every word there is a sign. Word order is the same as in spoken English.
- *Finger spelling.* This system is made up of an alphabet of 26 hand-formed letters that correspond to the regular alphabet. One hand is held in front of the chest and the other hand spells out the words, letter by letter.
- *Total* or *simultaneous communication.* As the name implies, this is a system in which communication combines both speech and a sign system (Photo 5–5).
- *Informal systems.* Pantomime, gestures, and body movements are accompaniments to speech used naturally by most speakers. Amer-Ind, American Indian Hand Talk (Skelly and Schinsky 1979) is a more formalized system that nevertheless is flexible and free of grammatical complications.

Which Method?

There is a longstanding controversy concerning which system to use in teaching language to a young child. Questions include: Is there a best way? Should the child be held to oral communication exclusively and allowed to do no signing of any kind? Is a combination method, such as total communication, the most effective? The total communication approach is favoured by those who have studied families in which there are hearing impairments. It was found that the parents signed with each other and with their infants who were hearing impaired in ways characteristic of hearing parents talking to their very young children. These children with hearing impairments seemed to go through stages of language acquisition similar to those of children who were developing normally. Bee (1992) suggests:

> a combination of sign language and spoken language works well for the child and for the relationship between the child and the parent. Not only is the child

exposed to a language at the normal time, but the child and parent can communicate with each other—something that is very difficult for a hearing parent who does not sign with a deaf child (p. 324).

There is good evidence that when emphasis is placed on oral language exclusively, children who are deaf have much more difficulty developing either speech or language than do children who are taught sign language, lip reading, and oral language at the same time (Moores 1985).

The final word on the subject is likely to be that the decision about **signing**, or speaking, or combining the two must be made in conjunction with the child's parents. The preschool teacher needs to accept the parents' decision and then work with them and a specialist in hearing impairment.

EARLY INTERVENTION WITH CHILDREN WITH HEARING IMPAIRMENTS

The importance of early language stimulation and training for infants and young children who are hearing impaired cannot be overemphasized. Language deficiencies among older children with hearing impairments may be the result of failure to begin language learning activities during the infant and toddler years. The longer the delay in starting language intervention, the less likely it is the child will develop fully functional language skills. Without preventive measures, even a mild hearing loss can result in a permanent loss in language ability.

GUIDELINES FOR TEACHERS

Throughout the years, preschool teachers have worked successfully with children with hearing impairments. Effective programming usually incorporates the skills of a specially trained early childhood consultant for the hearing impaired. The specialist should assist both teachers and parents in providing children who have hearing impairments with an education tailored to their special hearing loss. The following are guidelines from these specialists for working with children with hearing impairments.

1. Sit, kneel, or bend down to the child's level to talk. Look directly at the child when you are talking or communicating with him or her. Children with hearing problems need to be talked to face to face.

2. Talk in a normal voice. Avoid a loud or strained voice and do not over-enunciate. Overenunciation makes speech reading difficult.

3. Use gestures when appropriate, but avoid overgesturing. Too many gestures interfere with the child's efforts to speech read.

4. Use brief, but complete, sentences when the child who is hearing impaired has reached that stage of language development. As with hearing children, *holophrastic* and *telegraphic* language (Chapter 17) belong to particular stages of language development.

5. At group time, seat the child directly across from the teacher. This gives the child the best possible position for speech reading.

6. Face the light when talking to a child who has a hearing impairment. The light needs to be on the speaker's face, not the child's. Glaring light in the child's eyes interferes with bringing the speaker's face and mouth into full focus.

7. To get the child's attention, gently touch or tap a child on the shoulder or hand. Always be aware of the possibility of startling a person who does not hear and therefore may not see another person approaching.

8. When talking about something in the room, point to it, touch it, hold it up. (If the teacher picks up the scissors and demonstrates the cutting task while giving the instructions, the child has a better chance of understanding what is expected.)

9. Include children who are hearing impaired in all music activities. Provide many opportunities for them to participate by
   - putting their hands on various instruments so they may feel the vibrations;
   - allowing them to play the instruments;
   - having frequent rhythmic activities such as clapping, jumping, rolling, and twirling; and
   - pairing a child with normal hearing with a child who is hearing impaired for various musical games.

10. Involve children with hearing impairments in story time. Choose books with bright, clear pictures that tell the story. Gesture when telling the story, and use facial expressions that give clues to the moods in the story.

11. Keep to a regular schedule of activities each day. To feel secure, young children, and especially children with hearing problems (who often do not pick up on environmental signals), need to know what comes next.

12. Some children with impaired hearing make strange noises. They do not hear themselves but the noises often bother other children. Teachers must find subtle ways to help these children be quiet when necessary (perhaps gently putting a finger on the child's lips, and on the teacher's, in a "sh" gesture).

13. When a **manual interpreter** is present (unusual in an early childhood setting), allow the child who is hearing impaired and the interpreter to choose the most favourable seating.

Though many of the preceding guidelines focus on the child who has a hearing impairment, the early childhood teacher should constantly be working toward full inclusion—mainly, planning for group activities that will enable the full and equal participation of *all* children. Special adaptations can and should be planned, if necessary, so that a child who has a disability can participate in group activities as fully as he or she is able.

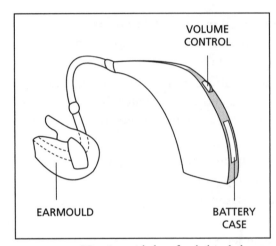

FIGURE 5–3 *Hearing aid that fits behind the ear.*

HEARING AIDS

Electronic hearing aids are a great help, especially for people with a conductive hearing loss. A hearing aid has three basic parts: a microphone, an amplifier, and a receiver (Figure 5–3). Most hearing aids are inserted into the ear canal or placed on the bone directly behind the ear.

In spite of the great benefits of hearing aids, problems occur. The fact that a child is wearing a hearing aid does not guarantee that the child is hearing. Teachers and parents need to be aware of possible minor breakdowns in the system, such as these:

- *Improperly fitting or damaged earmould.* If the **earmould** does not fit properly, it can cause irritation and discomfort. The same holds true if the earmould becomes chipped or cracked. A cracked or poorly fitted earmould also can make a squealing feedback sound, which can be extremely annoying.

- *Dead or feeble batteries.* Batteries die with amazing frequency. Teachers and parents know when batteries are dead because the child stops responding. However, batteries should be replaced well before they are dead so that children do not have to cope with periods of diminishing sound.

- *Switched-off device.* Teachers must check regularly to make sure a child's hearing aid is turned on. Young children tend to turn the devices off, sometimes repeatedly. This happens most frequently when they are first learning to wear their aid. Eventually, most children become accustomed to wearing the device and leave it turned on all the time. At this point, children can

PHOTO 5–6 *Teachers should check children's hearing aids at least once a day, more often with young children.*

begin to check its working order for themselves. Nevertheless, adults should continue to spot-check at least once a day (Photo 5–6).

- *Sore ears.* The earmould should never be inserted into a sore, cracked, or infected ear. At the first sign of irritation the child should see a health care provider.

Because so many things can go wrong with hearing aids, teachers, in conjunction with parents, should make sure that hearing aids are tested on a daily basis. They should receive special instructions from an **audiologist** on how to examine them to make sure that they are functioning properly.

BLINDNESS AND VISION IMPAIRMENTS

Children with visual disabilities tend to be classified as *blind* or as *low visioned*. For educational purposes, the American Foundation for the Blind (Chapter 4) provides the following definitions:

- **Blind.** Visual loss is severe enough so that it is not possible to read print—even with the strongest possible correction—requiring the child to be educated through the use of **Braille** (a system of raised dots that are "read" through fingertip touch) and other materials using touch or sound.

- **Partially sighted (low vision).** Residual vision is sufficient to allow a child to read large print or possibly regular print under special conditions and to use other visual materials for educational purposes.

Total blindness is the inability to distinguish between light and dark. Few children are totally blind. Most have some vision. Some can see the rough, general outlines of things, but no details. Others can distinguish light and dark or very bright colours. It should be noted that the usefulness of residual vision will be lost unless children are encouraged constantly to use whatever vision they have (Photo 5–7).

TYPES OF VISION PROBLEMS

Vision problems vary as to cause, type, and intensity. Vision problems often are grouped in terms of physiology, visual acuity, and muscular imbalances. Each of these categories will be discussed.

PHOTO 5–7 *Children should be encouraged to use their residual vision.*

Physiology

Physical problems resulting in impaired vision are fairly common. These may develop prenatally, or the damage can occur at the time of birth or any time thereafter. The cause may be diseases such as maternal rubella, inherited disorders, injury, or drugs taken by the mother during pregnancy. Even some medically prescribed drugs such as acutone (used to treat acne) may produce toxic reactions in the fetus.

Disorders that teachers are most likely to encounter include the following:

- **Cataracts.** A **progressive** clouding of the lens of one or both eyes.
- **Retinopathy of prematurity (retrolental fibroplasia).** Formation of a kind of scar tissue on the retina of one or both eyes. This is often caused by an overconcentration of oxygen administered to premature infants.
- **Glaucoma.** Gradual destruction of the optic nerve through a buildup of pressure caused by poor circulation of the fluids in the eye.
- **Retinal blastoma (cancer of the eye).** Infants may have had an eye removed in order to prevent the spread of cancer. A prosthetic eye can usually be fitted.
- **Cortical/cerebral visual impairment.** Vision loss is due to damage to the parts of the brain that receive and interpret the visual information from the eye. This type of impairment is often accompanied by other developmental disabilities.

Visual Acuity Problems

Acuity problems usually are caused by refractive errors (Figure 5–4). Simply put, refraction is the bending of light rays. When there is a malformation of the eye or certain parts of it, *refractive errors* can occur. These are the most common refractive errors:

- **Astigmatism.** A condition that often creates blurred vision.
- **Hyperopia.** Farsightedness, in which close-up objects are seen less clearly.
- **Myopia.** Nearsightedness, in which far-away objects are seen less clearly.

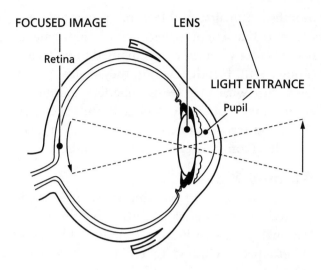

FOCUSED IMAGE   LENS

Retina

LIGHT ENTRANCE

Pupil

FIGURE 5–4 *Structure of the eye: refractory errors are common.*

Muscular Imbalances

When the major eye muscles are not working together, double vision as well as other problems may result. The following are among the most common:

- **Amblyopia.** A common term for this is lazy eye. In young children the brain may repress the image received from one eye, eventually destroying that eye's ability to function.

- **Strabismus.** People with strabismus are sometimes referred to in uncomplimentary fashion as cross-eyed or walleyed. When this condition exists, the two eyes are unable to focus together on the same image.

- **Nystagmus.** Characterized by quick, involuntary, jerky up-and-down or back-and-forth eye movements as the child tries to obtain a single image. These movements seriously interfere with the ability to see.

IDENTIFYING VISION PROBLEMS

Congenital blindness and severe low vision can be identified in the first year of life. It becomes obvious to parents that their infant does not look at them or at objects that they wave or offer to their child. Partial vision losses are more difficult to recognize. Often they go undetected until the child is in school. Even then, there are children with vision problems that are not identified until Grade 3 or 4, when the print in schoolbooks gets smaller, pictures are fewer, the print becomes more densely packed, and the children become aware that they cannot see what is being written on the blackboard.

On the other hand, many children with vision problems are first identified through routine screening tests in preschools and child-care settings. The *Snellen Illiterate E Test* for identifying visual acuity and muscle imbalance is widely used for young children, beginning at about 2 years of age. The *Denver Eye Screen Test* is an instrument that can be used with even younger children (as young as 6

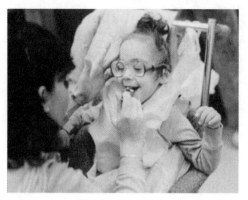

Photo 5–8 *Children with early and severe vision loss have little idea of what they are supposed to be seeing. They require guidance and support in how to explore objects.*

months). A major problem in trying to assess vision is that children with visual impairments have no idea what they are supposed to be seeing (Photo 5–8). In other words, they really do not know that what they see is imperfect and different from what others are seeing. Parents and early childhood teachers often are the first to suspect possible vision problems in young children.

Warning Signs

The following list of warning signs, or alerts, is adapted from material published by the (U.S.) National Society to Prevent Blindness. The alerts are grouped according to children's behaviour, appearance, or verbal complaints:

- rubs eyes excessively
- shuts or covers one eye
- tilts head, thrusts it forward
- has difficulty doing work or playing games that require close use of the eyes
- blinks excessively or becomes irritable when doing close work
- is unable to see distant things clearly
- squints, squeezes eyelids together, frowns
- has crossed eyes or eyes that turn outward
- has red-rimmed, encrusted, or swollen eyelids
- has inflamed, infected, or watery eyes
- has recurring sties
- has itchy, burning, or scratchy-feeling eyes
- is unable to see well
- experiences dizziness, headaches, or nausea following close work
- has blurred or double vision

If parents' and teachers' observations or a vision screening suggest a problem, the next step is for parents to get medical assistance. The best qualified consultant is a **pediatric ophthalmologist**. The ophthalmologist can arrange for the child to receive a test called *"Visual Evoked Potential."* This procedure involves placing surface electrodes on the child's scalp and then showing the child different visual patterns. This evaluation process measures involuntary brain activity and is very useful in identifying visual impairments in infants

PHOTO 5–9 *An ophthalmologist may prescribe eyeglasses for a child with vision problems.*

and young children. The ophthalmologist may also prescribe eyeglasses, medication, surgery, eye exercises, **occlusion** (covering) of one eye, or some combination of these (Photo 5–9).

A note of caution: If a screening test does not reveal a problem, but the symptoms continue, it is wise to refer a child for a medical checkup, anyway. Marotz (1983) explains that false positives can occur. This means that a child with a vision problem (or any other kind of problem) may pass the screening test. In the case of vision screening, there may have been unintended coaching by the examiner, or the child may have peeked around the occluder during testing. Test results (of all kinds) always should be regarded with caution, especially when a teacher or parent has reason to believe that a child's behaviours indicate a potential problem.

Children with severe visual impairments, especially school-age children with weak residual vision, may be referred to a low-vision clinic. The clinic can determine if the child will benefit from using magnifiers, telescopic lenses, specific electronic devices, or closed-circuit greatly magnified television. As children advance in the elementary grades, a number of other sophisticated reading and writing devices are available. (Sacks and Rosen [1994] provide interesting descriptions of many truly amazing vision-support devices.)

THE IMPACT OF VISUAL IMPAIRMENT ON DEVELOPMENT

Poor vision has a negative impact on overall development. Obviously, the more severe the visual impairment, the greater the developmental damage or delay. Much of what a young child learns comes from scanning the environment, then focusing and pondering what is going on. Learning comes, too, from watching others, imitating them, and observing what follows. Poor vision affects a child's language development, large and small motor development, and cognitive and social development. Why? Because the child's ability to interact with people, objects, and activities is seriously curtailed. For example, the child with vision problems may fail to recognize the presence of amusing events such as the kitten scampering about. Children with visual impairments may be oblivious to the consequences of their behaviour (the spilled juice staining the bedspread). They may be unable to enter into new experiences because they have no visual sense of what is going on. A card game such as Go Fish, for example, cannot be understood just by listening to it being played.

PHOTO 5–10 *Tactile exploration of the environment is essential for children with severe vision loss.*

It is likely that the inability to play freely is a great hindrance to the development of a child who has a visual impairment. When sighted babies begin deliberately reaching for and playing with nearby objects, infants who are blind remain passive. They continue to hold their hands at shoulder height, a posture typical of very young children (Fewell 1983). Not able to be visually stimulated by seeing play activities, babies with visual impairments play alone much of the time (Photo 5–10). In addition, they receive fewer invitations to play and so have fewer of the play challenges that sighted children exchange among themselves. Fewell and Kaminski (1988, 152) make the following observation about children who are blind:

> The cognitive, social, language, and adaptive skills that are acquired and practiced in the play of children as they prepare for higher order skills cannot be expected to arise from these natural childhood experiences. The facilitation of play in blind children appears to be a challenge for parents and teachers.

Effects on Language Development

After the first few months of life, language acquisition depends on discovering and identifying objects and actions. This is difficult for children who cannot see the objects and the actions. They must depend almost entirely on what can be touched or heard. This reduces their learning opportunities. Once the child with a visual impairment begins to understand how to explore objects and formulate ideas about them, language acquisition proceeds more rapidly. Nevertheless, it takes a child who is visually impaired at least a year longer to develop a full range of language skills. By school age, most are using language normally.

Effects on Cognitive Development

Children who are blind or low visioned generally lag behind sighted children in cognitive development and concept formation. For example, a sighted infant in play with adults will learn quickly that everyone has a nose. The infant who is blind will learn that they have a nose. The toddler who is blind can learn to identify his own nose and those of his parents, but may not be aware, unless taught, that all people have noses. Delays are more noticeable during the first three or four years of life. However, with adequate nurturing and early intervention, the preschool child who is blind can develop the functional skills for academic learning.

Effects on Motor Development

While a visual impairment is not the cause of delayed and imperfect motor development, it does exert a negative influence. The greater the vision loss, the greater the delays in reaching, crawling, and walking. In fact, a child who is blind does not develop the ability to localize sound and move toward it until the end of the first year (Fraiberg 1977). Many children who are blind do not walk until they are 2 years old. Motor development is further delayed by the child's inability to learn skills related to judging distance, direction, body position, and objects' positions in space. Thus, children who are blind often develop strange ways of walking and positioning themselves, because they have no visual reference points or models. It is therefore very important that children who are blind receive appropriate programming to facilitate developmentally normal body posturing and movement patterns.

Effects on Social Development

Young children with vision problems often are unable to participate in the interactions that build good social skills and interpersonal relationships. They may, because they are often focusing on listening to sounds in the environment, appear to be quiet and passive as infants. Parents, as noted earlier, must be helped to both stimulate and respond to their infant's developmentally different ways of interacting. Play skills, as mentioned above, develop more slowly in children who are visually impaired. Toys, for example, are used less creatively and play often is stereotyped because of the lack of visual models necessary for expanding the imagination. Furthermore, the young child with a visual impairment will often have more difficulty in interacting with peers because the child with a visual impairment is unable to pick up on the nonverbal cues in interactive play. For this reason, adult support in interpreting play is extremely important for the young child with a visual impairment.

INTERVENTION PROGRAMS

Early intervention programs serving infants and toddlers who are blind and visually impaired often focus on the parent as teacher. During the first year of life, as

PHOTO 5–11 *Specialists need to guide the child with a visual impairment in exploring new objects.*

with many early intervention programs for children with other special needs, programs for children with visual impairments are often home-based. A specially trained person visits the home on a regular basis. Throughout Canada, the Canadian National Institute for the Blind (CNIB) provides ongoing support to families of young children with severe visual impairments *as long as they are registered as visually impaired.* The visiting specialist provides information about the effects of vision impairment on all aspects of development and coaches parents in special techniques for interacting with their infant or toddler (Photo 5–11). The specialist also is likely to provide instructional play materials, demonstrate teaching strategies, and help parents record their child's progress.

In some areas there are intervention programs for older toddlers and preschoolers. The toddler program often includes parents. Older preschool children are likely to stay at school without a parent. Even so, parents should continue to be an integral part of their child's learning activities. Many school-aged children, depending on the severity of the vision problem and the child's progress, will be able to make the transition from a segregated early childhood or kindergarten classroom (if available) to an integrated setting. Other children, needing further specialized training, may continue in the segregated setting part-time. The remainder of the school day they participate in an integrated classroom.

Norma Kelly, Founder of the Ontario Foundation for Visually Impaired Children (1993), stated that before considering integrating a child with a visual impairment into a group setting, it is also important to determine

- the child's ability to track sounds; that is, can the child identify the teacher's voice and other voices?
- the child's level of preorientation and mobility skills; that is, can the child "map out" and travel the room safely?
- the child's comfort level and self-confidence in asking for help and questioning to seek clarification.

Many children who are blind or visually impaired learn to function perfectly well in an adequately staffed integrated program. When teachers model appropriate ways to interact with a child who is visually impaired, supporting their activity to build feelings of competence and independence, other children learn to do the same. They learn to call the child's name or touch the child's shoulder to attract his or her attention. They learn to put things directly into a child's hands, naming each object at the moment. They learn to help the child get about by describing things specifically: "Here are the lockers. Jenny's locker is the second one. You can put her truck on the bottom shelf." However, assisting a classmate who has a disability must never be a burden for the other children. Children who serve as helpers need to enjoy the job and feel special for being able to provide assistance.

GENERAL GUIDELINES FOR TEACHERS

A number of conditions causing visual problems are responsive to treatment procedures. It is important that teachers be alert to any signs that might indicate a change in a child's vision. It is the teachers' responsibility to alert parents and professionals if they note any changes.

A **resource teacher** or a specially trained consultant can help early childhood teachers arrange the classroom and develop curriculum activities that support the inclusion of a child with a visual impairment. This will ensure good learning experiences throughout the program for the child with a visual impairment (Photo 5–12). The broad goal of early education for such children is to strengthen their intact sensory channels and provide activities that require hearing, touch, taste, and smell.

The hardest part, for many adults, is to refrain from overprotecting a child who has little or no vision. Like all young children, children who are visually impaired need to explore their environment if they are to learn. In the process, they may bump into a wall, fall down, get up, start out again, have another mishap, and another, and another. To make sure the child does not come to unnecessary harm, the classroom and play yard must be kept safe and orderly. Pathways need to be clear of strewn toys and misplaced equipment that the child with a visual impairment (and the teachers and the other children) may trip over. Most importantly, children with impaired vision need to continue to be helped with their

PHOTO 5–12 *Use of trays helps to define the workspace for a child with a visual impairment.*

PHOTO 5–13 *A child with a visual impairment requires ongoing support in the development of orientation and mobility skills.*

mobility skills throughout the day (Photo 5–13). Learning to get about efficiently and safely on their own will be of prime importance throughout life. However, if furniture is to be rearranged, the child with a visual impairment should be alerted ahead of time and then physically guided over the new pathways. This enables the child to avoid the frustration of not knowing his or her way around and the embarrassment of bumping into things.

Teachers must also avoid the tendency to deny the child's right to learn self-defence and the right of possession. One way is to refrain from speaking out prematurely on behalf of the child. On many occasions, however, the teacher may need to supply the words: "Melinda, say, 'No! My eggbeater!' " Another time it may be necessary to tell the child who is visually impaired that he or she is about to lose a turn. For example: "Marcie, Violeta has been waiting for a turn on that swing. She is next. Violeta, tell Marcie, 'My turn.' " At this point, the teacher must be sure to follow through. It is important that the sighted child yield the swing, give back the eggbeater, or respond to any other reasonable request made by the child who is visually impaired.

WORKING WITH CHILDREN WHO ARE VISUALLY IMPAIRED

It is important to determine the degree of residual vision. Find out from the child's parents and the vision specialist what the child can see. Many children with visual impairments see shadows, colour, and large pictures or objects. Some children's **peripheral vision** may be their best vision; thus, a turned-away head does not necessarily signal inattention (Cook, Tessier, and Armbruster 1987).

Orientation and mobility skills should be a major initial teaching priority.

- Familiarize the child with the classroom layout and storage of materials, placing as many toys as possible on low shelves where they can be easily touched. Harrison and Crow (1993) suggest introducing the child to the room at a time when other children are not present. This allows the child to explore at his or her own pace. Depending on the individual child, this may need to occur over several days. (For further suggestions, see Harrison and Crow 1993.)

- Whenever changes occur, be sure to reorient the child.
- Put identifying material or subtle noisemakers on the floor, doors, room dividers, and lockers:
    - a wind chime near the door to the play yard
    - tile in the creative arts and sensory play areas, carpeting in the blocks area and large-group area
    - rough matting by doors to the outside
    - a patch of velveteen glued to the child's locker
    - cork or raised tape along certain walls or furniture
- Use specific words to tell the child what to do: "Put the book on the table"; or "I'm sitting by the piano. Bring your shoes to me." Avoid nonspecific phrases such as "Come here," "Put it there," "Be careful."
- Talk to the child about everything in the immediate environment. Give the names, over and over, for everyday objects such as ball, dog, cup, and brush. Naming the object is not enough. For a child who is visually impaired to understand the meaning of "watering can," for example, the child must hold one, feel what is inside, pour from it, and handle it empty and filled with water.

PHOTO 5–14 *Facilitating self-help/care skills in children with serious vision problems is a challenge for parents and teachers.*

- Give the child action words. Tell the child many times over what he or she is doing (Photo 5–14). "You are *running* in the grass." "You are *brushing* your teeth." "You are *drinking* juice."
- Help the child localize and sort out sounds. Tell the child what the classroom sounds are and where they are coming from: the guinea pig squeaking *by the window*; the faucet dripping *in the sink*; the fan whirring *up on the ceiling.* Help children learn to identify the sound of an eggbeater, the tick of a timer, the swishing of sandpaper blocks rubbing together. Play sound-guessing games. The teacher (or another child) can make the sound of one of several objects on a tray (tearing paper, closing a book, dropping a marble in a cup). The child who is visually impaired then must locate the correct object(s) by touch. To make the game challenging for sighted children, too, the teacher can turn away from the children while making the sound, or can make the sound under a cloth or in a large box open only on the teacher's side.

- Teach sounds that may signal danger in contrast to those that are simply frightening. The sound of the power mower in the playing field is something to stay away from. The drone of the vacuum cleaner signals something the child can help push. The fire alarm indicates STOP whatever is going on and stand by the door. The squeak of chains warns to stay back because the swings are in motion.

The teacher's goal should be to plan activities that involve all children, and incidentally are of specific benefit to the child with a visual impairment:

- Offer several opportunities each day to learn through smelling, touching, and tasting.
- Use actual objects, rather than plastic replicas, for teaching—for example, in a session on fruit, a real banana and orange should be used for feeling, cutting, peeling, smelling, tasting, and comparing.
- Plan cooking or baking experiences that involve measuring, smelling, tasting, touching, before-and-after cutting, mixing, and so on.
- Offer sorting activities.
- Use touch, hearing, smell, or taste to tell the difference between shapes, sizes, textures, and odours.
- Provide left-to-right training. Informal practice in working from left to right is a skill all preschool children need in preparation for reading English. The child who is visually impaired is no exception; Braille and other academic activities follow the same format. When using pegboards, for example, there can be teacher-initiated activities in which the child is encouraged to fill the board systematically by placing pegs in left-to-right and top-to-bottom progression.

Special considerations for children with visual impairments include

- using the child's name before speaking to the child, thus signalling that you are directing your statement to him or her;
- providing many physical prompts;
- making sure that teacher demonstrations take the form of subtle physical assistance and hand-over-hand guidance; and
- having the teacher guide and support the child from behind, gradually reducing assistance as the child masters the successive steps required to accomplish the task (see Chapter 20).

MANNERISMS OF CHILDREN WHO ARE BLIND

Rhythmical, seemingly purposeless mannerisms may occur almost continuously among some children who are blind, especially when they are left too long on their own (Photo 5–15). They may rock back and forth for long periods, poke their eyes, flip their hands about in front of their face, or spin around and around. These movements may be accompanied by strange noises or high-pitched squeals. It is speculated that these behaviours develop because of reduced stimulation. Lacking vision, infants receive less motivation and challenge from their environment. In turn, they do not learn to explore their environment the way sighted infants do. It is almost as if the strange behaviours were the infants' efforts to create their own stimulation and so have something to which to respond.

Whatever their causes, these behaviours can interfere with normal socializing. They make the child stand out as uncomfortably different. As teachers help children who have severe vision impairments learn appropriate play skills, the children will spend less of their developmentally valuable early learning time in

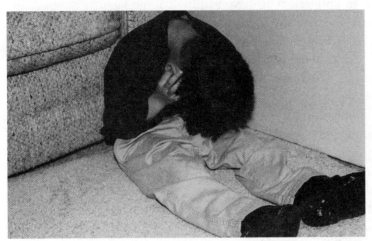

PHOTO 5–15   *Ritualistic behaviours are typical of children with severe vision loss.*

unproductive spinning, poking, and twirling. Other children can be of help, too, especially with prompts from the teacher. For example: "Come, Sarah, let's go and get Tammy and I'll pull you both in the wagon."

SUMMARY

Problems with hearing or vision greatly interfere with overall development. Infants who are blind or have an identified hearing deficit should receive early intervention services and programming in the first months of life. In fact, early intervention planning and programming should begin as soon as the condition is identified. It is important to include parents in this process. Children with vision and hearing impairments need to be educated in the most stimulating and enhancing environment possible. This may require a specialized setting, at least in the very early years, if the children are to develop basic skills necessary and prerequisite to adapting effectively to a group setting.

Hearing losses are classified in three ways: conductive hearing loss, sensorineural hearing loss, and problems originating in the higher auditory cortex. (Combined losses also occur.) The most devastating result of a severe hearing loss is interference with early speech and language development. Chronic ear infections, especially otitis media, which may come and go, are responsible for problems with both hearing and language. Infants who do not startle or blink their eyes in response to loud noises may be hearing impaired. A hearing loss may be suspected also in children who have acquired some language, especially if they ask for frequent repetitions or give a variety of other behavioural signs that they have difficulty hearing what is going on.

Specially trained teachers can teach speech to children with hearing impairments; also available are a variety of language systems, including American Sign Language (ASL). However, the long-standing controversy continues: Should the child be taught to communicate only through speech? Or should the child be allowed to use all forms of communication? Regardless of the child's special program, early childhood teachers are important agents in facilitating language development and cognitive learning in young children with hearing impairments. Part of the teacher's responsibility is to make sure each day that a young child's hearing aid is working.

Children classified as educationally blind are those who have no functional vision. For educational placement, children who are low visioned/partially sighted are those who will be able to learn through specially presented printed or other visual materials. In the preschool child, identification of a vision problem may be difficult, because screening tests cannot be relied on to identify all vision problems. Therefore, parents and teachers need to be alert to behavioural signs that a child may have a vision problem. If not identified and treated, poor vision has a negative impact on all areas of development.

Learning for children with visual impairments requires more time, more practice, more verbal mediation, and more encouragement from adults. Many early intervention programs serving infants and toddlers are home-based and focus on training parents as teachers. Young children, even those who are visually impaired, are readily accommodated in an early childhood classroom, if a specially trained consultant is available to assist the classroom teacher. It is important that teachers and parents restrain themselves from overprotecting the young child who is visually impaired. Children with vision problems need to learn how to be self-reliant in order to cope with daily challenges.

STUDENT ACTIVITIES

1. Locate a person with a hearing or vision loss (friend, schoolmate, grandparent, etc.). Talk with that person about the impact of the loss on everyday life.

2. Invite several of the above persons to come to class and demonstrate the use of their amplification or magnification devices. If appropriate, ask if members of the class might try the devices.

3. Simulate greatly impaired vision by playing blindfold games in class, such as moving about the classroom without mishap. Try moving toward one particular person based on recognizing that person's voice among several. Have several students blindfolded at one time and ask them to guess the source of sounds that you provide (closing a door, lowering a window shade, sharpening a pencil, and so on).

4. Prepare an identify-by-touch guessing game that children, both sighted and visually impaired, could enjoy together. Try it out with your classmates and have them critique it. Alter your game to include appropriate recommendations. Now try the game out with young children.

5. **Mix and Match**

   Select the one best match for each item in column I from column II and place that letter in the appropriate space in column I.

	I	II
—	1. otitis media	A. scar-tissue formation
—	2. amplification device	B. hearing aid
—	3. cochlea	C. vision screening
—	4. strabismus	D. blind at birth
—	5. American Sign Language	E. children's eye doctor
—	6. residual vision	F. crossed eyes
—	7. retinopathy of prematurity	G. partial sight
—	8. pediatric opthalmologist	H. inner ear structure
—	9. Snellen Illiterate E Test	I. may cause intermittent hearing loss
—	10. congenital blindness	J. ASL

REFERENCES

American Foundation for the Blind, 15 West 16th Street, New York, NY 10011.

Bee, H. 1992 *The Developing Child*. New York: Holt, Rinehart & Winston.

Cook, R.E., A. Tessier, and V.B. Armbruster 1987 *Adapting Early Childhood Curricula for Children with Special Needs*. Columbus, Ohio: Charles E. Merrill.

Fewell, K.K. 1983 "Working with Sensorily Impaired Children." In S.G. Garwood, ed. *Educating Young Handicapped Children*. Rockville, Md.: Aspen Systems.

Fewell, R.R., and K. Kaminski 1988 "Play Skills Development and Instruction for Young Children with Handicaps." In S.L. Odom and M.B. Karnes, eds. *Early Intervention for Infants and Children with Handicaps*. Baltimore: Paul H. Brookes.

Fraiberg, S. 1977 *Insights from the Blind*. New York: Basic Books.

Harrison, F., and M. Crow 1993 *Living and Learning with Blind Children: A Guide for Parents and Teachers of Visually Impaired Children*. Toronto: University of Toronto Press.

Horton, K.B. 1976 "Early Intervention for Hearing Impaired Infants and Young Children." In T.D. Tjossem, ed. *Intervention Strategies for High Risk Infants and Young Children*. Baltimore: University Park Press.

Kelly, N. 1993 Ontario Foundation for the Visually Impaired, Toronto. Interview.

Lowenbraun, S., and M.D. Thompson 1994 "Hearing Impairments." In N.G. Haring, L. McCormick, and T.G. Harry, eds. *Exceptional Children and Youth*. New York: Merrill.

Marotz, L.R. 1983 "The Influence of Health, Nutrition, and Safety." In E.M. Goetz and K.E. Allen, eds. *Early Childhood Education: Special Environmental, Policy, and Legal Considerations*. Rockville, Md.: Aspen Systems.

McCormick, L., and R.L. Schiefelbusch 1990 *Early Language Intervention*. Needham, MA: Allyn & Bacon.

McInnes, J.M., and J.A. Treffry 1982 *Deaf-Blind Infants and Children: A Developmental Guide*. Toronto: University of Toronto Press.

Moores, D. F. 1985 "Early Intervention Programs for Hearing Impaired Children: A Longitudinal Assessment." In K.E. Nelson, ed. *Childrens' Language*, 5, 159–196. Hillsdale, N.J.: Erlbaum.

Naremore, R.J. 1979 "Influences of Hearing Impairment on Early Language Development." In D.G. Hanson and R.S. Ulvestad, eds. *Otitis Media and Child Development: Speech, Language, and Education*. The Annals of Otology, Rhinology, and Laryngology 88: 54–63.

Peterson, N.L. 1987 *Early Intervention for Handicapped and At-Risk Children*. Denver: Love Publishing.

Sacks, S.Z., and S. Rosen 1994 "Visual Impairment." In N.G. Haring, L. McCormick, and T.G. Haring, eds., *Exceptional Children and Youth*. New York: Merrill.

Skelly, M., and L. Schinsky 1979 *Amer-Ind Gestural Code Based on Universal American Indian Hand Talk*. New York: Elsevier North Holland.

Turnbull, A.P. 1982 "Preschool Mainstreaming: A Policy and Implementation Analysis." *Educational Evaluation and Policy Analysis* 4, no. 3: 281–91.

6

Orthopedic and Health Problems

INTRODUCTION

Physical activity and general good health are critical to early development. Infants and young children who eat well, sleep well, and move about freely are likely to acquire a well-integrated range of cognitive, language, social, and physical skills. Problems with health and motor control, on the other hand, tend to interfere with everything a child tries to do or learn. Few have described the plight of the young child with physical impairments more sensitively than Caldwell (1973): "If he has any kind of a motor dysfunction he cannot get up to find something better, or at least, cannot move himself to a situation where the environment might make a better match with his own developmental state." Even casual observation indicates that innumerable times a day, able-bodied children will move about, rearranging their own learning environment.

Example:

> *A 9-month-old tires of playing with familiar toys. She crawls to the bookcase and soon discovers the fun of taking books off the shelf. This infant has found a challenge for herself and a match for her rapidly developing motor skills. (Of course, pulling books off the shelf may be viewed as mischievous by parents or caregivers. If so, they need to challenge themselves to find new play materials that both challenge the child and meet their adult standards of appropriateness.)*

In this chapter the discussion will focus on the two broad categories of physiological problems: orthopedic impairments and health impairments. Their definitions, given below, have helped reduce confusion about the meaning of the term *physically disabled.*

Orthopedic impairments relate to problems involving skeleton, joints, and muscles. Included are these problems:

- missing or malformed limbs
- clubfeet
- congenital hip dislocations
- damage caused by diseases such as polio and bone tuberculosis
- neurological disorders such as cerebral palsy and spina bifida
- **contractures** (muscular tightening) caused by fractures, burns, or amputations

Health impairments are defined generally as limited strength, vitality, or alertness due to chronic or acute health problems. Among them are the following:

- heart conditions
- epilepsy
- asthma
- leukemia
- sickle-cell disease
- diabetes
- hemophilia
- cystic fibrosis

Both categories represent somewhat artificial distinctions. Actual boundaries between physical disabilities and serious health impairments frequently overlap. Furthermore, neurological problems may complicate both. Orthopedic, health, and neurological dysfunction may all be present, as in cerebral palsy, spina bifida, and other childhood conditions.

This chapter will also consider the impact of nutritional problems on the development of young children.

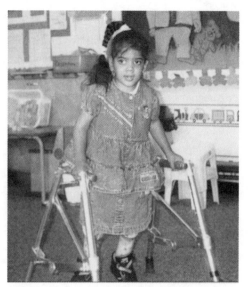

PHOTO 6–1 *Children with orthopedic impairments can participate when provided with specialized equipment.*

ORTHOPEDIC IMPAIRMENTS

Orthopedic impairment is a term that covers a wide range of problems. In general, it refers to any condition that interferes with the normal functioning of bones, joints, and muscles (Photo 6–1). The problems may be evident at birth—as with cerebral palsy or hip dysplasia, or they may be identifiable later, as in the case of muscular dystrophy.

CEREBRAL PALSY

Cerebral palsy (CP) has to do with "impairment of the coordination of muscle action with an inability to maintain normal postures and balance and to perform normal movements and skills" (Bobath and Bobath 1975, 29). CP is the most common source of physical disabilities among infants and young children. The basic cause of cerebral palsy is damage to the brain occurring before, during, or after the infant's birth. Cerebral palsy is a **nonprogressive** disorder resulting from oxygen deprivation (anoxia), injury, infection, hemorrhage (excessive bleeding), or malformation of the brain. Seldom can the exact cause be specified. The extent of the damage to the brain, and the corresponding impact on the child's ability to control physical movement, will determine how well the child will function. One way of classifying cerebral palsy is by type of **muscle tone**; the other is by how the various parts of the body are affected.

Classifications Based on Muscle Tone

Muscle tone may be described in terms of *hyper* (high) or *hypo* (low) muscle tension. The child who is *hypotonic* is one who has too little muscle tone. The result is an inability to move about or maintain postural control (the rag doll syndrome). Infants of this type often are referred to as "floppy babies." Many have difficulty simply holding up their heads. This deprives them of the learning experiences that most infants get from being held in an upright position. The *hypertonic* child is one who has taut muscle activity, preventing fluid movements.

PHOTO 6–2 *Hypertonicity causes muscles to tighten, as seen in this child's fist.*

- **Spasticity.** Most children with cerebral palsy fall into this category. They usually are considered hypertonic. Without early intervention a child may become locked into certain positions because muscles become permanently contracted. These muscle contractures may lead to the child's legs, arms, hands, fingers, or toes becoming irreversibly curled or clenched (Photo 6–2).

- **Athetosis.** Fluctuating or uneven muscle tone is called athetosis. Muscle control that goes from one extreme to the other (either too low or too high) is typical. Children with this condition tend to retain **primitive reflexes** past the normal time. This interferes with the development of **voluntary motor responses**. (See Thurman and Widerstrom 1990 for an excellent discussion of primitive reflexes.)

- **Ataxia.** A lack of motor coordination, ataxia is characterized by poor balance and a lurching kind of walk, reflecting lack of voluntary muscle control. Purposeful activity is extremely difficult. For example: A teacher's carefully organized collage materials are swept off the table as a result of involuntary muscle responses as the child strives to participate.

- **Mixed.** Approximately 30 percent of children with cerebral palsy have a mixture of spasticity and athetosis or ataxia.

Classifications Based on Body Parts

A second way of classifying cerebral palsy is according to the parts of the body that are affected. The following terms describe the location of the involvement:

- **Diplegia.** Involvement of all four extremities (legs and arms); in most cases, the legs are more severely affected.
- **Hemiplegia.** Only one side of the body is involved.
- **Paraplegia.** Involvement of the legs only.
- **Quadriplegia.** Involvement of both arms, both legs, trunk, and the muscles that provide head control.

The extent of motor impairment varies in children with cerebral palsy. Some children have disabilities so severe they cannot hold their heads still or straighten

PHOTO 6–3 *Children with cerebral palsy often have excellent cognitive and receptive language abilities.*

their arms or legs. Others have control problems so slight as to be scarcely noticeable. Many children with cerebral palsy, like children with other developmental problems, fail to meet major motor milestones at expected times. A distinction must be made, however. Children with general developmental problems usually have delays in all areas. In contrast, children with cerebral palsy may have developmentally appropriate cognitive and receptive language ability (Photo 6–3), but their motor skills, including those affecting speech production, may be poorly developed.

Young children with cerebral palsy, especially those with mild to moderate involvement, usually benefit from an inclusive early childhood classroom experience. All children with a motor dysfunction should receive ongoing evaluation. The parents and early childhood teachers should participate in developing a program for the child, while at the same time receiving appropriate training on physical management techniques and special programming strategies. The success of the early childhood program experience will depend on the teachers and child receiving adequate assistance and support from the interdisciplinary team, which includes a resource teacher, a pediatric physiotherapist, an occupational therapist, as well as a speech and language **therapeutic** consultant.

SPINAL CORD INJURIES

Spinal cord damage presents motor problems quite different from those associated with cerebral palsy. When the spinal cord is injured or severed, muscles below the point of damage become useless. Put simply, the muscles no longer receive messages from the brain. Sensations normally experienced below the point of injury no longer are transmitted back to the brain. It is important to note that *the brain itself is not affected*. However, because of interruption in **neural** communication between the brain and certain parts of the body, there are no sensations as to where the limbs are or what is happening to them. A child may suffer serious burns, cuts, or broken bones without knowing it. Parents, teachers, and caregivers of young children must learn to be the *sensory monitors* for the child's nonfeeling extremities and trunk (Tyler and Chandler 1978). It should be noted that regeneration (repair or renewal) of the spinal cord is not possible at this time.

PHOTO 6–4 *Children with spina bifida experience paralysis of the limbs below the area of spinal damage.*

The most familiar of the spinal cord injuries is spina bifida (**myelomeningocele** and **meningocele**). The damage comes from imperfect development of the spinal cord and spinal column during the first 30 days of fetal development. Children with spina bifida experience a number of problems in addition to paralysis of the affected limbs (Photo 6–4). The two most common problems are these:

1. *Hydrocephalus.* Blockage of the circulation of the spinal fluid in the cranial (brain) cavity. This is usually corrected through **shunting**, whereby tubes are surgically inserted in the back of the neck to drain spinal fluid from the brain to another area of the body, often the abdominal cavity (Canadian Paediatric Society 1992, 590). Without shunting, the spinal fluid will accumulate in the head cavity, enlarging the head and damaging the brain.

   Occasionally, shunts may become blocked. It is important that teachers be aware of the symptoms related to blocked shunts. These symptoms involve dizzy spells, nausea, sleepiness, and vomiting. The child's parents are the most appropriate resource for identifying their child's specific symptoms. Parents should also indicate to the teacher what action should be taken if any of these signs should occur.

2. *Incontinence.* Lack of bladder and bowel control. Many children with myelomeningocele do not feel the urge to urinate. Often they are unable to receive messages from the urinary sphincter muscles. The result is that the child has little or no control of urinary functioning. The same may be true of bowel activity. While these problems are difficult to overcome, many children who experience them can be helped. As the team evaluates the child's developmental skills, adaptive behaviours, and emotional strengths, members can determine the child's readiness to learn toilet skills and other everyday tasks.

MUSCULAR DYSTROPHY

Progressive weakening of the muscles is the major characteristic of muscular dystrophy and related muscular disorders. As children with muscular dystrophy get older, they lose their large motor skills first. Loss of fine motor skills comes later. Several types of muscular dystrophy exist; each type involves specific muscle groups. The most common is Duchenne's disease, a sex-linked disorder that affects only boys. In Duchenne's disease progressive muscle weakness begins at the hips and shoulders and gradually moves out to the arms and legs. Hand skills are often retained, even when the limbs are severely impaired. One child, for example, was able to string small wooden beads in complicated patterns if the beads were placed in a basket in his lap. However, when he ran out of beads he was unable to lift his arms to get more beads from the nearby table. While still mobile, and able to get around, a child with muscular dystrophy must be encouraged to move about the classroom frequently. Prevention of muscle contractures is a major goal of both therapy and classroom activity for these children.

OSTEOGENESIS IMPERFECTA

Brittle bones is the common term for this congenital condition. The child's bones do not grow normally in length or thickness and they break easily. Joints, too, are involved and may show excessive range of motion, as in children who can bend their thumb backward to touch the wrist. Dwarfism, dental defects, and hearing problems also may be associated with this bone disease. Oftentimes the child's hearing gets progressively worse, adding another dimension to teachers' planning. Generally, the child's cognitive skills are not affected, though a child may seem to be "behind" because of frequent hospitalization and absences from school.

OSTEOMYELITIS

Infection of the bones is the simple definition of osteomyelitis. It can be a crippling disease if not treated promptly and properly. Medication (antibiotics) and surgery are used to treat this condition in children.

HIP DYSPLASIA

This condition, also known as *congenital dislocation of the hip* (CDH), is the result of abnormal development of the hip joint. The head of the thigh bone (femur) may be out of the hip socket, or may move in and out at random. Interestingly enough, the condition is found much more often in females than in males. The hip displacement is usually diagnosed soon after birth and treated nonsurgically. Without treatment, the child will not walk normally, developing a waddling kind of gait.

JUVENILE RHEUMATOID ARTHRITIS

Arthritic conditions generally are associated with older people. However, young children also develop certain types of arthritis, especially juvenile rheumatoid arthritis. Chronic and painful inflammation of the joints and tissue surrounding the joints is a major symptom. Sitting for long periods (though less painful for the child than movement) causes further stiffening of the joints. Therefore, children with juvenile rheumatoid arthritis need both the freedom and the encouragement to move about a great deal, at home and at school. Symptoms often disappear by the time a child is 18 years old. The teacher's major goal must be to help the child keep his or her motor skills functional. Most children with juvenile rheumatoid arthritis are likely to be in total *remission* in 10 years or less (Miller 1975).

PHOTO 6–5 *Children may need adult support in learning how to handle their orthopedic equipment.*

PROGRAM IMPLICATIONS OF ORTHOPEDIC IMPAIRMENTS

It is generally agreed that early and appropriate intervention has a positive effect on the acquisition of motor skills in young children with developmental problems (Photo 6–5). Children with orthopedic disabilities, in spite of great individual differences, have basic classroom needs in common. These include

• the service of allied health professionals working as a team with classroom teachers;

• adaptive equipment designed to meet each child's physical needs; and

• environmental adaptations to facilitate each child's learning efforts.

Team Effort

The teachers' need for input from various health professionals in carrying out individualized early intervention programs has been discussed elsewhere in several contexts. A brief review, related to orthopedic and neurological problems, is presented here.

As noted repeatedly, good motor skills are critical to every aspect of children's development. The pediatric physiotherapist and/or occupational therapist, trained to focus on early motor skills, is often selected as case manager. The resource teacher, however, may be the key person in developing a specific program for the child. The resource teacher needs to work closely with the parents, teachers, and others involved in the care of the child, establishing and adapting goals and specific objectives as the child's skills and behaviours change. The resource teacher often is the person who must coordinate the roles and responsibilities of various members of the team involved in meeting the ongoing needs of the child. For example, in drawing up an intervention program for a child with cerebral palsy who also has a feeding problem, the resource teacher may make use of a nutritionist, a social worker, and perhaps a dentist to provide consultation or direct assistance. If the child also has a speech or language problem, the services of a speech and language pathologist, an audiologist, and a psychologist are likely to be enlisted.

The pediatric physiotherapist/occupational therapist needs to understand the goals of early childhood education and also needs to help teachers understand the goals of developmental therapy. As therapists and teachers share the knowledge base of their respective professions, there is "shared implementation and integration of children's daily therapy programs into the everyday format of the classroom structure" (Mather and Weinstein 1988, 7).

The ways in which a child who is physically disabled is positioned and helped to move about, at home and at school, are crucial to the child's development. Depending on the therapists' assessments, individual remediation activities are mapped out for each child. The classroom teacher should never be expected to put a child through stressful exercises. In fact, current practice tends to consider such exercises counterproductive where most children are concerned. Activities that are pleasant for both the child and the teacher (and often fun for other children as well) are the usual recommendations. **Under no circumstances should teachers initiate positioning exercises or remedial motor activities without specific guidance from a certified therapist.**

Adaptive Equipment

The pediatric therapist also guides teachers in the use of special mobility devices (Photo 6–6), demonstrates how *prostheses* are used, and shows ways in which to adapt regular play equipment. Some of the more common prostheses are discussed below.

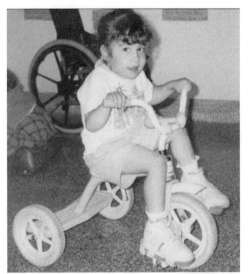

PHOTO 6–6 *Adapting the pedals of the tricycle, with straps and a frame to hold the child's foot in place, enables the child to join her peers.*

Mobility Devices

Braces, crutches, a walker, or a wheelchair are among the mobility devices prescribed for children who cannot move about easily. Young children with paraplegia may use a low, small-wheeled flat cart. They lie "tummy-down" on the cart and propel themselves from one activity to another by pushing with hands and arms. These are frequently referred to as scooter-boards or tummy-boards. For standup activities, these children are often fastened into a standing board—also known as prone-standers. Children with poor motor skills, even though they are able to walk, tend to fall more frequently than do other preschoolers. The falls are likely to distress adults more than they do the child. Usually, the child has become quite accustomed to falling down. Many children with physically handicapping conditions are given training in how to fall as well as how to get themselves up again. The latter is especially important. Adults must restrain themselves from "rushing to the rescue," picking the child up before he or she has a chance to get up independently. Adults who restrain themselves save the child from being unnecessarily and additionally disabled through *learned helplessness.*

Children with poor balance and poor motor control sometimes can hold on to and push a piece of play equipment as a means of getting about. A doll carriage or stroller, or a large wooden box with a handlebar attached, works well. If the box does not slide readily, wooden slats can be attached to the bottom. If the piece of equipment is too light, it can be loaded with bags of sand, thus providing a feeling of greater security. Teachers should never take the initiative in encouraging a child to walk without specific guidance from a pediatric therapist. Neurological and medical factors first must be evaluated by a physician or other accredited specialist before walking becomes part of the developmental programming for this child (Fallen and Umansky 1985).

Other children who lack precise hand control often need prosthetic devices such as on-head sticks to enable them to operate electrical typewriters, computers, and battery-operated toys. It is these devices that enable children who are unable to communicate by other means to communicate.

PHOTO 6–7 *Wedges are often recommended by therapists to promote proper positioning and support.*

Positioning Devices

Motor and neurological problems tend to be accompanied by muscular weakness that interferes with head and trunk control. Maintaining a sitting position becomes a problem as does grasping and hanging on to objects. The pediatric therapist can help teachers reduce the hampering effects of motor problems by recommending (even procuring) specially designed equipment such as **wedges**, **bolsters**, and **prone boards** (Photo 6–7). *Cautionary note:* The inappropriate use of adaptive equipment may do *more harm* than good. It is essential that therapists and resource teachers explain to teachers of young children the purpose of each piece of equipment, and guide the teachers in the proper use of the equipment for each individual child. Specialists must also help early childhood teachers be aware of situations that might arise and suggest precautions that should be taken while a child is using the equipment.

ADAPTING MATERIALS

Ingenious teachers have adapted almost every ordinary preschool material to fit the needs of children with motor impairments. A sampling of ideas follows.

Manipulative Materials

For children who must spend much of their time standing, or in a wheelchair, there are interesting materials that can be mounted on a board fastened to the wall. Wall displays allow children to grasp and manipulate objects they otherwise might not be able to manage. (These arrangements give a new dimension to materials for normally developing children, too.) Items that can be mounted on a playboard include the following:

- bolts, such as those used to lock doors
- bicycle bells
- light switches
- old-fashioned telephone dials
- doorknobs that turn

- clothespins
- metal boards with magnetic pieces
- mounted large-holed pegboards with large pegs

Creative Materials

For children with impaired fine motor skills, creative materials can be adapted in a variety of ways:

- Large crayons, chalk, and paintbrushes are available. Even these may be too small for some children to hang on to. If so, a section can be wrapped with layers of securely taped-down plastic material, enabling the child to get a firmer grip.
- Pencils, crayons, and coloured pens can be pushed through a small sponge-rubber ball. The child holds the ball to scribble and draw.
- Paper can be taped to the table. This prevents it from sliding away when a child is colouring, painting, or pasting.
- Magic markers or thick-tipped felt pens can be provided for children with weak hand and wrist control. They require less pressure than crayons but result in the rich, bright colours that please children.
- Fingerpaint, potter's clay, and water-play can be made available more frequently. These materials require a minimum of fine motor control but make a major contribution in the improvement and strengthening of small-muscle function.

Self-Help/Care Devices

Many devices (available through special education catalogues) assist children in feeding, grooming, and dressing themselves (Photo 6–8). In addition, low-cost adaptations can be devised:

PHOTO 6–8 *Many devices assist children in feeding.*

- Putting a small suction device (such as a soap-bar holder) under a child's plate keeps it from sliding out of reach or off the table.
- Building up a spoon handle by taping a hair roller or piece of foam rubber in place gives the child better control of the spoon.
- For a child who cannot hold a spoon, a cuff can be made that keeps the spoon in the palm of the hand. The cuff is a wide strap that has a pocket for the spoon and is fastened around the hand with a Velcro closure.

PHOTO 6–9 *Drinking equipment.*

- Velcro also can replace buttons, zippers, and snaps. In many cases, the Velcro can be put on over existing buttons and buttonholes.
- Other devices for feeling, touching, smelling, examining, and manipulating can be hung at the child's level from fixtures like those used in hanging mobiles. These fixtures can also be adapted so that they can be lowered or raised depending on the appropriate height for the individual child (Photo 6–9).

ADAPTATIONS OF THE CLASSROOM

Alterations may be needed in the classroom and play yard if children with motor impairments are to have a safe and appropriate learning environment.

Wheelchair Accommodation

Space to manoeuvre a wheelchair in and out of activities and to turn it around is essential. Toileting areas must be clear so that a child can wheel in and out of the bathroom easily, and pull up parallel to the toilet. Handrails mounted on the wall are needed so that the child can learn to swing from the wheelchair onto the toilet seat. Ramps can be constructed to facilitate movement in and out of the building and the classroom.

Railings

Attached in strategic places, indoors and out, railings help children with poor balance and faulty coordination move about more independently. Railings can serve all children. They can also be used as exercise and ballet bars.

Floor Coverings

Carpeting, if it is well stretched and securely nailed down, is good for children with mobility problems (Photo 6–10). It also provides a warm and comfortable play surface for the many activities that all children engage in on the floor. When carpeting is not possible, crutches must have nonskid tips and the shoes of a child with a motor impairment should have nonskid soles. Nonskid soles can be devised by gluing textured rubber onto the soles of a child's shoes.

Eye-Level Materials

Teachers need to ask themselves, "How does this room appear at a child's level?" Are there interesting things (such as manipulative wall hangings) for all children to

PHOTO 6–10 *Easily accessible equipment supports children's independence.*

watch, touch, work with? What is available at eye level for a child on a scooter-board or in a wheelchair, or one who gets about only by crawling?

Orderliness and Visibility

These concepts, and a number of others related to environmental arrangements, are discussed in considerable detail in Chapter 14. All are of major importance when designing learning environments for young children, and especially so when the program includes children with motor impairments.

HEALTH PROBLEMS

Most children are likely to have a variety of health problems during infancy and early childhood. For the most part these are relatively mild and do not interfere appreciably with growth and development. On the other hand, there are children who are chronically ill and have to live their everyday lives with serious health problems. These present the child and his or her parents and teachers with ongoing problems that must be dealt with throughout the developmental years.

ASTHMA

Asthma is among the most common of childhood's chronic diseases. During an attack the child has discomfort and tightness in the chest. Breathing may be laboured and may turn to wheezing. Depending on the child, attacks may be brought on by certain foods, pollens, dust, animal furs, air moulds, smoking and other environmental pollutants, as well as overexertion or emotional stress. When a child becomes asthmatic, stress will usually increase the severity of the condition. It is therefore important that teachers not overreact when a child has an attack.

Before the actual onset of an attack the child may begin to have a runny nose and/or a dry, hacking cough. Breathing (wheezing) may become loud and laboured. Lips and fingertips may take on a bluish look due to lack of air. When a child begins to have an attack in the classroom, the child should be encouraged to follow these steps:

1. rest and try to breathe easily

2. remain sitting in an upright position

3. drink warm water (avoid cold liquids)

If medication or special equipment, such as a Ventolin mask, is available for the child, this should be used as soon as it becomes apparent that the condition is increasing in severity. It is recommended that upon enrollment of a child with asthma, the teachers meet with the parents and obtain specific instructions as to how to recognize and respond to that child's condition. Furthermore, consultation with the child's physician and/or community public health nurse is advisable. If no special medication and/or equipment is available and a child appears to be having an asthma attack, it is important to quiet the child down, try to get the child into a relaxing, non-tension-producing environment, and observe to see if the symptoms subside. It has been suggested that having the child drink warm water at the first sign of a possible attack may prevent a full-blown episode. If the **symptoms** seem to be increasing in severity, the child should be taken to the nearest medical facility and the parents and physician notified immediately.

CYSTIC FIBROSIS

PHOTO 6–11 *Cystic fibrosis occurs most frequently in Caucasian children.*

Among Caucasian children, cystic fibrosis (Photo 6–11) is the most common of the inherited chronic diseases (in contrast to other racial groups, among whom it occurs infrequently). The disease is incurable. Generally, at this time, the child has a life expectancy of about 30 years. However, in recent years, new knowledge has been gained through research, and advances are opening the way for changes in this prognosis.

Cystic fibrosis is characterized by excessive mucus, progressive lung damage, and the body's inability to absorb fats and proteins appropriately. Children have trouble gaining weight and tend to have chronic coughs, an excessive appetite, and unusually salty perspiration. It is this excessively salty perspiration, detected through a medical sweat test, that confirms the diagnosis of cystic fibrosis.

The rate of deterioration varies from child to child. Symptoms may be minimal in one 5-year-old and severe in another. In general, teachers should encourage physical activity as long as the child is reasonably well. As the child gets older, health problems tend to worsen and more frequent hospitalizations are often required. Both the child and the family are likely to need considerable emotional support from teachers.

HEMOPHILIA

Another inherited disorder is hemophilia, experienced primarily by males. Females usually do not have the disease; they are the carriers or transmitters. Hemophilia occurs when the blood clots too slowly or not at all. As described by Apgar and Beck (1973, 295),

> the chief danger is not bleeding to death from accidental injury ... It is internal bleeding that poses the greatest threat to life and health. Bleeding into the joints, especially knees, ankles, and elbows can cause severe and constant pain, and eventually permanent crippling ... Internal bleeding episodes, particularly in children, can be triggered by what seem to be trivial bumps, falls and minor injuries. Often they occur without any known injury at all.

Dr. Apgar goes on to advise (1973, 297) that young children with hemophilia be encouraged to be as active as possible without exposing them to unnecessary risks.

> Active hemophiliacs in good physical condition seem to have fewer episodes of bleeding than inactive youngsters with a similar degree of clotting deficiency. Sometimes, an increase in physical activity results in a decrease in bleeding.

Despite some increased risk, most children with hemophilia grow up to lead normal adult lives. To ensure this outcome, teachers and parents must avoid treating an affected child as so special or so fragile that the child becomes excessively dependent or excessively concerned about personal health and well-being. Padding corners of furniture as well as the knees and elbows of the child's clothing will enable the child to move more actively without fear of damage from bumping into things.

LEUKEMIA

Leukemia is one of several forms of cancer to be found among young children. It is a disease that destroys bone marrow through an overproduction of white blood cells. It was viewed as a fatal disease up until a few years ago; recently, *chemotherapy* has proved very effective in the treatment of this condition in children. Fatigue, consistent aching of joints, and easy bruising are symptoms related to leukemia. They should be checked by a physician if they are observed in a child.

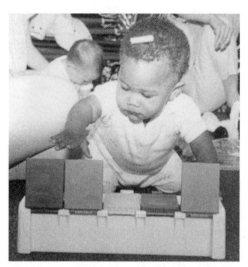

PHOTO 6–12 *Sickle-cell disease occurs mostly in black children.*

SICKLE-CELL DISEASE

Sickle-cell disease, another genetically transmitted disease, is found almost entirely among black children in varying degrees of severity (Photo 6–12). Apgar and Beck (1973, 128) suggest that in Africa the **genetic mutation** was probably an advantage—it offered protection against malaria. In North America, many generations later, this once-useful sickle-shaped red blood cell has led to a chronic health problem that can result in death during childhood. Leaving out the technical aspects of the explanation, what results is an insufficient amount of oxygen in the blood supply. A crisis is said to occur when a number of the "sickled" cells stick together and cause a blockage. The result is severe pain in the abdomen, legs, and arms; swollen joints; fainting; and overall fatigue. There is no cure for the disorder, but special therapy can help a child to adapt and lead a fairly normal existence.

Children with sickle-cell disease are often particularly vulnerable to infection. The decision to enroll the child in an early childhood program is a delicate one that should be reached jointly by parents, physician, and staff (Kendrick, Kaufman, and Messenger 1988). A child with a mild case of sickle-cell disease should continue to participate in regular preschool activities. Teachers can cooperate with parents and the physician in preventing a sickle-cell crisis by helping the child avoid fatigue, stress, and exposure to cold, and by making sure the child has an adequate fluid intake.

CARDIAC DISORDERS

Heart disease is a common term for cardiac disorders. Many heart defects result in death during the infant's first year. Others can be surgically repaired, allowing the child to lead a normal life. Children with cardiac conditions who reach school age are not likely to have life-threatening problems (Myers 1975). Reasons for congenital heart problems range from genetic abnormalities to maternal alcoholism.

Children with heart disease may complain of shortness of breath. Physical activity may be more tiring than it is for other preschoolers. Some children experience cyanosis, a blueness of the skin that is due to poor oxygenation of the blood. The child with continuing heart problems should not be pressed to participate in activities that bring on excessive fatigue. Actually, most children with cardiac problems are fairly reliable monitors of their own exertion tolerance. Children who have had complete surgical correction should have no difficulty participating in all preschool activities. Teachers, parents, and health care providers, however, need to exchange information on a continuing basis. Based on the current status of a child's condition, they should jointly plan activity levels for home and school.

JUVENILE DIABETES (MELLITUS)

Also known as insulin-dependent diabetes or Type I diabetes, this form of diabetes is one of the types most often found in young children. Diabetes is a genetic disease, regarded as the most common of the inborn errors of metabolism (see Chapter 4). The problem arises because the pancreas (a gland located behind the stomach) fails to produce enough of a natural chemical called *insulin*. Insulin is required if the body is to **metabolize** glucose (a form of sugar). Without insulin, cells cannot use the glucose already in the bloodstream. The result is insufficient nourishment to carry on the body's functions. Children with diabetes must receive insulin on a regular basis (usually twice a day). However, adverse reactions to insulin are a constant threat. One such threat is *hypoglycemia*, excessively low levels of sugar circulating in the blood. Another is *hyperglycemia*, too much sugar circulating in the bloodstream. This can result in diabetic coma (unconsciousness).

Katz (1975, 78) advises, "*If there is doubt, the situation should always be managed as a low sugar insulin reaction*, since the administration of sugar will cause no harm, while withholding sugar could have serious consequences." Teachers and caregivers will need to be involved in other ways too:

- careful regulation of food intake
- monitoring the child's exercise and activity level
- observing the child for changes in behaviour and signs of infection
- occasional urine testing

It is important that teachers, parents, and health care providers be in partnership and communicate regularly. This ensures the best possible care, with the fewest complications, for the child.

SEIZURE DISORDERS

The terms *epilepsy*, *seizure*, and *convulsion* are used somewhat interchangeably to describe disturbances in the normal electrical discharges in the brain. What happens, in simple terms, are *bursts of electrical energy*. These result in reduced or total loss of consciousness. Uncontrolled muscular movements, ranging from brief twitching of the eyelids to massive shaking of the entire body, accompany these bursts or episodes. These random motor movements have been categorized in various ways. The following is a classification that teachers are likely to find useful:

1. **Febrile seizures** are the most common. They occur in 5 to 20 percent of children under the age of 5. In general, the seizure is brought on by a high fever. Usually, it lasts less than 15 minutes and stops by itself. *Rarely are these seizures harmful* (Kendrick, Kaufman, and Messenger 1988), nor do children who experience them develop epilepsy.

2. **Absence (petit mal) seizures** are those where there is momentary loss of consciousness. This may occur many times a day with some children. The lapses are so brief that they may go unnoticed, even though there could be slight twitching of the eyelids, neck, or hands. The child often is accused of *daydreaming*.

3. **Tonic-clonic (grand mal)** *seizures* usually cause children to lose consciousness and fall to the floor with violently jerking muscles. They may stop breathing temporarily, lose bowel or bladder control, and bubble saliva about the mouth.

4. **Partial or psychomotor seizures**, found only rarely in young children, sometimes resemble a temper tantrum or an episode of bizarre behaviour characterized by lip-smacking, repetitive arm and hand movements, or aimless running about. Though there is the appearance of consciousness, the child is usually unaware of behaving strangely (Jacobs 1983).

A variety of medications are used to control seizures in children. The medication may have an adverse effect, causing the child to be drowsy or inattentive. An important role for teachers is to *observe* and *record* changes in the child's behaviour. Behavioural observations assist the child's physician in altering medication or dosage as needed. In general, the anticonvulsant medications prescribed for a child are effective in preventing seizures (Photo 6–13). Rarely does the early childhood teacher encounter a tonic-clonic (grand mal) seizure. However, it is important to know what to do should there be an episode. The following recommendations are adapted from material published by Epilepsy Ontario (1989).

PHOTO 6–13 *If seizures are not well controlled, a helmet may be recommended to protect the child from injury.*

1. Remain calm. Children will react the same way teachers do. The seizure itself is painless.

2. Do not try to restrain the child. Nothing can be done to stop a seizure once it has begun. It must run its course.

3. Clear the space around the child so that no injury from hard objects occurs and there is no interference with the child's movements.

4. *Do not try to force anything between the teeth.*

5. Loosen tight clothing, especially at the neck; turn the child's head to the side, wipe away discharge from the mouth and nose to aid breathing.

6. When the seizure is over, allow the child to rest.

7. Generally, it is not necessary to call for medical assistance unless the seizure lasts more than 10 minutes or is followed by another major seizure.

8. The child's parents are always to be informed of a seizure. Teachers and parents plan together on how future seizures are best handled for that particular child.

The child with epilepsy should not be restricted from participating in the full program unless specific limitations are imposed by the child's physician. It would be useful for the child's teacher to know what may trigger a seizure for this particular child, for example, flashing lights, fatigue, and so on.

A seizure episode can be turned into a learning experience for the children in the class. Teachers can explain in simple terms what a seizure is. They can assure children that it is *not catching* and that children need not fear for themselves or for the child who had the seizure. Epilepsy Ontario suggests that it is important that teachers help children understand, but *not pity*, the child, so that he or she remains "one of the gang." It is important that the child not feel self-conscious on regaining consciousness. Other children in the class should be encouraged to continue in their ongoing activities.

Making sure that the child receives the prescribed medication regularly and in the proper amounts is the best approach to preventing seizures. Teachers who are asked to administer medication must follow the guidelines described later in this chapter. In concluding this section on epilepsy, it seems important to reiterate two points. The first is a repeat of the cautionary note: *Never attempt to force anything between the child's upper and lower teeth.* This procedure, once thought necessary, was discontinued years ago. Children's teeth can be damaged and adults' fingers severely bitten. The second point that bears repeating is that *teachers should remain calm.* In the interests of everyone, a teacher must not panic. Young children rarely become unduly alarmed about anything if their teachers do not appear anxious or upset. Children's anxieties over a seizure episode are reduced almost immediately if adults are confident and matter-of-fact in assuring them that the child soon will be all right. In fact, the teacher's quiet care of the child having the seizure can be a valuable experience in human concern that is of benefit to all children.

AIDS (ACQUIRED IMMUNE DEFICIENCY SYNDROME)

AIDS stands for acquired immune deficiency syndrome. It is a disease that leaves a person open to contracting illnesses that a healthy **immune system** might otherwise overcome. It is caused by a human immunodeficiency virus (HIV). Individuals may be infected without knowing it and without showing symptoms of the infection. For example, there have been cases of AIDS being transmitted during routine blood transfusions to both adults and infants. Children who are infected may seem delayed or small for their age, or may display neurological problems, *before they display symptoms.*

AIDS is transmitted primarily through intimate sexual contact, blood-to-blood contact (as through shared hypodermic needles), or from an infected mother to her baby. It is estimated that one-third to one-half of the infants born to infected mothers will be infected. However, all infants of HIV-infected mothers will test positive for the disease in the first year or so of life. Why? Because the infant is still operating on its mother's **antibody** system while its own is gearing up and getting ready to function.

There is no evidence of casual transmission by sitting near, living in the same household with, or playing with a person with clinical AIDS (American Academy of Pediatrics 1990). According to Kendrick (1990, 270) and confirmed by the NAEYC Information Service (1991),

> HIV is not transmitted through urine, stool (diarrhea), vomitus, saliva (mouthing of toys and other objects) mucus, sweat, or any other body fluid that does not contain blood ... All children with HIV infection or AIDS should be admitted to the program as long as their own health and developmental status allows them to benefit from the program.

Typically, however, many children who have AIDS are quite ill and unable to be in a child-care program or a preschool classroom. Also, children with AIDS are highly vulnerable to all of the many childhood infectious illnesses; enrollment in an early childhood group of any kind may be against their best interests. For those children who are well enough to be in a program, strict hygiene procedures are required of caregivers:

• thorough handwashing,

• wearing disposable gloves when dealing with bodily secretions, and

• cleaning caregiving surfaces with bleach and water solution.

According to Best, Bigge, and Sirvis (1994):

Because these precautions constitute good hygiene for anyone who requires physical care, their universal adoption allows protection for care providers while preserving the privacy of the student with AIDS (314).

In an early childhood centre, no children or adults should be attending or working in the program if they have open, oozing sores that cannot be covered or kept under control with medication. Nor should they be in the program if there is any bloody discharge accompanying diarrhea. This applies to everyone, those with and those without known HIV infection. The foregoing recommendations are in accord with medical, technical, and legislative findings as reviewed by Dokecki, Baumeister, and Kupstas (1989) and the NAEYC Information Service (1991). Once again, a reminder: Information on AIDS/HIV is changing continuously. Therefore, it is essential that everyone working with infants, young children, and families keep abreast of current findings.

NUTRITIONAL PROBLEMS

OBESITY (OVERWEIGHT)

Obesity is not necessarily a handicapping condition. It is a developmental disorder that affects between 15 and 20 percent of the children and youth in North America. Unchecked, obesity may lead to significant long-term health problems, as well as social and psychological problems. Overweight children are often unable to keep up physically with their peers, and may be teased by others and/or excluded from play activities. This may lead to a poor self-image, decreasing physical fitness, and fewer opportunities to build satisfying social relationships (Marotz, Rush, and Gross 1993).

Fat babies do not necessarily become fat adults; substantial evidence exists, however, that overweight preschoolers are not likely to *outgrow* the problem. As weight increases, children move less vigorously and so continue to put on more weight. This further compounds both their physical and their psychological problems. The increase of obesity in children has risen dramatically in the past two decades. According to Brizee, Sophos, and McLaughlin (1990), the increase is thought to be associated with reduced physical activity and increased consumption of convenience foods and fast foods, which tend to be high in fat. Recent research indicates that genetics plays a major role in predisposing a person to obesity. Studies involving identical twins show that heredity accounts for as much as 70 percent of the factors causing obesity. The other 30 percent stems from environmental influences (Bouchard et al., 1990). However, there are two controllable factors that contribute to excessive weight gain that teachers can help to prevent:

- *Overeating.* The consumption of too many calories, or at least too many calories from the wrong kind of food. Often, an overweight person eats excessive amounts of foods with poor nutritional content, popularly known as junk food.

- *Underexercising.* Lack of physical activity often is given as a major reason for obesity.

All children, including those who are obese, need an adequate number of calories each day, but the calories need to come from the right kinds of foods—fruits, vegetables, grains, lean meats, fish, milk, and cheese. Through responsible menu planning, early childhood educators can introduce children to a variety of nutritionally sound foods.

Strangely enough, many children who are overweight are undernourished. The early childhood teacher can work closely with parents and a nutritionist or health care nurse to make sure that a child with a weight problem is getting a daily intake of appropriate foods in appropriate amounts (Photo 6–14). Teachers also can focus parts of the early childhood curriculum on helping children understand the role of good nutrition and exercise in everyday life.

Some children may require the concentrated supervision of a nutritionist or dietary specialist (Photo 6–15). Situations requiring intensive nutritional intervention vary. Sometimes patterns of excessive food intake may have been established unintentionally by parents

PHOTO 6–14 *Physical activity is important for all children.*

PHOTO 6–15 *Normal weight gain depends upon offering good food, cutting out empty calories, and then allowing children to eat only what they need.*

and caregivers. By providing an abundance of food, parents may seek to compensate for the many ordinary life experiences they are unable to provide for the child. For example, a parent who works long hours may lack the energy to interact with the child in the evening. Providing the child with a sugary treat not only pleases the child but alleviates the parent's feelings of guilt.

Physical activity is of major importance for all children. This is especially true for children who have a tendency to put on extra weight. These children should be monitored daily to ensure that they are encouraged to participate in gross motor activity. It is the responsibility of the early childhood teacher to make sure that the daily curriculum provides for ample outdoor activity.

Frequently, children with conditions that limit regular physical activity may require a diet with fewer calories. Children with other conditions, such as the genetic syndrome **Prader-Willi**, engage in uncontrolled and obsessive food consumption. Refrigerators must be kept locked. Food cannot be left out in the pet's dish. Teachers must keep uneaten food, even leftovers on other children's plates, securely out of the way of the child with Prader-Willi syndrome.

UNDERNOURISHMENT

Consuming too few calories is as damaging to a growing child as taking in too many. Many children with physical impairments burn far more calories each day than they are able to take in. One example is children with severe cerebral palsy. They use up tremendous amounts of energy on the unwelcome but constant and uncontrollable muscular reactions characteristic of their disability. Often these children are far below ideal body weight. The same disability and muscle impairment that burn so many calories also lead to other nutritional problems. Some affected children have trouble holding food in the mouth or chewing and swallowing. Parents, teachers, and caregivers need specialized help in learning to provide easy-to-swallow foods that are high in nutritional value (Photo 6–16).

While young children with physical disabilities may be undernourished due to eating difficulties, poor children also may be malnourished because their parents cannot afford to buy and prepare nutritious food on a daily basis. It is imperative,

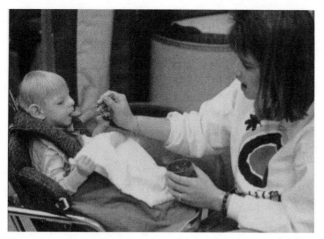

PHOTO 6–16 *Feeding can be a long and difficult process.*

therefore, that meals provided by child-care staff and parents, whether in centres or in private homes, follow Canada's Food Guide (1996) in detail. Many centres now offer breakfast as well as hot lunches and snacks. Elementary schools in impoverished areas may also provide breakfast and lunch for schoolchildren.

LEAD POISONING

A mineral known to be harmful, even lethal, if consumed in large enough doses, is lead. Toxic lead can come from certain kinds of painted pottery, old water pipes, even polluted air in some cases. The most frequent source of lead poisoning, however, is old school buildings, old houses, and old apartment buildings. Often they have coat on coat of flaking paint on top of crumbling layers of plaster. Such walls are a constant source of lead for the everything-in-the-mouth young child. Tiny amounts, consumed over several months, can lead to anemia, seizures, intellectual impairment, even death. Batshaw and Perret (1981) warn that the problem of lead poisoning will persist as long as there are dilapidated dwellings housing inquisitive children whose fingers find paint flakes (see Chapter 4).

HEALTH PROBLEMS AND CLASSROOM PRACTICES

Early childhood teachers sometimes feel anxious, inadequate, even threatened, when first asked to include a child with a serious health problem or a disabling physical condition in their class. However, teachers find that the more they work with children with disabilities, the more natural it seems. The NAEYC health manual (1991, 14) advises teachers:

> Having good information is one of the best ways to feel confident and in control. When you know what to do—whether it is taking a temperature, giving first aid, or keeping a child relaxed during an asthma attack—both you and the child are going to benefit from your knowledge. Lack of information often leads to panic in emergencies or improper care, such as spreading disease by not washing hands when necessary. You can provide the necessary care, remain calm, and maintain control.

Useful information for teachers comes from many sources in addition to parents and the interdisciplinary team members who are involved in the child's intervention program. Most important are up-to-date health records on each child and complete knowledge about a child's medication program. Teachers also must be sure they know what they will do in both routine and emergency situations related to specific health problems among the children in their class. Every time a child with a health problem is to be enrolled, teachers must have a careful briefing by both the child's parents and a health care professional before the child enters the program.

HEALTH RECORDS

A complete and frequently updated health record must be maintained on every child in the group. In order to provide the best possible support to the child and family, it should contain the following essential information:

- telephone numbers where parents and other emergency contacts can be reached at all times
- name of the child's regular physician, health care provider, or clinic, with address and telephone numbers
- permission slips authorizing emergency health care and transportation, and the administration of prescribed medications
- health insurance information, where relevant
- child and relevant family health history
- immunization information with dates
- results of medical assessment or physical and dental examinations and treatment
- results of special testing, such as vision or hearing assessments
- dated reports, signed by the attending teacher, on all injuries or illnesses that occur while the child is in the classroom, play yard, or on a school-sponsored excursion
- notations on allergies, special diets, treatment procedures, medications, prosthetic devices, or other health concerns
- notations on health-related communications with parents and health care providers, including referral recommendations and follow-up
- ongoing records of medications given to the child while at school

ADMINISTERING MEDICATION

Regulations regarding the administration of medication by teachers should follow provincial guidelines. These guidelines, as well as those for recording this procedure, differ from province to province. It is important that teachers familiarize themselves with the regulations in their specific area.

Teachers may be required to administer medication during program hours. All medication should be stored in a child-resistant container and labelled with the following information:

1. child's name
2. physician's name and phone number
3. name of the medicine
4. dosage to be given to the child
5. schedule for administering dosages

Requests for the administration of medication should be *put in writing and signed* by the parents. Each time medicine is given, *the time and date must be recorded* on the child's record sheet and initialled by the person who did the medicating. *Medication must be kept in a locked cupboard or refrigerator, and out of reach of all children.*

EMERGENCY CONSIDERATIONS

All programs serving young children should have carefully laid out plans for emergency situations. (See Kendrick, Kaufman, and Messenger [1988] for an excellent description of such plans.) When children with health problems and physical disabilities are enrolled, individual plans need to be formulated for each child. These include

- conferring with parents (or the child's doctor) to plan in advance for an emergency health crisis;
- understanding the cause of a crisis and how often it is likely to occur;
- learning how a child may behave before as well as during and after a crisis; and
- knowing what to do during and following the crisis, and understanding when to call for additional help.

Preventing a health crisis is important, too. For example, it is wise to prepare a list of classroom activities. Give this list to the child's parents or physician and ask them to indicate activities that should be avoided or modified. In addition, the other children need to be prepared for possible health crises of classmates. Teachers can give simple explanations. They also can assure children that the teachers will be able to take care of all of the children, not just the child who has the problem.

SUMMARY

Physical disabilities in children include a wide range of orthopedic and health impairments. Neurological involvement often accompanies both types of problems. The physical disabilities that teachers are most likely to encounter were described briefly in this chapter in terms of characteristics, causes, program recommendations, and the responsibilities of teachers, including crisis management, as needed.

Children with both orthopedic and health problems are likely to benefit from being enrolled in a regular early childhood classroom if the staff has adequate support. Resource teachers and other specialists must be used to support teachers in planning and implementing classroom activities. The specially trained resource teacher and/or physiotherapist is essential in cases of orthopedic involvement, though a variety of other disciplines also play significant roles, depending on the nature of the child's problems.

Teachers should never initiate any kind of therapeutic activity without specific instruction and supervision from a certified specialist. The specialist also learns from the early childhood educator how to accommodate therapeutic recommendations to the everyday activities and developmental principles of the preschool classroom.

Regular classroom activities, materials, and equipment often can be adapted to meet the needs of the child with a physical disability. A major responsibility of teachers is to help the child with a physical disability keep active and involved to the maximum extent possible. Teachers need to help children with physically handicapping conditions or disabilities learn how to do as much as possible for themselves so that their medical condition or disability does not take over their lives. Another responsibility of teachers is to prepare themselves to meet emergency situations. When teachers remain calm and quietly in charge, young children do not panic.

STUDENT ACTIVITIES

1. Divide into several groups of six or seven students. Select one person as a discussion leader and talk about disabilities or serious health problems that members have experienced firsthand or through living with a brother or

sister, close relative, spouse, or friend who has a disability. Discuss common experiences and attitudes.

2. Work with three or four other students in preparing a manipulative board to mount on the wall. Expand on the ideas suggested in this text. Be creative. Arrange for a tryout of the creation in one or more preschool classrooms.

3. Select a common preschool manipulative material and demonstrate ways in which it might be adapted so that a child with impaired fine motor skills could use it successfully.

4. Devise a game with beanbags, suitable for 4- and 5-year-olds, that would allow a child in a wheelchair to participate.

5. Select a possible crisis situation such as an asthma attack, insulin shock, or tonic-clonic (grand mal) seizure. Describe what you would say to a group of 4- and 5-year-olds who had witnessed such an episode for the first time.

REFERENCES

American Academy of Pediatrics 1990 "Lack of Transmission of Human Immunodeficiency Virus from Infected Children to Household Contacts." *Pediatrics* 85, no. 2: 1115–19.

Apgar, V.C., and J. Beck 1973 *Is My Baby Alright?* New York: Trident.

Batshwa, M.L., and Y.M. Perret 1981 *Children with Handicaps: A Medical Primer.* Baltimore: Paul H. Brookes.

Best, S.J., J.L. Bigge, and B.P. Sirvis 1994 Physical and Health Impairments. In N.G. Haring, L. McCormick, and T.G. Haring, eds., *Exceptional Children and Youth*, Sixth Edition. New York: Merrill.

Bobath, K., and B. Bobath 1975 "Cerebral Palsy." In P. Pearson and C.E. Williams, eds. *Physical Therapy Services in Developmental Disabilities.* Springfield, Ill.: Charles C. Thomas.

Bouchard et al. 1990 *New England Journal of Medicine* 322: 1477–82.

Brizee, L.S., C.M. Sophos, and J.F. McLaughlin 1990 "Nutrition Issues in Developmental Disabilities." *Infants and Young Children* 2, no. 3: 10–22.

Caldwell, B.M. 1973 "The Importance of Beginning Early." In J. Jordan and R.F. Dailey, eds. *Not All Little Wagons Are Red.* Reston, Va.: Council for Exceptional Children.

Canadian Paediatric Society 1992 *Well Beings: A Guide to Promote the Physical Health, Safety, and Emotional Well-Being of Children in Care Centres and Family Day Care Centres.* Toronto: Creative Premises.

Dokecki, P.R., A.A. Baumeister, and F.D. Kupstas 1989 "Biomedical and Social Aspects of Pediatric AIDS." *Journal of Early Intervention* 13, no. 2: 99–112.

Epilepsy Ontario 1989 *Epilepsy, Epilepsy, Epilepsy.* Willowdale, Ont.: Epilepsy Ontario.

Fallen, N.H., and W. Umansky 1985 *Young Children with Special Needs.* Columbus, Ohio: Charles E. Merrill.

Health Canada 1992. *Canada's Food Guide to Healthy Eating.* Minister of Supply & Services, Ottawa.

Jacobs, I.B. 1983 "Epilepsy." In G.H. Thompson, I.L. Rubin, and K.M. Bilenker, eds. *Comprehensive Management of Cerebral Palsy.* New York: Grune and Stratton.

Katz, H.P. 1975 "Important Endocrine Disorders of Childhood." In R. Haslam and P. Valletutti, eds. *Medical Problems in the Classroom.* Baltimore: University Park Press.

Kendrick, A.S., R. Kaufman, and K.P. Messenger 1990 *Healthy Young Children—A Manual for Programs.* Washington, D.C.: National Association for the Education of Young Children.

Marotz, L.R., J.M. Rush, and M.Z. Gross 1993 *Health, Safety and Nutrition for the Young Child.* Albany: Delmar.

Mather, J., and E. Weinstein 1988 "Teachers and Therapists: Evolution of a Partnership in Early Intervention." *Topics in Early Childhood Special Education* 7, no. 4: 1–9.

Miller, J.J. III 1975 "Juvenile Rheumatoid Arthritis." In E.E. Bleck and D.A. Nagel, eds. *Physically Handicapped Children: A Medical Atlas for Teachers.* New York: Grune and Stratton.

Myers, B.R. 1975 "The Child with Chronic Illness." In R. Haslam and P. Valletutti, eds. *Medical Problems in the Classroom.* Baltimore: University Park Press.

N.A.E.Y.C. 1991 *Health Manual.* Washington, D.C.

N.A.E.Y.C. Information Service 1991 Washington, D.C. Author telephone query.

Thurman, S.K., and A.H. Widerstrom 1990 *Infants and Young Children with Special Needs: A Developmental and Ecological Approach.* Baltimore: Paul H. Brookes.

Tyler, N.B., and L.S. Chandler 1978 "The Developmental Therapists: The Occupational Therapist and the Physical Therapist." In K.E. Allen, V.A. Holm, and R.L. Schiefelbusch, eds. *Early Intervention—A Team Approach.* Baltimore: University Park Press.

7

Social, Adaptive, and Learning Disorders

OBJECTIVES

After studying the material in this chapter, the student will be able to

- recognize the symptoms of anxiety disorders found in young children
- describe eating and toileting problems sometimes associated with behavioural disorders; discuss appropriate adult attitudes toward such problems
- provide a convincing argument against labelling or diagnosing a preschool child as learning disabled
- recognize the major warning signs in a preschool child that suggest the potential for learning disabilities related to later reading, writing, and math skills
- discuss the use and misuse of the term hyperactivity

INTRODUCTION

Disorders associated with behaviour and with learning have been linked to various developmental problems. The term *behaviour disorders* is widely used to classify a variety of social and emotional disturbances ranging from mild to severe. "Deviations from age-appropriate behavior that significantly interferes with the child's own development or with the lives of others" is a definition offered by Spodek, Saracho, and Lee (1984). The term *learning disorders* is often applied to children with normal IQs and reasonable adaptive functioning who nevertheless have difficulty learning to read, to write, or to do math.

A behaviour or learning disorder may be a child's major or *primary* problem, or it may be a lesser or *secondary* problem. There are children who perform normally in all areas of development who may exhibit one or more inappropriate behaviour patterns. In these cases, the behaviour disorder is the primary problem. In contrast, there are children with readily identified disabilities who also demonstrate inappropriate behaviours. Children who are blind, for example, may develop ritualistic, seemingly nonfunctional behaviours. These can take up so much of the child's time that they interfere with the child's acquisition of developmentally appropriate skills.

The inability, or lack of opportunity, to learn appropriate behaviours or to understand routine expectations may be the cause of secondary behaviour problems. The frustrations the child experiences in trying to perform normal developmental tasks and to engage in normal social exchanges is often a factor. Children with developmental problems tend to get relatively little positive feedback from parents, caregivers, and teachers; yet their maladaptive behaviours such as head banging, shrill squealing, or eye-poking draw a great deal of attention. Thus, the maladaptive behaviours become more dominant, making it even more difficult for these children to acquire necessary developmental skills.

When working with young children who present challenging or inappropriate behaviours, it is essential to keep in mind what is developmentally appropriate. Most 4-year-olds do not follow all directions, challenge adults occasionally, and can go from laughter to tears in a few seconds. The term behaviour disorder should be used with extreme caution when describing young children.

There is general agreement among most child developmentalists that preschool children (with few exceptions) *should not be labelled as emotionally disturbed*. Early development is characterized by constant change. Therefore, the label *emotionally disturbed* is premature, nonfunctional, and likely incorrect.

PHOTO 7-1 *Withdrawal is one form of anxiety disorder seen in young children.*

ANXIETY DISORDERS

Depression, fearfulness, and anxiety occur in young children, though to a lesser degree than found in preadolescents and teenagers. Common anxiety disorders in the early years revolve around separation problems, overdependence, and withdrawal (Photo 7–1), or avoidance of social contacts.

SEPARATION PROBLEMS

It is quite normal for infants and young children to be both fearful of strangers and unwilling to separate from a parent or major caregiver (Photo 7–2). The behaviour tends to peak between 12

PHOTO 7–2 *Saying goodbye to a parent may take extra time when a child is new to a program.*

and 15 months of age and then to lessen gradually. No consistent relationship has been found between the number of caregivers a child has had and the intensity of a child's protests over separation. In other words, a child who has had multiple caregivers is no less anxious about strangers than are children cared for by very few caregivers (Thompson and Lamb 1982). Children in families in which there is general instability may be especially fearful of strangers and, throughout the preschool years and beyond, have trouble separating.

Entering preschool or a child-care centre for the first time can be intimidating for young children. Young children with disabilities may experience even more anxiety. They are likely to have had fewer play experiences away from home than other children. Also, they often have been the focus of intensive adult care and concern to a degree that would be inappropriate in a school situation. The point is, separation anxieties are common. In general, they need not become a major problem if the first days of school are carefully planned by teachers and parents. (See Allen and Hart 1984, 181–99, for a detailed description of appropriate procedures.)

In a few instances, a child and parent may have prolonged and severe separation problems. At the least hint that the parent might leave, the child embarks on a full-blown tantrum. This severe reaction may have come about because the parent, after agreeing to stay, tried to slip away without saying goodbye. In these cases, teachers must involve parents in a plan to help the child learn to separate. Discussions of the problem should take place away from the classroom and out of the child's hearing. The situation can only worsen if the child is further burdened with the parent's and teachers' concerns. The separation process should focus on the parent's gradual withdrawal, usually over several days. The amount of time required depends on the child and the severity of the problem. Throughout the parent's separation efforts, teachers should encourage and appreciate the child's participation and active use of materials. Gradually, the teachers' support replaces the parent's support.

Occasionally, a child who likes coming to the program may use protest as a way to keep the parent at school. These children often engage in every activity and play happily as long as the parent stays. As soon as the parent tries to leave, however, the child makes a scene. Parents in these situations often complain about the child's behaviour. Yet, after saying goodbye they have a tendency to pause and look back, as if waiting for the child to begin a tantrum. (Maybe it is the parent who is having a separation problem?) In these cases, the teacher may have to assist the lingering parent in leaving swiftly with only a brief and matter-of-fact goodbye. The child almost always settles back into play after a token protest.

OVERDEPENDENCY

The early childhood teacher may be the target of a child's efforts to get extraordinary amounts of attention. Sometimes this is the child who has had separation problems, but not always. The overly dependent child may cling to a particular teacher, hang on to the teacher's clothing, and shadow the teacher's every move. Complaining, whining, and tattling may be accompanying problems. Working with a child of this kind requires the teacher to walk a fine line between giving too much attention and too little. Too much attention is likely to increase the child's dependency problems; too little may lead the child to feel unliked or rejected, or even distrustful of the situation.

To receive full benefit from the program, a child must be helped to relate to all teachers (Photo 7–3) and, eventually, to children. Once the child is familiar with the program and the routines, the *weaning* process can begin. As always, it is not a question of reducing the amount of attention; it is one of making decisions as to when to give attention in order to help rather than hinder the child's progress. Consider the following examples:

The teacher watches for those moments when the child is not clinging and immediately gives attention: "It looks as if you are enjoying that book. Let's read the pictures. What do you suppose is going to happen to the kitten?"

PHOTO 7–3 *Children need to learn to relate to more than one teacher.*

When a child is pulling at the teacher's clothing or person, the teacher should resist the impulse to react or respond. Hard to do, yes; but it is to the eventual benefit of both the child and the teacher. As always, preventive measures are best: as the child approaches, the teacher can reach out and put an arm around the child or take the child's hand before the clinging or clutching starts.

Teachers support the child in taking personal responsibility, beginning with nonthreatening situations: "If you want to play in the rocking boat I'll go with you while you talk to Sherri. If you ask, I know she'll stop rocking so you can get in."

Finding ways to get the child to allow another teacher to respond to his or her needs is another step in solving the problem. The teacher should choose those times when the child really wants something, as when one teacher says to another: "Ms. Singh, Charles wants the red truck. Will you get it out for him?" or to the child, "I can't read your book because I have to set up finger painting. Let's ask Mr. John to read it to you."

Occasionally, a teacher finds it flattering to be singled out for undivided devotion, and unintentionally reinforces the child's overly dependent behaviours. In these instances, both child and teacher need the help of other staff members.

Overly dependent, anxious children may also complain of headaches, stomach aches, or nearly invisible cuts and scrapes. Though the hurt is real to the child, it also has become a sure way of getting focused attention from an important adult. Most young children can be expected to have these kinds of complaints sometimes. When the complaints go on day after day, it is cause for concern. The first step is to check with parents to make sure that there are no physical problems. Classroom procedures then become the same as for other problem behaviours: minimum attention to the aches and scrapes, as well as additional attention when the child is actively engaged in play activities. This helps the child focus on the fun times at school.

WITHDRAWAL

Some children seem to be alone most of the time. They rarely engage in social play activities. Often they turn away when other children approach. In structured, large-group activities they may be there in body but are remote and not there in spirit. Teachers seldom express the degree of concern over these children that they do with children who act out. The behaviours of the withdrawn child are easily overlooked; those of the disruptive child seldom go unnoticed. Yet the withdrawn child may be in greater developmental jeopardy than the child who acts out.

Withdrawal problems and their causes may be so complex as to require clinical treatment and a segregated, therapeutic classroom. However, most children who are withdrawn whom teachers encounter in early childhood programs are likely to have less serious problems with less obscure origins. The cause may be a recent upheaval at home, such as a parent leaving or a serious illness in the family. It may be a change of neighbourhood where the new children's ways seem strange, even frightening or bullying. It may be the first venture of an only child or a child with a disability into a play setting with other children. These children may have been overprotected unwittingly, due to the parents' efforts to keep them from getting hurt or catching a childhood disease. There are also those children who are simply shy. All children experience shyness off and on to some degree. In some children, shyness becomes a longstanding habit. Whatever the cause, teachers usually can help these children become more involved.

Careful observation, as always, is the required first step. Specific questions need asking:

- Does the child engage in particular activities when playing alone?
- Are there materials and equipment that the child appears to enjoy or prefer? (Photo 7–4)
- Does the child spend time watching certain children or certain activities more than others?
- Is the child likely to leave an activity if certain children approach? Does the child avoid these children consistently?

PHOTO 7–4 *Does the child have a favourite toy or piece of equipment to use as a starting point?*

- Are some children less threatening for the child to sit next to in group activities or to play next to in parallel play situations?

When a child's preferences (and avoidances) have been noted, plans can be made to reduce the child's isolation. "Start small" is always the motto. Following are three examples of first approximations to social interactions for Jeanine, a child whose isolated behaviours were of concern.

On several occasions the teacher had observed Jeanine watching housekeeping play with apparent interest. The teacher arranged that he and the child together deliver additional materials to the activities in progress. The teacher announced: "Jeanine and I have brought some more birthday candles. We'll put some of them on the cake, too, okay?"

Jeanine seemed fascinated by the rocking boat. A quiet but friendly child asked the teacher for another ride. The teacher responded, "Yes, Jon, but let's give Jeanine a ride, too. Here, Jeanine, you sit across from Jon." Another time a third child is invited, who also is seated across from Jeanine. Then a fourth who sits next to Jeanine. In each of these early steps the teacher selected quieter, less rambunctious children to share the ride.

Jeanine was watching two children working with pegboards. The teacher said, "Jeanine, I'll put a pegboard down here for you." The teacher placed the pegboard at the end of the small table near, but not between, the other children. "All three of you can reach the basket of pegs." Having Jeanine take pegs out of a common basket was a step forward from the week before. At that time, the teacher had seated her near the other children but had given her a small basket of pegs of her own.

Sometimes, a shy child will focus almost exclusively on one or more of the adults in the program. Overdependency does not seem to be the problem; it is as if some children prefer the company of adults. They always find ways to sit next to the teacher. They linger during transitions to help the teacher clean up. They engage the teacher in long, one-to-one conversations. This may be pleasant for the teacher, but it does not promote the kinds of social development that come with learning to interact with other children. The teacher's job becomes one of consciously involving another child or two in the conversation or the cleanup operation. If no other children are about, the teacher should respond to the child pleasantly but briefly, and then move to an area where there are other children. Usually the shy child will follow. This increases the opportunity for the teacher to involve other children.

PHOBIAS

Fears that result in excessive and unrealistic anxiety about everyday happenings are called *phobias*. The individual with a phobia may go into a panic reaction at encountering a feared object or event, or at the mere thought of encountering it. For example, there are people who take unrealistic measures such as climbing 20 flights of stairs to avoid riding an elevator; or they walk a kilometre out of the way, every day, rather than pass a well-fenced yard in which there is a small, securely tied dog that barks at passersby. A certain amount of fear is normal. Fears are natural adaptive mechanisms in young children and are built in for survival purposes. No child should be laughed at or shamed for his or her fears. By the same token, children's fears should not be allowed to get blown out of proportion. As with all developmental issues, there is a fine line between too much and too little attention. Normal fears can become unrealistically stressful if adults are overly attentive to the child's fearful responses. On the other hand, not enough attention can make the child feel insecure and rejected. These feelings may lead to other kinds of maladaptive behaviours and stressful reactions.

EATING AND ELIMINATION DISORDERS

Eating problems associated with particular disorders, as well as overweight and underweight, were described in Chapter 6. Incontinence associated with spinal cord damage also was discussed. This section will look at several other eating and elimination disorders sometimes found among young children in group settings.

PICA

The uncontrollable eating of food and nonfood substances is called *pica*. Early childhood teachers may encounter children who are constantly tasting substances considered inedible: dirt, tar or grease, chalk, paper, fingerpaint, paste, play dough, or clay. Though often a health threat, frequent tasting of nonedible materials should not be confused with pica. Most young children take little tastes of materials. However, this should be discouraged, with an explanation to the effect that it can cause stomach upset. If the child continues, the problem usually is solved by removing the material with the simple statement: "I can't let you play with the play dough if you eat it. It will make you sick."

Children also may go on food jags. They insist on certain foods to the exclusion of all others. Except in extreme cases (or if too much pressure is put on the child to "eat right") the jag usually disappears in a reasonable time. Some children eat excessive amounts of a certain food. One 4-year-old was known to eat whole heads of lettuce, almost ravenously. At times this eating behaviour may indicate a nutritional deficit. Whenever a teacher is concerned about a child's eating, the parents and public health nurse should be consulted.

SOILING AND WETTING

It is not uncommon for early childhood teachers to encounter children who are not toilet trained, or are not reliable about getting themselves to the toilet in time. The same holds true for young children with developmental disabilities, many of whom may not be toilet trained when they reach preschool age. The reasons vary. Often, conflict has resulted in a toilet-training impasse between child and parents. In the early childhood program, where emotional involvement is at a minimum, toilet training usually can be accomplished quickly. Effective training guides are available including the well-known *Toilet Training in*

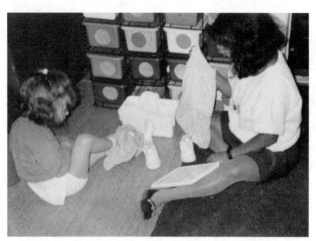

PHOTO 7–5 *Every child needs a change of clothing at school.*

Less than a Day by Azrin and Foxx (1974) and the Fredericks et al. (1975) program, *Toilet Training the Handicapped Child*. It is the rare child, even among children who are severely intellectually impaired, who cannot be trained to use the toilet.

Even after they are toilet trained, young children, including those with disabilities, may have soiling or wetting episodes on occasion. They often give clues of an impending accident by jiggling or clutching themselves. What is needed is a quiet instruction from the teacher, *before* the accident occurs: "Run in and use the toilet. I'll save the swing until you get back." When a toilet accident does occur, a child should never be ridiculed or made to feel guilty. Even the most conscientious child can slip up. Clothing should be changed matter-of-factly and the soiled clothing rinsed out and put in a plastic bag. Every young child needs spare clothes at school, rotated from home if possible (Photo 7–5).

Chronic soiling or wetting sometimes occurs in an older preschool or primary-age child who has been reliably toilet trained. Here are some possible reasons:

- Persistent wetting, especially in girls, may be related to chronic urinary tract infection.
- A child may have a recurring low-grade intestinal virus causing loose or runny bowels.
- Children with diabetes may have failure of urine control at times.
- Some children are anxious about using a strange bathroom, or may have been trained to greater privacy than is available at school.

Once in a long while, even when all physical disorders have been ruled out, a child may continue to have toileting problems. *Encopresis* (chronic soiling problem) and *enuresis* (chronic wetting problem) are the clinical names often assigned to such conditions. Though there are a number of possible reasons, earlier difficulties associated with elimination or toilet training may have become intertwined with anxiety, fear, and other emotional reactions. These can result in a child's unpredictable and hard-to-control soiling or wetting accidents. In these cases, as in all others, the clothes should be changed matter-of-factly, without reprimand or moralizing. Working together, teachers, parents, and the appropriate team member(s) can help a child with enuresis or encopresis gain reliable control.

SOCIAL/LEARNING ACCOMMODATION DISORDERS

Pervasive developmental disorders, **attention-deficit hyperactive disorders**, *and schizophrenia* are three conditions that, to varying degrees, interfere with the child's ability to

- initiate and maintain relationships with others;
- concentrate for any length of time; and
- assimilate new material into his/her existing framework of knowledge.

PERVASIVE DEVELOPMENTAL DISORDERS (PDD)

The disorders in this subclass are characterized by significant qualitative impairment in the development of

- reciprocal social interaction; and
- verbal and nonverbal communication skills.

Often there is a limited range of activities and interests, which frequently are stereotyped and repetitive. The severity and expression of these impairments vary greatly from child to child (American Psychiatric Association 1994).

Autism

Autism is the most severe form of pervasive developmental disorder. One of the earliest signs of autism is resistance to being held or cuddled. The infant tends not to mould to the mother's (or caregiver's) body, as do most infants. As toddlers and little children, children with autism treat others as *inanimate* objects. Rarely do these children make eye contact (Photo 7–6). Following rituals to excess and maintaining rigid requirements for sameness are typical. Changing the position of a piece of furniture or offering a drink from an unfamiliar cup may trigger a violent tantrum. Self-stimulating behaviours such as spinning, rocking, head banging, and self-biting are common. A pediatric neurologist (Coleman 1989, 25) rounds out the description as follows:

> These children may line up objects or toys for hours on end. They love to look at spinning objects such as wheels of toy cars ... When they begin to walk they may walk on their toes. When they are excited they may flap their hands or make finger motions in front or their eyes ... Another bizarre behavior of autistic children

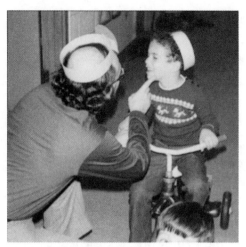

PHOTO 7–6 *Many children who are diagnosed as autistic rarely make eye contact.*

is their reaction to sensory stimuli. Many autistic children cover their ears to shut out vacuum cleaner sounds, the sounds of crying infants, or sometimes the most ordinary of sounds.

The language of children with autism (some do not develop language) often is strange. One child may have beautifully clear speech with complex language, but the message is so disorganized that it makes no sense. Another child may use language simply to express rote memorization. Many of these children can recite many commercial jingles heard on television, but they have no communicative language. In most instances, children with autistic behaviour lack appropriate intonation in their speech. One 4-year-old that one of the authors worked with for several years knew all the words to every stanza of over 40 popular songs and folk ballads. This same child had no social language except for a few stereotyped, **echolalic** (repetitive) phrases. To add to the mysteries of autism, some children with autism have been known to add, divide, and multiply complicated sets of numbers as rapidly as a calculator. (Savant was the name once popular for such individuals.) Others can read a newspaper, word for word, with expression; yet they do not understand a word they read (Batshaw and Perret 1981).

Getting the child whose behaviour is autistic to the point of being able to cope with an integrated classroom often depends on intensive treatment in a specialized setting, or having the child work with specially trained personnel at home prior to entering a regular program.

Schor (1983) states:

When observing the child, always be alert to the possibility of an undetected hearing or vision loss (unrecognized problems are common because children with autism tend to be resistant to clinical testing).

Classroom focus should be on language and self-help skills along with an individualized and systematic program aimed at reducing inappropriate behaviours and facilitating interactions with others.

Schor further suggests that when communicating with children who have autistic behaviours, it is important to keep these points in mind:

• Keep messages simple and direct.

• Use real objects and actions along with words—for example, show the child a shoe and demonstrate pulling the lace through.

- Emphasize spoken language by having the child ask for things by name rather than by gesturing.
- Pair adult attention with **tangible reinforcers** (small toys, stickers, music, or favoured foods, if all else fails) for planned learning programs.
- Establish and maintain a predictable environment that consistently uses the same schedules, language, behaviours, daily routines, classroom furnishings, and room organization.

In working with families of children who have autistic behaviours, it is important to support the parents in every way possible and to work with other members of the interdisciplinary team to help parents find **respite care**, as required by the family.

Another urgent need of parents is frequent assurance that the autism was not caused by a lack of love or caring on their part. Parents of children with autism often have been greatly wronged. Without valid evidence, for many years professionals implied that parents (more often than not, the mother) were somehow responsible for their child being autistic. According to Bee (1992), children are born with the disorder: "Whatever the specific origin, the evidence jointly points to the conclusion that autism reflects different brain functions of some kind" (p. 557).

CHILDHOOD SCHIZOPHRENIA

The child with schizophrenia frequently is described as cut off from reality. The major behavioural characteristics of schizophrenia as found in children include tantrums and repetitive or otherwise bizarre behaviours or postures. Other characteristics are rejection of and withdrawal from social contacts, and unpredictable mood swings. Children who are schizophrenic usually display normal language development, though the language may be used for noncommunicative purposes. Many of these children talk to themselves in a private language that no one can decode. Children with schizophrenia have been described as having more varied symptoms than autistic children and as being more likely to have contact with other people (Rutter, 1986).

ATTENTION DEFICIT/HYPERACTIVITY DISORDERS (ADHD)

Hyperactivity (or *hyperkinesis*) is a catchall diagnosis and label that is much overworked. It is used to refer to children who are highly active, energetic, impulsive, and distractible and who have a hard time waiting their turn or listening to

PHOTO 7–7 *Hyperactivity is used as a catchall phrase to refer to children who are highly active, energetic, impulsive, and distractible.*

instructions (Photo 7–7). These children may be described as showing "excessive motor activity." Regardless of particular behaviours, these children have two things in common:

1. Most adults find them troublesome.

2. Seldom is there to be found an identifiable physical or neurological cause for their high activity level.

Attention deficit hyperactive disorder (ADHD) is a term that has come into popular use over the past several years. It is classified as a subsection under Attention Deficit and Disruptive Behaviour Disorders by the American Psychiatric Association (1994), which no longer separates ADD (Attention Deficit Disorder) from ADHD (Attention Deficit Hyperactive Disorder). ADHD, according to the American Psychiatric Association's *DMS IV*, includes the following behaviours:

- Inattention
  a. fails to give close attention to details or makes careless mistakes in schoolwork, work, or other activities
  b. often has difficulty sustaining attention in tasks or play activities
  c. often does not seem to listen when spoken to directly
  d. often does not follow through on instructions and fails to finish schoolwork, chores ...
  e. often has difficulty organizing tasks and activities
  f. often avoids, dislikes, or is reluctant to engage in tasks that require sustained mental effort ...
  g. often loses things necessary for tasks or activities (e.g., toys ...)
  h. is often easily distracted by extraneous stimuli
  i. is often forgetful in daily activities

- Hyperactivity
  a. often fidgets with hands or feet or squirms in seat
  b. often leaves seat in classroom or in situations in which remaining seated is expected

   c. often runs about or climbs excessively in situations in which it is inappropriate

   d. often has difficulty playing or engaging in leisure activities quietly

   e. is often "on the go" or often acts as if "driven by a motor"

   f. often talks excessively

- Impulsivity

   a. often blurts out answers before questions have been completed

   b. often has difficulty awaiting turn

   c. often interrupts or intrudes on others (e.g., butts into conversations or games) (American Psychiatric Association 1994, 63–64)

The various behaviours described in each tend to be similar and overlapping, though the latter category tends to put greater focus on impulsivity, as well as difficulty in concentrating on the task at hand. Many of the same behaviours are also characteristic of young children diagnosed as learning disabled. The attention deficit disorder label, authoritative as it may sound, does little to lessen the problems associated with managing a young child who is constantly on the move.

Causes of ADHD.

Research has yet to reveal a specific cause of ADHD. Several hypotheses have been offered, one or two of which are backed up by fairly sound evidence. One is the possible role of genetic transmission. Bee (1992) reports a recent study in which one-fourth of the ADHD subjects had parents with a history of hyperactivity. Studies of twins also show possible genetic implications. Among identical twins, both are more likely to have hyperactivity, which is not the case among fraternal twins (Deutsch and Kinsbourne 1991). Researchers continue to work on the brain and its various functions, or misfunctions, to explain ADHD. A correlation has also been found between ADHD and a mother's smoking or drug and alcohol use during pregnancy.

MANAGING HYPERACTIVE BEHAVIOUR

The Hyperactive Label

The term *hyperactivity* is both misused and overused, especially where young children are concerned. As Bee (1992) states, "Two-year-olds are pretty good at doing; they are lousy at not doing. They see something, so they go after it; when they want something, they want it now!" Typically, children in preschool and

PHOTO 7–8 *Children in early childhood programs show a broad range of activity level.*

early primary classrooms show a broad range of activity levels (Photo 7–8). Some seem to be on the move continuously. Teachers often feel as if these children never settle into any activity for any length of time. Yet few are of medical concern because of organic problems. Only 1 to 3 percent of the children labelled hyperactive are truly hyperactive in the clinical sense (Trites and Laprade 1983). A child who can stay with any activity for several minutes at a time is not clinically hyperactive. As one pediatrician explains it: A child who passes the "TV test" (sits in front of a television set and attends to a favourite program) is not hyperactive. The child may be difficult to entertain, not interested in typical learning tasks, or perhaps worried and unhappy, but the child is *not* hyperactive in the medical sense (Holm 1978).

Even in cases of known organic involvement, the hyperactive behaviours must be dealt with as maladaptive behaviours, regardless of other treatment procedures.

Hyperactivity in young children places them at great risk for accidents because they do not anticipate the consequences of their actions. Also, adults become more frustrated by excessively active, impulsive children who must be watched constantly and so "the behaviour itself is problematic and will require training and reinforcement of more desired behaviour patterns" (Peterson 1987).

Medication

In assessing highly active children, it is argued that distinctions should be made between (1) the child whose high activity level is truly **organic**, and (2) the run-of-the-mill overly active child. The reason for making the distinction is that some children in the organic group may benefit from prescription drugs such as Ritalin or Dexedrine (but only if there is indisputable evidence of an organic disorder). However, the medication may have undesirable side effects, perhaps including weight loss, insomnia, or increased blood pressure (Holm 1978). Use of medication to control behaviour disorders should only be done under the guidance of a physician and only when there is clear evidence that it is the most beneficial treatment. Sometimes, it is parents and teachers who come to rely on the medication. In other words, they may become "addicted" to having the child on medication because the child is much less troublesome when medicated.

"Remember: drugs do not teach" (Cook, Tessier, and Armbruster 1987). Cook and her colleagues (1987, 141) follow that reminder with a number of excellent recommendations related to medication and children who are hyper-active.

> Teachers ... prepare the environment carefully, look for positive behavior to reward, and treat the child as one who is learning to develop self-control. Beware of the self-fulfilling prophecy: "Oh, you forgot to take your pill this morning. I guess this will be a bad day." Too many children and parents come to believe that the child's improved concentration is totally the result of medication. Without the child's effort, improvement would not be possible ... credit must be given where credit is due. Each time the child feels ... responsible for the improved behavior, the more likely he or she is to work toward self-control.

Special Diets

Special diets also should be viewed with skepticism. The controversial Feingold diet (introduced during the 1970s), for example, linked artificial food colouring and food additives with hyperactivity. Dr. Feingold (1975) asserted that many children labelled as hyperactive would improve if synthetic colours, flavours, and natural **salicylates** were removed from their diets. Research studies investigating his claims found no clinically significant differences between untreated groups of children and those on the Feingold diet (Conners 1980). True, no harm can come from feeding children foods that are nutritious and additive free. However, even if a curative diet is nutritious (and some are not), looking for a diet as the sole cure for a behaviour disorder often results in ignoring basic problems that require a different treatment (Worthington, Pipes, and Trahms 1978).

Classroom Management of Hyperactive Behaviour

Systematic classroom observation usually reveals one or more activities that engage even the most overly active child for 3 to 20 minutes at a time, several times a week. Such observations are important. They give teachers a place to start a positive behaviour-management program designed to increase the child's span of attention. Even brief focusing on an activity—any activity—sends a signal to teachers. Now is the time to give attention, while the child is engaged in a purposeful activity. This is in contrast to what teachers (and parents) often do—that is, giving their attention when the child is flitting about.

Teachers should watch for those times when a child is appropriately involved in an activity. It is then they should go to the child with a relevant comment, supportive interest, or a gentle challenge: "I bet you can fill that pail full of sand, all the way to the top. I'll watch while you do it." Few children can resist staying with a task when so challenged by an interested and responsive adult.

PHOTO 7–9 *Teachers should help children plan where they will play next.*

A child's span of attention often can be extended by calling attention to unexplored aspects of the activity or by asking questions. While supervising the water table the teacher might ask, "I wonder what would happen if we put a little yellow food colouring in the blue water?" (Or some nontoxic soap powder? Or a drop or two of glycerin?) At the finger painting table the teacher can pose questions such as "What can your thumbs do?" "The tips of your fingers?" "The backs of your hands?" An overly active child's "stick-to-it-iveness" may also be enhanced by offering additional but related materials: "Here are some new cookie cutters to use with the dough when you get it all rolled out. Do you want to start with the heart or the diamond?" Or, "The big doll looks as if it needs a bath, too." The key is always to offer the ideas and materials while the child is still engaged in the activity— before the child loses interest and leaves.

Overly active children, when they look as if they are getting ready to quit an activity, should be helped to plan where they will play next. Noting that a child is about to leave an area, the teacher can say, "Let's decide where you want to play now." If the child seems unable to make the decision, the teacher can offer choices: "There is room for you in the block corner or at the water table." Once a choice has been made, it is best for the teacher to accompany the child to the chosen area. If there is a teacher in the block area, for example, the first teacher can say something like: "Julie has come to work with blocks. Will you help her get started?" Otherwise, the accompanying teacher should help the child get involved (Photo 7–9).

To further reduce overactivity in young children, you may want to try the following ideas, which have proven useful. These suggestions are readily carried out in any early childhood program.

• Observe the child in various activities over several days. If observations indicate, for example, that a child's attention begins to wander after five or six minutes of music time, plan to end that child's participation as it gets toward the five-minute mark. A second teacher can quietly draw the child away and provide another activity before the child wearies of music. The child can be given crayons or a puzzle, or might assist the teacher setting up the snack tables. It is important that a special activity not be offered if the child has already disrupted the music group.

- Keep the classroom and play yard neat and orderly. Do not have too many materials out at any one time. Encourage the children to restore (tidy up) each play area before they leave it. A disorganized environment encourages disorderly behaviour, especially with overly active children.
- Alternate active and quiet experiences, large and small groups, teacher-initiated and child-initiated activities. (See Chapter 14 on environmental arrangements for guidelines on helping all young children focus more effectively on curriculum activities.) Extended free-play periods can be especially difficult for overly active children. The amount of free-play time and the number of play choices usually need to be limited.

When working with an overly active child, teachers frequently need to review the following questions:

1. Are the classroom activities interesting, varied, attractive, and lively? In other words, are they fun and are they challenging?
2. Are the activities a good match to the child's skill levels?
3. Are activities and interest centres adapted on a regular basis to reflect the changing interests and developmental levels of the children?
4. Is the child getting attention when focusing on an activity even for a moment or two, rather than for flitting about?

Working toward positive answers to these questions is essential in reducing hyperactivity. When behaviour-management strategies and knowledge of what is developmentally appropriate are laced together with care and concern for the child's well-being, hyperactivity inevitably lessens. The same four-pronged approach also works effectively with children who display a variety of other behaviour problems.

It is important to consider the following: "Most children who are diagnosed by competent mental health professionals as having attention-deficit hyperactivity disorder, do; but as early childhood educators, we must always ensure that our classrooms are developmentally appropriate and that children are not being inappropriately labeled because our classroom is inappropriate" (Landau and McAninch 1993, 49).

Learning Disabilities

Children with learning disabilities, to varying degrees and in varying combinations, may display the following learning disorders:

PHOTO 7–10 *Fine motor control is often more poorly developed in children suspected of having a learning disability.*

- constant motion and purposeless activity
- poor perceptual motor skills
- low tolerance for frustration
- frequent mood swings
- poor coordination, in both large and fine motor activities (Photo 7–10)
- distractibility and short attention span
- poor auditory and visual memory
- a variety of language deficits

From the above list, it is obvious that learning disabilities encompass a wide range of behaviour disorders. Efforts at clinical classification are continuing. Some textbooks discuss learning disabilities in conjunction with attentiondeficit disorders. Others may group learning disabilities with cognitive disorders or impaired mental functioning. Other classifications are motor dysfunction and impaired motor planning (sometimes associated with the term **minimal brain damage**). In this text, learning disabilities will be discussed as a separate category. The decision is based on the extensive overlap of learning disabilities with other behaviour disorders and related developmental problems. Providing a separate discussion may serve to clarify some of the issues. Nevertheless, the overlaps remain, as is confusingly evident in the sections that follow.

LEARNING DISABILITIES DEFINED

What is a learning disability? Two answers come immediately to mind: the first, the many things that it is; the second, the many other things that it is not. This is the official definition adopted in 1981 by the Learning Disabilities Association of Canada (1990):

> *Learning disabilities* is a generic term that refers to a heterogeneous group of disorders due to identifiable or inferred central nervous system dysfunction. Such disorders may be manifested by delays in early development and/or difficulties in any of the following areas: attention, memory, reasoning, coordination, communicating, reading, writing, spelling, calculation, social competence and emotional maturation.

> Learning disabilities are intrinsic to the individual and may affect learning and behaviour in any individual, including those with potentially average, average, or above average intelligence.

Learning disabilities are not due primarily to visual, hearing or motor handicaps; to mental retardation, emotional disturbance, or environmental disadvantage; although they may occur concurrently with any of these.

Learning disabilities may arise from genetic variations, biochemical factors, events in the pre- to peri-natal period, or any subsequent events resulting in neurological impairment.

This definition states clearly that a learning disability is not the result of these conditions:

- visual, hearing, or motor impairments
- mental retardation (intellectual impairment)
- emotional disturbance, or
- environmental disadvantages

We can say what a learning disability is not; what we cannot say is what it is. The confusion and indecision are not for lack of research. During the last 25 or 30 years, hundreds upon hundreds of studies have been conducted. Competent researchers in the field of psychology, neurology, education, and educational psychology have attempted to come up with definitive answers to the elusive question of how to define (and diagnose) learning disabilities.

Diagnosing learning disabilities in preschool children is difficult—perhaps impossible (Photo 7–11). As described in the formal definition given in U.S. law (PL 94-142), learning disabilities are related primarily to academic performance: "the imperfect ability to listen, think, speak, read, write, spell, or do mathematical calculations." Because most early childhood educators consider it developmentally inappropriate for preschool-aged children to be spending their school hours in such pursuits, we might ask whether young children should ever be considered learning disabled. "No," seems to be the logical response; yet not all teachers are comfortable with that, and for good reason. Many young children show behaviour patterns similar to those

PHOTO 7–11 *What is a learning disability? There is no agreed upon answer, especially where young children are concerned.*

associated with learning disabilities in older children. They may be distractible, easily frustrated, excessively active, or poorly coordinated. These behaviours already are interfering with their everyday learning activities in a variety of ways. A number of early childhood educators believe that it is in children's best interests to deal with these troubling behaviours during the preschool years, before they worsen and compound the child's problems. The type and timing of such intervention is a recurring issue in early childhood education.

PREDICTING LEARNING DISABILITIES

Is it possible that certain behaviours in a young child may be predictive of subsequent trouble with academic tasks? The answer seems to be "Yes," as long as it is understood that the judgment is based on *hunch* and educated guesswork. Teachers of young children frequently identify a child whose behaviours appear to put him or her at risk for learning disabilities and, perhaps, later academic problems. The next question: Is it possible that these worrisome behaviours can be eliminated, or at least reduced, before they have a serious impact on later academic performance? Again, the answer seems to be "Yes." During the past several years, early identification of potentially learning-disabled young children has gained strong support. Child developmentalists, parents, and professionals from other disciplines such as medicine and psychology believe that many of the learning, social–emotional, and educational problems associated with learning disabilities can be prevented or remedied if identification and

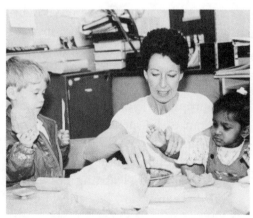

intervention are provided before the child enters school (Haring and McCormick 1990, 140) (Photo 7–12).

Caution is a necessary component in the identification of young children at potential risk for later learning disabilities. The first step is observation of the child in a number of activities. The next step is matching the observed performance to performance expectancies in all areas of development. At the same time, it must be remembered that all young children are different one from another, and all have much development yet to come. Another point is that young children often

PHOTO 7–12 *Teachers of young children frequently identify a child whose behaviours appear to put him or her at risk for learning disabilities and, perhaps, later academic problems.*

demonstrate marked differences or delays that are nevertheless within a normal range of development. These are some of the reasons for considering learning disabilities an inappropriate diagnosis for a young child. In most instances, it is more beneficial to the child to view early problems as developmental deviations calling for learning experiences that meet individual needs. Making such a decision also is a more economical use of professional energy than trying to decide whether to pin (or not to pin) the label "learning disabled" on a child.

PHOTO 7–13 *Readiness comes through appropriate early learning experiences and many unhurried opportunities to practise.*

SIGNS OF POSSIBLE FUTURE LEARNING DISABILITIES

A cue in older preschool children that learning problems may lie ahead is a lack of what are sometimes called *readiness* or **prerequisite skills.** As will be described in Chapter 19, these are skills thought to be necessary to academic success once the child enters grade school. However, simply waiting for the *unready* child to become ready rarely helps the child. Readiness comes through experiences, learning, and the opportunity to practise and master developmental skills (Photo 7–13). What follows are examples of particular deviations or delays in various areas of development that are thought to be related to potential learning disabilities.

1. Indicators of Visual-Sensory Gross Motor Difficulties

Many developmentalists, with Piaget in the lead, theorize that all early learning is sensorimotor based. Children about whom teachers express concern in terms of future academic performance invariably show some kind of sensorimotor problems. In addition, they often show generalized delay in reaching basic motor milestones and exhibit one or more of the following characteristics:

- *Imperfect body control* results in poorly coordinated or jerky movements and trouble with running, throwing, catching, hopping, or kicking.
- *Poor balance* may cause the child to fall off play equipment, fall down, or fall into furnishings or other people. (Inability to walk a balance beam is almost always a symptom in a kindergarten or Grade 1 child.)
- *Uncertain bilateral and cross-lateral movements* are often a telltale sign of future problems with academic tasks. The child with a bilateral problem may not

be able to use both arms simultaneously and/or in synchrony, as children do when catching a ball or jumping off a wall. Or a child may not use opposite legs and arms in opposing harmony (cross-laterality), as seen in agile children climbing to the top of a jungle gym. The clearest example of cross-laterality is crawling: left leg and right arm moving forward, alternating with right leg and left arm in forward movement.

- *Inability to cross body midline* has long been viewed as a possible predictor of future academic difficulty. In such cases the child has trouble using the right hand to work on a task where any part of the task lies to the left of the midpoint of the child's body or vision. The same holds true of the left hand and the right-side focus. A common example is a child painting on a large piece of paper at the easel. The child transfers the brush from the right hand to the left when painting on the left half of the paper and back again when painting on the right.

- *Faulty spatial orientation* interferes with children's ability to understand where they are in space, in relation to their physical surroundings. For example, a child may walk into a wall; poor orientation interferes with the child perceiving the wall as being *right there*. Or the child may gear up for a mighty jump only to land with frightening force because the ground was much closer than the greater height the child had anticipated. Putting clothes on wrong-side-up or backward, or having difficulty going up and down stairs, also may indicate problems with spatial orientation.

2. Indicators of Fine Motor Difficulties (Poor Fine Motor/ Eye–Hand Coordination Skills)

Problems in buttoning, lacing, snapping, cutting, pasting, and stringing beads are characteristics of older preschool children thought to be at future academic risk. Often these children are unable to draw a straight line or copy simple shapes such as a circle, cross, or square. When they manage to draw a crude imitation, the circle seldom is closed, the corners on the square are rounded or irregular, and the cross is crossed far off centre. Tasks of this kind and others, such as cutting with scissors, are virtually impossible for these children to master without extensive training and practice.

3. Visual-Perception Problems

Visual-perception problems refer to how well the child's processing mechanism handles the information that comes in visually—that is, how well the child makes sense of what is seen. Various aspects of perceptual motor skills will be described in Chapter 19; here the focus will be on other aspects related specifically to the current topic, learning disabilities, where problems take several forms.

PHOTO 7–14 *Visual discrimination and visual orientation skills go together.*

A problem in visual perception has nothing to do with blindness or impaired vision. In other words, there is no *physical* problem.

- *Visual discrimination* is the ability to look at objects or pictures and note how they are alike or how they are different. Children with visual-discrimination problems may have trouble sorting objects according to colour, size, or shape. They may not be able to match lotto pictures, copy block designs, or tell the difference between the smiling and the frowning clown pictures. Often they can be seen trying to fit a large object into too small an opening or container.

- *Visual orientation* is related to spatial orientation. The child may recognize three-dimensional objects such as a head of lettuce, a cap, or a paintbrush, but not recognize the same items in two-dimensional pictures (Photo 7–14). Another example of visual disorientation is recognizing objects in their normal or upright positions but failing to recognize them when they are turned over or lying sideways. One child insisted that an overturned wooden armchair was a cage; the moment it was turned right-side up, he labelled it as a chair. Even when the chair was turned over while he watched, he insisted it was a cage the moment it was overturned.

- *Visual memory* is obvious: remembering what was just seen, at least for a few seconds. Children with visual memory problems may not remember the name of the animal on their card, for example, even though the picture has been face down for only a moment. Or, in the familiar take-away game, they cannot recall what was removed even though there were only three or four articles on the tray when it was presented just a moment before.

- *Visual tracking* is skill in following objects visually. Children with tracking problems may have trouble keeping an eye on the ball, following the flight of a bird, or buttoning buttons, in order, from top to bottom. Visual-tracking ability is likely to be associated with reading skills, in that reading requires systematic eye movements from left to right and from top to bottom.

- *Visual–motor integration* is a skill that can also be thought of as eye–hand coordination. Children with these kinds of problems may have trouble with almost every motor task that requires vision: fitting appropriately shaped pieces into a puzzle box, cutting on the line, drawing around a form, or

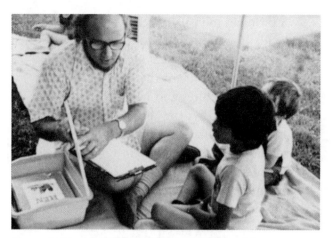

PHOTO 7–15 *A child may have trouble making sense out of what people are saying.*

tracing a simple shape. It is as if the child's hands cannot do what the eyes say needs to be done.

4. Auditory-Perception Problems

Many young children who seem to be candidates for future learning disabilities have trouble processing what they hear (Photo 7–15). Again, this is not a physical problem; deafness or being hard-of-hearing is not the cause of the child's problem. Basically, the problem results from the inability to tell the difference between sounds—lack of auditory discrimination. *Hat* and *mat* may sound the same to these children. Often, they cannot tell the difference between high and low musical tones, especially as the range lessens. Localization of sound is usually a problem, too. The child may have to look in two or three directions when trying to locate a whistler or a barking dog.

5. Language Deviations

Children at risk for learning disabilities frequently have trouble with receptive or expressive language, or both (see Chapter 17). Acquiring the more advanced grammatical forms and the ability to formulate organized sentences tends to come considerably later than for most children. While vocabulary is not necessarily more limited, trouble can arise, for example, when the child tries to recall a well-known word to describe a familiar concept. Carrying out directions that include common prepositions such as *in, on, under,* and *over* is often baffling. If the teacher says to put the block *on top of the box,* a child may look at the teacher questioningly while putting the object *in* the box. Many of these children have trouble repeating short sentences, rhymes, and directions. In addition, they often have difficulty imitating sounds, gestures, body movements, facial expressions, and other forms of nonverbal communication.

6. Cognitive Disorders

Trouble in organizing thoughts and processing information with logic is characteristic of many young children with potential learning disabilities. They tend to operate only in the here and now, with little or no ability to deal with any kind of abstract thought or events. While concrete thinking is characteristic of young children, most older preschoolers are able to deal with a certain amount of abstraction. For example, it is the rare 4- or 5-year-old who cannot relay a little information about the pet at home or the new swing set in the backyard.

Cognitively disorganized children may also have trouble carrying out simple directions or remembering what it was they were supposed to do, even while they are working on the task. Trouble generalizing from one event to another is common, too. A rule about no running indoors may not generalize to no running in the classroom, or in the halls, or in the library, even though all are indoors within the same building. Especially frustrating for adults is that the same mistakes are made again and again, simply because there is no carryover from one event to the next.

7. Perseveration

Perseveration (repeating the same act over and over, seemingly endlessly) is typical of many children who seem likely to develop a future learning disorder. These children appear unable to stop what they are doing of their own accord. A child may scrub back and forth with the same crayon, or draw the same shape for minutes at a time, until stopped by a teacher or parent. Some children chant the same words or make the same hand gestures repeatedly until someone succeeds in diverting them to something else. It usually is difficult for the perseverative child to change activities. Even when a change is accomplished, there may be carryover from the preceding activity. For example, the child who has been scrubbing with a crayon may have been moved into block play. Here the back-and-forth scrubbing continues on the floor, with the child using a block rather than a crayon to make the back-and-forth motions.

8. Deficit Social Skills

Children who appear to have the potential for later learning disabilities tend to have more than their share of social problems. They may be bullying or aggressive, withdrawn, or overly dependent. Their behaviour often confuses other children and so they have trouble making friends. When they do succeed in forming a friendship they tend to have difficulty keeping it. Sometimes the child puts too many demands on the friend, or has such inadequate play skills that the friend loses interest. Also, their impulsiveness may cause them to say and do inappropriate things. They may not foresee the possibility of negative consequences such as hurt feelings or the unintentional destruction of a friend's favourite toy. When a child loses two or three friends (for reasons the

PHOTO 7–16 *Rejection increases frustration, a sense of incompetence, and low self-esteem.*

child neither understands nor seems able to change), feelings of rejection are likely to follow. Rejection increases frustration, a sense of incompetence, and low self-esteem (Photo 7–16). These feelings, in turn, lead to a tendency to break into tears at the slightest provocation, to strike out for what seems to be little or no reason, or to withdraw even more.

PROGRAM CONSIDERATIONS

In concluding this section on possible learning disabilities in young children, one concept bears repeating. Characteristics associated with learning disabilities can be observed in all young children, at one time or another. Is there a preschool teacher anywhere who has not watched a child do a lovely painting only to see it overlaid from edge to edge and top to bottom with endless coats of paint? The teacher may mourn the loss of the painting (having mentally earmarked it for display at the parent meeting) but this once-in-a-while behaviour is no cause for concern, and should not (because it is an isolated event) be considered perseveration. As noted before, in connection with all developmental problems, one must look for *clusters of behaviours* and note the degree to which a behaviour occurs. Questions that are appropriate to ask are these: Are the behaviours happening excessively? Do they interfere with the child's development and general well-being? Age, too, must be a consideration. It is always a warning sign when a problem behaviour is extreme and persists significantly beyond appropriate age levels.

In working with children whose behaviours seem predictive of future learning disabilities, careful reexamination of the learning environment is essential (Chapter 14), as is a thorough review of effective teaching strategies. These strategies have been described throughout the text in regard to various developmental issues. Many of the strategies have special relevance in work with preschool children whose behaviour disorders put them at risk of future failure at school.

PHOTO 7–17 *Be patient. Provide a lot of support and encouragement.*

Strategies for Teachers of Preschool Children with Behaviour Disorders

- Be consistent in the use of positive reinforcement to increase behaviours that facilitate the child's development, thereby decreasing behaviours that interfere with development.

- Provide the child with encouragement and descriptive praise for each step forward, regardless of how small.

- Remember that every child has strengths and does positive things; concentrate attention on these rather than on the child's weaknesses and misbehaviours (Photo 7–17).

- Use **task analysis** to teach whatever skills the child is having trouble with, whether learning to imitate, to focus attention, to say "No" instead of hitting, or any other skill or behaviour.

- Give directions one at a time and allow adequate time for the child to comply. Verify the child's understanding of the request; rehearse (walk the child through) the required response as often as necessary.

- Teach new concepts and skills in short sessions with concrete materials that allow a child to use several sensory modalities: seeing, hearing, moving, and manipulating.

- Be patient. Children with learning problems may have to be told or shown many times in many different ways how to accomplish a simple task. Do not expect learning to generalize from one situation to another. Each situation seems new to the child.

- Help parents understand that their child is not being difficult or inattentive on purpose. Tell them of their child's accomplishments, no matter how small. To enhance the child's self-esteem, describe his or her accomplishments to the parent in the presence of the child, whenever possible.

SUMMARY

Teachers of young children may encounter a number of social and adaptive problems. These include
- excessive dependency on adults or general withdrawal from social contacts;
- fears that result in excessive and unrealistic anxiety about everyday happenings;
- withdrawal problems;
- eating problems—the most serious of which is pica, the eating of inedible substances (lead-based paint flakes are likely to pose the greatest risk: intellectual impairment, even death, may follow excessive eating of this toxic substance); and
- soiling and wetting that continues past the expected age for toilet training.

Social learning/accommodation disorders include these categories:
- pervasive developmental disorders (PDD), the most severe form of which is autism
- schizophrenia
- attention deficit hyperactive disorders (ADHD)

These are all conditions that require diagnostic assessment and specialized program support.

Learning disabilities are classified under a variety of headings, depending on the researcher's, the clinician's, or the teacher's theoretical background. Confusion arises at times because some definitions of learning disabilities refer to them as being specific to reading, writing, or math. For early childhood educators, this raises a number of questions. For example, is it ever appropriate to diagnose a preschool-aged child as learning disabled? If not, what about the many maladaptive behaviours (distractibility, short attention span, visual-perception problems, and many others) in some preschool children that resemble the behaviours of older children having serious problems with academic tasks? Is it not important to deal with these nonacademic behaviour disorders in the early years, before they become greater problems that are likely to have a negative impact on subsequent academic learning? The answer seems to be "Yes" and the question then becomes "How?" Strategies for teaching young children with all kinds of behaviour disorders and potential learning disabilities are found throughout this chapter and in the previous section.

Throughout this chapter there is a cautionary theme: behaviour problems of every type are common among young children. Every child exhibits a number of them during the developmental years. It is only when problems begin to become so excessive that they interfere with a child's developmental progress that they are of great concern. Even then, to label or classify prematurely a young child who has so much development yet to come often does the child a grave injustice. It is not how a child is classified, but how the child is cared for and taught, as an individual, that is the important issue in working with all kinds of behaviour and learning problems in young children.

STUDENT ACTIVITIES

1. Observe an early childhood classroom for one hour. Make brief anecdotal notes related to episodes of children showing short attention span (cite examples) and/or poor motor coordination. Discuss these with the teacher to see if the recorded behaviours are characteristic of the children you observed.

2. Analyze the preceding record to see if there are recurring patterns or particular behaviours that were repeated frequently. Assume you are the child's teacher. Draw up a set of guidelines that you might present to the other classroom teachers as possible ways to work with the child.

3. Select any one of the visual-perception problems described in the text. Design a learning activity for a one-to-one tutorial situation that would give the child with the potential problem practice in developing the skill or in overcoming the deficit. Adapt the same activity to a classroom game format that would be fun for normally developing children, while giving the child with the potential problem the opportunity to learn as part of the group.

4. Wear a watch (preferably one with a second hand) and observe an early childhood program during an entire free-play period (30 to 45 minutes). Consult with the teacher first to identify which child might be considered overly active. During the first half of your observation, record the types of activities that the child engaged in and the amount of time spent in each (also record time spent wandering about). Make the same recordings on a normally active child for the second half of the observation. Compare the observations and try to analyze the differences or similarities in the two children.

REFERENCES

Allen, K.E., and B. Hart 1984 *The Early Years. Arrangements for Learning*. Englewood Cliffs, N.J.: Prentice-Hall.

American Psychiatric Association 1994 *DSM IV*. Washington, D.C.: American Psychiatric Association.

Azrin, N.H., and R.M. Foxx 1974 *Toilet Training in Less than a Day*. New York: Simon and Schuster.

Bee, H. 1992 *The Developing Child*. New York: HarperCollins.

Coleman, M. 1989 "Young Children with Autism or Autistic-Like Behavior." *Infants and Young Children* 1, no. 4: 22–31.

Conners, C.K. 1980 *Food Additives and Hyperactive Children*. New York: Plenum Press.

Cook, R.E., A. Tessier, and V.B. Armbruster 1987 *Adapting Early Childhood Curricula for Children with Special Needs*. Columbus, Ohio: Charles E. Merrill.

Deutsch, C.K., and M. Kinsbourne 1990 "Genetics and Biochemistry in Attention Deficit Disorder." In M. Lewis and S.M. Miller, eds. *Handbook of Developmental Psychopathology*, 93–108. New York: Plenum.

Feingold, B.F. 1975 *Why Your Child Is Hyperactive*. New York: Random House.

Fredericks, H.D., V.L. Baldwin, D.N. Grove, and W.G. Grove 1975 *Toilet Training the Handicapped Child*. Monmouth, Ore.: Instructional Development Corp.

Haring, N.G., and L. McCormick 1990 *Exceptional Children and Youth*. Columbus, Ohio: Charles E. Merrill.

Holm, V.A. 1978 "The Pediatrician with an Interest in Child Development." In K.E. Allen, V.A. Holm, and R.L. Schiefelbusch, eds. *Early Interventions: A Team Approach*. Baltimore: University Park Press.

Landau, S., and C. McAninch 1993 "Young Children with Attention Deficits." *Young Children*, May, 49–58.

Learning Disabilities Association of Canada 1990 *Help Build a Brighter Future: Identification of Children at Risk for Learning Disabilities in Child Care Centres*. Ottawa: Learning Disabilities Association of Canada. Reprinted with permission.

Peterson, N.L. 1987 *Early Intervention for Handicapped and At-Risk Children*. Denver: Love Publishing.

Rutter, M. 1986 "Infantile Autism: Assessment, Differential Diagnosis and Treatment." In D. Shaffer, A. Erhardt, and L. Greenhill, eds. *A Clinical Guide to Child Psychiatry*. New York: Free Press.

Schor, D.P. 1983 "Autism." In J.A. Blackman, ed. *Medical Aspects of Developmental Disabilities in Children Birth to Three*. Iowa City: University of Iowa.

Spodek, B., O.N. Saracho, and R.C. Lee 1984 *Mainstreaming Young Children*. Belmont, CA: Wadsworth Publishing Co.

Thompson, R.A., and M.E. Lamb 1982 "Stranger Sociality and Its Relationship to Temperament and Social Experience during the Second Year of Life." *Infant Behavior and Development* 5: 227–28.

Thurman, S.K., and A.H. Widerstrom 1990 *Infants and Young Children with Special Needs: A Developmental and Ecological Approach.* Baltimore: Paul H. Brookes.

Trites, R.L., and K. Laprade 1983 "Evidence for an Independent Syndrome of Hyperactivity." *Journal of Child Psychology and Psychology* 24, no. 4: 573–86.

Worthington, B.S., P.L. Pipes, and C.M. Trahms 1978 "The Pediatric Nutritionist." In K.E. Allen, V.A. Holm, and R.L. Schiefelbusch, eds. *Early Intervention: A Team Approach.* Baltimore: University Park Press.

CHAPTER 8

Children Who Are Gifted and Talented

After studying the material in this chapter, the student will be able to

- define giftedness in young children and explain the factors that contribute to giftedness
- identify the characteristics of young children who are gifted
- give reasons why potential giftedness and talents may not be identified in young children with disabilities and children from different cultural backgrounds

INTRODUCTION

Children who demonstrate abilities that are advanced in one or more areas of development when compared to their peers of the same age are often described as gifted and/or talented. Furthermore, these children maintain this advanced state throughout their developmental years. In other words, children who are gifted continue to outperform children of the same age and socioeconomic status. Other children neither catch up to them nor overtake them.

Preschool children who are gifted are often not recognized as requiring specialized individual programming. It is important to note that in the United States some states now require the development of a formal Individual Education Plan (IEP) for gifted students, similar to that required for children with disabilities (Wolf 1994).

ORIGINS OF GIFTEDNESS

What is the source of giftedness, especially when it takes the form of high IQ and general intellectual competence? The child's environment seems to be a major factor. Children who are assessed as exceptionally bright are more likely to come from advantaged, middle-class families than from lower-class families.

Of equal importance is the genetic makeup of the child. It is when a child with the genetic predisposition for giftedness enters an enriched environment that giftedness is more clearly identified and encouraged. In general, better-educated families are better off financially. This enables them to provide the daily, taken-for-granted enrichment that is a key element in their children's performance. Given two children with equal genetic endowment, the child in the enriched environment almost surely would be observed and labelled as "brighter" than a poorly nourished child raised in an unstimulating environment. In other words, giftedness, most likely, is a combination of "good genes" and a stimulating environment (Freeman 1981). Standard methods used to identify gifted children are often culture- and class-bound and not sufficiently sensitive to recognize future performance potential.

CHARACTERISTICS OF YOUNG CHILDREN WHO ARE GIFTED AND TALENTED

Precocious is a term often used to describe young children who appear to be remarkably bright or unusually verbal. Precocious children tend to demonstrate outstanding talents, far beyond what would be expected for their age. The precocity may show up in some specialized areas such as painting or music or math. In the truly gifted child, the accomplishments seem to appear spontaneously, as a part of the child's own unique developmental process. Studies show that it is *unlikely* that these early and outstanding abilities emerge because of special training or parental pressure. In fact, parents of especially bright or talented children often are surprised when told of their child's remarkable abilities (Robinson 1981).

In general, the characteristics that identify young potentially gifted children appear to be a combination of advanced verbal skills, high levels of curiosity, and the ability to concentrate and remember. Many children who are gifted also seem to learn rapidly and to enjoy problem solving. The following list of specific clues to potential giftedness in a young child is adapted from Roedell, Jackson, and Robinson (1980) and Karnes and Johnson (1989).

The child who is potentially gifted

- has a large vocabulary that he or she uses appropriately; has an interest in words, and enjoys practising new words;
- uses language to give suggestions, express ideas, pass on information, and ask content questions: "How did the fox know the baby rabbit was there?";
- uses metaphors and analogies: "The moss on the tree is like an old man's beard";

Photo 8–1 *Preplanning is one characteristic of children who are gifted.*

- makes up songs and stories; invents rhymes; plays with the sound and rhythm of words;
- modifies his or her language to meet the comprehension level of younger children; uses language to handle conflicts and aggression in play situations;
- appears to understand abstract concepts such as time, family relationships (that Father can be both a husband and a brother), cause and effect (why the ice has melted), and connections between past and present experiences (Photo 8–1);
- uses blocks, play dough, or drawing materials to make interesting patterns; creates unusual and well-thought-out designs; thinks through the steps in what he or she is creating ahead of time;
- shows unusual speed in mastering new concepts, songs, and rhymes;
- is able to follow easily the steps in a task (for example, replicating a boat or hat that a teacher has demonstrated how to make);
- shows absorption in particular topics (for example, dinosaurs: pores over books and pictures about dinosaurs, memorizes their names and characteristics, learns to pronounce the difficult names);
- demonstrates complex classification and discrimination skills: spontaneously groups items such as toy cars, boats, airplanes, and trucks; arranges objects according to size and colour;
- is skilled in putting together new and difficult puzzles; appears to examine puzzle pieces first and then put them in place, rather than depending on trial and error;
- seems to have good orientation skills and a sense of spatial relationships: has some idea of how to get back to school when on a walk; manoeuvres wheel toys so as to avoid obstacles; keeps to his or her own space during dance and rhythmic activities;
- notices what is new and different in the environment (for example, rearrangement of equipment, a teacher's new hairstyle or new dress, a new drying rack);
- shows a sense of humour (tells about the new kitten falling in the fruit bowl); makes up jokes and riddles; and

- indicates awareness of feelings of others, both children and adults; may comment when a teacher is not feeling well or another child appears withdrawn or especially happy.

Obviously, no child is likely to show all of these traits; many, however, will show two, three, or more, in various combinations. What is also important is to note the child's ability to

- process abstract concepts (for example, comprehending the humour in a situation or understanding the quantity that a numeral stands for);
- comprehend consequences of actions;
- solve problems (for example, how to make a series of blocks balance; how to fit the pieces of a difficult puzzle together);
- learn new songs quickly;
- use a new toy, game, or computer program appropriately, with little learning time; and
- demonstrate curiosity in new situations, asking questions that show insight.

Some children demonstrate special talent in a specific area such as art, music, or psychomotor coordination. The following information, adapted from Saunders and Espeland's *Bringing Out the Best*, identifies a number of behaviour patterns in children that may indicate special talents in these areas. By recognizing special talent or ability, a teacher of young children may be able to develop and provide appropriately challenging and stimulating learning opportunities, ones that can be enjoyed by all the children, but that will enable the inclusion of those who are more advanced.

Children who have special ability in the area of art

- demonstrate eye–hand coordination that is developmentally advanced
- are able to include fine detail in pictures, clay, or play dough objects;
- are able to remember and replicate detail in objects, pictures, and scenes they have seen;
- recognize and respond to differences in textures and colours (hues and tones);
- show an interest in and respond to photos, paintings, and sculptures; and
- express their feelings, emotions, and moods in their drawings, paintings, and sculpted creations, such as in play dough, collages, etc.

Children who have special ability in the area of music

- often request and initiate music-related activities and show the ability to respond emotionally to different pieces or types of music;

- can label the name of a familiar song from hearing the tune or beat;
- can carry a tune when singing;
- can sing in key with a song that is within their range;
- can recognize the sounds of particular instruments within a group instrumental performance and can label the familiar instruments by name;
- dance, move, clap, and tap in time with music and rhythms;
- respond to poetry that has a rhythmical flow and rhyming words; and
- may spontaneously make up their own tunes, songs, or rhythmical chants.

Children with advanced psychomotor ability
- demonstrate a well-developed sense of balance: hopping, climbing on a jungle gym, showing early ability in gymnastics, skating, etc.;
- show advanced abilities in sport-related activities: can throw and catch a ball, dribble a basketball, skate, etc.;
- have advanced coordination as is evident in their running, jumping, climbing, and tumbling skills;
- compete easily with older children in sport-related activities; and
- are able to create vigorous dances involving active coordinated movement: rolling, jumping, hopping, twisting, etc.

PHOTO 8–2 *Children from different ethnic backgrounds often are not recognized as bright due to teachers' inability to understand the child's home language.*

MINORITY CHILDREN WHO ARE GIFTED

Many of the characteristics of children who are recognized as gifted relate to high-level language skills. Bright children from minority cultures and different ethnic backgrounds often are not recognized because they lack these middle-class language skills (Photo 8–2). This difference should never be interpreted to mean that a child has less potential. Rather, it is usually due to the fact that the child has had less opportunity to acquire sophisticated language. Often, the child's home-language skills, which are not observed, may be advanced (see Chapter 18).

In reviewing the work of a number of researchers, Karnes and Johnson (1989) note other influences that tend to work against the identification of gifted minority preschoolers. These are

- having the attitude that giftedness does not exist among children from low-income backgrounds;
- defining giftedness in ways that reflect only the majority culture's values;
- using identification procedures that are unfavourable to low-income and minority children (as will be discussed in Chapter 11); and
- providing few environmental opportunities for enhancing intellectual or artistic achievement in young and bright minority children. (No one can excel at anything without the opportunity to try.)

Clearly, there are children who are gifted in every ethnic and racial group at all socioeconomic levels. Thus, early identification and appropriate preschool education for children without economic advantages is critical as a means of identifying and nurturing those with special gifts and talents (Stile and Kitano 1991).

PHOTO 8–3 *The special talents of a child with a disability often go unnoticed.*

CHILDREN WITH DISABILITIES WHO ARE GIFTED AND/OR TALENTED

The fact that a child with a disability also may be a gifted child is often overlooked (Photo 8–3). A child with a learning disability may have superior intelligence or outstanding artistic or mechanical talents. The same is true of children who are deaf, children with cerebral palsy, or those with almost any other kind of developmental disability. The potential for intellectual or artistic giftedness in these children seldom receives much attention. Educational emphasis and energy tends to be narrowly focused on helping children overcome physical or sensory deficits. As Gallagher (1988) points out, rarely do we even search for potential giftedness in special populations.

Identifying children who are gifted among children with disabilities may be difficult. Conventional assessment instruments often fail to pick up on their strengths, let alone their giftedness. Wolfle (1989) suggests direct observation in a natural setting as a valuable way of discovering the special talents that a child with special needs may have. The importance of this recommendation is borne out by the following story of a situation that occurred with a 4-year-old in an integrated preschool:

Benjamin, blind since birth, had developed a number of unusual and repetitive behaviours that sometimes are observed in young children who cannot see. His preschool teachers noted, however, that the strange behaviours stopped whenever there was music in the classroom. Benjamin appeared to listen intently and always asked for more. One teacher began sitting down with Benjamin with musical instruments. One time it was a ukelele, then an auto-harp, another time a recorder. After a brief period of experimentation, Benjamin would "find" tunes he could play on any one of the instruments. Next the teacher took him to a classroom that had a piano. Again, with only limited exploration of the instrument, Benjamin began to improvise recognizable tunes. The teacher shared these experiences with Benjamin's parents, who were able to buy a piano. Benjamin spent hours at the piano and became an eager piano student. By the age of 16 he was regarded as a gifted young pianist.

Many young children with disabilities and sensory impairments have high potential for both intellectual and creative achievement. Attention needs to be directed toward these children in early childhood programs so that their curiosity and eagerness to learn are encouraged rather than allowed to wither. Karnes and Johnson (1987) argue that it is important to fund early intervention demonstration programs that focus on all young gifted children. These programs could provide training in identifying and nurturing the young gifted from every socioeconomic level. With early intervention and appropriate learning opportunities, children from minorities and children with all kinds of impairments, like all other children who are gifted, could be helped to realize their potential (Kirk and Gallagher 1986).

STRATEGIES FOR SUPPORTING YOUNG CHILDREN WHO ARE GIFTED AND TALENTED

It is important to *support* and *challenge* gifted children, while at the same time not draw attention in such a way as to give the children a false sense of importance or the message that they are expected always to achieve at the highest level. Too much "emphasis on success may result in children avoiding situations that may lead to failure" (Elkind 1981).

We must not forget the importance of supporting *all* areas of the young child's development. It should not be assumed that advancement in one area of development (for example, cognitive or language skills) necessarily precludes the need for support in another (such as gross or fine motor abilities).

Yewchuk and Jobagy (1991), in an article about the importance of recognizing the emotional needs of gifted children, state:

> Pressure to succeed, personal expectations, emotional sensitivity, lack of support from parents and peers—all may have a detrimental effect on the emotional development of the gifted child. Educators are finally becoming aware of the advanced academic needs of the gifted child, and programming is finally taking place. What is now required is that teachers and counsellors become aware of the social and emotional needs of the gifted child, as these can have a profound effect on the academic ability of the child.

Recent research seems to indicate that *truly* gifted children develop best in an environment that *recognizes* and *responds* to their special needs. Thus, very young children who show an interest in ideas and concepts beyond those of other children the same age should be encouraged and given opportunities to explore and expand their particular area of interest. Providing greater access to libraries, museums, and computer programs may enable these children to find answers to their questions and motivate them to further inquiry. Children who excel in psychomotor, music, and/or creative art abilities may need challenging and varied opportunities for expanding their particular talent. The child-care setting might provide obstacle courses, opportunities for creative dance, time for music improvisation, and materials for sculpting, constructing, and handicraft work. (For more extensive research information on gifted and talented children, see Klein and Tannenbaum, 1992.)

In the authors' experience, the following techniques and methods have worked successfully with young gifted and talented children:

1. Observe *all* children, especially those with identified special needs, for their unique strengths, abilities, and talents.

2. Plan small-group activities that may require all children, including the child who is gifted, to work as a team and to help each other reach a shared goal—for example, a cooking activity that requires eye–hand coordination for pouring and stirring; physical strength for beating and mixing, intellectual ability for interpreting a recipe, social skills for sharing, and language skills for reporting. Through activities such as this, all children take part and support each other.

3. Make sure you always have stimulating activities and materials available in your room (Photo 8–4). These may include
   - a terrarium-building activity;
   - new tapes for listening to;

PHOTO 8–4 *Make sure you always have something unique and challenging available.*

- a range of taped music and props for creative movement;
- tape recorders for children to use for their own compositions;
- computer programs that challenge creative thinking and prolem solving, abilities that do not simply require "yes/no" or "right/wrong" answers, and do not preclude opportunities for the child to play interactively with other children;
- different types of creative art materials (frequently augmented and changed) that allow opportunities to explore colour, form, and texture;
- new props that will stimulate creative role playing—for example, new hats, makeup, jewellery, uniforms, and supplies for "community helper" play; and
- opportunities for trips supported by specific preparation and follow-up activities.

4. Use volunteers who can provide unique learning experiences; often, they can help keep the gifted child intellectually stimulated and involved.

5. Help parents recognize ways in which they can support their child's talents. You might suggest

   - trips to exhibits, museums, street festivals, and building sites; and
   - hands-on experiences such as fixing broken things and exploring new media.

   As Wolfle (1989) points out, "The gifted child is a child who should be treated like a child … Like their peers, [gifted children] love drawing, going on field trips, playing in the housekeeping area, but seem to want to delve into everything deeper."

6. Develop interesting and enriching special program opportunities—for example, arranging for visitors with special skills, taking trips to interesting places and events, and locating people who will donate time or materials that will enhance learning opportunities for the whole class. Be sure to call on your parent group for contributions.

Kitano (1989) stresses that "offering learning activities at a range of levels hurts no one and helps gifted children, as well as many others." She urges teachers to be flexible and offer choices that will appeal to all children.

In conclusion, when programming for young children it is important to support all the developmental needs of the children in your group. The breadth of needs to which teachers must accommodate varies from group to group. The process of inclusion/integration, whether it is with a child who is developmentally delayed, has specific physical needs, or is developmentally accelerated in one or more areas, challenges the teacher to plan program and learning opportunities in which all the children can participate and from which all can benefit. The teacher should facilitate the inclusion of the gifted or talented child as a member of his or her peer group.

Whereas educational legislation for other areas of exceptionality is mandated in most provinces, services for young children who are gifted or talented receive no special consideration within legislation (with the exception of Ontario).

SUMMARY

Gifted and talented young children are those with exceptionally advanced skills in one or more areas of development. Characteristics that identify young potentially gifted children are a combination of advanced verbal skills, high levels of curiosity, and the ability to concentrate and remember. Many potentially gifted children from culturally different backgrounds and low-income families are not identified because of restricted learning opportunities and socially biased identification procedures. Many children with developmental disabilities are gifted; however, their potential often goes unrecognized because of the focus placed on overcoming their deficit areas.

It is of prime importance that teachers plan daily programs that provide a variety of new intellectually, challenging, and creative opportunities for play and learning.

STUDENT ACTIVITIES

1. Contact your provincial or local association for bright (or gifted) children. Find out what types of programs and resources this association offers.
2. Meet with a parent of a child who has been identified as gifted. Ask the parent to describe the skills and abilities that the child demonstrated when he or she was young. Indicate how this child was different from the child's playmates.

3. Observe a group of preschool children. List any instances of behaviour that you feel are signs of potential giftedness. Discuss your observations with the classroom teacher.

4. Have you or one of your brothers, sisters, or friends been described as gifted or talented? Describe the exceptional characteristics that led to such a label.

5. Contact your local association for learning disabilities to find out how they would identify children who are gifted or talented within the population they serve.

REFERENCES

Elkind, D. 1981 *The Hurried Child*. Reading, Mass.: Addison-Wesley.

Freeman, J. 1981 "The Intellectually Gifted." *New Directions for Gifted Children* 7: 75–86.

Gallagher, J.J. 1988 "National Agenda for Educating Gifted Students: Statement of Priorities." *Exceptional Children* 55, no. 2: 107–14.

Karnes, M., and L. Johnson 1987 "An Imperative: Programming for the Young Gifted/Talented." *Journal for the Education of the Gifted* 10, no. 3: 195–214.

Karnes, M., and L. Johnson 1989 "Training for Staff, Parents and Volunteers Working with Gifted Young Children, Especially Those with Disabilities and from Low-Income Homes." *Young Children* 44, no. 3: 49–56.

Kirk, S.A., and J.J. Gallagher 1986 *Educating Exceptional Children*. Boston: Houghton Mifflin.

Kitano, M.K. 1989 "The K–3 Teacher's Role in Recognizing and Supporting Young Gifted Children." *Young Children* 44, no. 3: 57–63.

Klein, P., and A. Tannenbaum 1992 *To Be Young and Gifted*. Norwood, N.J.: Ablex.

Robinson, H.B. 1981 "The Uncommonly Bright Child." In M. Lewis and L.A. Rosenblum, eds. *The Uncommon Child*. New York: Plenum.

Roedell, W.C., N.E. Jackson, and H.B. Robinson 1980 *Gifted Young Children*. New York: Teachers College Press.

Saunders, J., and P. Espeland 1991 *Bringing Out the Best: A Resource Guide for Parents of Young and Gifted Children*, Minjn.: Mn. Free Spirit.

Stile, S., and M. Kitano 1991 "Preschool-Age Gifted Children." *DEC Communicator* 17, no. 3: 4.

Wolf, J.S. 1994 "The Gifted and Talented." In N.G. Haring, L. McCormick, and T.G. Haring, eds. *Exceptional Children and Youth*, 456–500. New York: Merrill.

Wolfle, J. 1989 "The Gifted Preschooler: Developmentally Different but Still 3 or 4 Year Olds." *Young Children* 44, no. 3: 41–48.

Yewchuk, C., and S. Jobagy 1991 "The Neglected Minority: The Emotional Needs of Gifted Children." *Education Canada*, Winter.

section **IV**

PLANNING FOR
INCLUSION

CHAPTER 9

Partnership with Families

OBJECTIVES

After studying the material in this chapter, the student will be able to

- identify problems that are common among families of children with developmental disabilities
- outline the major components of an Individual Family Service Plan (IFSP)
- define the concepts enabling and empowering as related to families of children with developmental disabilities; explain the social significance of the concepts
- list a number of ways for teachers to communicate with parents
- draw up a format for holding a conference with the parents of a child with a serious problem; include planning and follow-up

INTRODUCTION

Family involvement has long been a tradition in early childhood education. With the advent of intervention programs for young children with developmental disabilities, family involvement now is viewed as essential (Photo 9–1). Contrast this with earlier times when parents were advised, almost routinely, to institutionalize a child who was impaired—sometimes at birth. Changes have come about because of the work of Wolfensberger (1972) on normalization and the activities of advocacy groups on behalf of the disabled. Professionals and parents alike agreed that institutions could not offer the individualized support and nurturing that were needed to facilitate early development.

Today, relatively few children are institutionalized; most live in their family's home, others may live in residential or group homes within their family's community. However, it was not until the 1970s that family support and involvement in their child's special education programs and intervention services was supported through provincial funding.

PHOTO 9–1 *Family involvement is essential in early childhood intervention programs.*

Turnbull and Turnbull (1988, 21) describe the shift:

> The pendulum has swung in many ways: from viewing parents as part of the problem to viewing them as a primary solution to the problem, from expecting passive roles to expecting active roles, from viewing families as a mother–child dyad to recognizing the presence and needs of all members, and from assigning generalized expectations from the professionals' perspective to allowing for individual priorities defined from each family's perspective.

The major trends examined in this chapter are the following:

- involvement of families in planning and implementing intervention services and educational programs for their infants and young children with developmental problems
- the rights and options of parents
- avoidance of professional intrusion into family affairs
- empowerment of the family
- parent roles and responsibilities in case management

As background, various aspects of family living will be touched on, starting with the many types of families in today's society. Having an infant with a disability and the impact this has on parents and on the family as a whole will be described. The rationale and justification for family involvement will follow, with emphasis on the family as a system of interactive, reciprocal relationships. Strategies that early childhood teachers engage in when working with parents of children with impairments will conclude the chapter. (Throughout the chapter, primary caregivers will be referred to as "parents," even though it is not always the case that the parent is the primary caregiver.)

FAMILY PATTERNS AND EXPECTATIONS

The makeup of families, and their expectations regarding the behaviour of family members, varies from family to family and from culture to culture. The emotional climate within families varies, too. Often it is characterized by the way parents interact with their children (which is not a one-way street, however, as we shall see later in the chapter).

The concept of **family uniqueness** recognizes that every family is a distinct collection of individuals who have come together to create a new whole. Although many families may share similar characteristics, it is important not to assume that these families share common beliefs and practices. For example, not all African-American families share common views on child rearing, nor do all Jewish families have the same priorities when it comes to early intervention goals, nor do all families headed by lesbian couples express their spirituality in similar ways. The concept of family uniqueness requires that practitioners learn how to work with families as individuals, how to communicate with families effectively, and how to develop cultural self-awareness to understand the ways our own beliefs influence our work (Harry 1992).

WHAT IS THE FAMILY?

Most children grow up in a family, but what does that mean? Who is *the family*? The idealized nuclear family of yesteryear with the stay-at-home, take-care-of-the-children mother and the outside-the-home breadwinner father no longer represents the typical North American family. In today's society, family often means a single woman with one or more children. The 1991 Canadian Census indicates that 13 percent of Canadian families were headed by lone (single) parents. Single mothers headed 82.4 percent of lone-parent families; 17.6 percent were headed by single fathers (Statistics Canada 1992).

Divorce and remarriage represent an increasingly common trend. The majority of divorced men and women remarry. When children are involved, the arrangement often is referred to as a *reconstituted* or *blended* family. It is not uncommon for *her* children, *his* children, and *their* children to be living under the same roof. Another variation is the rapid increase in dual-career families and in mothers of young children in the workforce. Baby sitters (and nannies) are often viewed as a regular part of the child's family. Children may also grow up in extended families, where combinations of parents, grandparents (Photo 9–2), aunts, uncles, and cousins live in the

PHOTO 9–2 *Grandparents are major caregivers in the families of many children.*

same household. Extended-family arrangements may also include living with friends. Two women with children may share expenses, household tasks, and child rearing; or a solo mother or father may have a live-in companion of the opposite or same sex. The extended-family concept has been taken one step further by Caldwell (1985): she suggests that the out-of-home infant- and child-care program often functions as an extended family. Licensed home day care and private baby-sitting arrangements, as well as care in a licensed child-care centre, are other options available to most families in Canada today. Finally, there are children who grow up in a series of foster homes, beginning as newborns.

FAMILIES OF CHILDREN WITH DISABILITIES

Whatever the makeup of a family, those with children with disabilities will feel the impact on family life. Some families say that they become more closely drawn together as they learn to adapt to a child's disability; others are less able to cope; and still others are pulled apart. At one point it was thought that the divorce rate was greatly increased among families with a child with disabilities. Research suggests (Wikler, Haack, and Intagliata 1984) that there are no differences in the divorce rate when social and economic factors are held constant.

Another important group that must not be forgotten are siblings. Many agencies provide support groups that give siblings opportunities to share information and coping strategies for dealing with the special issues associated with having a sibling with disabilities.

FAMILY ABUSE AND THE CHILD WITH DISABILITIES

Evidence does exist, however, that children with disabilities are more likely to be the target of family abuse (National Center on Child Abuse and Neglect 1980). One explanation is that infants and young children with developmental disabilities, through no fault of their own, often behave in ways that upset their parents. For example, some infants who have impairments have high-pitched, inconsolable crying that seems to go on night and day. Such crying appears to put healthy parent–infant interaction in jeopardy (Frodi and Senchak 1990). Other infant behaviours can have adverse effects, too. Consider these examples:

There may be difficulty with feeding, where the parent gets food into the child only after much time and effort and then, repeatedly, the child fails to keep it down.

Lack of responsiveness is sometimes seen in infants with sensory impairments. In many instances, it is difficult to tell whether the child's disability and resulting behaviours led to parental abuse or if the abuse caused the child's disability.

Peterson (1987, 424) describes this dilemma:

A normal child living in a stressful environment with an abuse-prone parent can become handicapped as a result of injury from abuse. On the other hand, a family with a handicapped child and without adequate support systems may incur enough stress to cause parents without abusive tendencies to abuse the child. In either case, the awareness of the potential problem of child abuse is crucial for educators who deal with young handicapped children and their families.

Adequate and appropriate support systems are a key factor in ensuring the well-being of families of children with developmental disabilities (Janko 1994). Support is often taken for granted when a family has regular income, extended health insurance, adequate housing, and caring family and friends. Even so, additional support is usually required as soon as it is identified that the newborn infant has serious developmental problems. Families do not plan to have a child with a disability. They expect a healthy infant who will grow slowly but surely into an independent and productive adult. From the start, parents of children with disabilities are faced with disappointments and adjustments. These will affect every member of the family and every aspect of the family's life together.

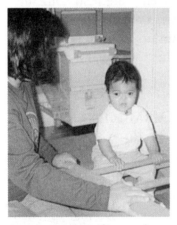

PHOTO 9–3 *Families need to adapt to the realities of caring for a child with disabilities.*

FAMILY ADJUSTMENT

Grief is the usual reaction when parents first realize that they have an infant with disabilities. Even when an older youngster comes to be diagnosed as having a disabling condition, grieving is the normal response of most parents. It is almost as if their child had died. In a way, it is so. The perfect baby or child that parents had planned for and expected will never be. In the process of grieving, parents may become angry, depressed, or overcome with unfounded guilt reactions. Or they may deny that anything is wrong, regardless of the child's appearance or behaviour. *These reactions are normal and expected.* At the same time, parents need help in working through these feelings. They need to begin the process of adapting to the realities of caring for a child with disabilities. Almost immediately, they will have to begin to make urgent decisions and solve complicated problems affecting the family unit (Photo 9–3). These might include the following:

- extensive (and perhaps painful or life-threatening) medical treatment and surgery; hospitalization that may occur repeatedly and for extended periods

- heavy expenses and financial burdens other than medical, such as the cost of special foods and equipment
- frightening and energy-draining crises, often recurring, as when the child stops breathing, turns blue, or has a major seizure
- transportation problems; baby-sitting needs for the other children; time away from jobs to get the child with a disability to consultation and treatment appointments
- lack of affordable, available, or appropriate child care for families with children who are developmentally disabled
- continuous day-and-night demands on parents to provide what are routine but difficult caregiving tasks (for example, it may take an hour or more, five to six times during a single day and night, to feed an infant with a severe cleft palate condition)
- constant fatigue, lack of sleep, little or no time to meet the needs of other family members
- little or no opportunity for recreational or leisure activities; difficulty (and additional expense) of locating baby sitters who are both qualified and willing to care for a child with a disability, especially if the child has severe problems (medical or behavioural)
- lack of, limited, or restricted respite-care facilities
- jealousy or feelings of rejection among brothers and sisters who may feel that the child with special needs gets all the family's attention and resources
- marital problems arising from finances, fatigue, differences about management of the child's disability, feelings of rejection by husband (or wife) who feels passed over in favour of the child

When these problems are further compounded by the social and economic effects of poverty, the subsequent development of the child with a disability as well as the growth and well-being of the rest of the family are doubly jeopardized.

Such problems suggest how nearly impossible it would be to provide effective intervention for a young child with a disability without including the child's family (Photo 9–4). It was Bronfenbrenner (1974; 1986) who convinced developmentalists of the range of environmental (and family) influences on a young child's development. The mother–child relationship, once thought to be the major determining factor, has proven to be but one of many. Innumerable strands of **reciprocal relationships**, both cultural and personal, are at work. They form the system, or *ecological niche*, into which the child is born and in which the child is reared. A child's ability to cope or adapt depends on understanding his or her

PHOTO 9–4 *Truly effective early intervention includes the parents.*

larger social system made up of family functioning, support of friends and community, and cultural beliefs.

THE INDIVIDUAL FAMILY SERVICE PLAN (IFSP)

Many early intervention programs in Canada have begun to put into place a service focused on the family. This is modelled after the requirements of the U.S. law PL 99-457, which amended the Education for All Handicapped Children Act (see Chapter 3). This U.S. legislation emphasizes family support, thereby recognizing that infants and young children are best served in the context of a strong and healthy family.

INDIVIDUAL FAMILY SERVICE PLAN COMPONENTS

The purpose of an IFSP—a term that some service providers use interchangeably with Individual Program Plan (IPP)—is to identify and organize resources to assist families in rearing their children who have developmental disabilities (see Chapter 11). These are some of its major features:

1. Help should be provided in a form that meets the unique needs of each child and family.

2. The IFSP should be an ongoing process that supports but *does not take the place of* parents' natural caregiving roles.

3. A major function of the IFSP is to preserve the principle that infants and toddlers are best served within the family.

4. Family-centred as well as child-centred services should be provided through an interdisciplinary team approach.

5. Family members must be equal participants in the team (Photo 9–5).

6. A case manager should be identified and assigned the task of coordinating services and keeping the program moving.

7. Specific steps assuring a smooth transition to the next intervention program should be described.

PHOTO 9–5 *Family members are essential members of the child's IPP team.*

Identification of Needs

Each infant and toddler with special needs should first receive an interdisciplinary assessment. In addition, the family should be asked to participate voluntarily in an interdisciplinary identification of its strengths and unique needs. Families should receive necessary services for their child even if they are unable to participate, or choose not to participate, in the identification process. Services designed to meet the assessed needs of the child and the identified needs of the family should be organized into an IFSP by their interdisciplinary team. The parents, **parent surrogates**, or an appointed guardian should be represented on the team. The family should be encouraged to invite an advocate, counsellor, or friend to assist or support them in presenting their position.

An important point, to be stressed again and again, is that the initial step in preparing an IFSP is *not* an assessment of the family. It is the family's *voluntary identification* of its strengths, resources, needs, and concerns, as these relate to *enhancing the development* of their child. Those who make up the intervention team need to recognize family problems that are beyond the scope of an early intervention program and advise the parents of appropriate resources.

Nonintrusiveness

Constant care is needed to ensure that families are benefited, rather than weakened or demeaned, by participation in the IFSP. Professionals involved in the IFSP process should not intrude into a family's life or lifestyle without the family's invitation to do so. Family members are not to be prodded into discussing private or sensitive matters. Personal information gleaned from professional probing usually has little or no bearing on the child's problems.

The out-of-family perception of a family's needs often misses the mark (Harry 1992). Instead, it is likely to represent the professionals' own biases and values. Emphasis in the IFSP should be on helping families identify their own needs and recognize their own abilities. Only when early intervention programs recognize and build on the diverse and unique strengths of each family will the IFSP concept fulfil its promise as a positive force in the lives of children with disabilities and their families (Dunst and Trivette 1989).

IFSP Evaluation

The IFSP should be evaluated at regular intervals by the team. The purpose of the evaluation and review is to appraise the progress made by the child and family toward the objectives spelled out in the IFSP. If progress is unsatisfactory, program revisions are in order.

Service Coordination (Case Management)

An interdisciplinary team approach to early intervention implies that a number of professionals are dealing with the same child and family. It is strongly recommended that one particular person be designated as **service coordinator (case manager)** (Photo 9–6). The service coordinator may be chosen because of his or her professional expertise in the child's primary problem or because it is anticipated that the service coordinator will have longer contact and more frequent involvement with the family. The communications specialist might be the service coordinator when the main concern revolves around speech and hearing; the physiotherapist when there are evident motor delays; and the nutritionist in cases of **failure to thrive**. In addition to providing clinical skill, the service coordinator needs to be a sensitive listener, a child and family advocate, and a linkage agent (getting families linked to needed services). In many areas, the resource consultant/resource teacher/early interventionist serves as the service coordinator.

Photo 9–6 *The appointment of the case manager, as well as his or her duties, is decided by the team.*

The service coordinator is essential to team functioning as well as to family functioning. Without a liaison or go-between, both the team and the family tend to become confused. When there is a duplication of efforts (the family may be put through three or four intake interviews, for example), intervention services lose continuity and coherence, and whole programs can fall into chaos and disintegration.

Generally speaking, the duties of the service coordinator/case manager are decided by each team. Assigned tasks might include these:

- coordinating the individual child's assessments and identification of family needs with prescribed services
- chairing team and parent conferences

- making sure that records are kept up to date, paperwork gets done, appointments are made (and kept)
- arranging the child's transitions to other programs and providing follow-up services
- serving continuously as a source of contact, interpretation, and support for the family

Parents, to the maximum extent possible, should have the opportunity to select their own case manager/coordinator. In some instances, family choice cannot be an option and a service coordinator must be assigned. A family that feels that its needs are not met adequately by the assigned case manager must be helped to find a more acceptable one.

Parents as Case Managers/Coordinators

Parents who wish to serve as their own case manager should be encouraged and supported by other members of the IFSP or IPP team. Training should be provided for parents in how the system and the network of backup services operate (Bailey 1989). Gathering together the necessary resources and assistance should not add to the family's burdens. Instead, the family should reap positive benefits and become stronger and more capable through the case-management process. Learning to take the responsibility for getting needed assistance is seen as one approach to reducing overdependency on the team service system. Parent associations for specific disabilities will often help parents to locate resources that will prepare them for their role in case management.

Program-to-Program Transitions

The interdisciplinary team should provide support for the child and the family during transitions from one program to another. The hallmark of effective early intervention is the child's graduation into a more challenging program—frequently a program that is in a different setting. The transition between programs calls for special kinds of planning and support. The focus of Chapter 12 is on planning and implementing transitions.

ENABLING AND EMPOWERING FAMILIES

A major public concern about the individual family service planning process was that it would promote increased dependency. Many feared that families would become less able to function independently. Out of this public concern grew the major philosophical thrust of IFSP, the *enabling* and *empowering* of families. Deal, Dunst, and Trivette (1989) suggest the following definitions of the terms:

Enabling families means creating opportunities for family members to become more competent and self-sustaining with respect to their abilities to mobilize their social networks to get needs met and attain goals.

Empowering families means carrying out interventions in a manner in which family members acquire a sense of control over their own developmental course as a result of their own efforts to meet needs. (p. 33)

The intent of the *enabling* and *empowering* concepts is to strengthen families without taking away their ability to cope. The IFSP aims to support and build on those things the family already does well. Professionals believe that this can be accomplished by providing families with the information and skills that will enable them to try to solve their own problems and meet their own needs. The case manager should play the pivotal role in fostering and overseeing the empowerment of families. "Case management may be considered effective only to the extent that families become more capable, competent, and empowered as a result of the help-giving acts of case managers" (Dunst and Trivette 1989, 99).

THE PARENT–TEACHER PARTNERSHIP

Parents and teachers should be partners in the facilitating of children's development. It is important that we recognize that parents must maintain the right to have the final word. They bear the ongoing and primary responsibility during the long years of their child's growth and development (frequently, many additional years when a child is disabled or developmentally delayed). Numerous research studies describe the benefits of active parent involvement in a child's early intervention program (Photo 9–7). Without it, children tended to regress or slip back once the program ended (Simeonson and Bailey 1990). Parent involvement has two major functions: (1) it provides an ongoing reinforcement system that supports the efforts of the program while it is under way, and (2) after the program ends, the child's gains are maintained and expanded upon as a result of the family's increased knowledge and confidence in their ability to support the changing developmental needs of their child.

PHOTO 9–7 *There are many benefits to active parent involvement in their child's intervention program.*

RATIONALE FOR PARENT PARTICIPATION

Many reasons can be given for encouraging parents' involvement in their child's early education and intervention program:

1. Parents are the major socializing agents for their child, as transmitters of cultural values, beliefs, and traditions (Photo 9–8).

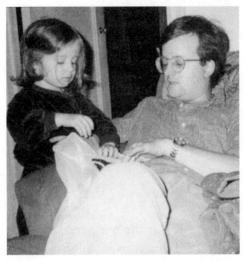

PHOTO 9–8 *Parents are the major socializing agents of their child.*

2. Parents know their child better than teachers or clinicians; thus, parents have a source of information that is available from no one else.

3. Family members can help the child transfer knowledge from school to home and neighbourhood: only a few hours a day are spent in school; many more hours are spent at home.

4. Consistency of adult expectations can be maintained. Young children become anxious when important adults do not agree on expectations. Confusion and even resistance may result if, for example, teachers expect a child to put on his or her own coat while parents always do it for the child.

5. Pleasing parents is important to young children, in that the parents are the source of many pleasant and necessary reinforcers for their young child—food, warmth, comfort, outings, playthings, and so forth.

6. Children with disabilities acquire developmental skills more quickly when parents learn to participate in home teaching (Shearer and Shearer 1977).

7. Involvement in an early intervention program offers parents access to support from other parents and a better perspective on their own child's strengths and needs.

DEGREE OF PARTICIPATION

The extent to which parents can be actively involved in their child's program depends on a number of factors:

- work schedule and job constraints
- additional young children at home who need care
- availability of transportation

- parental health (both physical and psychological)
- parental maturity and understanding of the child's needs
- attitudes and comfort level of the parent with medical personnel, teachers, and authority figures
- the program's ability to accommodate to the primary language of the parent

It is important to recognize that simply *maintaining a child's enrollment in a program is a form of parent involvement*. Lack of active participation does not imply lack of interest in the child or the program. Instead, as noted by Barber et al. (1988, 197), it may be a form of energy conservation:

> Family life with a child who has a disability is a marathon rather than a sprint. A crucial aspect of supporting families during the early years is to empower them with coping strategies that can help them to run the full course with their son or daughter and to avoid the trap of investing their energies heavily for a short period of time and then burning out.

COMMUNICATING WITH PARENTS

The teachers' approach to parents should be the same as the teachers' approach to children: respect and appreciation for individual differences in culture, values, attitudes, and learning styles. When mutual understanding can be established between parents and teachers, children are more likely to experience a good learning environment. Two-way communication is the centrepiece of understanding. Talking with—rather than to—parents is the basis for effective communication. Teachers should simultaneously try to share knowledge and obtain feedback. They should also try to share information that may address the expressed and unexpressed concerns of the parents. Unexpressed concerns may be one of the biggest obstacles to communication. With some parents, it may be a long while, for example, before they are able to talk about their child's impairments, or even to express openly that a problem exists.

Informal Exchanges

A tremendous amount of information can be exchanged during informal encounters. The quick conversations that occur in programs where parents pick up and deliver children are especially fruitful. To take full advantage of these, with as many parents as possible, arrival and departure time should be an extended period (20 to 30 minutes). One teacher is assigned specifically to these program periods (see the discussion of daily scheduling in Chapter 14). These brief exchanges often focus on specific issues such as the child's sleep patterns or relaying the physician's reasons for increasing a child's medication. Brief progress reports also can be given. For example:

- "Sissie can point to red, yellow, and blue now."
- "Keesha climbed to the top of the ladder box all by herself this afternoon."
- "Michael has hung up his jacket every day this week!"

Appreciative comments such as these, made by teachers to parents in the presence of the child, are important. Parents come to realize that seemingly small events have developmental significance. Children learn that their accomplishments have merit; otherwise, why would the teacher pass the news on? And why would both of these important adults, parent and teacher, look so pleased? Appreciative comments have another function, too. They serve as models for parents. Hearing them helps parents learn to put into words their own recognition and appreciation of their children's efforts.

Because they are public events, arrival and departure times should not be used to discuss concerns about a child (Photo 9–9), or problems with behaviour or learning. These moments should never be used to talk about anything not suitable for the child, other parents, or other children to hear. If a parent brings up a sensitive issue, the teacher should listen and make a quick note. As soon as possible the teacher should promise to telephone the parent to talk it over or to arrange a conference. The teacher should make a point of asking for a specific time to make the call. This is to ensure that the child is otherwise occupied. Any serious discussion between a parent and a teacher seems to get blown out of proportion in a child's mind if it appears that the adults are trying to keep the child from listening.

Photo 9–9 *Arrival and departure times are not the time to discuss concerns about the child.*

Parent Observations

In all programs for young children, parents should be welcome at any time. Since parents are the primary partners in their child's development, they have the right to see and question everything that goes on in the classroom. Firsthand observations offer one of the best ways of providing indirect parent education. Watching their child interacting with other children and adults, with materials and activities, provides insights that can be obtained in no other way. Against a background of children with similar developmental levels, parents will gain a better appreciation of their own child's skills and progress. Ideally, every parent observation is followed by at least a brief discussion with a teacher. If possible, the teacher should be the one who was in the activity area where the parent had observed for the longest period. When a conversation cannot take place on the spot, a follow-up telephone call is important. The follow-up conversation serves several purposes:

1. Teachers can answer questions that a parent may have about what she or he observed; teachers can also provide necessary explanations—for example, why certain play or group situations were handled as they were.

2. Teachers can help parents recognize the positive aspects of their own child's uniqueness and developmental progress.

3. Teachers can describe the appropriateness of individualized curriculum activities in enhancing the child's development and meeting their child's special needs.

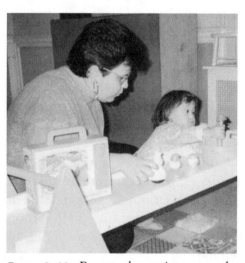

PHOTO 9–10 *Parent observations may be regularly scheduled events.*

Parent observations may be regularly scheduled or held on the spur of the moment (Photo 9–10). As noted, brief, informal observations should occur regularly as parents deliver and call for their children. When a formal observation is planned, it is best for teachers to provide some type of structure. A clipboard with a simple observation form works well. Parents are asked to note the child's activities, playmates, and special interests, as well as avoidances, if relevant. Focused observation helps parents note what is actually going on with their child. Taking notes helps parents see the subtleties of their child's involvement. This enables the parents to be a part of the programming process, while not interfering in their child's activities. Also, a parent engaged in close observation and note-taking tends to discourage the child from staying too close to his or her side. Because many parents find it difficult to observe due to their work schedules, videotaped observations may be used in place of on-site parent observations. Videotapes are also useful when parents need to turn to translators for interpretation. Follow-up discussions can then take place afterward.

Telephone Calls

Telephone calls help keep communication going between teachers and parents. When children arrive by bus and parents work, the telephone may become the chief means of maintaining contact. Telephone calls may be used for the same kinds of casual reporting as arrival and departure contacts. Many parents prefer that a convenient day and time of day be arranged in advance so that they can plan to have a few minutes to talk freely. When teachers' calls become a regular event, most parents welcome them; a call from school no longer signals trouble. Usually, the focus is on routine matters such as these:

- the outcome of a visit to the audiologist
- the progress of an illness
- the reason for an absence of several days

For children who are not picked up by their own parents, the teacher should phone to report any unusual happening at school: torn or soiled clothing; a scrape, fall, or rash; or an unexplained change in a child's behaviour. The teacher should always try to reach the parent before the child arrives home. This helps prevent misunderstandings that tend to occur when messages are relayed from the bus driver or another child's parent driving the car pool. The advance call also forewarns of unpleasant surprises, which are difficult for some parents to deal with when caught off guard. Finally, the teacher's call prior to the child's arrival protects the child. Young children often have difficulty explaining why something happened. They themselves may not understand it, may not perceive it accurately, or may not have the appropriate words of explanation. If the teacher is the first to reach the parent with potentially troublesome news, the parent has the opportunity to release anger or distress on the teacher, rather than the child. In addition, the call allows teachers to try to find out if parents consider it necessary to make changes in the program so as to reduce the likelihood of a recurrence of the incident.

Written Notes

If immediate reporting and feedback are not essential, written notes, sent home with the child, can be useful. Once a relationship has been established between a teacher and parent, a written note often is preferred to a telephone call. Parents can read the note at a convenient time. They are saved the sometimes annoying interruption of a phone call. The note may be a duplicated reminder of a meeting or an upcoming event. It may be a request, perhaps for additional clothing to be kept at school. It may be a report of an exciting breakthrough: "Lauren put on her shoes all by herself today." Parents appreciate a teacher's personalized recognition of their child, even in the form of such a one-line report. Notes of this kind give parents something specific and positive to talk about with their child (Photo 9–11). In addition, notes are one more way for teachers to help

PHOTO 9–11 *A written note sent home with the child might say, "Your child managed to eat by herself today."*

parents recognize the developmental significance of a child's seemingly routine accomplishments.

In our society, where English may be a second language for many families, audiocassette reports can be used as a substitute for written reports. These can then be interpreted by an individual of the family's choice, thus respecting the family's right to privacy.

The Two-Way Journal (or Communication Book)

Some settings take the brief written note idea a step further and set up a journal system. Parents and teachers both write in the journal. It travels back and forth between school and home on a frequent and fairly regular basis. Once such a system becomes established, it seems a relatively effortless but rewarding method for keeping the communication lines open between home and school.

Newsletters

A newsletter, duplicated and sent home with children, is appreciated by most parents. The major purpose of a newsletter is to describe the everyday events and learning activities that go on at school, from spring vegetable planting to the installation of a child-friendly computer. A newsletter also can serve as a reminder about situations that involve all families, such as colder weather and the need for warmer outdoor clothing. Newly enrolled children and families, teachers, and volunteers can be introduced in the newsletter.

A newsletter must be written at the reading level of the families receiving it. In many programs, newsletters need to be written in two or more languages. To ensure a simple and straightforward style, older children can be involved in the writing. All children learn from talking about what to include in a newsletter. Many children have fun dictating parts of it. Teachers must be sure to read the finished newsletter to the children before they carry it home. This enables the children to talk with their parents about the contents and prompt the parents to read the letter. In fact, a good rule for teachers is to inform children of every communication with parents—telephone calls, notes, and parent conferences. When a teacher says, "I called your father and told him how good you are at matching colours," the child realizes that good things truly are being reported.

PARENT–TEACHER MEETINGS

Meeting together has been the traditional form of parent–teacher interactions. Usually held on the premises of the school or program, the meetings provide opportunities for parents to see their children's work, interact with teachers, and compare notes with other parents.

Large-Group Meetings

Group meetings usually focus on issues of general interest, such as aspects of child development or the early childhood curriculum. A recognized expert in a particular area may be invited to speak. Parent meetings that draw the best attendance tend to be those based on the concerns and interests of the parents. Time for questions and open discussion is an important part of any parent–teacher get-together. An informal coffee hour or open house often precedes or follows the group discussion. Casual socializing helps parents get to know teachers and other parents better. Parents should have many opportunities to visit their child's classroom, where paintings, clay work, and woodworking projects can be on display. Toys, equipment, and teaching materials are often put out for parents to examine and manipulate. Many parents find that they can talk more easily with teachers when they can focus on materials. For shy parents, looking at materials can be a special benefit; it provides something to talk about with other parents. Parents of children with an identified disability should be encouraged to attend workshops or meetings offered by disability-specific organizations.

Parent Conferences

In addition to IFSP planning, regular parent conferences should be scheduled two or three times a year, more often in some instances. Conferences should have the purpose of building parent–teacher communications. A positive note must be established at the outset. Conferencing with parents requires a quiet place with comfortable seating. After greeting the parents cordially and exchanging social pleasantries, conversation should focus on a review of the purpose of the conference. This should be followed by a brief progress report. The report should combine both parent and teacher observations, interspersed with many examples of how the child is gaining (or has mastered) particular developmental skills, both at home and at school. Throughout, the teacher should ensure that the parents have opportunities to comment, ask questions, and express their concerns. The teacher might discuss with the parent strategies that could be tried both at school and in the home to address concerns that either the parent or school might have. The conference should close with a brief summary of the discussion, a restatement of long- and short-term learning goals for the child, and a restatement of the child's unique and valuable qualities. A date for a future meeting should be set.

In every parent conference, the focus must be on issues related to the child's development and learning. Teachers *should not* counsel parents on deeply personal concerns, regardless of the impact on the child. Teachers may, however, attempt to help the family find an appropriate resource.

PHOTO 9–12 *Teachers cannot help the child without the parents' help.*

Ethical issues are a concern of many teachers in their work with parents (Feeney and Sysco 1986). What should be done, for example, when a child has serious health problems that the parent appears to neglect? Or behaviour problems that parents apparently do not recognize? Before going into such a conference, the teacher must make extensive observations and when appropriate take frequency counts of the behaviour in question. The teacher should also consult with the other teachers. This will ensure staff agreement that a serious problem exists and that it cannot be handled through rearrangement of particular aspects of the program. No matter how carefully the teacher sets a positive note at the outset of such a conference, or how tactfully the teacher brings up the problem, parents may feel threatened. Inevitably, they feel that whatever is "wrong" with their child is their fault (or is perceived by teachers as the parents' fault). At first mention of their child's shortcomings, parents may feel alienated, defensive, and even angry. Little can be accomplished in that kind of an emotional climate. Teachers, therefore, should bring up difficult problems only when the child's present and future well-being is at stake and teachers cannot help the child without the parents' help (Photo 9–12).

It would be unconscionable for teachers not to bring up certain problems—for example, ongoing excessive drowsiness. The teacher must discuss this with the parents immediately. After brief greetings, the opening statements should have to do with the frequency of the problem as observed and documented. It should be pointed out to the parents how much the child is missing because of his lethargic state. At no point should the teacher back down. The teacher should advise the parent to consult immediately with the child's doctor. Should the condition continue, the teacher should contact the public health nurse or the case manager for support. Most feedback from parents is obtained indirectly. Much of it comes from incidental comments made during informal parent–teacher exchanges.

PARENT FEEDBACK

Most feedback from parents is obtained indirectly. Much of it comes from incidental comments during informal parent–teacher exchanges. Questionnaires are one way of getting feedback. Parents' responses are most useful if questions relate to specific aspects of the program. In addition, questions should be designed so that parents can rate the degree of satisfaction on each item, rather than having to give a yes or no answer. Suggestion boxes also can be helpful. Parents can make their comments anonymously if they are supplied with a form. They can fill it out at home and drop it in a box, unobserved. Teachers' responses to parents' suggestions can be posted on the bulletin board. If parents are given acknowledgment that comments are not only wanted, but acted on, they are more likely to continue to contribute their ideas and suggestions.

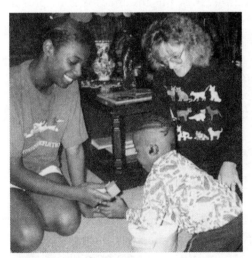

PHOTO 9–13 *Much can be learned from a home visit.*

HOME VISITS

Home visits have a long tradition of bridging the gap between school and home. Getting to know a family in its own setting enables teachers to work more effectively with children in the school setting (Photo 9–13).

According to Powell (1989, 97), "Home visiting programs represent an important strategy of parent-focused early education." Home visits require teachers to behave differently than they do in their own classrooms. In a child's home, teachers are no longer the central figure; the parents are. The teacher is a guest who needs to conform to the social and economic ways of the family.

Home visits provide excellent opportunities to observe children's ability to function in their own environment and to perceive the level of competence in functional skills. If a teacher is interested in a specific skill, he or she should plan the home visit around a naturally occurring time for that skill to be used. For example, if the parents have many questions about feeding, it would be advantageous to schedule the visit around a mealtime or snack time.

Caldwell and Bradley (1978) demonstrated how much can be learned about the child's developmental opportunities from a home visit:

- Are there toys (or household items converted into play materials)?
- Are there books and crayons?
- How do the children who are not in a program spend their time?
- Is the home excessively neat or excessively disorganized?
- How do parents respond to their children? To a particular child? If it is a child with disabilities, are the parents overly protective? Impatient with the child's shortcomings?

When home visits are scheduled on a regular basis, the visiting teacher usually brings learning materials. The teacher demonstrates the use of the materials with the child. Then the parent and child use the materials together, with the teacher providing feedback. The visiting teacher should also make suggestions and solicit parent suggestions as to how to expand and elaborate the learning opportunities within the routine of the family. In some instances it is helpful if parents are asked to make checks on a simple record sheet regarding various aspects of the child's progress.

Regardless of the approach, teachers always should remember the parents' role in their child's learning. Not only are parents the child's first teachers, they are also the child's most frequent teachers. With appropriate support, parents can make their home a significant learning environment for their children. Home is the place where all developmental skills can be practised over and over, in a real-life setting, with those who have a personal stake in the child's development.

SUMMARY

The family, regardless of its makeup, is a young child's most important teacher. While early childhood teachers are partners with parents in the teaching process, parents are always the primary partners. With children who have developmental disabilities, parents' involvement in their child's early intervention program is especially important. Involvement takes many forms. Simply keeping their child in the intervention program may be the only involvement some parents can manage.

An ecological approach to understanding early development is fundamental to the Individual Family Service Plan. The first underlying assumption is that children who are young and special can be helped best in the context of their family. The second is that family members are as likely to be in need of special services as is the child. The IFSP is to be an interdisciplinary team effort that includes parents as team members. A case manager is to be appointed to keep the program organized and running. The emphasis is on helping families become stronger and more able through the IFSP process.

The teacher–parent partnership is fostered in a variety of ways. A relationship that will benefit children is based on open communication and teachers' respect of the range of individual differences among parents. Many of the most effective teacher–parent exchanges are brief and informal chats, for instance, when a parent delivers his or her child, or observes in the classroom. Telephone calls, written notes sent home with children, newsletters, and group meetings keep the lines open between teachers and parents. Formal conferences are another means of communicating with parents, as are home visits. Teachers also may seek parent feedback about the program itself through questionnaires and suggestion boxes.

STUDENT ACTIVITIES

1. Select several classmates to role-play parent–child pairs during a program's arrival time. Take the role of teacher and initiate brief exchanges with the individual parents concerning a sleep problem, a child's new leg braces, a special painting a child has done, or a child's reluctance to play outdoors.

2. Prepare a one-page newsletter based on events that occurred in the classroom where you observe or practice-teach.

3. Find a family with a child with a disability. If they are willing, ask the parents to tell you about any special circumstances and caregiving arrangements they have had to deal with.

4. Select a partner to play the role of a parent who has a child with a disability. Demonstrate the kinds of nonintrusive questions you would ask to assist the family in identifying their needs and strengths.

5. Mix and Match

Select the one best match for each item in column I from column II and place that letter in the appropriate space in column I.

I

_____ 1. interaction with the family

_____ 2. respite care

_____ 3. blended family

_____ 4. case manager

_____ 5. parent feedback

_____ 6. ethical issue

_____ 7. parents and family

_____ 8. classroom activities report

II

A. newsletter

B. reconstituted family

C. reciprocal interactions

D. major socializing agents

E. relief caregiving

F. child abuse

G. questionnaire

H. FSP organizer

REFERENCES

Bailey, D. 1989 "Case Management in Early Intervention." *Journal of Early Intervention* 13, no. 2: 120–34.

Barber, P.A., A.P. Turnbull, S.K. Behr, and G.M. Kerns 1988 "A Family Systems Perspective on Early Childhood Special Education." In S.L. Odom and M.B. Karnes, eds. *Early Intervention for Infants and Children with Handicaps.* Baltimore: Paul H. Brookes.

Bronfenbrenner, U. 1974 *A Report on Longitudinal Evaluations of Preschool Programs, vol. 2: Is Early Intervention Effective?* DHEW Publication No. OHD 76 30025). Washington, D.C.: U.S. Department of Health, Education, and Welfare.

Caldwell, B. 1985 "What Is Quality Child Care?" In B. Caldwell and A. Hilliard, eds. *What Is Quality Child Care?* Washington, D.C.: National Association for the Education of Young Children.

Caldwell, B., and R. Bradley 1978 *Home Observation for Measurement of the Environment.* Little Rock: University of Arkansas.

Deal, A.G., C.J. Dunst, and C.M. Trivette 1989 "A Flexible and Functional Approach to Developing Individualized Family Service Plans." *Infants and Young Children* 1, no. 4: 32–43.

Dunst, C.J., and C.M. Trivette 1989 "An Enablement and Empowerment Perspective of Case Management." *Topics in Early Childhood Special Education* 8, no. 4: 87–102.

Feeney, S., and L. Sysco 1986 "Professional Ethics in Early Childhood Education: Survey Results." *Young Children* 42, no. 1: 15–20.

Frodi, A., and M. Senchak 1990 "Verbal and Behavioral Responsiveness to the Cries of Atypical Infants." *Child Development* 61, no. 1: 76–84.

Harry, B. 1992 "Developing Cultural Self-Awareness: The First Step in Values Clarification for Early Interventionists." *Topics in Early Childhood Special Education,* 12 (4), 333–350.

Janko, S. 1994 *Vulnerable Children, Vulnerable Lives.* New York: Teachers College Press.

National Center on Child Abuse and Neglect 1980 *Child Abuse and Developmental Disabilities. Essays.* (DHEW Publication No. OHDS 79 30226). Washington, D.C.: U.S. Department of Health, Education, and Welfare.

Peterson, N.L. 1987 *Early Intervention for Handicapped and At-Risk Children.* Denver: Love Publishing.

Powell, D.R. 1990 *Families and Early Childhood Programs.* Washington, D.C.: National Association for the Education of Young Children.

Shearer, M., and D.E. Shearer 1977 "Parent Involvement." In J.B. Jordan, A.H. Hayden, M.B. Karnes, and M.M. Wood, eds. *Early Childhood Education for Exceptional Children: A Handbook of Ideals and Exemplary Practices.* Reston, Va.: Council for Exceptional Children.

Simeonson, R.J., and D.B. Bailey 1990 "Family Dimensions in Early Intervention." In S.J. Meisels and J.P. Shonkoff, eds., *Handbook of Early Intervention,* 428–444. New York: Cambridge University Press.

Statistics Canada 1992 *Families: Number, Type, and Structure.* 1991 Census of Canada, catalogue no. 93-312. Ottawa: Supply and Services Canada.

Turnbull, A.P., and H.R. Turnbull 1988 *Families, Professionals, and Exceptionality: A Special Partnership.* Columbus, Ohio: Charles E. Merrill.

Wikler, L., J. Haack, and J. Intagliata 1984 "Bearing the Burden Alone? Helping Divorced Mothers of Children with Developmental Disabilities." In *Families with Handicapped Members: The Family Therapy Collection.* Rockville, Md.: Aspen Systems.

Wolfensberger, W. 1972 *The Principle of Normalization in Human Services.* Toronto: National Institute on Mental Retardation.

CHAPTER 10

Preparing Teachers for Inclusive Programs

Objectives

After studying the material in this chapter, the student will be able to

- describe the knowledge and training needed to work in early childhood inclusive programs with children who are developmentally disabled

- define developmentally appropriate learning experiences and justify the statement that all young children—disabled, normally developing, and gifted—need such experiences

- discuss early education arrangements for children who have severe and multiple disabilities

- compare *contingent stimulation, teachable moments, spontaneous teaching,* and *incidental teaching*; and identify developmental principles they have in common and their significance to children's learning

- list 10 or more characteristics found among the most effective teachers of preschool-aged children

INTRODUCTION

Qualified early childhood teachers should be the central element in programs for infants, toddlers, and preschool-aged children. These teachers should be supported by assistants who are trained, in the process of being trained, or by caregivers who have had on-the-job experience. Caregivers providing child care in family-home daycare settings should be supervised by qualified early childhood education personnel. Program quality is determined by the teachers' skills in managing the learning environment. Quality is further determined by teachers' personal attitudes about children and themselves, and by their beliefs regarding how children learn. In the inclusive classroom the need for quality teaching is critical. The developmental diversity among children calls for skilled and sensitive teachers who will respond to children's special needs with a range of individualized programs. At the same time, inclusive classrooms call for teachers who recognize that young children with developmental disabilities are more like normally developing children than they are different from them.

All children need learning activities geared to their level of development and interests. Normally developing children need such experiences; children who are gifted need them; children with developmental delays and disabilities need them. Effective early childhood teachers use a developmental approach as the basis for every aspect of their teaching. They recognize that all children have basic needs and all children have special needs. They recognize further that special needs cannot be met unless basic developmental needs also are met.

This section focuses on those general teaching skills and general developmental and behavioural principles that apply to all young children and all early childhood teachers. The point to be emphasized is this: *if children with developmental problems are to benefit from special approaches, learning activities must take place within a developmental framework.* In other words, teachers must make particular adaptations. These adaptations are then incorporated into each child's individual developmental program.

THE TEACHER EXPERIENCE IN AN INCLUSIVE SETTING

An early childhood program that offers an inclusive experience for children with developmental problems is both challenging and rewarding for teachers of children of varying ability levels. In such classrooms in early childhood settings, teachers encounter the richest and widest range of developmental likenesses and differences among children. Skilled teachers enjoy this diversity, once they are convinced of the underlying developmental similarities among children of varying ability levels (Photo 10–1).

No one professional can meet the needs of all the diverse learners in an inclusive early childhood program. Teachers in an inclusive classroom are members of a team of professionals who work together to meet the needs of all the children in the classroom. Each member of the team brings specialized knowledge to planning and implementing an appropriate developmental program for a child with special needs. Teamwork is especially important in providing the systematic and specialized instruction that is necessary to meet the needs of children with challenging behaviour or severe disabilities. The expertise that the early childhood educator brings to the team is how to create a classroom environment and learning activities that are fun, motivating, safe, interesting, responsive, and supportive.

PHOTO 10–1 *Skilled teachers enjoy the diversity found in working with children of varying abilities.*

To ensure successful inclusion, the challenge for early childhood teachers is to make adaptations that accommodate the developmental needs of the range of children in the group. Program adaptation is not a new or unusual challenge for early childhood teachers. Adjusting curriculum and teaching strategies to individual differences and developmental variations has long been the heart of early childhood education. The full implications of this philosophy tend to be overlooked, however, where children with a disability are concerned.

TRAINING PROGRAMS FOR EARLY CHILDHOOD TEACHERS

People who want to prepare themselves to work with exceptional children will find a range of training options.

- Some provinces have early childhood departments, child development and public health agencies, and university- or college-based institutes or centres that offer in-service and on-the-job training.
- Two-year colleges and vocational/technical schools often are sources of early childhood and special child teacher training programs.
- Some provinces have colleges that offer distance education courses in early childhood education and related areas.
- Workshops and seminars sponsored by agencies such as the Learning Disabilities Association Canada (formerly the Association for Children with Learning Disabilities), and the Association for Community Living (formerly the Association for the Mentally Retarded) are available in many communities.

SPECIALIZED TRAINING FOR EARLY CHILDHOOD TEACHERS

Post-diploma and degree programs offering specialized training for work with a range of developmental disabilities are available in a number of provinces. The Resource Teacher post-diploma program providing specialized training for early childhood education teachers in working with children with special needs and their families is an example of this type of program. With the expansion of the number of children included in community programs, the need for persons with additional knowledge and specialized training has greatly increased. If we are to be successful in accomplishing inclusion as an option for *all* children with challenging needs, greater financial support must be forthcoming from all levels of government.

DUAL PLACEMENTS AND COORDINATED TEACHING

Children with severe impairments should be provided with various kinds of inclusive experiences whenever they are possible and appropriate for the child and the child's family. For some children in specialized programs, this may mean frequently scheduled visits to regular classrooms. Other children may spend a part of each preschool or child-care day in an integrated setting. With careful coordination between the two teaching staffs—those from the specialized program and those from the regular early childhood setting—these arrangements can be of benefit to both the child with a disability and those who are developing normally.

Teachers do not need extensive retraining to provide effectively for children with developmental disabilities. What teachers do need is additional knowledge about the specific developmental problem of each child who is about to be enrolled (Photo 10–2). Teachers also need on-the-job experience with children with special needs, but should have continued support from specially trained staff such as resource teachers, resource consultants, and program advisers, as well as from the parents of each child with special needs. The kinds of information offered in this text may provide a useful and comprehensive starting point.

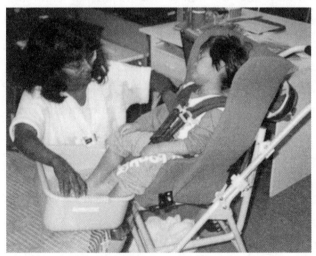

PHOTO 10–2 *To provide effectively for children with developmental disabilities, teachers need additional knowledge about the child's specific disability.*

It is important that early childhood teachers become aware of the special community support services available to families and child-care staff in their area. With written permission from the child's parents and the centre's supervisor, the child's teacher may find it helpful to contact one or more local services for a child needing special support. For example, if a 3-year-old is observed as having no verbal communication skills, the local hospital might be asked for an assessment by the speech pathologist. The speech pathologist might recommend a language stimulation program that might or might not be combined with signing.

In rural areas where specific agencies and organizations are often not yet established, it is helpful to contact the national organization needed (see Appendix C) and ask to be referred to the nearest local agency in your province or territory. Local elementary school principals and public health nurses are usually good sources of information on the availability of social services or special consultants in a given area. Some remote regions are visited once a year by a travelling clinic or team of consultants. Most of these consultants will give support if requested in writing prior to their visit. Retired specialists may also be willing to volunteer or offer support and advice. Any consultant services that are involved with the child's family in his or her home should also be consulted by the child-care centre.

Agencies and service organizations that focus on specific developmental problems can recommend or provide films, articles, books, and other kinds of information. (Appendix C offers lists of agencies and organizations.) These materials describe the disabilities and the problems that confront the child and family. If a child who has a visual impairment, for example, is to be integrated, it is imperative that teachers begin immediately to find out about blindness and how it affects early development. The Canadian National Institute for the Blind or any of several other organizations with expertise in the area of visual impairments, such as departments of health, are best able to provide helpful materials. To be truly effective, such materials are best used as background for information provided by the family. Parents, as noted in Chapter 9, are an important source of information about their children and their children's disabilities. No amount of special coursework or special training can take the place of the unique information that parents have to offer about their child with a developmental disability.

THE APPLIED DEVELOPMENTAL APPROACH

A CHILD IS A CHILD

It is true that early childhood teachers do not need extensive special training to teach in an inclusive early childhood setting. They do, however, need a particular mindset: seeing each child as a child, rather than as a "stutterer" or an

PHOTO 10–3 *A child is first of all a child.*

"epileptic" or a "Down syndrome child" (Photo 10–3). By viewing every child as first a child, teachers come to realize that many troublesome behaviours are not related necessarily to a child's disability. Blaming a child's tantrums or excessive shyness or aggressiveness on his or her disability is commonplace, but seldom justifiable. More accurate and certainly more helpful to the child is to view problem behaviours from the developmental perspective: as developmental commonalities, developmental irregularities, or cultural diversities that are seen in all children to a greater or lesser degree.

REVIEW OF DEVELOPMENTAL PRINCIPLES AND PRACTICES

Teachers who work with children with developmental problems need, first and foremost, a thorough foundation in normal growth and development. It is nearly impossible to recognize or evaluate many developmental deviations without an understanding of the range and variations of behaviours and skill levels found among both normal and special populations.

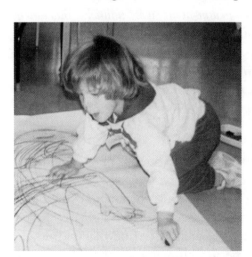

PHOTO 10–4 *Noting the sequence of developmental accomplishments is a key factor in working with young children.*

Developmental Sequences

Noting sequences of developmental accomplishments rather than chronological age is a key factor in working with young children (Photo 10–4). Effective teachers have learned that it is more useful to know that a child is moving steadily forward than to know that the child is above or below the so-called norm.

Example:

> *A 39-month-old child with Down syndrome is just beginning to pull up to a standing position. The child's teachers are predicting that she soon will be walking and are planning her program accordingly. How can the teachers be so confident? It's easy; they know this child has passed, in order (though late), each of the preceding large motor milestones.*

PHOTO 10–5 *Each area of development affects and is affected by every other area.*

Interrelationships Among Developmental Areas

Understanding the interrelatedness of developmental areas is important, too. Recognizing that each area of development affects and is affected by every other area is essential when teaching young children (Photo 10–5).

Example:

> *A 4 1/2-year-old boy with a developmental delay had refused solid foods throughout his life. Clinical findings indicated that the prolonged soft diet, requiring little chewing, had contributed to poorly developed muscle tone, hence poorly controlled movement of the mouth and tongue. The result was almost unintelligible speech, which in turn played a part in delayed cognitive and social development. Teachers and clinicians agreed that the child needed help in acquiring speech, social, and cognitive skills. They also agreed that even with treatment it was unlikely that there would be much improvement in any of the developmental problems unless the child learned to eat solid foods. That probably would not happen until the parents could be assisted in modifying their child's diet.*

Developmental Inconsistencies

Though not all children go through exactly the same sequence of development, there is a sequential pattern that most children follow: typically, they go from lying on their back or stomach to turning over, to sitting, to crawling, to pulling up, to standing, to walking. However, development is an irregularly paced process—even among normally developing children. A period of rapid development often is followed by an unsettled period known as a time of **disequilibrium**. During such periods, children seem to be developmentally disorganized: calm and capable one moment, screamingly frustrated (and frustrating) the next. Some children may even regress, or appear to go backward, for a while.

Example:

> *A 3-year-old with a 9-month-old sister competing for attention may revert to babyish ways. He displays tantrums for no apparent reason, loses the bladder control that seemed to be well established, demands the bedtime bottle that had been given up months ago. Teachers can help parents understand that their child is continuing to progress well in every other aspect of development and therefore it is unlikely that the current problems will persist. They might recommend that the parents attempt to give some individual time to this child, away from the baby who is perceived as getting so much attention. It may be agreed that there is no need for a clinical assessment of the child for the time being; that the situation is likely to be but a temporary regression to infantile behaviours. It is further agreed that both parents and teachers will continue to observe the child carefully in the event that the situation does not right itself within a reasonable period.*

Transactional Aspects of Development

Continuous interplay goes on between children and their environment. The process is referred to as the transactional aspect of development. The concept recognizes the young child as a dynamic individual who is affected by, and has an effect upon, almost everyone and everything that he or she comes in contact with (Horowitz 1987). Learning can be both positive and negative, reflecting the consequence of both direct and indirect or unintended teaching. It is easy for teachers to recognize their role in promoting intentional learning: they set up appropriate curriculum activities, respond to children positively, allow children to explore and experiment. Seldom, however, are teachers aware of inappropriate learning that may be promoted unintentionally. For example, the experience of having a single wagon or a single pegboard for a large group of 3- and 4-year-olds may teach more about shoving, pushing, waiting endlessly, and doing without than the fine and gross motor skills the materials were intended to promote.

A summary of a case study that illustrates efforts to help a child expand his attention span is given below. The situation demonstrates how an undesirable behaviour may be learned from the way teachers' well-intentioned efforts combine with the transactional nature of teacher–child interactions (Allen and Goetz 1982). In other words, the very behaviour you want to eliminate may be unintentionally reinforced by the way a teacher responds to the child.

> James was a 5-year-old who seldom stayed with an activity more than a moment or two. Teachers were constantly intercepting him, trying to settle him down, get him interested in something. As the weeks went by James continued to flit, more than ever, it seemed. What was he learning from the teachers' efforts? Certainly

not to focus his attention, which was their goal. Instead, he was learning, at some unrecognized level, that flitting about was a sure way to get the teacher-attention he needed and could not seem to get in any other way. Unfortunately, this constant flitting maintained a short attention span which interfered with James's acquiring other essential learnings.

Fascinating accounts of this transactional process are found in research studies that involve both normal infants and those who are disabled. One example is Fraiberg's (1974) comments on unsettling transactions between infants who are blind and their mothers. The infant's inability to see its mother's face interferes with its ability to respond to her smiles. The unresponsiveness often is perceived by the mother as rejection. Without her realizing it, her behaviour changes: she smiles less and less because her infant provides her with less delight. Both mother and baby, through no fault of their own, promote a mutual unresponsiveness. This comes at a critical developmental period when both need to be engaging in mutually reinforcing behaviours that lead to a strong parent–child attachment.

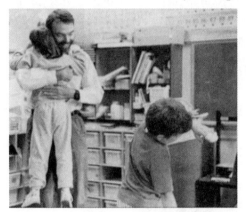

PHOTO 10–6 *Adult–child transactions have powerful potential for promoting healthy development.*

On the other hand, adult–child transactions have an equally powerful potential for promoting *healthy* development (Photo 10–6). Negative examples were cited here because of a general tendency for adults to overlook or underappreciate their everyday responses to children. Many of these responses carry the unsuspected potential for inappropriate learning emerging from routine interactions between children and adults. It must be remembered that children are learning *something*, for better or worse, from every environmental encounter.

Contingent Stimulation

Closely related to transactional processes is the principle of contingent stimulation. In the context of child development, *contingent* implies a kind of dependency or conditioning in which new learnings come about because of the responses of another. With young children, in particular, it refers to the ways in which parents and other significant adults respond to cues from the child. Adults who react to an infant's cooing, gurgling, and babbling stimulate the infant's continuing efforts to communicate. Contingent stimulation is readily observable in the simple give-and-take games that both parents and their babies initiate and take such delight in: peek-a-boo, pat-a-cake, chase-and-hide, and toss-the-toy-out-of-the-crib. According to Wachs and Gruen (1982), when adults make their responses at least partially contingent on what the infant or child says and does, specific developmental benefits result:

- Language development is earlier and better.
- Cognitive development is accelerated and richer.
- Self-esteem is much more evident.
- Attachments are more secure.

In the early 1970s, Burton White already was reporting similar benefits in his study of mother–child interactions. He was interested in discovering why some normally developing infants seemed to be more competent than other normally developing infants. For several years he observed mother and infant pairs from every socioeconomic level. He concluded that the key was not the *amount* of time that a mother spent with her infant, it was *when* she gave her attention. Mothers of competent children, he noted, seldom spent 10 or even 5 minutes at a time responding to their children. What they did do was to provide a great deal of *spontaneous* teaching—brief moments when they were totally focused on their child. These spontaneous mini-teaching episodes were usually in response to (contingent on) contacts initiated by the children (White 1975).

Readiness and Teachable Moments

In the White study it might be argued that the children, by contacting their mothers, were indicating a readiness for new learning. *Readiness* is a traditional idea that all but disappeared from child development texts for a time. It tended to be discredited because of its linkage with **developmental predeterminism** (now considered a questionable principle). In spite of that history, readiness is a useful concept when appropriately defined as a combination of genetic and environmental factors: *maturation, motivation,* and *opportunity.* When these three come together, the child is often ready to learn a new skill; in other words, *teachable moments* are likely to occur. Teachable moments are those naturally occurring opportunities when a child is most likely to learn a new skill. Consider the following two examples:

An infant reaches for the spoon while being fed, a cue that he or she is ready—that is, mature enough and has acquired the necessary perceptual–motor skills—to reach for and hold a spoon (though not always right-side up). The reaching also indicates readiness to begin to explore the difficult business of self-feeding. What is needed now is opportunity. Opportunity tends to come in the form of a patient adult who is willing, for many meals running, to scrub the floor, the high chair, and the child after every meal.

PHOTO 10–7 *Every day children show interest in exploring and acquiring new knowledge.*

Toddlers often get to the point where they hold their wet diapers away from their bodies, or they demand to be changed, or they step out of their wet diapers by themselves. These children, ranging anywhere from 15 to 40 months of age, are giving clear cues that they are moving toward the idea of learning to use the toilet.

The concepts of readiness and teachable moments are easily translated into classroom practice by observant teachers tuned to developmental difference among children. Every day children show interest in exploring and acquiring new knowledge (Photo 10–7).

Examples:

- *a 2-year-old trying to put on a shoe heel-to-toe*
- *a 3-year-old struggling to make an upside-down coat stay on the hook*
- *a 4-year-old asking, "Where did the ice go?"*
- *a 5-year-old trying to balance a teetering block structure*

In each case, based on knowledge of the individual child, the teacher makes decisions about how to use the moment to a child's best advantage.

INCIDENTAL TEACHING OPPORTUNITIES

Incidental teaching moments (Hart and Risley 1982) provide a well-organized format for making the best possible use of teachable moments. In many ways, incidental teaching is similar to contingent stimulation and White's notions about mothers who are spontaneous teachers. All three depend on child-initiated contacts. An incidental teaching episode, however, is *always* initiated by the child (Photo 10–8). The child approaches the teacher asking for help, materials, or information. Because the contact is child initiated, the teacher knows that the child is interested and therefore likely to be receptive to a brief learning activity about whatever it is that prompted the contact.

Incidental teaching moments represent the systematic application of principles compatible with both a developmental and a behavioural approach to early learning (Warren and Kaiser 1988). From the developmental point of view, the approach exemplifies:

- meeting a child where his or her interests lie;
- responding in a way that matches the child's skill level; and
- introducing the bit of novelty that provides challenge for the child.

PHOTO 10–8 *Incidental teaching is always child initiated.*

From the behavioural perspective, the incidental teaching process is a combination of the shaping, prompting, and reinforcement procedures central to effective teaching. (Reinforcement procedures, including shaping and prompting, will be discussed in Chapter 13.) In spite of being child initiated, every incidental teaching episode occurs in a planned environment, one that teachers have arranged so as to make good use of children's contacts.

The effectiveness of incidental teaching depends on teachers' efforts at:

1. providing an interesting classroom environment where children can be busy, active, and inquiring;
2. selecting appropriate objectives for each child that match his or her skill levels and interests;
3. answering a child's initiation of contact with a request for a response from the child related to a developmental objective for that particular child; and
4. responding to the child with whatever is most appropriate in terms of his or her initial contact.

These practices are illustrated in the following example having to do with a child with muscular dysfunction. One of the IPP objectives for André was to increase his ability to reach.

Teachers had observed André over several days and had identified a number of his play preferences. On the physical therapist's recommendation, the preferred materials were put in full view but out of reach. Whenever André asked for, or otherwise indicated interest in, a toy or material, a teacher held it out to him slightly out of reach, but close enough so that he could get it with a little effort. When he got his hands on the object his efforts were applauded: "You reached for the truck and now you are going to play with it." As André's reach improved, teachers gradually increased the distance. Later, to facilitate the development of overhead reaching, teachers held things just a bit above André's eye level. This, too, they increased gradually.

Further discussion of the process of incidental teaching will be postponed until Chapters 15 and 17. In those chapters, specific use of the procedures used with language and social developmental problems will be described.

Characteristics of Effective Teachers

In addition to a thorough knowledge of child development, several other traits characterize effective teachers in an integrated setting. True, teaching styles and interactions with children reflect a teacher's own unique personality; nevertheless, good teachers seem to have a number of characteristics in common. These are described in the following seven points.

1. Enthusiasm that Supports Learning

Teachers of young children need unlimited enthusiasm to support children's progress and accomplishments (Photo 10–9). This is especially important for

children with developmental disabilities. They may learn at a slower rate and in smaller steps than children who are developing normally. Thus, they tend to experience less sense of accomplishment and fewer feelings of success, both of which are incentives for learning. However, every child is quick to catch enthusiasm for almost any activity from a patient, skillful teacher who rejoices with the child over each step or partial step forward.

Enthusiasm is a reciprocal or mutually supportive process. The teacher's enthusiasm stems from the child's accomplishments, small as they sometimes are. The child's accomplishments, in turn, are supported by the teacher's skills and enthusiasm in promoting the child's learning. It is imperative, therefore, that teachers of young children know how to carry out task analysis, the process of

Photo 10–9 *Teachers must have unlimited enthusiasm.*

sequencing developmental tasks into small, **incremental steps**. Small-step successes give both child and teacher many opportunities to enjoy their work together. (Task analysis is based on behavioural procedures and will be discussed in Chapter 13.)

2. Consistency that Provides Security

The effective teacher is consistent and can be depended on to provide a predictable and stable environment. In addition to the teacher's being consistent, expectations also need to be communicated in ways that all children can understand. The teacher then can be confident about keeping to expectations, knowing that they are developmentally and individually realistic and understood by all. Consistency provides children with security, an especially important factor for children with developmental problems. Children who feel secure tend to be more self-confident. They learn to make sound judgments when they are sure of what is expected of them and know that things will remain the same unless teachers give fair warning.

Consistency does not rule out change. Children change throughout their developmental years. Teachers' expectations also must change. What remains consistent is the developmental appropriateness of the changing expectations and the teachers' care in communicating the changes to the children. Consistency, however, must never be confused with rigidity or inflexibility. An inflexible teacher is not an effective teacher.

3. FLEXIBILITY FOR SUPPORTING INDIVIDUALITY

The ability to be flexible, to improvise, to adapt an activity to individual or group needs at any given moment is a hallmark of effective teaching (Photo 10–10). A flexible teacher knows when to cut an activity short if it turns out to be too difficult or if it fails to hold children's interest. The opposite also is true. A flexible teacher knows how and when to extend and elaborate on an activity that has developed into an especially absorbing and worthwhile experience for one or more children. *Flexibility does not rule out consistency.* Truly effective teachers are a blend of consistency and flexibility. They are good judges of when to *bend the rules.* They know when to overlook a minor transgression when a child is trying to handle frustration or work through any other kind of learning experience, as in the following examples.

Jana's physical attacks on other children were frequent. Never had she been heard to tell anyone what she wanted; instead, she hit, grabbed, or shoved. One day, however, she stunned teachers by shrieking, "Get out, you stupid!" The rudely shouted command and name calling were directed at an approaching child who obviously meant no harm. The teacher, though regretting the verbal assault on a well-intentioned child, ignored the inappropriateness of Jana's response. Instead, the teacher supported Jana for talking, not hitting. This was done in the presence of the other child, to promote the child's understanding that Jana was learning to replace hitting with talking.

The teacher's flexibility indicated responsiveness to the most urgent priority for Jana as well as to the child who had been rebuffed. It let the child know that classroom expectations were operating, in spite of occasional exceptions. As for the unacceptable verbal behaviour, even if it should accelerate for a while, teachers should not be unduly concerned. When verbal requests dependably replace physical assaults, a new goal, polite requesting, can be written into Jana's IPP.

Photo 10–10 *Teachers need to be flexible enough to allow children to improvise and initiate.*

The second example focuses on a gifted 5-year-old and a blockbuilding activity.

The classroom rule was that block structures could be built only as high as the builder's head. Toward the end of the school year, a capable 5-year-old had discovered a balancing principle that enabled her to build the tower she was working on higher and higher. At one point she stood on a stool so as to continue building. (Technically, when she was standing on the stool, the blocks were not as high as the child's head.) The teacher's decision to be flexible about the height of the block structure was based on the purposefulness of the child's experimentation. The teacher's continuing presence conveyed consistency about classroom rules: that one child may not endanger another.

4. Ability to Build Trustworthiness

The more that children can trust the consistency of teachers' expectations, the more trustworthy children themselves become; hence, the more flexible teachers can be. Teachers who respect children and their need to develop **autonomy** can give children even greater freedom to explore and experiment with their own behaviour. The consistent teacher knows that children know what is expected of them. The teacher knows, too, that children usually can be trusted to stop themselves before a situation gets dangerously out of bounds. Consistency on the part of the teacher allows mutual trust to flourish as the school year progresses. DeVries and Kohlberg (1990, 37) summarize these ideas more formally within a Piagetian context:

> In a relationship of cooperation characterized by mutual respect, the adult minimizes his authority in relationship to the child and gives him as much opportunity as possible governing his own behavior on the basis of his interests and judgments. By exercising his ability to govern his own beliefs and actions, the child gradually constructs internally coherent knowledge, morality, and personality.

5. PROVISION OF POSITIVE CHILD-GUIDANCE TECHNIQUES

If children are to have a safe and healthy learning environment, teachers must set limits. Everyone needs limits, and especially young children who are trying

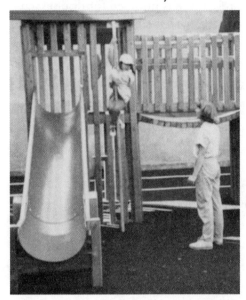

so hard to learn the many things expected of them. Limits, in the form of classroom rules, allow children to relax, to know that they can depend on someone else to make some of the decisions. Rules, in general, should be limited to health and safety issues and stated positively as much as possible (Photo 10–11). Limits should be established to cover situations in which

1. a child is likely to hurt himself or herself;

2. a child is likely to hurt another person; or

3. a child is likely to damage or destroy property.

Whatever rules there are *must be enforced.* Therefore, the number of rules should be kept to a minimum because enforcing rules is not an especially productive role for teachers.

A typical set of rules, designed to clearly govern teachers' decisions about situations in which children must be redirected, might include the following:

PHOTO 10–11 *Rules in general should be limited to health and safety issues.*

1. Children are not allowed to push other children when in high places.

2. Children are not to hit other children.

3. Children may not throw sand, toys, books, or other hard objects.

4. Teachers' cupboards (hopefully out of children's reach) are to be opened only by teachers.

5. Children are not to leave the classroom or play yard without a teacher or other authorized adult.

Rules should be stated to clarify the desired outcome behaviour; for example:
"The sand stays in the sandbox."
"Books are to read and look at."
"Those are the teacher's cupboards; children's cupboards are down there."

Only when a child fails to heed a reminder or redirection should the teacher give negative and emphatic commands: "Kelly, I can't let you throw sand." Rules apply to every child in the group. "No sand throwing" means *NO sand throwing.*

This includes children with developmental delays and limited cognitive abilities.

There should be no double standards. Double standards do the child with a special need a disservice by not helping him or her learn acceptable behaviour. Furthermore, double standards can lead to resentment and dislike among children who try to abide by the rules. Fortunately, there is no need for double standards. Every child can learn to abide by the few safety rules that are necessary in a classroom.

6. FACILITATING AND SUPPORTING CHILDREN'S EFFORTS

Though teachers must set limits and hold to them, their major role is that of *facilitator*, a person who makes things happen. A facilitative teacher recognizes that experiences, not teachers, are the best instructors for young children. Therefore, the facilitative teacher

1. provides a range of interesting and appropriate materials and activities;
2. presents these in ways that are attractive and conducive to children's learning;
3. offers the right amount and kind of assistance—not too much, but never refusing to assist;
4. is aware of what the next step is for each child on each developmental task; and
5. responds to children with ample feedback as to the effectiveness of each child's efforts (Photo 10–12).

Facilitation and support, in just the right degree, is especially important during children's play. As Gordon and Browne (1996) point out, it can be difficult for teachers to decide when to join children at play and when to remain outside the activity. The important question is "whether their presence will support what is happening or whether it will inhibit the play." In an inclusive classroom, teachers tend to find it appropriate to join in more frequently, but as unobtrusively as possible. Supportive teacher participation can go a long way toward fostering play relationships between children with or without disabilities, especially when the teacher quietly fades in and out, depending on the progress of the

PHOTO 10–12 *Provide encouragement and support for the child's efforts.*

PHOTO 10–13 *Teachers are program actualizers and integrators.*

activity. Children with special needs tend to have lower self-esteem; it is important for the teacher to work on supporting the building of self-worth and to offer opportunities for independence.

7. ABILITY TO TRANSLATE THERAPEUTIC RECOMMENDATIONS INTO AN APPROPRIATE PROGRAM

Supporting a child with special needs in an inclusive early childhood program includes environmental arrangement, curricular adaptation, and systematic use of teaching strategies to help the child be as effective as possible in interactions with the environment (Photo 10–13).

Example:

> *The speech therapist was working with a 5-year-old on beginning B, M, and P sounds. At the small-group breakfast table the teacher improvised a riddle game based on the therapist's objectives. The teacher described and gave the beginning sounds of various foods the children had encountered over the year. Children supplied the words or labels. The cues for the child in speech therapy had to do with such things as bananas, milk, and pears; butter, muffins, and plums. Everyone at the table participated and learned from the game and had fun with it. No one was the wiser (including the child with special needs) that speech therapy was going on.*

Classroom activities of this kind actualize and integrate the therapy sessions; in other words, they provide a bridge that allows the child to practise, **generalize**, and **consolidate** what is learned in therapy sessions to functional, everyday-life situations.

The foregoing discussion of the attitudes and attributes of effective teachers in an inclusive early childhood program is by no means complete. Teachers also need to know how to do these things:

1. integrate behavioural and developmental principles when teaching young children
2. work with parents and members of other disciplines
3. arrange and present materials and equipment
4. schedule the daily program to provide children with an appropriate balance of child-initiated and teacher-structured learning experiences

SUMMARY

In the inclusive classroom the need for quality teaching and appropriate learning experiences is critical. Children with developmental disabilities are especially in need of learning experiences presented by teachers who adapt developmental programs to children's special needs. Teachers who work with young children who are severely impaired should have the support of a resource consultant available to them. Many children with special needs may initially benefit from dual placements, with one program highly specialized to ensure the intensive treatment the child requires and the other providing opportunities to use newly learned skills as unplanned opportunities occur.

Early childhood teachers in an inclusive classroom do not need extensive retraining or a degree in special education. Knowledge about particular disabilities is available, as needed, through various training programs, organizations, resource centres, resource teachers/specialists who can assess children and consult with early childhood teachers, as well as from the parents of children with particular developmental disabilities. What teachers in an inclusive preschool or child-care setting need most is knowledge and experience in working with young children in general. To this end, this chapter briefly reviewed significant developmental principles and practices: developmental sequences, the interrelatedness of developmental areas, inconsistencies in development, the transactional aspects of the developmental process, and contingent stimulation.

Special mention was made of readiness and of spontaneous and incidental teaching opportunities. Use of incidental teaching moments is effective in teaching all children. It is especially effective when working with children with developmental problems. Because an incidental teaching opportunity is child initiated, it signals to a teacher that the child is ready and interested in learning whatever it is that he or she has contacted the teacher about. The teacher's responsibility is to be ready to take advantage of this teachable moment. Other characteristics of effective teachers in an inclusive early childhood program are: enthusiasm, consistency, flexibility, trustworthiness, the ability to limit children as necessary, and the skills for actualizing and integrating therapy-prescribed activities into the regular classroom program.

STUDENT ACTIVITIES

1. Locate and record the names and locations of several agencies in your community that provide resources for children and their families who need extra support. Select one and report on the kinds of materials they have available for teachers and for parents. Obtain samples, if possible.

2. Talk with teachers in an inclusive early childhood or child-care centre about their children with developmental disabilities and their families. Record their comments, concerns, and general attitudes about the children and their parents.

3. Observe a preschool session. Count the number of child-to-teacher contacts. Briefly describe those the teacher turned into a spontaneous teaching or incidental teaching episode.

4. Locate a program that serves children who are severely disabled. Ask your instructor to arrange an observation. While observing, list the special equipment and services provided for the children.

5. Think about a situation when you were a child and
   a. a teacher did something you felt was unjust, and
   b. a teacher did something that really met your needs.

   For each of these situations
   i. briefly describe the situation, identifying what characteristics of the teacher's behaviour had an effect on you,
   ii. indicate how it affected how you felt and responded, and
   iii. state what you think the teacher should have done.

REFERENCES

Allen, K.E., and F.M. Goetz 1982 *Early Childhood Education: Special Problems, Special Solutions.* Rockville, Md.: Aspen Systems. Reprinted with permission.

DeVries, R., and L. Kohlberg 1990 *Constructivist Early Education. Overview and Companion with Other Programs.* Washington, D.C.: National Association for the Education of Young Children.

Fraiberg, S. 1974 "Blind Infants and Their Mothers: An Examination of the Sign System." In M. Lewis and L.A. Rosenblum, eds. *The Effect of the Infant on Its Caregiver.* New York: Wiley.

Gordon, A.M., and K.W. Browne 1996 *Beginnings and Beyond. Foundations in Early Childhood Education.* Albany, N.Y.: Delmar.

Hart, B., and T.R. Risledy 1982 *How to Use Incidental Teaching.* Austin, TX: PRO-ED.

Horowitz, F.D. 1987 *Exploring Developmental Theories: Toward a Structural/Behavioral Model of Development.* Hillsdale, N.J.: Erlbaum.

Wachs, T.D., and G.E. Gruen 1982 *Early Experience and Human Development.* New York: Plenum.

Warren, S.F., and A.P. Kaiser 1988 "Research in Early Language Intervention." In S.L. Odom and M.B. Karnes, eds. *Early Intervention for Infants and Children with Handicaps.* Baltimore: Paul H. Brookes.

White, B.L. 1975 *The First Three Years of Life.* Englewood Cliffs, N.J.: Prentice-Hall.

CHAPTER 11

Identification and the Individual Program Plan (IPP)

Objectives

After studying the material in this chapter, the student will be able to

- explain this statement: Scores obtained on IQ tests given to young children must be viewed with caution, even skepticism
- discuss the role of the early childhood teacher in the identification of developmental problems and in the IPP process
- identify different observational recording techniques and give appropriate examples for application
- summarize each of the major components of an IPP

INTRODUCTION

The identification of developmental problems is a responsibility of everyone associated with infants and young children and their families. Though some provinces provide screening of newborn babies and follow-up home visits by public health nurses, there is no federal legislation in Canada that requires early screening and assessment of an infant's development. Recent research continues to support what many child development specialists have thought for a while now: that the early years have a lifelong impact on how the child develops, and that early identification of special needs is of extreme import in enabling early intervention and specialized programming. Early identification and intervention also help in the prevention of secondary handicapping conditions through individualized programming and educational planning.

The focus of this chapter is on these two issues: early identification of developmental problems and the delivery of special services through the IPP.

THE PROCESS OF EARLY IDENTIFICATION

Identification of developmental problems can take place any time from a few weeks after conception to adulthood (age 18). These years are formally recognized as the developmental period. Early identification of problems is not limited to the first 5 to 8 years of life. A child may be perfectly healthy up to age 12 or 15, then show first-time symptoms of a disability that has an impact on development (juvenile rheumatoid arthritis, for example). The older child is as much in need of early identification of an emerging problem as is a 2-year-old showing first-time symptoms of any kind. In both cases, early identification should lead to prompt treatment. In turn, prompt treatment can reduce the severity of the problem and prevent it from affecting other areas of development.

The identification of developmental problems or potential developmental problems involves several steps. These have been identified as screening, assessment, diagnosis, and evaluation. The first two of these steps in the identification process will be discussed in this section.

EARLY IDENTIFICATION

In Canada, because of the universal health care program, the identification of children who are developing outside of the norms falls mainly on the shoulders of the medical profession:

- the doctor or midwife who delivers the baby
- the nurses who observe the baby directly after birth
- the family physician and/or public health nurse who usually sees the child at regular intervals

Programs and services available through community public health departments, medical centres, and community early intervention services seek to identify those children who may require further assessment to ensure early identification of developmental problems.

Screening, based on various observation techniques and screening tools, is the process of identifying *possible* delays and deviations in a child's development indicating the need for assessment (Photo 11–1). Screening can be carried out by persons without highly specialized training. *Assessment* is the process used in the identification of development that may be deviating from the norm. Only persons who are specially trained and licensed are qualified to use the standardized evaluation instruments needed to carry out and interpret the findings of an assessment on a child. Specially trained early childhood resource teachers/

PHOTO 11–1 *Screening often involves direct observation of the child in the play environment.*

interventionists often are able to conduct informal functional assessments that can provide information to support appropriate programming. However, the use of standardized assessment techniques to obtain a more definitive diagnosis requires a licensed clinician.

SCREENING

Screening is important in the identification of developmental problems (or potential problems). In the United States, legislation was passed in the 1960s mandating states to conduct screening programs for young children on a community-wide basis, thus identifying children with potential developmental problems. (This program is known as Child Find.) The goal of this legislation was to provide easily administered, low-cost testing for as many children as possible. Children with obvious disabilities are usually not put through these screening procedures. They and their families are usually referred directly to the appropriate health care or social service agency. There is no parallel legislation across Canada, although some municipalities provide similar screening and assessment through departments of health and social services.

Screening tests describe a child's level of performance, but *only at the time at which the screening is conducted* (Allen and Marotz 1994). Comprehensive screening evaluates the child's current abilities, deviations, delays, and impairments in all areas of development. If problem areas are identified during routine developmental screening, clinical assessments are indicated. Several points should be emphasized:

1. Results from screening tests should not be confused with assessment. They do not constitute a diagnosis, and should never be used as a basis for planning an intervention program.

2. *Follow-through is essential.* "Identifying children with potential problems is only the first step; encouraging families to seek further assessment for their child is the next" (Hanson and Lynch 1989, 95).

3. Accurate results can be achieved only with **reliable and valid tests** developed specially for use with young children. There is a scarcity of such tests. In the absence of a valid instrument, testing is of no value (NAEYC [National Association for the Education of Young Children] 1988, 12).

PHOTO 11–2 *Parents have a wealth of knowledge about their child.*

Parents as Partners in Screening

Parents have a wealth of firsthand knowledge about their children (Photo 11–2). They know what their child can and cannot do in everyday life. Often, they are the first to suspect a problem, even if unable to specify its nature clearly. It is estimated that 65 to 75 percent of hearing problems in young children were noted first by their parents. The parents knew *something* was wrong. They did not necessarily recognize it as a hearing loss but they did report to the health care provider that their child acted strange or "talked funny."

A hearing loss, as well as a number of other subtle problems, may not show up during a routine medical checkup. When a problem cannot be pinpointed by the clinician, parents sometimes are led to believe that nothing is wrong with their child. They are often advised to go home and relax, to get over being so anxious. Ignoring parents' observations is not in the child's best interests, however. Neglecting a problem in its early stages may result in a long-range negative impact on development.

Cultural and Ethnic Differences

Family customs and language influence a child's performance on screening tests. A child's responses may be scored as wrong, even when, according to family values, they are right. The result may be an invalid (false) outcome, suggesting that the child is perhaps developmentally delayed or language impaired when in fact his responses conform to and reflect those of his family/home environment. These unjust procedures became dismayingly apparent in the early days of special education reform, when the "6-hour retarded child" came to be recognized. These were the children who functioned perfectly well in their own communities and in their own language but had few skills and little background for functioning in schools designed to accommodate only the majority culture.

To avoid similar errors, safeguards must be built into every step of the screening process. These include

- translating tests into the language or dialect of the children being tested and having the tests administered by persons skilled in that language;
- adapting test items and procedures so as to reward rather than penalize the strengths of the culture and the correctness of the responses of the culturally different child; and

- using more than one set of standardized norms so that a child may be scored in terms of the dominant culture's expectations as well.

PHOTO 11–3 *Several screening tests are available for assessing older infants as well as newborns.*

Types of Screening and Assessment Instruments

Early childhood screening tests take many forms. Some, like the *Peabody Picture Vocabulary Test*, focus on only one aspect of development and must be administered by a professionally trained speech pathologist. Others, such as the *Denver Developmental Screening Test* (DDST) and the *Diagnostic Inventory for Screening Children* (DISC), attempt to assess all developmental areas. These screening tests are primarily used in hospitals and early childhood centres.

Screening tests also are available that assess newborns and older infants (Photo 11–3), among them the *APGAR* and the *Bayley Scales of Infant Development*. Others assess vision (*Snellen Illiterate E*), hearing (*Pure Tone Audiometry*), and cognitive skills (the *Wechsler Preschool and Primary Scale of Intelligence*, or WPPSI).

A screening instrument noted for its interdisciplinary capabilities is the *DIAL* (Developmental Indicators for the Assessment of Learning). DIAL focuses on the classroom teacher as central to the screening process. The advantage is obvious: except for parents, no one knows or can interpret children's responses better. The *Battele* is a useful assessment tool because it is curriculum based. In other words, you can test a child, find the areas where the child lacks knowledge or ability, teach to that gap, and then retest to see if the missing information or skill has been acquired. The *DASI* (Developmental Assessment Screening Inventory) is useful for testing nonverbal children because it is strictly focused on evaluating performance. The *Brigance Diagnostic Inventory of Early Development* is also used by many agencies. (The latest edition of the Brigance covers the assessment of social and emotional development, as well as the range of other areas of development.)

Teachers also play a major role in screening for giftedness among young children. No single test identifies the young and gifted child. Several measures must be used. IQ scores, level of motivation, and creativity (which is difficult to define and measure) may be useful when backed up by a teacher's observations and knowledge of a child (see Chapter 9).

CRITERION-REFERENCED TESTS. Some screening instruments are criterion referenced; that is, a child's performance on each task is compared with a pre-selected standard (*criterion*). A child's performance is not compared with the performance of other children. Criterion-referenced test items might ask, for example, Can the child lace and tie his or her own shoes? Walk seven consecutive steps on a balance beam? Match five shapes and colours in one minute?

NORM-REFERENCED TESTS. With norm-referenced tests the question becomes: How well does the child do, *compared with other children of the same age*, on tasks such as counting pennies, naming letters of the alphabet, stacking six one-inch cubes? Norm-referenced tests provide standardized information intended to relate to children's abilities at various ages. In other words, the norm-referenced test provides scales that compare the performance of one child to the averaged performance of other children of approximately the same age. It must be recognized, however, that these tests tend to be less than reliable with young children (Cook, Tessier, and Armbruster 1987).

IQ TESTS AS SCREENING INSTRUMENTS. Most intelligence tests (IQ tests) are norm referenced. Tests such as the *Wechsler Intelligence Scale for Children* (WISC) and the *Stanford-Binet Intelligence Scales* are sometimes given to young children. The avowed purpose is to attempt to determine

- how much a child knows;
- how well the child solves problems; and
- how quickly a child can perform a variety of mental tasks.

The scores from IQ tests must be viewed with caution, even skepticism. A number of factors may lead to poor performance on an IQ test (or any other test, for that matter). The child may be tired, hungry, or unwell at the time. The child may be anxious about the unfamiliar testing situation and the unfamiliar person giving the test. The child also may be answering in ways appropriate to his or her own language or culture but inappropriate in terms of standardized test responses (recall the earlier discussion on cultural differences). Furthermore, some children are hampered by an unidentified developmental or sensory problem. A partial vision or hearing loss, for example, can interfere with a child's ability to respond appropriately; thus, the child's IQ score may falsely indicate an impairment of intellectual functioning.

IQ scores of young children *do not predict future intellectual performance* (Photo 11–4). In fact, they are not even good at assessing a young child's current intellectual capabilities. The major problem with IQ scores is that they do not account for the child's learning opportunities (or lack of learning opportuni-

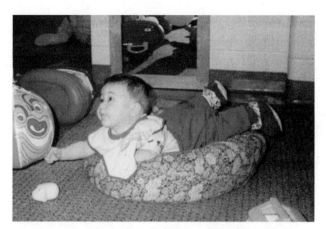

PHOTO 11–4 *The IQ scores of young children are often invalid. Furthermore, IQ scores do not predict later intellectual performance.*

ties). Neither do they reflect the quality of the learning experiences a child may have had. The use of a single test score to determine a child's intellectual competence must always be challenged. In fact, *more than one instrument* should be used in any screening program to ensure a valid picture of the child's development. As Perrone (1990, 13) points out:

> Teachers and parents have been told that tests have meaning, that they point out what children know and understand, that they can help give direction to instruction. The tests *don't* match the promise. Their contribution to the education of young children is virtually nil.

Who Does the Screening?

Screening programs may be conducted by professionals or **paraprofessionals.** Regardless of who is doing the screening, training in test procedures is important. Some screening tests, such as certain hearing tests and medical tests, should be administered only by members of that discipline. Other tests, such as the *Denver Developmental Screening Test* (DDST) or the *Snellen Illiterate E Test*, can be administered by a variety of individuals trained to use the instrument. Screening programs should be conducted by teams whose members are skilled in administering a number of tests. (For an excellent analysis and listing of screening and assessment instruments, see Thurman and Widerstrom 1990.)

Early childhood teachers and infant teacher/caregivers are key figures in the early identification process (Photo 11–5). It is essential that they take responsibility for recognizing and reporting warning signs that a developmental problem exists or may develop.

THE TEACHER'S ROLE IN EARLY IDENTIFICATION

The teacher's role is critical in the identification of developmental problems in infants and young children. It is teachers' recorded observations of children in many situations, over time, that provide a valid picture of each child's skills,

capabilities, and special needs. All children in a group should be observed and informally screened to ensure that the activities provided are developmentally appropriate. It is through this observation and comparison of all members of a group that the range of individual differences becomes evident and developmentally appropriate programs are planned (Hughes, Paasche, and Greer 1992).

PHOTO 11–5 *Early childhood teachers and infant caregivers are key figures in the early identification process.*

TEACHERS' QUALIFICATIONS

Teachers should have special qualifications and opportunities for experience in identifying children with developmental problems or potential problems. They have knowledge of early development. They understand its typical regularities and irregularities, which enables them to recognize developmental deviations. Teachers also should have had sufficient training to allow them to provide infants and young children with sound developmental activities that bring out the best in each child during the assessment process.

Teachers are further advantaged in that they see children in a natural environment. In the classroom, a child is likely to be comfortable and spontaneous. Furthermore, teachers can observe children of similar ages and interests; this enables them to compare each child's development in the context of a normal developmental range. Teachers also have extended periods of time and many situations and activities in which to informally observe children. Contrast this with clinicians such as the doctor, the audiologist, and the psychologist, who usually see the child only on brief and tightly scheduled visits. At these times the child may be ill at ease and behave quite differently than in a familiar home or school environment.

The Teacher as Observer

Observation, according to Irwin and Bushnell (1980, 62) is "both a scientific tool and an everyday skill of value to teachers and parents." The search for developmental problems should always begin with systematic observation of children as they work and play in the preschool or child-care centre. A NAEYC position paper (1988, 13) stresses that teachers' "assessment of young children should rely heavily on the results of their observations."

Observers must be *objective*—that is, they should write down only what a child actually does and says. *Subjective* recording, by contrast, occurs when teachers put their own interpretations on children's behaviour. Note the differences in the following statements:

- *Objective:* Susie smiled and laughed frequently throughout the morning; she cried only once.
- *Subjective:* Susie was happy and carefree today.
- *Objective:* Mark stamped his feet and screamed "No" each time he was asked to change activities.
- *Subjective:* Mark gets angry all the time.

PHOTO 11–6 *Systematically recorded observations are extremely useful in identifying possible developmental problems.*

Systematic Observations

Most teachers are used to observing children; few, however, record their observations in an organized way. Systematically recorded observations are extremely helpful for programming (Hughes, Paasche, and Greer 1992), and are often the key to effective identification of developmental differences (Photo 11–6). Each observation should start with these four parts:

1. child's name or initials (confidentiality of information is essential)
2. date and time of day
3. setting (and in some instances, names or number of children and teachers present)
4. name or initials of the observer

Teachers' observations take many forms. The questions teachers need to have answered determine the observation strategy they will select. In most cases, it is best if more than one person observes the child, especially if there is a hint of a serious problem. When two people agree they are seeing the same thing, personal bias and misinterpretation of a child's behaviour is reduced.

OBSERVATIONAL RECORDING TECHNIQUES

Discussed here is a sampling of the many kinds of observational techniques and records that are useful in working with young children. (For a comprehensive overview of observation strategies, see Bentzen 1985; Irwin and Bushnell 1980.)

1. Checklists

Checklists are a quick and effective way of collecting systematic information on one or many children. Teachers, aides, parents, and volunteers, as well as the children themselves, can record on checklists. Many young children recognize their own name when printed in large letters. If teachers need to know, for example, which 4- and 5-year-olds are using particular learning centres, they can post a list of children's names close by. Most children can make a mark by their name as they enter; the teacher can do it for those who cannot. At the end of the day (or week) teachers know which children are using which centres and which children are doing a great deal of coming and going (useful information in planning individual programs). Checklists can be as simple as the one just mentioned or they can be designed to give much more information, as in the Teacher Observation Form and Checklist (Figure 11-1). The most useful are checklists that teachers themselves design to answer their own questions about children and the program.

2. Frequency Counts

An effective way of making a recorded observation is simply keeping track of how often something happens. Teachers who are concerned about a particular behaviour need to know how often it takes place:

- excessively?
- infrequently?
- only under certain circumstances?

Every time the behaviour occurs, a tally mark is made on a piece of paper posted on the wall or carried in teachers' pockets. Over a period of several days the tally marks can provide significant information as to whether a given behaviour is actually a problem, as well as to how significant a problem it is.

FIGURE 11–1

TEACHER OBSERVATION FORM AND CHECKLIST

TEACHER OBSERVATION FORM AND CHECKLIST FOR IDENTIFYING CHILDREN WHO MAY REQUIRE ADDITIONAL SERVICES

Child's Name: _____ Birth Date: _____

Date: _____ Recording Teacher's Name: _____

LANGUAGE	YES	NO	SOMETIMES
Does the child:			
1. use two- and three-word phrases to ask for what he or she wants?	_____	_____	_____
2. use complete sentences to tell you what happened?	_____	_____	_____
3. when asked to describe something, use at least two or more sentences to talk about it?	_____	_____	_____
4. ask questions?	_____	_____	_____
5. seem to have difficulty following directions?	_____	_____	_____
6. respond to questions with appropriate answers?	_____	_____	_____
7. seem to talk too softly or too loudly?	_____	_____	_____
8. Are you able to understand the child?	_____	_____	_____

PREACADEMICS	YES	NO	SOMETIMES
Does the child:			
9. seem to take at least twice as long as the other children to learn preacademic concepts?	_____	_____	_____
10. seem to take the time needed by other children to learn preacademic concepts?	_____	_____	_____
11. have difficulty attending to group activities for more than five minutes at a time?	_____	_____	_____
12. appear extremely shy in group activities; for instance, not volunteering answers or answering questions when asked, even though you think the child knows the answers?	_____	_____	_____

MOTOR	YES	NO	SOMETIMES

Does the child:

13. continually switch a crayon back and forth from one hand to the other when colouring? _____ _____ _____

14. appear clumsy or shaky when using one or both hands? _____ _____ _____

15. when colouring with a crayon, appear to tense the hand not being used (for instance, clench it into a fist)? _____ _____ _____

16. when walking or running, appear to move one side of the body differently from the other side? For instance, does the child seem to have better control of the leg and arm on one side than on the other? _____ _____ _____

17. lean or tilt to one side when walking or running? _____ _____ _____

18. seem to fear or not be able to use stairs, climbing equipment, or tricycles? _____ _____ _____

19. stumble often or appear awkward when moving about? _____ _____ _____

20. appear capable of dressing self except for tying shoes? _____ _____ _____

SOCIAL	YES	NO	SOMETIMES

Does the child:

21. engage in more than two disruptive behaviours a day (tantrums, fighting, screaming, etc.)? _____ _____ _____

22. appear withdrawn from the outside world (fiddling with pieces of string, staring into space, rocking)? _____ _____ _____

23. play alone and seldom talk to the other children? _____ _____ _____

24. spend most of the time trying to get attention from adults? _____ _____ _____

25. have toileting problems (wet or soiled) once a week or more often? _____ _____ _____

*Question applies if child is 4 years or older.

VISUAL OR HEARING	YES	NO	SOMETIMES

Does the child:

26. appear to have eye movements that are jerky or uncoordinated?

27. seem to have difficulty seeing objects? For instance, does the child:
    • tilt head to look at things?
    • hold objects close to eyes?
    • squint?
    • show sensitivity to bright lights?
    • have uncontrolled eye-rolling?
    • complain that eyes hurt?

28. appear awkward in tasks requiring eye–hand coordination such as pegs, puzzles, colouring, etc.?

29. seem to have difficulty hearing? For instance, does the child:
    • consistently favour one ear by turning the same side of the head in the direction of the sound?
    • ignore, confuse, or not follow directions?
    • pull on ears or rub ears frequently, or complain of earaches?
    • complain of head noises or dizziness?
    • have a very high, very low, or monotonous tone of voice?

GENERAL HEALTH	YES	NO	SOMETIMES

Does the child:

30. seem to have an excessive number of colds?

31. have frequent absences because of illness?

32. have eyes that water?

33. have frequent discharge from:
    • eyes?
    • ears?
    • nose?

34. have sores on body or head?

GENERAL HEALTH	YES	NO	SOMETIMES
35. have periods of unusual movements (such as eye blinking) or "blank spells" that seem to appear and disappear without relationship to the social situation?	_____	_____	_____
36. have hives or rashes?	_____	_____	_____
wheeze?	_____	_____	_____
37. have a persistent cough?	_____	_____	_____
38. seem to be excessively thirsty?	_____	_____	_____
seem to be ravenously hungry?	_____	_____	_____
39. Have you noticed any of the following conditions:	_____	_____	_____
• constant fatigue?	_____	_____	_____
• irritability?	_____	_____	_____
• restlessness?	_____	_____	_____
• tenseness?	_____	_____	_____
• feverish cheeks or forehead?	_____	_____	_____
40. Is the child overweight?	_____	_____	_____
41. Is the child physically or mentally lethargic?	_____	_____	_____
42. Has the child lost noticeable weight without being on a diet?	_____	_____	_____

Example:

> *One teacher was concerned about John's safety because of what she thought were his frequent attempts to climb over the fence during outdoor play. The other teacher thought it seldom happened. An actual frequency count showed that the fence-climbing attempts occurred four or five times each play period. Teachers now could agree that there was a problem. They assessed the play yard and realized that there was not much for John to climb on. They began to set up climbing activities several days a week. John's fence-climbing dropped to one or no episodes per day. On days when no climbing activities were set up, John's fence-climbing was again high. The frequency counts gave teachers clues to the extent of the problem as well as to their success in reducing the unsafe behaviour.*

3. Duration Measures

A duration measure indicates how long an event or a behaviour lasts. This type of observation, like frequency counts, provides significant information that nevertheless is easy to collect. By simply noting a start and stop time on a child's activities, teachers can gauge such things as span of attention, how much time a child spends in either appropriate or inappropriate behaviours, and under what circumstances a behaviour (thumbsucking, perhaps) is most likely to continue unduly.

Example:

Teachers were concerned about Omar's poor attention span. They decided to find out how many minutes at a time he spent at various activities. Several days' observations indicated that he spent many minutes (15 to 20) with hands-on activities (painting, block-building, puzzles). In contrast, he had a short attention span—only a minute or two—for activities that required listening (music, stories, conversation). These duration measures were invaluable as teachers planned Omar's program, conferred with his parents, and participated in the team meetings.

4. Anecdotal Notes

These are brief, objective observations, each recorded individually on 3-by-5-inch notepad paper. The small-size paper ensures brevity. Anecdotal notes are recorded on each child in each area of development at regular intervals. See Figure 11–2 for an example of a motor note.

In looking back on three months of motor notes, Tina's teachers could see how helpful the physical therapist had been. The techniques she demonstrated when working with Tina helped teachers assist Tina in improving her motor skills. Furthermore, from a review of the social notes made during the same period, it appeared that Tina was most likely to get on the climbing frames if other children were there, too. Cognitive notes indicated that she had learned most of the names of the children with whom she climbed and often counted how many children were on the climber. The composite picture, made up of these brief anecdotal notes, is one of a child making steady progress within and across developmental areas.

FIGURE 11-2

EXAMPLE OF A MOTOR NOTE

Child: Tina   Observer: M.J.
Play yard   1/12/93

MOTOR DEVELOPMENT

Tina climbed up eight rungs of the climbing tower. On each rung she started with her left foot and brought her right foot up next to it before going on to the next rung. With each step up, she grasped the bar directly above with the alternate hand (left foot, right hand). In coming down she reversed the pattern.

5. Running Records

These are objective narrative recordings—attempts to write down everything that a child says and does for a period of time. Taken periodically, running records can produce a well-rounded picture of each child's overall behaviour and development. Running records are a useful form of observation; they also are the most time consuming. Unlike other written observations, a running record can rarely be taken by a teacher while supervising. However, a teacher can be released from direct work with children for an occasional 20 to 30 minutes to take a running record. Volunteers often are willing to relieve teachers for this purpose or take running records themselves. When there is a child that teachers are especially concerned about, volunteers' observations can be of great value.

6. Logs, Journals, and Diaries

Records of this kind are similar to the running record but less comprehensive. Written accounts may be kept in a loose-leaf notebook with a section for each child. (Some teachers prefer a separate folder for each child.) Notes are jotted down during class time or immediately after children leave for the day. The jottings may be general notes about a child or focused notes on some aspect of the child's behaviour (Photo 11–7). For example, teachers may need to know more about a child's outdoor activities before planning an individual program to increase play skills: With whom does Angelo play? Does he play on the climbing equipment? Ride the wheel toys? Build with outdoor blocks? Is he accepted into the play of other children? What other children? Are some play periods better than others? Why? The answers to these questions (or any others teachers may

PHOTO 11–7 *Observation notes may focus on identifying preferred activities and playmates.*

have about any child) provide clues for program planning.

7. Time Sampling

Time sampling has to do with periodic and momentary observations to determine the presence or absence of a behaviour. Is Leanne engaged most of the time with play materials? Does Marty engage mostly in solitary, parallel, associative, or cooperative play? Teachers look at the child in question at regular intervals. Usually it is only a brief glance, perhaps once every 2 minutes, or 5 minutes, or 15 minutes. On the other hand, they may take a quick look only 2 or 3 times a day at certain periods such as circle time. With each glance, if the behaviour is occurring, the teacher makes a mark on a tally sheet. It may turn out that Leanne, for example, was engaged with materials in only 3 out of the 15 samples. Might this be an indication that she needs different materials? Or help in extending her span of attention? As for Marty, he was playing alone in 5 percent of the samples, in associative play about 40 percent, and in cooperative play in the remaining samples—an appropriate balance for an almost-5-year-old.

8. Language Samples

As noted in Chapter 4, speech and language problems account for a major portion of developmental problems. Before treatment can begin, the current level of a child's skills first must be assessed. A good place to get information about a child's language is in the classroom. Here the child is doing what comes naturally, with familiar things to talk about and familiar people to talk with. Language samples are verbatim recordings (word for word, or sound for sound) of exactly what the child says or what sounds the child makes (Photo 11–8). If the child says "du gul," it is written "du gul" (phonetically) even if the observer knows the child is referring to "the girl." If the child is squealing "Eeeeee" and pointing to the juice, "Eeeeee" is what the observer writes down, not "Billy wanted juice." As an aside, it would be best for the observer to note the pointing along with the vocalization to show how Billy was able to communicate his need.

PHOTO 11–8 *The familiar classroom is a good place to obtain language samplings.*

EARLY IDENTIFICATION: CAUTIONARY NOTES FOR TEACHERS

Teachers' observations are of indisputable value in identifying developmental problems. Nevertheless, the information must be used with care, even caution. It can do a 3- or 4-year-old more harm than good to attach too much importance to a developmentally "normal" speech irregularity such as a lisp or mild stammering. Excessive concern, or pressure placed on a child with problems of this type, can be as damaging as failing to recognize a problem. It must be remembered, too, that some behaviours may not be what they appear to be. A child may seem to be hyperactive—constantly jumping up, pushing ahead of other children, or grabbing the book from which the teacher is reading. These behaviours actually may be the child's efforts to bring things into closer eye or ear range because of a vision or hearing deficit.

1. Teachers Should Avoid Making Diagnoses

Diagnosis implies decision making based on clinical expertise in interpreting **symptoms**. A proper diagnosis requires specialized expertise, often from several disciplines, to identify even fairly common problems. Blackman (1990) cites a number of such instances associated with food refusals in young children. Examples from teachers' classroom experiences are plentiful too, as in the following case:

Charles was a 5-year-old with delayed language skills. He had several maladaptive behaviours, including (but only on some days) crying and whining while hitting himself about the cheeks. Charles's parents had been told that the behaviours were signs of emotional disturbance. Teachers, however, observed times when there was no self-hitting and crying. They suggested that the parents get another opinion. The ultimate clinical diagnosis was abscessed back teeth with pain that flared up intermittently. Charles's "emotionally disturbed" behaviours ceased once the teeth were treated.

2. Teachers Should Avoid Labels

As emphasized in Chapter 4, labelling a young child as intellectually impaired, hyperactive, or emotionally disturbed can have disastrous effects. The intervention program tends to focus narrowly on what the label implies while overlooking the child's skills and strengths. Lost is the healthier individual who might have emerged if the stereotyping label never had been hung on the child. Such a loss very nearly occurred in a case study reported by Allen and Goetz (1982):

Maria was labeled early in life as retarded. Near her fourth birthday she was placed in an integrated preschool program where little was expected of her as a retarded child. However, a volunteer observed Maria's many problem-solving skills with materials and equipment. Intrigued by the volunteer's observations, the head teacher took several running records. These showed the same kinds of high level cognitive behaviors. Consultation with Maria's mother revealed that both she and Maria had been severely abused by the father before he left permanently two years earlier. Mother revealed further that she, too, had often suspected that Maria "wasn't all dumb." The staff helped Maria's mother arrange for a comprehensive reassessment by a child study team. Following the assessment, program changes (systematically reinforcing use of language and social interactions with children and teachers) were immediately put into effect. Within a year Maria was indistinguishable from any other child in the group in terms of mental functioning.

3. Teachers Should Avoid Raising Parents' Anxiety

Most parents know that their child has a problem even though they may be reluctant to admit it. The teacher's role is to help parents see their child more realistically without raising their anxiety unduly. Teachers should report to parents what the child *can do*, as well as what the child cannot yet do (Photo 11–9). This helps parents become better attuned to their child. It also provides an opening for teachers to help parents recognize the need to seek professional help so as to build upon the child's strengths. (See Chapter 9.)

PHOTO 11–9 *Carefully kept records and staff consultation are part of determining each child's developmental needs.*

4. Teachers Should Assist in Making Referrals

Early identification procedures are important for ensuring that children with developmental problems are referred for special services. Nevertheless, teachers should never refer a child directly, regardless of the severity of a child's problems. The teacher's role is to help parents recognize the need for intervention and/or treatment. The next step is linking the family to the needed services. This is accomplished more easily if a resource teacher or specialized program consultants are available to the program. If not, the teacher may have to play a more active role. Marotz, Rush, and Cross (1993) suggest: "A teacher who is familiar with local services, such as hospitals, clinics, health departments, medical specialists, private and public service agencies and various sources of funding can be helpful to parents in obtaining the comprehensive medical care and assistance the child needs."

5. Teachers Should Not Forget the Importance of Making Careful Judgments

Deciding if a behaviour is appropriate is sometimes difficult. The most important considerations, as noted earlier, are the behaviour patterns of the child's family and community. Often these are quite different from what the teacher is used to. Therefore, it is useful to ask the question: *Does the behaviour interfere with the child's willingness to engage in a wide range of learning experiences and social activities that are included in the developmental curriculum?* If the answer is "No," then it is not likely that teachers need to be overly concerned.

6. Teachers Must Remember that Each Child Is Different

It must be remembered, too, that no two children of the same age develop exactly alike (see Chapter 2). To expect uniformity is contrary to basic developmental principles. On the other hand, a nonintervention policy of expecting children to "grow out" of a developmental difference that has the potential for causing trouble is also dangerous. A "wait-and-see" attitude may condemn some children to unnecessary delays in treatment. Delay may lead to **cumulative deficits** that become increasingly difficult to overcome over the months and years ahead.

7. Teachers Should Determine Frequency of Behaviours

Many times, it is not the type of behaviour but the amount that is of concern. Almost all inappropriate behaviours are seen in children (and even in adults) at one time or another. Every young child cries, whines, sulks, clings, disobeys, and talks back (Photo 11–10). Rarely are these behaviours considered unusual, let alone harmful. They are a normal, even desirable aspect of the developmental process because they indicate a full range of emotional responses. Seldom are they cause for alarm unless

- a behaviour occurs excessively (children who frequently hit, bite, or kick others);

PHOTO 11–10 *Sulking is a developmentally normal behaviour in young children.*

- a behaviour is used constantly or exclusively in place of more developmentally appropriate responses (children who seem always to whine and cry for what they want instead of asking); or
- a behaviour interferes with significant learning experiences (hiding in a cubby much of the day, thereby withdrawing from classroom activities).

8. Teachers Should Be Aware of Environmental Factors

Situations outside the child often are responsible for the frequent occurrence of a maladaptive behaviour. One clue that indicates the likelihood of an environmental cause is that a behaviour occurs to excess under some conditions but not under other conditions. In these instances, it is probable that the environment, not the child, is at fault. Consider the following examples:

- A 4-year-old's inability to share may be caused by a shortage of attractive materials or equipment rather than by selfishness.
- The inability of a 7-year-old to cut on the lines may be due to faulty scissors.
- The unresponsiveness of an infant may change when the infant is exposed to appropriate activities.

THE INDIVIDUAL PROGRAM PLAN (IPP)

The Individual Program Plan (IPP) is an approach to providing services to individuals with special needs. "This approach involves a written IPP...and the IPP process of designing, implementing and evaluating that plan" (Galambos and Wilson-Whetstone 1989, 23). The written plan provides the structure and direction for the services and activities to be provided to the child and family by the early intervention program. (Note: *Individual Education Plan* [IEP] is sometimes used by service providers interchangeably with IPP to refer to the written plan in special education and early intervention.)

Teachers are essential throughout the IPP process: in their observations of children's behaviour; in their implementation of the classroom aspects of the individual programs; and in their evaluation. Linkage between classroom practice and the program recommendations by the child's IPP team should be carried out by the teachers. Furthermore, the ongoing evaluation of the appropriateness of each child's daily program is largely dependent on the teacher. In other words, teachers are central to the entire IPP process.

THE IPP TEAM

The IPP is developed by a team consisting of the child's parents or parent surrogates and professionals from the various disciplines involved with the child and family (such as resource teachers, early childhood teachers, physiotherapists, a speech and language pathologist, and/or the case coordinator). The types of teams and the disciplines involved are varied. Several models for IPP teams have emerged in the last few years:

- *Multidisciplinary.* Professionals working independently of each other in a parallel format; each professional is viewed as important but takes responsibility only for his or her own area of clinical expertise.
- *Interdisciplinary.* Professionals and parents collaborating in decision making around the program and service needs of each child and family, and relying on each other to build on the range of strengths found among different types of child development experts. (The term *interdisciplinary* will be used in this text.)
- *Transdisciplinary.* Professionals teaching each other through continuous staff development; joint team functioning; role release and role substitution; determining role definition (who does what) around the characteristics of each child and family; relying on each other to build on the range of strengths found among different types of child development experts.

COMPONENTS OF THE IPP

The IPP should be based on developmentally valid, nondiscriminatory assessment. Program and placement decisions are to be formulated from information from multiple sources: test scores, observation in situations in which the child is comfortable and at ease, and input from significant persons in the child's life (parents, grandparents, teachers, out-of-home caregivers). For an example of one aspect of a child's IPP focusing on motor skills, see Figure 11–3.

FIGURE 11–3

INDIVIDUAL PROGRAM PLAN (IPP)

Child's Name: Jason M.

Date of Birth: September 5, 19—
(C.A.: 2 yrs., 1 mon.)

Program: ABC Preschool

Conference Date: Oct. 12, 19—

Team Members Present:
  Mrs. M.—Parent
  Mrs. B.—Early Childhood Teacher
  Ms. G.—Resource Consultant

Area of Development: Gross Motor

Strength (present level of functioning):

 • pulls self to standing using furniture
 • stands momentarily without support, lowering to sitting
 • cruises around furniture
 • will take 10 steps with both hands held

Long-Term Goal: Jason will walk independently.

Short-Term Objectives:

 1. Jason will walk 10 steps with one hand held by an adult.
 2. Jason will take 4 to 5 steps without support, walking between familiar adults.
 3. Jason will walk independently for a distance of 10 feet.

Implementation Plan (services to be provided):

 1. Ms. G. will provide specific written suggestions to encourage walking, which can be implemented in the preschool and home environments.

2. Mrs. B. will provide daily opportunities for Jason to practise walking within the program routines.
3. Mrs. B. will maintain weekly communication with the family, for the purpose of sharing observations.

Evaluation: Ms. G. will conduct biweekly observations, documenting Jason's progress.

Next Conference Date: April 10, 19—

The completed IPP includes statements about

- the child's present level of skill development and the quality of performance;
- long-term (six months to one year) goals for the child and short-term objectives that will accomplish the long-term goals;
- specific services to be provided, with target dates and team member responsible for carrying out the service; and
- accountability (evaluation) to determine if objectives are being met.

These components will be discussed one by one. (Transition plans will be discussed in Chapter 12.)

1. Functional Assessment

Before an IPP is written, a child's developmental skills must be assessed. As described earlier, this is an information-gathering (nondiagnostic) process. It is not, however, a one-time operation; instead, it should be an ongoing process throughout the year so that the child's progress can be tracked and programs adjusted as needed. Ongoing assessment provides a comprehensive description—a developmental profile—of a child at particular points in time.

Depending on the results of earlier screening tests, the child may need to receive specialized assessments from specific disciplines (audiologist, nutritionist, physiotherapist/occupational therapist, and others). The early childhood teacher is responsible for collecting general information that often provides the "glue" for putting together the overall developmental picture of the child (Photo 11–11). As noted earlier, it is the teacher, working daily with a child, who is in the most advantageous position to assess the child's strengths and needs. Observing children play in the classroom gives teachers valuable information about a child's developmental skills and the effectiveness of intervention strategies. (Note: It is necessary to watch a child over several days and several play

PHOTO 11–11 *Teachers provide the "glue" that holds together the overall developmental picture of each child.*

episodes. Consecutive observations ensure that what is observed is representative of the child's everyday behaviours. See Bailey and Wolery 1989.)

Numerous assessment instruments have been developed over the past 20 years. (Appendix A provides a partial list of assessment tools.) In addition, there are developmental profile forms that many teachers of young children find even more useful. (NAEYC publishes one such profile designed especially for infant and toddler caregivers; see Lilly et al. 1987. For an example of a developmental profile, see Appendix B.) A separate chart or profile should be kept for each child. Periodic observations should be made and recorded for each child in all developmental areas: gross and fine motor skills; cognitive abilities; self-help/care; social and play behaviours; as well as receptive and expressive language.

The itemized skills on the profile are examples of behaviours characteristic of broad, general skills. A child may show an achievement in various ways. For example, an item in the 0 to 12 months preacademic square reads: "Puts blocks in, takes blocks out of a container." The basic skill is picking up and releasing an object within a prescribed space. An infant who can pick up a cookie, drop it in a cup, and then take it out should receive a passing score.

Highlight pens of several colours allow a quick readout of each child's status in all developmental areas. Items that the child passes in the initial assessment are lined through in one colour; a different colour may be used for each subsequent assessment. Skills that a child does not have are left unmarked. Inconsistent successes—responses that a child displays infrequently or *sometimes*—are especially important. They should not be lined through, but flagged, perhaps with an asterisk. These "sometimes" responses or **emerging skills** often indicate appropriate starting points for a specific intervention program.

A child's profile should be updated periodically on the basis of observations and notes made by teachers as they work with children. The updating usually reveals that each child has acquired some of the flagged emerging skills. Skills that were left unmarked in an earlier assessment often become a newly marked set of emerging skills. What the teaching staff has on hand at all times is a current visual profile of each child—that is, word pictures of overall functioning in relationship to developmental expectations for children of like ages.

PHOTO 11–12 *The pincer grasp is prerequisite to many fine motor tasks.*

Emerging skills show up clearly on the preschool profile. Mastering a skill in a particular area of development often depends upon specific achievements in other areas. For example, a child cannot perform certain self-help/care tasks such as buttoning and unbuttoning until the **pincer grasp** is well established (Photo 11–12). Developmental deficits also show up clearly. Deficits may accumulate because of unrecognized relationships among developmental areas. By keeping a child's profile up to date, teachers can pinpoint a deficiency in one area and so explain problems in other areas. Language disabilities, for example, often lead to poor play relationships because of the inability to express ideas and preferences adequately. Poor verbal skills also may delay cognitive development or have a negative effect on intellectual performance because inadequate language interferes with formulating and expressing thoughts.

The information about the child's performance in the early childhood setting is a valuable part in the overall assessment process. The early childhood teacher is able to provide information about the child's current skill level, as well as information about activities in which the child has interest and preference.

2. Goals and Objectives

LONG-TERM GOALS. The IPP should include written statements specifying expected learning outcomes for each child each school year. Long-term goals are usually presented as broad general statements about what can be expected of the child within six months to one year, depending on the child's age.

Example:

Erin will be able to
1. *move about the room independently throughout the day;*
2. *play cooperatively with other children during small group activities; and*
3. *use verbal skills to communicate her needs.*

Long-term goals centre on priorities essential to the child's overall development, as agreed upon by the child's IPP team. These sometimes are referred to as **functional goals** (Bailey and Wolery 1989). For every child, the number and kinds of goals will vary. Goals for a child should not be so numerous or so complex as to overwhelm the child and family; additional goals can always be added at a future date as required. Furthermore, self-sufficiency goals, as important as they are, should not rule out goals that help improve the child's self-esteem and enjoyment of life.

Example:

> *Melinda was a bright and lively child born with severely malformed hands. Even as an infant, it was obvious that she had a talent and love for music and rhythm. While long-term goals for this child must include learning to use a prosthesis on each hand (a major priority), her musical development is important, too. At least one goal related to music should be written into Melinda's IPP.*

SHORT-TERM OBJECTIVES. Every IPP should include a list of short-term objectives. These are mini-programs, step-by-step learnings that enable the child to achieve the designated long-term goals. Short-term objectives usually focus on skills or behaviours that can be measured (counted or timed) and acquired within one week to a month. The data gives objective evidence of a child's progress. Learning to wear and become adept at using her prostheses might be a long-term goal for the child mentioned above. Exactly how this is to be accomplished and how it is to be measured is spelled out in the short-term objectives. Enhancing the child's musical talents might also be worked into the goals and objectives.

Example:

> *Melinda will pick out tunes using single notes on the piano while wearing her prostheses, with encouragement from the teacher, for 15 minutes each day.*

The amount of time spent playing the piano and the numbers of tunes learned might be the measurable aspects of this objective. Furthermore, learning to play tunes on the piano is likely to be reinforcing for Melinda in her efforts at wearing her prostheses.

Objectives should answer the following questions:
- Who (child's name)?
- Will do what (desired behaviour)?
- Under what conditions (where, how, when, with what kinds of support)?
- To what degree of success (defines measure that determines success)?

Example 1:

> *May-lin is a 3-year-old child who has a very severe visual impairment. She currently is able to climb stairs, but places both feet on one stair before proceeding to the next stair. The goal set for May-lin was that she be able to navigate her environment.*

PHOTO 11–13 *Alternating feet is a step in the task analysis for stair climbing.*

After completing a task analysis (see Chapter 13) for stair climbing, it was determined that the next step in May-lin's program should be that she be able to climb stairs with alternating feet, using the railing for support (Photo 11–13).

The objective would be written as follows:
- Who? (May-lin)
- Will do what? (climb stairs)
- Under what conditions? (using alternating feet, while holding the banister)
- To what degree of success? (for a minimum of five consecutive steps)

Example 2:

Steven is a 3-year-old child with a diagnosis of Down syndrome. When requested, he uses single words to label objects, but only in imitation of an adult.

Steven's IPP team set the following goal for him: that Steven will speak in simple sentences to express his needs and wants.

The task analysis for this goal identified the use of single words to express needs and wants as the first step in a program for Steven.

The objective would be written as follows:
- Who? (Steven)
- Will do what? (use single words spontaneously)
- Under what conditions? (to indicate his preference when offered choices)
- To what degree of success? (each time a choice is offered)

Graphing (transferring the measurements to a chart, as shown in Figures 11–4 and 11–5) brings progress into focus. Displaying children's progress in graphic form is beneficial because it provides a visual record of change over time. Behaviour changes, even when slow, appear more clearly on a graph. The visual display also may help both teacher and child be more aware of progress and so feel more successful. Success always leads to increased motivation. Lack of progress also is readily apparent on a graph. In such cases the program can be changed promptly so as to improve the child's performance and decrease frustration for teacher and child.

FIGURE 11–4

MAY-LIN'S STAIR-CLIMBING PROGRAM.

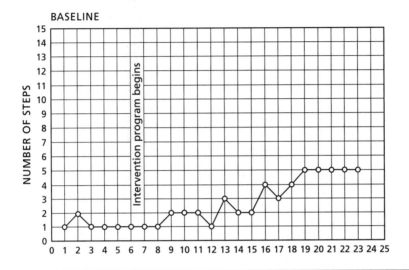

FIGURE 11–5

STEVEN'S VERBAL RESPONSE PROGRAM.

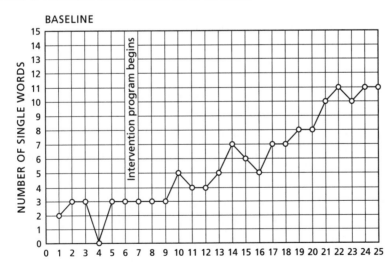

3. Implementation Plan

A statement of the specific intervention services and support services for the family should be included in the IPP. Depending on a child's problems, the plan might contain recommendations for

- the type of daily/weekly activities to be provided to the child in the early childhood program;

    (For example, in the case of Jason [see pp. 273–74], the IPP team identified that Mrs. B. will provide daily opportunities for Jason to practise walking within the program routines. In her observation notes, Mrs. B. identifies two activities that are of high interest to Jason. Each day when Jason wants to participate in these activities he will be supported in practising walking by the teacher to the areas in which his desired activities are taking place.)

- referral to a speech and language pathologist or a physiotherapist/occupational therapist (or both) (e.g., as might be appropriate for Steven [see p. 278]);

- referral to a community recreation program for increasing active participation in large motor outdoor activities (e.g., as might be appropriate for May-lin [see p. 278]); and

- assistance to parents in obtaining funding for a specific piece of equipment (e.g., a keyboard for Melinda [see p. 277]).

Projected starting dates should be specified for each service prescribed for the child, and the person responsible for carrying out the specific objective should be identified.

Example:

Josh will receive ongoing speech and language consultation services from the community speech pathologist beginning October 1.

The projected starting date assists the team members in implementing the plan. A reasonable length of time must be allowed for accomplishing the objectives and goals stated in the child's IPP.

4. Evaluation (Statement of Accountability)

At least once a year (more frequently for younger children) the individual program plan should be evaluated to see if the stated objectives are being met. Evaluations should be based on specifically described procedures such as developmental assessment results and written observations. In actual practice, evaluations should be conducted more often. As mentioned earlier, an in-place system of ongoing assessments simplifies the procedure. The Preschool Profile, for example, provides both ongoing assessment and program evaluation. Every item on the profile describes a specific child behaviour; its presence or absence can be noted by a teacher. Graphs also provide program accountability. By using the Preschool Profile to assess a child periodically and by keeping graphs of a child's progress, a convincing evaluation process is always in operation.

SUMMARY

The identification of developmental problems can take place any time beginning with the first several weeks after conception. The earlier a problem is identified, the more likely it is that it can be treated effectively and that associated problems can be prevented. All young children (except those with obvious disabilities) should be screened, for many differences are subtle and difficult to recognize.

Many kinds of screening instruments are available. Some are geared to overall development, some to specialized areas such as hearing and vision, some to particular ages or developmental domains. Whatever the test, for reliable results it must be given in the child's first language, with scrupulous regard for the customs of the child's family and the child's physical and biological state. More than one instrument should be used in the assessment process. Even then, the results of many tests must be viewed with extreme caution, especially IQ tests. Most early childhood educators view standardized IQ tests as being of little value when working with young children.

Teachers are major agents in the early identification process. Direct observation is a teacher's best tool in determining a child's developmental status and the suitability of specific classroom activities for the group and for individual children. Observation forms and checklists, especially those that teachers devise themselves, help teachers answer questions about children's behaviour and classroom practices. Teachers should always use their information with care and in the best interests of the child and family.

The Individual Program Plan is a major and logical outcome of early identification and assessment procedures. A child's teacher and parent(s) are an essential part of the IPP planning process along with other members of the interdisciplinary team. The IPP must be in written form. It should be based on nondiscriminatory tests and observations, and specify long-term goals and short-term objectives. Services that will be provided and their starting dates should be specified. Finally, the IPP should describe the accountability component: how the effectiveness of the implementation plan will be measured.

STUDENT ACTIVITIES

1. Arrange a sheet of paper so that you can take a frequency count of how often a child initiates a conversation with another child. While observing during free play, select one particular child and tally how many times that child initiates conversation with another child. Do the same on another day with a different child. Compare the observations.

2. Select a partner. Each of you, independently of the other, will take a half-hour running record of the same child. Compare your observations to see if you were seeing the same things. Critique each other's running record for objectivity.

3. Write to three early childhood centres in your province that integrate children with developmental delays and ask for copies of their IPP forms. Compare and contrast these with the IPP components as given in the text.

4. Make a photocopy of the Preschool Profile. Observe the same child for 30 to 45 minutes on three different days. Draw a horizontal line through the chart, indicating the child's age. Using a highlight pen, colour through the skills that you see the child engage in during your observations. (The skills may be on either side of the line.) When finished with the above activity show the profile to the child's teacher. Ask the teacher to discuss with you how well your profile assesses the observed child.

5. Plot the following data points on graph paper. (You can draw your own grid with pencil and ruler.)

   Number of times Leslie spoke to teachers:

Date	Frequency
Sept. 27	3
Sept. 28	11
Sept. 29	4
Oct. 2	0
Oct. 3	0
Oct. 4	7
Oct. 5	8
Oct. 6	8
Oct. 9	1
Oct. 10	2
Oct. 12	10

REFERENCES

Allen, K.E., and F.M. Goetz 1982 *Early Childhood Education: Special Problems, Special Solutions.* Rockville, Md.: Aspen Systems.

Allen, K.E., and L.R. Marotz 1994 *Developmental Profiles: Birth through Eight.* Albany, N.Y.: Delmar.

Bailey, D.B., and M. Wolery 1989 *Assessing Infants and Preschoolers with Handicaps.* Columbus, Ohio: Charles E. Merrill.

Bentzen, W.B. 1985 *Seeing Young Children.* Albany, N.Y.: Delmar.

Blackman, J.A. 1990 "From the editor." *Infants and Young Children: An Interdisciplinary Journal of Special Care Practices* 3, no. 1: iv.

Cook, R.E., A. Tessier, and V.B. Armbruster 1987 *Adapting Early Childhood Curricula for Children with Special Needs.* Columbus, Ohio: Charles E. Merrill.

Galambos, D., and P. Wilson-Whetstone 1989 *Individual Program Planning.* Oakville, Ont.: Sheridan College.

Hanson, M.J., and E.W. Lynch 1989 *Early Intervention.* Austin, Tex.: PRO-ED.

Hughes, A., C. Paasche, and M. Greer 1992 *An Early Identification Observation Process in Early Childhood Settings.* North York, Ont.: North York Interagency and Community Council.

Irwin, D.M., and M.M. Bushnell 1980 *Observational Strategies for Child Study.* New York: Holt, Rinehart and Winston.

Lilly, J.R., S. Provence, E. Szanton, and B. Weissbourd 1987 "Developmentally Appropriate Care for Children from Birth to Age 3." In S. Bredekamp, ed. *Developmentally Appropriate Practice in Early Childhood Programs Serving Children from Birth through Age 8.* Washington, D.C.: National Association for the Education of Young Children.

Marotz, L., J. Rush, and M. Cross 1993 *Health, Safety, and Nutrition for the Young Child.* Albany, N.Y.: Delmar.

NAEYC (National Association for the Education of Young Children) 1988 "Position Statement on Standardized Testing of Young Children 3 through 8 Years of Age." *Young Children* 43, no. 3.

Perrone, V. 1990 "How Did We Get Here?" In C. Kamii, ed. *Achievement Testing in the Early Grades: The Games Grown-ups Play.* Washington, D.C.: National Association for the Education of Young Children.

Thurman, S.K., and A.H. Widerstrom 1990 *Infants and Young Children with Special Needs: A Developmental and Ecological Approach.* Baltimore: Paul H. Brookes.

CHAPTER 12

Planning Transitions to Support Inclusion

Robin Hazel and Susan Fowler
with adaptations by Paasche, Cornell, and Engel

Objectives

After studying the material in this chapter, the student will be able to

- state the major goals of an early childhood transition plan
- identify possible accommodations that need to be made by children, families, and service providers during the transition process
- describe a transition-planning format that includes program and personnel responsibilities
- discuss ways to ease a child into a new program
- suggest support services that could assist a child in adjusting to a new classroom

INTRODUCTION

It is necessary to plan for the services required to assist young children as they move from one early childhood program to another, or on into an integrated school-board setting. Transition plans should be an essential element of the child's IPP, ensuring that services to meet the specific needs identified by the family are addressed. To formulate such plans, early childhood educators need to develop specific skills and procedures for facilitating both a child's and a family's transition into a new program.

As children and families move from one type of program to another, whether it is a new preschool program or a kindergarten program, they encounter new faces, new environments, and new procedures. Planning for these transitions into newness is critical. It is, however, an often neglected component of early intervention programming, especially for children who are moving into inclusive environments. Each change may require numerous accommodations on the part of the child, the family, and the service providers (Rice and O'Brien 1990). The child may need more time than his/her peers to adjust to the new environment, as well as learn how to play and work more independently. The family may need to alter their before-school child-care arrangements to fit the schedule of the new program. The early childhood teacher may need to redesign circle time to accommodate a new child with a specific disability.

If the child fails to make the necessary accommodations, or if the accommodations are made but do not last, the outcome may be an unsuccessful placement. The consequence of this is yet another transition; the implications are that either the individuals who were involved have failed or the educational system has failed (Johnson et al., 1989). Thus, planning for the changes required by the transition and developing ways to maintain the changes are critical components in ensuring a successful transition.

There are three specific steps to take when trying to ensure that a successful transition will be achieved:

1. identify possible problems that may arise during transition
2. plan strategies for supporting the child, the family, and the receiving teacher or teachers
3. maintain ongoing support following the transition

TRANSITION GOALS

The purpose of transition planning is to lay out a process that enables the family and the child to make a comfortable and positive change from one program to another. Ideally, the process produces a minimum of disruption in family routines, while supporting the child's developmental progress. The following is an example of the accommodations required of a child, a family, and a teacher during one transition program:

Abby, born with spina bifida, had gotten about in a wheelchair for most of her life. Psychological assessments indicated average to above-average intelligence. She had been in a private special education preschool and child-care centre since infancy. Both parents worked full-time. As Abby neared her fourth birthday, her parents decided she was ready to attend a regular preschool. Four months later, at the start of the school year, Abby was enrolled in a community preschool in the mornings while continuing her special class placement in the afternoons.

The new program was different in a number of ways from the special education preschool program. It had more group activities and less individualized attention. Abby's parents were concerned about her ability to pay attention and participate actively in large-group experiences. The dual placement meant also that the parents had to rearrange their daily schedules so that they could transport Abby from the morning program to the afternoon program. They realized that some days they would need to ask a friend or relative to provide midday transportation.

The community preschool teachers had concerns, too. They redesigned some of the materials and activities so that Abby would be able to participate during the first critical days of the transition. The teachers wondered, though, if they would have the time or energy to continue to adapt materials and learning experiences. They wondered, too, if they could consistently include Abby in large motor activities, given the demands on teachers' time made by a group of active 4-year-olds.

The success of the transition into the community preschool ultimately would be measured by the extent to which Abby, her family, and her teacher were able to manage the many accommodations required of them. It is the ability to handle and adjust to a range of accommodations (the transition's *sustainability*) that determines the success of a transition (Rice and O'Brien 1990).

TRANSITIONS IN PERSPECTIVE

The transition process requires systematic planning and evaluating (Photo 12–1). It also requires ongoing modification to keep it in tune with the needs of individual children, their families, and the service providers who are involved (Haines et al., 1991). The perspectives of all must be considered in identifying the accommodations needed. A particular mother, for example, may believe that she should be consulted about every aspect of her child's education, and that she should be the one to make the decisions about her child's transition to another program. In the same family, the father may believe it best to leave such decisions to the teachers. The professionals involved in the transition may have

PHOTO 12–1 *The transition process requires systematic planning.*

ideas quite different from either parent's about the decision-making process and who should decide what. Respect for, awareness of, and responsiveness to these several perspectives are critical for a successful transition for the child and the family.

THE CHILD'S PERSPECTIVE

A child's developmental progress is the main reason for a transition from one program to another. The change in services may be agreed on because of the child's age (entering kindergarten, for example, is usually based on chronological age). The change also may be called for on the basis of clinical evidence—an updated diagnosis or a change in diagnostic findings, as when an intermittent hearing loss is identified. Another factor may be that the child has acquired new and functionally significant skills. Whatever the reason, the child's ability to adapt to the next program is the central issue in determining the success of the transition (Haines, Rosenkoetter, and Fowler, 1991).

PHOTO 12–2 *A child may have problems transferring well-established skills used at home to the new environment.*

The accommodations required of a child during a transition will depend on the individual child and the *sending* and *receiving* programs. The child will need to make new friends, generalize old skills to new situations, and learn unfamiliar routines while attempting to explore a new environment. Children often have difficulty transferring even well-established skills to new situations (Photo 12–2). What looks like a similar set of expectations to professionals may not look at all the same to a child who has learned to respond to distinct cues or events that are not present in the new program. A child, for example, may be used to only one teacher or one particular type of instruction. That child may do well in a tightly structured, individualized program but have difficulty in a loosely structured program. Therefore, as professionals and parents prepare a child for a transition, they need to ask these three questions:

1. What will be different for the child?
2. What skills does the child already have that will be useful in the new setting?
3. What skills does the child need to learn before a transition is attempted?

A child's strengths and developmental differences or delays should be identified before the transition plan is developed. Which accommodations will be easy for the child? Which will be difficult? To answer these questions, each child must be assessed in terms of

- his or her current skills;
- the conditions under which the child demonstrates particular skills (Does the child demonstrate them at home but not at school, or vice versa?); and
- the skills the receiving program expects the child to have before entering the program.

THE FAMILY'S PERSPECTIVE

To ensure success, transition planning for a child must include the family. Because stress often is associated with change, transitions can be difficult for families (Turnbull, Summers, and Brotherson 1986). A family must adjust to differences between programs by adapting to new schedules, finding new services, and accepting new responsibilities. Families may have to educate new school personnel about their child's special needs. They may be expected to set new goals for their child. They may need to adjust to fewer contacts with their child's teacher. Plans for the family component in a child's transition will vary, depending on family structure, personality traits, and other characteristics.

Family Structure
- Who makes up the family?
- How do the parents define their family unit?
- Are the parents married?
- Divorced?
- Are they younger or older parents?
- How many other children are there in the family?
- What is the relationship of the extended family?
- What are the roles of the family members: wage earner? unemployed? decision maker? caregiver? housekeeper?

Family Characteristics
- What is the first language of the family?
- Its cultural/ethnic background?
- What are the family's beliefs and value systems?
- To what extent is the family involved with the community?

Nature of the Child's Disability

- What effect does the child's disability have on his or her ability to participate in family activities?
- Does the child's disability interfere with family members' activities and needs?
- Does it cause financial, emotional, and physical strain on the family as a whole, or only on particular family members?
- Do the child's problems pull the family together—make it stronger—as family members try to meet the needs of the child with disabilities?

Personality Traits

- Do family members talk about their feelings and fears?
- Do they focus only on the present (or past, or future)?
- Do they deal only with *the facts* of the situation?
- What appears to be the self-image of various family members?
- What seems to be their view of their lives compared to the lives of others? Do they face life with a sense of humour, a sense of resignation, a sense of getting even, a sense of hope? (Hazel et al., 1986)

PHOTO 12–3 *Successful transition planning depends on recognizing and respecting the diversity that each family brings to the planning process.*

Developing successful transition activities depends on recognizing the diversity that each family brings to the planning process (Photo 12–3). Each family has its own misgivings. Each family has to decide on the accommodations they are willing and able to make. In general, families are concerned about questions such as these:

- What services and supports will be available in the next setting, and how can they obtain these services and supports?
- How will their child adjust to the new program, both academically and socially?
- How will the new teacher or teachers adjust to their child, and vice versa?
- What changes in daily routines will be required?

Families need adequate time to address these questions if they are to make logical decisions about their level of involvement in the transition planning.

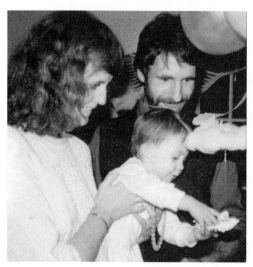

PHOTO 12–4 *Parents should be given the opportunity to help select learning goals for their children.*

Some families choose to let professionals make the decisions, while others want to make the decisions themselves; most families fall somewhere in between. According to Johnson, McGonigel, and Kaufmann (1989), parents should be given the opportunity to

- communicate their preferred role in the decision-making process;
- exchange information with the staff about their child;
- help select learning goals for their child (Photo 12–4);
- help in identifying potential placements;
- help make decisions based on their child's needs and the resources available; and
- participate in forming a relationship with the staff of the new program.

TRANSITION PLANNING

Planning is the key to successful transitions for the child, family, and teachers. As noted earlier, the accommodations required of everyone during a transition tend to be stressful. Careful planning reduces stress by putting the focus on specific issues related to the child's and the family's needs and preferences. When parents and professionals work as partners in developing a plan acceptable to all, it is likely that everyone will be more comfortable about what they are to do. It is likely, too, that everyone will find the time (or the help) necessary to accomplish the mutually agreed upon tasks.

Successful transition planning should be an ongoing and integral part of every child's program. Planning an individual transition requires ongoing commitment. Time must be built into the regular program schedule for staff and parent meetings, for visits to the sending and receiving programs, and for exchange of child and program information. Ten basic steps (described in the following pages) are identified as central to the transition-planning process.

STEP 1: COORDINATING THE TRANSITION

When several people work together to plan a child's transition, it is essential to appoint one person to coordinate efforts and take responsibility for getting things done. The transition coordinator may be the director of a program, a resource teacher, a consultant, an infant development worker, another member of the staff, or the case manager of the IPP or IFSP (Chapter 9). The professional background of the transition coordinator is likely to vary from child to child. An interdisciplinary team may rotate the coordinator's position among its members, depending on the child's and the family's special needs. Regardless of professional training, a major responsibility of the transition coordinator is to be familiar with

- the transition procedures of both the sending and the receiving programs; and

- the resources, placement, and service options available in the community.

STEP 2: VISITING ALTERNATIVE PROGRAMS

Early childhood professionals within a community need to be familiar with each other's programs. Familiarity creates understanding and cooperation. For example, the infant development worker should be familiar with the preschool options available in the child's community. He or she should therefore be able to inform the parents of the options available and support the parents in investigating the range of available settings. This provides parents with opportunities to become informed and better able to make the most appropriate choice with respect to their child and family. Similarly, when the community early childhood staff know what social and academic skills are expected from 5-year-olds by the local kindergarten teacher, they are better able to develop successful transition strategies. Learning about the specific expectations of a program or classroom helps the current teacher and the family decide if the child

- will be ready for the program under consideration;

- needs additional skills;

- is likely to need special help from the sending program prior to the transition; or

- will need certain changes in the receiving program in order to succeed.

The transition coordinator (or individual teachers) should visit the programs where their children are most likely to be enrolled. If possible, visits should extend through a full session. Only by sitting in on a program in its entirety can the observer become familiar with the schedule in action, the range and tempo of activities, and the teaching style.

PHOTO 12–5 *Coordinators can assist families in the transition process by arranging visits to new programs.*

Visits can be arranged by contacting the future program setting (Photo 12–5). An increasing number of school boards have an early childhood or kindergarten specialist whose job it is to arrange meetings to discuss a program-to-program transition.

While observing, the coordinator and parents should make written notes. Features of the program that might create problems for the child or family should be underscored. Observation notes often are arranged under the following headings:

1. *Environment/physical setting:* the physical arrangement of the classroom (including accessibility for the specific child), the number of teachers and aides, and the daily schedule

2. *Staff–child interaction:* what children and teachers do and how they interact

3. *Program approach:* the learning opportunities provided for the children and the range of available supports

4. *Parent involvement:* the range of opportunities for involvement/participation by parents within the program (see Figure 12–1—an example of a checklist that can be used by parents and professionals to plan for young children's transitions from one program to another).

STEP 3: HOLDING MEETINGS AMONG THE IPP TEAM

After the coordinator and family have visited several programs, the IPP team should meet and discuss the information obtained from the visits. Attention should be directed toward evaluating how each program may or may not be able to meet the priority needs of the child and his or her family.

Minor differences in approach are not likely to cause problems. However, when major differences exist, the staff of the child's current centre should consider adapting their program to reflect the expectations of the new setting.

FIGURE 12-1

CHECKLIST TO HELP ASSESS THE APPROPRIATENESS OF AN EARLY CHILDHOOD PROGRAM

THE PROGRAM APPROACH	APPROPRIATE FOR MY CHILD AND FAMILY?		
	YES	NO	UNDECIDED

General:

1. Activities are planned to promote the child's growth and development in all areas, e.g., social/emotional, intellectual, physical communication, and self-help.
2. Daily activities are planned based on the needs of the group.
3. The children are provided with a choice of activities.
4. The children are interested and involved in the activities.
5. The staff are open to consultation from other agencies.

Specific:

1. There is an appropriate balance of child-directed exploratory play and teacher-directed activities.
2. The room is set up to promote social interaction between children.
3. Sensory play experiences are a daily part of the program, e.g., water play, music/rhythms, or sand play.
4. The daily activities take into account children's interests.
5. The selection of toys and activities are appropriate for my child.
6. There is a balance between small-group, large-group, and individual activities.
7. The program activities address the priority areas in which my child needs to learn and develop.
8. There are opportunities for the staff to meet for information sharing and planning on a regular basis.

FIGURE 12–1 continued

Comments:

PARENT INVOLVEMENT

General:
1. Staff communicate with parents on a regular basis. I felt comfortable and welcomed by staff during my visit. The staff encourage full parent participation in their child's program.

Specific:
1. There are opportunities for parents to communicate with and get to know other parents.
2. Activities are planned that encourage parent involvement, e.g., meetings with guest speakers, social activities, etc.
3. The staff take into consideration the concerns of parents.
4. There is sufficient opportunity for parents to discuss their child's development with the staff.

Comments:

SOURCE: Metropolitan Toronto Association for Community Living, Early Childhood Services.

Step 4: Developing a Transition Plan

Ideally, the transition coordinator and the teacher meet with the family 9 to 12 months before the child's transition. This gives the family time to learn about and prepare for the transition. According to McDonald et al. (1989), "In a study from Alberta, Canada, on transition families participating in a home-based infant program, 64 percent indicated the need to begin transition planning 6 months to a year prior to the projected transition." A meeting should be held prior to the IPP meeting so that transition-related goals may be identified. The transition coordinator should introduce the topic of transitioning and explain the procedures. The family should identify their preferences, concerns, support needs, and other agenda items for their child. Next, the teacher should summarize the child's progress and include suggestions for future goals. The minutes of this meeting should be circulated in a written report.

After this meeting, the teacher and the family need to work together to develop ideas for specific goals related to the transition. To do this, the family will need to begin to identify their strengths and needs as well as the child's. For example, a child might work very well alone, but have difficulty working in group situations. If being able to work in group situations is important in the next setting, a transition goal would be to provide more opportunities for the child to experience group activities.

This meeting also is the point at which the family should begin to identify how much time they can devote to being involved; what they are able to do to prepare for the transition; and other issues they may want to address, such as the following:

- hours of operation
- program fees
- transportation arrangements

Figure 12–2 provides specific suggestions as to the kinds of information families like to have regarding their child's transition. Specific ideas on how families might help prepare their child for transition can be found in Figure 12–3.

A major task of the transition coordinator is to help the family determine the level of involvement best for them and to help the family develop appropriate strategies for reaching this goal.

FIGURE 12–2

TRANSITION INFORMATION FOR PARENTS

This list suggests information that families often like to have regarding their child's transition:

- prerequisite skills that will help the child in the new program
- general differences between the current program and the potential program(s)
- changes that may affect the child and family, such as daily schedule or transportation, and how best to prepare for the differences
- legislated rights with regard to the sharing of confidential materials
- the ways in which staff from both programs will be involved in the transition process
- additional assessments and evaluations that may be required

FIGURE 12–3

PREPARATION OF THE CHILD

Activities that help prepare preschool children as they make the transition from one program to another:

- Talk with the child about the impending changes.
- Provide opportunities for the child to make new friends.
- Teach the child to care for personal belongings.
- Teach the child to share toys and materials.
- Teach the child to use toys and equipment appropriately.
- Help the child acquire as many self-care skills and as much independence as possible.
- Encourage the child to ask for help when needed.
- Allow the child to practise working independently.
- Teach the child to follow directions.
- Read with the child more frequently, encouraging increased attention and involvement in the stories.
- Help the child learn his or her full name, address, and phone number.
- Help the child learn his or her new teacher's name and the name of the school.
- Take the child to visit the new program and the new teacher.
- Talk with the child about rules and activities in the new program.

STEP 5: RESPONSIBILITIES OF THE SENDING PROGRAM
Preparing the Child

PHOTO 12–6 *Many receiving programs expect children to be able to raise their hands to attract the teacher's attention.*

Classrooms in different programs vary greatly in their physical arrangements, the structure of learning opportunities, and the style, knowledge, and attitude of the teacher. To the best of their ability, teachers will want to prepare the child for the next environment, especially if it is quite different from the current one. For example, a child leaving a traditional preschool and entering a regimented classroom would be sure to benefit from learning some of the specific skills needed in the next classroom.

Once the transition goals have been identified, the sending program can devise activities for working toward those goals. The specific activities will depend on the skills needed for the next program. For example, if the receiving program is a kindergarten, the early childhood program can incorporate the following ideas into its current program:

- Gradually give children more responsibility for their personal and classroom possessions.
- Teach children to ask for attention in nondisruptive ways (4-year-olds learning to raise their hands, for example) (Photo 12–6).
- Help children learn to follow directions given to the group in general.
- Teach children to care for their toileting needs independently.
- Teach children the difference between boys' and girls' toilet facilities (if this differentiation is made in the new program).
- Gradually reduce the number of prompts from teachers to children during all kinds of tasks.
- Gradually increase the amount of time children work and play independently, without teachers' involvement.
- Teach children to line up and move in lines, if this is the practice in the new setting.
- Help children learn to complete one task before starting another.

- Teach children to recognize their printed name and to claim ownership of materials and possessions.
- Teach children to follow classroom routines and change-of-activity patterns (as much as possible, introduce the routines of the new program).
- Vary the length of activities.
- Vary the amount of help provided during and between tasks.
- Vary the type and number of instructions given to children.
- Teach everyday safety rules.
- Role play meeting new children and ways of making new friends.

STEP 6: PLACEMENT STAFFING

Several meetings may be necessary to determine the appropriate placement for a child. It is important that the transition coordinator, the teacher, and any other professionals who worked with the child attend these meetings (Photo 12–7). Personnel from the receiving program may include the transition coordinator, a member of the program's special service staff, and a teacher representing the classroom program. The family also must be present and be encouraged to invite others involved with the child (a grandmother who frequently provides care for the child, perhaps). Ideally, those from the receiving program would have observed the child in the current program prior to the placement meeting.

PHOTO 12–7 *The transition coordinator and the child's teacher are but two of the key people at the placement meeting.*

The group as a whole should discuss the child's overall performance and future needs. Information prepared by the sending teacher and the family regarding the child's abilities and progress toward transition goals should be circulated. This information provides the format for the discussion of what services the child needs and the potential sources of such services. There must be ample opportunity to ask questions, request further information, and receive clarification of particular issues. The service and placement decisions are based on the discussion at the meeting and on observations of the child. The child's parents should be equal partners in the decision-making process. When thinking about an appropriate placement, it is important to keep these considerations in mind:

- special services and supports available in the new program
- related services, such as transportation options between programs
- ratio of adults to children
- total size of group
- number of children in the group needing additional support
- availability of paraprofessionals, classroom aides, teacher assistants, or volunteers
- enrollment procedures and prerequisites
- the date on which the child can enter the new program
- classroom requirements (for example, special equipment)
- accessibility for children with physical disabilities
- medical or other clinical personnel available on the premises—if required

Once the appropriate placement has been determined, the parents, transition coordinator, and the teacher should meet with the new teacher, principal, or program director and the special service staff who will be involved with the child during and after the transition. The purpose of this meeting should be to review the child's current performance and special needs as well as future goals for the child. Arrangements also should be made for the receiving teacher to visit the sending program and for the child and parents to visit the new program.

STEP 7: TRANSFERRING RECORDS

Transferring a child's records can become a major problem. Sometimes records are not sent, do not reach the appropriate person, or are not read. A clearly defined process for transferring records needs to be made between the transition coordinators. Written procedures for transferring records assure that the right records are sent to the right persons in a timely manner. *Parental approval must be obtained before sending records of any kind to another person or program.* Parents must be informed about the records to be sent, whom they will be sent to, and when they will be sent. Ideally, parents should receive copies of any teacher reports that are to be sent to the receiving centre. The following questions can serve as a guide when planning the transfer of records:

- What method does each program use when getting parental consent for transfer of records?
- To what extent do the sending and receiving programs use the same types of records?

- What information collected by the sending program does the receiving program need?
- When and how will additional information be obtained?
- Who is responsible for sending the records?
- Who in the receiving program will accept and be responsible for the records?
- When and how will the records be sent?

Step 8: Child and Family Visit the New Program

A visit to the new program by the child and parents should be planned as early as possible, so that they can see what the new program is like. The transition coordinator can make the appointment. The visit should include a tour of the building, time to explore the classroom, and time for the child to play in the play yard (Photo12–8). It is of great value if the new teacher can arrange to spend a few minutes with the child and family. This kind of informal visit should help both the child and the family experience the new program and possibly reduce anxieties about the impending change. *The purpose of this visit is not for parents or teachers to discuss the child's specific needs or problems.* A meeting without the child must be scheduled when such issues can be discussed.

Photo 12–8 *The child should visit the new program and be given time to explore the environment.*

Step 9: Moving into the New Program

For some children, especially those with a developmental delay or specific disability, a full session in the new setting may be too much at first. Scheduling arrangements should vary, depending on each child. Program flexibility is critical when young children, with or without developmental problems, are starting a new program. Following are three suggestions for children who are not ready to start out independently or with a full session:

1. The child might attend the new program for only one hour a day for the first week or so; the time then can be extended. How quickly it is extended depends on how quickly the child adjusts.

2. The sending teacher, transition coordinator, or parent might accompany the child for the first few days. As the child becomes comfortable in the new classroom, adult support gradually can be withdrawn.

3. The child might continue to attend the old program part-time while starting to attend the new program the rest of the time.

With systematic planning and cooperation among staff and family, the new experience can be made comfortable for all children as they make the transition from one program to another. The following ideas are directed to teachers in the receiving program so they can help to make transitions easier on children:

- Talk with the children about the new program, how the children are growing up, and how the new program is different (and even a little scary, perhaps—but that it will be fun, too).

- Initially, provide additional time for free play so that children can become familiar with one another.

- Give simple one- and two-step instructions; gradually get children used to longer and more complex instructions.

- Vary the duration and type of activities more frequently at first.

- Vary the amount of teacher help during academic tasks, but always be available for a child who needs help.

- Throughout the transition period, review classroom rules and routines each day (more often for some children).

- Assign experienced children as *buddies* for new children.

STEP 10: SUPPORT SERVICES

During the first weeks—even months—of a new program, the child may need extra assistance. This may be in the form of support services offered by the transition coordinator, the previous teacher, or the special service staff. Many receiving teachers welcome such offers. Others are not interested. Whether the support services are provided depends on individual teachers. If a teacher is interested, the coordinator should plan to maintain communication. Four services that might be made available to the receiving teacher are described below.

PHOTO 12–9 *Meetings between the IPP coordinator, resource teacher, and classroom teacher often lead to solutions to problems.*

1. Teacher Conferences

Regularly scheduled meetings can be a critical part of the support services. They provide an opportunity for teachers to follow the child's progress. Suggestions can be offered as needed. During the first days of school in the new setting, the transition coordinator, who is familiar with the child's special needs and problems, can help. If trouble develops, the coordinator can suggest solutions based on the child's former program experiences. It is important that the coordinator also be available by phone, as problems can come up without warning.

Teachers sometimes want to schedule a few meetings with the transition coordinator after school, or they may want the coordinator to come and observe after the new child is enrolled. Sometimes the coordinator can provide the most help by simply listening quietly to a teacher describe the program day. Talking about a problem often leads to a solution (Photo 12–9). These meetings also can provide opportunities for teachers to express their feelings—both the frustrations and pleasures of working with a child with special needs.

2. Family Input

The child's family is a prime resource. Regular contact between the teacher and parents allows for the sharing of a child's progress, opportunities to express concerns, and identification of solutions.

3. Sharing Materials and Activity Ideas

Transitions can be eased if the new classroom offers experiences familiar to the child. The sending program might lend a favourite learning or play material to the receiving program. Something familiar to use or hang on to tends to promote a child's sense of security. With familiar objects and activities readily available during the first weeks of the transition, the classroom, the teachers, and classmates seem less strange.

4. Special Assistants

Providing a special assistant for short periods several times a week often helps both the receiving teacher and the child during the transition period. The special assistant can supplement the regular teaching activities in the classroom (which is especially useful when a child needs intensive instruction or supervision during the adjustment period, however long that may be). A special assistant can work individually with the specific child, or work with a small group that includes the child. Special assistants may be regular classroom aides, or they may be older children whose own learnings will be enhanced by working with younger children. Special assistants also may be arranged through parent groups, community volunteer agencies, and community college or university early childhood programs.

MAINTAINING A POSITIVE PLACEMENT EXPERIENCE

The process of successful inclusion of a child with a disability may not always be a consistently smooth experience. Problems may arise if the early childhood teachers have not been part of the planning process and therefore may be unsure of the objectives or threatened by the developmental needs of the child, as well as the expectations placed on them with respect to the child. This can make teachers feel inadequate or frustrated, and may lead to a certain amount of resistance. It is important at this point to get support for the teachers. Early childhood teachers should be encouraged to obtain help in overcoming difficulties of this type if and when they occur. The case manager, transition coordinator, and/or early interventionist/resource teacher should be contacted for support and help in resolving any problems that arise.

It is important to involve all of those working with the child in developing an effective team problem-solving approach. Here are six steps to include in effective team problem solving:

1. Identify the specific issues that are of concern, and state them.
2. Gather all information that has a bearing on the situation.
3. Identify and state all possible options for resolution (brainstorm).
4. Agree on the most appropriate option.
5. Agree on a specific plan of action.
6. Set up a schedule for an ongoing group review of the process.

SUMMARY

For children with special needs and their families, a successful transition from one program to another is critical to the child's long-range progress. The number and type of accommodations made by children, families, and service providers during periods of transition, and the sustainability of these accommodations, are critical factors in a successful transition. Transition planning should involve a minimum number of disruptions for the child, the family, and the teacher, and yet sustain the child's progress.

The various perspectives of child, family, and professionals must be considered if the accommodations that each must make are to be recognized and planned for. To increase the likelihood of successful transfer from one program to another, systematic transition planning should be a component of all inclusive early childhood programs. Planning should begin within a few weeks of a child's enrollment and continue throughout the year and into the next program for as long as necessary. Transition planning requires a number of steps. As a starting point, representatives—one each from the sending program and the receiving program—are appointed to serve as transition coordinators. Once selected, the coordinators are responsible for visiting other programs and becoming acquainted with classroom practices and staff. The coordinators need to learn the expectations of the other programs and how they differ from their own. Next the coordinators work with their own classroom staff to help minimize the differences between programs for the child who will be in transition.

Parents need to be included throughout the transition process. The parents and transition coordinators must discuss how to make the transition; together, they write a specific transition plan. The plan should meet with the approval of everyone: parents, administrators, and teachers. At the time the child is actually transferred, careful pacing is required. Moving through changes too rapidly tends to be upsetting for any young child, and especially for a young child with developmental problems. One recommendation is that the child's time in the new program be increased gradually.

As the child enters the new program, the receiving teacher needs to know what support services are available if needed (and wanted). Possibilities for support services include consultations with the staff from the sending program, from special service staff members in the current program, and from the family. There also may be loans of materials from the sending program and supplementary teaching in the form of special assistant services. It is the rare child, even one with a severe disability, who cannot be helped to succeed in a carefully selected new program. Changing from one program to another can and should be a positive experience for the child, family, and teachers. Careful, individualized planning and sufficient time are required.

STUDENT ACTIVITIES

1. Interview a centre supervisor who has integrated children with special needs. Find out what steps were taken and who was involved throughout the transition planning process.

2. Write a summary report on a preschool child with an identified special need who will soon be entering kindergarten. Include what you believe the student's strengths and needs are, regarding transition.

3. Interview the family of a kindergarten child with special needs. Ask them to describe the issues they faced during their child's transition into an out-of-home program (family daycare or a full- or half-day program in a centre).

4. Meet with the parents of a child with a special need who has recently been placed in an early childhood program. Find out what role the parents play and what adjustments the family had to make.

5. Talk with an early childhood teacher who has had children with special needs integrated into her group. Find out what adjustments she had to make and what supports were provided.

REFERENCES

Fowler, S.A. 1982 "Transition from Preschool to Kindergarten for Children with Special Needs." In K.E. Allen and E.M. Goetz, eds. *Early Childhood Education: Special Problems, Special Solutions.* Rockville, Md.: Aspen Systems.

Fowler, S.A. 1988 "Transition Planning." *Teaching Exceptional Children* 20, no. 4: 62–63

Haines, A.H., S.E. Rosenkeotter, and S.A. Fowler 1991 "Transitional Planning with Families in Early Intervention Programs." *Infants and Young Children*, 3: 38–47.

Hazel, R.A., P.A. Barber, S. Roberts, S.K. Behr, E. Helmstetter, and P. Guess 1986 *A Community Approach to an Integrated System for Children with Special Needs.* Baltimore: Paul H. Brookes.

Johnson, B.K., M.S. McGonigel, and R.K. Kaufmann 1989 *Guidelines and Recommended Practices for the Individualized Family Service Plan.* Chapel Hill, N.C.

Johnson, T.E., L.K. Chandler, G.M. Kerns, and S.A. Fowler 1986 "What Are Parents Saying about Family Involvement in Transitions? A Retrospective Transition Interview." *Journal of the Division for Early Childhood* 11, no. 1: 10–17.

McDonald, L., G. Kysela, S. Siebert, S. McDonald, and J. Chambers 1989 "Transition to Preschool." *Teaching Exceptional Children* 22, no. 1: 4–8.

Metropolitan Toronto Association for Community Living 1992 "Choosing an Early Childhood Program: A Checklist for Parents." Toronto, Ont.

National Early Childhood Technical Assistance System, and Washington, D.C.: Association for the Care of Children's Health.

Rice, M.L., and M. O'Brien 1990 "Transitions: Times of Change and Accommodation." *Topics in Early Childhood* 9, no. 4: 12–14.

Turnbull, A., J. Summers, and M. Brotherson 1986 "Family Life Cycle: Theoretical and Empirical Impressions and Future Directions for Families with Mentally Retarded Members." In J. Gallagher and P. Vietze, eds. *Families of Handicapped Persons: Research, Program and Policy Issues.* Baltimore: Paul H. Brookes.

section **V**

**IMPLEMENTING
INCLUSIVE EARLY
CHILDHOOD
PROGRAMS**

CHAPTER 13

The Developmental Behavioural Approach

INTRODUCTION

The developing child is in a state of continual behaviour change. Developmental/behavioural changes range from the simple to the complex. They come about because of physical growth, maturation, experience, and observational learning (modelling). The changes are orderly. They take place in accordance with specifiable theories of behaviour and predictable biological sequences.

Basic developmental principles have been discussed specifically in Chapter 2, and elsewhere throughout this text. This chapter will provide a brief analysis of behavioural principles, especially those that have particular relevance for teachers of young children. It will focus on reinforcement procedures, discipline and punishment, task analysis, and modelling, with emphasis on adult social reinforcement. Positive reinforcement practices are emphasized as the first and preferred approach to effective discipline.

EARLY EDUCATION: DEVELOPMENTAL AND BEHAVIOURAL PRINCIPLES: A BLEND

Effective early childhood teachers rely on developmental principles and also show an awareness of behavioural principles when deciding how to program for young children. They know that one of the best measures of the effectiveness of their teaching is change in children's behaviour.

DEVELOPMENTAL AND EDUCATIONAL INFLUENCES

A developmental-behavioural approach to teaching has been evolving for at least 40 years. By the middle of the century, developmentalists were in the majority. Researchers such as Gesell et al. (1940) believed that development was independent of experience, a natural *unfolding* of innate or inborn abilities. The role of teachers (and parents) was neither to unduly restrict nor to push the child. Then came theorists like Hunt (1961), who argued that development was *not* independent of external influences. Rather, it was controlled to some unknown extent by environmental experiences. Hunt was greatly influenced by Piaget (1952). Piaget had theorized that though there was a natural progression that was developmentally based, changes in a child's thinking (cognitive structure) were direct results of exploration of the environment. Hunt went one step further. He suggested that learning depended on a good *match* between the child and the experiences available to the child.

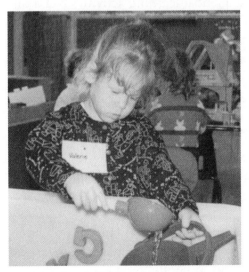

PHOTO 13–1 *Activities should match the child's skill level.*

The Problem of the Match

In early childhood education *the problem of the match* became a central issue. Teachers were trained to provide play materials and learning opportunities that attracted and held children's attention. At the same time the materials were to include new and intriguing elements (Photo 13–1). These were to be just a bit beyond the child's current skill level. Providing exactly the right match was the way to produce pleasure and continuing eagerness (motivation) to learn. There was no need for teachers or parents to push. The *joy of learning*, often referred to as *intrinsic motivation*, would take over. Children would seek out additional learning of their own accord, simply because they wanted to.

Learning from Success

The role of environmental influences also was central to the developmental ideas of Bijou (1959). He believed the results (consequences) of a child's behaviour were the crucial element. According to Bijou, children tend to learn the behaviours that result in success and positive consequences. They avoid those that result in failure or negative consequences. Teachers were trained to present tasks step by small step, and to provide positive consequences for each successful step. The result: a learning environment in which children had frequent success and were motivated to learn more.

Environmental Arrangements

Arranging the learning environment so as to help a child take a next step in skill development is a long-established and fundamental principle in early childhood education. Following are three examples from different periods in the history of early childhood education.

- Friedrich Froebel (1782–1852), hailed as the founder of the kindergarten movement, is likely to have been the first to propose that early learning experiences be broken down into their smallest components. Froebel also argued that young children need hands-on experiences: materials to enjoy, examine, and manipulate.

- Maria Montessori (1870–1952) was a champion of the educational potentials of deprived, disabled, and developmentally delayed children. She spent her life demonstrating systematic and sequential learning activities based on what she called *didactic materials*. Many of these materials, as well as her ideas about a prepared environment, are central to today's early education practices for both children who are developmentally disabled and children who are developing normally.

- John Dewey (1859–1952) is often given the title of founder of the *progressive education* movement. He, too, put major emphasis on the learning environment, especially as represented by the teacher, who was to respond, support, and guide children's exploration of everyday materials.

In each of these approaches to early education, the route to sound learning reflects similar principles, a developmental and behavioural blend that includes these elements:

1. a prepared learning environment matched to children's current skill levels (in behavioural terms, preparing the environment is referred to as the *arrangement of antecedent events*, a topic yet to be discussed)

PHOTO 13–2 *Materials and activities should be sequenced to provide both success and challenge.*

2. materials and activities sequenced in small enough segments so as to provide both success and challenge (Photo 13–2)

3. emphasis on learning through play and active involvement with appropriate materials

4. responsive teachers who serve as guides and facilitators

BEHAVIOURAL PRINCIPLES AND PRACTICES

Misinformation, faulty implementation, and abuse of behavioural practices have led to a "knee-jerk" reaction in many early childhood educators whenever the behavioural approach is mentioned, according to Wolery (1994) who goes on to say: "The behavioral perspective, although often seen as stressing the impact of the environment, in fact proposes that learning occurs from dynamic interactions between children and their environment" (p. 98). He goes on to say, "Particularly beneficial are those child-environment interactions that are initiated and directed by children and in which they are highly engaged" (p. 99).

The behavioural approach to early intervention is based on arranging the environment and implementing teaching strategies in ways that enhance children's learning opportunities. While the approach is important in working with all children, it is particularly important in facilitating learning among children with developmental deviations, delays, and deficits.

ALL CHILDREN CAN LEARN

In an inclusive classroom, the most significant and useful behavioural principle for teachers is one that bears repeated emphasis: *All children are teachable.* Every child can learn. Some children learn faster than others. Some children learn more than others. Some children learn some things easily, other things only with great effort or not at all. Some children learn from one type of approach, others from a different approach. But all children can learn. This well-established concept is documented by several decades of behavioural research. Bijou and Cole (1975, 3) summarize:

Traditionally, an individual who did not learn what was presented was considered incapable, indifferent, unmotivated, or lacking. The behavioral view on the other hand is if the student does not learn, something is lacking in the teaching situation.

PHOTO 13–3 *Start with what the child can do.*

To make the *teachability* of all children a day-by-day reality, teachers need to understand and practise basic behavioural principles. In the inclusive classroom these procedures are especially important. Each child can be provided with a responsive and reinforcing learning environment matched to his or her developmental level and special interests. Children who are gifted can be provided with learning opportunities that neither push nor hold them back, but instead foster their interests and talents. Children with developmental problems, though they may learn more slowly or with greater effort, need to be provided with a responsive and reinforcing learning environment matched to their developmental skill levels. The essence of the approach is to start where the child is, developmentally, and build from there (Photo13–3).

Children who have severe disabilities may have few observable behaviours to build on. Skilled observation is important here. Teachers need to be able to pick up on subtle cues that indicate a child's possible interest and awareness (Beckman et al. 1986). For example, a child's eyes may widen as the caregiver approaches the crib, even though the child cannot raise or turn her head in the caregiver's direction. In some instances, teachers, parents, and caregivers themselves may have to decide what should be the starting point for learning. An example might be a child with multiple impairments who displays few behaviours of any kind. Simply getting the child to look in a given direction may be a first priority. Even to accomplish this, a teacher often has to structure the environment so as to evoke (trigger) an attending response from the child: the sight or fragrance of a favourite food or the sound of a loud bell—whatever will attract the child's attention and give the teacher a behaviour to reinforce and expand upon.

REINFORCEMENT PROCEDURES

Reinforcement procedures come from research related to **operant conditioning**, **behaviour modification**, and **learning theory**. Volumes of studies demonstrate that behaviour is triggered by antecedent events and then increases or decreases according to its consequences (reinforcers). The principles can be put into a simple ABC format:

A: *Antecedent event* (that which precedes or comes before a behaviour—see Photo 13–4)

B: *Behaviour* (response of the individual)

C: *Consequence* (that which follows a behaviour)

A and C are environmental events, planned and unplanned, that both precede and follow a behaviour.

Example:

A	B	C
Teacher slices apples	*Child looks and says, "I want apple"*	*Teacher hands child a slice of apple*

The child's request (B) was triggered by seeing the teacher slicing the apple (A). It is likely the child will ask for an apple (B) every time the teacher is cutting apples (A), because the request resulted in a piece of apple being given to the child (C).

PHOTO 13–4 *Antecedents are what the adult does before expecting the child to perform.*

If specific learning (B) is to occur (or not to occur as in the case of inappropriate behaviours) then A and C must be decided on and systematically arranged. In simple terms, A is what teachers do *before* they would have a child respond. This includes the selection, arrangement, and presentation of activities and materials (and playmates, in some instances). Then, C (consequence) is what teachers do immediately following a child's behavioural response, such as providing or withholding reinforcers (the next topic to be discussed). Whatever adults do in A and C (or fail to do) will have some kind of an effect on the child's behaviour and learning (Allen 1974).

Reinforcement is a response to a behaviour that increases the likelihood that that behaviour will occur again. Reinforcement takes two main forms: *positive* and *negative*. Reinforcement, as we will see, may also be both *external* and *intrinsic*. In this text, the focus will be mainly on positive reinforcement because of its value in working with young children.

1. Positive Reinforcement

In simple terms, a positive reinforcer is a pleasant consequence to a behaviour; therefore, it has a high probability of increasing whatever behaviour preceded it.

(Note: In the following examples, A refers to *antecedent*, B refers to child's *behaviour*, and C refers to social *consequences*.)

Example 1:

    A: *Teacher announces it's time to tidy up so children can go outside.*
    B: *Ari runs over and begins to put toys away.*
    C: *Teacher praises Ari for being such a good helper.*

Example 2:

    A: *Teacher says it's time to tidy up so children can go outside.*
    B: *Ari runs over and begins to put toys away.*
    C: *Teacher tells Ari he can have the first pick of the toys outside.*

Reinforcers that are usually successful with young children are

- toys, play, and other favourite activities; and
- the attention of certain adults.

Different children like different things. A reinforcer for one child may be of little value to another. Hugging is a good example. It is generally assumed that all children like to be hugged. Not true: some children may be selective as to whom they like to be hugged by. Therefore, hugging may not be an effective reinforcer for these children.

2. Negative Reinforcement

Negative reinforcement is defined as strengthening of a behaviour through the avoidance of an unpleasant consequence.

Example 1:

    A: *Teacher asks children to tidy up.*
    B: *Patrick continues to play.*
    C: *Teacher says, "If you don't tidy up, you won't be allowed to play outside."*

Example 2:

    A: *Teacher says, "If you don't tidy up, you won't be allowed to play outside."*
    B: *Patrick tidies up.*
    C: *Patrick goes out to play.*

In the above examples, the teacher wants Patrick to tidy up. She threatens to remove something the child likes if he doesn't comply. Because Patrick wants the thing that the teacher states she will remove, he complies with the behaviour she desires. It should be noted that overuse of negative reinforcement as a child-management technique places the teacher in a power role that may lead to fear in the child, and for this reason should be avoided.

PHOTO 13–5 *Intrinsic reinforcement: a sense of pleasure, satisfaction, and self-esteem.*

3. Intrinsic Reinforcement

Positive inner feelings of pleasure and personal satisfaction describe intrinsic reinforcement. This form of reinforcement comes from working on or accomplishing a task; discovering something new; or solving a problem (Photo 13–5). For those who love to play with water, playing with water is always intrinsically reinforcing; that is, the very act of playing with water provides hour after hour of pleasure, stimulation, and satisfaction. For children who fear getting wet, there is little or no intrinsic reinforcement; water-play is taxing, something to be avoided. The same holds true whether it is tricycle riding, blockbuilding, or working with puzzles.

4. External Reinforcement

One reinforcer that is both powerful and universally appealing to young children of every culture is adult social reinforcement. Adult social reinforcement is made up of the attention of significant adults: parents, teachers, grandparents and other family members, and nurturing caregivers. Generally, adult attention is readily available and potentially plentiful. More than 30 years of research provides conclusive evidence that adult attention is likely to increase those behaviours that it immediately and consistently follows. The opposite also is true: when adult attention is consistently and immediately withheld (ignoring the behaviour) or withdrawn, the child's behaviour decreases. The following excerpt from a case study points up the appropriate and systematic use of teachers' attention in helping a child acquire a needed behaviour—improved attention span.

Concerns about James's lack of attention span led teachers to make a series of observations. It was obvious that James was getting a great deal of attention from teachers, yet there was no increase in his attention span. Teachers agreed, therefore, to focus their attention on James only on those moments, no matter how brief, when he was engaged with a material or activity. They agreed, further, not to interact with him just as he was leaving an activity or when he was flitting about. That is, they refrained from doing what they usually did at those times, which was to attempt to steer the child into an activity. Teachers consistently held to their plan as to when they would provide attention and when they would withhold it. James's span of attention soon began to increase.

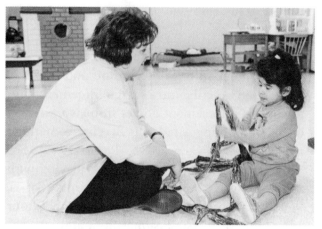

PHOTO 13–6 *The essence of a reinforcement procedure is responding to children in positive and encouraging ways.*

Many research studies demonstrate how powerful teachers are as sources of reinforcement for young children. Most important, the studies indicate how simple reinforcement procedures may bring out the best in each child. All that has to be done is what good teachers do so well: responding to children in encouraging and positive ways, and providing materials and activities matched to children's interests and skill levels (Photo 13–6). The following are brief descriptions of everyday teacher behaviours that serve as powerful reinforcers for almost any young child:

- *Verbal responsiveness.* Example: producing relevant comments, interested questions, answers to children's questions, exclamations of approval such as "Great!" and *descriptive praise* that focuses on some aspect of what the child is accomplishing, such as "Paula, you laced your shoe all by yourself!" (Note: In addition to the term descriptive praise, the terms *encouragement* and *effective praise* are also in common usage. For a discussion of these forms of adult attention, see Hitz and Driscoll 1989; also Allen and Hart 1984.)

- *Physical proximity.* Example: quietly standing or sitting close to a child and showing genuine interest by watching, nodding, smiling, or listening.

- *Physical contact.* Example: touching, hugging, holding a child's hand, tussling, rocking, or otherwise physically comforting a child. (Teachers must note and discuss the occasional child who avoids or shrinks from adults' touch.)
- *Physical assistance.* Example: providing support on the climbing frame, pushing a swing, helping a child achieve balance on a walking beam, etc.
- *Providing things that children want.* Example: providing a favourite nutritional snack, play materials, activities, mini-excursions such as a ride in the elevator or crossing the road to watch the carpenter.

PHOTO 13–7 *On occasion, it may be necessary for a teacher to ignore a child's behaviour or withhold attention.*

WITHHOLDING OR WITHDRAWING REINFORCERS

Another form of adult social reinforcement, much less pleasant to practise, is taking away (withdrawing or withholding) something that is important to a child—a favourite toy, activity, playmate, or the attention of an important adult. Withholding reinforcement is used when an inappropriate behaviour is not decreasing in spite of teachers' efforts. (Recall the staff's first efforts to redirect James, with the resulting increase in flitting about.) Though punishment itself will not be discussed until later, withdrawing/withholding reinforcement, in one sense, is a form of punishment (Photo 13–7). It has less damaging side effects than physical or verbal punishment, however. It is also more effective. Equally important, it cuts down on the emotional conflict between adult and child that so often accompanies other forms of punishment. In early childhood settings, withholding attention and other reinforcers can be accomplished in several ways:

1. Teachers may ignore an incident and act as if they do not see the undesirable behaviour (as long as the child is not endangering himself or others). Ignoring can be accomplished by turning away for the moment, and showing interest in another child or activity.
2. Teachers may remove materials or equipment if a child continues to misuse them.
3. Teachers may remove the child from play with other children or from an activity.

It will be stressed again and again in this book that in a well-arranged and developmentally appropriate early learning environment, the need for any kind of negative procedure should be rare. Hence the rationale for including in this text an entire chapter (Chapter 14) on appropriate environmental arrangements and the consequent positive effect on children's behaviour.

INCOMPATIBLE BEHAVIOURS

Incompatible behaviours are two or more responses that cannot occur together. An inappropriate behaviour cannot occur at the same time that an appropriate behaviour is occurring. For example, it is impossible for children to walk and run at the same time. Therefore, if the rule is "No running in the classroom," teachers should turn their attention (social reinforcement) to children who are remembering to walk. The child who runs, after a first reminder, receives no further teacher attention until the running stops (withholding attention). Here are some other examples: listening is incompatible with talking out loud; making a neutral comment is incompatible with teasing; waiting for the cookie basket to be passed is incompatible with snatching cookies. In other words, whenever a child is not behaving inappropriately, he or she is engaging in some kind of appropriate behaviour (even if it is only standing and watching for a moment). Recognizing this gives teachers the opportunity to respond to something appropriate rather than wasting their time and emotional energy on behaviours that are inappropriate.

Withholding attention from behaviours that are maladaptive or inappropriate need not (and should not) result in a child getting appreciably less adult attention. Misbehaving children tend to be attention seekers; ignoring them along with their inappropriate behaviours often results in more varied and even greater inappropriateness as they increase their efforts to get attention. The strategy is for teachers to attend to other, more appropriate (or at least, less objectionable) behaviours in which the child engages. The best behaviours for teachers to reinforce are those that are incompatible with the inappropriate behaviours. James, once again, will be the example:

> James's constant flitting about the classroom prevented him from focusing on any one activity. In other words, flitting and focusing are incompatible behaviours. Teachers therefore stopped attending to his flitting and instead paid attention to those moments, brief as they might be, when he became engaged in an activity. The teacher in charge of the activity provided interest and support as long as James was engaged. When he left, that teacher and the others immediately turned their attention elsewhere, until such time as he lingered again, even briefly, with

another activity. As noted earlier, James's attention span soon began to show rapid and marked improvement.

Support the Child When the Child Is Doing Something Positive

One problem that often occurs in early childhood settings is that the focus on punishment is too strong. Adults tend to remain fairly neutral until a child does something the adult considers inappropriate. *Then* the child is likely to get a great deal of attention, but of a punishing kind that will do little to eliminate the unacceptable behaviour. It is important to respond positively to a child who is engaged in positive/appropriate behaviours (Photo 13–8).

PHOTO 13–8 *It is important to respond positively when children are engaged in positive behaviours.*

DISCIPLINE VS. PUNISHMENT

The goal of discipline is self-discipline. Discipline techniques used by teachers should support the child in developing control of the child's own behaviour. As children mature, they become more aware of the range of consequences that may result from their actions, enabling them to adapt their behaviour on their own.

Discipline is most effective when it is based on anticipation. Through their observations of children and their knowledge of child development, teachers can anticipate potential trouble spots and deal with them *before* they occur. In other words, adults prevent mishap; hence the term *preventive discipline* (Harris and Allen 1966).

Preventive discipline depends on what teachers do and say to forestall trouble (in behavioural terms, this is referred to as *arranging antecedents*). How you arrange the learning environment can be one form of preventive discipline (see Chapter 14). By placing the drying rack next to the easel, for example, teachers help children avoid the many problems (and tension-provoking reminders) associated with carrying a dripping painting across the floor. By providing a parking place for wheel toys (instead of letting children abandon them "mid-road") teachers help children avoid injuring others or getting into angry exchanges as to which child really owns a piece of equipment. The point to be underscored is this: *Environmental arrangements are a major determinant of children's behaviour and of*

Photo 13–9 *By placing a learning centre away from other areas of activity, children can focus more easily.*

children's learning (Photo 13–9). Preventive discipline accomplishes the following:

1. It communicates to children how to behave according to developmentally appropriate expectations, and then facilitates children's efforts to do so.

2. It makes it easy for children to learn the vast number of behaviours and skills necessary to grow up to be confident and competent in a world that expects so much of young children and the adults who care for them.

3. It helps children avoid unnecessary and ego-deflating errors that squander children's time and self-esteem.

4. It assures a positive environment in which teachers enjoy teaching and children enjoy learning.

Punishment, in terms of its common definition, consists of those adult behaviours that emotionally or physically hurt children—scolding, nagging, yelling, ridiculing, criticizing, isolating, slapping, shaking, and spanking. As noted earlier, punishing children is *not* an effective way of managing them. True, punishment often stops an undesirable behaviour at the moment. However, it usually is a short-lived victory for the adult and one that tends to backfire. Yelling at children is an example. Most children will stop, for the time being, whatever they are doing that is causing them to be yelled at. That behaviour, however, is almost sure to return, again and again, under various circumstances, and often as soon as the adult who was yelling at them leaves the scene.

In many instances, punishment has undesirable side effects. In the yelling example, the behaviour that the adult does not like is stopped at the time. This reinforces the adult for yelling at the child. The result? The adult yells at the child all the more. In addition, the adult is modelling yelling, literally teaching inappropriate yelling behaviour to the child: "Children who are yelled at yell back on other occasions. So, to a considerable degree, you get back what you give" (Bee 1989, 476).

The same holds true of spanking or other forms of physical punishment. Some children who are spanked frequently, or otherwise physically punished, become highly aggressive (Bandura 1973). Other children react very differently.

Some behave as though they were tightly coiled springs. They often behave well at home or school but once out from under adults' eyes they seem to explode into a range of forbidden behaviours. Still other children appear troubled, turn inward, hold back, become passive. It is as if they fear that whatever they do will result in ridicule, criticism, or some form of physical punishment. In general, punishment leads to loss of self-confidence and self-esteem. Frequently punished children (either verbally or physically punished) do not feel good about themselves or their world. Such feelings have a negative effect on all aspects of their development.

STOPPING A HARMFUL BEHAVIOUR

All children must be stopped (that is, have limits set) on occasion. A child who is endangering himself or herself or others, or causing serious disruptions at home or in the classroom, must be controlled. For many children, a reminder or a mild verbal reprimand is enough. This is especially effective in classrooms and homes where preventive discipline is practised, where children receive adequate amounts of positive attention for the good things they do all day long. When a child does not respond to ordinary reminders, the teacher may need to use a firmer tone of voice and more definitive words.

Example:

"No! Janie, I can't let you push Tammy off the tricycle. That can hurt Tammy."

When none of this works, the child may have to be removed from this activity—a form of discipline *that seldom needs to happen.*

WITHDRAWING THE CHILD

Clare Cherry (1983, 137) uses the term *renewal time.* She states that "time out is a widely used term, but it tends to be overused, as it can be applied to many different kinds of situations. It often characterizes punitive isolation." Cherry goes on to say: "I prefer the term renewal time. It is easy to say and it means what I really want—a chance for the inner self to become renewed, as opposed to the whole self being 'out.'"

In this form of discipline, the message given to the child is that he or she needs some time to calm down and to gain some inner control. Examples of renewal time are contained in these statements:
- "Playing alone for a little while will help you settle down."
- "You may read a book quietly or play quietly, but you need time by yourself because you were hurting (disturbing, etc.) other children."

- "You need some time to calm down. You were getting too wild and excited. You need to play quietly on your own for a while until you are calmer."

Giving choices also empowers a child:

- "You need to sit and watch; or you can play quietly somewhere."

The goal (as it should be with all forms of discipline) is to help children become self-managing.

The process to follow in positive discipline is this:

1. Tell the child what is problematic about the child's behaviour, explaining why you are asking him or her to change what he or she is doing.
2. If the child does not respond, the teacher needs to tell the child again, this time explaining the limit that the teacher is going to have to place on the child.

Example:

> *A child is throwing sand at another child. The teacher says, "Please don't throw sand, Tony. If you throw the sand it could get in someone's eyes and hurt them." Tony continues to throw the sand. The teacher then says, "Tony, if you keep on throwing sand, I am going to have to ask you to leave the sandbox. I don't want any of your friends to get hurt."*

The teacher clearly explains to Tony *what* is wrong in his behaviour, *why* she feels that this behaviour cannot continue, and the *limit* she will have to place if he does not stop the behaviour on his own.

Basic guidelines for placing limits include the following situations:

1. The behaviour is harmful to the child himself or herself (this includes physical hurt as well as situations in which a child may be becoming overly stimulated emotionally).
2. The behaviour is likely to be harmful to another child.
3. The behaviour is likely to harm property.

Children often realize that they have made a mistake in self-management, but may not yet have developed the inner control needed to change their behaviour. When they are asked to leave a play situation, the adult is letting them know that it is important to work on developing this control if they want to remain in their chosen play situations. To help children remember, the teacher can talk with the children about what happened and how they could have handled the situation more effectively.

Time-Out

Time-out should be used only as a last resort. It is the extreme form of withdrawing reinforcement. *Time-out* means removing the child from all reinforcement,

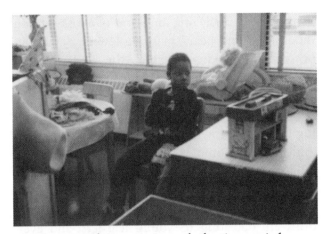

PHOTO 13–10 *If time-out is used, the time period should be short.*

including teacher attention, other children, materials, and equipment. *Time-out should be used only with the permission of the parent and the consultants.* It should be reserved for seriously inappropriate behaviours that have not responded to less severe forms of behaviour management. Children who do not comprehend verbal and problem-solving strategies for changing behaviour may need time-out to define the limits being set.

(Note: In many provinces there are specific guidelines that must be followed for use of specific behavioural practices, including time-out.)

On those occasions when time-out has to be used, the time-out period should be short (Photo 13–10). *Never should it exceed three minutes*; one minute is usually enough. If a child is making a disturbance in time-out, the one- to three-minute release rule still applies, beginning when the child has quieted down. *A written plan that monitors the frequency and duration of time-out should be maintained.*

An important reminder: Children do not learn *what to do* in time-out; they learn only *what not to do.* If children are to learn how to work and play with each other and with materials, they need to be involved (Schickedanz, Schickedanz, and Forsyth 1982). It is in the classroom, *not in time-out,* that teachers can help children learn appropriate ways of responding. Good teachers seldom need to use time-out or any other punishment procedure when preventive discipline is the practice and all children receive adequate amounts of positive attention. It must be remembered, however, that what is an *adequate amount* will vary from child to child, depending on individual differences.

TASK ANALYSIS

Task analysis is a teaching procedure that grew out of the behavioural concept of *shaping* new responses (Photo 13–11). It is a particularly important teaching strategy to use when a child is unable to accomplish a task within a time period that is considered developmentally appropriate for a child of his or her chronological age. Shaping of behaviour is the process of reinforcing *successive approximations* (a series of small steps) toward the eventual mastery of a complex

PHOTO 13–11 *In task analysis (identifying the step-by-step procedure), teachers should watch the performance of an accomplished child.*

behaviour. In analyzing any kind of a task—tying shoes, counting bears, printing letters, defending possessions, making friends—the first requirement is to break the task down into its step-by-step components. The steps must be small and logical. They also must be in sequence, progressing from the known, simple, and easy to the more difficult and complex. Small steps provide frequent opportunities for success. Many small steps, and therefore many small successes, help the child avoid unnecessary frustrations. Too many frustrations are defeating to young learners, and even more defeating for children who are developmentally disabled.

OBSERVATION AND TASK ANALYSIS

In preparing to analyze a task, early childhood teachers often find it helpful first to watch a young child perform the task. It is especially instructive to watch a child who has only recently mastered a particular skill. The child's motor coordination and general approach to the problem are likely to be more finely sequenced and developmentally appropriate than those of an older child or an adult performing the same task. When adapting a procedure to an individual child, the starting point is determined by observing that child. The rule is to start where the child is, with what the child can do. This provides the child with a successful experience at the start. It also enables the teacher to make positive comments immediately, thus getting the new learning off to a good start.

It is true that the first step may be far removed from what is seen as the end behaviour. Many times it is nothing more than a child standing and watching an activity that has been targeted as a developmentally necessary skill for that child; this, however, is but a first step, an opportunity for a teacher to reinforce a first approximation to a more complex skill. A teacher can stand companionably close, watch with the child, and comment briefly on some aspect of the activity. Task analysis and the reinforcement of successive approximations to a child's use of climbing equipment are illustrated in the abbreviated case study and learning sequence detailed in Appendix D. (In that case study, standing and watching are the first approximations to helping a child learn to use climbing equipment.) Additional examples of task analyses are provided in other chapters, whenever relevant.

PROMPTING, CUEING, AND FADING

Step-by-step learning often needs to be accompanied by, and reinforced with, physical and verbal assistance referred to as *prompting and cueing*. Prompts and cues help all children, and especially children with developmental problems, acquire a skill they may be having trouble with. *Fading* is the process of gradually and systematically reducing assistance (the prompting and cueing) as much and as soon as possible without interfering with the child's progress. The goal is for the child to learn to perform the task as independently as is feasible. To illustrate these procedures, the task of learning to hang up a coat is described here:

1. The teacher accompanies the child to the cubby or locker and gives verbal cues: "Here is your locker. Here is the hook for your coat."

2. The teacher explains and demonstrates: "This is the loop that keeps your coat on the hook. It goes over the hook like this."

3. Taking the coat off the hook but holding it open, the teacher prompts, "Can you find the loop?"

4. When the child finds the loop, the teacher says, "Right. Now you can put your finger into it, just as I did."

5. The teacher continues, "Now, slip the loop over the hook." If the child cannot yet coordinate the necessary movements, the teacher guides the child's hand (provides a **manual prompt**).

6. After a few tries the teacher is able to withdraw physical assistance the instant before the loop goes over the hook and so can say to the child, "Look at that! You hung up your coat. Good for you."

In this example, physical assistance was gradually reduced while verbal prompts and cues and positive comments were continued. As the child got better at the task, verbal help was also reduced, but only as the child showed near mastery of each step. Some tasks and some children need even smaller, more specific steps and special kinds of assistance.

Manual prompting is a common form of special assistance leading to skill mastery. Manual prompting (Photo 13–12), sometimes referred to as *hand-over-hand*, consists of positioning the adult's hand around the child's and actually putting the child through the motions. Once the child has the feel of the movements, manual prompting is gradually reduced.

Teachers must guard against overwhelming children with directions when helping them learn a complex task. Directions, like rules, should be kept to a minimum. They should be given only if the teacher is prepared to help the child carry through with additional prompting, cueing, and physical assistance. As with rules, *directions are more effective if worded positively*. It is more informative and helpful to say, "Hold tight with both hands" than it is to say, "Be careful. Don't fall." The latter statements provide children with no information about what they *should* be doing. In all cases, the primary goal is to encourage children's independence, especially in children with developmental disabil-

Photo 13–12 *In manual prompting, the teacher places a hand around the child's in order to guide the child's movements.*

ities. Therefore, teachers provide just enough assistance to ensure children's success but not so much as to promote overdependence. And now a few words of caution: Slow down. Be patient. Adults best promote children's independence by waiting, allowing children adequate time to figure out what they are going to do next and how they will do it. This is in contrast to what happens all too often: The adult says "Put on your sock." They young child is still trying to figure out which is the open end of the sock when the adult grabs it and expertly puts it on the child's foot. What message does this convey to the child?

Amount and Timing of Reinforcement

How much reinforcement is enough? The answer varies from child to child and task to task. Almost continuous reinforcement—feedback—may be needed when a child is beginning to learn something new. Every time the new behaviour (or an approximation to the new behaviour) occurs, the adult tries to respond in some way. At times, smiling and nodding may be all a teacher can take the time to do (Photo 13–13). As in the shaping and prompting examples, adult attention is gradually reduced as the child becomes more able. The goal, always, is that the child's success (intrinsic motivation) takes over, keeping the child eager to continue learning. To accomplish this, a balance must be achieved:

PHOTO 13–13 *There are many instances when the teacher provides a nod or a smile.*

not so much adult attention that the child becomes dependent, but enough so learning continues until the skill is well established and intrinsically reinforcing.

PRAISE AND ENCOURAGEMENT

Praise and encouragement, because they are so central to children's learning, will be discussed in several places in this text. They are mentioned here because of their relationship to step-by-step learning. Praise statements, like prompts and cues, need to be specific. It is of little value, in terms of children's learning, to make statements such as "Good boy," "Good work," "That's nice," "What a pretty picture." In contrast, saying *what it is that is good* gives the child specific feedback, which is always an aid to further learning (Photo 13–14). When the teacher says, "You're matching all the red blocks and the red squares. Good for you," the child knows exactly what it is that he or she is doing well. Such information is useful to the child in learning the rest of the colour-matching task. Furthermore, the focus is on the child's efforts, rather than strictly on outcome or product.

Rarely if ever should teachers make statements such as "*I like* the way you tied your shoes" (or patted the baby, or shared a cookie, or any of the other good things children learn to do). Contrast the above statement about shoe-tying with this one: "Risa, you tied both shoes all by yourself! That must make you feel really happy." The first statement implies that a child should be working to please others and needs to depend on external sources as a measure of personal worth. The second praise statement recognizes the accomplishment in a way that encourages the child to feel good about himself or herself. A child's confidence, self-esteem, and love of learning are thus nurtured.

LEARNING THROUGH IMITATION

Social learning theorists demonstrate that many kinds of learning take place without direct reinforcement from anyone or anything outside the child.

PHOTO 13–14 *Descriptive praise: "You got your coat off all by yourself."*

Children watch and then imitate; that is, they model their behaviour after others. The involvement and self-feedback the child experiences (intrinsic motivation) lead to learning. Specific labels for this kind of learning are *observational learning* or *modelling* (Bandura 1977).

Children learn both appropriate and inappropriate behaviours by watching what is modelled on television, in the classroom or neighbourhood, and by parents and family members. Teachers of young children are powerful models for classroom behaviour. For example, teachers who believe that children should not sit on tables should not sit on tables themselves. Teachers who do not believe that children should yell at them should not yell at children. "Do as I say but not as I do" *cannot* be the rule.

The skills spontaneously modelled by older or more skilled children serve as motivation for other children. Normally developing young children are always eager to learn. It is almost inevitable that they will try things they see more mature children doing. To facilitate learning through imitation in less-skilled children, teachers can provide descriptive praise or feedback to the more-skilled child: "Maria, you are getting down all by yourself, slowly and carefully, one foot and one hand at a time." An approving statement of this kind serves several purposes:

1. Maria is encouraged to appreciate her own individuality and to value her own skills and capabilities.

2. An indirect lesson is provided for children within hearing distance who may not yet have achieved Maria's level of climbing skills.

3. The teacher's words, "slowly and carefully, one foot and one hand at a time," suggest to them what they might try, in their own way, as they work at becoming proficient climbers.

Not all children know how to imitate, however. Some children need specific instruction; in other words, they must first learn *how* to imitate before they can learn *through* imitation. In these instances, teachers need to provide specific kinds of assistance, as will be described in Chapter 15.

COMPETITION IS INAPPROPRIATE

Descriptive statements, such as those about Maria's climbing, carry no implications that any one child is better than another. Promoting competition among young children establishes an uneasy learning environment. Children cannot appreciate the process of learning, or their own uniqueness, if adults imply that they should try to be better than someone else. The only competition that enhances development occurs when a child's progress is approvingly measured against that child's own earlier performance (Brophy 1981). For example: "You are really learning colours. Now you know all the colour names of all the blocks."

The foregoing is a much abbreviated sketch of learning through modelling. The practice will be further examined in subsequent sections where the focus will be on teaching particular skills.

SUMMARY

Developmental concepts such as the "problem of the match" and "learning from success," as well as behavioural principles, have blended into today's well-articulated early childhood teaching practices. The effectiveness of an early education program is demonstrated by changes in children's behaviour. To have healthy development, ongoing changes in behaviour must occur. The blend of developmental and behavioural principles and practices is good for all children and particularly important in inclusive preschools where the range of skill levels is extensive. The blend of practices demonstrate that all children are teachable; if a child is not learning, the blame is placed squarely on the program, not the child.

In the behavioural perspective, systematic reinforcement procedures—if imposed within a developmentally appropriate structure—account for children's learning (or failure to learn). The principles can be put into an ABC format: A stands for what happens first, or antecedents (that which precedes the child's behaviour); B stands for the child's behaviour; C stands for consequences, or reinforcement (that which follows the behaviour). Reinforcements (consequences) are negative or positive. Positive reinforcement is the teacher's best tool. It is readily available through teachers' assistance, genuine interest, and positive reactions to each child and each child's activities. Positive reinforcement also resides in the interesting and appropriate materials and activities provided by teachers.

In some instances, reinforcers must be withheld or withdrawn so that a child does not get attention for behaviours that are detrimental to his or her development. When teachers must withhold reinforcement for an inappropriate behaviour, it is important that they double their efforts to give the child positive attention for useful behaviours. When they do so, inappropriate behaviours are likely to be *crowded out* by more appropriate ones.

Preventive discipline supports appropriate behaviour by guiding children before problems occur.

Renewal time involves removing a child from a situation that he is not able to cope with and directing him to a quiet area where he can play on his own until he is able to rejoin the group. This is the preferred form of withdrawal.

Time-out is used only in those infrequent situations where systematic positive practices have failed to produce necessary behaviour changes.

Punishment is the least desirable and least effective of all forms of child management. Though the punished behaviour may stop for the moment, it usually returns again and again. Frequent punishment has many undesirable side effects, including heightened aggressiveness and diminishing self-esteem.

Other educational practices related to reinforcement procedures include task analysis and learning through observation (modelling), a principle derived from social learning theory. Task analysis is the process of breaking a learning task into small sequential steps for those children who need special help in the form of reduced frustration and more frequent successes. Step-by-step learning is further facilitated with prompting and cueing, which is reduced gradually as the child gains mastery of a task. Children also learn by watching others—for example, by modelling their behaviour on that of a more skilled child. In every kind of learning situation, teachers provide encouragement and descriptive praise to the degree that is appropriate for individual children.

Teachers should never promote competition. Competitiveness among children has no place in early childhood education.

STUDENT ACTIVITIES

1. Observe for one hour in an early childhood classroom. Write down every example of adult social reinforcement that you see and hear.

2. Imagine a child engrossed in painting at the easel or at a table. List 10 positive statements you might make that recognize the child's worth and efforts.

3. Discuss with several of your classmates how they felt as little children when they were punished, and what they believe might be the long-term effects, if any. What experiences did they have with preventive discipline?

4. For several days, watch an older child brush his or her teeth. Do a task analysis of the activity, starting with the child's approach to the sink.

5. Talk with the parents of a preschool child. Ask what behaviours, both positive and negative, they feel their child may have learned through imitation or modelling from family or television or at school. (If you have a preschool child of your own, examine your own reactions.)

6. **Mix and Match**

   Select the one best match for each item in column I from column II and place that letter in the appropriate space in column I.

	I		II
_____	1. Gesell	A.	modelling
_____	2. intrinsic motivation	B.	didactic materials
_____	3. Bijou	C.	hand-over-hand
_____	4. Montessori	D.	joy of learning
_____	5. positive reinforcement	E.	shaping
_____	6. incompatible behaviours	F.	standing and sitting
_____	7. manual prompts	G.	developmentalist
_____	8. successive approximations	H.	behaviourist
_____	9. observation learning	I.	pleasurable consequences

REFERENCES

Allen, K.E. 1974 "Behavior Modification Principles." In J.C. Cull and R.F. Hardy, eds. *Behavior Modification in Rehabilitation Settings.* Springfield, Ill.: Charles C. Thomas.

Allen, K.E., and B. Hart 1984 *The Early Years: Arrangements for Learning.* Englewood Cliffs, N.J.: Prentice-Hall.

Bandura, A. 1973 *Aggression: A Social Learning Analysis.* Englewood Cliffs, N.J.: Prentice-Hall.

Bandura, A. 1977 *Social Learning Theory.* Englewood Cliffs, N.J.: Prentice-Hall.

Beckman, P.J., C.C. Robinson, B. Jackson, and S.A. Rosenberg 1986 "Translating Developmental Findings into Teaching Strategies for Young Handicapped Children." *Journal of the Division for Early Childhood* 10, no. 1: 45–52.

Bee, H. 1989 *The Developing Child.* New York: Harper and Row.

Bijou, S.W. 1959 *Learning in Children.* Monographs of the Society for Research in Child Development, 24.

Bijou, S.W., and B.W. Cole 1975 "The Feasibility of Providing Effective Educational Programs for the Severely and Profoundly Retarded: Educating the 24-Hour Retarded Child." Paper presented at National Association for Retarded Citizens, New Orleans.

Brophy, J.E. 1981 "Teacher Praise: A Functional Analysis." *Review of Educational Research* 51, no. 1: 5–32.

Cherry, C. 1983 *Please Don't Sit on the Kids.* Belmont, Cal.: Pitman.

Dewey, J. 1950 *Experience and Education.* New York: Macmillan.

Froebel, F.W. 1911 *The Education of Man.* (Trans. W.N. Hailmann). New York: Appleton.

Gesell, A., H.M. Halverson, B. Thompson, F.L. Ilg, B.M. Castner, L.B. Ames, and C.S. Amatruda 1940 *The First Five Years of Life. A Guide to the Study of the Preschool Child.* New York: Harper and Row.

Harris, F.R., and R.E. Allen 1966 *Undersix: Children in Preschool KCTS Television Series and Viewer's Guide.* Seattle: University of Washington.

Hitz, R., and A. Driscoll 1989 "Praise or Encouragement? New Insights into Praise: Implications for Early Childhood Teachers." *Young Children* 43, no. 5: 6–13.

Hunt, J. McV. 1961 *Intelligence and Experience.* New York: Ronald Press.

Montessori, M. 1912 *The Montessori Method: Scientific Pedagogy as Applied to Child Education in "Children's Houses."* (Trans. A.F. George) New York: Frederick A. Stokes.

Piaget, J. 1952 *The Origins of Intelligence in Children.* New York: International Universities Press.

Schickedanz, J.A., D.I. Schickedanz, and P.D. Forsyth 1982 *Toward Understanding Children.* Boston: Little, Brown.

Wolery, M. 1994 *Designing Inclusive Environments for Children with Special Needs in Early Childhood Programs.* Washington, D.C.: N.A.E.Y.C.

Arranging the Learning Environment

After studying the material in this chapter, the student will be able to

- explain how classroom and play-yard facilities and program scheduling influence children's learning in an inclusive setting

- list a number of things that teachers can do to increase the safety of indoor and outdoor learning areas for children with disabilities

- discuss the major issues involved in planning a program schedule for children in an inclusive setting

- describe how to plan smooth transitions and describe the types of learning opportunities available to children during transitions

INTRODUCTION

In today's society, the environments provided by early childhood programs will influence, even determine, the development of countless numbers of children. Those environments and the way they are arranged also will determine how effectively teachers will teach and the kinds of messages children will get about themselves and others. According to Harms (1989, 232):

> The environment that adults create for children is a powerful tool for teaching. Through the way we structure children's surroundings, we communicate our values, provide guidance about how children are to behave in the environment, and influence the quality of their learning. Teachers of young children need to become aware of the constant influence the environment has on the children in their care.

THE INCLUSIVE ENVIRONMENT

In an inclusive setting, environmental arrangements assume special importance because of the range of differences among children.

PHOTO 14–1 *Indoor and outdoor play space should be arranged so that children with disabilities can be included easily in all activities.*

Teachers should arrange play spaces and activities, both indoors and out of doors, so that children with disabilities are included easily and naturally (Photo 14–1). By doing so teachers convey a powerful message about human values: *All types of children can play together and have fun.* Having fun together is likely to be the best avenue to genuine inclusion of children with disabilities with their nondisabled peers. Many children in wheelchairs can join in the exuberant activity of a lively beanbag toss and other group games. Wolfensberger, best known for his concept of *normalization* (1972), recommends bringing as few pieces of special equipment as possible into the classroom. His argument is that they brand the children who use them as too different. True, many children with developmental disabilities cannot function without certain types of special equipment. Wolfensberger argues that only what is essential for the child to enter into classroom activities should be used. Therapeutic equipment is available that is fun for all children, however: huge medicine balls, tumble tubs, balance beams, portable stair-climbing apparatus, trampolines, and the like. (Specialized equipment and specific environmental adaptations will be discussed in subsequent chapters under the various disability headings.)

Teachers must always keep in mind that children with disabilities are first and foremost children. Their basic needs are essentially no different from those of all children, just more pronounced, as the following examples show:

- Loud and distracting noises are difficult for most children; for children with hearing impairments such noises may be intolerable.

- Moving about safely, in an environment free of clutter, slippery floors, or rumpled rugs, contributes to the safety and security of every child; for children with limited vision or orthopedic problems, an environment free of obstacles protects against serious injury.

PHOTO 14–2 *Minimizing clutter and confusion enhances the ability of all young children to concentrate on the task at hand.*

- Minimizing clutter and confusion enhances the ability of all young children to concentrate on the task at hand; for children with attention or learning disorders, reducing distractions may be the only way to promote learning (Photo 14–2).

Regardless of special problems, a well-planned learning environment is a necessary context for meeting developmental needs. It is unacceptable to provide one kind of environment for normally developing children and a different kind for children with problems. As Olds (1979, 94) points out:

> Wheelchairs, braces, crutches, and caregivers can support a body as it grows, but they cannot provide sustenance for eyes, ears, hands, brains and muscles that become limp, useless, and restless with passivity and disuse. [Those who] prevent the special needs child from experiencing the activity and risk-taking essential for normal development, simply retard and prejudice a disabled child's chances for a positive developmental outcome.

Teachers also need to use guidance procedures (discipline) that will reduce prejudice and promote positive outcomes in children with developmental problems. Helping children with disabilities learn to behave appropriately reduces the behavioural differences that often set them apart from children who are developing normally. The most efficient way to accomplish this is by arranging the learning environment in ways that prompt acceptable behaviour in all children. Such arrangements are one aspect of preventive discipline, which was discussed in Chapter 13.

ARRANGEMENTS FOR LEARNING

A program setting, even the newest, most lavish, does not guarantee quality learning experiences. The physical plan may contribute to quality, but it does not ensure it. As Gordon and Browne (1996) point out, the *environment* is more than a plant; it is the physical and human qualities that combine to create a space in which children and adults work and play together.

Setting up and maintaining an effective early learning environment puts teachers' knowledge of child development to the test. Classroom and play-yard arrangements must be sensitive to developmental sequences and individual differences. Early childhood teachers must know what to do when one child is experiencing learning difficulties, another is not making developmental progress, and a third is hampered by behaviour problems. Teachers must recognize that the first move is to step back and take a look, to observe the child in the context of the daily program. Necessary changes in the environment can then be made.

Rearranging the location of learning centres changes the way children "orbit" in a room. This in turn changes children's interaction patterns, stimulating involvement in new areas and often bringing about positive changes in group or individual behaviour patterns.

PLANNING THE ENVIRONMENT FOR LEARNING

The first step in planning an early learning environment is specifying the kinds of learning opportunities that will be offered. Most programs, including inclusive settings, plan three broad types of experiences: learning through self-help/care routines, through teacher-guided learning opportunities, and through free play-discovery learning opportunities. Each of these will be discussed in terms of physical arrangements.

1. Self-Help/Care Routines

These are skills related to socially prescribed routines such as toileting, dressing, eating, cleaning up, and doing one's share of classroom chores. *Mastery*, the ability to perform a task, is tied closely to the child's emerging sense of independence and competence. During toddlerhood and the early preschool years, teachers systematically guide children through each step of each routine until the various skills become *automatic*. In an inclusive setting, children with developmental problems (including older preschoolers) often need teachers' help in learning basic self-help/care skills. Much of the help can be provided indirectly, by arranging the environment so that all types of children can work and play together throughout the program day (Photo 14–3). This social blend

PHOTO 14–3 *The learning environment can be arranged so that children of every skill level can work and play.*

assures a variety of good models, through observation of children who already have mastered the sequenced steps of many developmental tasks (see Chapter 13).

Other environmental arrangements that promote self-help/care skills among children with special needs are appropriately sized furnishings and accessories. Hooks, washbasins, toilets, and drinking facilities that can be reached and operated by a child allow children to help themselves. Children with special needs can learn to take care of many of their own needs through various environmental arrangements. Consider the following examples:

- Cork or raised tape placed along certain walls and pieces of furniture will help a child with a severe visual impairment independently find his or her way around a room.
- A prearranged comfortable and secure place to go to remove leg braces, as needed, frees a child of having to wait for an available adult.
- Large knobs or rungs on children's furniture facilitate the opening of drawers and doors.
- Teaching a child how to adjust the volume on his or her hearing aid reduces the amount of time the child is uncomfortable or not "tuned in."
- Having everything in the classroom and play yard in good working order reduces frustrations and increases children's initiative and independence.

The latter point is especially important. Few situations make a child with special needs—or anyone else, for that matter—feel more incompetent than a doorknob that spins aimlessly, a faucet that will not turn off, a drawer that will not open. These experiences are especially devastating for children with developmental disabilities; they have to do more than their share of coping as it is. When something cannot be made to work, children often do not realize that it is the equipment and not themselves that is at fault. To the child who already is coping with a disability, it may add one more frustration to accomplishing an everyday task. *Induced incompetence* is the term Olds (1979) uses to describe the effects of poorly functioning equipment on children with developmental disabilities.

WASHROOM FACILITIES. Learning to toilet themselves is a developmental goal for most children during the early years. In designing a washroom, the following should be taken into consideration:

- Toilets and sinks should be of appropriate size and height.
- Adequate space should be provided for maneuvering crutches or a walker, or for pulling a wheelchair parallel to the toilet or up to the sink.
- A handrail should be installed that will enable the child to steady himself or herself.

- A hollow block or small footstool should be provided for a child's feet to rest on, thereby reducing insecurity and fear of falling off the toilet.

All children should be guided in developing self-help/care skills in going to the toilet and washing and drying their hands afterward. (Special adaptations for teaching toileting to children with developmental disabilities will be discussed in Chapter 20.)

In programs for toddlers or children who are developmentally delayed, teachers need to be immediately available to the children's washroom. For preschoolers who have become fairly trustworthy in handling their toileting needs, it is best if the washroom is accessible to all activity areas. Accessibility from the outdoor play area is especially important so that children can get to the washroom in a hurry as they often need to do. School-age children can be expected to use a washroom out of sight of teachers, even down the hall. A teacher, nevertheless, needs to be available near the door where children leave and return.

PHOTO 14–4 *Each child needs his or her own cubby.*

CUBBY AREAS. Cubbies or coathook areas (Photo 14–4) in early childhood centres should be as near as possible to the outdoor exit and the washroom. This location helps children keep track of coats and mittens as they come in to use the toileting facility. If there are no distractions en route, many children can be responsible for toileting themselves during outside play periods. This arrangement may put the cubbies at some distance from the door through which children arrive and depart for home. However, this distance need not be a problem if the traffic lane from the entry door to the cubbies is free of obstacles and clutter.

SLEEPING AREAS. The sleeping area in all-day programs must be carefully planned and free of distractions. Placement of cots should

- be consistent—in the same spot every day—and so provide a sense of security for the child; and
- take into consideration an awareness of the specific needs of individual children—for example, a space to maneuver walkers or crutches independently, or a quiet corner without distractions for an overly active child.

2. Teacher-Guided Learning Opportunities

Teacher-guided learning opportunities (also referred to as large- and small-group activities and one-on-one teaching or instruction periods) should be available throughout the program day (Photo 14–5). The teacher's intent is to support learning of skills that children need but cannot learn solely from a self-guided exploration of the environment. A teacher-guided activity might comprise stories, songs, fingerplays, discussions on care of materials, demonstrations of gentleness with animals, opportunities for children to learn names of objects, basic directionality and number concepts, and so on. These activities may be formally planned learning experiences or they may arise spontaneously out of a child's immediate interest or need (see *incidental opportunities* in Chapter 10).

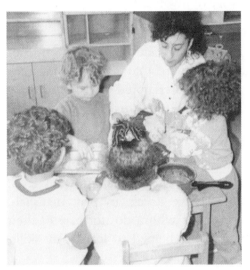

PHOTO 14–5 *Teacher-directed activities are interspersed throughout the program day.*

Children with developmental disabilities sometimes need more teacher support in approaching and maintaining involvement in activities. They may have trouble initiating their own play idea or getting into the play of others. What they may need most is brief but frequent teacher guidance on how to join and participate in play activities. (Such methods will be discussed in Chapter 15, on social skills.) They also may need teacher-guided activities related to skills that normally developing children seem to acquire almost spontaneously. Pointing at objects might be an example. Most children need no help in learning to point; usually they have to be taught not to point. Children with perceptual-motor problems or cognitive limitations often need direct instruction in learning to point.

In arranging the location for teacher-guided activities such as story reading or music and movement group time, a first consideration is ease of transition to and from other activity areas. Children can change activities more readily if teacher-planned interest centres and activities can be approached (and seen) from all other play areas. Furthermore, seeing that an attractive activity is starting up often serves as a cue. When a teacher wishes to draw the children together for a group activity, children should be warned a few minutes ahead of time that they will need to be tidying up "in five minutes."

Children still in the process of tidying up a play area may need some teacher support in completing the task before moving on to the group activity. The teacher supporting the group activity can find subtle ways to involve a child with a shorter attention span when he or she is no longer able to attend to this activity without disrupting the group. It is then appropriate to send the child to a different activity area or teacher for alternative involvement.

3. Free Play-Discovery Learning

Free play-discovery learning includes child-initiated activities, free nonstructured time periods, and other opportunities to explore a range of learning centres set up by teachers. These should be given uninterrupted blocks of time in a well-planned play environment, both indoors and outdoors. The processes of exploration and experimentation are fundamental to early learning. It is through play that children discover their world and themselves. Play provides opportunities for children to apply their own ideas as well as the learning they have acquired in teacher-supported activities. At every developmental level, children need opportunities to play and to have access to play materials. Children with developmental disabilities, many of whom do not play of their own accord, or even know how to play, must be helped to learn play skills. (Teaching children to play will be discussed in Chapter 15.)

Very young children and some children with developmental problems do not always benefit from *large* blocks of unstructured time. They may spend too much of their developmentally valuable time unengaged or inappropriately engaged because of their limited skills or short span of attention. For these children, brief teacher-structured activities are easily interspersed during free play learning periods. Learning to point, mentioned earlier, will be used as an example.

PHOTO 14–6 *Each block has its own space.*

Baillie needed to learn to point. During a free play period, the teacher in the immediate area noticed Baillie standing about, seeming not to know what to do with herself. The teacher took her companionably by the hand, and said, "Let's go pointing" (an improvised game Baillie enjoyed). While keeping her eye on the other children, the teacher walked around the area with Baillie for a minute or so, having her point to well-known objects. The teacher then helped Baillie point to what she would like to do next and followed up by having the teacher in that area help her settle in.

Free play-discovery learning areas work well when they radiate from the location of teacher-supported learning centres and activities. Where these activity centres are placed is determined by furniture, storage, and the cleanup requirements of each area (Photo 14–6). Tables that are used for lunch and for sensory activities are likely to determine where puzzles and other fine motor materials are to be used during other periods. A large rug in the manipulative area often is suitable for group activities such as music and rhythms. Transitions from small-group to large-group activities can be eased by placing individual carpet squares on the rug in a circle or semicircle (as place markers for individual children) at the start of the transition.

Teachers' selection and grouping of materials indicate clearly how each area is to be used. Children, and especially very young children and children with varied developmental problems, should not be given mixed signals. For example, some children are likely to think that it must be all right to colour in the library books if crayons are left on the bookshelves. In contrast, the examples that follow offer environmental signals dictating appropriate behaviours:

- The block area should contain only those items related to block play. Accessory items to be incorporated into block play (cars, trucks, dollhouse furniture, zoo animals) should be grouped, rotated regularly, and displayed in the same area, on shelves separate from but adjacent to the block storage shelves.

- The block area needs to be clearly separate from other areas. Ideally, it will consist of a large open space free of furniture or equipment except for shelves filled with materials related to block play. The shelves and a floor marker such as tape, a painted line, a piece of very low-pile tightly stretched carpeting (glued or fastened down) are useful for marking off the block play area. Boundaries such as this act as guidelines for reminding children of the range of space in which their activity can safely expand. Different play and learning centres should be separated by clear paths.

- Manipulative materials should be displayed only in the manipulative area. Each material should be

PHOTO 14–7 *Learning centres should be set up so that they are distinct.*

given a distinct place, with related parts grouped together (hammer, individual tins of nails, and hammering board; pegs and pegboards; large, *unstrung* wooden beads and plastic-tipped laces). The display tells the child what to expect of the material and how to use it. This is particularly important in groups in which there are children with attention deficits or lower cognitive functioning. A broken or incomplete set of play materials should never be put out for children. (It is better to have no puzzles than puzzles with even one missing piece.)(Photo 14–7.)

PRINCIPLES OF PLANNING EARLY LEARNING ENVIRONMENTS

Cutting across all aspects of environmental planning are certain basic principles. These include safety, visibility, ease of movement, versatility of equipment, teachers' availability, and structured flexibility.

PRINCIPLE 1: SAFETY

Safety in the preschool classroom and play yard is a major consideration on two scores. One is preventing accidents and injuries. The other is fostering independence. Independence comes about only in a safe and secure environment where children know that adults can be depended on to protect them from harm and from harming themselves. Teachers should make sure that area rugs have nonskid backing or are glued or fastened down. A skidding rug is a hazard for all children and teachers and is especially hazardous for children who are blind or orthopedically disabled. Teachers also should make sure that materials and equipment are nontoxic, free of cracks and splinters, and in good working order. It is frustrating for any child to try to steer a wheel toy that has a bent axle; for a child with limited motor skills it may lead to a serious accident. This can discourage the child from making further efforts to join in outdoor play. If the accident involved other children, avoidance of the child with special needs may follow. The children who were hurt (and their parents) usually do not understand that it was the equipment that was at fault, not the child with the developmental problem.

Order and Organization

Clutter and disorganization are incompatible with safety. Teachers must make sure that *everything has a place* and, when not in use, *everything is in its place*. A child with a visual impairment needs to know that the dough and cookie cutters and rolling pins (with no potentially hurtful things mixed in) are always to be found, for example, in the lower left corner of the housekeeping cupboards. Logical arrangements contribute to the child's independence; they enable the child to put materials away when finished with them, a responsibility of every child. The ongoing *restoration* of play areas is especially important in inclusive classrooms. The child mentioned above, who is visually impaired, needs to be confident that a rolling pin that rolled off the table earlier will not be left there for him or her to fall over later.

PHOTO 14–8 *Teachers help children restore play areas.*

Teachers who routinely help children restore play areas after each use provide children with valuable lessons in common courtesy as well as regard for the physical safety of children with impairments (Photo 14–8). By the same token, regard for others also must be the concern of the child who uses special equipment. The child with an orthopedic disability needs to learn how to position his or her crutches when they are not in use so they do not fall about, endangering others. A child who uses a wheelchair only part of the time must learn to park it in an agreed-upon place, not abandon it haphazardly.

Matching Children and Equipment

A critical aspect of safety has to do with matching equipment and materials to the skill levels of the children in the group. Wheel toys, all oversized, for example, pose a safety hazard for younger, smaller children. They also are a hazard for children with developmental problems who may not be able to exercise good judgment in selecting suitable equipment. In many instances, the poor judgment is simply lack of experience. Children with developmental problems often have been overprotected by well-meaning adults concerned that they not hurt themselves. Children with disabilities, if they are to develop independence, must learn to take risks. Learning to take risks, however, can be accomplished only where children are protected from becoming too frightened or seriously harmed.

Safe Outdoor Environments

Outdoor play, in a safe and carefully arranged play yard, is an essential aspect of a quality program for young children. It is here that children practise physical skills such as running, jumping, ducking, pumping, climbing, and kicking. They learn to throw, catch, and bat and combine these skills into games. The outdoors also provides opportunities for children to learn voice and tone modulations— shouting, chanting, whistling, imitating a siren—all without causing discomfort for others.

Outdoor equipment (as well as indoor gym equipment) needs to be simple yet versatile. It should include ladders, planks, jumping boards, and simple climbing frames. There should be walking boards of various widths placed at different heights and combined with small portable climbing frames, ladders, and gang-planks with side rails. Equipment of this type can be arranged and rearranged to meet the needs of children with delayed motor skills as well as advanced children. The arrangement in the outdoor area can be elaborate yet simple at the same time. Children just beginning to try out their gross motor coordination can be as well served as daring children in need of constant challenge.

PRINCIPLE 2: VISIBILITY

A major function of early childhood education is encouraging children to explore and experiment with materials and equipment. This means that children are going to be taking risks as they try out new skills; therefore, they need to be visible to teachers at all times. Some of children's experiments will work, others will not; but all provide teachers with opportunities to teach. A 6-year-old who decides to try jumping off a swing in motion, for example, presents a teaching opportunity. A teacher may make suggestions concerning speed and a jumping-off point suitable for a first attempt. Also, the teacher is alerted, ready to catch the child who does not heed suggestions or whose timing goes awry.

Visibility is especially critical in working with children with developmental problems who cannot always gauge their own limitations. At the first indication that a child is about to attempt something dangerously beyond his or her capabilities, the observant teacher can intervene immediately. The child's efforts can be redirected to provide encouragement for continued work on the skill, but in ways more suited to the child's skill level.

PRINCIPLE 3: EASE OF MOVEMENT

Children and teachers need to be able to move about freely (Photo 14–9). Movement is enhanced when traffic lanes are unobstructed and have adequate space to maneuver trucks and doll carriages or wheelchairs and crutches. Traffic lanes, free of obstructions and unpleasant *surprises* (unmopped puddles of water on the floor, an abandoned doll carriage, an upturned rug edge) are critical,

PHOTO 14–9 *Teachers can support children's efforts in developing new skills.*

especially for children with limited vision, as well as those on crutches or in wheelchairs. Ease of movement within interest centres is important, too. Crowded activity areas, where children's movements are restricted, inevitably lead to conflict and aggression, as well as overstimulation for children with attention deficit disorders. Problems are prevented by providing additional attractive interest centres. Small groups, of varying developmental levels, then have space to play together, or side by side.

PRINCIPLE 4: TEACHERS' AVAILABILITY

Teachers who are readily available are the key to a safe and comfortable early learning environment. Young children are learning *something* each of their waking moments. Teachers, therefore, must be available where they are most needed throughout the program day to facilitate learning. When children can move independently between activities, undistracted by inappropriate or unsafe activities, teachers can teach rather than police.

PRINCIPLE 5: STRUCTURED FLEXIBILITY

To meet the range of developmental levels found within a group of young children, the learning environment must be well structured. At the same time it must be flexible and adaptable (Photo 14–10). A structured environment, where rules and expectations are consistent, provides a secure yet freeing framework. Children can explore and test limits, and teachers can react spontaneously to the infinite variations in children's learning.

Systematic advance planning and logical revision of arrangements are essential to both program structure and program flexibility. Both are based on teachers' periodic assessments of their programs. A widely used assessment instrument is the *Early Childhood Environment Rating Scale* (ECERS) (Harms and Clifford 1983). It is designed to give an overall picture of space, materials, activities, daily schedule, and supervision. Another instrument, the "Preschool Assessment of the Classroom Environment" (PACE) (McWilliam and Dunst 1985) also is useful. It has been tested in classrooms that include children with

PHOTO 14–10 *Learning environments must be well set up, flexible, and adaptive.*

and without disabilities. (For additional environmental evaluation tools, see Appendix A.)

Much more could be said about arranging appropriate learning environments for young children. Softness (Prescott, Jones, and Kritchevsky 1972), aesthetics (beauty), privacy, lighting variations, built-in lofts, display of children's work—these are but some of the additional dimensions that teachers need to be aware of.

SCHEDULING

Specific principles must be addressed when planning daily, weekly, seasonal, and year-long activity schedules for both children and teachers in an inclusive setting. Two major scheduling factors are individual differences among children and their changing skill levels over time.

Accommodating Individual Differences

To determine the sequence of activities, teachers must be sensitive to individual differences among children and to their special needs and preferences. Teachers should strive to maintain a global perception of the overall plan of the day, of the room setup, as well as of the specific opportunities for learning. This process should vary during the year as teachers get to know children better and as children become more skilled in all areas of development (Photo 14–11). The length and type of classroom activities and amount of outdoor time often differ from fall to winter, winter to spring, and spring to summer. In the fall, for example, children may need longer active play periods outdoors as they adapt to new children, new adults, and a group experience. In the winter, the colder weather and bulkier outdoor clothing may limit the range of activities available to some children with special needs, such as those with cerebral palsy, spina bifida, and other conditions that may affect physical coordination.

In the spring, more time can be spent outdoors because the weather will be warmer. This provides excellent opportunities for extended time in small-group and independent play activities. A summer schedule should provide more outdoor time. (Note: Don't forget hats, sunscreen, and other recommended measures, such as shaded areas for activities, needed to protect the sensitive skin of young children.)

PHOTO 14–11 *Child-directed activity periods can be extended as children become more experienced.*

Many activities can be brought outdoors in warm weather. Easel painting and work with clay, for example, take on entirely different dimensions when done out in the fresh air. When basic components of the program are moved out of the indoor classroom and onto permanent outdoor tables, they give teachers and children a refreshing change of pace.

Varying Activity Levels

Periods of high physical activity should alternate with periods of quiet activities. Most children are subject to a kind of *energy spillover* from active play periods. Therefore, learning experiences that require children's concentration should not be scheduled immediately following vigorous free play. A way around this is to insert a brief "cooling down" period, perhaps by spacing books at regular intervals on the circle area where a group music activity will be held. (Books should always be available to children, even during free play periods. If children are taught proper care of books from the start, their misuse during this transition activity is unlikely.) As children assemble by ones and twos, they can look at books until the rest of the children have assembled and the music activity begins.

Orderly Sequences

Activity periods should generally follow an orderly and predictable sequence. Most young children have trouble accepting any departure from what they are used to. Change in routines may be even more difficult for very young children and children with developmental problems. Children with pervasive developmental disorders (PDD) and attention deficit disorders (ADD) frequently become overly attached to the daily schedule. Commonplace routines become rituals and must be held constant. Change is intolerable for some children; the unexpected may drive the child into a frenzy. Even so, all children (and most adults) feel more secure knowing what comes next. According to Read, Gardner, and Mahler (1986, 87):

A fixed sequence to parts of the program gives a child confidence in himself because he knows what to expect. He can predict the order of the day. The order need not be rigid; it should be flexible. It should also be modified from time to time, for a trip or special event. Flexibility can be predictable, too.

PHOTO 14–12 *Teachers should give advance warning to prepare children for a change in activity.*

Giving Advance Notice

Children do not give up on activities easily; teachers, therefore, should give warning well in advance of an activity change (Photo 14–12). As stated earlier, several minutes before a transition, the teacher should advise the children: "Soon it will be time to put away the blocks and get ready for snack." It comes as no shock, then, when the teacher announces a few minutes later: "Time to get the blocks on the shelf; I'll help you get started." Ample time must be allowed for children to finish each activity and accomplish each routine. All children need the satisfaction that comes with task completion. Very young children and those who move slowly or with difficulty often need additional time. Therefore, activities and transitions should be scheduled so that all children can move at their own pace, whether fast or slow. A child who has a physical disability may require additional time to get from one place to another. This need should be recognized and the child should be appropriately cued when transitions are about to occur. It is demeaning to a child's efforts, even insulting, to carry a child who, given enough time, could walk from snack to music.

APPLICATION OF SCHEDULING PRINCIPLES

Schedules vary. They are determined by the type of program, number of teachers, and number and type of children. Never should one early childhood program be ruled by another program's schedule. Neither should it be ruled by the big hand of the clock. It is *sequence of activities* and *allocations of ample time* for children's learning needs and interests that is the critical element. The actual number of minutes spent in stories or transitions or snack is irrelevant (Photo 14–13). The schedule of activities outlined below, and the accompanying clock

PHOTO 14–13 *The specific number of minutes spent in an activity is irrelevant.*

times, are *suggestions* only. (In full-day child-care settings, early morning, late afternoon, and mealtimes and naptimes all require special planning. The comments in each time slot and program activity suggest the potential learnings and relationships inherent in each activity.

SAMPLE DAILY SCHEDULE FOR A HALF-DAY PROGRAM

8:30 A.M. to 9:15 A.M. Arrival

The ideal arrangement is one in which a teacher receives children over an extended period of time. This allows the teacher opportunity to provide a brief health check, give personal greetings, and engage in a short conversation with each child and adult. As the parent leaves, the child can be given assistance in learning self-help skills as needed—using nose tissues, storing belongings, turning coat sleeves right-side out. Once the self-help/care routine is accomplished, the receiving teacher can plan with the child which learning centre he or she will work in first.

Arrival time is also a good time for letting a child know that the teacher has planned something special with that child in mind. Or, it may be that the teacher has set a requested material aside for the child's use, or has remembered to look up the answer to a question the child and teacher had pondered the preceding day. Daily exchanges such as these assure children that they are coming into a stable and caring environment where teachers see them, hear them, and respond to their individual needs and preferences.

8:30 A.M. to 9:45 A.M. Free Play-Discovery Learning

The amount of time each child spends in the first free play-discovery learning period will vary, depending on time of arrival. Children who arrive early often are ready to be among the first to start the transition to the next activity. Many programs find that this first period works well as an outdoor period. Children and teachers are saved one transition requiring undressing and dressing for outdoor play. Whether indoors or out, teachers should have arranged a variety of play and work options before children's arrival. Learning centres should be set up taking into consideration the range of difficulties within the group. In implementing a truly inclusive curriculum, teachers should plan learning opportunities in which all children can participate equally.

To promote large motor activities, for example, simple or complex mazes and obstacle courses can be set up to accommodate children on crutches, in a wheelchair, or on a "tummy board" (one child called it his *crawlagator!*). Such activities are fun for all, not just the child with motor problems. Art and "mark-making" activities can be done on plastic sheets on the floor to accommodate a child who may find it difficult to stand at an easel or sit at a table. Collaging can be done on sticky surfaces, such as the back side of MacTac. This allows a child who hasn't got the fine motor coordination for gluing to participate in collaging.

9:45 A.M. to 10:00 A.M. Transition

Restoring, or cleaning up, of activity areas by children (with teachers' help) is a major focus of transitions. Play materials need to be put back on shelves or in containers, wheel toys should be parked, dress-up clothes should be hung up or folded away. All children can help. Even so simple a task as holding a container for other children to put Lego blocks into is important for (for example) a child with cerebral palsy. Shared cleanup activities promote a sense of belonging. Shared cleanup also provides a way for children to learn about the social responsibilities inherent in community living. Children who restore play areas learn to respect materials and equipment. They also learn to take pleasure in leaving an attractive environment for other children to enjoy. As children finish their part of the cleanup they move at their own pace into self-help routines such as removing outdoor clothes, toileting, hand washing, and nose care (Photo 14–14). A mid-program snack usually follows.

10:00 A.M. to 10:20 A.M. Snack and Small-Group Interaction

Adults and children should eat *together* in small groups. Small groupings, with participating adults, provide children with needed assistance as they practise finger or spoon feeding, pouring, drinking, and using utensils. Snacktime is a good time for teachers to model everyday social skills. It also gives children unpressured opportunities to practise the courtesies that society requires of all: passing, sharing, polite requesting, and acknowledging.

Conversation, too, provides important opportunities for learning during snacktime. All children can be helped to participate. Even nonverbal children can join in with gestures and vocalizations. Though conversational activities appear to be spontaneous, many teachers find they need to come prepared with conversation *starters* or with specific concepts that children can be helped to develop as they

PHOTO 14-14 *In self-help/care routines, children should be allowed to move at their own pace.*

talk together. A teacher who starts a conversation with "Guess what I saw on my way to school this morning" is sure to elicit at least one response that other children can be helped to build upon.

10:20 A.M. to 10:50 A.M. Enriched Learning Opportunities

At this time the teacher has opportunities to introduce new interest areas and expand on learning opportunities set up earlier in the day. This can be done by adding a few new props to the dramatic play area; adding soap to the water in the water table or changing the colour of the water in it; placing new objects next to the scale; setting up a new art interest area; or putting out a new puzzle, game, or range of table toys. This is also a time when special activities such as cooking, group collages, and planting or nature projects might occur. Children should be allowed to choose activities according to their own preferences, as long as there is space available.

The following are examples of activities and materials that should be frequently available (two or three at a time) for young children:

- easel or mural painting, fingerpainting, and occasional specialty painting activities (see Mayesky, Neuman, and Wlodkowski 1990)
- crayons, chalk, "magic markers"
- potter's clay
- paste, paper, collage materials
- wood gluing, sewing and beading, mobiles, and stabiles

All children can learn to use these materials; some will need more prompting from the teacher, especially in the beginning.

> Multiply handicapped children can learn to work with purpose, with an end product in view. They discover that hands are tools for making objects. The sense of achievement is a giant step toward a form of independence. (Schattner 1971)

It should be noted that most developmentally appropriate learning opportunities enhance children's perceptual motor skills, support social interaction, stimulate the use of speech and language, and also may involve opportunities for problem solving. One hurdle faced by educators is that many early childhood programs have responded to public pressure for "learning" by "emphasizing academic skill development with paper-and-pencil activities that are developmentally inappropriate with young children" (Bredekamp 1987, 1). More appropriate learning activities are those that provide opportunities for classifying and categorizing, and stimulate the learning of language and concepts relevant to such tasks: *same as, different from, bigger than, in front of,* and so on.

Other goals include opportunities for children to begin to develop task-orientation skills (focusing on the job at hand) and a lengthening span of attention. These two skills, basic to all learning, can be acquired only if the cognitive activities are interesting and matched to each child's current skill levels. Children with behaviour and attention disorders or cognitive delays are in special need of activities related to task orientation and lengthening attention span. Like all other children, they, too, can develop these skills when provided with enjoyable tasks.

11:20 A.M. to 11:30 A.M. Transition

Children and teachers tidy up the room. Children needing help in going to the washroom can be given special attention and support at this time. Others use the toilet as needed.

11:30 A.M. to 12:00 Noon. Music, Rhythms, Stories, Departure

As children finish their discovery learning activities they gradually move into a large-group activity. The first part of this period can be a time for finger plays, songs, chants, and rhythmic activities such as jumping, rolling, and tiptoeing to music (Photo 14–15). Children with the shortest span of attention for large-group activities can be drawn off first to a small-group story. This process continues until two or three story groups are in progress and all children are engaged in a teacher-conducted story activity. As stories end, children and teachers can talk about what went on at school that day and what to look forward to on the next day of school or over the weekend. In many settings, music, stories, and departure time can be conducted outdoors when the weather is fair.

PHOTO 14–15 *Time for finger plays, songs, and rhythmic activities.*

11:50 A.M. to 12:00 Noon. Departure

Children leave the story groups, a few at a time, to go to their cubbies. Some children, those with developmental disabilities perhaps, need extra time or assistance. These children are intermixed in this staggered process so that the teacher's assistance can be divided effectively. As children put their outdoor clothing on, they greet the person who picks them up and say goodbye to the teacher who is supervising departures. The remaining two or three children may return to a story location or can use crayons at a nearby table for the few minutes before they are picked up.

(Note: In full-day child-care programs, the morning schedule should contain essentially the same format as indicated above, moving the time frames up to accommodate the earlier hours of arrival and the need to begin washing up and preparing for lunch at about 11:30 or 12:00. The full-day schedule also needs to include routines for washroom use, eating, preparing for naptime, and arising from naptime.)

SCHEDULED TIME FOR TEACHERS

Teachers need scheduled times to carry out their own responsibilities and to have planned breaks during each session. Such time is not a luxury; it is essential. When children are present, teacher's focus *must* be on teaching, *not* on preparing materials, *not* on cleaning up, *not* on discussing children's learning needs. A block of paid preparation time necessarily is scheduled before children arrive. Paints are mixed, teacher-structured activities are set up and positioned for use, the play yard is arranged. At the end of the session, teachers again need time for a final cleanup of each play area. Scheduled time for frequent, even though brief, staff meetings is also important. This can be most difficult to arrange in full-day programs, but it is not impossible. Here teachers discuss the events of immediate concern and the needs of individual children. Even the best of teachers are significantly less effective if they do not have scheduled, uninterrupted times to talk together about children's needs, staff–child relationships, and alterations in the physical setting or daily schedule. Failure to recognize the need for paid staff time for planning and preparation may well be one aspect of the current child-care staffing crisis described by Daniel (1990).

TRANSITIONS

In a quality program, a smooth transition appears effortless. The effortlessness is deceptive, however. It is the result of considerable planning, knowledge of each

PHOTO 14–16 *Children should be well focused, especially during routine and transition times.*

child, and attention to a multitude of details. Transitions should be used for teaching and for helping children learn about their own capabilities. At no time should children be waiting about idly or in rigidly enforced silence (Photo 14–16).

The underlying principle of smooth transitions is that each child moves individually, at his or her own pace, from one activity to the next. The individual differences among children provide the gradual movement between activities for the group as a whole. Different children, because they use materials with different levels of involvement, will finish cleanup at different times. Different children, because of different levels of self-help skills, will move through the cubby area routine and into discovery learning at different times. The different learning needs of children in different activities should prompt teachers to hold children for different lengths of time. Arrangements such as these are ideal for all children—for very young children, for children with developmental disabilities, and for normally developing and gifted children.

A developmentally appropriate curriculum cannot be carried out unless there is an adequate ratio of teachers to children. This is especially true in an inclusive early childhood program: the ratio of children to teachers must be increased as the number of children with developmental disabilities increases. NAEYC supports this position in the following statements:

> Implementation of developmentally appropriate early childhood programs requires limiting the size of the group and providing sufficient numbers of adults to provide individualized and age-appropriate care and education. (NAEYC 1985)

> Even the most well-qualified teacher cannot individualize instruction and adequately supervise too large a group of young children … Younger children require much smaller groups. Group size, and thus ratio of children to adults, should increase gradually through the primary grades. (Bredekamp 1987)

> There may be a problem in some provinces in which the size of the groups for young children is not legislated. In many of those provinces where legislation does exist, group size may be too large for successful inclusion of children with

special needs. The range of differences in group size for 4- and 5-year-olds varies, depending on the province or territory, from a maximum of 6 to a maximum of 30 children per group. (Childcare Resource and Research Unit 1993)

SUMMARY

Early childhood environments determine how well children learn and how well teachers teach. For children with developmental disabilities, a normal (least-restrictive) environment is the most suitable, with adaptations made for special needs. Teachers who provide a well-arranged learning environment communicate to children what it is that children can do in any given area. Children are less likely to transgress or behave inappropriately if the equipment is well prepared.

The environment should be planned in terms of the types of learning that go on throughout the program day: self-help/care skills, teacher-structured activities, and discovery learning. Teachers can arrange for activity areas that support the various kinds of learning in terms of six basic principles: safety, visibility, ease of movement, activity concentration, teachers' availability, and structured flexibility. Periodic assessment of all aspects of the environment is critical to advancing each child's development.

A daily schedule that is based on children's individual needs and differences furthers the benefits of the well-arranged classroom and play yard. Each segment of the daily schedule (in planned and predictable sequence) provides valuable opportunities for teaching and learning throughout the program day. All children are given advance notice when activity changes are scheduled; children with learning impairments often need extra advance warning and special help in dealing with departures from established routines. Regularly scheduled staff meetings, brief though they may be, allow teachers to teach more effectively.

Transitions are designed to enable children, from the most delayed to the most advanced, to move at their own pace between program activities. Transitions characterized by idle waiting about or rigidly enforced quiet are developmentally inappropriate.

STUDENT ACTIVITIES

1. Observe one child during free-play time in a preschool classroom. Track the pattern of the child's movement through activities over a 45-minute period of time. Indicate the activity areas in which the child was involved and the length of time spent in each, and list the areas the child did not approach.

2. Observe a preschool classroom and draw a rough sketch of the floor plan; indicate location of furnishings, activity areas, doors, and windows. Which areas will accommodate a child in a wheelchair, crutches, or walker? Which will not? Resketch the floor plan showing possible modifications that might better accommodate a child in a wheelchair.

3. Select any five activity areas in an early childhood program for 3- and 4-year-olds (music, easel painting, water play, to suggest a few). With three or four other students working with you as a teaching team, draw a basic plan for presenting these activities. Now decide among you what changes might be introduced into each structure to better serve both developmentally delayed children and gifted children.

4. Observe three different self-help routines in a child-care centre. Describe the strengths and weaknesses of each for developmentally disabled children according to the guidelines discussed in this chapter.

5. Draw up a daily schedule for a group of sixteen 4- and 5-year-olds who are in an inclusive full-day child-care program. Assuming three or four of these children have impaired motor skills and somewhat limited cognitive skills, indicate special schedule adaptations that might be needed.

REFERENCES

Bredekamp, S. 1987 *Developmentally Appropriate Practice in Early Childhood Programs Serving Children from Birth through Age 8.* Washington, D.C.: National Association for the Education of Young Children. Reprinted with permission from the National Association for the Education of Young Children.

Childcare Resource and Research Unit 1993 "Child Care Information Sheets: The Provinces and the Territories." Toronto: Childcare Resource and Research Unit, Centre for Urban and Community Studies, University of Toronto.

Daniel, J. 1990 "Child Care: An Endangered Industry." *Young Children* 45, no. 4: 23–26.

Gordon, A.M., and K.W. Browne 1996 *Beginnings and Beyond. Foundations in Early Childhood Education,* 4th ed. Albany, N.Y.: Delmar.

Harms, T. 1989 "Creating Environments for Growing and Learning." In A.M. Gordon and K.W. Browne. *Beginnings and Beyond: Foundations in Early Childhood Education,* 2nd ed. Albany, N.Y.: Delmar.

Harms, T., and R.M. Clifford 1983 *Early Childhood Environment Rating Scale.* New York: Teachers College Press.

Mayesky, M., D. Neuman, and R.J. Wlodkowski 1990 *Creative Activities for Young Children.* Albany, N.Y.: Delmar.

McWilliam, R.A., and C.J. Dunst 1985 "Preschool Assessment of the Classroom Environment," unpublished scale. Family, Infant, and Preschool Program, Western Carolina Center, Morganton, N.C.

NAEYC 1985 *Guidelines for Early Education Programs in Associate Degree Granting Institutions.* Washington, D.C.: National Association for the Education of Young Children.

Olds, A.R. 1979 "Designing Developmentally Optimal Classrooms for Children with Special Needs." In S.J. Meisels, ed. *Special Education and Development.* Baltimore: University Park Press.

Prescott, E., E. Jones, and S. Kritchevsky 1972 *Day Care as a Child Rearing Environment,* vol. 3. Washington, D.C.: National Association for the Education of Young Children.

Read, K.B., P. Gardner, and B. Mahler 1986 *Early Childhood Programs: A Laboratory for Human Relations.* New York: Holt, Rinehart and Winston.

Schattner, R. 1971 *An Early Childhood Curriculum for Multiply Handicapped Children.* New York: John Day.

Wolfensberger, W. 1972 *The Principle of Normalization in Human Services.* Toronto: National Institute on Mental Retardation.

CHAPTER 15

Facilitating Social Development

Objectives

After studying the material in this chapter, the student will be able to

- defend this statement: *The degree to which parents and caregivers respond appropriately to an infant's cues may be a major factor in determining that child's social development.*
- define social skills and explain their importance in the overall development of young children, especially children with developmental problems
- outline the steps or phases that infants and children go through in acquiring social skills; explain the importance of this knowledge to teachers in an inclusive/integrated setting
- describe the possible impact of a disability on early social development
- list at least 10 ways a teacher can help children with developmental delays learn appropriate play and social skills

INTRODUCTION

Social development depends on each individual acquiring a wide range of social skills. These are the many behaviours that help people live together in a family and in a society. These skills must be learned by all children: those with disabilities, those who are developing normally, as well as those described as gifted. How well they are learned depends on the quality of the interpersonal relationships in the child's everyday life. Only through interacting with others can infants and young children learn the social skills (as well as the accompanying language and intellectual skills) necessary for healthy development. Only through interacting with others can young children get feedback about their social competence.

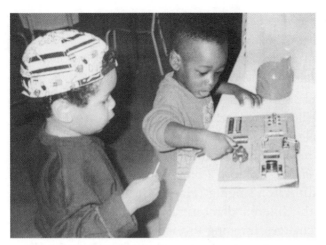

PHOTO 15–1 *Taking turns is an important early learning skill.*

Interpersonal relationships are reciprocal; that is, there is mutual responding or *turn-taking* (Photo 15–1). During the early months and years, social interactions depend on the child's ability to give and receive social messages. Children with developmental problems may fail to respond to social signals, or they may give too few appropriate signals. Either situation reduces feedback and may lead to negative responses; both situations will interfere with emerging social development. It is not unusual for the social delays in children with disabilities to become a greater problem than the problems associated with their primary disability (Bailey and Wolery 1989).

No child, simply because he or she has a developmental disability, should be excused from learning acceptable social skills. To exempt the child from this type of learning does the child a grave injustice. Normally developing children seem to acquire social skills spontaneously, or with only brief episodes of informal coaching. Children with developmental problems often need systematic help; appropriate social behaviours may have to be taught directly, over a considerable period of time. How teachers can help young children whose development differs from the norm acquire such a **repertoire** of behaviours is the focus of this chapter. First, however, social skills will be examined from a developmental perspective.

SOCIAL SKILLS AND OVERALL DEVELOPMENT

Though discussed as an independent topic, social skills are never truly separate from other areas of development. Each influences all others. The following example, typical of the social activities of normally developing 4-year-olds, illustrates the close interrelatedness of skills.

John ran to Aaron, who was sitting on the edge of the sandbox filling cake tins with sand.

John began: "Let's decorate cakes. Here's some decorations," and poured small plastic rings into Aaron's cupped hands. Aaron replied: "Too many," handing a few back. "That's plenty."

John smiled at Aaron and began alternating rings around the edge of his sand cake while singing "Now a blue one, now a yellow one."

Aaron stuck twigs into his sand cake and pulled a ring down over the top of each twig. Then he sang "Happy Birthday" several times, each time naming a different classmate.

A number of developmental skills can be identified in this play interaction. Both large and small motor skills are evident: running, pouring, catching, picking, and placing. Cognitive skills include arithmetic concepts of *some, too many,* and *plenty,* as well as colour recognition, naming colours, and understanding such concepts as *decorate* and *alternate* ("now a blue one, now a yellow one"). Memory was obvious, too, with Aaron singing "Happy Birthday" and recalling several classmates' names. Both children demonstrated good communication skills in the form of verbal exchanges, listening to each other, and smiling.

These developmental skills were in addition to, and blended with, high-level social skills such as

- each child initiating his own ideas;
- following suggestions from each other;
- sharing materials; and
- role playing (cake decorators).

PHOTO 15–2 *It is important that all children be helped to learn social skills.*

This exchange between two normally developing children shows the developmental complexities that work *for* some children but *against* others. In the John and Aaron episode, each child was helping the other to learn and each was spontaneously reinforcing the other for a variety of skills and responses. *Spontaneous* peer reinforcement may not always happen for children with developmental disabilities; instead, their poorly developed play skills often lead to rejection. A negative cycle can then be set in motion. A continuing lack of skills shuts out further opportunities to learn. Lack of learning opportunities results in little positive feedback. The combination sometimes sets up emotional reactions which, as noted a moment ago, may cause as much developmental interference as the disability itself. It is important, therefore, that young children with (and without) developmental problems be helped to learn *appropriate* social skills (Photo 15–2).

APPROPRIATE SOCIAL SKILLS: WHAT ARE THEY?

One definition of *appropriate social skills* is that they are *prescribed* ways of behaving: they are *expectations* of particular groups as to how group members will conduct themselves in private and in public. Prescriptions for what is socially appropriate vary from community to community and society to society. Variations exist even within the tight circle of home, early childhood centre, and neighbourhood. Confusing choices often result, especially for young children.

Examples:

Five-year-old Doug had learned that he could get almost anything he wanted from his parents and teenage brothers through his tantrums. The same behaviour in the neighbourhood and preschool did not pay off. Children taunted, "Crybaby, crybaby" and ran off leaving him shrieking.

Rebecca painted with obvious enjoyment during the first week of school. One day she began to cry, pointing to a small paint smudge on her sleeve. The teacher assured her it would wash out and that the apron protected most of her dress. Rebecca would not return to the easel, even on subsequent days. What emerged were confusing social expectations between home and school. Teachers had assured Rebecca that it was all right if paint got on clothing; at home, she was scolded if her "good school clothes got all dirty."

Lynn spent much of her time playing in the streets with older, aggressive children. There she learned to hit, run, dodge, grab, and kick, the social skills necessary to that particular street setting. In the preschool, these same behaviours were considered socially unacceptable. Lynn had to learn to restrain the aggressive behaviours at school but to keep them ever ready when playing in the street.

These examples, described by teachers, are from real life. They point out how difficult it is to specify what is appropriate. In each instance, children were exhibiting social skills relevant to given situations in their lives. Yet, they also were receiving contradictory signals about the inappropriateness of those same behaviours in another context. Most children learn to deal with such contradictions. They find ways to adapt their behaviour to the expectations of various situations (a social skill necessary, for all of us, at every life stage). Such adaptations tend to be more difficult for children with developmental problems. They are likely to have trouble learning to discriminate when a behaviour is appropriate and when it is inappropriate. It is not easy to understand, for example, why it is all right to brush one's hair over the bathroom sink but not over the kitchen sink.

Photo 15–3 *Children need to be able to trust and enjoy adults outside their immediate family.*

Rather than attempting to define a term like *social skills* it may be of greater value to list the various aspects of these skills. The major social skills to be learned during the early years relate to getting along with others:

- interacting with children and adults, in a variety of ways, at home and away from home

- trusting and enjoying known adults outside the immediate family (Photo 15–3)

- recognizing and protesting inappropriate advances from known or unknown adults within or outside the family

- attending to self-help/care needs at home and in public places with consideration for others

- sometimes initiating play ideas with children, at other times following other children's lead

- participating in group activities through listening, taking turns, and contributing to group effort

- sometimes putting aside individual needs and interests so the needs and interests of the group may be met

- working and playing independently as well as cooperatively; learning to be alone without feeling isolated or rejected

- using language as the powerful social tool it is for persuading, defending, reasoning, explaining, solving problems, and getting needs and preferences attended to

- acquiring attitudes of acceptance toward all types of individual differences

Acquiring Social Skills

Social skills are learned behaviours. Children's learning of a full range of social skills—*the socializing process*—cannot be forced or hurried. Mastering such skills is a major occupation of the developing child. Refinement of previously learned social skills and the learning of new ones continues throughout life (a sign of true maturity!).

TEMPERAMENT AND EMOTIONS

The development of social skills, as noted earlier, is influenced by home, school, and community expectations, and by the interpersonal relations within these environments. A child's set of emotional reactions, or more precisely, **temperament**, also exerts influence (Photo 15–4). Based on differing behavioural patterns and ways of responding, Thomas and Chess (1977) described three types of infants: *easy, difficult,* and *slow to warm up.*

Easy babies tend to be lively but not excessively so; they are fairly calm in their reactions to the unexpected and are open to new experiences such as trying out unfamiliar foods. They tend to be regular in their eating and sleeping habits. In general, they are happy and contented.

Difficult babies are likely to be irritable, easily upset, vigorously resistant to the unfamiliar. They cry more frequently and they cry in a way that grates on parents' and caregivers' ears (and nerves). Biological rhythms (eating, sleeping, and elimination patterns) are difficult to regulate; the child is often labelled as spoiled.

Slow-to-warm-up infants show few intense reactions, either positive or negative. They seldom are outright resistant to new experiences but neither are they eager to sample the unknown. For example, instead of fighting off a new food, they may simply not swallow it. They store it in one cheek or let it quietly slide out of their mouth. *Passive-resistant* is a term used to describe this type of behaviour.

PHOTO 15–4 *A child's temperament influences social development.*

These personality or temperament traits may have genetic linkage. However, this is difficult to demonstrate and also relatively unimportant. What is important is that babies respond differently to what may be similar circumstances (as when they are in the same infant-care program). These personal behaviour patterns appear to persist into childhood, affecting how others respond to a child. Parents and caregivers play a role in the persistence of personality traits. Behaviours that one caregiver reacts to as constituting a difficult temperament might not be perceived as at all difficult by another caregiver. That person might describe the child as an eager, active, happy-go-lucky runabout.

Granted that every child's social responses are influenced by temperament, the fact remains that all social behaviours are learned. They can be

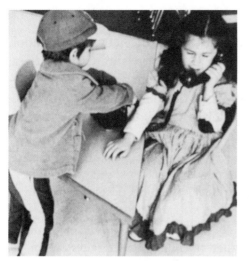

PHOTO 15–5 *Social skills are made up of observable behaviours.*

seen and heard and sometimes felt, as when one child pats or strikes another. Social skills are observable ways of behaving (Photo 15–5). Like all behaviours, they can be eliminated, strengthened, or modified. This is true even of those responses labelled *emotional*. These, too, can be eliminated, strengthened, and modified. Think about it. Is it not through their behaviours that we know children's emotional state? That we know if they are feeling good about themselves? Sympathetic toward others? Hostile? Generous? Fearful?

Picture the following:

- three children jumping on a jumping board, smiling and talking
- two children laughing while they divide cookies
- a 5-year-old running from a snarling dog
- two children walking together with arms entwined

Such behaviours provide specific clues as to which children are feeling happy, frightened, or loving. They provide clues, too, as to how well the children's social skills are developing. Each of the responses was *learned* through social interactions with the child's physical and interpersonal environment. By carefully observing children's behaviours (facial expressions, bodily postures, gestures, verbalizations) children's emotions can be recognized and dealt with in ways that strengthen both their emotional development and their social skills.

SOCIAL REINFORCEMENT

The development of appropriate social skills begins with infant bonding, attachment, and the establishment of basic trust. As the child matures, the further development of social skills depends almost entirely on the amount and type of social responsiveness available to the child when still young. All children need opportunities to interact with others in a give-and-take fashion. Most newborns *come equipped* with social behaviours that attract and hold the attention of significant adults. In the typical situation, the baby cries and someone comes and provides comfort. The baby is soothed and stops crying. The caregiver is pleased. This puts in motion a reciprocal system that is socially and mutually reinforcing for both infant and adult. Even the newborn is highly skilled at taking turns. Bee (1992) puts it this way:

PHOTO 15–6 *Infants soon learn that smiling makes good things happen.*

As early as the first days of life, the baby sucks in a "burst-pause" fashion. He sucks for awhile, pauses, sucks for awhile, pauses, and so on. Mother enters into this "conversation," too, often by jiggling the baby during the pauses. The conversation looks like this, suck, pause, jiggle, pause, suck, pause, jiggle, pause. The rhythm of the interaction is really very much like a conversation and seems to underlie many of the social encounters among people of all ages. The fascinating thing is that this rhythm, this turn-taking, can be seen in an infant one day old.

Adult Responsiveness

Social reinforcement, in the form of adult responsiveness, is a crucial factor in determining how well a child's social skills will develop. The following is a pertinent excerpt from a U.S. Department of Health and Human Services (1980, 11) pamphlet, *Infant Care*:

When your baby first smiles, you pay attention to him and smile back. When he smiles again, you smile back and pay attention to him again, and talk to him and cuddle him. He soon learns that when he smiles good things happen to him [Photo 15–6], and so he learns to do a lot of smiling when you are around. In just the same way, when you pay attention to his first cooing and gurgling sounds, your smile, your voice, and your fondling reward him. He coos and gurgles more and more frequently … The same holds true for all kinds of social behaviors in the infant and young child. When you respond to something your child does by giving attention, a smile, a kind word, or by fondling or joy, your baby will do that thing more and more frequently. If you ignore it, it will happen less and less.

Contingent Stimulation

The process of adult reinforcement is sometimes referred to as *contingent stimulation*. The degree to which parents, caregivers, and family members respond appropriately to the infant's cues may be a major factor in determining a child's development (Photo 15–7). As noted in Chapter 11, when there is at least partially contingent stimulation (responding) from significant adults, infants

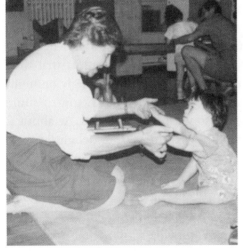

PHOTO 15–7 *Contingent social stimulation facilitates an infant's development in all areas.*

and young children develop better. Language skills develop earlier and children have more advanced cognitive abilities, greater self-esteem, and more durable attachments.

THE IMPACT OF DEVELOPMENTAL PROBLEMS

A potentially responsive early environment cannot *guarantee* that a child will develop necessary and appropriate social skills. Through no fault of parents or caregivers, children with developmental problems often are deprived of stimulation and reinforcement because of their own limitations. Consider these examples:

1. An infant who is deaf cannot hear the crooning, loving sounds that its mother makes during bathing, dressing, and feeding routines. Thus, the infant does not make the lively responses typical of an infant with normal hearing. The infant's lack of responsiveness reduces the mother's efforts to interact. To further compound the situation, an infant's hearing loss often goes undetected during the developmentally crucial early months. Not realizing that her infant has an impairment, the mother may take the infant's lack of interest in her conversation as rejection; unwittingly, she may respond less positively to the child as well as less often. Social reciprocity, the give and take of the system, goes awry. This puts the child's social development as well as cognitive and language development at risk.

2. Infants who are blind also are at high risk for poorly developed social skills. According to Fraiberg (1974), they do not engage in the **mutual gaze** interactions that appear to be crucial to the attachment process between parent and child. Mothers of babies who are blind often report that they feel rejected when their infants do not look at them. Interestingly enough, Fraiberg noted that 4-week-old babies who are blind did begin to smile just as the sighted babies did. But then, something happened. At about 2 months, when sighted babies were smiling with increasing delight at their mother's face, the babies with visual impairment were smiling less frequently and more tentatively. Gradually, the mothers in Fraiberg's studies on infant blindness seemed to withdraw psychologically from their babies, even though they continued to give physical care.

These examples do not imply that children with developmental disabilities cannot learn appropriate social skills. Quite the contrary: they can and do. With the help of relevant members of the interdisciplinary team, parents learn to recognize in their infants alternative kinds of signalling and responding behaviours.

An infant who is blind, for example, may begin to thrash about at the sound of the mother's approaching footsteps. The child's mother comes to value this response in the same way she would value a welcoming smile from a sighted infant. Another example: the infant who is deaf may *snuggle* in when picked up. The mother learns to respond by stroking the child rhythmically—better yet, by stroking *and* singing or crooning. Though the baby does not hear the singing, it usually gives pleasure to the mother. The singing also may transmit subtle vibrations from mother's chest or throat that further stimulate the infant's responsiveness.

Overstimulation and overresponding may also interfere with an infant's ability to make use of a responsive environment. Overstimulation often occurs among fragile infants—those who are premature or of very low birth weight. They are easily overloaded with (what are for them) too many signals coming in from the environment. Their underdeveloped nervous systems simply cannot handle the *rush* and so the infant *shuts down*, withdraws, may become rigid, and even rejecting of loving pats and cuddling. In a sense, the infant is "unavailable to its environment, becoming unable to obtain information or give feedback and, in turn, causing the parents and other caregivers to feel less competent and effective" (Bennett 1990, 36). The opposite is true of the overresponding infant. In some instances, an infant with a central nervous system (CNS) disorder, for example, may have an involuntary but rigid arm extension when attempting to turn its head into nursing position. The infant's strong-arming may be perceived by the parent or caregiver as rejection or obstinacy, a reaction that interferes with establishing a warm relationship (Taft 1981).

These illustrations point out, once again, the need to identify a developmental problem as early in infancy as possible. Early identification, followed by interdisciplinary intervention for infant and family, is a key factor in preventing other problems (insecure attachment, for example) that invariably compound the original problem for the child who has a disability.

SOCIAL SKILLS IN SEQUENCE

In inclusive programs, teachers will encounter children who are functioning at many levels of social competence. To work effectively with these children, some of whom will have developmental problems and others who will not, teachers must have a thorough understanding of the sequence of social development during the early years.

During the first year of life, infants' social responding is directed to parents, brothers and sisters, grandparents, and to all frequent and regular caregivers. If all goes well, strong **affective** bonds are established between the infant and significant individuals in the infant's life. Somewhere in the middle of this period a child may begin to show **separation protest** and then fear of strangers. The stranger-anxiety may last until 18 months or so. Generally speaking, this shyness disappears of its own accord if the child is not unduly pressured. Even so, during this reluctant period, infants appear to be somewhat interested in outsiders and to have moments of responsiveness to strangers. From the safety of the grocery cart in the supermarket or the pack on father's back, many babies will smile at a smiling stranger. From the security of a highchair in the restaurant, infants often follow each other with their eyes. They even laugh at each other's antics. Hammering on the highchair tray or throwing spoons to the floor appears to be a hilarious and mutually enjoyable pastime for a pair of infants, total strangers though they may be.

Photo 15–8 *Early intervention programs offer many types of experiences for young children.*

The Role of Early Learning Programs

Infant, toddler, and preschool programs play a crucial role in the development of appropriate social skills (Photo 15–8). Opportunities to learn social skills should be available throughout the day in the varied activities that teachers present and the ways teachers present them during self-help/care routines, teacher-structured activities, and free play-discovery learning activities. Toddlers, for example, need many opportunities to gradually gain the skills required for being a member of a group. Therefore, a group story time should be flexible and short, involving only brief periods of sitting in a loosely structured group. Group time for toddlers should be flexible, allowing them to participate spontaneously.

Older preschool children, on the other hand, need to begin to learn how to identify with a group: sitting quietly when someone is talking and following directions given to the group. At the same time they need to learn how to function as individuals within a group by making contributions of general interest and by practising ways of interrupting tactfully. School-aged children, who have learned group membership skills, need help with finding ways to organize and influence group activities. They also need to learn ways of responding in positive ways to the ideas and suggestions of others, both when agreeing and disagreeing. These patterns in the development of social skills can be guidelines as teachers work with all types of children in the integrated setting.

PLAY

Through play, young children become interested in each other. At first, they do not see each other as personalities or playmates. A fellow 18-month-old, for example, is something to be pushed or poked, prodded or ignored. It is not unusual to see one toddler shove a doll buggy directly into another toddler. It is as if the first child regards the other as just one more obstacle to be gotten out of the way. When the second child falls down and cries, the first child may look surprised, appearing not to connect the two events, the pushing down and the crying.

A next step (referred to as *parallel play*) in the development of early social skills comes out of interest in the same materials. Often this leads to shrieks of "Mine!" as each child tries to hang on to the same toy. The following is an amusing example of evolving social skills centred on the use of the same play materials:

PHOTO 15–9 *One stage in social development is to focus on materials rather than on other children.*

Two boys, just under 2 years of age, were in the housekeeping area. One child was busily taking cups and plates from the cupboard and putting them on the table. The other child was just as busy, taking them off the table and returning them to the cupboard. It took several alternating trips back and forth before either noticed they were at cross purposes. The discovery led to mutual fury and clamour: "Mine! Mine! Mine!", almost in unison.

A next stage (known as *associative play*) continues to focus on materials and equipment rather than on other children (Photo 15–9). There is, however, some independent *interacting* on common projects such as raking leaves, heaping them into piles, and hauling them off in separate wagons. At this stage young children also begin to run, jump, climb, and ride wheel toys in small packs. These spontaneous groupings seem to be based on common activities rather than on friendship. Then comes a cooperative stage: children actually play together and engage fairly regularly in a give and take of materials and ideas.

Cooperative play leads into the next higher order of social skills, that of forming more or less durable friendships. Other children now are valued both as personalities and as companions in play. Friends are preferred playmates and are first on the birthday invitation list. Friends are also to quarrel with, to make up with, and to threaten not to invite to your birthday party.

The Importance of Play

Play is the major avenue for early learning of every kind. Even in infancy, most children seem to play spontaneously and apparently effortlessly. In play-oriented early childhood programs, children appear to be self-propelled as they move through the curriculum. They learn new skills and practise them in the course of self-initiated play activities. They participate in group activities and join eagerly in teacher-initiated play opportunities. Almost every skill that children master is mastered through play.

GUIDED PLAY

Children with developmental disabilities may need more adult support in learning how to play. The play of children with hearing impairments is less social and more solitary than that of children who are hearing normally. However, children with a severe hearing loss, even those with serious language deficits, have been reported as having imaginary playmates (Mogford 1977). As for children with severe visual impairments, Rogers and Puchalski (1984) report significant delays in their symbolic play (make-believe, pretend, using one object to represent another—as when a doll blanket becomes a magic cape). Children with autistic behaviours or limited cognitive skills also tend to be lacking in symbolic play skills. The deficit may lead to inappropriate use of materials such as hammering the cookie cutters with the rolling pin or breaking the crayons into little pieces.

Photo 15–10 *Children with developmental disabilities have fewer play skills.*

In general, children with developmental disabilities have fewer play skills (Photo 15–10). Often they hang back, not knowing how to get into other children's play. Or, they try to gain entry in inappropriate ways—for example, crashing a truck into housekeeping play—which leads to rejection. It is essential, therefore, that children who do not know how to play be taught. Teaching children to play may seem contrary to tradition. Yet, no child should be deprived of this powerful avenue for learning and the many enjoyable experiences that come with it.

Strategies for teaching and supporting the development of play skills include the following:

1. physically guiding the child to a play activity and helping him or her to settle in

2. orienting the child toward the material or equipment and handing the material to the child to establish physical contact

3. putting a clothespin (or some other object) into the child's hand, and moving the hand so that it is directly above the container into which the object is to be placed

4. verbalizing to the child what he or she is doing: "You have a clothespin in your hand. You can drop it in the can."

5. rejoicing over the smallest accomplishments: "Look at that!" or "Did you hear that! You dropped the clothespin in the can." (In the beginning it does not matter that the child is involved only because the teacher's hand is around the child's hand, manually shaping the child's response.)

6. arranging for the child to be near other children in a given activity, thereby enabling the teacher to point out and describe what other children are doing and so begin to promote imitation (Photo 15–11)

PHOTO 15–11 *Arranging for a child to work or play near another child facilitates social development.*

7. gradually helping other children join in activities, once the child has acquired a semblance of a play skill (two children might drop clothespins into the same can)

8. providing social reinforcement for the play: "It looks as if *you two* are going to fill that can full of clothespins!"

9. moving the child slowly but steadily toward group play by building small groups of two, then three *nonthreatening* children who participate with the child with the developmental problems in simple play activities such as tossing beanbags into a box

(For more in-depth information on factors affecting peer interactions of children with disabilities, see Guralnick 1990.)

As a child with a developmental disability begins to play more spontaneously, teachers continue their assistance, but in a less directive fashion. For example, when helping a group of children decide where to play after music time, the teacher reviews the options for each child. The child with the developmental problem is helped to choose after several other children have made their choices. Because the child has heard the choices reviewed several times and has heard several children choosing, making a choice becomes easier. It is helpful, too, for the teacher to pair the child who has a special need with another child who has chosen the same activity. This provides a good model for the less skilled child both in locating the activity and in getting off to a good start.

Activities must be planned carefully so that children with developmental problems can experience maximum success. When a child with a severe visual problem is participating in an art activity, the teacher might describe and physically help the child locate materials by guiding his or her hand:

"Here is the big circle to paste the little circles on. The little circles are here in the basket. Here is the paste, by your right hand. The sponge to wipe your fingers on is next to it. Corliss is working across the table from you." (This promotes the activity's social aspect.)

Along with helping the child with developmental problems, teachers also need to help all children learn to be explicit about what they are doing in certain situations. For example, it can be disconcerting for a child who cannot see to have materials moved from the rehearsed location. Yet telling the other children not to touch his or her materials may cast a negative shadow on the child who has a special need. Instead, children can be taught the simple social skill, the courtesy (due all children) of stating what they are doing whenever they use or change another person's materials: "Kelly, I need some of your paste. I'm going to move it over here [guiding Kelly's hand] so we can share, okay?"

Gentle Insistence

Not all children with developmental problems are eager to play, nor do they want to be taught to play; they may even avoid play materials and would-be playmates (Photo 15–12). These are the children who sometimes need to be gently pushed (perhaps pressured a bit) just to get them to try a play activity that teachers know will be of developmental benefit to them.

Example:

Jolene was a somewhat solitary 3-year-old with cerebral palsy. An instructional objective written into her IPP by the interdisciplinary team was that Jolene learn to ride a tricycle. The physical therapist adapted a tricycle by adding a trunk support and stirrups. Jolene, however, would not get on. Teachers' coaxing intensified her resistance until just the sight of the tricycle set her to crying. The teachers were ready to give up—but not the physical

Photo 15–12 *Some children may avoid playing with other children.*

therapist, who impressed on them the therapeutic value of tricycle riding for this particular child. The therapist maintained that this preschool treatment would promote more general development, as well as motor coordination, than any number of clinic sessions.

After talking it over with Jolene's parents, a plan was agreed on: one teacher would lift Jolene onto the tricycle and support (and comfort) her while the therapist put Jolene's feet in the stirrups and pulled the vehicle from the front. This they did, with Jolene crying louder and louder at first. The teacher continued to support her physically and to comfort her while the therapist moved the tricycle gently forward. Gradually, Jolene quieted.

Within a few days she stopped resisting the riding sessions. Furthermore, and much to the teachers' relief, she appeared to be enjoying the sessions. Six weeks later, Jolene was riding her specially fitted tricycle independently, in the company of other children.

Giving in to Jolene's anxieties (as well as the teachers') would have been to deprive Jolene of learning a play skill central to both her mobility and her social development.

INCIDENTAL SOCIAL LEARNING

As in the above instance, there are times when it is not only appropriate but even urgent to teach play skills directly. Most of the time, however, teachers can promote social interactions fairly easily by being alert to what goes on naturally among children. More frequently than we tend to realize, brief, positive interactions occur between children with and without developmental disabilities: smiling, handing materials, moving aside, helping to pick up the pieces of a dropped puzzle, and so on. Teachers can quietly comment about these commonplace interactions: "Martin, when you held the door open for Corey it was easy for him to get his wheelchair through. See how he is smiling at you?"

When the teacher makes similar comments to Corey, both children are introduced to a higher level of socialization. The result may be interaction between the two (see Chapter 10).

Children's concern or anxiety about another child's disability also offers opportunities for incidental social learning. A teacher may notice a child looking obliquely at the black patch over another child's eye; or witness one child showing reluctance to hold another child's malformed hand; or overhear a child expressing fear about *catching* the paralysis of the child in a wheelchair. The children's concerns are genuine, and not to be shushed or ignored. They provide opportunities for teachers to promote social learning and interactions. Often the teacher and the child with the disability can respond together. Using the eye patch case as an example, the teacher might first acknowledge the one child's concern and then help the second child explain. If the child with the eye problem is not at that verbal stage, the teacher can explain and ask for the child's corroboration (Photo 15–13). "The doctor put the patch on one eye so your other eye can learn to see better, right?" The explanation can be expanded further, depending on the interest and comfort level of both children. The teacher should always work to reassure the concerned child that the disability is not catching and that there are many, many things the other child can do. Often the two children can be guided into a joint activity at that point.

Photo 15–13 *Teachers should acknowledge a child's concern over another child's eye patch.*

A child's first tentative steps toward joining a play situation is another form of incidental social learning that teachers need to note and reinforce. The child who stands and watches may be nearly ready to interact. A teacher might watch with the child for a moment or two at a time, while commenting on the activity: "It looks as if Bart is making cookies and Cami's making a pie." Another time, sensing the child's readiness, the teacher might help the child actually get into play: "Matt is bringing more cookie cutters for everybody to use." The teacher also can prompt the other children directly or indirectly.

Example:

> *Josh, a child with Down syndrome, had a drum in his hand but was standing apart from a small group of children who were experimenting with rhythm instruments. Teacher: "It*

sounds as though you need a drummer in your band." (pause) Teacher: "You could ask Josh. He has a drum." If Josh joined in, the teacher could then provide reinforcement to all, as a group: "What a good band! Mary and Meg and Fouad and Josh and Karen, your music sounds really good." (It is best not to make specific mention of the children having invited Josh into the group; this could make Josh stand out unnecessarily as being so different as to need special treatment.)

Incidental social learnings can be expanded even further through play activities already in progress. Teachers need to reinforce the interaction, but subtly, to avoid distracting either child. Depending on the situation the teacher might

- move closer, kneel down, watch with interest, but avoid eye contact to keep from interrupting the children's mutual focus;
- smile and nod if either child turns toward the teacher, but while keeping the teacher's focus on the activity, not the child;
- bring additional materials to extend the play, placing them close to the activity (with or without comment, depending on the situation); and
- make encouraging comments that further promote joint effort: "Missy and Sam, you are building a long, long road. It looks as if it's going to go all the way to the gate!"

Facilitating Affection and Friendship

Teachers can promote positive social interactions between children with disabilities and those without disabilities through *affection* or *friendship* training (McEvoy, Twardosz, and Bishop 1990). These researchers suggest that group games, songs, and rhythmic activities can be adapted to promote interaction. In such activities as the *Hokey Pokey, If You're Happy and You Know It,* or *The Farmer in the Dell,* teachers can readily change the words to promote both physical and verbal exchanges as when the farmer *hugs* his wife (Brown, Raglund, and Bishop [1989] published a manual that describes how to adapt typical songs and games to promote social interactions).

Twardosz and her colleagues (1983) offer three reasons to explain the effectiveness of the affection procedure in promoting social interactions between children with special needs and those without. One is the pairing of two children of differing abilities in a pleasurable experience. A second has to do with desensitization—children getting used to each other and inevitably less wary of differences. And the third, children are given opportunities to practise affectionate behaviours in a nonthreatening and supportive situation.

PHOTO 15–14 *Sharing and turn-taking is the foundation for good play exchanges between children.*

SHARING AND TURN-TAKING

Sharing and taking turns are the foundation for good play exchanges between children (Photo 15–14). Yet these skills are the most difficult to learn. Why? Because they involve *giving up something;* and giving up anything is contrary to the young child's perfectly normal **egocentric** view of the world. As noted earlier, "Mine! Mine! Mine!" is the clarion call of every healthy child at one stage of development (at least in our country). With adult support, patience, and many unpressured opportunities to learn, most children eventually cooperate when a teacher says: "Mary, two more turns around the driveway and then its Sara's turn." The teacher can say this in many different ways to each child, over the weeks and months: "Sara, watch. Mary is going around the driveway two more times; then it will be your turn. Let's count." Or, "Mary, Sara has waited a long, long time for the tricycle you were riding, so she gets a long turn, too. I'll call you when she's through."

Gradually reducing the amount of available material is another way to teach sharing. As always, it is the teacher who makes it happen. Conflict among children is avoided when the teacher plans such a step carefully, monitors the situation, and helps children work it through.

Examples:

A teacher might put out fewer but larger portions of playdough to encourage children to divide their dough with latecomers to the activity. With the teacher's help, some children (certainly not all) will be able to break off a part of their dough; when two or three children do this, and the newcomer has an adequate amount to work with, the teacher can then reinforce the act of sharing. A spinoff is that children who did the sharing have provided good models for the children not yet able to share.

Several individual baskets of coloured wooden cubes might be poured into one larger basket. The children must then share common but plentiful material. Again, the teacher must be there to teach, partly by assuring the children there is plenty for all. If one child is accused of taking more than his or her share, the teacher might suggest that each child take no more than five cubes at a time (thus teaching counting, concurrently).

A child who has great difficulty sharing may be put in charge of a plentiful but uncontested material, perhaps tickets for snacks, or for a "train ride" (chairs lined up), or tickets "just because." The tickets may be nothing more than a quantity of small squares of coloured paper—irresistible, nonetheless, to most young children. As the child passes out the tickets, the teacher can comment what a good job he or she is doing of giving away tickets, but remarking also: "You have a lot left."

It is the responsibility of the teacher to promote and respond to friendly interactions between two children, thereby making spontaneous sharing somewhat easier. When two children decide to work on a puzzle together, the teacher might reinforce the friendly interaction by sitting down briefly and watching the children work. When two children are using a wagon together, the teacher may spend some time pulling them around. Teachers can also point out situations that involve friendly interactions: "Martha and Jay, you really have a long train now that you have hitched all your cars together." In addition, teachers help children wait for a turn or a material by offering alternates until the preferred material is available.

Self-Assertion

The problem may be the reverse with some children. They may give up too easily or fail to defend themselves or their possessions. All children need to learn to stand up for their rights. It is especially important that teachers find ways to help children who have disabilities fend for themselves; otherwise, some may resort to trading on their disability to get what they want ("You shouldn't take my doll because I can't walk as good as you").

The following is an example of how a teacher might help a child with severely limited vision assert her rights:

Five-year-old Lisa, blind since birth, was playing with an interlocking floor train. Bart took one of her cars. Lisa, touching her train, realized a car was missing. She began to rock back and forth, whining and poking at her eyes. The teacher said, "Lisa, Bart has your car. Tell him to give it back." The teacher turned to Bart: "That car is Lisa's. Be sure to hand it back when she asks you for it." By not retrieving the car, the teacher helped both children: Lisa, to learn about the rights of possession; Bart, to recognize that all children have rights that are to be respected.

MATERIALS AND EQUIPMENT

The materials and equipment available to children greatly influence their learning of social skills. Paints, crayons, and scissors, for example, are most commonly used in nonsocial but constructive play activities (Rubin and Howe 1985).

Materials that have proven to be good socializers include
- housekeeping and dress-up play materials;
- mural-painting and collage-pasting materials (several children work on the same piece of long paper);
- unit blocks and large hollow blocks;
- trucks, cars, and airplanes;
- Lotto and other simple board games;
- musical instruments; and
- puppets.

When small groups gather, there need to be sufficient materials to go around, thus inviting each child's participation. It is also a good idea to have some duplicate materials. A child with a developmental problem then has the opportunity to use the same material as another child and so learn appropriate usage through imitation. On the other hand, too much or too many different materials tends to promote solitary play. For example, a wheel toy for every child defeats a major goal of most programs—that of promoting sharing and turn-taking. A practical ratio is about one wheel toy to every three or four children; all kinds of inventive doubling-up games and cooperative ventures can be the result, such as wagon and tricycle trains.

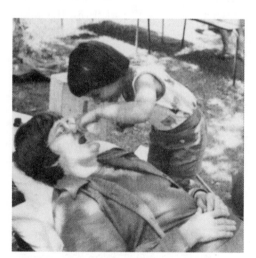

Photo 15–15 *Young children learn many things by watching other children and adults.*

Imitation and Modelling

Young children learn many behaviours and skills by watching other children and adults (Photo 15–15). Using these observations, they imitate what they have seen. For this reason, adult behaviour in interacting with, and in the presence of, children is very influential in determining the behaviours and attitudes a child will develop. Teachers of young children who model acceptance of children with special needs are helping shape patterns of acceptance within their early childhood group. Furthermore, providing children who have developmental problems with models for appropriate behaviours, especially social behaviours, supports a major argument in favour of inclusion. It must be stressed, however, that the inclusion of all children does not automatically lead to their learning appropriate play behaviours and social skills. From the start of the integration movement it has been apparent that *spontaneous* social interactions among children, with and without developmental problems, occur infrequently (Allen, Haring, and Hayden 1970). Teachers play a major role in promoting interaction. They *make it happen* by

- arranging the environment so as to ensure interactions between disabled and nondisabled children;
- reinforcing children, in general, for playing together; and
- reinforcing children with developmental problems when they imitate appropriate behaviours.

Each of these practices is discussed in detail in various sections of the text. Here let it be stressed that if children with disabilities are to learn from other children, they must be involved in a wide range of play activities. Once again, the teachers, through *modelling, guiding, responding,* and *developing activities* designed specifically to facilitate play interactions through small-group experiences, play a major role in supporting the development of social skills. Such activities might include

- pasting projects (collage), where children perhaps decorate a big carton for storing sand toys;
- a giant-size pegboard, with children taking turns putting in pegs from their own baskets; and
- a big picture book to look at together, each child pointing to a preselected character when it appears (more verbal children can tell what their character is doing).

At times, teachers may decide which children should play together in which activities. This ensures the inclusion of a child with disabilities in an activity with children best suited to that child's skill levels. The grouping can be done on the basis of mutual interests, temperament, or abilities. Wagon trains, mentioned earlier (several wagons and tricycles hitched together in separate pairs) can be introduced. This wagon-riding game (and many others that teachers can devise) allows a child who cannot walk, the excitement and enjoyment of being involved—perhaps sharing a wagon ride with a normally developing child. The child with the disability is an integral part of a spirited outdoor social activity. A rocking boat also promotes closeness and interaction as children synchronize their efforts to make it rock. A note of caution: Children who are just beginning to interact with other children usually should not be paired with overly rambunctious children.

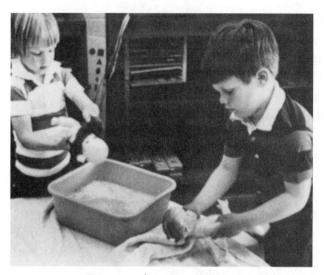

PHOTO 15–16 *Discovery learning activities provide social learning experiences.*

Free play-discovery learning periods are especially good times for promoting social learning through imitation and modelling (Photo 15–16). Teachers need to provide several interest centres and several attractive activities where interaction is almost automatic: the water table, the dough table, a simple cooking experience. Easily conducted science and math experiences promote interactions, too—for example, when a few children go into the yard together to pick up leaves to sort by size, type, or colour into baskets. The key issue is that *interactions occur and are pleasurable* for both the normally developing children and children with developmental problems. "Play experiences that are fun and enjoyable are likely to lead to a happier and more satisfying peer relationship" (Li 1983).

Peer Tutoring

Peer tutoring is the act of one child *modelling for and helping* another child to complete a task successfully. As discussed in Chapter 1, children who are nondisabled also may act occasionally as teachers for children with disabilities. Sometimes these peer tutoring episodes occur spontaneously, as when

- one child helps another to rearrange and separate his or her fingers when putting on mittens;
- a child indicates which cube goes where when two children happen to be involved in sorting colour cubes for storage; and
- another child at the table shows the child pouring from a pitcher how to steady it with the other hand so as to pour slowly and prevent the juice from overflowing the cup.

Teachers also can plan child-teaching-child events. Such peer-teaching episodes are appropriate to any part of the program:

- At music, two similar instruments might be provided, with the normally developing child designated to help the child with deafness recognize when and with what force to join in.

- During cognitive learning activities, the teacher could have two children work together, asking the sighted child to help the child who is visually impaired learn to put the wooden shapes into a form board.
- During free play-discovery learning a teacher might ask a child with language limitations to show a child wearing a prosthesis how to make a tunnel "just like yours."

In every instance, teachers should pair children carefully so as to ensure an appropriate match of skills and temperament. It is important that the child with a disability and the nondisability child enjoy and benefit from the interaction. Never should either child feel burdened; never should either child's learning opportunities in any other area be curtailed. When carefully managed, peer tutoring should be of benefit to both children. The child with developmental problems has the opportunity to learn through play from someone who is a master at play—another child. The peer-tutor model practises and refines his or her own developing skills and learns a new and higher-order social skill, that of teaching or imparting knowledge. Hartup (1983) suggests even greater gains: the tutor gains in self-esteem because of the increased status that comes with being teacher. The tutor also gains in sensitivity, in that a certain amount of nurturing is required when teaching a less able peer. Furthermore, it appears that child tutors undergo positive behavioural and attitudinal changes toward the children with disabilities who are being tutored (Franca et al., 1990).

PHOTO 15–17 *The rules apply to all children: No child is allowed to crash wheel toys into others.*

Optimal Standards for Play

Children who are developing normally have the ability to be good models for the simple, everyday, acceptable play behaviours expected of children in an early childhood program. Appropriate use of materials and equipment is one example. *All children* need to learn to use community property responsibly. *No child* can be allowed to paint on the walls, crash a tricycle repeatedly (Photo 15–17), deface books, or waste materials. It is especially important for children with developmental problems to learn respect for materials and equipment, and to learn it in the company of other children, whenever possible. Otherwise, they may be viewed as unwanted playmates, disrupters of play activities, people to be disliked or avoided. Let it be stressed, once again, that classroom rules (whatever they may be) apply to *all* children. There should be no double standards. To allow any child to repeatedly and unduly disturb or distress other children does the disturbing child a grave injustice. He or she is likely to be shunned, disliked, and excluded from play activities. Exclusion from play activities and play models closes the major avenue a teacher has for helping children learn appropriate social skills.

SUMMARY

Children with developmental delays and disabilities, like all young children, need to learn how to get along with others. To do this, they must learn appropriate social skills. Such learning may be more difficult for children with developmental problems. Like all other skills, social skills are dependent on every other area of development, one or more of which may be impaired in some children. Notwithstanding, children of all developmental levels can and do master basic social skills as prescribed by their respective families, schools, and communities.

Even though affected by each child's temperament, all social skills are learned behaviours. They depend largely on reciprocal responsiveness between the child and significant adults, starting with the first hours and days of life. However, children with certain developmental disabilities may not be able to engage in the give and take typical of normally developing children. For them, the entire socialization process may go awry unless special help is provided for them and their family by relevant members of the child's IPP team. Enrollment in an inclusive early childhood program can help too, to advance social skills learning for children with developmental problems.

Play is a major medium in early learning, especially in learning social skills. Not all children know how to play; some may even be reluctant to try. In such instances, the children should be taught, using firm but gentle insistence if need be. This ensures that all children have both the fun and the incidental learning opportunities that are available only in play.

Learning social skills through imitating normally developing children is a major argument in favour of inclusion. For modelling to take place, children with disabilities and those without must interact. Teachers should promote interactions among all types of children by arranging both the physical and the social environments. They also should encourage peer tutoring (modelling and helping), sometimes planned in advance, more often incidental in occurrence. Both the normally developing child and the child with developmental problems can benefit from peer tutoring.

STUDENT ACTIVITIES

1. Observe in a child-care centre that has a wide age range, from toddlers to kindergarten-age children, if possible. Record anecdotal notes (Chapter 11) on three different children at three different age levels, displaying three different but developmentally appropriate social skills; during your observation, note any inappropriate play skills you see. Explain why you consider them inappropriate.

2. Visit a preschool, public school, or child-care centre that includes children with developmental disabilities. Observe for 30 minutes one of the children who has a disability. Record the social skills the child displays; analyze your observations and list the social skills you feel the child lacks in terms of his or her age and developmental level.

3. While making either of the above observations, list the indoor and outdoor play materials and equipment that seem to promote the most and the best cooperative play. Note in particular if children with developmental problems are using the equipment. If not, try to decide why not.

4. Work with another student or two as a teaching team and make plans as to the kinds of activities or materials you might present to promote sharing among 3-year-olds, some of whom have a developmental delay.

5. Assume you are working with a 4-year-old with a cognitive delay and few play skills. You feel it is important that this child learn to play with blocks. How might you go about teaching block play to this child? Be specific. Select a classmate to be the child and demonstrate your teaching strategies in class. How might you include another child to help in teaching block play? Demonstrate.

REFERENCES

Allen, K.E., N.G. Haring, and A.H. Hayden 1970 *Building Social Skills in the Preschool Child*. Seattle: Media Services, Child Development and Mental Retardation Center, University of Washington. Film.

Bailey, D.B., and M. Wolery 1989 *Assessing Infants and Preschoolers with Handicaps*. Columbus, Ohio: Charles E. Merrill.

Bee, H. 1992 *The Developing Child*. New York: Holt, Rinehart & Winston.

Bennett, F.C. 1990 "Recent Advances in Developmental Intervention for Biologically Vulnerable Infants." *Infants and Young Children* 3, no. 1: 33–40.

Brown, W.H., E.U. Raglund, and N. Bishop 1989 *A Socialization Curriculum for Preschool Programs that Integrate Children with Handicaps.* Nashville, TN: Vanderbilt University.

Department of Health and Human Services 1980 *Infant Care.* DHHS Publication No. (ODDS) 80-30015. Washington, D.C.: U.S. Government Printing Office.

Fraiberg, S. 1974 "Blind Infants and Their Mothers: An Examination of the Sign System." In M.L. Lewis and L.A. Rosenblum, eds. *The Effect of the Infant on Its Caregiver.* New York: Wiley.

Franca, V.M., M.M. Kerr, A.L. Reitz, and D. Lambert 1990 "Peer Tutoring among Behaviorally Disordered Students: Academic and Social Benefits to the Tutor and Tutee." *Education and Treatment of Children* 13, no. 2: 109–28.

Guralnick, M. 1990 "Social Competence and Early Intervention." *Journal of Early Intervention* 14, no. 1: 3–14.

Hartup, W.W. 1983 "Peer Relations." In P.H. Mussen and E.M. Hetherington, eds. *Carmichael's Manual of Child Psychology*, 4th ed. New York: Wiley.

Li, A.K.F. 1983 "Pleasurable Aspects of Play in Enhancing Young Handicapped Children's Relationships with Parents and Peers." *Journal of the Division for Early Childhood* 7 (June): 87–92.

McEvoy, M.S., S. Twardosz, and N. Bishop 1990 *Affection Activities Procedures for Encouraging Young Children with Handicaps to Interact with Their Peers.* Education and Treatment of Children, 13, 297–73.

Mogford, K. 1977 "The Play of Handicapped Children." In B. Tizard and D. Harvey, eds. *Biology of Play.* Philadelphia: J.P. Lippincott.

Rogers, S.J., and C.B. Puchalski 1984 "Development of Symbolic Play, in Visually Impaired Infants." *Topics in Early Childhood Special Education* 3, no. 4: 57–63.

Rubin, K.H., and N. Howe 1985 "Toys and Play Behaviors: An Overview." *Topics in Early Childhood Special Education* 5, no. 3: 1–9.

Taft, L.T. 1981 "Intervention Program for Infants with Cerebral Palsy: A Clinician's View." In C.C. Brown, ed. *Infants at Risk, Assessment and Intervention: An Update for Health-Care Professionals and Parents.* Johnson and Johnson.

Thomas, A., and S. Chess 1977 *Temperament and Development.* New York: Bruner/Mazel. Reprinted with permission from the authors and publisher.

Twardosz, S., V.M. Norquist, R. Simon, and D. Botkin 1983 *The Effect of Group Affection Activities on the Interaction of Socially Isolated Children.* Analysis and Intervention in Developmental Disabilities, 13, 311–38.

Vaughn, S.R. 1985 "Facilitating the Interpersonal Development of Young Handicapped Children." *Journal of the Division for Early Childhood* 9, no. 2: 170–74.

Wachs, T.D., and G.E. Gruen 1982 *Early Experience and Human Development.* New York: Plenum.

CHAPTER 16

Facilitating Positive Behaviours (Managing Problem Behaviours)

Objectives

After studying the material in this chapter, the student will be able to

- identify possible causes of behavioural problems
- identify behaviour problems that are developmentally normal
- explain what factors determine when a behaviour problem requires special attention
- list positive strategies for preventing (and reducing) behaviour problems in the preschool classroom
- outline a plan for behavioural change for an individual child in a group setting

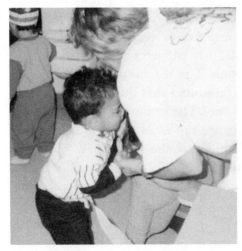

PHOTO 16–1 *All children misbehave once in a while.*

INTRODUCTION

All young children engage in maladaptive and inappropriate behaviours at least once in a while (Photo 16–1). It is one way that children learn the difference between appropriate and inappropriate ways of behaving. It is how they are learning what to do (and not do), where, and when.

The inability and/or lack of opportunity to learn appropriate behaviours, or to understand routine expectations, may be the cause of secondary behaviour problems. The frustration the child experiences in trying to perform normal developmental tasks in normal social exchanges is often a factor. Children with developmental problems often get little positive feedback from parents, caregivers, and teachers. Sometimes behaviours that may be self-stimulating in origin, such as head banging, shrill squealing, or ritualistic rocking, draw a great deal of adult attention. Thus, the repetitive behaviours are reinforced by the adult attention, which tends to increase the undesirable behaviour, which in turn blocks the acquisition of developmentally appropriate behaviour patterns.

Developmentally Normal Deviations

At what point is an inappropriate behaviour a problem behaviour? A behaviour disorder? An emotional disturbance? There are no easy answers to these questions because so many factors influence a child's development. The range of individual differences among children further complicates matters. However, it is safe to assert that preschool children (with but few exceptions) *should not be labelled as emotionally disturbed*. Early development is characterized by constant change. Therefore, the label *emotionally disturbed* is premature, nonfunctional, and likely to be inaccurate. The issue is summed up neatly by Peterson (1987, 272), who says, "How one judges deviance, normality, and hence pathology in a young child is highly influenced by social values and by the perspective of the individual who attempts to make the determination."

Rarely is there a normally developing child who has never had a tantrum or an irrational fear, or who has not balked at being separated from a parent. Rarer still are children who are never moody or withdrawn, aggressive or antisocial, argumentative or oppositional. Most young children retreat or respond negatively or aggressively to situations that are new, frightening, or beyond their understanding. Replacing a long-time favourite caregiver with a stranger, for example, may trigger a run of maladaptive behaviours. The reactions usually are temporary (assuming that the new caregiver is a good one). The untoward behaviours disappear once the child gains understanding and confidence about the new event. A child also may exhibit inappropriate behaviours when overly tired, hungry, or coming down with an illness (Photo 16–2). These minor disruptions are not likely to become fixed patterns of behaviour unless they are the only way a child can be sure of getting adult attention.

Photo 16–2 *A child may exhibit inappropriate behaviours once in a while.*

TEMPERAMENT

Behaviours that sometimes are viewed as inappropriate may be a reflection of the child's basic personality. Some children seem to be born with a temperament that makes them easy to manage, others with a temperament that makes them more difficult. An interesting aspect of this proposition is what Thomas and Chess (1985) call *goodness of fit*. These authors suggest that it is not the child's temperament itself that determines behavioural outcome. Instead, it is how the child's personality characteristics match the demands of the environment, especially the expectations of parents and caregivers. Consider, for example, a child who is active, independent, constantly curious, and into everything. This child may be seen as troublesome, a behaviour problem, and a candidate for frequent punishment by overworked parents who hold high standards for order and routine. On the other hand, energetic, creative parents might view the temperament of this active, into-everything child as highly desirable. They might go out of their way to reinforce, nurture, and respect the child's efforts at exploration and experimentation.

Young children labelled as intellectually impaired, as well as those who have been labelled as emotionally disturbed, often exhibit behaviour problems. A common tendency is for adults to excuse these behaviours, explaining that the child "can't help it" or "doesn't know any better." Making such excuses is neither fair to the child nor sensible. All young children, regardless of their developmental level, should be supported in learning basic social requirements. Early childhood programs that fail to provide such learning opportunities do these children a serious injustice. Other children can come to dislike and reject them. This may result in a further increase in the acting-out child's maladaptive behaviours or lead to excesses of aggression or withdrawal.

WHEN IS BEHAVIOUR A PROBLEM?

Occasional episodes of maladaptive behaviours are seldom cause for concern. Only when a behaviour or a pattern of behaviours becomes excessive is it a problem. This raises the question: How much is *too much*? For classroom purposes, it is useful to define excessive behaviour as that which interferes seriously with a child's (or other children's) ability to engage in normal everyday activities. Consider the following situations:

A 4-year-old who has a brief tantrum once or twice a month is not likely to be a worry. The 4-year-old who has tantrums several times every day over minor frustrations is cause for concern.

PHOTO 16–3 *Thumb sucking need seldom be considered a problem unless it seriously interferes with a child's participation in learning activities.*

Thumb sucking is seldom a problem except for the occasional child whose thumb sucking is so continuous that the child seldom engages in activities that require two hands (Photo 16–3).

Biting others is a fairly common, but unacceptable, behaviour, even among toddlers. In the interest of safety, the biting has to be controlled, but the toddler seldom is viewed as having a serious behaviour disorder. On the other hand, a 5- or 6-year-old who bites others, even infrequently, almost always is of concern.

CONDUCT DISORDERS

Conduct disorders have been described in the American Psychiatric Association's *Diagnostic and Statistical Manual of Mental Health Disorders (DSM-IV)* as "a repetitive pattern of behavior in which the basic rights of others or major age-appropriate societal norms or rules are violated..." (American Psychiatric Association 1994, 66). In young children, conduct disorders may include aggressiveness, disruptive behaviours, noncompliance (disobedience), temper tantrums, and the inability to share. In an early childhood program, these behaviours seem to be fairly evenly distributed among children who have and those who have no handicapping conditions.

AGGRESSIVENESS

Aggressiveness, like so many other terms that we apply to children, is difficult to define. What is considered aggressive by one group of people, one parent, or one teacher may not seem noteworthy to another group, another parent, or another member of the teaching team.

Conflict and Ethical Issues

Almost any child displaying continuing aggressiveness creates conflict among teachers, among parents, and among children. Often the child's problem spreads into conflict between teachers and parents, with children caught in the middle. Ethical issues always are at stake. Take the case study of 4-year-old Eric, presented to readers of *Young Children* by the NAEYC Ethics Commission (1987):

Eric was described as a large and extremely active child who often frightened and hurt other children. His parents felt that his behaviours were typical for boys his age. Other parents were complaining about Eric. The teachers were becoming stressed and tired, their patience wearing thin. In readers' responses to the ethical issues in this case study, a sense of conflict prevailed (Feeney 1988, 48):

> Values that conflict in this case are the needs of the group (for safety and serenity) versus the needs of the individual (to be responded to appropriately, to express anger and frustration). Also in conflict are the family's need for a program for their child and the teachers' need for an environment that fosters mental and physical health.

Two major principles were inferred from the responses:

1. Children's safety must be the teachers' highest priority.
2. The rights of every child in the classroom should take precedence over the needs of an individual child, especially when that child's behaviour hurts others.

Responses were conflicting as to whether the child should be banned from the classroom. Caldwell (1988, 50), in her comments, suggested: "It is probably a tactical error to insist the child leave the group until 'his behavior improves' … No matter what the underlying causes are, some of the elicitors of the outbursts are sure to be found in the group experience, so Eric will eventually have to work things out in that setting." The authors of this text agree. Reducing aggressive behaviours while maintaining the child in the group is not easy. However, it can be done, and done safely. Furthermore, problems need not get out of hand, as Eric's had gotten to be, if the unacceptable behaviours are dealt with at the outset, before they reach crisis proportions.

Managing Aggressiveness

An individualized program based on behavioural procedures designed and monitored by a behaviour therapist is imperative in helping a young child whose aggressive behaviours are truly troublesome. Always, and this should be stressed, *the behaviour management program is in addition to and concurrent with the teachers' best efforts at understanding the child's feelings*. It is in addition to finding legitimate ways for the child to "blow off steam." It is in addition to working with parents to help alleviate the child's stress, frustrations, anxieties, or lack of self-esteem. The child who kicks, hits, and knocks children about, either physically or verbally, invariably needs more adult attention. However, attention should never be given at the moment the child is hurting another child. At a different time, the teacher should encourage the child to talk about the situation, the angry feelings, and what he or she might do "next time." They might even rehearse alternative and more acceptable responses.

Young children often behave aggressively because they feel left out or do not know acceptable ways of getting into play (Photo 16–4). Children with disabilities may lack the play skills or the verbal niceties that would make them desirable playmates. In both cases the teachers' responsibility is twofold. One responsibility is to take the initiative in helping the child acquire the necessary play and social skills. (Review Chapter 15 for teaching strategies.) The second is to watch for the child to show approximations to more appropriate play and interact with the child pleasantly and positively at those times. (Review Chapter 13 on behavioural practices.)

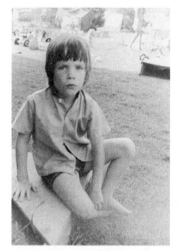

PHOTO 16–4 *A child may lack play skills.*

When a child with a history of aggression hurts another child, the teacher should turn his or her full attention to the child who has been hurt or attacked. *The child who did the hurting should receive no adult attention at that time; however, that child may need to be prevented from further aggressive behaviour.*

A child who is frequently and severely aggressive may need to be removed from the group temporarily for each aggressive episode. This step is taken only when other forms of working with the child are not having the needed effect. No child can be allowed to hurt other children repeatedly. When more positive methods have failed, time-out (Chapter 13) is a nonaggressive way to help a child learn that he or she absolutely cannot attack other children. Time-out is an intrusive management strategy. It should be used only with children who have been identified as having a significant behaviour problem. *The use of time-out is a decision that should only be made jointly, among teachers, a behavioural consultant from the interdisciplinary team, and the child's parents.*

Provincial regulations need to be reviewed in this context. In Ontario, for example, the Ministry of Community and Social Services has regulated the use of behaviour management practices, including the use of time-out. (See the Ontario Child and Family Services Act, 1992.) In extreme behaviour problems, when it is decided that a form of time-out is to be used, it should be done in consultation with the resource teacher, or a special consultant, and the parent. The procedure and process should be decided on, documented, and then clearly explained to the child.

Moving a child into time-out should be done with a minimum of adult attention. The teacher should accompany the procedure with a firmly spoken

"No," followed by a brief but equally firmly spoken statement: "I cannot let you hurt children." No other attention is given to the child at that time. One, two, or three minutes later, depending on the situation (but never more than three minutes later, even in the most distressing cases) the teacher should go to the child, briefly inform the child of the problem that led to his being pulled from the group, help him understand some positive behavioural alternatives, and encourage him to verbalize his feelings rather than use physical aggression. The teacher should then help the child return to the group, stating something to the effect of: "Let's try again. Where would you like to play?" When returning the child to play the teacher should be sure not to lecture or moralize, or try to extract promises from the child "to be good." What does seem to work is making a suggestion regarding a next activity: "There's room for you at the water table. I'll help you get started." A successful start is often the key to a successful play experience, especially if a teacher checks in frequently with favourable and interested comments.

PHOTO 16-5 *Give attention to children when they are behaving appropriately.*

DISRUPTIVE AND DESTRUCTIVE BEHAVIOURS

Every early childhood classroom, at one time or another, has a child who seems bent on upsetting the program. These children interfere with teacher-directed activities and with other children's projects. Music periods are interrupted by the child making inappropriate noises, faces, and comments, or running aimlessly about the room (Photo 16–5). Books are tossed around recklessly and toys are unnecessarily damaged. The child tramples other children's sand structures, topples their block towers, soaks their clothes and hair at the water table, swears at them or calls them names. The list of possible misdeeds is long. What early childhood teacher has not seen them all at one time or another?

Need for Attention

Children who behave in these ways have learned that this behaviour is a sure way of getting adult attention. These children often have low self-esteem and other stresses in their lives. Like the overly active child, they are greatly in need of large amounts of attention from important adults. These children appear to feel that when they are behaving appropriately they are ignored (which is often the case), and when they misbehave they get immediate attention (which also is often the case). Research indicates that young children are seven times more likely to get teachers' attention when they are behaving inappropriately than when they are behaving well (Strain et al., 1983). Therefore, the refrain that has been heard, and will be heard, again and again in this chapter and elsewhere in this text is *give attention to children when they are behaving appropriately.*

An interesting dilemma is that teachers and parents usually feel that the child who is acting out is getting a great deal of attention, even a disproportionate amount compared to other children. This is likely to be true. The problem is that adults are giving large amounts of time-consuming attention, but lavishing it on the very behaviours that are bothering them. They also are spending large amounts of unproductive time correcting the havoc created by the child. *Half as much of that time directed toward the child when not misbehaving would go twice as far toward producing a more constructive environment* (Photo 16–6). The first step in remediation, therefore, is for adults to make several observations of the child. They are almost always amazed at how much of the time the child's behaviour is appropriate, and how rarely this draws adult attention.

PHOTO 16–6 *Teachers should recognize and support children's positive play.*

Mastering Routines

Many disruptive children have never understood or mastered classroom routines and expectations. They need to be *walked through* routines, one step at a time. For example, at the easel a child may need to be shown, and then asked to practise, how to return each paintbrush to the paint pot of its own colour. A first step may be for the teacher to remove all paint containers but two. This makes it easy for the child to "do it right." It also allows the teacher to give specific, descriptive feedback: "Great! You remembered to put the red paintbrush back in the red paint pot." Lengthy verbalizations must be avoided, or the important message will get lost. (For example, teachers must not yield to the temptation to follow up with explanations about keeping the colours nice and clear for other children,

PHOTO 16–7 *As the children paint, the teacher can make appropriate comments.*

and so on. Such expectations can be discussed in small-group sessions, when necessary.) As the child paints, the teacher can make appreciative comments, when appropriate, about the brightness of the colours or how beautifully the child combined red and blue on the paper to make another lovely colour (Photo 16–7).

Redirection

Disruptive acts that damage the classroom, equipment, or other children's learning experiences cannot be allowed. With most young children, simple, positive redirection is best. Statements such as "Paint stays on the *paper*," "Walk *around* Mark and Judi's block tower," or "Tricycles stay *on the path*" are all that is required. Other children, especially those with a history of disruptive behaviours, may pay little attention to subtle redirection. When the child ignores redirection, what is often needed is a clear and firm statement about limits as well as expectations: "I cannot let you paint on the walls. The paintbrushes stay at the easel." If the child persists, either the material or the child should be removed, depending on the situation.

Before resorting to time-out for disruptive behaviour, teachers must have done everything possible to modify both the classroom environment and their own responses.

NONCOMPLIANCE

Refusing to do what an adult asks, or ignoring an adult request, is a frequent and typical behaviour of many young children. This is seldom a serious or unmanageable problem unless it becomes a child's habitual way of responding to adults. In those instances the child often is labelled *noncompliant* or *oppositional*. The following three episodes, recorded in less than an hour, are characteristic of one 4-year-old's habitual noncompliance, which was not being effectively dealt with:

Father: Michael, hang up your coat.
Michael: No, you do it.
Father: All right, but you pick it up off the floor and hand it to me.

Michael: You pick it up. (Michael started playing with a truck in the cubby next to his. Father hung up the coat, said goodbye, and left.)
Teacher: Michael, let's pick up the blocks.
(Michael ran to his locker and sat in it, looking at a book he had brought from home.)
Teacher: OK, Rachel, you pick up the blocks.
Teacher: Michael, it's time to come in.
Michael: Not coming in (while continuing his climb to the top of the climber).

The first step in dealing with noncompliance (or any other problem behaviour) is collecting specific information through several systematic observations. The second step is consultation with parents and appropriate team members. It must be determined that the child does not have a hearing loss or a problem with receptive language (Photo 16–8). Innumerable children with these kinds of undiagnosed problems have been labelled noncompliant or disobedient (and have received undeserved punishments as a consequence). Others have been inappropriately labelled as "mentally retarded" or "emotionally disturbed" because they failed to do what they were told. The injustice is that it is often impossible for these children to follow directions without special intervention.

PHOTO 16–8 *Refusing to follow an adult's request is a typical behaviour of many young children.*

Prevention Strategies

Oppositional children frazzle teachers' and parents' patience. However, most noncompliance (as well as other behaviour problems) can be reduced to manageable proportions through *preventive discipline* (Chapter 13) or anticipatory discipline. Basic to this form of discipline is systematic observation of the child to determine what triggers the inappropriate responses. Once trouble spots are identified, teachers can plan ways to handle the situations *before* a problem develops. The essence of the strategy is the now familiar behavioural approach, this time with emphasis on rearrangement of antecedents (remember those? whatever it is that occurs before the child turns resistant or otherwise inappropriate, Chapter 13). In other words, the question becomes: What is it about the environment, including adults' behaviour, that prompts a child's resistance?

Considerable space was devoted to preventive discipline in Chapter 13. That information should be reviewed whenever planning for and dealing with children who are oppositional. A number of related strategies also are effective with all kinds of behaviour problems, extreme and mild, and with all children, including those with disabilities.

Strategies for Supporting Positive Behaviour

GIVE ADVANCE WARNING. Give children ample warning before bringing an activity to an end, especially a play activity. Provide a clue as to what comes next: "Soon it will be time to come in and get ready for snack." To the child who always resists coming indoors: "Sara, you can be the last one in today." The offer, however, is made before the child has lined up her oppositional arguments. (This tactic might be called taking the wind out of the child's sails.)

REDUCE OVERLOAD. Check frequently to make sure the child is not overloaded with directions, expectations, and picky rules (Chapter 10). Even a compliant child may develop some noncompliance if overwhelmed with rules and instructions.

GIVE CLEAR DIRECTIONS. Make requests and give directions clearly and briefly (Photo 16–9). Adults tend to say things like: "We're going in to get washed for snack so don't forget to hang up your coat when you take it off, but first put your truck in the shed and shut the door." (This was an actual word-for-word recording of a teacher's verbalization in an integrated childcare classroom.) Such a jumble of directions is confusing to any child, and sets up even greater opposition in a noncompliant child. The way to help a child through such a routine is to give advance warning that it will soon be time to go indoors. When the time comes, give directions one or two at a time in the order in which they are to be carried out (in this case, parking the truck and then shutting the shed door). (To review giving instructions to young children, see the more detailed discussion in Chapter 19.)

PHOTO 16–9 *Teachers should provide children with advance warning and clear instruction.*

ALLOW CHOICES. All children, and particularly noncompliant children, need to be offered, as often as possible, opportunities to make choices:

- "Do you want to sit here with Ms. Bobbie? Or over there with Mr. Paul?"
- "Would you like to put the cups or the napkins on the table?"

- "Whom are you going to ask to help you decorate the window?"
- "It's a warm day. You can decide if you want to wear your sweater outdoors."

Choosing and making decisions helps a child develop a sense of responsibility and independence. It also reduces the child's feelings that he or she is always being told what to do.

Adults must be careful of the kinds of choices they offer young children. Whenever an adult offers a choice, the adult must be prepared to honour it. The teacher does not ask, "Would you like to park your wagon and come in for music?" unless it is permissible for the child to stay outdoors and play with the wagon during music. The child should not be offered an option that, in this case and all too many others, the teacher had no intention of honouring. What usually follows will be conflict, argument, confusion, or a power struggle, depending on the child. The more appropriate approach, once the earlier warning has been given, is for the teacher to say: "Time to come indoors for music. You can park your wagon by the door or in the shed."

Focus the child's attention. Teachers can reduce confusion for all young children by making sure that children are paying attention before giving instructions. To ensure a child's attention, follow these steps:

1. Precede every request by speaking the child's name: "Gail, the pegs go in the basket."
2. Get down to the child's level (the half-kneel, an almost automatic posture among preschool teachers, works well. See Photo 16–10).
3. Look into the child's face and speak directly to the child. In some cases it is necessary to check the child's understanding by getting verification: "Where does the puzzle go?"

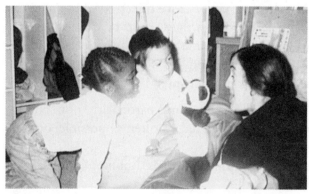

Photo 16–10 *Speak to the children at the children's eye level.*

4. Demonstrate, as needed, and hold a rehearsal: "Jon, turn the pages like this. Now you try it."

Give adequate time to comply. An instruction should not be repeated until the child has had ample time to comply. Teachers often give the instruction a second time (even a third time) while the child is gearing up, getting ready to comply to the initial request. When enough time has been given and it becomes obvious that the child is not going to comply, the direction should be offered a second time. The teacher's voice quietly conveys the expectation that the child will do it this time. The child should not be coaxed or nagged, bribed or offered a reward. Following the second request, when there is no compliance after a reasonable period, the teacher should turn away to do whatever else needs doing. The child should not be permitted to go on to another activity until the coat is picked up, the book is put away, or whatever else was requested. (See the example that follows.)

SHOW CONSISTENCY AND FIRMNESS. When giving directions to children who are noncompliant, teachers need to be matter-of-fact, firm, and consistent. They also must be quietly confident of their own authority. If a teacher says, "Raoul, you may go to the woodworking table as soon as your blocks are picked up," then Raoul must do just that—pick up blocks before going to woodworking. The teacher who gives this direction to Raoul should then alert the other teachers that Raoul has a job to do in the block corner before he can play elsewhere. If other children are busy putting blocks away, the teacher should push a fair share aside for Raoul to take care of. At this point, the contingency can be restated clearly and simply: "Raoul, this is your share of the blocks to put away. You can go to woodworking as soon as you finish." It is appropriate for the teacher to offer to help the child: "As soon as you get started, I will help you put the blocks away."

PHOTO 16–11 *Teachers' behaviour serves as a model for the children.*

DEMONSTRATE SOUND JUDGMENT. Teachers must always remember that their behaviour serves as a model for the children in their care (Photo 16–11). The teacher who shouts at the children "Be quiet!" or who handles the children roughly is modelling the very behaviours that teachers do not want to see. Furthermore, because consistency is important, teachers must not set a requirement that children may not be able to carry out. In the preceding example, it would be unwise for the teacher to tell Raoul that he could not go home until the blocks were picked up, especially if he came to school in a car pool or by school bus. Drivers cannot spare that kind of time. In such instances, the teacher should provide an option: "Raoul, the driver will be here in a few minutes. How about getting your blocks picked up before he comes?" If the child says "No" or ignores the request, the teacher should accept it. The teacher's authority is *not* undermined, and an argument that the teacher could not have won in any event is forestalled.

TEMPER TANTRUMS

Young children who have frequent, full-blown temper tantrums require special help. The advice often given is for adults to ignore the tantrum. While that is good advice, it may prove nearly impossible to carry out. Parents report that they repeatedly tried ignoring their child's tantrums, and "it didn't work." The reason it did not work is because most adults give in long before the child gives in.

A child with a history of tantrums whose outbursts are suddenly ignored may go to even greater extremes of behaviour—having tantrums of increasing fury and duration. As a tantrum becomes more violent, the adults who are trying to ignore the tantrum get increasingly anxious; finally, they can no longer restrain their concern for the child. They go to the child and provide attention in one way or another. As this pattern is repeated, the tantrums become worse.

The child learns two damaging lessons from such experiences: (1) that it takes ever greater and more prolonged fury to break down the adults' defences; (2) the defences invariably do break down and the adult eventually will provide some kind of attention. This leads to deepening trouble for both the child and the adults who are involved. Therefore, while ignoring tantrums is the surest way of ridding the child of such behaviour, most adults need help and support in carrying out such a program. Any one of several professionals on the interdisciplinary team usually are qualified and willing to work with parents and teachers in managing a child's tantrums.

Management of Tantrums

Difficult as it may be, tantrums can be handled at school. It takes careful planning among teachers, parents, and a psychologist, nurse, or other member of the child's IPP team. All of the teachers in a room should be trained by a specialist on how to handle a child's tantrums. At the start of a tantrum, one teacher should take responsibility for the child who is having the tantrum. The child may need to be removed to a separate place where injury is not likely to occur and where the child is unable to break or destroy anything. Though not always available, a small, bare, carpeted room is best. The teacher should withhold all attention while the child is having the tantrum. However, the teacher (or another adult) must stay close by (immediately outside the door is preferable, unless there is a legal requirement that an adult remain in the room). When the tantrum has stopped, the teacher should wait a moment and then return the child to a play activity *with no lecturing or moralizing*. Studies indicate that tantrums first get worse, but then disappear within a week or less if adults can be totally consistent in carrying out these procedures (Allen and Goetz 1982).

Lesser tantrums often are handled by the teachers in the classroom. Like major tantrums, lesser ones will probably accelerate briefly when attention is first withheld. It is best if all of the teachers have an agreed-upon process for managing a child's tantrums, so as to provide consistency of procedures. The teacher(s) not involved in the management of a tantrum should focus on the rest of the children, who may become uneasy as the tantrum escalates. These teachers can provide a special story, game, or record to keep the children occupied and diverted. Sometimes children can be taken on a walk around the building or to the gym or library while the tantrum is going on. The children should always be assured that the child who is throwing a tantrum will be all right and is being well cared for by their other teacher.

Teachers and parents must recognize that tantrums always are an indication that the child is experiencing stress, anxiety, frustration, or other upset. Underlying causes must be sought and the preschool or child-care program studied for changes that might be made to help the child. In the meantime, and along with the other efforts, the tantrums must be brought under control. Otherwise, the tantrums themselves prevent the child from benefiting from the changes being made on his or her behalf.

PHOTO 16–12 *Children in group settings have frequent opportunities to learn to share.*

INABILITY TO SHARE

It is questionable that the inability to share and take turns is a problem serious enough to include in a discussion of behaviour disorders. Many of today's children, who have been in group care since infancy, learn to share early and readily (Photo 16–12). However, the issue continues to be of concern to many early childhood teachers; therefore, even though discussed earlier in Chapter 15, other aspects of learning to share and take turns will be explored here.

PHOTO 16–13 *Having sufficient materials supports learning to share.*

Sharing and taking turns are learned behaviours. It is suggested that developmentally, the *egocentric* young child needs to establish a sense of *mine* before accommodating to the concept of *thine*. For many young children, the learning does not come easily. It may be especially difficult for certain children with developmental problems. What follows are suggestions for helping all types of young children learn to comply with these social expectations.

- Keeping plentiful materials is one key to helping young children learn to share (Photo 16–13). In all early childhood programs, there should be duplicates of the most popular materials. Large sets (Lego, for example) can be divided into two or three smaller sets. These are distributed among individual baskets or boxes, enabling several children to have their very own. A side effect is that spontaneous trading of particular pieces often emerges.

- Interest centres need to be attractive and located in various parts of the classroom and play yard. With several attractive setups, children do not need to stand around waiting. The teacher can advise, "You could play at the water table or the woodworking bench for a while. I'll call you when there is room on the bouncing board." It is important that the teacher remember to alert the child when space becomes available. By that time, of course, the child may not want to change activities, but the teacher's part of the bargain has been kept.

- A game-like atmosphere can help children learn to wait and take turns. For example, the teacher might use a kitchen timer and advise: "When the timer rings, it is Barry's turn"; or "It will be Mario's turn with the big rolling pin when the timer goes off."

Older preschool children can look at the clock with the teacher and understand: "When the big hand gets to 5 it will be your turn." Or they can agree among themselves: "There's no room at blocks right now, but you can go there first right after music." Children and teachers also can count turns: "Aviva, you can have two more turns around the track. Then it will be Susie's turn. She has waited a long time for a turn. Susie, you and I will count."

Children must be stopped when they knock other children off equipment because they want a turn, or when they use force to get or keep the toys they want. As with other forms of aggression, the teacher states the case clearly and firmly: "I cannot let you take Maria's doll" or "I cannot let you knock Jerry off the swing." At the same time, the teacher helps the other child hang on to a possession by encouraging specific verbalizations such as "Tell Nonie, 'That's my doll. Give it back,'" or "Tell Claude, 'You can't have the swing till I'm through.'" At that point, the teacher makes sure the doll is returned or the place on the swing is recovered. If necessary, the teacher physically assists in the return.

SUMMARY

This chapter presented a variety of strategies to support positive behaviours found in young children. The chapter also described a number of behaviour problems sometimes labelled as "acting-out" behaviours. Many of these behaviours are perfectly normal. They tend to be trial-and-error responses, a part of children's efforts at learning to discriminate between acceptable and unacceptable ways of responding to the expectations of their own home, school, and community. Seldom are acting-out behaviours cause for serious concern unless they become excessive to the point of threatening the child's well-being or the rights and safety of others.

Most behaviour problems can be managed through careful arrangement of the environment: materials, activities, space, routines, expectations, and adult attention—especially when adult attention is focused on all of the good things each child does each day. When a child's behaviour causes damage or injury, the child must be stopped; it is unethical to do otherwise. In extreme cases, where the child has not responded to careful rearrangement of the environment, temporary use of time-out may be needed. Brief time-out periods must always be used in conjunction with other procedures, including acceptance and understanding of the child's stresses and special attention to the child's appropriate behaviours.

STUDENT ACTIVITIES

1. Select two or three fellow students and form a classroom teaching staff whose concern is a 4-year-old overly aggressive child. Work together to formulate a guidance plan for this child. Prioritize the steps in your plan, beginning with the steps you will take before undertaking direct intervention with the child.

2. Select a partner; one of you play the role of the teacher, and the other, a noncompliant child. Demonstrate several ways the teacher might work with this child to obtain compliance *before* the child balks at a request. Reverse roles and play out several ways of helping a child share a wagon.

3. Divide a sheet of paper into five columns. Head each column with terms commonly used to describe children's acting-out behaviours: aggressive, destructive, disruptive, noncompliant, tantrum. Observe during a free-play period and put a mark in the appropriate column each time one of the behaviours occurs. Circle the mark if a teacher responds in any way. Figure out the ratio of teacher responses to child behaviours. Analyze to see if certain behaviours draw more teacher attention than others.

REFERENCES

American Psychiatric Association 1994 *Diagnostic and Statistical Manual of Mental Health Disorders (DSM-IV).* Washington, D.C.: American Psychiatric Association.

Caldwell, B.M. 1988 "Ethics Commission Member's Comment." *Young Children* 43, no. 2: 50.

Feeney, S. 1988 "Ethics Case Studies: The Aggressive Child." *Young Children* 43, no. 2: 48–51. Reprinted with permission from the National Association for the Education of Young Children.

NAEYC Ethics Commission 1987, *Young Children* 42.

Ontario Child and Family Services Act 1989 Ministry of the Attorney General, Queen's Printer for Ontario, Toronto.

Peterson, N.L. 1987 *Early Intervention for Handicapped and At-Risk Children.* Denver: Love Publishing.

Strain, P.S., D.L. Lambert, M.M. Kerr, V. Stagg, and D. Jenker 1983 "Naturalistic Assessment of Children's Compliance to Teachers' Requests and Consequences for Compliance." *Journal of Applied Behavior Analysis* 16, no. 2: 243–49.

Thomas, A., and S. Chess 1985 "The New York Longitudinal Study: From Infancy to Early Adult Life." In R. Plomin and J. Dunn, eds. *The Study of the Temperament: Changes, Continuities, and Challenges.* Hillsdale, N.J.: Erlbaum.

CHAPTER 17

Facilitating Language, Speech, and the Development of Communication

---

Objectives

After studying the material in this chapter, the student will be able to

- define *language* and explain how it develops
- outline in developmental order the major steps in language development and give examples of each step
- explain the difference between receptive and expressive language and discuss the developmental significance of each
- list a number of ways (including augmentative communication systems) in which teachers can help children with language delays expand their communication
- discuss dysfluency among young children and describe appropriate responses from teachers and parents

---

INTRODUCTION

Learning language is a complex developmental task, yet most children accomplish it easily. In fact, children seem to have fewer problems learning language than researchers do defining it. **Language** is a system that enables individuals to express ideas and communicate them to others who use the same code. **Speech** is the sounds of a language, the ability to communicate verbally. Speech depends on articulation, the ability to produce sounds distinctly and correctly.

Generally speaking, language—whether written, spoken, or body—is a complicated symbol system used for communication. The *symbols* used in language are words, signs, gestures, and body movements that stand for something other than the movements themselves (that is, the symbols represent ideas). It is the

397

mutually agreed upon meaning of symbols that enables a group to communicate with each other.

Communication is the exchange of thoughts and ideas, feelings, emotions, likes and dislikes. While speech is the major form of communication, there are other forms:

1. *Gestures and body language.* These may be used alone or with speech. Holding up a hand with fingers upright and palm facing another individual almost universally indicates "Stop." To make the command doubly emphatic, the spoken word may accompany the action. Touching conveys messages such as irritation or caring, as when an adult grabs a child's arm forcibly, or gently brushes the hair out of a child's eyes.

2. *Printed words.* Books, letters, and directives allow communication without speech or one-to-one contact.

3. *Art forms.* Creative acts and products such as music, dance, paintings, and the like are also powerful forms of communication.

Photo 17–1 *Imitating sounds is an early step in learning to talk.*

The code of every language is based on informally transmitted *rules* about grammar (word order) and word meaning (semantics).

In spite of its complexity, most children acquire language with relative ease. One psychologist has suggested that it would be virtually impossible to prevent normally developing children from learning to talk (Flavell 1985, 248) (Photo 17–1). Furthermore, once children begin to talk, there seems to be no stopping them.

Communicating with others is the essential purpose of language. It functions as both a social and cognitive activity. Allen and Hart (1984) describe the interrelationship: Language serves as a social skill for interacting with others, for expressing needs and ideas, and for getting help, opinions, and the cooperation of others. It serves also as a cognitive skill for understanding, inquiring, and telling about oneself and one's world.

LANGUAGE ACQUISITION

In order to recognize language and speech that deviates from the norm, it is essential that one is knowledgeable about the normal sequences of language development, as well as theories that seek to explain how children acquire language.

1. THE IMITATION AND REINFORCEMENT EXPLANATION

PHOTO 17–2 *Language acquisition depends upon a combination of factors, including the ability to imitate.*

Children learn from imitating the speech and language habits of others (Photo 17–2). In turn, they receive feedback (reinforcement). This theory had great popularity a decade or more ago. Today, there continues to be considerable agreement that imitation and reinforcement play an indisputable role in language acquisition. It is acknowledged, at the same time, that these processes cannot account for the tremendous variation and creativity in a young child's language. Children's choice of words and their sentence construction frequently bear no resemblance to anything an adult would say.

Motherese

The research on *motherese* is cited as both evidence and partial explanation of the role of imitation and reinforcement on early language development. Motherese is defined as certain patterns of speech found in virtually all adults who care for young children. Adults, especially mothers, and even older brothers and sisters, tend to simplify and slow their speech when talking to the very young (Snow and Ferguson 1977). They speak in higher-pitched voices, use short and grammatically simple sentences, and repeat words and phrases. It is not that parents have figured out that talking this way is the best way to teach language. Unconsciously, most adults seem to have found that this is an effective way to get their children to *understand* them. It also appears to be the best way to keep a young child's attention (Bee 1992).

2. THE MATURATION OR INNATENESS EXPLANATION

There was a time when it was believed that language was not a learned skill, but that it unfolded or emerged as a pattern within the developmental processes. The child was viewed as having a kind of built-in mechanism that made language learning an almost automatic process. The major flaw with this approach was that it did not take into account the child's emerging cognitive skills. Most developmentalists believe that cognition cannot be left out of a language-acquisition explanation, because cognition strongly influences the content of what children say.

3. THE COGNITIVE EXPLANATION

The child's language, from this point of view, *may* start with some kind of a built-in mechanism. However, the process is far from automatic. It is closely tied to the child's cognitive level of development. Increases in cognitive sophistication enable children to bring increasing order and precision to their language.

4. THE INTEGRATED EXPLANATION

Language acquisition, most likely, is a combination of the above explanations. Kuczaj (1982) is credited with combining the explanations into a three-part format:

1. the maturationally determined mechanism for learning language (innateness)
2. the input, or quality and timing, of the child's early language experiences
3. the use the child makes of input; the strategies the child devises for processing spoken language and then reproducing it

Bee (1992) suggests, "For psychologists and linguists, the child's rapid and skilful acquisition of language has remained an enduring puzzle" (p. 296).

Regardless of differences of opinion, it appears that healthy newborns arrive with a potential for language. According to McCormick and Schiefelbusch (1984), they come equipped to learn to talk and the environment teaches them how. There is no dispute that language skills are developed through participation in language activities. Early language activities, for the most part, are informal and spontaneous. They occur during daily routines, casual play, and impromptu social exchanges. Such interactions, *in the everyday world*, are the main ingredients of language development. When language is not developing properly, the child is put at great developmental risk. As Warren and Kaiser (1988) point out, the educational and social consequences may persist for years to come.

SEQUENCES IN LANGUAGE ACQUISITION

Language and speech acquisition, as in all areas of development, occur in a sequential order. They follow a step-by-step pattern from children's early primitive sounds and movements to the complex expression and fluent speech characteristics of their home language.

PRELINGUAL COMMUNICATION

Language development begins in early infancy, long before the first words appear (Photo 17–3). Known as the preverbal, or more accurately, *prelingual*

PHOTO 17–3 *Language development begins long before the infant's first words.*

stage, the infant's language is characterized by body movements, facial grimaces, and vocalizations. During this period, the foundations for communicative language are established. The earliest efforts take the form of crying, then cooing, then babbling.

Crying

Healthy newborns spend most of their time sleeping. When they are awake, crying is a major form of communication. It is an infant's most reliable way of ensuring that its needs are met. Infants' cries tend to vary. Many parents seem to distinguish one cry from another and become skilled at anticipating hunger, discomfort, or their infant's need for company.

Cooing

By 2 months of age most infants are cooing—that is, making a string of single vowel sounds such as "eeeeeeeeee" or "aaaaaaaaaa." Characteristically, the sounds indicate well-being or pleasure. Cooing increases as parents and caregivers respond with smiles and similar sounds. These early *conversations* between infant and parent seem to promote the infant's awareness of turn-taking as a way of interacting vocally with others.

Babbling

At about 6 months of age, infants begin to combine consonant and vowel sounds. These they repeat over and over: bu bu bu bu, gu gu gu gu, da da da da, ma ma ma ma. Ma ma ma and da da da are purely coincidental, in spite of parents' jubilation that their infant is now calling them "by name." It is no wonder that da da and ma ma become shaped so rapidly. Their sounds are *consistently reinforced* by the parents' expressions of delight upon hearing them. Babbling, like all other aspects of language, is readily affected by adult attention. In a classic study conducted many years ago, Rheingold and her colleagues (1959) demonstrated that when adults smiled at a babbling baby, patted its tummy, or responded with similar sounds, the babbling increased.

Self-Echoing

Infants who have been babbling for a while begin to sound as if they are having conversations with themselves. They repeat a sound several times, pause as though listening to what they have to say, then repeat the sound again. This sequence makes it appear that infants are echoing their own sounds; hence the occasional use of the term *echolalia* (Rathus 1988). (It should be noted that the term echolalia is more commonly used in describing the speech patterns of children diagnosed as having autism. See Chapter 7.)

Intonation

During the latter part of the echolalic period, a new characteristic appears. Infants' vocalizations begin to be marked by intonation—that is, the rising and falling variations in pitch that resemble the speech of the adults with whom they have been communicating. "Learning the tune before the words" is the way Bates, O'Connell, and Shore (1987, 299) describe this period.

FIRST WORDS AND SENTENCES

Every aspect of early language development is exciting. Major accomplishments for the child are found in making first words and then sentences. Once these are mastered, language development progresses with giant strides.

Vocabulary

As babbling increases, first "words" begin to emerge. Parents often miss out on these first words because they are hard to recognize. In the beginning, infants tend to vary the sounds. They appear to be unsure, at first, which combination of vowels and consonants to settle on when referring to a particular object or action. After the milestone of the first recognizable word, somewhere around the first birthday, new words follow slowly. Months go by before there is a real burst in vocabulary growth. The sequence goes like this:

- During the three or four months following the first words, the child may acquire fewer than a dozen new words.
- A rapid increase in vocabulary, up to about 50 words, often comes between 14 and 18 months.
- Between 18 months and the second birthday, a normally developing child is likely to have learned between 250 and 300 words.
- After the age of 2, children acquire hundreds of new words a year.
- At age 6, many children have a vocabulary of 14 000 words.

Receptive and Expressive Vocabulary

The words a child learns are of two types, receptive and expressive. Receptive vocabulary refers to the words and concepts a child comprehends. Expressive vocabulary is made up of the words the child uses to communicate verbally.

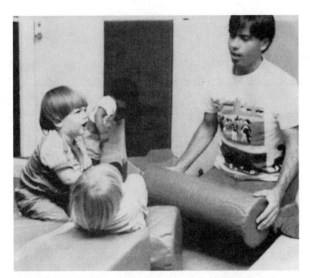

PHOTO 17–4 *Normally developing children under-stand most of what is said to them.*

RECEPTIVE LANGUAGE. Throughout life, people understand more words than they use when speaking (Photo 17–4). By the end of the fifth year, the typical child, as noted above, understands approximately 14 000 words. However, that same child is likely to have many fewer words (2500) in his or her expressive vocabulary.

Receptive language always *precedes* expressive language. Before speaking his or her first words, it is obvious that an infant understands much of what is said. Most infants squeal with delight when a parent says, "Let's go to the park"; or a caregiver says, "Time for applesauce" (if that happens to be a favourite food of the moment). Later, good receptive skills are demonstrated when a toddler runs to her grandfather as he calls out, "Where's my favourite little girl?"

EXPRESSIVE LANGUAGE. Words and sentences that an individual speaks (or signs, for those who are deaf) come under the heading of expressive language. Gestures, grimaces, body movements, written words, and various art forms are included under the same heading. Expressive language takes two forms:

PHOTO 17–5 *Checklists help teachers assess children's language skills.*

1. initiative—the individual starts a communicative interaction with another

2. responsive—the individual answers or behaves in some way in response to another's verbal initiation

Both initiating and responsive language skills are essential to effective communication. Figures 17–1 and 17–2 provide examples of these language skills (Allen et al., 1972). Simple checklists of this kind are important assessment tools (Photo 17–5). They can be thought of as *probes* or mini-tests. When the answer to a question is *yes,* a teacher has evidence of the child's progress. *No* indicates the need for follow-up to see if a problem exists. *Sometimes* suggests an emerging skill that is likely to benefit from specially focused learning activities.

FIGURE 17–1

Child's Expressive Response Behaviours

	NO	YES	SOMETIMES
DOES THE CHILD RESPOND:			
• to your voice by looking?	_____	_____	_____
• to "What do you want?" by pointing?	_____	_____	_____
• to "Give me the —," or	_____	_____	_____
• "Find the —" when there are no gestural cues?	_____	_____	_____
• when there are gestural cues?	_____	_____	_____
• to "Do you want it?" by nodding? with words?	_____	_____	_____
• to "What do you want" with words?	_____	_____	_____
• to "Tell me about" with sentences?	_____	_____	_____
• to "What is it for?" with phrases or sentences?	_____	_____	_____
• to commands to get two different objects?	_____	_____	_____
• to directions for two different actions?	_____	_____	_____
• to questions with four- to five-word sentences?	_____	_____	_____

Early Sentences

Children's progress in putting words together to form sentences is as rapid as vocabulary growth during the early years. Learning to combine words in a particular order pays off. It enables the child to convey more complex thoughts. This aspect of language acquisition is known as the development of syntax. It has several stages, beginning with the holophrastic language.

FIGURE 17-2

CHILD'S EXPRESSIVE INITIATING BEHAVIOURS

	NO	YES	SOMETIMES
DOES THE CHILD INITIATE BY:			
• making sounds in combinations?	_____	_____	_____
• making "talking sounds" to get attention?	_____	_____	_____
• using inflectional patterns to ask questions?	_____	_____	_____
• pointing to items he wants?	_____	_____	_____
• asking for items by name?	_____	_____	_____
• talking in phrases that sound like words?	_____	_____	_____
• telling you what he sees in two- and three-word phrases?	_____	_____	_____
• telling you what happened?	_____	_____	_____
• telling you where something is?	_____	_____	_____
• "telling about," using adjectives?	_____	_____	_____
• asking why?	_____	_____	_____
• "telling about," combining sentences with *and*?	_____	_____	_____
• asking how?			

Holophrastic Language

Whole phrase is an easy way to remember the meaning of the term *holophrastic*. At this stage, the child uses a single word to convey an entire thought. The intended meaning, however, is as unmistakable as a complete sentence. Holophrases always occur in reference to something the child sees, hears, smells, tastes, or feels. In other words, what the child is experiencing provides the environmental context for the intended meaning. The child's intonation or voice inflection also contributes to the meaning, as do gestures such as pointing or looking up. The single word "Doggie," depending on context, inflection, and gesture, can be readily understood to mean any of the following:

- "I want to play with this dog." (while toddling after the dog)
- "See the dog." (while pointing to a dog)
- "Where did the dog go?" (while looking outside)
- "Is that a dog?" (while pulling the fur on a stuffed animal)

During this period the child may use the same word for several objects or events. For example, *doggie* may mean *all* furry four-legged creatures; *bye-bye* often means both the absence of someone as well as someone leaving.

Telegraphic Speech

Toward the end of the second year, the child begins to speak in simple two-word sentences. These sentences convey grammatical meaning even though many words are left out. Hence the term *telegraphic,* because of the similarity to the way telegrams were written. Few parents or caregivers mistake the intent of telegraphic statements or demands. The following are several such *sentences,* recorded from an 18-month-old:

- "Mama purse?"
- "Daddy bye-bye."
- "Me want."
- "All done!"

These abbreviated two-word phrases are an important milestone in language acquisition. They indicate that the child is learning the word order (syntax or grammar) of the language. Without appropriate word order, words cannot convey meaning, especially as sentences get longer. Most of us would agree that without conventional word order it would take a while to figure out what the child wants.

THE DEVELOPMENT OF LANGUAGE COMPLEXITY

Language acquisition progresses rapidly in normally developing children between 2 and 5 years of age (Photo 17–6). Children learn to

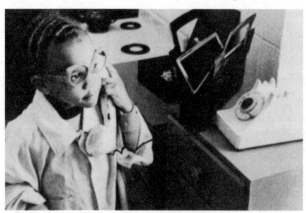

PHOTO 17–6 *Language learning is rapid in children between the ages of 2 and 5 years.*

- use all forms of questions: *Who? Where? What? When? How?* and the seemingly never-ending *Why?*;
- transform positives to negatives: *can/cannot, will/won't, is/isn't*;
- change verb forms, as required, to convey particular meanings: *run/ran, I will go/I went, It is raining/ It has rained*;
- classify objects or animals: at first all dogs were just "dog"; now *this* dog is a collie-type of dog while *the other one* is a poodle-type of dog;

- indicate "more than one" through the use of plurals: *boy/boys, kitty/kitties, toy/lots of toys;*
- convey ownership: *mine!, hers, ours, theirs, Daddy's.*

(See Allen and Marotz 1992 for more detailed age-by-age analysis.)

Overregularizations

The years of rapid language development are characterized by several kinds of errors. Developmentally, these should be thought of as misconstructions, rather than as errors. They represent children's *best efforts* to apply the complex rules of the language to the situation at hand. Often the misconstructions occur because children are trying to regularize the irregular. This leads to *overregularization* (Rathus 1988). Many children will say *digged* instead of *dug* for a while. When they say *digged,* they are relying on an earlier learning that called for adding *ed* to a verb to indicate action in the past. These children, as yet, have no understanding of such things as irregular verbs. In a sense, *digged* is right. The child is applying the rule correctly. The child is wrong only in not having learned when *not* to apply it.

Young children also mix up and overgeneralize various forms of plurals. They may say *feets* instead of feet, *mouses* or *mices* rather than mice, *gooses* rather than geese. According to Rathus (1988, 277), such *errors* aid rather than hinder language learning:

> *Overregularization does represent an advance in the development of syntax.* Overregularization stems from accurate knowledge of grammatical rules—not from faulty language acquisition. In another year or two, mouses will become boringly transformed into mice, and Mommy will no longer have sitted down.

When such *errors* occur, adults should, without emphasis or comment, simply use the correct form—"Yes, the mice ran away." The child should not be criticized or corrected directly. Children should not be made to feel self-conscious or cute, regardless of how charming or amusing an adult may find the misconstructions. Unless undue attention is focused on the situation, these perfectly normal irregularities will self-correct in good time.

By the end of the fifth year, the development of syntax is nearly complete. Most children will be using all but one or two of the conventional grammatical structures. They will be adept at creating and using compound and complex sentences and will have a minimum of 2500 words in their expressive vocabulary. Furthermore, they will continue to add new words to their vocabulary throughout their lives.

Teachers can expect 5- and 6-year-olds to understand most of what is said to them, *but only if they have had exposure to the vocabulary being used.* Adequate vocabulary depends on a child having been raised in an adequate language environment. Some children are not so privileged. For example, a child who knows colour names may be unable to follow the directions in a colour-matching activity. Why? Because the word *match* (or the concept *match* in a task-related context) is not in the child's vocabulary. A teacher, several times a day, may have to teach the vocabulary related to given tasks. Failure to do so may result in some children being unable to catch on to what is expected of them.

Nonverbal Communication

Though the primary focus of this chapter has been on verbal skills, children's efforts to communicate nonverbally are important, too. Adults need to be aware of what children do, as well as what they say (Photo 17–7). This is especially important with children who have language problems or delays. A child who shrugs, scowls, smiles, flinches, or looks off into space is communicating. Teachers and parents should try to respond to such efforts as often as possible. A responsive language environment is crucial to the development of communication skills.

Signs of Possible Problems in Speech and Language Development

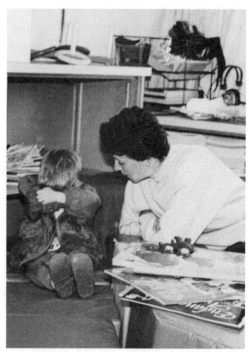

Photo 17–7 *An essential skill for teachers is recognizing what children communicate nonverbally as well as verbally.*

As in all areas of development, the rate at which children develop language varies from child to child. Children who are in families where another language is spoken in the home may be slower in developing English (Photo 17–8). Children who have hearing problems will almost always demonstrate a delay in language development, as well as some mispronunciation of sounds and words once they do begin to speak. (When the model for speech is heard inaccurately or unclearly, the child's speech will reflect what he or she hears.) Children who have muscular problems in tongue and jaw control (commonly occurring in children with cerebral palsy), or who have physiological problems in the hard or soft palate in the mouth, will also have

PHOTO 17–8 *Children whose first language is not English may be slower to develop English.*

problems in speaking. Early childhood teachers should be alert if they notice a cluster of any of the following symptoms. The following list, from the Middlesex-London Health Unit (1990), was provided by the Thames Valley Children's Centre:

• child never makes attempts to vocalize sound

• child does not make any sounds

• child is embarrassed and disturbed by his speech at any age

• there is concern about a child's dysfluency (stuttering)

• child's voice is monotone, too loud or too soft, too high or too low for his age and gender, or has a poor quality

• child sounds as if he is talking through his nose or as if he has a cold

As an infant:

• child babbles normally until 8 months of age and then stops

As a toddler:

• child uses mostly vowel sounds in his speech at any age after 1 year

• child does not recognize any familiar objects or does not follow any simple commands by 12 months of age

• child is not talking by 18 months of age

• child is not combining 2 or more words to express ideas by 22 months of age

As a preschooler:

• child is difficult to understand after age 3

• child is still not using a variety of 3- to 4-word sentences by age 3

• child uses sentence structure that is noticeably faulty at age 4

At school age (age 5+):

• child has language which is disordered and irrelevant

• child cannot tell stories in sequence

• child has naming difficulties

• child does not appear to comprehend discussion

If an early childhood teacher feels that there is some concern about how a child's speech is developing, he or she should seek the advice of a consultant. Regardless of the cause of a speech or language delay, it is important that a child not be made to feel self-conscious in any way about his or her speech. Teachers need to develop programs that encourage and enhance opportunities for verbal interaction.

The Teacher's Role in Facilitating Language Development

Teachers have a major role in facilitating language development in infants and young children. The foundation for building children's language and communication skills, according to Schwartz et al. (1993), is the social communicative context of the environment. This means that in the inclusive classroom, teachers will engineer a social context where people are sensitive to children's attempts to interact with others and where the physical environment and the people in it make communication easy and enjoyable for children. In this context, teachers and children become partners who share responsibility for selecting and maintaining communicative interaction. It is most important to make sure that the environment is arranged so as to prompt both children's language and an appropriate degree of teacher responsiveness (not too much and not too little).

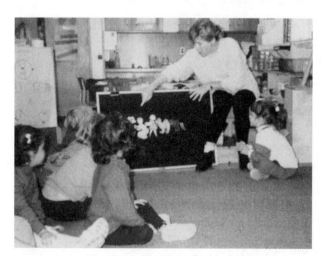

Photo 17–9 *Teachers should make sure that there is plenty to talk about.*

Arranging a Language-Learning Environment

To promote language development, teachers should arrange the learning environment so that every child has many opportunities to talk. Teachers should also make sure that there is plenty to talk about (Photo 17–9). Activities should be arranged so that both materials and teachers are responsive to children's language efforts. The basics of arranging an effective early learning environment are covered in Chapter 14.

Teachers' skills and attitudes are discussed in Chapter 10. A brief review of a few of these concepts as they relate specifically to language acquisition are discussed in the following sections.

Teachers' Expectations

The environment should be consciously arranged so that children are (1) expected to communicate, and (2) have frequent reasons for communicating. Using language then becomes an unpressured yet integral part of all classroom activities. Teachers should also provide a relaxed atmosphere in which children are allowed plenty of time to say what they want to say. Highly verbal children should be helped to learn to listen, so that less assertive or less verbal children have a chance to talk, too.

Teachers themselves should work at being good listeners and alert responders. They should answer children in ways that indicate that they really are interested and genuinely want to hear more. One of the ways that teachers may convey interest is by responding with *open-ended* questions. It is better to avoid questions that can be answered *yes* or *no,* or have only one right answer. When a child says, "We went to Grandma's yesterday," the teacher might reply, "And what did you do at Grandma's?" Contrast that response with: "Did you have a good time?"

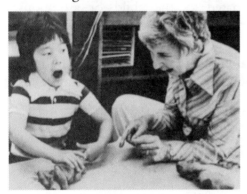

PHOTO 17–10 *Some children may need more adult input, prompting, and encouragement.*

While teachers need to be good responders, it is important that they not talk too much. Rarely can children maintain interest in an overly long and wordy response. Nor can they remain interested in a response that goes off on a tangent to fit the adult's perception of where the conversation should go. Children learn language by engaging in conversation, by using interactive communication with peers and adults. *Teachers do not need practice in talking,* children do. In an effective early learning program, talking is going on all the time, but it is children who are doing most of the talking. Teachers are serving as facilitators, sometimes prompting, sometimes questioning, sometimes reflecting a child's thoughts back to the child (a sure signal to the child that the teacher is really listening). Children with language delays may need more adult input, prompting, and encouragement (Photo 17–10).

The Role of Questions

Questions, asked or answered, are an important part of language acquisition. A child who turns away without responding when someone says, "Hi, how are you today?" quite effectively ends the exchange. Rieke, Lynch, and Soltman (1977) point out that if this happens frequently, teachers, family, and playmates may stop trying to communicate. The child loses out on two important sources of learning:

Photo 17–11 *Children need activities that prompt language.*

1. the language play and practice that facilitates language acquisition (Photo 17–11)

2. the necessary information that most children get through everyday verbal exchanges

Teachers should ask questions *only* if they expect (and are willing to wait for) answers. If an answer is not forthcoming, the child should be helped to formulate one. It may be a simple verbalization or gesture originated by the child, or a response modelled after one the teacher provides. In any event, the child is expected to respond. Children, both normally developing and those with developmental problems, will soon fall quite naturally into the routine of responding, if teachers' expectations are realistic and consistent.

It cannot be overemphasized that teachers should not talk *at* children excessively; on the other hand, they do need to be responsive when children initiate interactions.

Activities

Children need to have many things to talk about. They need novel materials to ask questions about. They need excursions, preferably simple ones such as a visit to the house under construction across the street, so as to practise verbal recall. They need easily managed picture books that enable them to "read" the story. They also need active play for prompting language of every kind. For children in need of special help with language skills, the importance of materials and equipment that require physical activity cannot be overemphasized; puppets, manipulative materials, and props that stimulate social interactive play are especially effective.

PHOTO 17-12 *Adults should respond to children's initiations.*

Incidental Learning and Teaching

Hart and Risley (1982) have demonstrated conclusively that incidental teaching is an effective strategy for improving language. Their research focused on both normally developing children and children with developmental delays. Incidental teaching is defined as a child-initiated interaction between an adult and an individual child. This should occur when the child is engaged in free play or some other child-initiated activity (Photo 17–12). The child may be seeking information, assistance, materials, feedback, or reassurance. The adult can make use of this naturally occurring interaction to promote a brief but immediate learning situation. Furthermore, this teaching opportunity should be perfectly matched to the individual child's learning requirement of the moment. The child is initiating this interaction based on an interest and a need. The essential feature in incidental teaching is that *the child initiates the contact.* The more frequently a child initiates interaction with a teacher, the more opportunities there are for the teacher to teach and for the child to learn. It is important, therefore, that each child have opportunities for interactions with teachers. To ensure such frequency, teachers need to be

- readily available and eager to foster learning according to each child's individual skill level;
- interested in what the child is offering or inquiring about, as well as prompt and positive in making a response (the response may be verbal or it may be an action: giving physical assistance or giving additional materials and equipment);
- conscious of keeping the contact brief and focused on the child's expressed interest; and
- warm, receptive, and able to show their enjoyment of interaction with the child.

During an incidental learning situation the teacher should never

- tell a child "No, that's wrong"; or
- criticize, reprimand, drill, or lecture.

The whole point of incidental learning is to have the child find the encounters so pleasant, and so rewarding, that he or she will return to the teacher again and again for more teaching and more learning.

Example:

> *Emily, a 4-year-old with a language delay, held a paint apron up to the teacher. The teacher knelt down, smiled, and waited, giving Emily time to make a request. Emily remained silent. After a moment the teacher said, "Emily, what do you need?" (The teacher did not anticipate Emily's need by putting the apron on for her.) When Emily did not answer, the teacher asked, "Emily, do you want help with your apron?" Emily nodded. "Tell me 'apron,'" prompted the teacher. Emily made a sound somewhat similar to apron and the teacher said, "Yes, apron. Here, let me put it over your head. Now, I'll tie it." The teacher's last sentence modelled tie, the next word that would be expected once Emily had learned to say apron.*

> *Had Emily not said apron, the teacher should still have put the apron on Emily, verbalizing a description of the procedure in simple language at the time.*

A child should never be scolded, nagged, or coaxed. If teachers introduce pressure into incidental learning opportunities, many children stop making the contacts. Some children turn to communicating their needs less appropriately through whining, crying, or sulking. Children who are most in need of the highly individualized help that makes incidental teaching so effective are usually the first to be put off at any sign of pressure.

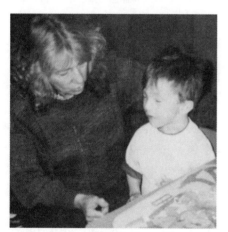

PHOTO 17–13 *Articulation refers to the production of speech sounds.*

SPEECH IRREGULARITIES

Speech irregularities, or dysfluencies, are perfectly normal. Most children, 80 percent or more, will show some kind of dysfluency during their early years. These irregularities should not necessarily be viewed as worrisome. For a time, the ability to formulate thoughts and ideas is greater than the child's ability to pronounce words correctly or to organize the words into sentences that make sense. The irregularities that early childhood teachers are most likely to encounter are discussed in the following sections.

ARTICULATION ERRORS

Articulation refers to the production of speech sounds (Photo 17–13). Perfectly normal articulation errors are likely to occur as young children work at mastering the complex sounds that make up everyday speech. Misarticulations usually are classified as omissions, substitutions, additions, or distortions.

- *Omissions.* Sounds are left out, often at the beginning or end of words: "That's my agon (wagon)," "Here's the broo (broom)."
- *Substitutions.* Interchanging sounds such as b and v: "Put the balentines on the vack seat," or replacing one sound with another: "wabbit" for "rabbit."
- *Additions.* Inserting sounds not part of a word: "warsh" (wash) or "Notta now" (Not now).
- *Distortions.* Deviations in speech sounds usually occur because of tongue misplacement or missing teeth, as is the case with many 6-year-olds: "schwim" for "swim" or "tink" for "think."

LISPING

Rarely is lisping (pronouncing *s* as *th*) considered a worrisome problem in preschool children. Seldom does it persist. Exceptions may be those few cases where the child's lisp has been showcased by adults who think it is cute. If lisping should continue into the primary grades, parents usually are encouraged to seek consultation.

DYSFLUENCY

Stuttering is a common word for dysfluency or fluency disorders. *Cluttering* is another term also used to label a fluency problem. (Both terms are losing favour among developmentalists and speech and language clinicians.) *Dysfluency* better describes children's excessive repetition of particular sounds or words, noticeable hesitations between words, extra sounds, or the undue prolonging of a sound. Such speech irregularities are common, even normal. To label a young child as a *stutterer* is unwise, in part because of the self-fulfilling consequences, as discussed in Chapter 11. It is also unrealistic. Most children outgrow their dysfluency (Prins 1983). For those few who do not outgrow their stuttering it may be, in some cases, that too much attention was focused on the dysfluency during the child's early years.

SUPPORTING CHILDREN WITH SPEECH IRREGULARITIES

A developmentally common speech irregularity seldom needs to turn into a major problem. Teachers and parents can help to forestall such a consequence by practising preventive dos and don'ts.

What adults can do:

1. Make sure the child is getting good nutrition, adequate rest, and many more hours of active play than television each day.

2. Provide comfort, care, and support; reduce tensions as much as possible (difficult, but not impossible, even in this hurried world).

3. Have fun with the child and with language; inject humour, simple rhyming activities, and simple riddles into everyday routines. Music activities are also effective.

4. Discipline with calmness, firmness, and consistency; avoid harshness, ridicule, or teasing.

5. Offer activities where the child can be successful and develop self-esteem.

6. Be sure that no one is creating undue pressure, such as trying to change a child's handedness.

What adults should not do:

1. Do not correct or nag the child; avoid saying, "Slow down," "Take it easy," "Think before you speak."

2. Do not call attention to dysfluencies directly or indirectly; the child could become all the more tense when an adult focuses intently with exaggerated patience, a forced smile, or a rigid body, waiting for the child to "get it out."

3. Do not interrupt a child or act hurried; young children need plenty of time when trying to put their ideas into spoken language.

4. Do not compare a child's speech with another child's, especially if the comparison is unfavourable to either.

These suggestions are well summarized by what one group of speech and language specialists call *benevolent neglect* (Rieke, Lynch, and Soltman 1977). Benevolent neglect is based on accepting common errors. To correct a child unnecessarily undermines the child's confidence as a speaker. If children are to improve their language skills, they must keep talking. Children who fear that they will be criticized each time they speak will speak less and less. Rieke and her colleagues offer adults an important rule: *Never force a child to repeat anything that you have understood* (p. 43).

REFERRAL

The importance of not overreacting to perfectly normal speech and language irregularities cannot be overemphasized. On the other hand, if a genuine problem exists, it needs to be identified as early as possible and an intervention program put into effect immediately. The early childhood teacher may be the first to perceive a possible problem. (See Chapter 11 on the teacher's role in early identification.) Whenever a teacher is in doubt as to whether a child has an actual problem, parents should be counselled (and assisted, if need be) to seek help. Parents often have the feeling that *something* may be wrong. On the other hand, it is common for parents to become so accustomed to their child's speech that they do not realize how poor it actually is. Speech, language, and hearing (audiology) clinicians who specialize in young children provide the most reliable testing and consultation.

THE REFERRAL PROCESS

The necessity of referral to a speech pathologist for consultation, assessment, and/or therapy may be determined by consulting Figure 17–3.

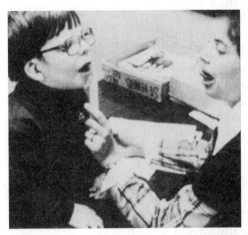

PHOTO 17–14 *Speech therapy is sometimes necessary.*

INTERVENTION

Young children who are diagnosed as having specific speech and language problems need an individualized intervention program (Photo 17–14). For best results the early childhood teacher and the therapist must work together. Therapy sessions in which a child works exclusively with a therapist tend to be short, sometimes a half-hour or less, once or twice a week. Everyday preschool and child-care sessions provide opportunities for teachers to transfer the goals of a child's prescribed program (IPP). This in turn provides opportunities for the child to have ongoing practice in the use of new skills.

Treatment may be largely ineffective unless short and infrequent therapy activities are coordinated with classroom and home activities. Whatever is taught in therapy sessions should be integrated into the child's everyday activities.

Therapists can promote classroom cooperation by informing teachers regularly about the goals and strategies used in the child's treatment. The particular skills the therapist is working on and the progress the child is making should also be discussed. Therapists should also work with the teacher and the child in the classroom itself. They can demonstrate specific strategies for the group setting where the usefulness of language is obvious to the child.

FIGURE 17–3
SPEECH AND HEARING CHECKLIST FOR THE FAMILY PHYSICIAN

			YES	NO
Birth to six months	Does the child:	• startle to loud, sudden noises	____	____
		• sometimes stir or awaken when sleeping quietly and someone makes a loud noise?	____	____
		• Does the 3-to-6-month-old child stop moving when called?	____	____
Six to twelve months	Does the child:	• turn toward a sound or when his name is called?	____	____
		• babble, laugh, or make sounds like "ga-ga," "ma-ma," or "ba-ba"?	____	____
Twelve to fifteen months	Does the child:	• repeat sounds?	____	____
		• understand some simple phrases such as "come here," "don't touch"?	____	____
		• recognize the telephone or the doorbell ringing, etc.?	____	____
Fifteen to eighteen months	Can the child:	• say four to six different words?	____	____
		• tell you what he wants by pointing and saying a word?	____	____
		• understand phrases such as "give me that," when gestures are used?	____	____
		• recognize the names of common objects such as "ball," "table," "bed," "car"?	____	____
		• use the names of familiar things such as "water," "cup," "cookie," "clock"?	____	____
Eighteen to twenty-four months	Can the child:	• use two-word combinations?	____	____
		• say about twenty or more words?	____	____
		• use words to express physical needs?	____	____
		• follow simple directions such as "sit down," "give me the ball"?	____	____

FIGURE 17-3 Continued

			YES	NO
		• point to an appropriate picture when you say, "Show me the dog (hat, man, etc.)"?	___	___
Two to three years	Can the child:	• use three-word sentences?	___	___
		• tell a story or express his feelings in words?	___	___
		• remember some recent events?	___	___
		• count to three?	___	___
		• tell you his first and last name?	___	___
		• Can people outside the family understand 40–50% of what he says?	___	___
Three to four years	Does the child:	• use four- to five-word sentences?	___	___
		• tell the story?	___	___
		• ask a lot of questions?	___	___
		• repeat a sentence of eight to nine syllables ("we are going to buy some candy")?	___	___
		• name three colours?	___	___
		• use plurals such as "toys," "balls"?	___	___
		• Can he repeat three or four numbers?	___	___
Four to five years		• Can he define four or more common words or tell how the objects are used (e.g., hat, dish, apples)?	___	___
		• Can he name a penny, a nickel, and a dime?	___	___
		• Do people outside the family understand 80–90% of what he says?	___	___
		• Does he like to look at books and have some read to him?	___	___
		• Does he use *I, me, you, he,* and *him* properly?	___	___

SOURCE: The Ontario Association of Speech-Language Pathologists and Audiologists, 410 Jarvis St., Toronto, Ontario M4Y 2G6.

The foregoing does not imply that teachers or parents are expected to become language specialists. They can, however, readily learn simple procedures for facilitating individual children's speech and language development. This means that the teacher needs to develop a program in which all children are involved and that provides opportunities for the child with speech problems to practise the necessary sounds. The teacher should model correct pronunciation and support the efforts of all children. Programs such as the Hanan Early Language Parent Training Program (Grolametto, Greenberg, and Manoloson 1986) may be useful.

Manoloson et al. (1995) encourage parents to respond and play interactively with their child. They state that parents and teachers should "allow your child to lead" (be able to drop their own agenda in favour of the child's); "adapt to the moment" (be able to enter into the child's play); and "add new experiences and words" (expand on what the child is doing or saying) (pp. 238–52). They also discourage the parent or teacher from taking on the role solely of an "entertainer," "director," "reporter," or "watcher," stressing that when a teacher takes on these roles, the child is not given adequate opportunity to practise language (pp. 40–41).

AUGMENTATIVE COMMUNICATION SYSTEMS

Some children with severe disabilities do not acquire speech easily; others use some words but have such poor articulation that their speech is largely unintelligible. For these children, an augmentative communication system may enhance their ability to communicate. *Augmentative communication systems* include: gestures signs, symbols, prerecorded words and phrases, pictures, and under special circumstances, voice synthesis. For preschool children, most augmentative systems use either sign language (Zeece and Wolda 1995) or a picture/symbol exchange (Bondy and Frost 1994). *Before* introducing an augmentative system as a primary communication method, a speech and language pathologist should be consulted. When selecting an augmentative communication system, the issue of *intelligibility* is important: Will the people in the child's environment be able to understand and communicate with the child using the system? Many young children with severe disabilities do not have the fine motor skills necessary to use sign language effectively. For these children, a picture- or symbol-based system may be a better choice.

Children using augmentative communication systems should be encouraged to use their systems in all different environments and activities including snack time, on the playground, during circle-time activities, and during free play. Using

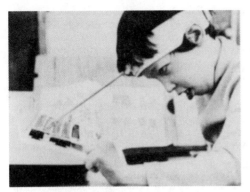

PHOTO 17–15 *Communication boards may be activated by a pointer attached to a headband.*

the system across activities will promote generalization and improve communication skills (Photo 17–15).

In inclusive programs, a simple sign system whose complexity can be geared up or down offers a tremendous boost to language and communication development for all children. Signing is both *functional* and *fun* for children who are preverbal or nonverbal, learning a second language, gifted and in need of ongoing challenge, or shy about speaking up. Signing also is successful with children with cognitive and behavioural disorders.

SUMMARY

Learning to use language for communication is probably the most complex of the developmental tasks mastered by infants and young children. Explaining how children do it has been the subject of thousands of research studies as well as major, and often conflicting, theoretical formulations. In spite of disagreements about how children accomplish this difficult task, most children do, and with little apparent effort. Without specific instruction, children move through the developmental sequences in speech and language acquisition, from crying, cooing, and jabbering to producing complex sentences and many-syllabled words in their first five or six years. Most speech and language irregularities come and go, and appear to be self-correcting unless the child is pressured.

A number of young children have problems speaking or learning the language; some children have trouble with both. Problems may range from the developmentally normal delays and dysfluencies to serious problems requiring the services of a speech and language specialist. An undiagnosed hearing loss is always a possibility and needs to be ruled out first before diagnosing a language delay or impairment in a young child. A stimulating classroom environment with interesting materials and activities and support for social interaction between children, coupled with incidental teaching, has proven effective in enhancing the speech and language skills of all children at all levels of language development.

Teachers' knowledge of normal development and their skill in observing children are essential to identifying children with language problems. It is important that teachers discriminate between language that is developmentally delayed or deviant and language that is culturally different.

STUDENT ACTIVITIES

1. Listen to a child between 3 and 6 years of age. Record 25 spontaneous language samples in the child's home or classroom. (Review language sampling techniques in Chapter 11.) Decide if the child's language is developing normally, is accelerated, or delayed. Substantiate your decision.

2. Write down or tape-record at least 15 verbal responses of adults while they are caring for a child or children between 1 and 3 years of age. Is there evidence of motherese? Give examples.

3. How would you increase the language skills of a 3-year-old who came up to you with a sweater in hand and said, "My sweater"? List ways to do this.

4. Work in small groups of four or five. Appoint a recorder. Generate as many ways as possible, including nonverbal, to let a child know you are interested in his or her new shoes and want to hear more about them.

5. Select a partner to act as a parent of a 3-year-old who says to you, the teacher, "I'm really concerned. Ryan has been stuttering the last two weeks." Counsel this parent.

6. Rearrange the following in appropriate sequence (from earliest to most complex normal language development).

   a) telegraphic speech

   b) grammatical overregularizations

   c) crying

   d) vocal intonation

   e) holophrastic speech

   f) echolalia

   g) complex sentences

   h) babbling

   i) first words

   j) cooing

REFERENCES

Allen, K.E., and B. Hart 1984 *The Early Years: Arrangements for Learning.* Englewood Cliffs, N.J.: Prentice-Hall.

Allen, K.E., and L.R. Marotz 1982 *Development Profiles: Prebirth to Eight.* Albany, N.Y.: Delmar.

Allen, K.E., J.A. Rieke, V. Dmitirev, and A.H. Hayden 1972 "Early Warning: Observation as a Tool for Recognizing Potential Handicaps in Young Children." *Educational Horizons* 50, no. 2: 43–55.

Bates, F., B. O'Connell, and C. Shore 1987 "Language and Communication in Infancy." In J.D. Osofsky, ed. *Handbook of Infant Development,* 2nd ed. New York: Wiley.

Bee, H. 1992 *The Developing Child.* New York: Holt, Rinehart and Winston.

Bondy, A., and L. Frost 1994 "The Picture Exchange Communication System." *Focus on Autistic Behavior* 9 (3), 1–19.

Flavell, J.H. 1985 *Cognitive Development,* 2nd ed. Englewood Cliffs, N.J.: Prentice-Hall.

Grolametto, L., J. Greenberg, and H.A. Manoloson 1986 "Developing Dialogue Skills: The Hanan Early Language Parent Program." *Seminars in Speech and Language,* vol. 7, no. 4: 367–82.

Hart, B., and T. Risley 1982 *How to Use Incidental Teaching for Elaborating Language.* Lawrence, Kans.: H & H Enterprises.

Kuczaj, S.A. II 1982 "On the Nature of Syntactic Development." In S.A. Kuczaj II, ed. *Language Development,* vol. 1. *Syntax and Semantics.* Hillsdale, N.J.: Erlbaum.

Manoloson, A., B. Ward, and N. Dodington 1995 "You Make the Difference in Helping Your Child Learn." The Hanen Centre, Toronto, Canada.

McCormick, L., and R.L. Schiefelbusch 1984 *Early Language Development.* Columbus, Ohio: Charles E. Merrill.

Middlesex-London Health Unit 1990 *Safe Healthy Children: A Health and Safety Manual for Childcare Providers.* London, Ont.: Middlesex-London Health Unit.

Ontario Association of Speech-Language Pathologists and Audiologists. "Speech and Hearing Checklist for the Family Physician." Brochure. Reprinted with permission.

Prins, D. 1983 *Treatment of Stuttering in Early Childhood. Methods and Issues.* San Diego: College-Hill Press.

Rathus, S.A. 1988 *Understanding Child Development.* New York: Holt, Rinehart and Winston.

Rheingold, H.L., J.L. Gewirtz, and H.W. Ross 1959 "Social Conditioning of Vocalizations in the Infant." *Journal of Comparative and Physiologic Psychology* 52, 68–73.

Rieke, J.A., L.L. Lynch, and S.L. Soltman 1977 *Teaching Strategies for Language Development.* New York: Grune and Stratton.

Schwartz, T.S., B. McBride, I. Pepler, S. Grant, J.J. Carter 1993 *A Classroom-Based Curriculum for Facilitating Communicative Independence in Young Children with Special Needs.* Paper presented at the Division of Early Childhood Conference, San Diego, Dec. 1993.

Snow, C.E., and C.A. Ferguson 1977 *Talking to Children.* Cambridge, England: Cambridge University Press.

Warren, S.F., and A.P. Kaiser 1988 "Research in Early Language Intervention." In L.S. Odom and M.B. Karnes, eds. *Early Intervention for Infants and Children with Handicaps.* Baltimore, Md.: Paul H. Brookes.

Zeece, P.D., and M.K. Wolda 1995 "Let Me See What You Can Say; Let Me See What You Feel!" *Teaching Exceptional Children* 27 (2): 4–10.

Bilingualism and Second Language Development

*Merylie Wade Houston**

Objectives

After studying the material in this chapter, the student will be able to

- identify current issues in Canada that relate to first and second language learning in young children
- discuss the importance of supporting first language development within the context of an English- or French-speaking early childhood program
- describe the potential consequences of the loss of the child's first language to the young child and family
- list ways in which teachers can support the growth of the child's home language, in both the preschool and the home environments
- describe programming that supports the learning of English as a Second Language

INTRODUCTION

Sao Chan refuses to speak Chinese to her parents at home. She gets upset if they address her in their native language when they pick her up at kindergarten; and if they speak Cantonese to her, she answers in English. Her teachers call her Susan.

Ebrahim's family have been told that, if they want their son to do well in school, they must speak only English to him at home. His mother and grandmother try their best with the limited English they know.

---

* Merylie Wade Houston is a Professor and Coordinator of Early Childhood Education at Seneca College, Toronto, Ontario. Parts of this chapter were originally published in Ruth Fahlman and Kenise Murphy Kilbride (1991), *Families and Teachers: Partners for Children* (Ryerson Press, Toronto, Ontario).

PHOTO 18–1 *Many children in Canada enter early childhood programs with their early language development in a language that is not English.*

Omi is considered to be a severe behaviour problem at his child-care centre. The teachers don't know what to do with him. Omi won't do anything but ride the tricycles. When he is invited to paint or play with puzzles or join in group activities, he answers back very rudely. And, on top of that, many of the younger boys are now following him and doing everything he does.

Increasing numbers of children in Canada are entering childcare, nursery school, or kindergarten with their early language development in a language that is not English (Photo 18–1). Immigration projections (Employment and Immigration Canada 1996; Statistics Canada 1992a) predict that these numbers will continue to increase, particularly in large urban centres. In these cities, children not born in Canada, or born to families that have immigrated recently, may soon represent a large portion or even a majority of the child population. Concerned early childhood educators often cite children's lack of English as the single biggest language problem in their centres.

Speaking a **home language** other than English is *not* a "special need." But because many teachers see it as a problem, because it is so prevalent, and because there is so little help available, it is important to spend some time dealing with it here.

Note that we are talking about children who have a language; it just doesn't happen to be English. "This is Mi Ryung. She speaks Korean," not "This is Mi Ryung. She doesn't speak English." Notice the difference?

The examples at the beginning of this chapter point out that the issue is not only one of spoken language. Body language, cross-cultural communication, self-image, and respect for cultural values are only a few of the areas we need to address. This chapter discusses these and related issues, and describes ways in which teachers can support the learning of English as a Second Language as well as the growth of children's home language.

(Note: Although Canada has two official languages, most of the discussion in this chapter is about the use of English. Much of the information applies also to the French as a Second Language situation, where French is the dominant language of the surrounding community as well as of the preschool setting. The terms *heritage language* and *minority language* refer to languages other than English and French.)

Learning and Teaching Language

Why Teaching English as a Second Language Is So Important Now

It is not new to have English as a Second Language (ESL) children in preschool centres, but the recent steep increase in their numbers is changing the educational needs of all of the children and families involved. In fact, although families with a first language other than English or French may very soon be in the majority in many urban areas (Statistics Canada 1992b), the term *minority language* continues to be used to refer to the relationship to the dominant language—in most of Canada, English. The term *Other First Language* (OFL) is a more appropriate term to use.

At the same time as numbers of OFL children are increasing, research is teaching us new things about the learning of first and second languages. It used to be thought that children "naturally" learn new languages, and that if only the parents would speak English at home, their children would do just fine.

It is now being shown that such advice is not only wrong, it can be damaging to the children and families involved.

The Importance of Language Learning

Much of the assessment done on children by classroom teachers is based on language ability. Certainly, the articulate child is instinctively thought to be intelligent and creative. Teachers, along with families and others, frequently are impressed by and pay attention to a verbal child. Chapter 17 discusses the interrelationship between cognitive development and the development of language. Because of the perceived connection between increasing cognitive structures and language maturity, it has always been assumed that it was important to help children develop skills in English as quickly as possible. The inability to speak English has been treated as a deficit by teachers. Skill in speaking a first language has seldom, or ever, been taken into consideration by the practitioner in evaluating a child. So a "good" teacher has always been one who has worked toward teaching children English as quickly as possible.

THE EFFECT OF PRESCHOOL SECOND LANGUAGE TRAINING

When a child learns English in preschool after starting to learn a different language at home, the English usually develops *instead of* rather than *in addition* to the first language (Wong-Fillmore 1991). This is referred to as subtractive bilingualism, and it leads to a loss of whatever skill the child already had in the first language. In a home with parents and other family members who may speak only the first language, the child quickly loses the ability to communicate. This is a high price for families to pay for sending their child to daycare or preschool—loss of the ability to talk to their child. If parents and older family members cannot use their traditional language to transmit their culture and values, they have (to a large degree) lost the ability to raise their child, and may therefore lose the connection between generations (Photo 18–2). These social reasons alone seem to require that the child continue to learn and use the family's language. There are other good reasons, too.

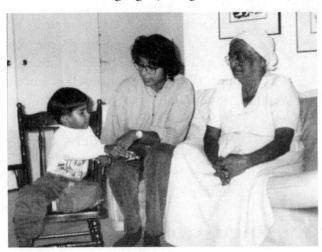

PHOTO 18–2 *Use of home language enables the generations within the family to communicate with one another.*

It is important to support the use of the home language because of evidence (Cummins 1984; Skutnabb-Kangas 1981) that the more children speak their first language, the better they learn English. The reason for this is that learning a language teaches our brain what language is: what it is for, how it works, how it is structured. That skill can then be applied to the learning of another language. The more highly developed the child's skill is in the first language (L1), the more skill he or she has available to use in learning the second (L2). So continuing to speak the first language actually helps the child to learn English. The later the introduction of English, the stronger the knowledge of and practice in the first language will be. Remember the difference between the 2-year-old's telegraphic speech and the 6-year-old's compound and complex sentences, as outlined in Chapter 17.

Another reason for maintaining the development of the first language is that we need language in order to think (Cummins 1981). Cognitive learning is

PHOTO 18–3 *Social language can be picked up quickly through mimicking.*

closely linked to both receptive and expressive language. Children's ability to think in their L2 will not catch up to the same ability in their L1 for five to seven years, although we may sometimes be misled by their fluent social language. Social language is surface language, and it can be picked up quickly, through mimicking (Photo 18–3). Teachers often protest, "Language isn't the problem, he can talk all right," because they have noticed the child's relatively fluent surface language. This will not reflect the child's ability to express concepts for many years, however.

How Bilingual Preschool Education Works

With what we know at present, probably the best way to educate preschool children who have first languages other than English is in a bilingual setting. Concepts are presented in the first, or home, language, thus developing the child's cognitive strengths, and then are reinforced in English. In this way, comprehension and English language development are combined.

(Note: Bilingual education should not be confused with *French Immersion*. Children in French Immersion programs are taught in French, by francophone teachers. The children's home and community language is usually English, and they are learning French as an additional language.)

In an optimal setting for bilingual education, the teacher shares the children's language and culture. There are many communities across Canada where the population shares a common language, culture, and/or religion, and where such bilingual programs are thriving. There, children are able to become truly bilingual and reap the additional cognitive benefits of being able to think in two languages.

Children who learn two languages in this way learn to **code switch**—to move from one language to the other depending on the situation they are in. Children who speak an English dialect also code switch—for example, from Jamaican patois to Standard English. Teachers and parents often worry that the children will become confused, but if both languages are taught well and valued, this doesn't seem to happen. Although Bee (1992) admits that there may be a drop in IQ during the period of initial introduction of the second language, this quickly corrects itself. Hakuta and Garcia (1989) find that the higher the degree of bilingualism, the higher the level of cognitive development.

There are two major difficulties that stand in the way of delivering bilingual education: the expectations of parents, and the reality that many schools have children who speak a number of different home languages.

CAN PRESCHOOL BILINGUAL EDUCATION BE DONE?

Many parents are hesitant to register their children in a bilingual preschool program. They know that, in order to be successful in "big school," their children will need a good command of English, and they want them to start to learn it now. Parents are prepared to try to switch to the use of English in the home if it means that their children will do better at school. And both the parents and the children quickly recognize the connection between language and power. The "power" language, in many parts of Canada, is English. So children themselves will sometimes refuse to speak the home language after they have started school. If the parents speak an English that is not as "good" as the teacher's, the children may lose respect for their parents, for their heritage, and ultimately for themselves. It is essential that the teacher do some good parent education, so that the parents understand why learning only English at a preschool age will be harmful both to their children's learning of English and to their future use of the first language.

The second reason that explains why there are not many successful bilingual preschool programs is that most communities and schools in Canadian cities reflect a number of different language groups. The Mount Pleasant Neighbourhood House preschool in Vancouver has 15 different languages among the 30 families involved (McMurter 1992). It is, of course, unreasonable to expect one teacher to be able to speak and teach in several languages.

In spite of these problems, we must find ways to

- support the growth, not just the maintenance, of the children's first languages;
- show that we support and value the families' cultures and languages, in order to build the self-esteem of the children;
- show that we support and value the families' cultures and languages, so that the other children recognize their value;
- teach new concepts in the children's first language(s) in order to continue to develop their critical thinking skills as well as to support the learning of English; and

- deliver a first-rate early childhood education program to all children in spite of the fact that many of them and their families will come to us without a word of English.

Supporting the Child's First Language

The unilingual teacher can do much to encourage a child in the learning of his or her first language:

Photo 18–4 *Work toward hiring staff who reflect the language and culture of the community.*

- Strongly encourage the family to continue to use their first language at home.
- Work toward the hiring of staff who reflect the language, cultural, racial, and religious backgrounds of the children and their families (Photo 18–4).
- Introduce new concepts in the child's first language wherever possible.
- Help the families to help their children make the leap from home to school by letting them know the learning skills needed to "make it" in your classroom, such as speaking up, answering questions, and waiting their turn.
- Show respect for the families' values by adjusting your expectations to reflect those of the home—for example, helping children wait until you are free to listen if interrupting adults is frowned on by the community (Hendrick 1992), or honouring the request of Chinese-Canadian parents that their child not have ice-cold drinks in the winter or play in water.
- Show respect for the families' backgrounds by reflecting them in the toys, books, dramatic play materials, posters, music, food, and so on in *daily* use in the classroom.
- Don't just allow, *encourage* the children to use their home language in play, especially "pretend" play.

USING FAMILIES FOR INFORMATION AND ASSISTANCE

Language, as we learned in Chapter 17, is nonverbal as well as verbal. Body language and gestures vary in meaning from group to group. Most of us are aware of the teaching of some groups, including some West Indian and Chinese families, to show respect to a teacher by avoiding eye contact. This can be more than confusing to a teacher who uses eye contact as a measure of social development. The common hand gesture used to beckon a child may be insulting to some, if it is their gesture for calling a dog. The "O.K. sign"—a circle made with forefinger and thumb—commonly used in Canadian dominant culture, may be

PHOTO 18–5 *Your best source of information is the child's family.*

extremely rude to others. Teachers should be encouraged to take any available courses on cultural knowledge. Because there is variation among any group of people on any given subject, and in order to avoid stereotyping, *your best source of information is the family of the child* (Photo 18–5). A good way to ask is: "How do you do it in your family?"

A lot can be learned by visiting the child in the home. This author conducted home visits with a number of Japanese-Canadian families whose children were in her preschool program. During these visits the different expectations of behaviour for boys and girls became clear. Boys were expected to be much more aggressive than girls, never to cry, and to belong to a group. The group leader, usually the oldest and smartest boy, was the direct authority for the others and was also responsible for their behaviour. Omi, described at the beginning of this chapter, clearly was playing this role with the group. Painting, collage, and most seatwork was considered by this group to be "girls' work." Recognizing that these cultural factors affected the children's behaviour and learning led to an overhaul of the program's curriculum.

ADDITIONAL MEASURES TO SUPPORT FIRST LANGUAGE DEVELOPMENT

1. Learn the correct pronunciation of the child's name. We have no right at any time to change or Anglicize a child's name, unless the request is initiated by the parent. Some names may be difficult to pronounce at first, but learning to pronounce them phonetically with the family's help opens the first door to a good working relationship. Morrow (1989, 20–23) tells us

PHOTO 18–6 *Parent involvement in the centre is important for all children.*

that it is critical to learn both the child's and the adults' names and correct forms of address. This is especially true of children from Southeast Asian countries whose names and manner of addressing others are so very different from Western traditions.

2. Children need to see their families become part of this new child-care world (Photo 18–6). Find out the family's interests and abilities and invite them to participate in the program, not for "culture days" but just as you would any other parent. Remember that this will be hard at first since the culture of the classroom, as well as the language, is likely to be alien. Plan a specific job to be done. If no family member is available during the day, ask if parents could serve on the advisory board, sew bookbags, help with bookkeeping, or contribute snacks. Be careful not to ask parents with other first languages only when there are menial or housekeeping tasks to be done.

3. Fill your room with books, tapes, and records in the children's heritage languages. They are available at some bookstores and at children's libraries. Families, community associations, churches, synagogues, or mosques will often donate books outgrown by older children. Visitors to the native country, or a relative there, may also be sources for purchases or donations. You may not be able to read the books, but the families can. That is a special talent you need to acknowledge. If parents are willing to tape-record a reading of the book, ask them to ring a bell when it is time to turn the pages.

   It is important to use the same standards you would always use in selecting the books to read: choosing for age appropriateness, good illustrations, and other usual criteria.

4. Learn a few basic words and phrases in the child's first language (*hello, drink, Mommy will be back soon, Daddy, Grandma, do you need to go to the toilet?* etc.). With the families' help, display some phrases on the bulletin board and in your newsletter, and incorporate them into children's songs. *The Newcomer Preschool* (Dotsch and McFarlane) will give you other good ideas, and some examples of phrases.

5. Ask the families to save boxes and cans for the housekeeping corner that reflect the foods, language, and calligraphy of the home.

6. At New Year's, which may be in September (Rosh Hashanah), October (Diwali), March (Now–Ruy), January (Chinese New Year), or many other times of the year, ask all the families to find a calendar that they can obtain for free that reflects their language, culture, or religion. Put the calendars up and use them.

7. Don't assume that you know how much and what the children know: what their previous experience and body of knowledge are. Ask the families. They are your best resource.

8. Find translators ("graduated" parents, or people from local school, church, community, or government organizations) and use them for parent meetings, interviews, and messages. This is not the parents' responsibility; it is yours. Try not to use older children to translate for their parents. This violates the natural order of authority between the generations. Families often take great pride in the linguistic abilities of their children, but be careful to check, especially when dealing with guidance and educational issues. Do not use other parents when private information is being shared. The interpreter must be acceptable to the family, both for confidentiality and for professional status. All families have a right to understand and be understood when their children's well-being is at stake. This is not a gift. It's a right.

FIGURE 18-1

IN-THE-HOME SUGGESTIONS FOR FAMILIES

What Can Families Do to Help

- Read and tell stories to your child in your first language. Stories include your own family saga, where you are from, and funny things that people have said and done.

- Borrow books from the child-care centre or the public library. Take your child to get his or her own library card. Even infants and toddlers can have a library card. It's free. Ask the librarian about books in your first language.

- If you still have relatives or friends in your first language country, ask them if they can send books for your child. After they are outgrown, consider donating them to the child-care centre. If you travel, remember to look for books.

- Talk to your child in your first language and point out interesting things to them. Also read signs, labels, and posters to them when you are out.

- Offer to translate simple books into your family's first language for the preschool or child-care centre, either in print, on tape, or by telling a story to the other children.

- When your child is old enough to register for elementary school, ask the school for information on Heritage Language or International Language classes in your first language.

PROGRAMMING TO SUPPORT THE LEARNING OF ENGLISH

Now that we have built in protection for the child's first language, we need to look at ways to support the learning of English. (Note, however, that the following programming guidelines are equally pertinent to the learning of French as a second language.)

PHOTO 18–7 *Use gestures and hugs to reassure children.*

The first question that teachers often ask is: "How long does it take for a child to learn English?" The answer depends on several variables: the child's opportunity and willingness to interact with competent English speakers; how similar the first language is to English; and the child's age. Dotsch (1992, 24–26) has shown that, for immigrant and refugee children, both previous positive experience in a child-care setting and the lack of a serious traumatic experience help speed up language acquisition. In general, it takes at least three months before children begin to understand what is said to them, two years before they can carry on a conversation, and a full five to seven years before they can think in a second language (Cummins 1981).

During the first three or four months when the child is unable to understand what you are saying, you should remember that words without understanding are just noise. Terrifying noise. Remember how important it is to use gestures and hugs to reassure a new child, while gradually introducing words (Photo 18–7). Several things help facilitate language learning:

1. *Scaffolding your language.* It is important, at first, to support the words you use with gestures, actions, facial expressions, objects, or pictures to reinforce meaning. Without the context of meaning, the child hears only noise; he or she cannot isolate and identify the sound of the word and remember it. As the child acquires more receptive language, the gestures and actions can be slowly reduced so that the child becomes more dependent on the sound of the word rather than the gesture. Any early childhood teacher knows how to "perform" for children. An ESL teacher must be even more of a "performer." Exaggerate and keep the language very simple; but you can get carried away with the silliness. If you're lucky, the children will giggle. That brings us to the second point in second language learning.

2. *Using the affective component.* Simply put, this means that if you show the children that you like them, they are more likely to like you back. And if they like you, there is more motivation to try to communicate with you,

so they will acquire a second language more quickly. It helps if staff develop a special relationship with each child, right from the beginning. As each new child joins the group, one staff member can become the child's special friend to help with this transition.

3. *Planning good programming.* Finding out where children's interests lie and developing exciting, interesting programming promotes speech. If nothing of interest is going on in the room, what is the children's motivation to talk? We don't teach English to preschool children, we provide an enriched language-learning environment and then motivate children to want to communicate. (See *Multicultural Early Childhood Education—A Resource Kit* [Kilbride 1990] for more ideas.)

4. *Taking the necessary time.* Remember, it can take months before children begin to understand meaning, and years before they may feel comfortable talking to you. Don't force children to talk before they are ready. That's not the way to build trust. But when they do speak, respond with warm reinforcement.

THE ENRICHED LANGUAGE-LEARNING ENVIRONMENT

Keeping in mind our goals to support the first language and to introduce the second language, how does this all come together in early childhood education programs?

The ideal language-learning classroom is well staffed, busy, messy, bright, and stimulating, just like any other ideal classroom. With a slight change of emphasis your room can meet all the needs of the child who speaks a first language other than English.

- *Plan time for one-to-one and small-group work.* Try to organize your staff so that one or two adults establish a warm, personal relationship with each child, and can spend some time each day in one-on-one interaction with that child. Small-group work often gives the second language child the encouragement and opportunity to speak without the competition of first language children (who always know the words first). Take advantage of any opportunity to be alone with the child during washroom and other caretaking times.

- *Turn off the tape player and other background noise.* Turn off the radio or tape player during time when you are working on building language. Save tapes and records for small-group time when they can be listened to and concentrated upon. Consult with the parents to select music from the child's own

PHOTO 18–8 *The ideal classroom is well staffed, busy, messy, and bright.*

cultural background that can be played, when appropriate, during unstructured time.

- *Use caretaker speech.* Caretaker speech directs the child's attention to the immediate environment, labelling everything, speaking simply and slowly, asking rhetorical questions, repeating and expanding on the child's words (McLaughlin 1984). "What's that? It's a ball. Ball. Can you throw me the ball? It's a red ball." The level of caretaker speech matures as the child's command of the language increases.

- *Use sensory activities for talking and interacting.* Join the child at the sand or water table, or model together with play dough or clay. The soothing, open-ended nature of these activities makes it possible to participate fully without language, while helping the child relax and be receptive to new words about feelings, textures, and temperatures. This is often a good time to encourage the child to label in their first language, teaching you (Photo 18–8).

- *Allow "non-teaching" quiet time.* Learning a new language is exhausting. All children need time to be alone with their own thoughts. They need relaxing creative play time without teacher interference when they can speak their home language alone or with others, or, if they choose, play with English-speaking classmates. Culture shock can leave a child in such a state of stress that the new language can make you seem even more alien and the environment even more threatening. Allow silence.

- *Encourage peer play with English-speaking children.* Don't isolate the ESL children from their peers. As children they need to hear native English-speaking children speaking child talk. Saville-Troike (1976) has shown how English use expands as soon as a fluently English-speaking child joins the group. It is also important that the children hear you speaking to children with English as a first language.

  Research also shows that the number of English interactions in dramatic play increases when a teacher supports the play. This more intense involvement by the teacher in dramatic play is one of the few areas where the role of the teacher should be different with children who speak a first language other than English.

- *Set a good example.* Be a good language model. Speak good, correct, if simple, English. Dotsch (1992, 24–26) tells us to slow down a little, but not to talk louder, or the children might think that you are angry at them. Remember that the children's receptive English (what they can understand) is always more advanced than their expressive language (the language they speak).

- *Use songs for transition times and routines.* Be consistent in the language used for routines. Avoid saying "Tidy up, please," one day, "It's time to tidy up now" the next, and "Put the toys away" the third day. Songs provide an easy way to use the same words, rhythm, and tone each time. A simple song for tidy-up time, for snack, for washing hands, sung by all the staff, provides the child with an aural (heard) cue that immediately connects words and action.

- *Sing lots of songs and use finger plays with actions.* If you have large-group or circle time, establish a set of "old favourites," simple finger plays, songs, and games with gestures to support the meaning of the words. Children find this repetition comforting. Children will often sing before they speak. Remember singing "Frère Jacques" years before you knew any French? (Even your accent was probably pretty good.) Singing in a large group is less threatening, especially to a shy child, or one whose culture doesn't encourage drawing attention to oneself. And singing provides practice in the rhythms of a language.

   This is another good area to involve the families. Ask a family member to teach all of you—the teacher, too!—a new song in another language. Sometimes children's songs in other languages can be found on tape or compact discs. If you can't handle the whole song yet, try to get help to translate the chorus of a favourite song into several languages that represent your group. Songs that include counting are particularly easy to use (or adapt) for this purpose. (Paul Fralick's [1989] *Make It Multicultural—Musical Activities for Early Childhood Education* may help you get started.)

- *Program for language.* Most children like technology, and can use a simple calculator or adding machine even without words. Let children operate the tape recorder themselves. If you can get a typewriter or computer, try writing books; Polaroid pictures of a field trip give you great material (did you remember the tape recorder?). Invest in an inexpensive set of walkie-talkies. Even though they never push the right button, many kids will talk into a walkie-talkie, or will listen. Don't interfere too much; just let them go. Old microphones or a TV console—sans tube!—are terrific language-stimulating additions to your dramatic play area.

   Making old-fashioned tin-can telephones is a great fine motor activity, and what good are they if you don't talk? Get a child to hold one and

Photo 18–9 *Activities in the science area require materials that can be labelled.*

listen to you saying silly things. You'll need enough cans and string for everyone, of course. If your room ends up looking like a spider's web, what a good challenge to talk as we try to get untangled!

In many areas, Bell Canada has donated old telephones to schools. If you are handy—or maybe a parent is—telephones can be hooked up to each other so that you can actually hear through the earpiece.

Attitudes change quickly in all children when language and related technology are added to your programming. Children whose first language is English need language stimulation, too.

- *Plan easily followed activities.* Plan lots of activities in science (planting, magnets) or cooking (Photo 18–9). These subjects require materials and procedures that can be labelled and demonstrated, but also followed visually. While building vocabulary, the participatory nature of these activities builds feelings of success and increased self-esteem.

Photo 18–10 *While building language skills, remember the child's other needs.*

- *Read out loud.* Read books, read instructions, read calendars, read street signs. Read to the children every chance you get. Making the connection between written symbols and words is the basic preliteracy skill needed for reading. Read in natural situations; don't overwhelm the children.

- *Continue to provide for other needs* (Photo 18–10). While building language skills, remember that the child's other needs—social, emotional, physical—are the same as those of any other child. Of course, language and other needs go together: "What a big jump!" "Where's my hug?"

FIRST NATIONS LANGUAGE ISSUES

Most of the discussion in this chapter also applies to children and families who speak Native languages in Canada, but there are some issues that are special to this group. Socially and economically, for complex historical reasons, and as a result of racist attitudes, Native Canadians are frequently disadvantaged within the larger society. It is important that all early childhood educators pay special attention to the education needs of the founding peoples of our country. The term Native people, as used here, refers to status Indians, non-status Indians, and Inuit people.

BACKGROUND

There are 50 different Native languages in Canada, belonging to 11 ancestral language groups: the Algonquian, Athapaskan, Iroquoian, Salishan, Eskimo-Aleut, Wakashan, Tsimshian, Siouan, Haidan, Tlingit, and Kutenaian families of languages. Some of these language families contain only one language, while others contain a number of distinct languages: one Algonquian language, for example, is Cree, which is spoken by 22 percent of Native-language speakers in Canada. Cree itself has a number of dialects. Kutenaian and Tlingit, on the other hand, each contain a single language with fewer than 500 speakers (Burnaby 1982).

The number of speakers of Native languages as a first language is diminishing. On some reserves, 100 percent of the population are Native-language speakers. But among Native people in Vancouver, for example, only 18 percent speak their Native language in their homes (Frideres 1988). And the average age of these speakers is over 40. If only the older generation speaks a language, the language dies as the last speaker dies. Huron was last spoken early in this century. Once a Canadian Aboriginal language is lost, there is nowhere else in the world to go to get it back.

It is a common pattern to have elders who speak only the Native language, a middle-aged group who speak both the Native language and an official language (English or French), and a younger generation who only speak the official language. It is obviously difficult for elders to pass on oral traditions and cultural values to children if they do not share a language.

Most families feel that their children must be able to speak, read, and write English or French in order to survive in Canada. Education is seen as the key to doing well. But it must be admitted that education has not done its job for Native children in the past. Educators are now looking at language issues as being part of the key to making changes that will enable children to be more successful in school while maintaining traditional values and identity.

Early Childhood Response

Native groups and early childhood educators across Canada are beginning to develop preschool programs designed to meet the needs of the children and families in their communities (Photo 18–11). The National Indian Brotherhood, in the document *Indian Control of Indian Education* (1972), outlines three objectives for these programs:

1. that the program contribute to the child's general success in school achievement

2. that the program contribute to the child's sense of his or her identity as a Native person

3. that Native languages be preserved and maintained

Photo 18–11 *Provide stimulating program activities designed to meet the needs of the children and families in their community.*

Child-care centres such as Winnipeg's Nee Gawn Ah Kai (Children of Our Tomorrows) more than meet these objectives. Native staff are able to speak Cree to support children who have recently arrived from the North without English. Staff are working to develop a bilingual program to teach the language to children whose families have lost it. Meals include bannock and other traditional foods. Traditional values are an integral part of the curriculum because the staff are members of the community.

There are few curriculum materials available to support such teaching. Families and communities must work together to develop materials and the training to use them. Early childhood education training programs must also change to reflect these needs (Photo 18–12).

One such program is at the Arctic College of Iqaluit, which has recently developed and taught the first early childhood education program in the Northwest Territories. The skill of the students as well as of the elders in the community of Nunatta has been used to design a program that supports language and literacy in both Inuktitut and English (McNaughton and Stenton 1992, 20–21). The early childhood values of cooperation, noncompetitiveness, teaching by example, and respect for the child's freedom mesh very well with

PHOTO 18–12 *Families and communities should work together to develop curriculum materials.*

Inuit traditional child-rearing practices. Colwell and Wright (1992, 18–19), however, point out that another value, the prohibition on expression of feelings, has made children susceptible to substance abuse, and has contributed to a high suicide rate. Working through these conflicts between early childhood and cultural practices is a challenge to all culturally sensitive programs. The Meadow Lake Tribal Council of northern Saskatchewan and the School of Child and Youth Care of the University of Victoria are working together to develop a training program that recognizes that both the First Nations and the traditional educational system have important contributions to make (Pence et al., 1992, 15–17).

Whether in a northern community, a small town, or an inner-city preschool, programming must support the children's development of their identity as Native persons. The family's traditional language forms an essential part of that identity.*

SUMMARY

Children do not just "pick up" a new language. Our school systems are full of children with no real, solid language base. It takes a relaxed child with high self-esteem, a good language modeller with a lot of appropriate animation, and an environment that fosters first language retention to make the new language acquisition possible.

By supporting first language development, by building in family involvement, and by using good second language teaching strategies, early childhood educators can help make sure that the children in their care not only retain their first language, but mature in its use; not only learn English as a second language, but achieve total command. It all starts in preschool.

---

*Additional relevant readings are included in the reference list at the end of this chapter.

STUDENT ACTIVITIES

In reference to the case examples at the beginning of this chapter, complete the following exercises.

1. Explain why Sao Chan refuses to speak Cantonese to her parents at home. Discuss the implications of her attitude. List five things that you could do to help. What advice would you give to her family?

2. Ebrahim's family want him to learn English as soon as possible. In a small group of three or four, role play a family interview in which the teacher discusses first and second language learning. What support people should be present at such an interview?

3. Work in small groups of four or five. Generate as many examples as possible of children's behaviour that is affected by cultural expectations. Start with Omi's situation. Pass your group's list of examples to another group. Using the new list passed to you, identify the issues involved in each behaviour and discuss how you would handle it as a teacher. If you cannot identify the cultural issues involved in each behaviour, indicate the resources that would help you.

4. Arrange to do an observation in a child-care centre that has some children who speak a home language other than English. Using one room as your source, list examples of (a) programming that supports home language maintenance, and (b) programming that supports the learning of English as a Second Language. List five program activities that would enrich the language-learning opportunities in the room.

REFERENCES

Bee, H. 1992 *The Developing Child.* New York: Holt, Rinehart & Winston.

Burnaby, B. 1982 *Language in Education among Canadian Native Peoples.* Language and Literacy Series, Ontario Institute for Studies in Education. Toronto: Ontario Institute for Studies in Education.

Chud, G., and R. Fahlman 1985 *Early Childhood Education for a Multicultural Society: A Handbook for Educators.* WEDGE Publishing. Vancouver: University of British Columbia.

Colwell, K., and P. Wright 1992 "Arctic Realities: Developing Early Childhood Training for Inuit Students." *Multiculturalism* 14, nos. 2, 3.

Cummins, J. 1981 *Bilingualism and Minority-Language Children.* Language and Literacy Series, Ontario Institute for Studies in Education. Toronto: Ontario Institute for Studies in Education.

Cummins, J. 1984 *Bilingualism and Special Education: Issues in Assessment and Pedagogy.* Clevedon, Avon, England: Multilingual Matters.

Cummins, J. 1985 "Bilingualism in the Home." *Heritage Language Bulletin* 1, no. 1.

Derman-Sparks, L. and the ABC Task Force 1989 *Anti-Bias Curriculum: Tools for Empowering Young Children.* Washington, D.C.: National Association for the Education of Young Children.

Dotsch, J. 1992 "Newcomer Preschool Children: Their Cultural and Linguistic Adaptation to Childcare Settings." *Multiculturalism* 14, nos. 2, 3.

Dotsch, J., and J. McFarlane n.d. *The Newcomer Preschool: A Resource Book for Teachers.* Toronto: Ministry of Culture and Recreation, Ontario.

Employment and Immigration Canada 1991 *Immigration Statistics.* Canada Immigration Group, Statistics Division. Ottawa: Supply and Services Canada.

Fralick, P. 1989 *Make It Multicultural—Musical Activities for Early Childhood Education.* Hamilton, Ont.: Mohawk College.

Frideres, J. 1988 *Native Peoples in Canada: Contemporary Conflicts,* 3rd ed. Scarborough, Ont.: Prentice-Hall Canada.

Hakuta, K., and E.E. Garcia 1989 "Bilingualism and Education." *American Psychologist* 44, no. 2.

Hendrick, J. 1992 *The Whole Child,* 2nd Canadian ed. Toronto: Maxwell Macmillan.

Houston, M. W. 1992 "First Things First: Why Early Childhood Educators Must Support Children's Home Language While Promoting Second Language Development." *Multiculturalism* 14, nos. 2, 3.

Houston, M. W. 1995 "Tell Me a Story (Then Tell It Again)." *Interaction,* Spring.

Kilbride, K.M. 1990 *Multicultural Early Childhood Education—A Resource Kit.* Toronto: Ryerson Polytechnic Institute.

McLaughlin, B. 1984 *Second-Language Acquisition in Childhood,* vol. 1, *Preschool Children,* 2nd ed. Hillsdale, N.J., and London: Erlbaum.

McMurter, J. 1992 "Thirty Preschoolers—Fifteen Languages." *Multiculturalism* 14, nos. 2, 3.

McNaughton, K., and D. Stenton 1992 "Literacy, Leadership, and Practice: One Formula for Effective Early Childhood Education Training." *Multiculturalism* 14, nos. 2, 3.

Morrow, R.D. 1989 "What's in a Name?" *Young Children* 44, no. 6.

National Indian Brotherhood 1972 *Indian Control of Indian Education.* Ottawa: National Indian Brotherhood.

Pence, A., V. Kuehne, M. Greenwood-Church, M.R. Opekokew, and V. Mulligan 1992 "First Nations Early Childhood Care and Education: The Meadow Lake Tribal Council/School of Child and Youth Care Curriculum Development Project." *Multiculturalism* 14, nos. 2, 3.

Ramsey, P. G.1987 *Teaching and Learning in a Diverse World: Multicultural Education for Young Children.* New York, N.Y.: Teacher's College Press.

Saville-Troike, M. 1976 *Foundations for Teaching English as a Second Language.* Englewood Cliffs, N.J.: Prentice-Hall.

Skutnabb-Kangas, T. 1981 *Bilingualism or Not: The Education of Minorities.* Clevedon, Avon, England: Multilingual Matters.

Statistics Canada 1992a *Mother Tongue: 20% Sample Data.* 1991 Census of Canada, catalogue no. 93-333. Ottawa: Supply and Services Canada.

Statistics Canada 1992b *Profile of Census Tracts in Toronto. Part A.* 1991 Census of Canada, catalogue no. 95-353. Ottawa: Industry, Science and Technology Canada.

Wong-Fillmore, L. 1991 "When Learning a Second Language Means Losing the First." *Early Childhood Research Quarterly* 6: 323–46.

York, S. 1991 *Roots and Wings: Affirming Culture in Early Childhood Programs.* St. Paul, Minnesota: Redleaf Press.

CHAPTER 19

Facilitating Cognitive Learning

Objectives

After studying the material in this chapter, the student will be able to

- make a case against prescribed paper-and-pencil tasks in preschool programs; describe, instead, the learning activities that should be emphasized
- suggest ways that teachers can help young children with developmental problems learn to focus their attention on cognitive activities
- explain the concept of readiness and how to relate this to maturation and learning theories
- describe basic cognitive functions needed by all young children
- identify ways that teachers can help children, including those with special needs, become involved in group cognitive learning activities

INTRODUCTION

The terms *academic* and *preacademic* are sometimes used to describe cognitive activities in programming for preschool-aged children. These terms are viewed as inappropriate among many early childhood educators. The use of these terms implies approval of a "pushed-down" elementary school curriculum for young children. Terms such as *cognitive, sensorimotor activities,* or *intellectual experiences* are considered more positive alternatives.

The selection and presentation of a wide range of early learning activities appropriate for use in an inclusive early childhood program are covered in this chapter.

A SOCIAL/ECONOMIC/EDUCATIONAL ISSUE

The terms *preoperational* and *readiness* are commonly used to describe the cognitive skills and abilities of children who are no longer infants, but are not yet reading, writing, and doing arithmetic (Wolery and Brookfield-Norman 1988, 109). Though called preoperational or readiness skills, these skills, in a very real sense, are preacademic skills for preschool-aged children. They are the skills most necessary for young children to acquire during the preschool years if they are later to engage with eagerness and confidence in formal academic activities.

Many parents, striving for what they perceive as best for their children, believe that early formal instruction in reading, writing, and math will help their children "succeed" in school. Preschools and early childhood centres are pressured to demonstrate that children are doing more than playing, that they are learning "something worthwhile." This pressure has led to some early childhood programs emphasizing paper-and-pencil tasks and workbook exercises. *Such activities, however, represent an inappropriate and ineffectual teaching format for young children. They also are contrary to philosophical beliefs about appropriate early learning experiences.* As Bredekamp (1987) points out:

Children need years of play with real objects (Photo 19–1) and events before they are able to understand the meaning of symbols such as letters and numbers … Throughout early childhood, children's concepts and language gradually develop to enable them to understand more abstract and symbolic information.

This is certainly true. It is especially true for children with more-aware families that seem automatically to provide day-long opportunities for the development of their children's concepts and language. But what about young children whose family situations cannot provide them with the kinds of stimulation and learning opportunities that support concept and language development? Schickedanz and his colleagues (1990, 12), in a well-reasoned and timely article, ask if the movement to "ban academics in preschools" is not ill-advised in that it further delays those children who need it most. These children are denied opportunities to get the same kind of intellectual underpinnings that the majority of children get as a part of everyday family life. "For children who do not get academic learning at home, academically stimulating preschools are an opportunity equalizer" (Schickedanz et al., 1990).

PHOTO 19–1 *Children need years of play with tangible objects.*

These authors suggest further that "preschoolers are ready for academic content—lots of it," and draw on their research for evidence. They offer a long list of cognitive-type activities that a young, middle-class child is likely to engage in almost daily with family members, usually the mother. Their conclusion is that it is the teaching methods, not academics per se, that is the early childhood centre's problem; that cognitive skills learning *can be embedded* in experiences that are appropriate for young children. In other words, academic learning is not an either/or situation. This is the approach exemplified in this text. Young children can have both: Bredekamp's "years of play with real objects and events" *and* cognitive kinds of learning experiences within the context of playful and appropriate activities that "preserve childhood" (to borrow a phrase from Greenberg [1990]).

PHOTO 19–2 *Cognitive activities are a part of most preschool activities.*

In truth, by whatever name—cognitive, language, sensorimotor, intellectual, academic, or preacademic—such activities are an integral part of most early childhood programs (Photo 19–2). However, we want to emphasize this: *The learning experiences for preschool-aged children should never be presented in the form of workbooks, ditto sheets, prescribed paper-and-pencil tasks, or rote memorization. Such activities are not appropriate in any early childhood curriculum or for any preschool-aged child, regardless of developmental level.* The focus must always be on enjoyable activities that promote children's effective use of language, the development of their social interaction skills, their emerging abilities to formulate concepts, and their interest in, and curiosity about, the world around them.

COGNITIVE EXPERIENCES AND YOUNG CHILDREN

Skills related to concept development can be observed from infancy on, even in children with developmental disabilities.

Children with disabilities may place anywhere along the developmental continuum in cognitive functioning. A child who has severe motor disabilities may be advanced in some areas of cognitive development.

Many children with disabilities never realize their cognitive potential; others excel far beyond their nondisabled peers. This chapter, therefore, will emphasize *starting where the child is* and working from there, step by step, to approach the subject through a focus on planning cognitive activities that will benefit all children.

In early childhood programs of every description, daily learning opportunities and experiences are the rule, rather than the exception. The teacher's role in these situations is to observe children's developmental levels, recognize their emerging interests, and then plan learning opportunities that challenge them to think and that stimulate curiosity and learning. The teacher first sets the scene and then follows the children's lead. Based on those leads, teachers should guide and then support children in exploring learning opportunities.

PHOTO 19–3 *Teachers should respond to children's questions and signs for further information.*

DIRECT TEACHING

Teachers should always respond to children's interest, questions, and signs of readiness for further information (Photo 19–3). Most importantly, teachers should guide, pose open-ended questions, and prompt children to use skills and information they already have. It is in cognitive activities that the teacher is most likely to engage in a limited amount of direct teaching. On occasion, teachers will suggest to children what they might try doing, or how to approach a task. Whenever possible, however, teachers should combine direct teaching with an indirect and facilitative approach—for example, posing questions that encourage a child to think and try out alternative ways of doing something.

Example:

> *A child asks, "What's that?" pointing to a picture of an unfamiliar animal. The teacher might begin by asking, "What do you think it looks like?" and then, taking the child's answer, saying, "Let's read what it says here" (modelling that one learns answers through reading), and reading the word possum.*
>
> *The teacher engages in direct teaching by reading possum, the name in the caption below the picture. After reading the name, the teacher might ask the child to describe this animal. The teacher then expands on what the child has said, and then reinforces the child's response: "That's right; it is a possum." If the child (and the other children) still seem interested, the teacher can take advantage of this teaching opportunity by opening another book*

with pictures of familiar animals and help the children find a somewhat similar animal (a woodchuck) and discover the likenesses and differences between it and the possum.

Cognitive activities can be presented in structured settings. However, it is far more effective for learning to occur informally as an outgrowth of children's exploration and through teacher-prepared developmentally appropriate learning opportunities and activity centres that are set up and expanded on throughout the day.

Example:

A child with limited cognitive skills is learning to button his coat. After completing the buttoning, the teacher then expands on the activity by counting the number of buttons.

This is done informally, in the context of an activity that has meaning for the child. In an approach of this type, the learning that takes place often goes unlabelled and unrecognized as "real learning." Thus, the learning vs. play argument persists in spite of decades of research indicating that children's learning and play are inseparable in early learning.

EARLY LEARNING: EAGERNESS AND ANTICIPATION

Most children are born ready and eager to learn. Preserving and promoting this innate interest to explore and seek answers has been a goal of early childhood educators for a long time. Rather than drill and instruct, the role of the early childhood teacher is to *help children observe, ask, and find out more about things that interest them.* Therefore, children of all developmental levels, from the most delayed to the most gifted, need activities that support awareness, curiosity, and the urge to question. Activities that involve sensory experiences—touching, seeing, hearing, tasting, and smelling—are essential. In other words, children need a learning environment where they are free to explore and experience materials and activities through their senses in their own way, at their own pace (Photo 19–4). Children with visual and hearing deficits need such experiences, too, if their eagerness to learn is to be preserved. However, they often need a teacher's encouragement and guidance in learning to use and develop their other senses and abilities to the best possible advantage.

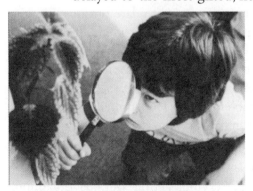

PHOTO 19–4 *Teachers should arrange the environment to support children's innate interests.*

As Katz and Chard (1989) put it, "Children's minds should be engaged in ways that deepen their understanding of their own experiences." At the same time, preschool teachers can advance, *indirectly* but significantly, children's anticipation of learning to read, write, and do math. Teachers can do this by writing out a child's story or questions and reading them back to the child, or helping the child to find the answers or make measurements. They can help children keep a log by writing down what each child dictates about observed changes— for example, in a plant's growth. With these kinds of preacademic activities, most children, when they reach the primary grades, are ready and eager to learn to read about, tell about, write about, even measure their experiences. Teachers must convince parents, administrators, and policymakers who may be pushing for workbooks and other paper-and-pencil tasks of the benefits of an enriched, supportive preacademic environment that is flexible enough to be developmentally appropriate for all the children in the group (Wolery 1994).

Valuing Today's Learning

An important goal in planning cognitive activities is recognizing that today's living and learning is important to overall development. Enjoyable and challenging readiness activities contribute to an everyday sense of well-being and accomplishment. The immediate developmental value of these activities is not to be questioned, even though they contribute to long-term, school-related accomplishments. Everything that is recommended for infants and young children—good nutrition, quality child care, medical attention—has the same dual purpose: to foster everyday well-being and long-term development.

Expecting children to engage in activities that do not relate to their interests or developmental level can stifle children's eagerness to learn. Children seldom enjoy or master tasks that are a poor developmental match (Hunt 1961). True, countless numbers of children survive the mismatch during their early years and go on to function adequately during their school years. But other children, and especially those with developmental problems, may feel immense frustration, resulting in difficulties such as the following:

1. poor self-esteem and lack of trust in their ability to learn
2. a dislike of school, schoolwork, and teachers
3. school-related avoidance behaviours (crying, acting out, daydreaming, withdrawing, and chronic stomachaches)

In cases where a child's major disability is an intellectual impairment, it is important to identify the child's current level and rate of learning in deciding what type of tasks are an appropriate match. (See Chapter 11 and Appendix C.) The length of time and number of steps into which a task is broken down depends upon the individual child. It may take one child several weeks to learn what another child can learn in a day.

READINESS AND PREACADEMIC ACTIVITY PLANNING

Since preacademic skills are a mix of many developmental skills, each skill could be labelled a *readiness skill*. Some readiness skills are directly related to future academic performance, while others are indirectly related (large motor skills, for example). A readiness skill might be described as the underlying prerequisite behaviour a child needs to learn in order to perform a particular task.

When a child shows developmental irregularities or delays, the cause often is cited as immaturity: "The child is not ready. Let's wait and see." This puts many a child "on hold" during a critical developmental period and proves disastrous for young children who are at biological or environmental risk. The result may be further delay in development and a worsening of the child's problem.

Children with special needs often have difficulty acquiring readiness skills on their own. Teachers must identify the missing skills in each child and then teach them, step by step. Behaviours that might delay or interfere with learning include these:

- short attention span
- limited ability to imitate
- perceptual motor inefficiency (see Photo 19–5)
- inadequate fine motor controls (eye–hand–wrist coordination)
- limited ability to formulate concepts
- poorly developed short-term and long-term memory
- inability to follow instructions

All preacademic skills are intertwined with each other and with all other areas of development. This interrelatedness is the essence of the *whole child* concept of development. For example, when children are recalling their trip to the zoo, all skills come into play and even overlap, as the teacher helps children discuss and act out what they saw, heard, and did. This interrelatedness of developmental skills also makes a convincing argument against an academic, subject-matter approach in the education of young children.

PHOTO 19–5 *Teacher support is often needed when children have perceptual motor inefficiencies.*

ATTENTION SPAN

Attention span is the length of time an individual is able to concentrate on an activity or event. The ability to simultaneously *focus* on certain aspects of the environment and *ignore* others is essential. When working with a puzzle, a child needs to be able to focus on the frame board and the puzzle pieces while ignoring other children's play activities. As stressed in Chapter 14, children's ability (or inability) to focus their attention is strongly influenced by classroom arrangements.

Example:

> *Jeri, a normally developing 3-year-old, picked up a completed puzzle from the table, dumped it out, looked at it briefly, and tried to put in a piece. She then picked up a second puzzle and dumped it out also. Next, she picked up a nearby truck and ran it through the puzzle. Leaving the area with the truck, she went to the sand table. There she picked up some sifters, sifted for two minutes, and then went over to look at the fish.*

Jeri's "short" attention span can be related to activities that may have been developmentally too advanced (the puzzle she chose), an environment that was too stimulating for her (she just couldn't focus in on any one thing), and perhaps how the room was arranged, as well as the fact that no teacher stepped in to support her interest in any one area.

A child cannot be successful (or even interested) when materials are overly difficult or poorly arranged (the puzzle and the truck on the same table) (Photo 19–6). Many children have the potential for longer periods of attention, yet they do not stay with activities because the materials are developmentally inappropriate or set up in inappropriate ways.

It is true that attractiveness of materials and the ways in which they are presented are important factors in determining how involved a child will become with an activity. Even so, there are children who have trouble becoming involved on their own, regardless of the attractiveness of the setting. They need help from teachers in getting started. Once their attention is engaged, however, they too learn to focus. Bailey and Wolery (1984, 133) suggest several ways in which teachers can help children who are delayed and those who

PHOTO 19–6 *The child's ability to focus attention is strongly influenced by classroom arrangements.*

are developing normally to focus their attention:

- Provide materials that are appealing and colourful, can be manipulated, and have built-in feedback, such as a jack-in-the-box.
- Offer participation as a privilege rather than a responsibility.
- Give children an immediate role: "Julie has the punch to punch the train tickets."
- Instruct or prompt an activity: "I'll help you start a fence at this end. Where shall I put my first block?"
- Identify children's preferences for materials; preferred materials result in longer involvement.

Further strategies for increasing children's interaction with learning activities were discussed in Chapter 7 in the section on overly active children and attention deficit disorders.

IMITATION AND MODELLING

As noted in several other chapters, the ability to *imitate* is essential to all learning. When trying to learn a new skill such as driving a car, jumping rope, or pronouncing a new word, the first step, usually, is watching and listening to others. The next step is to try to imitate the behaviour that was observed. This process—observing and imitating—is repeated until the learner is satisfied with his or her performance (or decides to abandon the effort). Most infants and young children imitate spontaneously. They do not have to be taught, but they do need good models and opportunities to practise. The many peek-a-boo games, fingerplays, action songs, chants, and rhyming games found in most cultures probably were devised (unintentionally) to motivate imitation in infants. Such activities, popular in most early childhood programs, are there for the same reason (Photo 19–7).

A distinction should be made between *learning through imitation* and *learning to imitate*. Children who do not imitate spontaneously must be taught, if they are to learn other developmental skills. However, the inability to imitate often

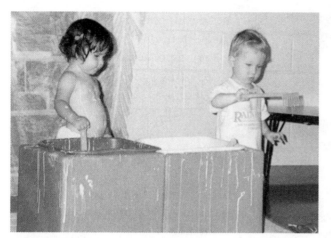

PHOTO 19–7 *The ability to imitate is essential to all learning.*

goes unrecognized and so becomes the cause of continuing learning difficulties. When a child with developmental problems is enrolled in a group, an informal assessment of imitation skills should be a priority. (A simplified version of a game such as Simon Says can tell a teacher a great deal about a child's ability to imitate.) If imitation skills are lacking, initial teaching priorities should be concentrated in that area. Bailey and Wolery (1984) make the following suggestions for teaching children how to imitate:

- Imitate the child. Imitating the child's vocalizations and gestures often stimulates the child and also reinforces the child's further efforts.
- Provide models appropriate for the child's level of development. If a child at 7 years of age is functioning more like a 3-year-old, then behaviours typical of the younger age should be the starting models, with special concentration on those behaviours the child already has.
- Provide whatever assistance is needed to help the child learn to imitate. Placing a mirror in front of the child, for example, allows the child to judge the accuracy of his or her imitations.
- If necessary, be directive in teaching the child to imitate. Physically put the child through an imitative response. (The teacher points to the child and says, "Marla, point to the circle," while stretching out the child's index finger and placing it on the "point to" object. An encouraging and descriptive comment follows: "Marla, look at that! You're pointing to the circle!")
- Make imitating a rewarding and playful experience; learning to imitate should be fun.
- Provide positive feedback and encouragement for approximations (first efforts) to an imitative response. (When a child finally points to an object, even though it may not be the one requested, respond positively: "You're pointing to a blue truck. Good for you. Now let's find the red one and you can point to it, too.")

PHOTO 19–8 *Perceptual motor skills are made up of understanding sensory messages and translating them into appropriate action.*

PERCEPTUAL MOTOR SKILLS

Perceptual motor skills are made up of two closely related processes (Photo 19–8). One has to do with *understanding* sensory messages: what is seen, heard, touched, tasted, or smelled. The second is the translation of the messages into appropriate actions. Generally, more than one sense is involved in a response; this is referred to as *sensory integration*. The following are three examples of perceptual motor skills coupled with sensory integration:

1. A 2-year-old stops her play and turns at the sound of an engine. She looks up, moves her eyes back and forth, and then points to an airplane. This child is exhibiting integrated visual (seeing) and auditory (hearing) skills resulting in appropriately matched motor responses of turning, scanning, and pointing.

2. A 4-year-old picks up a bar of cocoa butter, smells it, bites off a corner, and then spits it out while making a wry face. The child is expressing appropriate smell and taste perceptions and responding with relevant perceptual motor responses: the cocoa butter smelled like candy, and she took a bite. It tasted more like soap than candy, however, and so she spit it out while making a face indicating an unpleasant taste.

3. A 5-year-old, during group time, reaches into the Mystery Bag and verbally identifies unseen objects by touch.

Every preschool activity involves various forms of perceptual motor skills. Outdoors there is climbing, jumping, riding wheel toys, watching a caterpillar creep, splashing in puddles. Indoors there is blockbuilding, playing with table toys, painting, working with clay, colouring, cutting and pasting. Music and stories and dramatic play provide opportunities to rhyme, pantomime, and pretend. Such play activities help young children, those with disabilities and those with no disabilities, to develop perceptual motor skills essential to everyday living.

Children with impaired perceptual motor skills often receive incomplete or distorted messages from the world around them. In some instances, children

PHOTO 19–9 *An activity that promotes fine motor control and perceptual motor skills simultaneously.*

have become nearly immobilized because they are so distrustful of moving about. Their distrust stems from having received faulty sensory messages. For example, children with impaired depth perception are sometimes hurt and badly frightened by stepping off into unanticipated space. Thus, children with sensory problems need special activities, adapted materials, and additional support in using their intact senses. Some of these adaptations were described in Chapter 14 on environmental arrangements and in earlier chapters on specific disabilities; others will be described later in this chapter.

Fine motor skills (eye–hand coordination, use of the fingers, hands, and wrists) are closely related to perceptual motor skills. Both are important in learning self-help/care skills (Chapter 20) as well as in learning to use all kinds of tools: paintbrushes, hammers, crayons, and eventually pencils for printing and then writing. Practice in fine motor control is embedded in many early childhood activities. The same activities that enable practice of fine motor skills have important cognitive, social, and language components. Here are some examples:

- water-play—pouring, squeezing, measuring
- blockbuilding—stacking, bridging, balancing, putting away
- art activities—painting, hammering, woodworking, clay, cutting, pasting, crayoning, and so forth (Photo 19–9)
- housekeeping—dressing dolls, pouring "tea," stirring "soup," and setting the table

Manipulative materials, sometimes referred to as *table toys*, are especially good for promoting fine motor control and perceptual motor skills simultaneously. Among the most useful are these:

- wooden beads and strings with metal or plastic tips
- puzzles and parquetry blocks
- picture dominoes and lotto games
- nesting and stacking cups, kitty-in-the-keg, form boxes
- pegs and pegboards, hammer and nails set
- Montessori graduated cylinders and colour boards

When appropriately matched to children's skill levels, manipulative materials ensure practice sessions that are informal and fun for all children. They also can be used successfully by children with developmental disabilities, because they are so readily adaptable. The following examples demonstrate how manipulative materials can be adapted or specially presented for a child who needs special support.

- For fine motor skill development, wooden beads are especially useful. Offer only the largest wooden beads with a stiff wire on which to string them; a straightened coat hanger with ends wrapped with tape works well.
- For a child who has delays in cognitive as well as fine motor development, select puzzles with few pieces and each piece a recognizable object.

    Adaptation of materials is also important. For example, when a child has mastered the simple puzzles but the next ones seem too complex, teachers need to be inventive. Here is one suggestion. Several of the inside pieces of more difficult puzzles can be taped down from underneath with a strip of Scotch tape doubled back on itself. These pieces remain in the frame when the child turns the puzzle out. Less is required of the child; fewer pieces have to be replaced to complete the task and the job is simplified because finding the fit for border pieces is usually easier. The task gradually can be made more difficult by taping down fewer and fewer puzzle pieces. The advantage to this procedure is that each time the child completes the task there is always the reward of seeing the completed puzzle. (The foregoing example, by the way, is an excellent illustration of a teacher's creative efforts at task analysis.)

- When handing out nesting cups, present only four or five of the largest nesting cups.

    1. Put them out in a straight line, in order.

    2. Hand them to the child, one by one, to ensure successful nesting from the outset.

    3. Then let the child begin to pick up the cups, but continue to present them in order.

    4. Gradually randomize the order of presentation, but revert to fewer cups, temporarily.

    5. As the child becomes proficient, cups can be added, one at a time.

    For a child with a more severe impairment, every other cup might first be presented so as to maximize size differences; the drawback is that the child does not get the quality of sensory feedback that is achieved when the cups are nested in precise order.

CONCEPT FORMATION

Concepts and *concept formation* are difficult terms to define without becoming overly technical. For the purposes of this text, concepts will be defined as internal images or ideas (mental activities) that organize thinking. Concepts enable us to make sense out of our world. Concepts developing in preschool-aged children include this grouping:

- colour
- texture
- size
- shape
- weight
- same vs. different
- directionality and position in space, such as *up, down, inside, outside, on top of, under, over*

PHOTO 19–10 *By continuously formulating new concepts, young children impose order on all of the things they must learn.*

By continuously formulating new concepts, young children impose order on all of the many things they must learn (Photo 19–10). Skills related to concept formation include discrimination, classification, seriation, understanding of spatial and temporal relationships, memory, and ability to follow directions.

1. Discrimination

Concept development depends on the ability to *discriminate*—that is, to perceive likenesses and differences among related objects and events. Put even more simply, it is the ability to "tell things apart"; to specify "same or different"; to match objects, sounds, or ideas in terms of one or more attributes (characteristics). Opportunities to practise making both simple and complex discriminations are found throughout the preschool day:

- At music time the teacher introduces a song that asks: Who is wearing sandals? Boots? Running shoes? Blue socks? Striped socks? No socks?
- A variety of sorting tasks are usually available, such as putting the yellow pegs in one compartment and the blue pegs in another.

- Unit blocks often are put away according to the size and shape drawn on the shelf.
- A patterned string of wooden beads may be presented for children to copy—a small round blue bead, a big square red bead, a long green bead. This is repeated several times. This task is complex in that the beads vary on three dimensions: shape, size, and colour.

It should be noted, too, that the fine motor and perceptual motor skills are demanding. It might be that a child could make the necessary discriminations but not have the fine motor skills for stringing the beads. This is an instance where the teacher would need to make an adaptation in materials, perhaps providing a wire rather than a string for threading the beads. A child with more severe physical limitations might participate by identifying the next bead, and another child or adult can place it on the wire.

Discrimination tasks can be adapted to fit any developmental level. For children who are functioning at a higher level, the bead-stringing task can be made more complex by introducing number concepts as well as colour, space, and shape: repetitions of three small round blue beads, two large square red beads, one long green bead. Or, it can be made very simple for a child who is developmentally at a lower level of functioning, such as alternating a square red bead with a square blue bead; or simpler yet, having the child select and string only large blue beads (with only large red beads in the basket as distracters). Adaptations for individual differences are unlimited.

2. Classification

The process of imposing order on objects and events is another major characteristic of concept formation. This skill is sometimes described as the ability to classify—that is, to form categories. In other words, children learn that cats, dogs, and squirrels have certain characteristics in common: fur, four legs, a tail, and so on. On the basis of these shared attributes, the creatures all fall into the category of *animal*. Each category is subject to further breakdown, as the child's experiences broaden. Dog becomes a category by itself when the child learns to discriminate among different kinds of dogs—poodles, collies, Airedales. Learning to classify, like learning to discriminate, can be taught.

3. Seriation

Seriation is the process of arranging objects and events along orderly and related dimensions (a prerequisite skill is the ability to make fine discriminations) (Photo 19–11). Everyday examples include these:

- tall, middle-sized, shortest; and eventually, "These tall ones are taller than those tall ones"

PHOTO 19–11 *The arranging of objects in a prescribed order is an example of seriation.*

- first, last, next-to-last
- happy, sad; "saddest one of all"

Seriation experiences, like those in the preceding list, help children learn to make comparisons about quantities, time and space, and affect (feelings). Learning to tell about what happened in the order of occurrence is another seriation skill that many older preschoolers begin to master.

Example:

> *"Yesterday we went to Grandma's. We got to play in the attic. Then we had dinner but first Grandma made us wash our hands and face 'cause we got so dirty. After dinner Grandpa read to us and then it was time to go home and I slept in the car."*

Many early childhood activities lend themselves to seriation practice and to endless adaptations for children with limited abilities. For example, children can retell a story that has just been read, or teachers can ask, "What comes next?" when reading a familiar story. Sequenced picture cards (commercial or teacher-made) are also useful. The cards tell a story when arranged in proper order: the first card may show a child digging a hole in the ground, the second shows planting a seed, and the third, pulling up a carrot. For more advanced children, the series can be longer and more complex, including pictures related to watering, weeding, and sprouting. For the very limited child, the teacher might use just two pictures, a child climbing up on a stool and then jumping down. At first, the teacher and child can alternate placing the cards, with the teacher stating what comes first and what happens next.

4. Understanding of Spatial and Temporal Relationships

Learning how objects and events are related to space, to time, and to the child is another aspect of concept formation. Spatial and temporal (time) concepts include this grouping:

- on, in, under
- in front of, behind, next to
- in between, in the middle, second from the end

- yesterday, today, tomorrow
- soon, after a while, later, not yet

Many children seem to learn such concepts automatically. However, there are children with and without developmental problems who need direct instruction. Spatial and temporal concepts are best taught as children themselves are moving about in space and time. For example, each child must learn to recognize his or her body-occupying-space in relationship to the body-space of others. This may not come easily and certainly it does not come early. Toddlers, as mentioned in Chapter 15, may "plough through" other toddlers as if they did not exist.

PHOTO **19–12** *Active play is especially helpful in children's development of spatial awareness.*

Active play is especially helpful in developing children's spatial awareness (Photo 19–12). Outdoors, a teacher might comment, "Hamid, you climbed so high. You are on top of the ladder box." If the child is having difficulty forming spatial concepts, the teacher should do an immediate follow-up: "Where are you, Hamid?" and wait for the child to respond. If the child does not respond, the teacher models the words high, on top. When the child repeats the statement, the teacher corroborates: "That's right, Hamid. You are high; you are on top."

Learning to understand time is more difficult for most children. "Yesterday is eons away and tomorrow can be expected any minute" (Cook, Tessier, and Armbruster 1987, 187). As with spatial concepts, time concepts are most effectively learned in relationship to play and everyday activities. Short and more immediate time intervals are better understood in the beginning:

- "Time to come in *after* you run around the track two more times."
- "Snack comes *when* we finish this story."
- "We will get back *in time for* lunch."

5. Memory

The ability to remember what previously has been experienced and learned is a skill necessary to all new learning. Two kinds of memory are required: long-term and short-term (being able to remember what took place some time earlier as well as what happened in the immediate past). Tasks requiring rote memorization are inappropriate for young children and of doubtful value for children of any age. Activities that encourage children to practise remembering within their everyday work and play activities are the kind that foster learning. Such activities might include

- conversational questions *of interest to the child* (with teacher prompts, after a suitable pause):
  - What did you have for breakfast? ... (orange juice? cereal? anything else?)
  - Where does your kitten sleep? ... (in a basket?)
  - What was the caterpillar doing on the leaf? ... (crawling? chewing on the leaf?)
- remembering each other's names and teachers' names, and using these names appropriately
- remembering where materials are stored so as to get them out and put them away properly
- telling what object or objects have been removed in games such as "cover the tray"
- story- and picture-reading activities, as mentioned under *seriation*
- leaving the bathroom in prescribed order for the next children who will be using it

For children with cognitive, neurological, or related problems the teacher often begins memory training by telling the child what comes next: "The paper towel goes in the basket." The teacher follows up immediately: "Where does the paper towel go?" The child has to remember only long enough to repeat the information (or comply). A child's memory system may be activated more slowly if he or she is delayed; therefore, it is important to give adequate time to respond. In teaching paper towel disposal, for example, the teacher must allow adequate time for the child's memory to become charged and produce action.

6. Ability to Follow Instructions

The ability to follow instructions and carry out requests is important. Children with language, cognitive, or neurological impairments often have trouble with such tasks. Whenever a child has repeated difficulty, teachers should ask themselves the following five questions:

1. Does the child hear (or see) well enough to know what is expected?
2. Does the child have the vocabulary necessary to understand the request?

3. Does the child understand the concepts (understand *match* when the teacher says: "Match circles of the same colour")?

4. Is the child able to imitate the behaviours expected, as when the teacher demonstrates how to fold a piece of paper in half?

5. Are the instructions too complicated or given too rapidly? Too many at one time?

Three- and four-step directions, spoken in rapid sequence, are more than most young children (let alone children who are developmentally delayed) can manage. It is true that a few older preschoolers might be able to carry through on "Would you be so good as to go to the sink and wet a sponge—I think there's one under the sink or in the bathroom—and then wipe up all that messy paint on the floor and halfway up the table legs?" Many others would be completely lost. A few might try to carry out the last step in the direction (the only thing they remember) by rubbing at the paint on the table leg with their hand, perhaps.

PHOTO 19–13 *When giving directions to young children, teachers should get down to the child's eye level.*

The younger the child in age, experience, or developmental level, the simpler directions should be. *It is important that teachers take nothing for granted about what children understand.* For very young children and for children with developmental problems, directions should be given one at a time. The process works best when

• the teacher gets down to a child's eye level and speaks directly to the child (Photo 19–13), and

• the language used is clear and free of unnecessary words or explanations.

The following is an example of the last-mentioned point, based on the confusing and complex set of directions quoted above:

"Marty, we're going to have to get this paint wiped up. Would you go to the sink (enough of a pause to let the child start moving toward the sink) and find a sponge?"

When Marty has the sponge in his hand, the teacher gives the next direction: "Now, wet the sponge." If the teacher wants to make sure that the child does not cross the room dripping water all the way, an intermediate instruction should be given: "Squeeze some water out of it."

Some children might not know what the teacher expects, so the teacher says, "Like this," pantomiming how to squeeze a sponge. "Now, let's go over and wipe up the paint on the floor."

When that is accomplished, the teacher can draw the child's attention to the paint on the table legs.

Instructions should be accompanied by gestures—for example, pointing when asking a child to put the car on the shelf.

Most children who are developmentally ready can learn to follow instructions if they are allowed to begin with one-step directions like those in the example. When the child has mastered one-step directions, it is logical to move to two- and then, perhaps, three-step directions. In an inclusive setting when teaching how to follow complex directions or instructions, it is often a good idea to pair a child without a disability with a child who has disabilities.

Example:

"Judi and John, will you get the chalk and the small chalkboards and put them on the big, round table?"

PREREQUISITES FOR READING, WRITING, AND MATH

Other cognitive skills and activities are more closely associated with reading, writing, and math. Here is a list of a few such skills, those sometimes seen in early childhood programs:

* "Reading" a series of pictures on a page from left to right and top to bottom. (Many picture books and board games are set up to promote this kind of prereading visual organization in children.)
* Pencil or crayon activities that begin to show some degree of eye–hand control (scribbling large swirling circles upon circles; making the marks that children often describe as "writing"; experiencing occasional success at writing one's own name).
* Freestyle cutting with scissors (Photo 19–14). Some children spontaneously try to "cut on the line."
* Counting a row of objects from left to right (or top to bottom, as in coat buttoning) by touching each in turn (one-to-one correspondence).
* Grouping objects in sets of two, three, or four.
* Identifying groups of objects as the *same, more,* or *less.*
* Understanding that different but similar sounds are not the same. (Numerous songs, fingerplays, poems, and teacher-improvised games contribute to this learning.)

PHOTO 19–14 *Freestyle cutting is a prewriting skill.*

None of these tasks is easily accomplished. They require at least minimal competence in the underlying skills discussed earlier in the chapter. However, all of them can be taught, to some degree. All can be sequenced so as to facilitate children's learning. Learning to cut on the lines will be used as an illustration:

Julio was a highly distractible 7-year-old with uncertain fine motor skills. Using a pair of specially designed scissors that allowed him to put his hand over Julio's, the teacher helped Julio learn to hold the scissors and then to "cut" the air with them. Next, the teacher prepared strips of paper about 1.5 cm wide with heavy lines drawn across them at 2 cm intervals. The teacher held up a strip and instructed Julio to open his scissors. The teacher then inserted the strip between the scissor blades, in contact with one of the black lines, and said, "Cut." It was a simple matter for Julio to close the scissors. Success was immediate and evident: a cleanly cut piece of paper came off with each contact. To add interest to the task, the teacher soon switched to strips of brightly coloured paper, feeling that Julio would not now be distracted from his cutting task by the variations in colour. Julio's cuttings were put into an envelope to either take home to play with or paste into a "picture" at school.

PLANNING AND PRESENTING LEARNING OPPORTUNITIES

A successful early childhood program depends on careful planning, whether the learning opportunities are informal and incidental or teacher-initiated. How the materials are presented and how children are grouped also determine the success of the learning activities.

GROUPING CHILDREN

A preschool class with as many as 15 to 20 children is best divided into three or four small groups for teacher-supported activities. The number of teachers, or assistants, that are available usually determines the number of groups. Group size can be increased as children become more skilled and more experienced. The closer children with developmental problems get to their kindergarten year, the greater is the benefit of having opportunities to work in larger groups, as long as that is appropriate for the developmental level of the child. Younger children and children with developmental disabilities continue to need more support and attention from teachers.

GROUP COGNITIVE AND INTERACTIVE ACTIVITIES

An overall goal for early childhood settings is to help children be interested, comfortable, and appropriately challenged. To ensure that children do participate actively in all activities, the following arrangements are suggested. These are especially important with children who are developmentally delayed, overly active, or have trouble staying on task.

Short Periods

Teacher-directed activities should be limited to short periods: three, four, or five minutes in length. This time period can be lengthened if the interest and involvement of the participating children is maintained. Activities should always be concluded *before* children lose interest.

Nonthreatening Materials and Activities

Start with materials that children enjoy and are familiar with (the problem of the match, once again): crayons; simple puzzles and manipulative materials; pictures of everyday objects to talk about, match, and group. Such materials allow most children to feel comfortable and competent, right from the start.

Preferred Materials and Activities

Noting what materials and activities are preferred by which children is important. These can be presented several days in a row to firm up the child's comfort and competence. Preferred materials also are useful as takeoff points for increasing the complexity of learning tasks, and expanding them as a child is ready.

Readiness to Expand Learning Opportunities

If a child has become inattentive or frustrated, the teacher needs to observe the child in the context of the learning situation. Often, the problem resides not in the child but in the learning environment. Changes may need to be made in the materials or activities so they more closely match the child's interests and ability level. It is best to have additional materials immediately at hand to expand activities and create new interest.

Advance Preparation

Before children arrive, all materials for the daily program should be assembled and handy to the learning centres (Photo 19–15).

PHOTO 19–15 *Teachers should arrange materials before children arrive.*

ENJOYING COGNITIVE LEARNING

Cognitive activities should be enjoyable for children and for teachers. When preacademic activities are fun and developmentally appropriate, children will be eager to participate in the learning experiences. Eagerness to participate invariably promotes successful learning in children. Successful learning is enjoyable for teachers in that it represents a teacher's success as a teacher. With that kind of reward (motivation) teachers tend to put more and more of themselves into their teaching. The result? Their teaching gets ever better and their enjoyment increases proportionately. A positive and mutually reinforcing system is activated for both children and teachers.

SUMMARY

Stimulating learning for young children involves a range of informal, nonacademic, cognitive, language, social, motor, and perceptual motor tasks. These are a part of most early childhood programs. Preacademics or readiness activities *should not* include drills and workbooks or paper-and-pencil tasks. Promoting children's day-by-day integration of developmental skills and fostering their eagerness to learn is the major value of the learning activities that take place in the early childhood years.

Readiness and preacademic skills can be taught if they do not come about in due course through normal developmental processes. In other words, a child's short attention span or inability to imitate or follow instructions is not ascribed to immaturity. Instead of a "wait-and-see" approach, some skills can be encouraged through a step-by-step approach, thereby avoiding a further and additionally damaging developmental delay. In addition to attention span, imitation skills, and following instructions, other specific preacademic skills include perceptual motor and fine motor skills, memory, and the ability to formulate concepts. Certain prerequisites for reading, writing, and math skills may also be subsumed under preacademics, but these are child-initiated, not teacher-directed "seatwork" activities.

Small-group activities, based on a variety of learning opportunities, are offered in most early childhood programs. When activities are attractively arranged and appropriately presented, most children, including children with developmental problems, enjoy them, especially if teachers help the children acquire whatever prerequisite skills they may lack. The most important aspect of all activities is that they be enjoyable to both children and teachers. Enjoyment leads to feelings of success, which lead to further enjoyment in learning and in teaching.

STUDENT ACTIVITIES

1. Observe a preschool or early childhood program for interest centres and learning opportunities. Describe the various cognitive learning opportunities that are available to the children.

2. Observe one particular child in a group, preferably a child with a developmental disability or delay. Describe the kinds of adaptations that teachers made to enhance this child's learning. If you saw no such adaptations, suggest what might have been done.

3. Select three of the manipulative materials listed (or materials of your own choosing). Demonstrate for the class ways the materials might be presented or adapted to match the skills of a child who is gifted and a child with delayed cognitive development.

4. Observe a teacher for 20 minutes. Write down everything the teacher does that relates to facilitating children's cognitive learning.

REFERENCES

Bailey, D.B., and M. Wolery 1984 *Teaching Infants and Preschoolers with Handicaps.* Columbus, Ohio: Charles E. Merrill.

Bredekamp, S., ed. 1987 *Developmentally Appropriate Practice in Early Childhood Programs Serving Children from Birth through Age 8.* Washington, D.C.: National Association for the Education of Young Children.

Cook, R.E., A. Tessier, and V.B. Armbruster 1987 *Adapting Early Childhood Curricula for Children with Special Needs.* Columbus, Ohio: Charles E. Merrill.

Greenberg, P. 1990 "Why Not Academic Preschools?" *Young Children* 45, no. 2: 70–80.

Hunt, J. McV. 1961 *Intelligence and Experience.* New York: Ronald Press.

Katz, L.G., and S. Chard 1989 *The Project Approach.* Norwood, N.J.: Ablex.

Schickedanz, J., S. Chay, P. Gopin, L. Sheng, S. Song, and N. Wild 1990 "Preschoolers and Academics. Some Thoughts." *Young Children* 46, no. 1: 4–13.

Wolery, M.R. 1994 "Implementing Instruction for Young Children with Special Needs in Early Childhood Classrooms." In M. Wolery and J.S. Wilbur (eds.), *Including Children with Special Needs in Early Childhood Programs.* Washington, D.C.: National Association for the Education of Young Children.

Wolery, M.R., and J. Brookfield-Norman 1988 "Pre-academic Instruction for Handicapped Preschool Children." In S.L. Odom and M.B. Karnes, eds. *Early Intervention for Infants and Children with Handicaps.* Baltimore: Paul H. Brookes.

CHAPTER 20

Facilitating Self–Help/Care and Independence Skills

Objectives

After studying the material in this chapter, the student will be able to

- explain why it is important developmentally that all children, including those with disabilities, learn self-help/care skills

- describe ways in which a teacher can help young children learn necessary self-help/care skills

- discuss the concept of helpful and not-so-helpful "kindness" when assisting young children in their efforts to achieve greater independence

- write a task analysis for common self-help/care activities

- demonstrate forward and backward chaining in teaching a self-help/care skill

INTRODUCTION

A major goal of inclusive early childhood programs is balance: *ensuring that children do things on their own (without help) and ensuring that they are not left out because they cannot do something* (Wolery 1994, 154). Two basic principles guide quality programs, according to Wolery:

1. the principle of independence—that children be encouraged and allowed to do as much as possible for themselves in learning environments designed to support their endeavours; and

2. the principle of participation—that children with special needs be a part of all activities and that adaptations be made to encourage a child's participation to the maximum extent possible.

While these two principles apply to all early childhood curriculum areas, they are especially relevant in helping children with special needs acquire the self-help/care skills that are the focus of this chapter. These skills, when adequately learned, enable individuals to manage personal needs and to *adapt* their behaviours to social expectations.

The terms *self-care* and *self-help skills* are used interchangeably. They describe the ability of individuals to manage personal needs and to adapt their behaviours to social expectations. The specific skills and adaptive behaviours that children are required to learn are determined by the culture in which they live. Though patterns differ, all cultures prescribe ways of eating, toileting, dressing, behaving sexually, sleeping, resting, and keeping public places orderly. An individual's competence in self-help/care and adaptive skills may be the distinguishing factor between those who are considered intellectually impaired (mentally retarded) and those who are not. Recall the AAMR definition of mental retardation (Chapter 4). Essentially, it says that regardless of IQ scores, an individual is not to be considered intellectually impaired (mentally retarded) if he or she displays adequate

- personal independence,
- social responsibility, and
- functional skills for daily living based on his or her age and the expectations of the culture.

The individual's skill in these areas is generally assessed through checklists, developmental profiles, and the professional judgment of teachers and clinicians. Expectations vary according to age level. In infancy and early childhood, the expected behaviours are those commonly associated with normal developmental processes. These include sensorimotor skills, communication skills, social skills, and self-help/care skills. This chapter focuses on the latter.

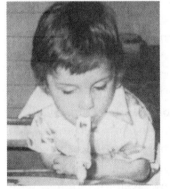

PHOTO 20–1 *Children with disabilities can learn independence in many different ways.*

SELF-HELP/CARE SKILLS AND THE CURRICULUM

Competence in self-help/care leads to greater independence. Therefore, helping young children develop a full range of self-help/care skills is a major curriculum goal in early childhood programs. The goal holds for all children, including (and perhaps, especially) for children with disabilities. Children with developmental problems need to learn to live as independently as possible with their disability (Photo 20–1). The more proficient they become in caring for their personal needs, the more likely it is they will be able to be included in integrated/inclusive classes (Spodek, Saracho, and Lee 1984, 229).

Self-help/care skills are learned behaviours. This means that they can be taught. Traditionally, the family had major responsibility for teaching self-help/care skills. Early childhood programs provided backup assistance. In recent years, as infants and children are being enrolled at younger and younger ages in all-day child-care programs, the pattern has been reversing. Early childhood teachers often have the major responsibility for initiating self-help/care training. In addition, and especially for children with developmental problems, schools themselves are assuming increasing responsibility. This trend can be attributed to

- improved teaching strategies derived from behavioural principles; and
- the presence of increasing numbers of children with developmental disabilities in early childhood programs.

An early childhood program can be a comfortable place for children to learn self-help/care skills. Teachers are trained to help children carry out these tasks. It is an established part of the teacher's job and time commitment. For many parents, already overburdened with responsibilities and stresses, teaching self-help/care skills may be just one more frustrating and time-consuming task among many. If their child is developmentally disabled, the demands may be overwhelming. Furthermore, the resistance and stress often associated with teaching certain self-help/care skills (toileting, for example) can lead to emotional conflict between parent and child. It is almost as if the parent's own self-esteem is damaged if the child is not acquiring all of the socially approved self-help/care skills. Teachers do not have that kind of personal involvement in the child's performance. They do not feel pressured to push for early performance. Instead, whether a child has a disabling condition or not, most preschool teachers know that time and effort are saved by slowing the pace and expecting less when teaching any new skill.

Even when parents are able to assume the major responsibility for teaching self-help/care skills, early childhood educators often find themselves involved. Frequently, they are asked by the child's IPP team to play a supporting role. This is good for children, parents, and teachers. Parents must be involved if children are to have ample opportunities to practise the self-help/care skills that occur most frequently and most naturally in the home setting. A number of studies leave little doubt that such a parent–child alliance works well for children with developmental problems. Supporting parents during their child's training usually results in more positive outcomes for both the child and the parent.

In any event, for many young children today, and for many more young children in the foreseeable future, teachers are and will be a significant source of self-help/care learning. Thus, teachers become an important factor in children's development. This may be especially true in the development of children with disabilities. Bailey and Wolery (1984, 334) describe the benefits:

> Teachers who do so (teach self-care skills) not only increase children's ability to care for themselves, allowing them to function independently, but also decrease the number of behaviors that point out the differences between handicapped and typical children. For example, a child who is six years old and does not feed herself is more obviously different from typical children than the six-year-old handicapped child who does.

PRINCIPLES OF TEACHING SELF-HELP/CARE SKILLS

Eating, dressing, toileting, and care of the classroom and play yard are significant program areas in the early childhood curriculum. Self-help/care activities are best learned within the context of the program throughout the day. These skills can take up a significant share of both the teachers' and children's time and energies, and so ample time must be built into the schedule to effectively accommodate these skills.

Interrelatedness of Self-Help/Care Learning

Opportunities for learning self-help/care skills need to be integrated with every other part of the curriculum. Mealtimes, for instance, can be arranged to promote a variety of curriculum goals in addition to those directly associated with eating.

Example:

> *If conversation during meals is acceptable in the culture, several small tables may be set up to promote child–child and child–teacher conversations at these times.*
>
> *Information sharing and concept learning, as well as self-help/care learning, can be carried out at mealtimes as teachers and children informally discuss names, colours, and textures of foods, their origins and nutritional value.*
>
> *Mealtimes provide opportunities for the **generalization** of cognitive skills presented in preacademic/readiness activities. Knowledge about the concept green, for example, can be extended by drawing attention to foods such as peas, broccoli, and lettuce, or by asking children to think of other foods that are green.*
>
> *Perceptual motor skills can be practised—lifting and pouring from a pitcher, filling a glass to a certain level, cleaning up spills (Photo 20–2), passing the pitcher, handle first, to the adjacent child.*

Self-help/care routines such as eating provide a variety of other opportunities for learning, in addition to these. One might be learning about sequence (what comes before and after eating); another, learning to estimate how much

PHOTO 20–2 *Spilling and mopping up are parts of self-help/care mastery.*

food to take relative to one's own hunger or, perhaps, to the amount of food available. The ability to estimate is necessary for all young children. It is important, for example, that a child be able to estimate how long it is safe to wait before going to the bathroom!

Opportunities to practise language also occur during self-help/care routines. There are opportunities to learn the names and functions of the objects and actions that are a part of everyday lives: clothing, furnishings, and working parts of equipment, such as toilets that flush and sinks that drain. Learning to comprehend and follow directions given by the teacher is a language skill that can be practised during self-help/care routines. The opportunity for verbal expressiveness, such as when children are encouraged to state their preferences, seek help, or explain to another child how to hang up a coat, occurs frequently throughout a program day. In addition, self-help/care activities provide occasions for children to learn language that is somewhat abstract (not supported by the activity at hand). During the arrival routine, a child telling the teacher about what happened to Grandmother's dog is an example of this.

INDIVIDUALIZING SELF-HELP/CARE PROGRAMS

Effective self-help/care programs allow children to participate individually. Young children, as noted repeatedly, function at different levels of motor, social, and cognitive ability. They need differing amounts of time and assistance in completing self-help/care tasks. Some children, both disabled and nondisabled, learn self-help/care skills early and with ease; others have varying degrees of difficulty. Inconsistent levels of competency may exist within the same child. Depending on the skill, one child may master some self-help/care skills well in advance of the normally expected time, while others do so much later.

Building Independence

The preschool years are the prime time for children to learn self-help/care skills. Children are striving for independence during these years (Photo 20–3).

PHOTO 20–3   *In one way or another, children are in constant pursuit of independence.*

They are eager to help themselves. They work hard at it if adults allow them to operate at their own pace. They constantly watch and attempt to imitate the self-help/care efforts of older children and adults. Furthermore, they are willing to practise; in fact, they insist on practising, practising, and practising. Think about older babies learning to walk. They take a few steps, fall down, get up, take a few more steps, fall down, over and over again. Once the falling-down period is past, they are even more insistent about practising their walking. It seems, for a while, as if every waking moment is given over to the task. A toddler's perseverance and physical energy seem never-ending. It is the parents and caregivers who run down and become exhausted.

Examples:

> *A toddler's discovery of how to unlace shoes often leads to a continuous process of lacing and unlacing his or her shoes a dozen to 15 times a day.*
>
> *The perseverance of a 2-year-old in pushing, pulling, tugging, shoving, dragging a kitchen chair over to the kitchen sink. Why? To get a drink of water, "all by myself."*
>
> *The 3-year-old's struggling, twisting, and turning in a mighty effort to get an undershirt on without help. The shirt, of course, may end up inside out or back to front, but that is all right. Learning that shirts have a right and wrong way of being worn comes later and requires much finer discrimination skills than the child possesses at this point.*

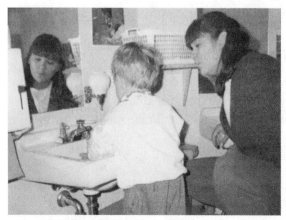

PHOTO 20–4   *Independence in hand washing builds feelings of success.*

Building In Success

All children need to experience the joy and self-esteem that come from mastering self-help/care skills. Such pride of accomplishment can be seen on the face of a 2-year-old who finally gets the chair in position to get that drink of water. It can be heard in the gleeful shout of the 3-year-old: "Look what I did! I got my shirt on all by mysel" or the quiet pleasure of the 5-year-old who finally learns to tie shoes (never mind the lopsided bow or the dangling laces). It can be seen also in

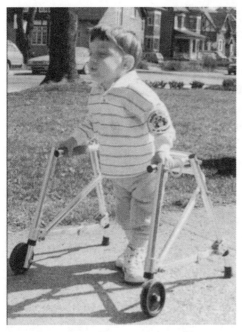

Photo 20–5 *Walking with a walker increases independence.*

the self-importance of the 6-year-old who learns to make jam sandwiches, not only for himself, but also for his little sister. Such experiences help children feel successful and in better control of their lives (Photo 20–4).

Though children with severe impairments may sometimes be the exception, most children with developmental disabilities can learn self-help/care skills. Like normally developing children, they, too, feel good about themselves simply by getting the shirt on, inside out or backward. Not all children with disabling conditions are able to verbalize their accomplishment. They may not be able to say, "Look what I did!" but their facial expressions leave little doubt as to their feelings of satisfaction.

It is true that getting about in a wheelchair, with leg braces, or with a walker is bothersome (Photo 20–5). Such disabilities need not prevent independence, however. What does interfere with independence is not being taught how to manage routine matters such as toileting, dressing, and eating. Having to ask for help over and over, every day, is the real burden. It is troublesome, both for the person with the disabilities and for those who must stop what they are doing (often reluctantly) to give help. Constantly having to seek help gets to be embarrassing, especially during adolescence.

Self-Help/Care Skills and the Teacher

As noted earlier, teaching self-help/care skills has become an integral part of the early childhood program. As with all other curriculum areas, specific principles and guidelines determine when and how teachers facilitate such learning.

Letting the Child Do It

"Me do it! Me do it!" What parent or early childhood teacher has not heard that refrain from a red-faced, frustrated, struggling 2-year-old? The urge to do for oneself is strong in normally developing young children. Though not expressed as aggressively, perhaps, the urge also is there in children with developmental problems. At least, it most likely was there at one point in the child's developmental history. Children with disabilities often try to do things for themselves, and these efforts often go unrecognized. Adults tend not to expect children with developmental and physical disabilities even to try to learn self-help/care skills. Also, the earliest strivings for independence may have been snuffed out by well-meaning family members and caregivers who could not bear to watch the child struggle. In many instances, children with disabilities become further handicapped because of learned dependence.

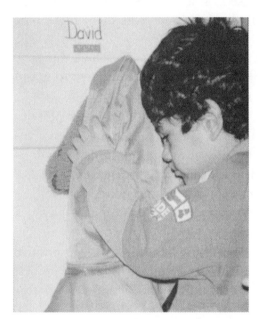

PHOTO 20–6 *Learned helplessness can be prevented by letting children with disabilities do as much as possible for themselves.*

PROVIDING ASSISTANCE

Not all adults know how to help a child with developmental disabilities (or a child *without* developmental problems, for that matter). Misplaced kindness leads many adults to take over. They do too much for children. They do things for, or to, a child that the child could do, given enough time and space. What happens when a teacher or parent steps in and expertly zips up the zipper that the child has been working on so intently? Or reties the shoe the child has just tied with so much effort? Or whips off the wrong-side-out sweater the child is crowing about having gotten on "all by myself"? Unintentionally, and even without words, a negative message is conveyed. It is as if the adult were saying, "You are too slow," "You aren't good enough," "Can't you do anything right?" Such "assistance" often sets up patterns of conflict between adult and child; or it may have the opposite result. The child learns to be passive—that is, just sitting or standing about—while the adult does more and more for the child. This can lead to *learned helplessness*, another way a child can become overly and unnecessarily dependent (Photo 20–6).

In early childhood programs such adult "helping" may be the result of understaffing. If teachers have too many children to look out for, they may feel that they cannot take the time to let a child make repeated efforts to fasten his or her jacket while other children are waiting to go outdoors. More frequently, however, such "helping" comes from teachers' lack of confidence in their own skills.

This is common among teachers who are just learning to work with young children, especially children with developmental problems. Inexperienced teachers do not know what to do in many situations. They find themselves feeling helpless. By doing things for the child, the teacher feels busy and needed, more competent, and more successful. It is not only the inexperienced who feel obligated to help, however. Many adults feel uncomfortable and hardhearted if they let a child struggle.

To prevent learned helplessness, even the kindest and most well-meaning assistance must not be unnecessarily pressed on a child. Kindness to children with developmental disabilities lies in finding ways to assist them in helping themselves.

- Kindness is guiding a child's arm and hand so that he can reach all the way down into his wrong-side-out coat sleeve. It is demonstrating how to grasp the edge of the cuff. It is helping the child learn that he can pull the cuff through, discovering that he can make a coat sleeve come right-side out.
- Kindness is putting a rubber suction cup under the plate of a child with cerebral palsy so that the plate stays in place while he works at feeding himself.
- Kindness, in the case of a 6-year-old just learning to walk with crutches, is laying her clothes out within easy reach. When everything she needs for dressing herself is at her fingertips, she is more likely to manage happily and well on her own.

Another aspect of kindness is to provide ample encouragement and positive feedback to children who are trying to take care of their own needs. The best way to do this is to tell children exactly what it is they are doing right (descriptive praise). Children need encouragement in the form of immediate feedback when they are successful, or getting closer to a successful performance. They need to know, too, that their efforts are appreciated. Children thrive on statements like the following:

- "You poured your milk nice and slowly. Not a drop got on the table!"
- "Look at you! You've already buttoned three buttons. Only two to go."
- "You remembered again today to rinse the soap off your hands and to turn the water off. You sure are getting good at washing your hands all by yourself."

At the same time, kindness is not expecting children to do what they are not yet able to do, or to perform tasks that are too complex for their developmental level. No child learns efficiently when overly frustrated or when encountering too-frequent failure. Teachers, therefore, must know when to help, how to help, and how much to help.

PHOTO 20–7 *Many children at an early age are able to grasp a spoon and get it into their mouth.*

KNOWING WHEN TO HELP

Knowing when and how to help depends on several teaching skills discussed earlier (Chapter 10). Among these are an understanding of developmental sequences, readiness, and the interrelatedness of developmental areas. Consider the following examples:

Because a 2-year-old managed to get a chair to the sink to get a drink of water does not mean that the child can turn the water on. Large motor skills (in this instance, shoving a chair into place) generally precede fine motor skills (here, the eye–hand–wrist control needed to turn on the water). The adult needs to anticipate the possible outcome of the less than fully developed fine motor skills. Assistance, if needed, should be offered before *the child becomes overly frustrated at not being able to get a drink. After all, great effort went into getting the chair in place.*

Many children, at an early age, are able to grasp a spoon and get it into the mouth. That is no guarantee, however, that a filled spoon will remain right-side up and so deliver food into the mouth. Usually, adult help is needed at this point so that the child can learn to keep the spoon upright, loaded, and on target (Photo 20–7).

Assistance should be given as subtly as possible. This helps preserve children's pride in their own efforts. In the first example, the adult might loosen the faucet just to the point where the child can make the water flow. In the second, a teacher might quietly place a hand around the child's hand after the spoon has been filled, and then remove the helping hand as the spoon enters the mouth. This kind of unobtrusive assistance gives the child a sense of accomplishment while learning a difficult task.

Occasionally, there is a child who gives up without trying, who makes excessive demands for adult assistance. It is likely that such a child is in need of extra attention. Teachers must find ways to give the needed attention; at the same time, they must avoid giving in to excessive demands. The alternative is to watch for times when the child is doing a task independently and then give warm and positive attention.

When Children Can't

It is true that children need to be encouraged to do for themselves as much as possible; nevertheless, teachers must be prepared to make exceptions. A child may ask for help with a task that he or she has already mastered. Children, too, have their "off" days. Like adults, they become tired, upset, or feel unwell. All children—including those with disabilities—can be expected to be dependent at times. They need to know that it is all right to ask for help, to say, "This is too hard. I can't do it by myself." A child should never be ridiculed or belittled for asking for help, no matter how simple the task. Children who have been helped to feel competent most of the time rarely seek help unnecessarily. Usually, they will ask for assistance only when they truly feel, at the moment, that a task is too much for them to do by themselves. In such situations, it is important that help be given immediately, but in just the right amount. The adult should never take over. Instead, the role of the adult is to help the child find a way to resolve the impasse, as in the coat-sleeve example cited earlier. The child should always feel that there is more help available if the problem is not solved on the first attempt, or even on the second or third.

PHOTO 20–8 *First the teacher asked, "What do you need?"*

GAME-LIKE ASSISTANCE

One way to keep a child involved and successful in a self-help/care situation is to create a game-like atmosphere. The exchange that follows is focused on Robert, who was born with cerebral palsy. He had recently passed his sixth birthday and was finishing his third year in an integrated early childhood program. Throughout the sequence, the teacher can be seen giving just the right amount of appropriately timed assistance and feedback in order to keep Robert involved. Interactions between the teacher and the child are followed by interpretive comments (in italics).

1. Robert put his foot, in an unlaced shoe, in the teacher's lap.
   Teacher: Hi, Robert, what do you need? (Photo 20–8)
   Robert pointed to his shoe.
   Teacher: Tell me what you need.
   Robert: Tie my shoes.

Children need practice using language. The teacher, therefore, required Robert to ask for what he needed. In working with children with no language, or more delayed language, the teacher probably would have settled for one word or even the simple gesture of raising the foot and pointing to the untied shoe. In the latter case, the teacher might respond, while tying the shoe, "You are showing me that your shoe needs tying." Because Robert had the ability to verbalize his need, he was asked to do so.

2. Teacher: All right, but first you need to lace them.

   The teacher began to sequence the task for Robert by reminding him that the shoe first had to be laced. A subsequent time, the teacher might ask Robert to tell what needed to be done before the shoe could be tied. Learning to state the order in which a complex task is to be accomplished is a skill step that gives the child experience in thinking through ordered sequencing for all tasks. Note that the teacher did not require Robert to stop and say, "Please." The teacher chose to focus his efforts on the self-help/care task itself rather than on social niceties.

3. Robert: No, you lace them. I don't know how.

   As he said this he kept his eyes on two favourite playmates who seemed to be about ready to start the transition to putting on coats for outdoor play.

   With Robert's refusal to lace his shoes, the teacher reassessed the situation. It was immediately obvious that Robert did not want to be left behind when his friends went out to play. Yet the teacher knew they would be gone long before Robert, with his less-developed fine motor skills, could lace his shoes by himself. What to do?

PHOTO 20–9 *The teacher had the child pull the lace through.*

4. Teacher (smiling): Robert, you are kidding me. Every day I see you lacing your shoes. But sit down here on the floor and I will help you.

   The teacher knew that Robert could lace his shoes and felt that it was not good for him to get away with saying he was not able to do it. On the other hand, his eagerness to be ready to play with his friends was important, too. The teacher decided, therefore, to let him know she knew he could tie his own shoes, but to give him assistance, nevertheless.

5. Robert sat on the floor. The teacher inserted the tip of one lace partly through an eyelet, while instructing Robert.

   Teacher: Robert, you pull it through (Photo 20–9).

Having Robert sit on the floor gave him a firm base and the necessary balance for lacing the shoe. The teacher did the part of the job that would have given Robert the most difficulty, getting the lace started into the eyelet. The task the teacher held Robert to could be done quickly and with immediate success, thus giving promise that the shoe was that much closer to being laced.

6. As Robert pulled the first lace through, the teacher said, "Great! You got that one through. Now hand me the other lace." The lacing continued in this fashion until only the top pair of holes was left.

   With each step, the teacher gave Robert encouragement, positive feedback, and a cue for the next step in the sequence ("Now hand me the other lace").

7. Teacher: I bet you can do the last two by yourself. Here, I'll hand you the laces this time.

   Robert: I know which ones. I can do it.

   With the job so close to being finished, the teacher sensed that it would not be difficult for Robert to complete it. Hence, the friendly challenge to Robert to take the responsibility.

8. Teacher: Look at that, Robert. All done! You finished the lacing all by yourself. Here, let me tie your shoes and you will be all ready to play.

   The teacher then called to Robert's friends.

   Teacher: Robert's ready to go out, too. Wait while he gets his coat on, okay?

   Because task completion is important to children's learning, the teacher gave specific praise: "Robert, you finished the lacing all by yourself." Then the teacher made sure that Robert's efforts really paid off—she had his friends wait for him. Also, no suggestion was made that Robert work on shoe tying, even though it was a task on his IPP. That would be saved for another time. Instead, the teacher tied the shoes quickly so that there would be no further delay (Photo 20–10).

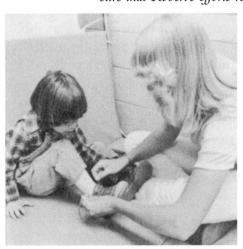

PHOTO 20–10 *Quickly, the teacher tied the lace.*

Robert was a child who had made good progress in acquiring self-help/care skills in spite of his disabilities. Other children with developmental problems may have learned to do much less for themselves. Many cannot put on their own coat. They cannot feed themselves or take care of their own toileting needs. Some children cannot ask for what they need. In these cases, the teacher's job is more exacting and the need for a specific task analysis (Chapter 13) is even more crucial.

VARIED APPROACHES: PUTTING ON A COAT AS AN EXAMPLE

Self-help/care skills can be taught in different ways. If a teacher finds one approach unsuccessful, another should be tried, and then another, if need be. Teaching a child to put on a coat, for example, can be accomplished in several ways. The usual way (often the most difficult for young children) is to have the child reach behind and put in one arm at a time. Another way is to place the coat on the floor or on a table, with the child facing the opened-out coat. The child puts both arms into the sleeves and tosses the coat over his or her head. A third way is to hang the opened coat on a chair. Because this procedure seems to work best for young children, it will be described step by step.

1. Place the coat on a child-sized chair. Arrange it so that it looks as if a child had slipped out of it while sitting on the chair.
2. Have the child sit on the chair (on the coat).
3. Point to one of the armholes and ask the child to look at the armhole.
4. Guide the child's arm into the armhole.
5. Give positive, specific feedback and then a cue as to what comes next: "There! You have one arm in. Now let's look at the other armhole."
6. Repeat for the other sleeve.
7. The child, at this point, may spontaneously shrug the coat over his or her shoulders. If not, the teacher can move the child's arms up and forward to make it slide on easily.

MATURATION AND LEARNING: TOILET TRAINING AS AN EXAMPLE

As noted at the outset, all self-help/care skills are learned. It follows, then, that all self-help/care skills can be taught. Starting too early dooms the child and the adult to failure. Success depends, in part, on physiological maturity, especially of the **sphincter muscles** when toilet training a child.

Toilet training, once thought to be totally dependent on maturation, can be *task analyzed* and taught in its component parts. With some children, *each part*, in turn, may need to be task analyzed and taught step by step. Ordinary toilet training includes many steps. It starts with getting into the bathroom, pulling the pants down, and getting up onto the toilet. It concludes with getting off the toilet, pulling clothes up, and flushing. What could be more simple? Yet, for many young children, both disabled and nondisabled, one or more of the steps may present great difficulty. Even the seemingly simple task of getting on and off the toilet may need to be broken down into smaller steps. For sure, using toilet tissue effectively is a challenge for all young children! Several commercial toilet training programs have been developed for children with disabilities (Azrin and Foxx 1971; Fredericks et al. 1975; Snell 1978). Basically, the programs involve the same procedures that have been discussed here, with even greater emphasis on small steps. The programs also provide information on toilet training **nonambulatory** children and those with other special problems. (Children who are on seizure medication, for example, must not be given large quantities of liquids.)

Step-By-Step Planning

In teaching any self-help/care skill the teacher must know exactly where each child is in that particular skill sequence. This can be accomplished by asking a simple question about each step: can the child do it? If yes, the teacher can proceed to the next step; if no, the teacher figures out the substeps appropriate for that child at that point in the sequence. Figure 20–1 shows the procedure for the first two or three steps in the toilet-training tasks listed above.

FIGURE 20–1

Skill sequence for independent toileting.

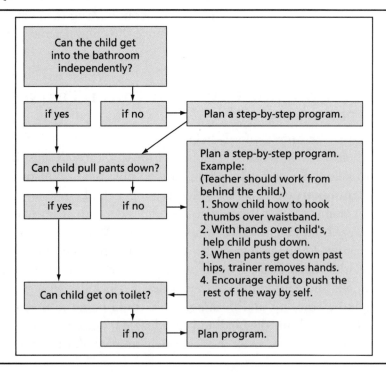

Chaining

Self-help/care tasks such as toileting, shoe lacing, and feeding oneself are all examples of tasks composed of a set of smaller behaviours (skills), chained (sequenced) together and organized into what seems to be a single task. When the chaining concept is adapted to teaching self-help/care skills, the child is helped to learn one response, one link of the skill chain at a time. Once the child is performing the first component in the chain, the next step, or link, is introduced. Single components of the chain are added one by one until the child can perform all of them, in order, from start to finish. Step-by-step learning can be made easier if the child can see the entire chain being performed (see learning through observation and modelling, Chapters 11, 13, and 19).

On many tasks, forward chaining and backward chaining are equally successful. The choice depends on the particular task and level of skill the child displays. In forward chaining, the teacher helps the child learn the first step in the chain, then the second, and so on. In *backward chaining*, instruction begins with the last step and progresses in reverse to the first component.

The child in the following example of zipping has fairly well-developed fine motor skills; the teacher, therefore, has broken the task into only six component parts (a six-step task analysis). The steps are suitable for teaching the task with either a forward or a backward chaining approach. Throughout both forward and backward chaining, the teacher will demonstrate or provide manual prompts (Chapter 13) as needed.

PHOTO 20–11 *Step 5 in backward chaining for learning how to zipper.*

Step 1. With both hands, the bottom front edges of the coat are brought together at the bottom.

Step 2. The zipper foot is inserted into the zipper catch.

Step 3. The zipper foot is seated in the catch by pushing up and down with opposing movements of each hand.

Step 4. The tab on the zipper is grasped between thumb and forefinger.

Step 5. The bottom of the coat at the zipper catch is held with one hand while the zipper tab is pulled to the top, with the other hand holding the zipper tab (Photo 20–11).

Step 6. The zipper tab is pushed down firmly into locked position.

In backward chaining, the child would first master step 6, then 5, and so on, back to step 1. The major advantage of backward chaining is that the child is always reinforced by task completion, even in the first lesson. Accomplishing the last step sends a reinforcing message to the child that the time has come to get on to something more interesting. At some point, for most children, the chain becomes one integrated skill that scarcely needs thinking about.

SPECIAL CONSIDERATIONS

In the zipping task above (and in many other dressing and self-help/care tasks) it is important that the adult work from behind the child. This ensures that the teacher's hands are performing the hand and finger movements in the same way that the child will be expected to reproduce them. Young children do not have a well-developed sense of spatial orientation, nor do they have a concept of reversibility. Teachers' demonstrations, therefore, must be conducted from the child's perspective. For this reason and others, the use of lacing, buttoning, and zipping boards for children to practise on has been questioned. It is too confusing for many children to try to reverse and transfer the motions learned in practice sessions to their own bodies (Cook, Tessier, and Klein 1992).

A word about the importance of suitable clothing when learning self-help/care skills: Children who are being toilet trained need underpants (and outer pants) with elastic at the top so that they can be pulled down easily. Children who are learning to dress themselves can learn more easily if their clothing has big, sturdy zippers that work, large buttons and unrestricted buttonholes, and simple fastenings such as Velcro on belts, shoes, and overalls. When children are having prolonged difficulty in learning to dress themselves, temporarily providing clothing a size or two too big is sometimes a help. Obviously, teachers should never presume to tell parents how to dress their children. On the other hand, parents often welcome suggestions that help their children learn more easily.

THE MATCH: PROGRAMS MUST MEET THE CHILD'S DEVELOPMENTAL NEEDS

A mandate for all teachers is to exercise additional ingenuity whenever a child seems unable to learn a task matched to his or her developmental level and prerequisite skills. If a child is not learning, the program should be re-examined, not the child. The teacher may need to change or adapt the sequence, the size of the steps, the motivation, or the task itself until the child succeeds. Teachers must have faith that all children in an inclusive early childhood program can learn an adequate range of self-help/care skills (see Chapters 10 and 13).

SUMMARY

The term self-help/care skills means the ability to take care of one's personal needs in a socially acceptable way. Traditionally, families had the major responsibility for teaching self-help/care skills to children; in recent years, early childhood teachers are increasingly involved. Opportunities for learning and practising self-help/care skills should be integrated with every part of the curriculum. Throughout the day, children need to experience the sense of independence, the pleasure, and the feelings of self-esteem that come from mastering self-help/care skills.

A child's disabilities need not prevent the learning of self-help/care skills. Adult helpfulness and genuine kindness encourage children with disabilities to learn ways to do things for themselves. Children who are trying to master a self-help/care task need ample encouragement and feedback as to exactly what it is they are doing right. Knowing when and how to help depends on teachers' knowledge of developmental sequences, readiness, and the interrelatedness of developmental areas. Many skills, once thought to be totally dependent on maturation, can and should be taught, especially to children with developmental problems.

Teaching self-help/care skills can be done in a lighthearted, game-like fashion using a variety of approaches. If one method does not work, another should be tried (and another, if need be). Specific step-by-step planning—that is, task analysis—is usually necessary to teach self-help/care skills effectively. Most self-help/care tasks can be thought of as chains of many smaller responses. Self-help/care skills can be taught through either forward chaining or backward chaining. The major advantage of backward chaining is that the child always has the satisfaction of completing the task, even in the first teaching episode. It must be remembered that when children fail, teachers and caregivers need to re-examine the program goals set for these children.

STUDENT ACTIVITIES

1. Observe a preschool or child-care centre during arrival or departure time, a toileting period, or a meal or snack time. List 10 or more self-help/care tasks and adaptive behaviours in which you see children engaged.

2. When you next wash your hair, take note of what you do. When finished, write down what you did, step by step, starting with the decision to wash your hair and ending with it arranged as you always wear it.

3. Select one of the major steps in the toileting sequence (or any other self-help/care skill) and analyze it into its component parts (do a task analysis). Write a 6-to-10-step program for teaching that subskill to a 4-year-old who has a serious hearing loss but has no other impairments.

4. Ask a fellow student to role-play a child who cannot tie a shoe. Teach the task to the "child."

5. Assume that "learning to count five or more objects" is written into the IPP of a 4-year-old. Give examples of how teachers might integrate this learning task within several self-help/care routines.

REFERENCES

Azrin, J.B., and R.M. Foxx 1971 *Toilet Training in Less Than a Day.* New York: Simon and Schuster.

Bailey, D.B., and M. Wolery 1984 *Teaching Infants and Preschoolers with Handicaps.* Columbus, Ohio: Charles E. Merrill. Reprinted with permission.

Cook, R.E., A. Tessier, and M.D. Klein 1992 *Adapting Early Childhood Curricula for Children with Special Neets.* Columbus, Ohio: Charles E. Merrill.

Fredericks, H.D., V.L. Balwin, D.N. Grove, and W.G. Moore 1975 *Toilet Training the Handicapped Child.* Monmouth, Ore.: Instructional Development Corp.

Snell, M.E., ed. 1978 *Systematic Instruction of the Moderately and Severely Handicapped.* Columbus, Ohio: Charles E. Merrill.

Spodek, B., O.N. Saracho, and C.L. Lee 1984 *Mainstreaming Young Children.* Belmont, Cal.: Wadsworth.

Wolery, M. 1994 "Implementing Instruction for Young Children with Special Needs in Early Childhood Classrooms." In M. Wolery and J.S. Wilbur (eds.), *Including Children with Special Needs in Early Childhood Programs.* Washington, D.C.: National Association for the Education of Young Children.

CHAPTER 21

Intervention with Infants and Toddlers

Ann Atkinson Witte* with adaptations by
Paasche, Cornell, and Engel

Objectives

After studying the material in this chapter, the student will be able to

- define the term enabling environment as related to infant/toddler caregiving and describe how this environment might be adapted for infants with developmental problems

- outline several requirements for providing infants with a safe, healthy, and well-supervised environment

- describe several components of a responsive infant/toddler learning environment and give one or more examples of each component

- explain the parents' and the teacher/caregiver's roles in promoting infant learning through sensory stimulation and discuss special considerations related to working with infants with sensory impairments

INTRODUCTION

Healthy infant/toddler (birth to 2 1/2 years of age) development does not "just happen," even with babies who are born full term and normal in every respect.

A well-known study by Klaus and Klaus (1985) showed that even when only a few hours old, the newborn's attention moves from the outer contours of the

---

*Ann Atkinson Witte is an Assistant Professor in the Department of Human Development and Child Studies, Oakland University, Rochester, Michigan. As a special educator and an early childhood educator, Professor Witte has taught in hospital-, centre-, and home-based programs for infants, toddlers, and preschoolers with and without disabling conditions.

parent's face to the parent's eyes and mouth. Fostering mutual responsiveness is essential and all-important.

PHOTO 21–1 *The care of large numbers of infants in early childhood settings is a relatively new trend in our society.*

The care of large numbers of infants and toddlers by those other than natural parents or the extended family is a relatively new trend in our society (Photo 21–1). Single-parent families are increasingly common and double incomes are an economic necessity for many young families. In 1990, 57 percent of preschool-aged children in the United States had mothers who worked outside the home; 53 percent of these children were under 1 year of age (Edelman 1990). It is projected that as many as 65 percent of mothers of young children in the United States will be in the labour force by the year 2000. The Canadian situation parallels the situation in the United States. The number of infants in need of special services also is increasing rapidly, because of the social and economic factors discussed in Chapter 4.

In the United States, federal legislation—PL 99-457—recognizes infant intervention as an important national option. Title I of the law authorizes services for at-risk infants and those with developmental problems, from birth through 2 years of age. There is no comparable federal legislation on infant intervention in Canada at this time. However, in the early 1970s, responding to pressure from parents, a few provinces began to fund programs that provided mainly in-home support services for infants with special needs. As suggested by Brynelsen (1990), the major difference between the development of infant services in the United States and Canada was that in many Canadian communities, programs were started on parents' initiative in partnership with the professional community.

Over the years, infant development/early intervention programs have been established in most Canadian provinces and territories. However, the lack of sufficient ongoing research and coordination and the lack of provincial databases (with the exception of British Columbia, Alberta, Saskatchewan, Ontario, and Newfoundland) have meant that such services have developed mainly in isolation from one another (Brynelsen 1990). Skills in working with and programming for infants and toddlers is included in many early childhood education training programs.

In this text, the terms teacher/caregiver, educator, and infant teacher will be considered as interchangeable. When discussing at-risk infants and infants with developmental problems, the term interventionist also will be used. The role played by parents is of prime importance in the infant's and toddler's development. Brynelsen (1990) states: "It is the parents' involvement and the daily interactions and activities they provide that bring change, not only for the infant, but for themselves as parents."

RESPONSIVE AND ENABLING CAREGIVING

Newborns are vulnerable to negative environmental influences. Inadequate nurturing, inappropriate stimulation, or insufficient medical and nutritional care can do great damage. Some infants are more vulnerable than others; all infants, however, are vulnerable to some degree, even those who are healthy and responsive at birth. Development is at its most critical stage when infants are most dependent on others to meet all of their needs. When adults fail in their caregiving responsibilities, an infant's development is put in jeopardy.

Extremely low birthweight infants, as well as those who are medically fragile or at high risk, usually require intensive caregiving.

The goal of infant/toddler care is the healthy development of the child. The guidelines for infant/toddler care outlined in this chapter are based on developmental principles relevant to all infants and toddlers, those with and those without disabilities. The guidelines are intended to assist the teacher/caregiver in responding most efficiently, most effectively, and most appropriately to each infant on a day-to-day basis. The responsible adult in caring for infants/toddlers must believe in the ableness of the infant/toddler with a disability (Photo 21–2), and in his or her own ability to serve as an interventionist in responding to the infant/toddler's strengths at whatever level they exist.

Whether the infant/toddler is developing normally or in an atypical manner, the teacher/caregiver's responsibilities are similar. The focus should be on providing an environment in which daily routines, play activities, and the teacher/caregiver's responsiveness are geared to the responsiveness and skill level of the infant/toddler. Such an environment is not only

PHOTO 21–2 *Caregiver philosophy: believing in the ableness of each infant.*

developmentally appropriate, it also is an enabling environment because it accomplishes the following:

- It encourages the infant/toddler to respond and adapt to environmental experiences by helping the infant/toddler regulate biological rhythms (sleeping, eating, elimination) and psychological state (soothability, excitability, responsiveness).
- It helps the infant/toddler learn to maintain a balance between approaching and avoiding environmental events (stimuli). Infants and toddlers accomplish this when caregivers help them learn to respond in mutually satisfying ways.
- It promotes the infant's or toddler's emerging abilities to differentiate simpler, more specific responses among global undifferentiated responses. These differentiating skills come as teachers/caregivers foster

    a. the infant's sense of control; and

    b. the use of various senses to experience the environment in many different ways.

- It facilitates the infant's or toddler's efforts to initiate new responses to people, objects, and events. The foundation for new responses is provided by the teachers/caregiver's support of the child's efforts to initiate activities in ways that lead to more complex behavioural and emotional patterns.

    In summary, the environment should be:

- interesting and gratifying to each infant/toddler,
- responsive to and manageable by each infant/toddler,
- challenging to each infant/toddler, and
- supportive of each infant/toddler's emerging autonomy.

Interacting and responding can occur naturally when caregiving routines are viewed as a time for warm, responsive, sharing of looks, smells, smiles, laughs, songs, touches, gestures, movements, and playfulness such as in peek-a-boo and other **contingency-type games**.

Caregiving routines also are a time for words. Adults must never forget that talking time is all the time. It is important to describe and explain the events taking place in the infant/toddler's world. Providing verbal connections helps the child develop an understanding of the relatedness of actions, objects, and people.

PHOTO 21–3 *Teachers/caregivers should provide appropriate learning activities chosen to support each child's development.*

ARRANGING AN ENABLING ENVIRONMENT

It is important to determine whether a caregiver is providing for and responding to infants and toddlers in developmentally appropriate and enabling ways (Photo 21–3).*

A Safe Environment:

To ensure an overall safe environment for infants/toddlers, environmental needs must be met. The following guidelines should be incorporated in caregiving plans.

- Fresh air and well-regulated heat, humidity, and cooling conditions are maintained.
- Electrical outlets are covered, extension cords are not exposed, and hazardous substances are kept out of children's reach.
- Floors are covered by securely laid and easy-to-clean carpeting.
- Cribs are sturdy with vertical bars and horizontal rails that meet the regulations of Consumer and Corporate Affairs, Canada, and are finished with non-toxic paint or varnish.
- Low steps and climbing structures are well padded and safe for exploration and development of motor skills.

A Sanitary and Healthy Environment

Guidelines for limiting injuries and the spread of infectious diseases include:

- Diapering, sleeping, feeding, and play spaces should be separated to ensure sanitation and provide both quiet, restful areas and lively activity areas.
- Because infants and toddlers mouth toys, it is important that all toys be clean and disinfected with a bleach solution (1 part chlorine bleach to 10 parts water), and left out to dry. This must be done at regular intervals.

---

*The section on Infant/Toddler Health and Safety makes use of descriptions and recommendations from Bredekamp, 1987, *Developmentally Appropriate Practice in Early Childhood Education*, N.A.E.Y.C. The guidelines reflect the *Accreditation Criteria and procedures of the National Academy of Early Childhood Programs.* For further information, see Kids Care National Program, Consumer and Corporate Affairs Canada, 50 Victoria Street, Hull, P.Q. K1A 0C9.

- Toys should be safe, washable, and too large for infants and toddlers to swallow.
- Each infant/toddler must have his or her own crib, bedding, feeding utensils, clothing, diapers, pacifiers, and special comforting objects.
- Diaper changing areas must be easily and routinely sanitized after each diaper change.
- Infants should be dressed appropriately for the weather and the type of play they engage in.
- Each personal item should be labelled with the infant/toddler's name.
- Staff should be healthy and take precautions not to spread illnesses or infectious diseases.
- Caregivers must wash their hands before and after each diaper change and the feeding of each infant.
- Adults must be aware of the symptoms of common childhood illnesses and diseases, of children's allergies to foods or other substances, and of potential hazards in the environment.
- Written records must be maintained on each infant/toddler. Immunizations must be current. Up-to-date emergency information must be immediately at hand.

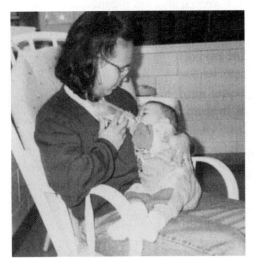

PHOTO 21–4 *Infants must be held with their bodies at an appropriate angle when being fed from a bottle.*

Additional information on safety and health considerations can be found in the Canadian Paediatric Society publications, *Well Beings* (1992) and *Little Well Beings* (1994).

A Well-Supervised Environment

Infants and toddlers must always be under supervision; safe adult–infant/toddler ratios must be maintained at all times. The required ratio depends on regulations that have been established by each province/territory.

- Infants must always be held with their bodies at an appropriate angle ("head above heart") when being fed from a bottle (Photo 21–4).
- Infants/toddlers who can sit up should be fed in groups of one or two with a caregiver/ teacher to provide assistance.

- Safe finger foods are encouraged. Only healthy foods should be offered. Eating should be treated as a sociable, happy time.

All objects must be large enough and smooth enough to be mouthed, since infants/toddlers (until they reach a mental age of 18 months or more) suck, bite, or chew just about everything they come in contact with. To prevent objects from becoming lodged in the throat, mouth, ears, or nose, a general rule of fist is that infants/toddlers have access to no objects smaller than their own fist (Photo 21–5).

A Responsive Environment

PHOTO 21–5 *Rule of fist: Infants have access to objects no smaller than their fist.*

No matter how safe, sanitary, and well-supervised a setting may be, an infant/toddler will not thrive developmentally unless the environment actively engages and responds to the child. By its very nature, a responsive environment encourages and supports active exploration by providing individual infants/toddlers with opportunities and options for

- gaining free access to what is happening in the environment;
- making appropriate choices;
- engaging in experiences that evolve from a simple to a more complex level; and
- creating an impact on their environment.

Toys and Learning Materials for Infants/Toddlers

The following list is adapted from the NAEYC (Bredekamp 1987, 37). Appropriate infant/toddler toys include:
- busy boards
- balls and clutch balls
- vinyl-covered pillows to climb on
- large beads that snap together
- nesting bowls
- small blocks
- shape sorters
- music boxes and musical toys and bells
- squeeze toys that squeak
- rattles, spoons, and teethers

- rubber dolls
- heavy cardboard books
  Other things that infants/toddlers find interesting include these items:
- mobiles and wind chimes
- pull toys, small wagons, and "ride them" cars, trucks, etc.
- toy telephones
- various types of containers (cups, boxes, pans)
- washable squares of cloth (60 cm x 60 cm) of different colours and textures

Be sure that all toys, and especially mobiles, are seen (and used) from the infant/toddler's perspective. Audiotapes can provide another source of stimulation from earliest infancy.

Active contact with play materials allows infants/toddlers to experience some control over their environment. Hearing the chiming of a musical rattle when it is shaken or seeing a rubber toy that the infant had held under water float to the surface teaches the child the effects of his or her actions. All infants and toddlers, including those with disabilities, need to have opportunities to manipulate objects and experience control. Remember, it is much more interesting and motivating for a child to bat a mobile or ring a bell than it is to watch someone else bat a mobile or ring a bell.

Interaction Between Infants/Toddlers and the Environment

Infants/toddlers usually respond to the following types of stimulation.

SENSORY STIMULATION

Toys and materials that stimulate the senses include those that encourage the infant/toddler's developing abilities to see sights, hear sounds, touch and feel textures, and move the body in and through space. Starting soon after birth, infants are learning to use their abilities to see, hear, taste, smell, and move about. These emerging skills enable them to be active participants in sharing a variety of experiences with others in their world.

VISUAL STIMULATION

Faces, contrasting black and white designs, geometric patterns, and muted and bright colours all are of interest to babies. The activities of people close by provide an additional source of visual stimulation. Of even greater interest is the child's own reflection! (See Photo 21–6.) For this reason, unbreakable mirrors designed to hang in cribs make excellent "toys." Try also to provide the infant classroom with at least one shatterproof mirror large enough for a child to see his or her entire body and observe what that body can do. Materials that change

PHOTO 21–6 *All infants need the opportunity to explore their mirror image.*

predictably are excellent attention-getters, especially when the child can help bring about the change, as in stacking blocks and watching them topple.

Infants/toddlers also should be able to observe routine events such as these:

- people coming and going in and out of the classroom door
- older children playing out-of-doors
- trucks, cars, and people (on bicycles, in strollers, on foot) passing by a window
- trees blowing in the wind, birds feeding at a bird feeder, squirrels climbing

Inside the classroom there should be mobiles and pictures placed within the infant/toddler's line of vision. Changing the position of these materials regularly allows children to focus on different elements. Important, too, are pictures of the infants/toddlers themselves, and life-sized pictures depicting familiar objects and events. These serve as stepping stones between concrete and representational thinking.

AUDITORY STIMULATION

Children enjoy hearing sounds: peoples' voices, various types of instruments, different forms of music, and the sounds of everyday happenings, such as household and other environmental noises. It is the rare infant who does not turn to the whir of the blender, to birds singing or scolding, to street noises such as sirens and the screeching of brakes. Remember that sounds occurring together with an intriguing sight provide opportunities for the young child to integrate several sensory modalities. This occurs when the infant/toddler hears a chirping bird and turns to watch and point as the bird flies to a nearby bush.

Infants/toddlers are sensitive to and interested in different voice tones and inflections, singing, and reading voices. Infants/toddlers also enjoy making and being encouraged to make sounds. They like to hear reproductions of their own voices and sound-making efforts.

Musical instruments including tambourines, triangles, drums, and cymbals, as well as more familiar baby rattles and bells, should be introduced in such a way that the infant/toddler can "play" with them. By wiggling a body part, for example, the infant/toddler can cause the instrument to produce sound. In this way, the child enjoys another way in which to "communicate" with the surrounding world.

Remember, also, that adults serve best as language models when they simply and clearly describe or explain events and describe the infant's responses as events occur.

TACTILE STIMULATION

Infants/toddlers, if they are to thrive, need the significant emotional experience that comes from being held and cuddled. Most infants and toddlers also like to experience the furriness of a stuffed animal, the fluffiness of a lambskin rug, the smoothness of a cool sheet, and the soft roughness of a terrycloth towel. Infants/toddlers also enjoy feeling the water in their bath and the dewiness of grass under knees or feet. Many kinds of experiences with natural materials (for example, simply touching nontoxic leaves, large shells, stones, or pine cones) can become pleasant learning activities for older infants/toddlers, but only if each is closely supervised at all times.

KINESTHETIC STIMULATION

Infants/toddlers tend to respond either by getting excited or becoming calm when they are held and walked, or when they are rocked in a cradle or a hammock-like swing. If the stimulation is excessive, the infant/toddler may react by shutting down all systems (going to sleep or "blanking out") or by overactivating all systems (crying and writhing). When the stimulation is pleasurable and manageable, most infants/toddlers become relaxed, yet alert; or, if already tired, they drift off into a normal sleep state.

Extensive research supports the conclusion that infants/toddlers who do not move about and explore their environment are less able to organize and represent their experiences internally. This is especially true of infants/toddlers with neuromuscular conditions affecting their balance and movement, and of infants and toddlers with visual or hearing impairments. These children, without special help, tend to engage in few exploratory moves. The parent and caregiver/teacher's task is to provide movement experiences that are challenging, yet result in relatively

PHOTO 21–7 *Teachers/caregivers support children's developmental and appropriate movement experiences.*

few frightening falls, bumps, or otherwise unpleasant experiences (Photo 21–7). (For a more detailed discussion of caregiver/teacher practices in these situations, see Chapter 8.) As a teacher/caregiver helps an infant/toddler build confidence in moving about and exploring the environment, the child is likely to show increasing interest in physical activity, and may even come to enjoy "rough-and-tumble" play. It must be remembered, however, that infants should never be rocked, shaken, or swung roughly, lifted rapidly and abruptly, or thrown into the air. Infants and toddlers cannot adjust posturally to quick extremes of motion. Serious injuries to the head, brain, neck, and back may result.

Integrating Sensory Modalities

Some infants/toddlers appear to enjoy all kinds of movement experiences; others may be overly sensitive, sometimes in one sensory modality more than another. Still other infants/toddlers may be able to use comfortably only one sense at a time. An example is the child who likes to listen to a music box, but only if allowed to look away from the action. Great distress may occur if an adult tries to coerce such a child into listening and looking at the same time. It must be remembered, too, that how the caregiver/teacher perceives and responds to a sensation is not necessarily the way an infant or a toddler will react to the same sensation. It is best, therefore, for the parent or teacher/caregiver to introduce a new experience when the child is in a calm state, in familiar surroundings. Experiences that cause distress should be modified or stopped and reintroduced under different circumstances or when the child is more developmentally advanced.

Adapting Play and Learning Materials

As noted earlier, all children benefit from manipulative materials that promote maximum independence and enable them to produce some change or effect on the environment. The task of the teacher/caregiver is to make materials accessible and also figure out adaptations so that all children can explore, manipulate, and control play materials and everyday objects (Photo 21–8). Musselwhite (1986) offers several strategies for increasing access to play materials for children with poorly developed motor skills:

- Place toys on a tray.
- Fit the child with a Velcro mitt and attach strips of Velcro to toys to make them more accessible.
- Attach toys to playboards or wall surfaces.
- Suspend toys from activity frames.

PHOTO 21–8 *Teachers make materials accessible so that all children can explore and manipulate.*

- Attach objects to blankets or mats with Velcro loops (especially good for children who spend much of their day lying down).

Once play materials are accessible to the child, adaptive play goals should focus on these aims:

- increasing the duration of the child's play
- encouraging various kinds of manipulation of play materials
- introducing a wider range of toys and manipulative materials
- reducing a child's dependence on prompting from the caregiver.*

Infant/Toddler Biological Rhythms

It is sometimes difficult to synchronize the infant's or toddler's biological "schedule" with the schedule of other family members and with other children and adults in the infant-care setting. The process of learning to adapt to the time frame of others is not easy. Infants and toddlers must gain control of some kind of a rhythm for themselves before they can adjust to the rhythms of others. Caring for infants and toddlers in ways that harmonize with their immediate needs will result in a greater number of positive interactions. The child will be responding from his or her own strengths and sense of "having it together." It follows, quite naturally, that a baby who is calm and relaxed is more likely to be a cooperative baby. Stress for everyone can be reduced if caregivers are patient. They must allow time for the infant's or toddler's internal clock to become regulated before they impose the scheduling expectations of others.

---

*An additional source of information on adaptive play is *Lekotek,* a worldwide system of resource centres and play libraries for children with special needs and their families. (Such facilities are often called toy-lending libraries or centres.) According to Mary Sinker (Program Director for the National Lekotek Center in Evanston, Illinois), "Good toys function like masterful, ever present teachers." *Toys for Growing: A Guide to Toys That Develop Skills* (Sinker 1986) is a price-coded book that categorizes play materials according to areas of development. A range of toys is described, from simple rattles, balls, and puzzles to toys activated by electronic or battery-operated devices. Similar information is available from the Canadian Association of Toy Libraries and Parent Resource Programs (TLRC Canada), 101-30 Rosemount Avenue, Ottawa, Ont. K1Y 1P4.

PHOTO 21–9 *The daily routines are prime times for teachers/caregivers to interact playfully with an infant.*

TIMES FOR SHARING AND LEARNING

The daily routines of feeding, diapering, bathing, dressing, and helping an infant/toddler relax or go to sleep are prime times for a teacher/caregiver to interact calmly and playfully with the infant/toddler (Photo 21–9). When an infant cries, for example, it usually is a signal that the infant needs something: food, diapering, comforting, company. Crying is usually the infant/toddler's way of both losing control and attempting to gain control. Trust develops when an infant's cries are answered in a prompt and caring way.

When comforting an infant/toddler, the adult may be able to soothe with movement, sounds, sights, or touching. Rocking (gentle movement), soft singing (sounds), a favourite toy (sight and texture), and/or a gentle rubbing or patting (touch) will often successfully pacify a baby. Sometimes an infant is signalling the need for warmth, security, or food. The appropriate caregiving response, then, may be gentle swaddling, loosely wrapping the infant in a soft blanket for a short time, being careful that circulation to limbs is not restricted. For infants with neuromuscular problems, swaddling often provides additional comfort by relieving the discomforting effect of twitching or jerking limbs or muscles. In the event that the baby is hungry, it is important that the feeding activity be made a happy and sociable time.

Feeding times may be difficult for infants with particular types of disabilities. Mealtimes are likely to be less stressful if a relaxed attitude is maintained. This can be accomplished through appropriate positioning in a specially adapted chair, or by seating the infant/toddler securely in the adult's lap.

Any behaviour shared between the infant and adult lays the foundation for the more sophisticated games of peek-a-boo or pat-a-cake, in which infant and adult each plays an interactive role (Photo 21–10). The parent or teacher/caregiver should always encourage and provide the opportunity for the infant/toddler to further explore anything confusing or frustrating about a situation. They must also be sensitive to the efforts that an infant/toddler makes toward controlling a game.

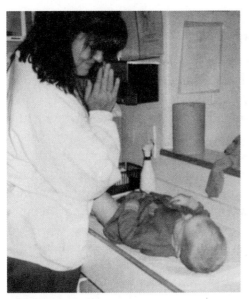

PHOTO 21–10 *Interacting and responding can occur naturally.*

INFANT/TODDLER INTERVENTION

The goal of infant/toddler intervention is twofold: to enable infants and toddlers to explore and master their environment, and to encourage them to use their capacities and abilities in ways that are individually meaningful and productive. Table 21–1 identifies behaviours typical of the 1- to 3-month-old, with corresponding suggestions for responding appropriately to the behaviours. The table illustrates and emphasizes the importance of appreciating and nurturing everything that an infant can do, at each point in his or her development. When an infant does not respond in ways described in the table, it is likely that special intervention may need to be considered.

RESPONDING TO THE INFANT/TODDLER'S DEVELOPMENT

Teacher/caregiver sensitivity is critical in recognizing the developmental accomplishments of the infant/toddler with disabilities. Their achievements often seem so small when measured against those of healthy infants. However, the developmental gains of these infants, minimal as they may seem, must be viewed as "major victories and sources of pride and pleasure" (Provence 1990, 2). To properly appreciate these victories, teachers/caregivers need to recognize that the potential for positive development exists in all developmental areas for every infant/toddler. Teachers/caregivers need to be aware, too, that the strengthening of one area, through appropriate intervention procedures, usually contributes to development in other areas.

A major responsibility of the infant teacher/caregiver/interventionist is to appreciate all aspects of development, both evident and emerging. Infants/toddlers with developmental problems exhibit a wide range of competencies and incompetencies. Developmental sequences follow the same pattern for all children. However, anything that interferes with a young child's development may reduce his/her ability to utilize information.

TABLE 21–1

CHARACTERISTIC BEHAVIOURS WITH APPROPRIATE CAREGIVER RESPONSES: 1- TO 3-MONTH-OLD INFANT

INFANT BEHAVIOURS

Motor	Cognitive	Language	Personal-Social	Perceptual
Reacts with eyes by following objects and sounds	Studies your face, attentively watches your actions; somewhere between 4 and 8 weeks, while doing so, a smile will gradually appear	Listens to and responds to sounds by changing physical behaviour; a still child may begin to wriggle while an active child may be calmed	Comforts self and is content to be alone for limited periods of time (5 to 15 minutes)	Discriminates mother's face from stranger's face when other clues such as voice, touch, or smell are available
The eye muscles are assuming control and the baby is increasingly able to turn the eyes independently of turning the head; the child uses the eyes to locate and follow light, bright objects, and objects that move; the human face is the most interesting object of all to the infant	Babies have a natural capacity for attention and will become bored if they spend a lot of time awake and alone; early smiles act as an insurance policy against neglect and for pleasant social contact (Leach 1987)	From birth, babies can hear; loud, sudden sounds can frighten and startle a baby, eliciting protective reflexive movements, while rhythmic sounds tend to be soothing and relaxing; the sounds most attended to by babies are those of people talking —it is as though babies are programmed to listen to the voices of their caregivers	As dependent on parents and other caregivers as the baby is, "it is important that they respect that it is the baby who quiets himself, recovers his equilibrium and lays a foundation for maintaining integration as he goes" (Murphy and Small 1989, 5); it is the role of the caregiver to respect the baby's efforts to comfort and calm self	It is healthy for babies to develop different patterns of trust and mistrust; they learn to feel safe with certain people in certain situations; an excessive lack of trust in others or their surroundings can inhibit children from expressing their needs and discovering the necessary resources to cope with them

TEACHER/PARENT/CAREGIVER BEHAVIOURS

Motor	Cognitive	Language	Personal-Social	Perceptual
Hold or suspend an attractive object within 8 to 10 inches above the baby —when object is slowly moved, baby will begin to follow; talk to baby from various places in the room— respond encouragingly as the baby attempts to turn the eyes and perhaps the head to locate the source of your voice	Keep the baby close by you when awake by propping in a carriage with a pillow under the mattress (a safe-guard against suffocation), in an infant seat, or on a rug or mat; while your chores and tasks may be tedious to you, their sounds, sights, and movements are intriguing to an infant	Talk to your baby about all the things you are doing; describe what objects look like and what they do; explain what is happening now and what is about to happen	While remaining available and ready to respond, allow the infant short periods of time to be alone or in your presence without your interacting directly with the baby; do respond discerningly and supportively, ensuring that whatever is sooth-ing to the baby is available (e.g., soft toy, rhythmic music, or the baby's own hand —suckably close to the mouth)	By being a consistent primary caregiver who responds to the baby in consis-tently comfort-ing ways, you are helping the baby recognize not only who you are, but who he or she is—the basis for establishing attachment

Generally speaking, one sense cannot fully compensate for another. A child who is visually impaired may become highly skilled at identifying objects and events through touch. That information, however, is never as complete as it would be if the child also were using vision. Even when the various sensory systems appear to be intact, there may be problems due to imperfect sensory integration (Hanson and Hanline 1984). For example, the infant may hear a teacher/caregiver's voice but be unable to orient his or her eyes or head movements in that direction. With problems of this type, the teacher/caregiver's role is to provide learning experiences and intervention activities based on the guidelines outlined earlier for responsive and enabling caregiving.

ENABLING THE INFANT TO RESPOND AND ADAPT

Infants with developmental problems, delays, and disabilities may be less responsive and less vocal than their normally developing counterparts. Studying 15 mothers and their infants with disabling conditions, including Down syndrome, brain injury, blindness, and various congenital disabilities, Stone and Chesney (1978) reported the following disturbances in behaviours commonly associated with attachment:

- delayed or infrequent smiling or vocalizing
- tenseness, limpness, or unresponsiveness when handled
- little effort to get the mother's attention

PHOTO 21–11 *Teachers/caregivers need to be available to support the child's initiations.*

Similarly, premature and low birthweight babies often have trouble forming attachments because of reduced physical strength or immature neurological development. It is important to recognize that lack of infant responsiveness contributes to less effective responding by others. Parents and teachers/caregivers, therefore, need to be available and ready to respond in kind when an infant initiates an interaction or responds to stimulation from the environment (Photo 21–11). If the infant/toddler smiles spontaneously, the adult smiles back; if the infant/toddler smiles again in response to the adult's smile, the caregiver smiles once again and perhaps adds an affectionate pat or word.

Responding in kind may not be simple, especially when an infant/toddler has limited abilities. For example, low birthweight infants with medical complications usually are considerably less responsive than healthy infants. Yet, Brachfield, Goldberg, and Sloman (1980), in their parent–infant research, found that parents of these infants seem to try to compensate by providing more physical and playful contacts than do parents of full-term, healthy infants. Many of the parents appear not to understand the need to lower the number and the tempo of their reactions to match the infant's activity level. Instead of responding calmly and soothingly on those infrequent occasions when the infant is able to initiate an interaction, the parent reacts too actively, verbally and physically, thereby overwhelming the infant to the point that he or she may shut down.

Clearly, responsible adults need to find a middle ground. In some instances, it is best to wait for the infant to make an overture and then respond at a matching level of activity. In other instances, it may be better if the teacher/caregiver watches for signs of receptiveness and then initiates a simple activity such as smiling and gently clapping the infant's hand against his/her own hand. More often than not, infants will signal "enough is enough" by averting their gaze and then looking back when they are ready for further activity (Curry and Johnson 1990). Teachers/caregivers must, in order to meet the needs of the infant/toddler, develop the following skills:

- general sensitivity to the infant's need for stimulation as well as for quiet

- responsiveness to the infant's specific signals, such as fussing and turning away

- talking and playing with the infant in ways that actively encourage development

ENABLING THE INFANT TO MAINTAIN PSYCHOLOGICAL BALANCE

Weak reflexes or the absence of muscle tone may interfere with an infant/toddler's ability to control his or her responses to the environment. Some infants/toddlers have difficulty becoming aroused, while others become too easily overaroused. For example, the predisposition to respond to the parent or teacher/caregiver's face with matching facial expressions may overflow and engage the infant's entire body. Als et al. (1982, 42) describe the reaction:

> A newborn is drawn to the animated face of the interacting caregiver. His attention intensifies, his eyes widen, eyebrows rise, and mouth shapes toward the interactor. If the [infant's] dampening mechanisms of this intensity are not established, as in the immature organism, the whole head may move forward, arms and legs may thrust toward the interactor, and fingers and toes will extend toward him. The response, which generally is confined to the face, will early on involve the total body in an undifferentiated way.

Such activity "overflow" often characterizes the behaviour of infants with developmental problems. Other examples of dysfunctional infant responses include the following:

- extreme sensitivity, or marked lack of sensitivity, to everyday occurrences

- early reflexes and behaviour patterns that persist, making it difficult for the child to initiate, stop, or redirect his or her own behaviour

- exhaustion as a result of having to spend disproportionate amounts of energy in trying to control or direct neuromuscular activity (as in the child with cerebral palsy); or excessive energy expended in trying to seek out and process new learnings

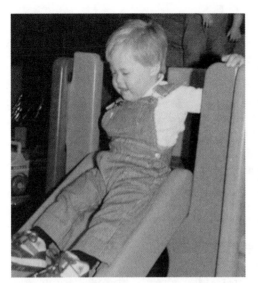

PHOTO 21–12 *The toddler is learning to become an active participant.*

Among the jobs of the teacher/caregiver is assisting the infant/toddler in becoming an active participant in appropriate learning opportunities in the immediate environment (Photo 21–12). Another is communicating with the infant/toddler in ways that let the child know that his/her messages are being heard and respected.

ENABLING THE INFANT/TODDLER TO DIFFERENTIATE RESPONSES

An infant/toddler with developmental problems may retain undifferentiated social, cognitive, and communication responses longer than is typical of a normally developing infant/toddler. In social development, for example, the infant who may deviate from the norm may not show the selective interest in parents or caregivers that is seen in most 2-month-olds. Unable to receive information through one or more of the senses, this infant may withdraw from his or her immediate world or overreact to it. Either response can prevent the infant from becoming actively interested in what is going on. In turn, this prevents the infant from attaining a sense of self and from forming effective relationships with others. As a result, the infant may

- respond in a global, all-or-nothing way;
- resist changes and transitions to other activities or settings; or
- resist adaptations, extensions, and opportunities to interrelate or to combine elements and experiences.

It takes skill and insight for a teacher/caregiver to help an infant/toddler learn to modify what he or she is able to do. As a first step, the teacher/caregiver can help the infant/toddler process incoming stimuli. For example, a puppet or toy that looks, feels, and sounds unusual might elicit a total approach or a total withdrawal reaction. If the infant can experience first the touch and then the sound of the object, the experience may become a manageable one. With some infants, an effort to touch the puppet still may spread throughout the child's entire body. When the child is therapeutically positioned in a manner that inhibits much of the overflow (see Finnie 1975), the infant's energy can be directed at making controlled arm movements that allow the infant to success-

PHOTO 21–13 *Provide opportunities for the infant to explore objects of interest.*

fully reach for and touch the puppet. By helping the infant inhibit some responses so that others can be functional, the teacher/caregiver has enabled the infant to differentiate and effectively use an appropriate response from among his or her outgoing responses.

Once infants/toddlers develop some strategies for controlling their responses, parents and teachers/caregivers can help them develop a greater and more varied range of behaviours. Parents and teachers/caregivers can do this by creating opportunities for the infants to seek out, explore, and manipulate whatever interests them (Photo 21–13). The best learning opportunities occur when the new experience is a natural outgrowth of an old and familiar one. Extensions of earlier experiences need to be gradually introduced while remaining rooted in what the infant/toddler already knows. Parents and teachers/caregivers can assist in several ways:

- Providing many slightly different opportunities for the infant to do the same thing. For example, there can be balls and blocks of many sizes, plastic cups of different shapes, chairs of different designs, and mechanical switches that are activated in different ways. If the child already walks confidently on a smooth, flat surface, this ability can be challenged by putting out a bumpy mattress to walk on. If a child with seizure problems has to adjust to wearing a helmet for head protection, happier experiences can be offered as starters, perhaps wearing different kinds of hats in preparation for adapting to the helmet.

- Offering new experiences similar to previous experiences and using familiar materials to ease transitions. An infant/toddler may find bathtime pleasant when sitting in a special seat in the bathtub. Using the same seat when introducing the child to the pool is likely to help the child adapt to being in water in a different setting. Another example: Many infants and toddlers are comforted by a special crib toy or blanket when going to sleep at home. If so, coping with going to sleep at the child-care centre often is made easier if the infant/toddler brings the same toy or blanket (or its duplicate) from home.

- Changing one dimension of an experience. When toddlers are going outdoors to play on the grass, a teacher/caregiver can take along familiar play materials—balls, for example. As a toddler starts to play with the toys "in the same old way," the toys are likely to respond differently by not moving as freely on the grass. As a result, the toddler must internalize this new information about the toys and how differently they react in different settings. Such experiences motivate a child to explore the newly exhibited properties of balls (and other play materials) as teachers/caregivers transfer the toys from one situation to another.

ENABLING THE INFANT/TODDLER TO INITIATE NEW RESPONSES

An infant/toddler with a developmental problem often uses energy to maintain internal equilibrium, making it more difficult to acknowledge external events. Or, if the infant/toddler should become aware of external stimuli, the awareness

tends to be one-dimensional—that is, the infant/toddler addresses only one source of input while ignoring the others. On the other hand, an infant/toddler may use only one sense, such as vision or hearing, to experience an object. For example, an infant/toddler may be so engrossed in watching an activity that any sounds or speech accompanying the action do not register (Photo 21–14). Also, an infant/toddler may respond with one sense but not integrate the response with other sensory input. The child may look or touch, but not put the two behaviours together so as to gain more complete information. Infants and toddlers with perceptual–motor problems, for example, may follow the movement of an

PHOTO 21–14 *Infant fully engrossed in an activity.*

object with their eyes. They may not, however, try to reach for or grasp the object as it moves out of visual range—indicating, perhaps, an inability to integrate and coordinate looking with touching.

INFANT/TODDLER INTERVENTION: AN ONGOING CHALLENGE

As previously indicated, teachers/caregivers who work with infants and toddlers with developmental problems are challenged with providing a day-by-day learning environment that supports interactions between each infant/toddler and his or her world. To develop individual strengths and reduce the impact of the developmental problem, teachers/caregivers should provide a variety of sit-

PHOTO 21–15 *All infants/toddlers need to integrate experiences across several areas of development.*

uations and activities that engage the child as a participant. Infants/toddlers especially need to integrate experiences across several areas of development. For this reason they often seem compelled to look at and touch and suck on an object. Such achievements need to be viewed not as ends in themselves, but as abilities that enable the child to recognize the functions of objects and to participate in daily experiences (Photo 21–15). Teachers/caregivers who delight and share in very young children's discoveries, ideas, and perspectives of the world are likely to promote in them a sense of a "benevolent, orderly world worthy of their attention" (Bredekamp 1987, 18).

SUMMARY

Social and economic factors, as well as legislation related to infant/toddler intervention services, are resulting in greatly increased numbers of infants and toddlers being cared for by individuals other than their parents. This shift away from parents' full-time care of their own infants/toddlers is generating a need for a greatly increased number of infant/toddler teachers/caregivers/interventionists—trained individuals who are able to provide an appropriate and enabling learning environment for both normally developing and disabled infants and toddlers.

Providing appropriate care and promoting sound learning experiences are based on a teacher/caregiver's knowledge of infant/toddler development and what constitutes a safe and healthy day-to-day environment for infants and toddlers. It is based also on a teacher/caregiver's ability to implement this knowledge by providing responsive caregiving in an enabling and engaging environment.

Responsive teaching and caregiving means that each infant's and toddler's unique ways of responding are recognized, respected, and nurtured in developmentally appropriate ways. Only by observing what an infant/toddler is doing and how the infant/toddler responds to overtures from others can parents and teachers/caregivers decide how best to respond to individual abilities and needs. Experiences should not be imposed on infants and toddlers; the adult should patiently try to engage the child's active participation, as an initiator as well as a responder.

All infants and toddlers—those who are developing normally and those with disabilities or other developmental problems—need a safe, healthy, well-supervised, and engaging environment. However, even in such an environment, disabling conditions such as sensory impairments, motor or neurological dysfunctions, and severe health problems can thwart the infant/toddler so that his or her efforts may be ineffectual, misdirected, or misinterpreted. The infant/toddler may experience no consistent outcome or results to promote a sense of accomplishment and confidence. For these infants and toddlers it is especially important that parents and teachers/caregivers respond in enabling ways. That is the challenge for the teacher/caregiver early interventionist.

STUDENT ACTIVITIES

1. Observe a wide-awake infant between 3 and 8 months of age for 45 minutes in a setting where there is at least one adult. (This may require more than one observation session.) Record the following:
   - what behaviours the infant engages in
   - which behaviours are directed to others in the environment
   - how many of the infant's overtures were responded to
   - how the infant's behaviours were responded to

2. Based on your written observation, write a simulated report for the caregivers. Commend them specifically on what they were doing that was developmentally appropriate and enabling; describe observed situations in which they might have responded or been more appropriately responsive.

3. Think about a caregiving/teaching routine—diapering, feeding, bathing—and list the kinds of infant learning experiences that a teacher/caregiver can weave into the routine.

4. Visit an infant/toddler care centre. Diagram the space, noting which activities occur, where they occur, and how teachers/caregivers were distributed.

5. Select a classmate to participate in a role-playing situation. One of you will initiate responses typical of a 3- to 6-month-old; the other will play the caregiver/teacher role and respond "in kind." Reverse roles and do the same for a 9- to 12-month-old infant and his or her teacher/caregiver.

REFERENCES

Als, H., B.M. Lester, E.Z. Tronick, and T.B. Brazelton 1982 "Toward a Research Instrument for the Assessment of Preterm Infants' Behavior (APIB)." In H.E. Fitzgerald, B.M. Lester, and M.W. Yogman, eds. *Theory and Research in Behavioral Pediatrics,* vol. 1. New York: Plenum.

Brachfield, S., S. Goldberg, and J. Sloman 1980 "Parent–Infant Interaction in Free Play at 8 and 12 Months: Effects of Prematurity and Immaturity." *Infant Behavior and Development* 3: 289–305.

Bredekamp, S. 1987 *Developmentally Appropriate Practice in Early Childhood Programs Serving Children from Birth through Age 8.* Washington, D.C.: National Association for the Education of Young Children.

Brynelsen, D. 1990 "Historical Perspective on Infant Development Programs in Canada." Paper prepared for presentation to the Atlantic Conference, Halifax, N.S. May.

Canadian Association of Family Resource Centres 1990 TLRCC Canada, Ottawa, Ont.

Canadian Paediatric Society 1992 *Well Beings.* Toronto: Creative Premises.

Canadian Paediatric Society 1994 *Little Well Beings.* Toronto: Creative Premises.

Consumer and Corporate Affairs, Canada. Kids Care National Program.

Curry, N.E. and C.N. Johnson 1990 *Beyond Self Esteem: Developing a Genuine Sense of Human Value.* Washington, D.C.: National Centre for Education of Young Children.

Edelman, M.W. 1990 "Closing Address." National Association for the Education of Young Children Annual Conference, Washington, D.C.

Egeland, B., and A. Sroufe 1981 "Attachment and Early Maltreatment." *Child Development* 52: 44–52.

Finnie, N.R. 1975 *Handling the Young Cerebral Palsied Child at Home,* 2nd ed. New York: Dutton.

Hanson, M.J., and M.F. Hanline 1984 "Behavioral Competencies and Outcomes: The Effects of Disorders." In M.J. Hanson, ed. *Atypical Infant Development.* Baltimore: University Park Press.

Klaus, M.H., and P.H. Klaus 1985 *The Amazing Newborn.* Reading, Mass.: Addison–Wesley.

Leach, P. 1987 *Your Baby and Child.* New York: Knopf.

Lewis, M. 1984 "Developmental Principles and Their Implications for At-Risk and Handicapped Infants." In M.J. Hanson, ed. *Atypical Infant Development.* Baltimore: University Park Press.

Murphy, L.B., and C.T. Small 1989 "The Baby's World." *Zero to Three* 10, no. 2: 1–6.

Musselwhite, C.R. 1986 *Adaptive Play for Special Needs Children: Strategies to Enhance Communication and Learning.* San Diego, Cal.: College-Hill Press.

Provence, S. 1990 "Interactional Issues: Infants, Parents, Professionals." *Infants and Young Children* 3: 1–7.

Stone, N., and B. Chesney 1978 "Attachment Behaviors in Handicapped Infants." Mental Retardation 16, no. 1: 8–12.

APPENDIX A

SELECTED LIST OF SCREENING TOOLS AND ASSESSMENT INSTRUMENTS FOR USE WITH INFANTS/TODDLERS AND YOUNG CHILDREN

Section I, below, describes screening tests designed to call attention to possible developmental problems. Neither the test items nor the results should be used for program planning. Where the test results yield information regarding a child's potential deficiencies and delays, further assessment and evaluation is indicated.

SECTION I: SCREENING TOOLS AND ASSESSMENT INSTRUMENTS

Apgar Scoring System
The purpose of the APGAR (1953) is to measure the newborn's physical responsiveness, development, and overall state of health at 1, 3, 5, and 10 minutes following birth. The infant is rated on a scale of 1 to 10. A low APGAR score indicates a handicapping or stressful condition that may be life threatening and that calls for immediate medical attention.

Bayley Scales of Infant Development
The Bayley Scales (1969) yield separate scores for mental development and for motor development. However, research indicates that an infant's scores on the tests do not reliably predict later IQ performance. The main benefit of the Bayley is to identify very young children who may have significant developmental problems.

Battelle Developmental Inventory (BDI)
This instrument is behaviourally based and provides information about a child's functioning in five major domains: personal-social, adaptive, motor, communication, and cognitive.

The BDI is suitable for children from birth to age 6. It provides information that can be used in the development of Individual Program Plans.

Brazelton Neonatal Behaviour Assessment Scale with Kansas Supplement

The Brazelton measures the infant's physical maturation and responsiveness and is appropriate for evaluating infants throughout the first month of life. The Kansas Supplement allows the examiner to rate the quality of the infant's responses in terms of best responses and modal (more typical) responses.

Denver Developmental Screening Test (DDST)

The purpose of the DDST (developed by Frankenberg et al. 1975) is to quickly determine the developmental deviations in children from birth to 6 years of age. The screening test covers gross motor, fine motor, language, adaptive, and personal-social skills. DDST scores should not be used as a basis for program planning but rather to indicate areas where follow-up assessment is indicated.

Developmental Indicators for the Assessment of Learning (DIAL)—Revised

The purpose of this screening instrument is to identify potential learning problems in the areas of gross motor, fine motor, concept development, and communication skills. The DIAL, geared to screening children in the 2 to 5 age range, is an especially useful tool for teachers in early childhood settings.

Diagnostic Inventory for Screening Children (DISC)

The Diagnostic Inventory for Screening Children (DISC) is designed to identify children in need of further diagnostic evaluation. The DISC focuses on eight skill areas. It provides developmental scales from 1 month to 5 years of age within each of the eight areas. This tool is often used by professionals and teachers because of the ease with which it is administered.

Developmental Profile

This revised instrument (Alpern, Boll, and Shearer 1980) is designed to screen the development of children from birth through 9 years of age. Test items focus on physical, self-help, social, academic, and communication skills. The results of the test are expressed in terms of a developmental age or DQ (developmental quotient). Outcome scores determine if there is a need for further assessment.

Vineland Social Maturity Scale (Doll, 1984 Revision)

Described as covering birth to maturity, the Vineland attempts to evaluate progress toward social maturity, competence, and independence. The scores are translated into social age and social competence.

REFERENCES

Alpern, G., T. Boll, and M. Shearer 1980 *Developmental Profile II*. Aspen, Colo.: Psychological Development Publications.

Amdur, J., and M. Mainland 1984 *Diagnostic Inventory for Screening Children (DISC)*, Child Family Clinic, Kitchener-Waterloo Hospital, Kitchener, Ont.

Apgar, V. 1953 "A Proposal for a New Method of Evaluation of the Newborn Infant." *Current Researches in Anesthesia and Analgesia* 32: 260–67.

Bayley, N. 1969 *The Bayley Scales of Infant Development*. New York: The Psychological Corporation.

Brazelton, T.B. 1973 *Neonatal Behavioral Assessment Scale*. Clinics in Developmental Medicine, No. 50. Philadelphia: J.B. Lippincott.

Frankenburg, W., J. Dodds, and A. Fandal 1975 *Denver Developmental Screening Test*. Denver, Colo.: Ladoca Publishing Foundation.

Mardell-Czudnowski, C., and D. Goldenberg 1983 *Developmental Indicators for the Assessment of Learning—Revised (DIAL–R)*. Edison, N.J.: Childcraft Education Corp.

Newborg, S., J.R. Stock, L. Wnek, J. Luidubaldi, and J. Svinicki 1988 *Battelle Developmental Inventory: Examiner's Manual*. Washington, D.C.: Riverside Publishing Company.

Sparrow, S.S., D.A. Balla, and D.V. Cicchetti 1984 *Vineland Adaptive Behavior Scales*. Circle Pines, Minn.: American Guidance Service, Inc.

SECTION II: INSTRUMENTS SUITABLE FOR INDIVIDUAL PROGRAM PLANNING

Brigance Developmental Inventory of Early Development

This inventory assesses children (birth to 7) in personal-social, motor, adaptive, communication, and cognitive areas of development. The results provide developmental age levels in each domain. The inventory is useful in deciding on instructional objectives for individual children.

Callier-Azusa Scale, G Form

This scale assesses children who are deaf and blind and have multiple handicaps. It can be used with infants as young as 6 months and focuses on the major developmental skills.

Developmental Programming for Infants and Young Children

This instrument yields information about the developmental status of children birth to 3 years of age in six areas: fine motor, gross motor, language, cognition, social, and self-help. It is especially useful in making interdisciplinary team assessments and intervention decisions.

Hawaii Early Learning Profile (HELP)

This profile, based on a developmental milestones model for all areas of development, includes tasks and skills suitable for children from birth through 3. Many interdisciplinary teams find this profile useful in identifying problems and prescribing intervention strategies.

Learning Accomplishment Profile (Early LAP and Infant LAP)

These profiles assess children in the birth-to-6 age range and provide guidelines for individual programming in large and fine motor skills, self-help, social, language, and cognitive development.

Portage Guide to Early Education

The Portage Guide includes a checklist to assess developmental performance in the birth-to-6 age group and offers 580 lesson plans or activity cards for building skills in all areas of development.

Preschool Language Scale

This scale assesses both receptive and expressive language in children from 1 through 7 years old. A Spanish version of this scale is available.

Uniform Performance Assessment System (UPAS)

To be used with children from birth through age 6, the assessment system is based on criterion-referenced tests in the areas of preacademic, communication, social, self-help, and motor skills.

Note: Other types of developmental screening tests, such as vision and hearing tests and a host of others, are available. However, in these specialized areas, where gross screening tests may fail to reveal a serious but subtle problem, it seems best to leave such screening to specially trained professionals.

REFERENCES

Brigance, A.H. 1978 *Brigance Diagnostic Inventory of Early Development*. Billerica, Mass.: Curriculum Associates.

Furuno, S., K. O'Reilly, C. Hosaka, T. Inatuska, T. Aleman, and B. Zeisloft 1979 *Hawaii Early Learning Profile (HELP)*. Palo Alto, Cal.: VORT Corp.

LeMay, D., P. Griffin, and A. Sanford 1981 *Learning Accomplishment Profile: Diagnostic Edition (Revised)*. Winston-Salem, N.C.: Kaplan School Supply.

Schafer, D.S., and M.S. Moerschm, eds. 1977 *Developmental Programming for Infants and Young Children* vols. 1–3. Ann Arbor, Mich.: University of Michigan Press.

Shearer, D.E., J. Billingsley, A. Froman, J. Hilliard, F. Johnson, and M. Shearer 1976 *Portage Guide to Early Education—Revised.* Portage, Wis.: Portage Project.

Stillman, R. 1982 *Callier-Azusa Scale.* Dallas, Tex.: Callier Center for Communication Disorders.

White, O., E. Edgar, N. Haring, J. Affleck, A. Hayden, and M. Benderesky 1981 *Uniform Performance Assessment System (UPAS).* Columbus, Ohio: Charles E. Merrill.

Zimmerman, I., V. Steiner, and R. Pond 1979 *Preschool Language Scale.* Columbus, Ohio: Charles E. Merrill.

SECTION III: ASSESSING THE DEVELOPMENTAL ENVIRONMENT

Early Childhood Environment Rating Scale (ECERS) 1980

According to the authors, the ECERS was "designed to give an overall picture of the surroundings for children and adults in preschool settings, including the use of space, materials, and activities to enhance the children's development, daily schedule, and supervision." The scale assesses both infant and preschool environments. The Infant Toddler Environment Rating Scale (ITERS) (Harms, Cryer, and Clifford, 1990) and the Day Care Home Environment Rating Scale (DCHERS) (Harms and Clifford, 1983) also are environmental rating scales for infant and toddler centres and for family daycare homes. The intent of each is to determine the quality of care in a child's environment.

Home Observation and Measurement of the Environment (HOME)

The HOME survey is designed to evaluate the physical environment as well as the social, emotional, and cognitive support available to a child in his or her home. Two versions of the HOME are available, one for children birth to 3 and the other for children 3 to 6.

Preschool Assessment of the Classroom Environment (PACE)

This scale (McWilliam and Dunst 1985) assesses classroom organization, staffing and scheduling patterns, instruction strategies, and program evaluation. PACE was designed for programs serving children (birth to 6) with developmental disabilities.

REFERENCES

Caldwell, B., and Bradley 1978 *Home Observation and Measurement of the Environment.* Little Rock, Ark.: Center for Child Development and Education, University of Arkansas.

Harms, T., and R.M. Clifford 1980 *Early Childhood Environment Rating Scale.* New York: Teachers College Press.

Harms, T., R.M. Clifford, E. Padan-Belkin 1983 *Day Care Home Environment Rating Scale (DCHERS).* Chapel Hill, N.C.: Homebased Day Care Training Project.

Harms, T., and R.M. Clifford 1990 *Infant/Toddler Environment Rating Scale (ITERS).* New York: Teachers College Press.

McWilliam, R.A., and C.J. Dunst 1985 "Preschool Assessment of the Classroom Environment," unpublished scale. Family, Infant, and Preschool Program, Morgantown, N.C.: Western Carolina Center.

Preschool Profile

	GROSS MOTOR SKILLS	FINE MOTOR SKILLS	PREACADEMIC SKILLS	SELF-HELP SKILLS	MUSIC/ART/ STORY SKILLS	SOCIAL SKILLS AND PLAY SKILLS	UNDER-STANDING LANGUAGE	ORAL LANGUAGE
0–12 months	Sits without support. Crawls. Pulls self to standing and stands unaided. Walks with aid. Rolls a ball in imitation of adult.	Reaches, grasps, puts object in mouth. Picks things up with thumb and one finger (pincer grasp). Transfers object from one hand to other hand. Drops and picks up toy.	Looks directly at adult's face. Tracks objects (follows them smoothly with eyes). Imitates gestures: e.g., pat-a-cake, peek-a-boo, bye-bye. Puts block in, takes block out of container. Finds block hidden under cup.	Feeds self cracker: munching, not sucking. Holds cup with two hands, drinks with assistance. Holds out arms and legs while being dressed.	Fixes gaze on pictures in book.	Smiles spontaneously. Responds differentially to strangers and familiar persons. Pays attention to own name. Responds to *no*. Copies simple actions of others.	Looks at people who talk to him. Responds differentially to variety of sounds: e.g., phone, vacuum, closing doors, etc. Responds to simple directions accompanied by gestures: e.g., *come, give, get*.	Makes different vowel sounds. Makes different consonant-vowel combinations. Vocalizes to the person who has talked to him. Uses intonation patterns that sound like phrases: e.g., intonations that sound like scolding, asking, telling.
12–24 months	Walks alone. Walks backward. Picks up object without falling. Pulls toy. Seats self in child's chair. Walks up and down stairs with aid.	Builds tower of 3 cubes. Puts 4 rings on stick. Places 5 pegs in pegboard. Turns pages 2 or 3 at a time. Scribbles.	Follows one direction involving familiar actions and objects: e.g., *Give me (toy). Show me (body part). Get a (familiar object).* Completes 3-piece formboard. Matches similar objects.	Uses spoon, spilling little. Drinks from cup, one hand, unassisted. Chews food. Removes garment. Zips, unzips large zipper. Indicates toilet needs.	Moves to music. Looks at pictures in book, patting, pointing to, or naming objects or people. Paints with whole arm movement, shifts hands, scrubs, makes strokes.	Recognizes self in mirror or picture. Refers to self by name. Plays by self; initiates own play activities. Imitates adult behaviours in play. Plays with water and sand. Loads, carries, dumps. Helps put things away.	Responds to specific words by showing what was named: e.g., toys, family members, clothing, body parts. Responds to simple directions given without gestures: e.g., *go, sit, find, run, walk.*	Asks for items by name. Answers *What's that?* with name of object. Tells about objects or experiences with words used together (2–3 words): e.g., *More juice.*

	GROSS MOTOR SKILLS	FINE MOTOR SKILLS	PREACADEMIC SKILLS	SELF-HELP SKILLS	MUSIC/ART/ STORY SKILLS	SOCIAL SKILLS AND PLAY SKILLS	UNDER-STANDING LANGUAGE	ORAL LANGUAGE
24-36 months	Runs forward well. Jumps in place, two feet together. Stands on one foot, with aid. Walks on tiptoe. Kicks ball forward. Throws ball, without direction.	Strings 4 large beads. Turns pages singly. Snips with scissors. Holds crayon with thumb and fingers, not fist. Uses one hand consistently in most activities. Imitates circular, vertical, horizontal strokes.	Matches shapes. Stacks 5 rings on peg. in order. Demonstrates number concepts to 2 (i.e., selects set of 1 or 2; can tell how many, 1 or 2).	Uses spoon, no spilling. Gets drink unassisted. Uses straw. Opens door by turning handle. Puts on/takes off coat. Washes/dries hands with assistance.	Participates in simple group activity: e.g., sings, claps, dances. Chooses picture books, points to fine detail, enjoys repetition. Paints with some wrist action, makes dots, lines, circular strokes. Rolls, pounds, squeezes, pulls clay material.	Plays near other children. Watches other children, joins briefly in their play. Defends own possessions. Engages in domestic play. Symbolically uses objects, self in play. Builds with blocks in simple lines.	Responds to *put it in* and *put it on*. Responds by selecting correct item: big vs. little objects; one vs. one more object. Identifies objects by their use: e.g., *Show me what mother cooks on* by showing stove, or *Show me what you wear on your feet* by showing shoe.	Asks questions. Answers *Where is it?* with prepositional phrases: e.g., *in the box, on the table.* Answers *What do you do with a ball?* e.g., *throw, catch.* Tells about something with functional sentences that carry meaning: e.g., *me go store* or *me hungry now.*
36-48 months	Runs around obstacles. Walks on a line. Balances on one foot 5 seconds. Hops on one foot. Pushes, pulls, steers wheeled toys. Rides (i.e., steers and pedals) trike. Uses slide without assistance. Jumps over 15 cm (6") high object, landing on both feet together. Throws ball with direction. Catches ball bounced to him.	Builds tower of 9 cubes. Drives nails and pegs. Copies circle. Imitates cross.	Matches 6 colours. Makes tower of 5 blocks, graduated in size. Does 7-piece puzzle. Counts to 5, in imitation of adults. Demonstrates number concept to 3.	Pours well from pitcher. Spreads substances with knife. Buttons/unbuttons large buttons. Washes hands unassisted. Cleans nose when reminded. Uses toilet independently. Follows classroom routine with minimum teacher assistance. Knows own sex. Knows own age. Knows own last name.	Knows phrases of songs. Listens to short simple stories (5 minutes). Painting: names own picture, not always recognizable; demands variety of colour. Draws head of person and one other part. Manipulates clay materials: e.g., rolls balls, snakes, cookies, etc.	Joins in play with other children; begins to interact. Shares toys, takes turns with assistance. Begins dramatic play, acting out whole scenes: e.g., travelling, playing house, pretending to be animals.	Responds to *put it beside* and *put it under*. Responds to commands involving 2 objects: e.g., *Give me the ball and the shoe.* Responds to commands involving 2 actions: e.g., *Give me the cup and put the shoe on the floor.* Responds by selecting correct item: e.g., hard vs. soft objects. Responds to *walk fast* by increased pace, and to *walk slowly* by decreased pace.	Answers *Which one do you want?* by naming it. Answers *if/what* and *what/when* questions: e.g., *If you had a penny, what would you do? What do you do when you're hungry?* Answers questions about function: e.g., *What are books for?* Asks for or tells about with grammatically correct sentences: e.g., *Can I go to the store? I want a big cookie.*

	GROSS MOTOR SKILLS	FINE MOTOR SKILLS	PREACADEMIC SKILLS	SELF-HELP SKILLS	MUSIC/ART/ STORY SKILLS	SOCIAL SKILLS AND PLAY SKILLS	UNDER-STANDING LANGUAGE	ORAL LANGUAGE
48–60 months	Walks backward heel-toe. Jumps forward 10 times, without falling. Walks up/down stairs alone, alternating feet. Turns somersault.	Cuts on a line continuously. Copies cross. Copies square. Prints a few capital letters.	Points to, names 6 basic colours. Points to, names 3 shapes. Matches related common objects: e.g., shoe, sock, foot; apple, orange, banana. Demonstrates number concept to 4 or 5.	Cuts food with a knife; e.g., sandwich, celery. Laces shoes. Knows own city/street. Follows instructions given to group.	Sings entire songs. Recites nursery rhyme. "Reads" from pictures (i.e., tells story). Recognizes story and retells simple facts. Painting: makes and names recognizable pictures. Draws a person with 2–6 parts.	Plays and interacts with other children. Dramatic play: closer to reality; attention to detail, time, and space. Plays dress-up. Builds complex structures with blocks.	Responds by showing penny, nickel, dime. Responds to command involving 3 actions: e.g., *Give me the cup, put the shoe on the floor, and hold the pencil in your hand.*	Asks *how* questions. Answers verbally to *Hi* and *How are you?* Tells about something using past tense and future tense. Tells about something using conjunctions to string words and phrases together: e.g., *I have a cat and a dog and a fish.*
							Above items are selected from *The Sequenced Inventory of Communication Development,* University Press, University of Washington, 1975.	
60–72 months	Runs lightly on toes. Walks a balance beam. Can cover 2 m (6'6"), hopping. Skips. Jumps rope. Skates.	Cuts out simple shapes. Copies triangle. Traces diamond. Copies first name. Prints numerals 1–5. Colours within lines. Has adult grasp of pencil. Has handedness well established. (i.e., child is left- or right-handed).	Sorts objects on one dimension: i.e., by size or by colour or by shape. Does 15-piece puzzle. Copies block design. Names some letters. Names some numerals. Names penny, nickel, dime, quarter. Counts by rote to 10. Can tell what number comes next.	Dresses self completely. Learns to distinguish left from right. Ties bow. Brushes teeth unassisted. Crosses street safely. Relates clock time to daily schedule.	Recognizes rhyme. Acts out stories. Draws a person with head, trunk, legs, arms, and features. Pastes and glues appropriately. Models objects with clay.	Chooses own friend(s). Plays simple table games. Plays competitive games. Engages in cooperative play with other children involving group decisions, role assignments, fair play. Uses construction toys to make things: e.g., house of Lego pieces, car of rig-a-jig.	See Preacademic Skills.	Child will have acquired basic grammatical structures, including plurals, verb tenses, and conjunctions. Following this developmental ability, the child practises with increasingly complex descriptions and conversations.

This profile is a working draft only and was prepared by the Communication Disorders Specialists Linda Lynch, Jane Rieke, Sue Soltman, and teachers Donna Hardman and Mary O'Conor. The Communication Program was funded initially as a part of the Model Preschool Center for Handicapped Children by the U.S. Office of Education, Program Development Branch, Washington, D.C. Experimental Education Unit (WJ10) of the College of Education and Child Development and Mental Retardation Center, University of Washington, Seattle, Wash.

APPENDIX C

SOURCES OF INFORMATION, SUPPORT, AND TRAINING MATERIAL FOR TEACHERS AND PARENTS OF CHILDREN WITH DEVELOPMENTAL DISABILITIES

CANADIAN AND NORTH AMERICAN PROFESSIONAL ORGANIZATIONS

Alexander Graham Bell Association for
the Deaf
3417 Volta Place NW
Washington, D.C. 20007

American Association on Mental
Retardation (AAMD)
1719 Kalorama Road NW
Washington, D.C. 20009

American Cleft Palate Foundation and
Parent Committee
Louisiana State University School of
Medicine, Department of
Audiology and Speech Pathology
Shreveport, Louisiana 71130

American Foundation for the Blind
15 West 16th Street
New York, New York 10011

American Speech, Hearing, and
Language Association (ASHA)
10801 Rockville Pike
Rockville, Maryland 20852

Association for Bright Children
Suite 100, Box 156
2 Bloor Street West
Toronto, Ontario M4W 2G7

Association for the Neurologically
Disabled of Canada
59 Clements Rd.
Etobicoke, Ontario M9R 1Y5

Autism Society, Canada
129 Yorkville Avenue
Suite 202
Toronto, Ontario M5R 1C4

Canadian Association for Community
Living (formerly
Canadian Association for the
Mentally Retarded)
4700 Keele Street
Toronto, Ontario M3J 1P3

Canadian Association of the Deaf
2435 Holly Lane
Ottawa, Ontario K1V 7P2

Canadian Association for People Who
  Stutter
P.O. Box 2774
100 City Centre Drive
Mississauga, Ontario L5B 3C8

Canadian Cerebral Palsy Association
880 Wellington Street, Suite 612
Ottawa, Ontario K1R 6K7

Canadian Cleft Lip and Palate Family
  Association
170 Elizabeth Street
Toronto, Ontario M5G 1E8

Canadian Council for Exceptional
  Children
1010 Polytek Court, Unit 36
Gloucester, Ottawa, Ontario K1J 9J2

Canadian Cystic Fibrosis Foundation
2221 Yonge Street, Suite 601
Toronto, Ontario M5S 2B4

Canadian Diabetes Foundation
78 Bond Street
Toronto, Ontario M5B 2J8

Canadian Down Syndrome Society
12837 76th Avenue, Suite 206
Surrey, British Columbia V3W 2V3

Canadian Hearing Society
271 Spadina Road
Toronto, Ontario M5R 2V3

Canadian Hemophilia Society
1450 City Councillors, Suite 840
Montreal, Quebec H3A 2E6

Canadian Mental Health Association
970 Lawrence Avenue West, Suite 205
Toronto, Ontario M6A 3B6

Canadian National Institute for the
  Blind (CNIB)
1929 Bayview Avenue
Toronto, Ontario M4G 3E8

Council for Exceptional Children
  (CEC)
1920 Association Drive
Reston, Virginia 22091-1589

Epilepsy Association of Canada
2099 Alexandre-Deserve
P.O. Box 1560, Station C
Montreal, Quebec H2L 4K8

Epilepsy Foundation of America
4351 Garden City Drive
Landover, Maryland 20785

Juvenile Diabetes Foundation of
  Canada
89 Granton Drive
Richmond Hill, Ontario L4B 2N5

Learning Disabilities Association
  Canada
323 Chapel Street, Suite 200
Ottawa, Ontario K1N 7Z2

Muscular Dystrophy Association of
Canada
150 Eglinton Avenue East, Suite 400
Toronto, Ontario M4P 1E8

National Association of the Deaf
National Association of Parents of the
Deaf
814 Thayer Avenue
Silver Springs, Maryland 20910

National Blindness Information Center
1346 Connecticut Avenue NW, Room
222
Washington, D.C. 20036

National Information Center for
Handicapped Children and Youth
(NICHCY)
P.O. Box 1492
Washington, D.C. 20013-1492
(NICHCY is a free information centre
and materials development program for
anyone in need of particular kinds of
information about handicapping conditions and the lives and needs of those who
are handicapped. NICHCY answers
questions and sends materials in response
to requests made by mail.)

National Society for Children and
Adults with Autism
1234 Massachusetts Avenue NW, Suite
107
Washington, D.C. 20005

Prevent Blindness America (previously
National Society to Prevent
Blindness)
500 Cast Remington Road
Schaumburg, Illinois 67173

SpeciaLink
P.O. Box 775
Sydney, Nova Scotia B1P 6G9

Spina Bifida Association of America
343 South Dearborn, Suite 319
Chicago, Illinois 60604

Spina Bifida Association of Canada
633 Wellington Crescent
Winnipeg, Manitoba R3N 0A8

United Cerebral Palsy Association
1000 Elmwood Avenue
Rochester, New York 14620

APPENDIX D

TASK ANALYSIS: LADDER-CLIMBING SEQUENCE

PLANNING PROCESS

1. Assess Child's Abilities and Needs

Before a task can be selected for a child to perform, a careful assessment of the child's current abilities and skills must be completed.

Example of a case history:

> *Matthew was soon to be 4 years old. He was a pale, slow-moving child who seldom played with other children. He rarely engaged in the vigorous outdoor play activities typical of the rest of the group. Teachers agreed, based on a series of observations, that it would help Matthew's overall development if he were to learn to use the climbing equipment. However, he resisted all of their efforts to involve him in climbing activities. Below is a condensed account of the step-by-step procedures that resulted in Matthew's becoming not only an active climber but a more sociable 4-year-old. (For a detailed case history, see K.E. Allen and E.V. Goetz,* Early Childhood Education: Special Problems, Special Solutions *[Rockville, Md.: Aspen Systems, 1982].)*

2. Set a Goal, Objectives, and Task

a. Set a goal: Set a goal and then identify the task to be performed by the child. The goal in the above example might be developing motor skills for outdoor play.

b. Identify objectives: For example, the child will independently climb up to the top of the slide in the playground.

c. Set the task: The task in this case is climbing a ladder.

3. Determine the Sequential Steps Necessary for Performing the Task

The child follows this sequence of steps when climbing a ladder:

1. looks at ladder
2. approaches ladder
3. places hands on rungs of ladder
4. places dominant foot on lower rung

5. pulls body up with arms while at the same time pressing down with the dominant foot
6. places other foot on bottom rung
7. moves dominant hand up one rung
8. moves dominant foot up to the next rung
9. repeats above steps

4. Decide on an Implementation Plan

Develop a plan and decide on how this plan will be carried out. Teachers need to agree on the following:

a. the step in the sequence with which to begin

b. the teaching strategies that are most appropriate for this child

c. the type of reinforcement to be provided

d. when and where the task will be performed

5. Implement the Plan

A short ladder with broad steps was set up against play equipment that Matthew often wandered past. A teacher was stationed near the ladder, supervising children playing in the area.

Whenever Matthew wandered by, the teacher spoke to him and chatted with him. Often he drew closer, watching the children climbing about. When he stopped watching the children and looked as if he were about to move away, the teacher became busy with the other children.

As Matthew stopped to chat more frequently and for longer periods of time, he sometimes leaned against or put his hand on the ladder. Soon the teacher began to chat with Matthew only when he was touching the ladder.

Next, whenever Matthew was leaning on the ladder, the teacher made up a game, placing one of Matthew's feet on the lowest rung and then taking it off. Matthew delighted in the game. Soon he was putting his own foot on the ladder.

Before long, Matthew himself was putting both feet on the bottom rung of the ladder. The teacher then changed the game to feet on and off the second rung.

In this game-like atmosphere, where the teacher provided both physical and verbal reinforcement, Matthew was soon climbing up and down the ladder.

The ladder was later moved to different locations. Matthew continued to climb on it with only occasional attention from teachers. It appeared that the activity itself had become fun for Matthew and therefore self-reinforcing.

The next step was to place the ladder against another big piece of climbing equipment. As Matthew began to make the transition from the familiar ladder to the big piece of equipment, teachers once again provided an abundance of physical and verbal support.

By the ninth day of the program Matthew was spending more than half of the outdoor play time in a variety of climbing activities. At midyear he was as active and involved outdoors as any child in the group. Presumably, vigorous outdoor play with other children had become a pleasurable activity that would continue to be self-reinforcing.

BECOMING AWARE OF BABY AND YOU: EXAMPLES OF WAYS TO INTERACT WITH YOUR BABY

MONTHS OF AGE	MOTOR	COGNITIVE	LANGUAGE	PERSONAL/ SOCIAL	PERCEPTUAL (ESSENTIAL EXPERIENCE)
Birth to 3 months	Lay on side or stomach, often nuzzle, cuddle, stroke baby gently. Rhythmically rock in rocking chair. Slowly move object in 180° arc for baby to follow with eyes. Hold in different positions: head lifted to shoulder, face forward or to side.	Expose to soft toys and musical ones. Place rattle in hand—gently pull, change from hand to hand. Carry baby with you, preferably in front carrier.	Look at and establish eye contact when talking with baby. Smile, talk, and sing to baby. Smile, talk, and sing in direct response to baby's sounds, movements, and cries—from different places in room. Encourage sucking and tongue activity. Imitate baby's sounds.	Respond to needs when baby cries. Hold baby, especially when feeding. Respond with animated expressions to your baby. Smile at your baby. Play with and enjoy your baby.	Assist baby in staying calm and interested in his/her surroundings—internal regulation.
3–6 months	Massage baby, rubbing arms, legs, and body with lotion. Gently bounce on knee (while supporting upper body). Hold in standing position. Anticipate that baby will soon be rolling—tummy to back and back to tummy—crawling, and sitting. Place on blanket with freedom to roll.	Provide different views from crib. Put bells on booties. Put patterned sheet on bed. Provide objects to be picked up and reached for—with both arms. Provide mirror so baby can look at reflection. Attach toy to string for baby to pull.	Talk about occurrences as you take baby outside, to store, etc. Play music and recordings of nursery rhymes. Imitate baby's sounds. Encourage child to locate sound source with eyes and to imitate your sounds. Provide soft dolls and animal toys to elicit vocalizations.	Respond to baby's smiles, coos, and gurgles. Respect baby's attitudes toward strangers. Respond as consistently as possible to attention-seeking behaviour.	Assist baby in making a rich, deeply multisensory investment in the animate world—attachment.
6–9 months	Provide small items to be picked up with "swipe" motion. Allow baby to crawl (avoid walkers when appropriate). Assist child in attempts to sit up (place pillows so child isn't hurt by fall). Offer toys barely beyond hands to encourage reaching.	Position baby so able to watch you. Provide mirror for baby to see self and others. Provide mouthable (chewable, suckable) objects to manipulate and explore, passing hand to hand.	Call baby by name. Imitate baby's *da-da, ma-ma,* and *ba-ba*. Wave bye-bye, play pat-a-cake. Sing nursery rhymes with accompanying simple actions aimed at involving baby. Use gestures and hand signals and accompanying words.	Support baby's efforts at independence (e.g., let hold spoon). Offer small amounts of liquid from a spoon in preparation for drinking from a cup. Provide small pieces of soft finger foods for self-feeding. Explore the house—together. Label and talk about body parts.	Assist your baby to achieve purposeful "communications" and differentiated responses to the world.

MONTHS OF AGE	MOTOR	COGNITIVE	LANGUAGE	PERSONAL/ SOCIAL	PERCEPTUAL (ESSENTIAL EXPERIENCE)
9–12 months	Explore space moving around, under, and over furniture. Let baby "unwrap" items (use paper or cloth; be sure paper doesn't go in mouth). Roll a ball to baby, retrieve, and repeat. "Baby safe" surroundings for crawling and standing child. Be ready to catch child as she pulls self to standing, stands momentarily, and walks holding on to furniture, etc.	Place toys in container baby can dump and refill. Play "cause-and-effect" games, tailoring your response to baby. Hide toys or ticking clock and help baby find (baby can watch as you hide the object!). Clap hands together, bang toys together —together! Push buttons with one finger.	Talk with baby in front of a mirror and acknowledge yourselves. Read books and tell baby simple stories. When child offers you an object—accept, comment upon, and give it back. Respond to speech sounds. Introduce "no-no" consistently.	Enjoy and admire your baby's "antics" (e.g., wearing basket or empty box as hat!). Play "where's baby?" hiding behind furniture. Let baby try to feed self, hold cup, wash with cloth or sponge. Use baby's name when giving simple commands, directions, or requests. Refer to self as "mama" or "da-da."	Assist your baby to initiate complex, organized assertive, innovative, integrated behavioural and emotional patterns.
12–15 months	When someone is available to watch, let child crawl up and down stairs. Crumple paper into balls and throw. Lift child up to touch toys that are high and out of reach. Provide opportunities to shovel sand and empty into bucket. Take short "walks" together.	Provide photos or pictures of familiar events you and your baby are engaging in. Provide "toy" or real (when safe) objects to use to imitate your actions (telephone, broom, etc.). Introduce water and sand play when you can supervise.	Provide words for actions. When child is trying to do something new, provide models and verbal directions. Play games where you enact action words. Try to understand baby's feelings and say words for those feelings; express your feelings with words. Record words baby uses. Attempt to interpret baby's gestures (shaking head for "no-no" and holding out arms to be picked up).	Plan plenty of time for undressing and make it easy. Make cleanup time a game—gradually expect more and more cooperation. Help child to express feelings in socially acceptable ways. Provide small amounts of liquid in a small cup. Provide safe bits of finger foods for self-feeding.	

Adapted from Irving Preschool Educational and Diagnostic Center, 1982.
For further information, see S. Greenspan and S. Porges, "Psychopathology in Infancy and Early Childhood: Clinical Perspectives on the Organization of Sensory and Affective-Thematic Experience," *Child Development* 55 (1984), 49–70.

APPENDIX F

CURRENT INFORMATION ON PROVINCIAL AND TERRITORIAL SERVICES AND RESOURCES

Note: Statistical information for this section comes from the following sources:
- The Childcare Resource and Research Unit 1997 (in press)
- Child Care in Canada: The Provinces and Territories (draft), Childcare Resource and Research Unit, University of Toronto

PROVINCE: ALBERTA

CONTACT:

Day Care Programs
Alberta Family and Social Services
10035–108 Street
Edmonton, Alberta T5J 3E1
(403) 427-4477

STATISTICAL INFORMATION:

Number of licensed/regulated spaces (1995)
Infant and preschool 43 262
School-age 12 878
Family daycare 7826
Special needs children 400

PUBLICATIONS:

Integrated Day Care Programs: guidelines to assist children with special needs in mainstream daycare centres or family day homes (guidelines are currently being updated)

OTHER RESOURCES:

Early Intervention, Office of the Commission for Children and Families, Alberta Family and Social Services

Handicapped Children's Services, Alberta Family and Social Services: provides assistance to families with children with disabilities

Program Funding Unit, Alberta Education: for individual programs to meet educational needs of children with severe disabilities, ages 2 1/2 to 6 years (service available for a maximum of 3 years)

COMMENTS:
Children's services are being redesigned.

PROVINCE: BRITISH COLUMBIA

CONTACT:
Community Support Services Division
   Ministry of Social Services
   614 Humboldt Street,
   3rd Floor
   Victoria, British Columbia
   V8V 1X4

STATISTICAL INFORMATION:
Number of licensed/regulated spaces (1995)
Centre-based (full-time). 15 106
Family daycare 15 917
Children with special needs. 1111

PUBLICATIONS:
Supported Child Care: the report of the Special Needs Day Care Review in British Columbia (1993)

The Government's Response to Supported Child Care: The Report of the Special Needs Review in British Columbia (1994)

Program Guidelines: Early Intervention Programs (1993; revised 1995)

Community Support Services Policy Manual: Services for Children with Special Needs (1996)
- Infant Development Program
- Special Needs Day Care Program
- At Home Respite Benefits
- Child and Youth Care Worker Services for Families with Children with Special Needs
- Behavioural Support for Children with Autism
- Parent Support for Families with Children with Special Needs
- Professional Support Services for Children with Special Needs

COMMENTS:

British Columbia is working toward a more inclusive approach to serving children with special needs in typical child-care programs. The term "supported child care" is used to describe the service delivery model.

PROVINCE: MANITOBA

CONTACT:

Manitoba Family Services
   Child Day Care
   2–114 Garry Street
   Winnipeg, Manitoba 43C 1G1
   (204) 945-2197

STATISTICAL INFORMATION:

Number of licensed/regulated spaces (1995)
Full-day infant/toddler/preschool . . . 8282
School-age 3255
Family daycare 3111
Children with special needs 625

PUBLICATIONS:

The Community Child Day Care Standards Act, Manitoba Regulation 69/86 updated in 1993; contains definitions of "child with disabilities" and "special needs."

Children with Disabilities Program Guide (1990)

COMMENTS:

Funding for children with disabilities is provided through the Children with Disabilities Program. Children with special needs are integrated into many child-care centres but most do not receive additional funding. No special training is required for staff working with children with disabilities.

PROVINCE: NEW BRUNSWICK

CONTACT:

Office for Family and Prevention Services
   New Brunswick Department of Health and Community Services
   P.O. Box 5100
   Fredericton, New Brunswick
   E3B 5G8
   (506) 453-2950

STATISTICAL INFORMATION:
Number of licensed/regulated spaces (1995)
Centre-based 7838
Family daycare 114
(Included in above: 220 children with special needs in regulated child care)

PUBLICATIONS:
Day Care Regulations 83 to 85

Day Care Facilities Standards

Standards of Early Intervention Programs

OTHER RESOURCES:
Collaborative efforts within the Department of Health and Community Services resulted in seven major initiatives increasing healthy pregnancy outcomes:

1. enhanced prenatal screening and intervention

2. enhanced postnatal screening and intervention

3. re-targetting preschool clinics

4. home-based early intervention services

5. integrated daycare services

6. social work prevention services

7. home economics services

COMMENTS:
Screening is done to identify "priority" infants and preschool children and their families.

Priority preschool children are those at risk of a delay in school readiness. They may be physically or intellectually challenged or may live in families facing multiple social risk factors.

PROVINCE: NEWFOUNDLAND AND LABRADOR

CONTACT:
Direct Home Services Program
  Department of Social Services
  Government of Newfoundland and Labrador
  P.O. Box 8700, Confederation Building
  St. John's, Newfoundland
  A1B 4J6

Statistical Information:

Number of licensed/regulated spaces (1995)
Centre-based full-time. 2946
Centre-based part-time 759
Centre-based school-age 479

(Included in above: 318 children with special needs in regulated child care)

Publications:

- The Family and Rehabilitative Services Policy Manual
- The Direct Home Services Program Procedures Manual
- Direct Home Services Program Intervention Description Brochure

Other Resources:

Department of Health: public health nursing, health services at hospitals (i.e., physiotherapy, speech and language), pediatric physician services

Department of Education: some school boards offer early supports to children who will be attending in the coming year

Department of Social Services: daycare programs

Comments:

No written policy regarding children with special needs but fee subsidies may be available for children with special needs integrated into child-care centres. Currently, new child-care strategies are being designed.

Territory: Northwest Territories

Contact:

Early Childhood Programs
   Department of Education, Culture and Employment
   Government of the Northwest Territories
   Yellowknife, Northwest Territories
   X1A 2L9
   (403) 920-8902

Statistical Information:

Number of licensed/regulated spaces (1995)
Centre-based 1182
Family daycare 104

(Included in above: 14 children with special needs)

PUBLICATIONS:

Child Day Care Act and Regulations

Education Act (includes provision for child-care givers following completion of the daily school program)

COMMENTS:

The Student Support Division of the Department of Education, Culture and Employment may support "at risk" children as with the early intervention programs. Specialized equipment or services required in order to help the child participate in an early childhood program are also available.

PROVINCE: NOVA SCOTIA

CONTACT:

Department of Community Services
    Prevention and Child Care
    P.O. Box 696
    Halifax, Nova Scotia B3J 2T7
    (902) 424-3788

STATISTICAL INFORMATION:

Number of licensed/regulated spaces (1995)
Full-time 6892
Part-time 3584
Family daycare 169
Children with special needs 120

PUBLICATIONS:

Day Nurseries Act and Regulations (1989) (currently being revised with special consideration being given to a section governing facilities providing care for children with special needs)

Integration of Children with Special Needs in Day Care (1989) (presently under revision)

COMMENTS:

Currently modifying all program information being sent to child-care centres to include children with special needs.

Currently updating provincial early childhood education training standards to reflect an inclusive model for delivering services to children and families.

PROVINCE: ONTARIO

CONTACT:
Child Care Branch
  The Ministry of Community and Social Services
  Room 476, 4th Floor, Hepburn Block
  80 Grosvenor Street
  Toronto, Ontario
  M7A 1E9
  (416) 327-4865

STATISTICAL INFORMATION:
Number of licensed/regulated spaces (1995)
Centre-based 128 093
Family daycare (estimate) 18 072
Child-care resource centres 185

PUBLICATIONS:
- Day Nurseries Act
- Ontario Child Care Review (1996)
- How to Improve Ontario's Child Care (working paper, 1997)
- Making Services Work for People: A Framework for Children and People with Developmental Disabilities (April, 1997)

COMMENTS:
Ontario anticipates a major change in child-care legislation in 1997–98, which will result in a child-care system different from the existing system. Changes being discussed include shifting the management of all child-care services from the provincial government to local municipalities and adjusting the provincial/municipal cost-sharing arrangements.

PROVINCE: PRINCE EDWARD ISLAND

CONTACT:
Provincial Consultant for Early Childhood
  Health and Community Services Agency
  4 Sydney Street
  Charlottetown, Prince Edward Island
  C1A 7N8
  (902) 368-6513

STATISTICAL INFORMATION:
Number of licensed/regulated spaces (1995)
Infant (full-time) 64
Preschool (full-time) 1624
School-age (part-time) 568
Special needs 55
Kindergarten/nursery (part-time) . . . 1549
Family daycare 28

PUBLICATIONS:
Resource Manual for Case Conferences

COMMENTS:
Prince Edward Island and other Atlantic Provinces cooperate with the Department of Education, Atlantic Provinces Special Education Authority in Halifax to arrange for special services for preschool children with visual or hearing impairments. The same resource manual is used by the five regional health authorities working with the provincial early childhood associations to hire special needs consultants who develop action plans for any preschool child with special needs.

A special needs focus group was expected to release a report in January, 1997, with recommendations for written policies on services to young children with special needs. This report will include a requirement for specialized training for staff working with children with special needs.

PROVINCE: QUEBEC

CONTACT:
l'Office des services de garde à l'enfance
100 Sherbrooke Street East
Montreal, Quebec H2X 1C3
(514) 873-2323

STATISTICAL INFORMATION:
Number of licensed/regulated spaces (1995)
Infant/toddler/preschool
  centre-based 48 009
Family daycare 17 871
Children with special needs 1135

PUBLICATIONS:
(Unavailable at this time)

COMMENTS:

In November, 1996, major policy changes to the provision of child-care service were announced, including:

1. Facilities for 22 000 more children in child-care centres, and 60 000 more in family settings, both under the auspices of the Child Care Services Branch.

2. Nonprofit centres and agencies to be converted into agencies that will provide a range of services. Each centre board will be able to administer up to three separate centres and family settings with up to 100 places.

3. Tax credits and financial assistance will gradually disappear. Parents will pay $5.00 per day, with the difference to be made up by higher child-care services subsidies.

4. Free services for disadvantaged 4-year-olds gradually will be introduced starting in Montreal, September, 1997, with twenty-two hours of activities per week.

5. Full-day service for 5-year-olds in kindergarten will start in September, 1997 throughout the education system. (Barthioume, 1997)

The above changes are being introduced so rapidly that the profile of child-care services may change radically during the next five years.

Barthioume, Daniel. "The Development of Early Childhood Services in Quebec." *Interaction* (Summer, 1997): 4–5.

PROVINCE: SASKATCHEWAN

CONTACT:

Child Day Care Branch
   Saskatchewan Department of Social Services
   1920 Broad Street,
   Chateau Towers, 11th Floor
   Regina, Saskatchewan
   S4P 3L8
   (306) 787-0443

STATISTICAL INFORMATION:

Number of licensed/regulated spaces (1995)
Infant 235
Toddler 709
Preschool. 2783
School-age. 926
Family daycare 2613
Children with special needs 216

PUBLICATIONS:

The Child Care Act 1989–90, Chapter c-7.3

The Saskatchewan Child Care Regulations, June 1995

The Child and Family Services Act

COMMENTS:

Staff working with children with special needs are required to have additional training.

The Individual Program Planning approach is used.

TERRITORY: YUKON TERRITORY

CONTACT:

Child Care Services Unit
   Department of Health and Social Services
   Yukon Territorial Services
   P.O. Box 2703
   Whitehorse, Yukon
   Y1A 2C6
   (403) 667-3493

STATISTICAL INFORMATION:

Number of licensed/regulated spaces (1995)
Infant/toddler 230
Preschool. 419
School-age. 189
Family daycare 222
Children with special needs 35

PUBLICATIONS:

New Child Care Regulations (regulations implemented in 1995)

COMMENTS:

A child is designated "special needs" on the assessment of a child-care professional and must have an individual Program Plan.

No segregated child-care programs exist in Yukon.

APPENDIX G

TALKING WITH CHILDREN ABOUT DEATH AND DYING

WENDIE BRAMWELL*

INTRODUCTION AND BACKGROUND

Early childhood education programs provide young children the opportunity to acquire skills that help them find their way through the ups and downs of growing up. Early childhood educators provide foundations for helping children learn to communicate with one another, for expressing their feelings, and for acquiring the art of compromise when disagreeing. Even so, one critical area is invariably overlooked in early childhood teacher-training programs: Death. It is a topic that causes many of us to look away, to redirect the conversation, or to answer with short, uncomfortable comments. We have been raised to avoid talking openly about death and dying because it is painful and personal. Yet, by keeping too great a distance from the topic of death we are ignoring an important part of living for ourselves and for our children.

As educators, many of us avoid dealing with the topic of death by convincing ourselves that children are too young to understand its complexities. Some of us may assume that children are immune or should be sheltered from the pain and grief associated with loss. But how can we ignore a topic of such vital importance? How many children in our classrooms experienced the death of a family member, friend, or pet during the school year? Have we not overheard conversations about shootings and violence from our very young children? Has a child in our school not died sometime during the school year? Has a teacher or staff member died? Seldom is there a school year when children are not confronted with at least one of these circumstances.

It is becoming increasingly important to understand responses to death as we move toward inclusion in early childhood programs, especially as we include children with more severe medical problems. Children with special needs and their families have a higher risk of confronting death and dying due to accidents, frequent hospitalizations, medical complications, and fragile health conditions (Kudrajavcev, Schoenberg, Kurland, and Groover 1983). As classrooms welcome all children, teachers and staff must expand their own understanding and appreciation for life as well as for death.

---

*Wendie Bramwell is an early childhood educator and currently works on an early intervention training project at the University of Washington and as an instructor of early childhood special education classes at Bellevue Community College.

ESTABLISHING GROUNDWORK

It may be difficult for early childhood educators to know where to begin in offering guidance to young children on the topic of death and dying, subjects that have preoccupied philosophers and theologians for thousands of years. Yet, we must begin somewhere. A two-pronged approach may work: understanding the developmental levels of children's comprehension of death, and understanding our own feelings and views about death.

DEVELOPMENTAL CONSIDERATIONS

Understanding the developmental context of a child's notion of death is an easier task than examining our own values and beliefs. With a sweep of the hand, children are often dismissed from family discussions and arrangements dealing with death. Sometimes this may be appropriate yet it excludes children from a process that can help their understanding and healing. How can we know what will be best for a child? We can begin by listening carefully to children to gain insights into their thoughts. The 6-year-old who exclaims that he will "cling to the couch if death comes" has a very different concept of death from the 9-year-old who matter-of-factly answers that death means "You have had your life."

Interpreting what children say will be more meaningful if we understand the developmental stages of children's concepts of death. Current evidence acknowledges that even children under the age of 5 do understand death on some level. Kubler-Ross (1981) reports that her 4-year-old child buried a dog in the fall. Suddenly the child said, "This is really not so sad. Next spring when your tulips come up, he'll come up again and play with me." This 4-year-old's notion that things do not remain dead is reinforced over and over in children's stories. Snow White and Sleeping Beauty arise from the dead by being kissed. Tinkerbell is clapped back to life and the Beast is revived because of Beauty's pure love.

Allen Mendelson, in the *Young and Special* (1982) video series entitled "Let's Not Even Talk About It," describes the reaction of children in his class to the death of Bryan, their 4-year-old classmate. "Death is not finite for most 4-year-olds and that would come out over a period of days; 'Bryan's not here again today.' And it was my job to say, 'Right. And Bryan will never be here again because he died.' The reality took awhile for different children. 'Oh, he's not at school today, he's dead, but maybe he will be here tomorrow.'"

Between 5 and 7 years of age, children begin to understand the permanence of death but may think of it as a person, a "deathman," who will come and remove them bodily from their environment. This varies greatly from culture to culture but there is evidence that many children of this age fear that death has a form that can take them away.

Consistent with their sense of invincibility, young children talk about eluding death. They assert that they can run, hide, stomp or destroy whatever form death might take. They also rationalize their safety from death. When a 7-year-old classmate died in a drowning accident after slipping into the lake from an icy deck, children were overheard saying things like, "I don't have a deck" or "I don't even know where the lake is" or "My shoes are the kind that don't slip."

By middle childhood most children can grasp the four subconcepts of death as outlined by Essa and Murray (1994): finality, inevitability, cessation of bodily functions, and causality. Although cognitively understanding what has happened, children of this age may feel guilty or responsible for what has happened. They may be anxious about their future. In the book *How It Feels When a Parent Dies*, Jill Krements (1981) reports the words of a 9-year-old whose father has died. "I was worried that my mother might have to go back to work and there would be somebody new picking me up from school every day." When 8-year-old Stephen learned that his father had died in a plane crash, the first thing he asked his mom was if he "could keep Skippy and Shadow, our dog and cat, and could we keep our house." Thoughts such as these make the needs of the older child far different from those of the younger child who simply doesn't understand what it means to die.

Beyond the developmental context of death there are other important factors that influence children's understanding. Children who are critically ill or who have experienced a death close to them at a young age have an earlier and deeper understanding than their same age peers (Kubler-Ross 1983). Clearly, cultural and religious influences also greatly affect a child's perception of death and its significance. For example, each year families in Mexico celebrate the "Night of the Dead (La Noche de Muertos)." Families clean gravestones, prepare favorite dishes of deceased family members and set up a vigil for spirits who will return for this particular evening. Shops are filled with humorous, whimsical skeletal figures participating in mundane daily activities. Greg Palmer, in *Death: The Trip of a Lifetime* (1993), interviews the Lucas family in Mexico about the celebration of death. Mrs. Lucas explains, "The Night of the Dead is good for families. It gives us a reason to talk about death with our children so they are used to it before it happens to one of us. They are not afraid of it. And they get a feeling for the family, too. That it's not just the living, it's still my mother and my husband's brother and the baby they did not know."

INTROSPECTION

If young children have an imperfect understanding of death, do we then conclude that adults have a "perfect" understanding? No. Even though most adults understand death on a conceptual level, each successive experience with death contributes to a deeper understanding, even appreciation of death. Death, like every part of living, is a topic about which adults continue to increase their understanding throughout their lifetime.

Essa and Murray (1994) report, "Adults who explore and give thought to their own feelings about death find it easier to help children understand and cope with death." Teachers have been taught to turn to books, offer handouts or bring in experts when a need arises for new information, but death requires more introspection than most other topics. If we look at our own early experiences with death we can begin to understand what has shaped our current beliefs. We need to recognize what was comforting, what was missing in terms of comfort and explanations, what contributed most to fears or what contributed most to being able to cope. These remembrances will help us take the first step toward helping children.

Adults who have the opportunity to talk about death often will reveal what is important to know and understand about children. One adult student vividly remembered her first kindergarten friend. They held hands, played together at recess, and shared lunch. Her friend stopped coming to school and no explanation was ever offered for her absence. It was only much later that she learned the child had died. The sense of loss and confusion still permeated her telling of this incident. Friendship, throughout her life, always felt risky because her first experience had been so distressing. Another adult who lost someone she loved through a violent crime remembers being criticized for talking about the event with a detachment that her listeners associated with indifference. She explained that the only way she could talk about the event was to remove herself emotionally because it was too painful to live through the feelings each time.

All too often, we do not talk about death until someone close to us dies. Grief intermingles with unresolved feelings about deaths in the past and the task of supporting children becomes diluted with our own turbulent feelings. If we are to offer the very best guidance to children, we must first understand our own feelings and memories by talking with others. With insights gained from such experiences, we might more easily grasp the importance of clear and accurate information for children. We also may have a deeper understanding of the child who appears to be able to shrug off the death of a loved one as though it were "no big deal."

GRIEF AND MOURNING

Rituals associated with death have taken many forms throughout the ages and across cultures but their purpose remains the same: to acknowledge death and the accompanying feelings and to provide the bereaved with a community in which they can express and share their grief. Children often create their own rituals when a pet dies. Beloved objects are placed with the pet before burial, a choice site in the yard is selected and often tiny pebbles or flowers mark the site, in imitation of the adult rituals. If we look carefully at these gestures we begin to understand that children are seeking the same sense of closure that adults seek from rituals. When we exclude children from ceremonies associated with dying we are creating what Doka (1989) calls "disenfranchised grievers"—children who are discouraged or even prevented from displaying their grief.

Adults need to create opportunities for children to express their thoughts and feelings. Sometimes this happens in traditional religious observances where friends and family gather together to honor and remember the deceased. At other times families may prefer to create their own rituals that allow children the chance to talk about death as this family did:

> The oak piano bench was draped with a lace table cloth. Carefully arranged on it were a rose, a candle, a precious stone, a crocheted granny square and a photo. The bench was pulled close to two couches that faced one another. Sitting on the couch were five children ages 7 to 14 who had been brought together to commemorate their grandmother who had died after a long illness. Other family members and a grief counselor were also assembled in the dim light, talking about memories and thoughts and listening to one another. There were awkward but poignant silences but gradually the children started to talk. There was an outpouring of sadness and guilt and unexpected associations. The pets who had died in previous years were discussed in detail. There was some anger about the perceived expectation to cry and be sad. There was guilt that the expected tears did not readily flow. There were sweet memories of shared moments and there was a great sense of emptiness at the loss.

Grief manifests itself in unique ways for both adults and children. Adults who sanction, encourage and respect the ways in which children express loss are helping to move children out of the category of "disenfranchised grievers." The stages of grief that Kubler-Ross (1969) has identified (denial, anger, bargaining, depression, and acceptance) describe many of the feelings that cycle through one's grieving experience. Yet there are behaviors that come out of grieving that seem so disconnected from the experience of loss that it is hard to recognize them as grief-related. Some children act out in angry, violent ways saying hurtful and hateful things about the people closest to them. Some have disruptions in their sleeping and eating habits. Others have a difficult time in school focusing and remembering. As parents, and as teachers of young children, we need to accept these feelings and try to understand them. We can best accomplish this by becoming more introspective about our own feelings about death. The more aware we are of our own feelings, the better prepared we will be to respond to children's expressions of grief.

GRIEF AND FAMILIES OF CHILDREN WITH DISABILITIES

As our awareness of different stages and manifestations of grief increases, so will the realization that events other than a death can send us into a grief cycle. Loss of many kinds, a separation or divorce, a move or a job change are a few of the life events that may evoke a grieving response. Ken Moses (1987) suggests that parents of children with disabilities experience a grieving process that is strikingly similar to that of people who experience a death. Working with groups of parents, Moses saw anxiety, anger, denial, guilt, depression, and fear expressed over and over again. Gradually he came to understand that the parents were grieving the *loss of the dream* of what their child was to have been for them.

"Disability shatters the dreams, fantasies, illusions, and projections into the future that parents generate as part of their struggle to accomplish basic life missions. Parents of impaired children grieve for the loss of dreams that are key to the meaning of their existence, to their sense of being. Recovering from such a loss depends on one's ability to separate from the lost dream and to generate new, more attainable dreams."

Families who are dealing with the kind of loss associated with a child with disabilities have complex and often conflicting feelings that surface and resurface throughout the years. As early childhood educators, we will find ourselves listening and responding to this type of grief as our centers and classrooms become inclusive. If we listen and respond to their needs, we will recognize dynamics that affect all family members. For example, brothers and sisters of children with disabilities are often misunderstood or overlooked as families meet the needs of their child with disabilities. While the parents adjust to the challenges of a special needs child, siblings often feel the child is receiving a disproportionate amount of attention. We can understand why guilt and depression, even anger, are not uncommon feelings under these circumstances.

Children and adults who have experienced a death and families with children who have disabilities are connected by their common experience of loss. We connect best with others when we share similar meaningful experiences. Although confronting the issues of loss can be painful, failing to do so can be isolating and ultimately self defeating. By exploring the topic of death and dying teachers of young children can achieve a deeper understanding of an important part of children's lives.

REFERENCES

Doka, K.J. (1989). *Disenfranchised Grief.* Lexington, MA: Lexington Books.

Essa, E.L., and Murray, D.I. (1994). Young children's understanding and experience with death. *Young Children, 49*(4), 74–81.

Evans, P.M., and Alberman, E. (1991). Certified cause of death in children and young adults with cerebral palsy. *Archives of Disease in Children, 66*(3), 325–329.

Eyman, R.K., Grossman, H.J., Chaney, R.H., and Call, T.L. (1990). The life expectancy of profoundly handicapped people with mental retardation. *The New England Journal of Medicine.* 323:584–589.

Krementz, J. (1981). *How it feels when a parent dies.* New York: Knopf.

Kudrajavcev, T., Schoenberg, B.S., Kurland, L.T., and Groover, R. (1983). Cerebral palsy—trends in incidence and changes in concurrent neonatal mortality: Rochester, MN, 1950–1976. *Neurology, 33*(11), 1433–1438.

Kubler-Ross, E. (1981). *Living with Death and Dying.* New York: Macmillan.

Kubler-Ross, E. (1969). *On Death and Dying.* New York: Macmillan.

Kubler-Ross, E. (1983). *On Children and Death.* New York: Macmillan.

Mendelson, A. (1982). *Young and Special*, a Video Based Inservice for Mainstreaming Preschool Children, "Let's Not Even Talk About It." Circle Pines, MN: American Guidance Service.

Moses, K. (1987). "The Impact of Childhood Disability: The Parents' Struggle." *WAYS.*

Palmer, G. (1993). *Death: The Trip of a Lifetime.* New York: Harper Collins.

GLOSSARY

Acute: in reference to the sudden onset of an illness: usually of short duration; a chronic problem may have acute episodes periodically.

Adaptive: able to meet the expectations of the community for common behaviours such as self-help/care skills and basic social skills such as knocking before opening a closed door.

Advocacy group: a group of individuals who work together for a particular cause; the Epilepsy Association works to ensure equal access, opportunity, and acceptance within society for persons with epilepsy.

Affective: refers to the expression of feelings or emotions.

Amino acids: one of the chief components of proteins; amino acids are obtained from the individual's diet or are manufactured by living cells.

Amniocentesis: a medical procedure to determine if genetic abnormalities are present in the developing fetus; can be done about the 16th week of pregnancy (gestation).

Anemia: a reduced number of red blood cells usually resulting from inadequate nutrition; often characterized by listlessness and pale appearance of the skin.

Anoxia: a shortage of oxygen to the brain. Oxygen deprivation can cause physical damage to the brain before, during, or at any time after birth. Anoxia is one of the major causes of physical and/or cognitive dysfunction.

Antecedents: events that come before a behaviour. In behavioural psychology, the antecedent is the stimulus that causes a response. Consequences are the events that follow a behaviour.

Antibody: a substance, manufactured either by the body or artificially, to help the body fight diseases of various kinds.

Attachment process: the building of positive and trusting bonds (emotional and physical) between individuals, usually infant and parents or major caregivers.

Attention deficit/hyperactivity disorder (ADD/ADHD): behaviour that is characterized by consistently short attention span, inattentiveness, distractibility, impulsivity, and heightened levels of movement and physical activity (hyperactivity).

Audiologist: a specially certified professional who focuses on hearing testing and hearing impairments.

Auditory: refers to what is experienced through hearing.

Auditory brainstem response: a procedure that measures the brain's response to high-frequency sound.

Autonomy: behaving in a way that is self-directing; acting and reacting independently; the ability and willingness to make choices and decisions.

Behaviour modification: a system by which particular environmental events are systematically arranged to produce specified behaviour changes.

Biological insult: interference with or damage to an individual's physical structure or functioning.

Braille: a system of writing for the blind that uses patterns of raised dots that are read by the fingers.

Case manager: the member of the IPP team who assumes responsibility for coordination of the program and services for the child.

Cerebral palsy: a condition that affects muscular control. It is caused by damage to various parts of the brain. Its effects range from very mild (nonincapacitating) to moderate (involving fine and/or gross motor skills), to pervasive (involving almost all areas of the body's physical activity).

Chorionic villus sampling (CVS): a test for genetic abnormalities. It can be done between the 9th and 11th week of gestation; at this writing, amniocentesis is considered the safer procedure, resulting in fewer miscarriages.

Chromosomal disorders: include a number of developmental conditions that result from deviations in the formation of the chromosomal pair at the time of conception.

Chronic: in reference to a health problem of long duration and frequent recurrence.

Cochlea: a snail-shaped structure in the inner ear that allows hearing to occur.

Cochlea implant: a device, surgically placed by opening the mastoid structure of the skull, that allows electrical impulses (sound) to be carried directly to the brain.

Code switch: moving from one language and its cultural expression to another, depending on the situation.

Conductive hearing loss: refers to problems in the mechanical transmission of sounds through the outer or middle ear, which in turn reduce the intensity of sound vibrations reaching the auditory nerve in the inner ear.

Congenital: refers to a physical condition that originates during the prenatal period.

Congenital anomaly: a developmental deviation from the norm, present at birth.

Consequences: a response that follows the actions or behaviour of a child.

Consolidate: refers to bringing together several new developmental skills and applying them, as a package, to everyday living.

Contingency-type games: "if/then" interactions, as in peek-a-boo (the caregiver drapes a towel over his or her face and the baby lifts it and looks under it.

Contracture: a permanent tightening of muscles and joints.

Cumulative deficits: compounded results of developmental problems; an undiagnosed hearing loss can result in an accumulation of additional problems (language, cognitive, and social).

Cumulative effect: an adding or accumulation of consequences.

Deficit curriculum model: an approach that focuses on a child's disabilities and delays and tries to remediate (cure) what is wrong with the child; in contrast, the developmental model builds on a child's strengths and works through the problems within a developmentally integrated curriculum.

Developmental disabilities: a range of conditions that interfere with any aspect of the normal development of the child.

Developmental predeterminism: an approach that proclaims in advance how a child is going to turn out by making predictions based on both racial and family genetics without regard for culture and experience.

Didactic materials: manipulative materials in which the child's errors and successes are self-evident; the material, not the teacher, provides the information. Montessori was the originator of many such materials.

Disequilibrium: lack of balance or harmony; used to describe a child who seems to be experiencing temporary developmental irregularities.

Dysfluency: in speech patterns, hesitations, repetitions, or omitted or extra sounds.

Dysgraphia: difficulty with or inability to express thoughts in writing, and/or to identify the written symbols of language.

Dyslexia: an impaired ability to read; may also refer to an inability to understand what is read.

Earmould: that part of an amplification device (hearing aid) that is fitted to the individual's ear.

Echolalic: describes a condition in which language is characterized by repetition of words and sentences that do not convey meaning. This condition is often associated with autism.

Egocentric: in reference to young children, implies a restricted view of the world—mainly from one perspective only, the child's own.

Enzymes: complex proteins that produce specific biological-chemical reactions in the body.

Failure to thrive: refers to undersized infants whose bodies, for various reasons (organic, genetic, or environmental) either do not receive or cannot use the nurturance necessary for proper growth and development.

First trimester: the first three months of prenatal development.

Functional: with reference to children's learning, those skills that a child uses in daily living.

Generalization: the spread of a learned response from the training situation to everyday, real-life situations.

Generalize: with reference to children's learning, the application of what has been learned in one situation to a variety of related situations.

Genetic mutation: an alteration in the chromosomal materials (genes) that control inherited characteristics.

Handicapping condition: any physical condition or disability that makes it difficult for the individual to function within a given environment in the same manner as the majority of people.

Higher auditory cortex: the section of the brain that processes sound.

Home language: usually refers to the child's first language, the language a child hears in the home environment; often referred to as "mother tongue."

Hydrocephalus: a condition that occurs as the result of a buildup of cranial spinal fluid in the head; if not corrected (shunted), can lead to an enlargement of the head and, ultimately, pressure on and deterioration of the brain.

Hyperactivity: *See* **attention deficit/hyperactivity disorder.**

Immune system: that aspect of body functioning responsible for warding off diseases.

In utero: Latin for "in the uterus."

Incremental steps: a series of steps, often very small, in which each new step adds something to the preceding ones in a regular order.

Interdisciplinary: refers to several different professions working together on a common problem, sharing information and exchange roles, depending on the case.

Irreversible developmental damage: a condition, such as a missing arm or Down syndrome, for which there is no known means of restoration to normality. The irreversibility of the condition does not mean the individual cannot find ways of compensating and living a full life.

Jargon: the terms and forms of speech peculiar to particular professions and therefore not easily understood by persons outside those professions. To a medical person, a URI is what most people refer to as a common cold.

Learning theory: emphasizes the dominant role of environment and reinforcing experiences in all learning. Social learning theory adds other dimensions—that learning also occurs through observing and imitating and that individuals can generate their own satisfactions (intrinsic reinforcement).

Manual interpreter: an individual who translates spoken language into sign language for those who are deaf.

Manual prompt: positioning the teacher's hand around the learner's and actually putting the learner through the motions (may also be referred to as "hand over hand").

Meiosis: the process of cell division that produces reproductive cells in which one member of each chromosome pair is passed on to the new cell.

Meningocele: similar to myelomeningocele except that the protrusion is limited to the covering of the spinal cord and usually causes little or no neurological impairment.

Metabolism: the chemical process within living cells by which energy is manufactured so that the body can carry out its many functions.

Minimal brain damage (MBD): a condition in which the child demonstrates normal or near normal intelligence accompanied by minor behavioural deviations suggesting a mild neurological abnormality that often cannot be pinpointed.

Mitosis: the process of cell division for all cells except reproductive cells.

Multidisciplinary: refers to members of various disciplines working independently but exchanging their findings about a case; each concentrates on his or her own discipline.

Muscle tone: the interaction between central nervous system and motor activity; the term does not mean the same thing as muscle strength. Without muscle tone there is no voluntary movement.

Mutual gaze: the steady looking at each other's face that goes on between normally developing neonates and their parent or primary caregiver.

Myelomeningocele: a congenital protrusion of the spinal cord through the vertebrae; paralysis and lack of sensation below the protrusion (usually the lower trunk and legs) are often the result.

Neural: refers to the nerves and nervous system.

Neurological: refers to the functioning of the nervous system.

Nonambulatory: unable to walk.

Nonprogressive: in terms of diseases or other health problems, refers to a condition that does not get worse but stays "as is."

Normalization: refers to the care and education of the disabled in as culturally normal a way as possible, with services provided in regular community facilities rather than in segregated institutions.

Occlusion: an obstruction; as used here, something to prevent vision. An occluder is the object the examiner uses to prevent a child from seeing (usually one eye at a time).

Operant conditioning: a teaching strategy in which the child's behaviour is shaped as the result of a planned response designed to reinforce a specific behaviour.

Organic: refers to a condition within the individual's own body or neurological system.

Oromuscular dysfunction: weak or faulty movement or muscles controlling the mouth and tongue.

Orthopedic: refers to problems involving the bones and joints.

Paraprofessional: a trained person who works under the guidance of a more qualified professional.

Parent surrogate: someone appointed to act in place of a parent.

Pathologist: a certified professional who focuses on disease or impairments; a speech pathologist specializes in speech-related problems.

Pediatric ophthalmologist: a physician who specializes in disease and malfunctioning of the eyes during the developmental years.

Perinatal: occurring or existing at the time of birth.

Peripheral vision: that degree of vision available at the outer edges of the eyes.

Pervasive developmental disorder (PDD): a serious disturbance that affects a child's social-language interaction and/or ability to engage in imaginative play.

Pincer grasp: the act of picking up a small object using the forefinger and thumb (a developmental skill that does not appear until the latter part of the infant's first year).

Postnatal: occurring or existing after birth.

Prader-Willi syndrome: a genetic disorder characterized by obesity, short stature, disorders in sexual development, and a tendency toward behavioural and cognitive disabilities.

Prenatal: occurring or existing prior to birth.

Prerequisite skills: skills that must be acquired before a next higher level skill can be achieved. Children must be able to stand before they can walk, and walk before they can run.

Preventive discipline: a child management procedure for arranging the environment in ways that reduce the occurrence of maladaptive behaviours and increase the occurrence of appropriate behaviours.

Primitive reflexes: the responses the infant is born with, such as grasping, stepping, rooting, and sucking. Most of these disappear around 4 months of age and are replaced by similar but voluntary behaviours, as in the sucking response.

Progressive: in terms of health and functioning, refers to a condition that gets steadily better (or worse).

Prosthesis: a replacement for a missing part of the body.

Punishment: a negative action administered by an adult in response to a child's undesirable behaviour.

Reciprocal relationships: interactions between individuals in which each person gives and receives in response to the giving and receiving of the other.

Reflexive behaviours: involuntary body reactions to specific kinds of stimulation (a tap on the knee produces the knee jerk). Infants are born with a number of reflexes that should disappear as the nervous system matures.

Reinforcement: a general term for a consequence, an event, or procedure that increases or maintains the behaviour it follows; high grades are reinforcement for good academic performance.

Reinforcers: consequences that increase the likelihood that a behaviour will occur again. Reinforcers are specific to individuals: candy is a reinforcer for many children but not for others.

Reliable and valid tests: Reliability relates to consistency—how accurate, dependable, and predictable a test is. Validity refers to how accurately a test measures that which it purports to measure. For example, a score on a verbal IQ test for a child with an undiagnosed hearing impairment is not likely to be valid. The test does not measure the child's intelligence but rather how well the child's faulty hearing allows for interpretation of questions.

Remission: in reference to health conditions, a temporary or permanent relief from the condition.

Repertoire: in describing social behaviour, the sum total and range of an individual's social skills.

Residual hearing: the degree of hearing of a deaf or hearing impaired person.

Residual vision: vision remaining after disease or damage occurs to a person's visual system.

Resource teacher: a professional with special training and expertise in planning and implementing developmentally appropriate programs for children who have developmental problems.

Respiratory distress syndrome (RDS): a problem commonly found among premature infants because of the immature development of their lungs. It may also occur in about 1 percent of full-term infants during the first days of life.

Respite care: temporary caregiving that enables the regular caregiver (usually the mother) to get some relief and time away from the individual who is sick or disabled.

Rote memorization: the act of memorizing things without understanding them; being able to recite something that has little or no meaning for the one who has memorized it.

Salicylates: chemical compounds commonly known as salts of various kinds.

Scaffolding: the process of supporting words with gestures, actions, facial expressions, objects, and/or pictures to reinforce meaning.

Sensorimotor: Piaget's term describing the first major stage of cognitive development, from birth to about 18 months, when the infant moves from reflexive to voluntary behaviour.

Sensorineural hearing loss: a loss that involves a malfunctioning of the cochlea or auditory nerve.

Separation protest: the fussing or displeasure that an infant displays between 8 and 12 months (approximately) when the mother or principal caregiver tries to leave.

Service coordinator: *See* **case manager.**

Shunting: a process for implanting a tube (shunt) into the brain to allow proper circulation and drainage of fluids from within the skull into one of the body cavities.

Signing: manual communication systems such as finger spelling or ASL (American Sign Language).

Sphincter muscles: those muscles that determine bowel and bladder control (the retention and release of urine and fecal material).

Standardized IQ test: a measure of intellectual performance based on averages that have been established by testing large numbers of individuals of the same age (ideally of the same socioeconomic background, too).

Standardized norms: norms based on a large number of averaged scores of children of similar age on the same test items. For example, the average 17-month-old can build a tower of three cubes.

Stigmata (stigma): an identifying mark or characteristic; a diagnostic sign of a disease or disability.

Subtractive bilingualism: developing a second language (English) that replaces the first language (home language), causing the first language to cease to develop.

Symptom: a sign or indication that there may be a problem. (Sneezing and a runny nose often are symptoms of an allergy.)

Tactile: refers to that which is learned or perceived through touch.

Tangible reinforcers: material things that the individual likes; in children, favourite foods and drinks, toys, stickers, and so on (older children usually like money).

Task analysis: the process of breaking down a complex task into smaller units so that learning can occur more easily.

Teachable moments: a specific point in time when a child's level of readiness and interest come together to create the best milieu for new teaching.

Temperament: an individual's psychological makeup or personality traits. Of interest to the caregiver is how temperament influences an individual's responses to different situations.

Therapeutic: refers to specific treatment strategies for disease and disabilities.

Threshold: the physical or psychological point at which an individual begins to respond to certain kinds of stimulation.

Visual acuity: how well an individual is able to see; clarity of vision.

Voluntary motor responses: those motor movements that the individual controls, in contrast to involuntary or primitive reflexes (such as sucking and grasping), which are inborn.

Wedges, bolsters, and prone boards: therapeutic positioning devices prescribed for use by physiotherapists and occupational therapists in treating children with impaired motor skills.

INDEX

To the owner of this book

We hope that you have enjoyed *Exceptional Children,* Second Canadian Edition, and we would like to know as much about your experiences with this text as you would care to offer. Only through your comments and those of others can we learn how to make this a better text for future readers.

School _____ Your instructor's name _____

Course _____ Was the text required? _____ Recommended? _____

1. What did you like the most about *Exceptional Children?*

_____

_____

_____

2. How useful was this text for your course?

_____

_____

_____

3. Do you have any recommendations for ways to improve the next edition of this text?

_____

_____

_____

4. In the space below or in a separate letter, please write any other comments you have about the book. (For example, please feel free to comment on reading level, writing style, terminology, design features, and learning aids.)

_____

_____

_____

Optional

Your name _____ Date _____

May ITP Nelson quote you, either in promotion for *Exceptional Children* or in future publishing ventures?

Yes _____   No _____

Thanks!

You can also send your comments to us via e-mail at
college_arts_hum@nelson.com

PLEASE TAPE SHUT. DO NOT STAPLE.

TAPE SHUT

TAPE SHUT

FOLD HERE

Nelson

MAIL ✈ **POSTE**

Canada Post Corporation
Société canadienne des postes

Postage paid	Port payé
if mailed in Canada	si posté au Canada
Business Reply	**Réponse d'affaires**

0066102399   **01**

0066102399-M1K5G4-BR01

```
ITP NELSON
MARKET AND PRODUCT DEVELOPMENT
PO BOX 60225 STN BRM B
TORONTO ON M7Y 2H1
```

TAPE SHUT

TAPE SHUT